C
POC[

John Hobbis Harris Major (Retd)
Author and Publisher

The contents of this publication does not negate the individual's responsibilites to
check such information in the approprite Cadet Pamphlet

ISBN 1-874528-13-6

THE CHARTER OF THE ARMY CADET FORCE

THE ARMY CADET FORCE IS A NATIONAL VOLUNTARY YOUTH ORGANISATION.
IT IS SPONSORED BY THE ARMY AND PROVIDES CHALLENGING MILITARY, ADVENTUROUS AND COMMUNITY ACTIVITIES.
ITS AIM IS TO INSPIRE YOUNG PEOPLE TO ACHIEVE SUCCESS IN LIFE WITH A SPIRIT OF SERVICE TO THE QUEEN, THEIR COUNTRY AND THEIR LOCAL COMMUNITY, TO DEVELOP IN THEM THE QUALITIES REQUIRED OF A GOOD CITIZEN.

THIS AIM IS ACHIEVED BY:-

a. PROVIDING PROGRESSIVE CADET TRAINING, OFTEN OF A CHALLENGING AND EXCITING NATURE, TO FOSTER CONFIDENCE, SELF RELIANCE, INITIATIVE, LOYALTY, AND A SENSE OF SERVICE TO OTHER PEOPLE.

b. ENCOURAGING THE DEVELOPMENT OF PERSONAL POWERS OF PRACTICAL LEADERSHIP AND THE ABILITY TO WORK SUCCESSFULLY AS A MEMBER OF A TEAM.

c. STIMULATING AN INTEREST IN THE ARMY, ITS ACHIEVEMENTS SKILLS AND VALUES.

d. ADVISING AND PREPARING THOSE CONSIDERING A CAREER IN THE SERVICES OR WITH THE RESERVE FORCES.

THE MOTTO OF THE ARMY CADET FORCE IS:-

INSPIRE, TO ACHIEVE

The Cadet Training Centre, Frimley Park, Camberley, Surrey

CONTENT

CONTENT

CONTENT

PERSONAL DETAILS

Surname ....

Other Names ....

Home Address..

.... Post Code...

Date of Birth   /   /   Nat Insurance
No...

Blood Group.......... Home Telephone No ....

Next of Kin Relationship.. Tel No...........................

Address... Post Code ....

Email Address ....Mobile Phone No...................................

Religious Denomination ....

Relevant Medical Information, Allergies, etc ....

School Attending/Employer ....

....

Date Joined................................. Date Passed Basic Training ....

Enrolled on .... at ....
Sponsors:-
         1 ....

         2 ....

Signed... Detachment ....
         Officer i/c

Unit .... Date ....

THE BANNER OF
THE ARMY CADET FORCE

The Banner of the ACF was first presented on 9th Feb. 1960 at the Tower of London, by his Royal Highness the Duke of Edinburgh as Colonel in Chief, on the Occasion of the Centenary. A new banner was presented by His Royal Highness the Duke of Edinburgh at the Chapel of the Royal Hospital, Chelsea on 27th March 1982. The original Banner was laid up in St. Peter's Church, Frimley, Surrey in July 1982 where it may be seen to this day.

THE CADET PRAYER

O God our heavenly father, who hast brought

us together as members of the Army Cadet Force;

help us to do our duty at all times,

and be loyal to each other.

May all that is good and true prosper among us;

strengthen us to defend the right; and bless our work

that it may be acceptable to thee.

Chapter 1

GENERAL INFORMATION

INTRODUCTION

The first Cadet Pocket Book was published over twenty years ago. It is designed to help you learn or revise correctly and safely. With its help, you will attain a high standard in the Army Proficiency Syllabus (APC) subjects. Some of the contents do not relate directly to APC training, but it does relate to you as a person and the way you will develop as a young adult. Cadet Instructors will find the Pocket Book an invaluable aid when planning lessons.

RESPONSIBILITIES

This chapter contains advice on what is expected of you by your Officers and Adult Instructors. Like you, they are volunteers; the Army Cadet Force is their hobby.

Your Detachment will only be as good as you and other Cadets make it. Your Detachment Commander and Adult Instructors are there to encourage and train you. Work as a team - even if you do not particularly like someone; let's face it, it could be useful to learn how to work with people you do not like! Being a member of the ACF gives you opportunities to grow in knowledge and experience.

THE ENROLMENT CEREMONY

The first few weeks you parade at your Detachment you will take part in your Basic Training. Providing you attend regularly, you will be ENROLLED in about six to eight weeks. You are then officially allowed to wear the Cap Badge of the Regiment or Corps to which your Detachment is affiliated.

The format of the Enrolment Ceremony varies, but usually your OC will have invited your parents or guardians, and possibly the Padre to help officiate in the ceremony. Normally, each Cadet being enrolled has two friends from the Detachment who are appointed as his/her 'sponsors'. They will help you through this milestone in your Cadet career. The Enrolment Ceremony serves as a reminder to the other Cadets of their commitments to their Detachment and the ACF. The Enrolment Ceremony is personal to the Cadets taking part. Usually not more than two cadets are enrolled at a time.

GENERAL INFORMATION

It is not a photo opportunity for the PRO or local press to be involved in a publcity stunt, it is very much a personal matter for all the Cadets.
Many County ACF's allow Cadets to join after their 12th birthday this is a young age to measure up to becoming a member of your Detachment and therefore will need to be made welcome straight away. Their Sponsors have a special responsibility to se that this is carried out.

YOUR DETACHMENT COMMANDER WILL EXPECT YOU TO:

1. Be smartly turned out both in uniform and in your normal clothes.
2. Wear your uniform correctly - keep it clean and well pressed.
3. Walk tall, don't slouch - you can look ten centimeters taller!
4. Read and comply with notices and orders put up on the notice board.
5. Obey orders - if they seem unfair, obey them and complain after.
6. Remember your good manners.
7. Look after new recruits; make them feel part of the Detachment.
8. When your Detachment is "Open to recruit" encourage those who you feel would make good Cadets to attend a Detachment Parade.
9. Be ALERT, be SAFETY and SECURITY CONSCIOUS AT ALL TIMES
10. Treat other peoples property with respect ; prevent damage and vandalism.
11. Never be afraid of doing more than you have been asked to do.
12. Keep fit, play and work hard, take part in sports and games.
13. Work in the Detachment as you SHOULD DO at home - be prepared to help with the 'chores' without having to be asked.
14. Be tidy; do not rely on others to clean up after you.
15. Be on time - five minutes before time!
16. Remember to let your Detachment Commander know in good time if you are unable to attend a weekend/camp etc. Just not turning up is not good enough, nor is it good manners.

BE A "FULL MEMBER"

Whenever events, parades, sporting events, weekend training, Annual Camps are planned, your Detachment Staff and others at Company and County/Sector level will have spent many hours in planning a full and interesting programme.
This is all organised for your benefit.

GENERAL INFORMATION

What does being a **"Full Member"** mean?
Like your Detachment Commander and Adult Instructors, you have other responsibilities outside the ACF, with the time you have available for Cadets, put maximum effort in to becoming a good Cadet.
A good Cadet is a *full member*, and is expected to:

1. Take an active part in the life of the Detachment and make the progress required not only in training but also as a person.
    2. Help others who find it difficult to learn new skills.
3. Look after new recruits; make them feel part of the Detachment.
4. When your Detachment is "Open to recruit" encourage those who you feel would make good Cadets to attend a Detachment Parade.
5. Be ALERT, be SAFETY and SECURITY CONSCIOUS AT ALL TIMES

THE CADET AND THE COMMUNITY

A part of the Army Cadet Force Charter reads:
"To inspire young people to achieve success in life with a spirit o f service to the Queen, their country and their local community, and to develop in them the qualities required o f a good citizen".
As an individual, a Cadet, you are a CITIZEN. You live in this country, in your own town, city or village. You have family, friends and are part of the community you live in. Every community depends upon people who are prepared to work towards making it a better place to live.
During your training, depending on how your Detachment staff plans it, you should be taking part in various projects and activities in your local community.
This is an excellent opportunity to meet the local "Movers and Shakers", Civic dignitaries such as the Mayor, local Councillors and those who actively support and work for the community in many ways, through business, profession or charitable work.
It also presents the opportunity for them to meet you and the other Cadets in your Detachment. The impression you make is reflected on you and your Detachment - let it be a good one!
If you are taking part in the Duke of Edinburgh's Award Scheme, you may chose to undertake community project work as part of your award.
Getting involved in the community can often be difficult and demanding, but it can also be great fun and very rewarding.
You may find that you continue working in the community long after you have left the Cadet Force.

GENERAL INFORMATION

KNOW WHO's WHO IN YOUR COMMUNITY

This will bring you and your unit into close contact with the
community in which you live.

You will meet new people in a variety of situations, some may be
employers, others local councillors, professional people like doctors,
solicitors or accountants.

It will all present opportunities for them to get to know you, your unit
and the Cadet Force and of course for you to get to know them.
What impression you make on them will be very important, as it is
always said that first impressions are lasting impressions. Were you
helpful, did you go out of your way to help, did you have good
manners, they will ask you again, what will be their lasting impression
of you and your Detachment?.

YOUR WELFARE AND SAFETY

The purpose of the following information is to make you aware of what
laws there are for your protection and how they are put into action.

Welfare

The Children Act 1989

This Act is designed to ensure that children (up to the age of 16 years)
and young persons (up to the age of 18 years) are treated properly.
What does it mean within the ACF? Firstly, it means that Adults who
express an interest in working with the Cadets are vetted to try and
prevent people who might wish to harm young persons physically or
mentally from joining the ACE Secondly, it means that the adults in the
ACF must think at all times of your welfare and safety. It is termed
"Duty of care".

There are systems and procedures in place on a County or Sector level
that provide a 'listening ear' for any problems there may be. It is
confidential, but you should be aware that serious problems will be
passed on to trained personnel for further action.

What do you do?

If something has happened that makes you feel really bad, share it; talk
to an Officer or Adult Instructor you get on well with, it is pretty
certain that they will have experienced something similar.

- If you feel that you are not being treated properly, talk to a person
  you can trust. Be truthful, enlarging on the truth will not help you.
- In your cadet activities, there could be some training that you feel
  you just cannot cope with; you know you will fail.

Give it your best, you've tried and that is not failing.

GENERAL INFORMATION

SAFETY

All Officers and Adult Instructors have to comply with official safety requirements. There are strict safety rules all cadet activities. If these rules are followed, the risk of someone being injured is reduced.
Failure to follow the safety rules can lead to disciplinary action and possibly court proceedings particularly if someone is injured.

How does this work?

Your APC syllabus contains safety training where required.
When you are out on exercise, there are briefings to inform you of how, what, when and where. Before you receive your briefing, the Adult Instructors and Officers have carefully planned the activity and have had their briefings, including the safety aspects.

What do you do?

- Remember your safety rules ALWAYS follow them
- Watch the more junior Cadets, ensure they follow the safety rules
- Listen, (take notes if necessary), when you have your briefing
- Do not fool around at the wrong time
- Know the telephone numbers of: Your Detachment Comdr and other Adult Instructors. Your Company/Area Comdr and Cadet County HQ. Out on exercise - the mobile number(s) to call in an emergency, not forgetting the Tel No of the Camp you are at.

ANNUAL CAMP

For many years the Army Cadet Force and the Combined Cadet Force have enjoyed the training camps provided by the Ministry of Defence. Annual Camp has always been the highlight of the cadet year. You should always make a special effort to attend. It is a time when all the training you have received during the year is put into practice in 'the field', by taking part in exercises and expeditions. You will be a full time Cadet for the duration of camp and is an ideal opportunity to make new friends and learn new skills. Another opportunity Annual Camp offers you is the chance to be in a very different part of the country, perhaps for the first time in your life. Try and find out as much as you can, what the area is famous for, what is made there, local customs and history.

Many counties, depending upon the location of the camp have "Open Days", when parents and friends visit the camp. The day is often planned as a Sports Day, with demonstrations and displays, many of which are organised by the Cadets. Some events are set up to involve visitors making it an entertaining day.

GENERAL INFORMATION

ANNUAL CAMP "DO'S and DON'TS

The following information should make your camp enjoyable by helping you get the most out of it and keeping you our of trouble.

Remember that while you are under the supervision of your Officers and Adult Instructors they are responsible for your SAFETY and WELFARE.

This applies to ANY Cadet activity no matter where it is. Annual Camp like weekend training means you are away from home; your Officers and Adult Instructors are responsible for you even whilst you sleep! The rules, instructions and orders given by your Officers and Adult Instructors are there to protect you. Make sure you follow the rules, if you are an NCO, make sure that you set an example by complying and seeing that they are properly carried out.

BEFORE CAMP - PREPARATION

1. Save up for camp - be ready to pay your camp fees when asked. (Note: if you have difficulty in this, see your Detachment Commander, help may be available).
2. Get to know when and where you are going as soon as possible.
3. Get to know the programme and what you are to be doing.
4. Practice some of the training that you will be carrying out at camp, particularly those you are not very good at.
5. Get your OC to provide a map of the camp and surrounding area, build up a picture in your mind of what it will be like.
6. Do a project on places of interest, special features of the countryside, the people, industries and other interesting information.
7. Do you have any friends or relatives in the area - if so you may be able to visit them?
8. Check that your uniform fits you properly, if not try and get it changed early enough to give the Quarter Master a chance to help you.
9. Check all your kit for camp. Make a list of all your needs, get it organised well before hand. Your OC will give you a checklist for camp; you may find the Annual Camp Check List at the end of this section useful.
10. Do your own packing. If you have never packed before, ask for a demonstration. Do not start packing the night before you are due to leave.
11. Have your MEDICAL CERTIFICATE (sometimes known as the FFI form - Free From Infection), make sure it is correctly completed and SIGNED by your parent or guardian. Put it into your coat pocket when leaving home for camp.

GENERAL INFORMATION

MEDICAL CERTIFICATE

You will be given a Medical Certificate for your parent/guardian to complete and sign before you go to annual camp. Procedures vary; you may have to hand it back to your Detachment Commander, or hand it to the Adult in charge of your coach. (see page 1-15 for Certificate)

The reason for this form being a requirement is that the Ministry of Defence cannot entertain certain risks and these must be eliminated by regulations, for example:

1. Condition - **Epilepsy**. Not allowed to undertake such activities as Rock Climbing, Swimming, Shooting, Canoeing, Orienteering, and Expeditions in Wild Country etc.

2. Condition - **Asthma**. Whether or not they are receiving any form of therapy is not allowed to undertake activities involving strenuous activity.

3. Condition - **Diabetes**. Those dependent on Insulin treatment may not undertake activities involving irregular meals or long periods of exertion.

4. Condition - **Heart problems.** These are of such a variable nature that a cadets' medical practitioner must judge them individually. Should any doubts exist on a Cadets' ability to undertake all the activities listed below, a doctor should be consulted by the parent or guardian before the certificate is signed.

EXAMPLES OF PHYSICAL & SPORTING ACTIVITIES

Rock Climbing, Canoeing, Hang Gliding, Hill walking on Expeditions, Life Saving, Parachuting, Par ascending, Sailing, Rafting, Offshore and Windsurfing.

Skiing: Cross Country and Downhill, Water Skiing, Caving, Sub-Aqua Diving. Athletics, Boxing, Circuit Training, Cricket, Cross Country Running, Cycling, Mountain Biking, Football, Rugby, Hockey, Judo, Orienteering, and Swimming.

IMPORTANT NOTICE - INSURANCE

The Ministry of Defence and the Army Cadet Force Association have insurance policies for Cadets who may have an accident.

THIS INSURANCE IS ONLY VALID IF YOU ARE TAKING PART IN AN ACTIVITY THAT IS PLANNED AND ORGANISED AS PART OF YOUR CADET TRAINING.

WARNING

Therefore if you decide to organise an expedition or exercise WITHOUT AUTHORITY and as a result someone is injured, they would NOT be covered by insurance.

GENERAL INFORMATION

CLAY TARGET SHOOTING
The important facts
Even clay shooting novices can talk like seasoned professionals with this guide to the sport Clay target shooting, also known as clay pigeon shooting, began in 1921 when the shooting of real pigeons was made illegal

The sport has several names but is formally known as 'inanimate bird shooting'

The clays are made from a mixture of pitch and chalk, and are designed to be flung from traps at high speed.

Clays in the air are called 'BIRDS'.

A successfully struck clay is called a 'hit' or a 'kill'

Shooters must have an extremely keen eye because a clay target is just 110mm in diameter

Different clays pose the shooter different problems. Clays that scuttle along the ground are known as 'rabbits' while those that fly through the air are called 'game'.

The trajectory of the clay known as the 'mini', meanwhile, is likened to a flying bumblebee

In trap shooting the clay targets are launched at different angles, speeds and trajectories away from the marksman

In Skeet shooting targets are fired from two trap houses positioned 40 metres apart. Competitors must shoot from each of the seven positions

Traps come in all sorts of different shapes and sizes. They launch different targets in singles or pairs to distances of up to 100 metres

SAFETY FIRST
ACF Counties who set up Clay Target Shooting will have sent an Officer or Adult Instructor on one of the Clay Target Associations Safety Officers Training Courses. This course has been adapted by the Army Rifle Association for instructors to qualify for the Clay Target Shooting. This enables them to teach Cadets how to shoot safely. It also authorise them to organise and run Clay Target shooting events.

In August 2007 was the inaugural Cadet Clay Target Shooting competition, which was run under the auspices of the Council for Cadet Rifle Shooting.

Each of the 15 teams of four cadets from all four Cadet Forces had to compete in two disciplines: the Saturday 'flush' and Sunday's '50 bird sporting competition'.

GENERAL INFORMATION

Teamwork IS The key to success
The flush requires teamwork while the 50 bird event is different - that part of the competition is all about reaction,"

THE THRILL OF CLAY SHOOTING
There is no doubt about it Clay Target Shooting is great fun but remember *carried out safely*. The thrill of pressing the trigger of your 12 bore shot gun, seeing your shot going after the clay into the sky and then it shatters in a puff of grey powder, then a split second after a second clay is airbourne, you lock on, apply pressure to the trigger and BANG! another shattered clay and a puff of grey dust.
It will take some practice to get to the stage of not missing a clay!! but with dedication you will make it happen.
Outside the Cadet Forces there are many Clay Shooting Clubs in the country, which if you joint them will give more time on the range to become proficient.

CLAY SHOOTING - THE FUTURE IS BRIGHT
Due to the enthusiasm and great interest in this activity plans are already being made for next year. To the future this event and the spirit engendered makes it an obvious choice for an annual competition for the cadet Forces and a popular event at Annual Camps.

PAINT BALLING
This is not a recognised 'sport' where the participants 'fire paint balls directly at each other, however, where your County has the use of a **close quarter battle** range and the necessary weapons and equipment, then firing at the targets - not individuals - as presented is permitted. In addition that you have been trained in the safety aspects of Paint Balling. Be aware it can be dangerous activity outside the ACF control and remit. It is subject to special insurance being taken out by your County ACF for it to be practiced by you.

GENERAL INFORMATION

ON YOUR WAY TO CAMP

When traveling by coach or public transport: **"Do Not: "**

- Make unnecessary noise to the annoyance of other travellers
- Leave your kit unattended, or in a place dangerous to others.
- Cause problems for coach drivers or those responsible for you.
- Do not deliberately spill drinks, leave litter or cause damage.
- Go wandering off without permission.

WHEN AT CAMP - DO THE FOLLOWING:

1. Put most of your spending money in the camp bank (if available) or other means of safe keeping organised by your adult staff at camp.
2. Listen and make note of the camp Standing Orders for Security, Fire and Safety instructions. Strictly observe 'Out of Bounds' notices.
3. Read daily routine orders and comply with them.
4. Write, phone or email home to let them know you have arrived safely and remember to keep in touch.
5. Remember to wash yourself every day. Leave the ablutions as clean as you would wish to find them.
6. Clean your kit daily, wash out dirty socks and underclothes - remember to rinse them properly or you will get sore!
7. Carry out all duties and "chores" cheerfully and properly.
8. Help others - especially the junior cadets who are away from home AND at camp for the first time.
9. Be polite to people you meet in the area, particularly the civilian staff in the camp and those who run the cookhouse and the camp NAAFI.
1 0. Watch out for bullying or signs that another Cadet is really unhappy. If you see it, report it.
1 1. Be safety conscious, report any suspicious persons or events.
12. Pull your weight - work hard, play hard, keep your bed space clean and tidy. Most important of all, ENJOY CAMP

WHEN AT CAMP DO NOT:

1. Make work for yourself and others by dropping litter or leaving kit lying about.
2. Leave the toilets or washbasins in a dirty state; you will probably have to clean them.
3. Never wander off on your own, or in a group without telling anyone where you are going.
4. Be a nuisance to local residents by being noisy or 'fooling about' in the streets or other public places.

GENERAL INFORMATION

5. Hitchhike in uniform - it is not approved of.
6. Stay out of camp later than permitted, without first having asked for special permission.
7. Leave valuable items of personal kit lying about, lock them away safely.
8. Do not touch or pick up strange objects on the training area, (remember Camp Standing Orders).
9. Get involved with 'trouble makers' - unless you do not want to have an enjoyable camp, and get a bad name for your behaviour.
10. Be tempted to 'do drugs' in any form.
11. Get involved with local 'trouble makers' outside camp, who will try to create problems bringing dis-credit on the Cadet Force, just don't get involved.

SELF TEST QUESTIONS

1. When was the first Cadets Pocket Book published,
2. Are your Officers and Instructors fulltime employed in the ACF.
3. What is the training you do in your first few weeks as a Recruit.
4. When do you get 'Enrolled' and what does it mean to you.
5. How soon can you wear your cap badge.
6. What Regiment or Corps is your Cap Badge
7. At the enrollment ceremony who will have been invited.
8. What are 'sponsors' and what is their purpose.
9. What should the enrollment ceremony mean to other Cadets.
10. What is important to you personally about the ceremony.
11. Your Detachment Commander expect a great deal from you,how many of those 'expectations' can you name.
12. What is meant by being a 'FULL MEMBER of your Detachment.
13. What is the Cadet Charter, can you recite it.
14. What do you understand by the term "Movers and Shakers".
15. How does your Detachment support your community.
16. What charity work do you help with.
17. What is the main purpose of the Childrens Act 1989.
18. If you have a bad experience who do you report it to.

(Self test questions continued on page 1-16)

GENERAL INFORMATION

ANNUAL CAMP KIT CHECK LIST	
COMBAT TROUSERS	
COMBAT JACKET	
SHIRTS - TWO	
JUMPER	
BUNGEES (6)	
BRASSARD	
BERET	
BELT- WORKING	
BOOTS AND CLEANING KIT	
THICK SOCKS (AT LEAST 3 PAIRS)	
SPORTS KIT (INCLUDING SWIM KIT)	
TROUSER ELASTICS (TWO SETS)	
KNIFE, FORK, SPOON AND MUG	
CIVVIES	
WASHING KIT (INCLUDING SHAMPOO & SOAP)	
HAIR GRIPS, SCRUNCHIES, HAIRNETS, MAKE UP ETC.	
TOWELS (I LARGE, I HAND)	
PILLOW SLIP	
UNDERWEAR	
WASHING POWDER/LIQUID (WRAP TO PREVENT LEAKS)	
POCKET NOTEBOOK AND PENCILS	
NEEDLE AND COTTON	
STRONG PADLOCK AND 2 KEYS	
WEBBING	
TORCH	
SCISSORS AND STRING	
POCKET MONEY	
PERSONAL FIRST AID KIT	
ANY MEDICATION YOU MAY NEED	
YOUR FFI (Free From Infection) FORM (Duly Signed)	
BOYS - IF YOU SHAVE - YOUR SHAVING KIT.	

CHAPTER 2

THE ARMY CADET FORCE PAST & PRESENT

THE EARLIEST DAYS

The Cadet Force can trace its' beginnings to 1859. At that time there was a threat of a French invasion. Few units of the British Army were at home; most of them were serving in India after the Indian Mutiny. Due to the threat of invasion the Volunteers were formed. History was repeated in 1940 when there was the threat of invasion from the German Army.

THE VOLUNTEERS

The formation of the Volunteers – ancestors of the Territorial Army, saw the start of the Cadets. In 1860 at least eight schools had formed units. Volunteer units formed Cadet Companies. One of these, the Queen's Westminsters, paraded their cadets when Queen Victoria carried out a review of the Volunteers in 1860.

The Cadet movement continued, it was seen as being of great value to the boys who lived in the terrible conditions of the London slums.

OCTAVIA HILL – SOCIAL WORKER

One of the most respected social workers of that time was Miss Octavia Hill. She realised that cadet training was of great benefit to these boys; as a result, the Southwark Cadet Company was formed to introduce the boys of the area to the virtues of order, cleanliness, teamwork and self-reliance. The story goes that she had contacts at the Woolwich Garrison and persuaded them that the boys who were living rough on the streets could be accommodated in the stable haylofts at the Barracks. No doubt there were as many rats and mice there as on the streets, but at least it would be dry and warm; and they got fed regularly!

At the age of 26 she collected rents in Paradise Place, one of the most notorious slum areas in London. She was angry and upset to see families living in such terrible conditions that she decided to make it her mission in life to find or provide better housing for the poor.

Today, as a result of her tireless energy and work there is a thriving

THE ARMY CADET FORCE - PAST & PRESENT

Octavia Hill Housing Trust that now has 1300 homes in the London area.

Another passion in her life was the creation of open spaces in built up areas to bring "Healthy gifts of air and joy of plants and flowers". Her public campaigns to save recreational open space accessible to all, led to the creation of the National Trust.

Cadets today can be justly proud that the voluntary spirit of Octavia Hill is part of our history and heritage.

THE OCTAVIA HILL MUSEUM AND SOCIETY

The memory of this lady and her life's work is preserved in the Octavia Hill Birthplace Museum. The museum is organised and staffed by the members of the Octavia Hill Society, who, true to the traditions and spirit of Octavia Hill are all volunteers giving their time supporting the museum and staffing it.

The Army Cadet Force is well represented; a model of an Army Cadet was recently added to the display. Every Cadet should make the opportunity to visit the museum, which is located in the Cambridgeshire town of Wisbech, at **1 South Brink Place, PE13 1JE** It is always advisable to check the opening times before making a visit. If your Annual Camp is on the Stanford Training Area it is quite near for you to make a visit.

THE BOER WAR

At the start of the Boer War, about fifty schools had Cadet Corps (the forerunners of the Combined Cadet Force). Many 'Open Units' (forebears of the present Army Cadet Force) had started in the larger cities.

AFTER THE BOER WAR

In 1908, the Volunteers were converted to the Territorial Army, Public Schools and Universities were asked to provide units of the Officer Training Corps. Cadet Corps were formed in schools and 'open units' for those who had left school. The title Cadet Force was introduced and the administration was taken over by the Territorial Army Associations.

THE FIRST WORLD WAR

In 1914, the Great War, there was a massive expansion of the Cadet Force. The War Office took over the administration, and continued until 1923 when control and administration reverted to the Territorial

THE ARMY CADET FORCE - PAST & PRESENT

Army Association. In that year, 1923 the government ceased to recognize the Cadet Force taking away all financial support. This was a very difficult period for everyone, but the voluntary spirit that had been its greatest strength in the early days came to the surface. Individuals had to find the funding for everything. The wearing of Regimental badges and buttons was forbidden. It was a difficult and unhappy time for the Cadet Force.

THE AMERY REPORT

In 1957 a special Government Report (The Amery Report), was published. It concerned the future of the ACF in the immediate post war years. Many changes were made; Frimley Park, the Cadet Training Centre, was founded. The ACFA was one of the youth organisations given massive grants from the King George VI Memorial Trust Fund. As a result of this the Cadet Officer and Instructor courses that are run at Frimley are called the KG VI Leadership Courses.
Cadet training took on a new direction, the war was over and National Service was about to cease. It then became more important to develop the Cadet as a person, more responsible for their actions, guiding and developing them through their training to become good citizens.

THE DUKE OF EDINBURGH'S AWARD SCHEME

It was a happy coincidence that the Duke of Edinburgh's Award Scheme started soon after the Adventurous Training was introduced into the ACF. As a result of this the ACF became involved in the Award Scheme as an operating Authority, right from the start.
Thre are many benefits to be gained by taking part in the Award Scheme. It is recognised world wide for any individual who has achieved an award.

ADVENTUROUS TRAINING INTRODUCED

With the emphasis on this change of direction, Adventurous Training was introduced as a subject in the cadet syllabus. Special grants were made available to County Territorial Army Associations to set up County Adventurous Training Centres. Many Counties took advantage of this and set up Adventure Training Centres in their counties. Hopefully, many of you still have the opportunity to go on weekend training.

Quarter Guard. Christ's College, Brecon, Cadet Corps 1898.
Annual camps were an established feature of the Volunteer Force
and the custom soon spread to cadet units. Sometimes a camp
would be organised by an individual unit, but increasingly
combined camps became the order of the day. The first Public
Schools Cadet Camp was held at Churn Downs in 1889.
The competitive element in these camps gave a useful incentive to
training, drill and shooting competitions being keenly contested.
Each unit in turn had to provide the camp quarter-guard and
again there was keen rivalry to produce the smartest turn-out.
The quarter-guard of Christ's College Cadet Corps is illustrated.
They wear dark blue field service caps and scarlet tunics with
white collars and cuffs. Trousers are of dark blue serge with a
scarlet welt down the outside seams. The bugler to the left carries
the wing epaulettes of a bandsman. Belts of white buff leather are
worn and the guard is armed with the cavalry version
Martini-Henry rifles.
The Christ's College Cadet Corps was formed in 1895 and
became affiliated to the 1st. (Brecknockshire) Volunteer Battalion,
South Wales Borderers. By 1908 it was down to only 35 cadets
and was disbanded. It was revived in 1916 as a cadet corps but
again disbanded in 1921. Finally, it re-formed in June 1937 as a
unit of the Officers Training Corps.

THE ARMY CADET FORCE - PAST & PRESENT

Frimley and Camberley Cadet Corps 1909.

Surrey is a county which has always been strongly represented in the ranks of the Cadet Force. The Frimley and Camberley Cadet Corps was formed in 1908, largely at the instigation of a Miss G. M. I. Reynolds. Acting very much in the tradition of Octavia Hill Miss Reynolds became concerned at the Cadet Corps lack of recreation facilities for older boys in her bible class. Her subsequent efforts led to the formation of a cadet corps. The uniform illustrated was worn by the corps between 1908 and 1912, yet it has a curiously modern ring. A brown jersey was worn with a contrasting red collar, perhaps not so much a concession to informality as a means of providing a cheap uniform in days when the full cost had to be met locally. The real attraction for boys would be the slouch hat, an item of headgear which the South African War had made popular in both volunteer and cadet units.

The cap badge took the form of the letters F&CCC in brass. The equipment worn was limited to a brown leather belt with brass clasp and a white haversack.

There was no lack of initial support for this unit and in 1909 Lord Roberts became its President. Curiously, official recognition did not come until 1912. In the same year, the unit became affiliated to the 5th. (T.F.) Battalion Queen's Regiment with appropriate changes in. uniform and badges. The corps was fortunate in its location and adapted to the lean inter-war years better than most. The Royal Military College at Sandhurst was able to assist during this period with both instructors and second-hand uniforms. Since that time, the unit has survived and prospered; today it has close links with the 2ndCadet BN The Queen's Regiment, Surrey ACF.

Card No 11

THE ARMY CADET FORCE - PAST & PRESENT

NATIONAL CADET ASSOCIATION (BNCA)

Trying to keep the Cadet Force alive and at the same time trying to win back government support, brought about the formation of the BNCA. By 1932 the BNCA had gained recognition and achieved some measure of success. It was allowed, under the guidance of the Territorial Army – to run the Cadet Force.

THE SECOND WORLD WAR

Shortly after the start of the war, (1939-45), saw a massive expansion of all the Cadet Forces, not only the Army Cadets and the Sea Cadets, they were joined by the newly formed Air Training Corps. By 1942 the War Office, known today as the Ministry of Defence, took over the administration of the ACF once again, giving it support beyond its members wildest dreams.

Uniforms were provided free, they had rifles issued, although they were from the Boer War period! See the illustration below.

This was the Martini Henery Rifle. The actual rifles issued were the Cavalry version being much shorter and more suitable for the Cadets to handle. They were for drill purposes only, which means they had their firing pins removed so could not be fired.

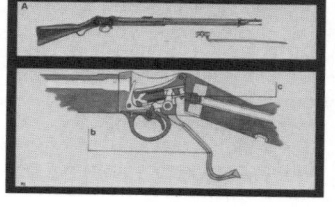

Annual Camps were set up and assistance given to help run them and train the Cadets.

The accommodation was mostly in bell tents, there were no beds only sacks that the cadets filled with straw (called a palliasse) as a mattress to sleep on the duck boards in the tents. They were not very comfortable, especially when it rained as it usually does at Annual Camp.

The War Certificate 'A' parts 1 and 2 was introduced as the Proficiency Tests for training, with the red star worn on the arm of uniforms similar to your APC red and blue stars today. At that time if a Cadet passed his Cert 'A' Part 2 it was an exception rather than the rule as the standards were very high.

At one period there were more than 140,000 Army Cadets. The biggest problem was to find officers and instructors to run the Detachments, most able bodied men were already in the forces or committed members of the Home Guard or other Emergency Services, taking what spare time they had.

THE ARMY CADET FORCE - PAST & PRESENT

Wiltshire Army Cadet Force 1943.

During the early part of the Second World War, existing cadet units maintained their position, though many Cadet Force officers were lost to the forces, Home Guard or Civil Defence. In April 1941 responsibility for cadets was tranferred to the Home Guard Directorate, with the subsequent provision of increased cash grants, free uniforms and equipment. From January 1942 a massive expansion took place, assisted by Cadet Committees formed in each County area. A new title of 'Army Cadet Force' was introduced, to distinguish Army Cadets from the Sea and Air Cadet units which were forming. The original target for A.C.F. strength was fixed at 150,000 but by mid 1943 over 170,000 army cadets were serving. The age range was fixed at fourteen years to seventeen years.

Assistance with training came from a variety of sources. The Home Guard did a great deal, providing both instructors and weapons. Equally, local army units often gave help and at a more official level the army provided 'Travelling Wings' of some half dozen officers and N.C.O.'s for instruction and revision sessions. The pre-war Certificate 'A' examination of the O.T.C. was adapted as War Certificate 'A' and became the training aim. Camps were enthusiastically attended and in the summer of 1942 an estimated 100,000 cadets went to camp for a week.

We show a member of the Wiltshire A.C.F. wearing battle-dress. Distinguishing features of cadet uniform included a deep blue backing to the peak flap of the khaki field service cap, also a printed shoulder title with the words CADET FORCE in black on a khaki background. The cap badge of the parent unit was worn, along with slip-on regimental titles of khaki cloth on the shoulder straps. The red star which denoted a pass in Certificate 'A' was worn on the left sleeve.

The background to the picture is the site of Stonehenge.

THE ARMY CADET FORCE - PAST & PRESENT

FORMATION OF THE ARMY CADET FORCE ASSOCIATION

In 1945 the British National Cadet Association changed its name to the Army Cadet Force Association, having spent some considerable time planning to meet the peace time needs of the A.C.F.

Growing in importance was the role of training for citizenship. An equally important factor was the continuation of National Service and the need to offer some form of pre-service training.

Some shrinkage of the A.C.F. took place immediately after the war and there was a further loss of some 100 school units in 1948 when they opted to join the newly organised Combined Cadet Force.

In 1956 the Amery Committee was set up to report on the future organisation and training of the Cadet. The recommendations have provided the basis for all subsequent training with their equal emphasis on the development of character, the introduction of Adventure Training and leadership, and the acquisition of soldierly qualities. The ACF were one of the organisations to join the 'pilot' scheme for the introduction of the Duke of Edinburgh's Award in the same year gave a firm direction to much of the thinking in the report. One important recommendation led to the establishment in 1959 of the Cadet Training Centre at Frimley Park.

ACF ONE HUNDRETH ANNIVERSARY

In 1960 came the centenary celebrations of the Army Cadet Force. Many Parades were held up and down the country when the newly presented Standard of the ACF was presented by His Royal Highness the Duke of Edinburgh

Another highlight of the year1960 was a review of the ACF and CCF in the grounds of Buckingham Palace Majesty the Queen and His Royal Highness, the Duke of Edinburgh.

In the period from 1960 to the mid 1980s some counties had enrolled girl cadets, initially as a pilot scheme, now of course they make as valuable contribution to the success of the Army Cadet Force.

NEW RIFLES INTRODUCED

1986 was a special 'milestone' in our history with the introduction of the L98. A1 Cadet GP Rifle made especially for the Cadet Forces.

The L81A2 Cadet Target Rifle was reintroduced to encourage more target shooting in the Cadet Forces. Initially there were some probems which have now been rectified. There is an ever increasing number of teams who compete at Bisley and Pirbright each year.

THE ARMY CADET FORCE - PAST & PRESENT

1994 saw the replacement of the .303 Bren LMG. This was a much loved weapon by those who were marksmen. It had proved its worth in battle from the North African desert, the jungles of the far East . It was a simple action, easy to strip and clean.

The Light Support Weapon (LSW) is the 5.56 Rifle (SA 80) with refinements making it ideal as the Section Fire Team weapon.

For a number of years Cadets spent their pocket money buying 1958 pattern webbing equipment in order to be up to date with the same appearance as the Regular Army Soldier.

To everyones delight 1958 Pattern webbing equipment was eventually issued to all County ACF's. At first it raised a few problems as the Cadet could put so much in all the different pockets and pouches that they were unable to lift it off the ground. This was solved by introducing sets of scales to check that the weight was under the permitted amount - one quarter of their own body weight.

The illustration of the Royal Irish Ranger Cadet on the next page shows him wearing Barrack Dress. Cadets on parade always looked so smart in their Barrack Dress instead of combat kit, regretfully, however these were withdrawn.

In the year 2002 during an Annual Camp a female cadet was involved in an accident as a result of which she lost her life. As a consequence of this tragic accident questions were asked as to who was responsible for and in charge of the Army Cadet Force.

The short answer was it was unclear at the time and to a great extent each County ACF *did their own thing*. The Ministry of Defence through HQ Land Command officially took over the ACF in the UK.

At about this time TAVRA's (Territorial Army Volunteer Reserves Association) were re-named RF & CA (Reserve Forces & Cadet Association).

Many changes in the movement have been made and it might be said that the ACF is now more professional in its outlook and attitudes due in part to the Health & Safety regulations that have tended to restrict the level of many activities.

Royal Irish Rangers.

In the pre-war years, the authority of the various bodies controlling British cadets did not extend to Northern Ireland. Therefore, apart from some O.T.C. units, there is little early evidence of cadet activity.

The Northern Ireland A.C.F. was formed in January 1943 and organised into battalions of the three Irish infantry regiments; the Cap badge Royal Inniskilling Fusiliers, the Royal Ulster Rifles and the Royal Irish Fusiliers. After the war, cadet units became affiliated to the newly constituted Territorial Army units and a variety of cap badges were worn.

Strengths rose during the fifties with a greater emphasis on adventure training and the Duke of Edinburgh's Award Scheme. In 1968 the detachments affiliated to the three infantry regiments were re-badged to the new combined regiment, the Royal Irish Rangers. Despite the limitations imposed by civil unrest, the A.C.F. in Northern Ireland is thriving and has 79 detachments supervised by 108 officers, 129 adult instructors and the number of cadets exceeds 1,700 cadets.

We show a cadet sergeant in barrack dress. Which was dark green trousers in a strong material. A woolly pullover and stable belt. He wears the distinctive dark green bonnet or caubeen of the Royal Irish Rangers, complete with green hackle. The brassard on his right arm carries an A.C.F. flash in white and green, dark green chevrons and various proficiency badges. In the background is Carrickfergus Castle.

THE ARMY CADET FORCE - PAST & PRESENT

DIRECTION OF THE ACF
INTRODUCTION

This Chapter explains how the Army Cadet Force is directed, organised and supported. It is important for you to have an understanding of this to realise how much is done for you, by whom it is done and the need to for you to make an effort to show how much it is appreciated.

The Charter of the ACF combines two mutually supporting themes - firstly as a youth organisation, designed to help you develop as an individual and a citizen, and secondly for you to identify with and understand the Army, as the ACF is modelled on some of the methods used by the Army.

As a national youth organisation the ACF is represented by the Army Cadet Force Association (ACFA).

The ACF is not a part of the Armed Services in any way.

THE ROLE OF ACFA

The ACFA has three main roles, they are as follows:

1. To direct activities outside military training in which the ACF is involved as a Youth Service. National Sporting events. Duke of Edinburgh's Award. National Shooting Competitions. Commonwealth Cadet Forces.
2. To advise the Ministry of Defence on all matters of policy. This is a very important role on your behalf.
3. To maintain the spirit of the Army Cadet Force throughout the UK, to act very much in the same way as a Regimental Headquarters does.

ACTIVITIES OF THE ACFA

As mentioned in the History of the ACF, the Army Cadet Force Association was formed from the BNCA - the volunteers - who "kept the flag flying" when the government of the day was giving them a difficult time.

As far as the "members" of the ACFA are concerned it is in many respects similar to a Regimental Association, keeping them informed of all that is going on, providing insurance schemes for non military activities.

It is a source of information, that is of course, if you keep in touch by joining the Association and paying your annual subscription.

All Officers and Adult Instructors in the ACF are expected to be members of the ACFA, although anyone can join by writing to the Membership Secretary, **ACFA, Holderness House,5 1-61 Clifton Street,London EC2A 4DW. Email: Editor @armycadets.com.**

THE ARMY CADET FORCE - PAST & PRESENT

ARMY CADET MAGAZINE

As a member of ACFA you will be sent the official magazine of the Army Cadet Force, the ARMY CADET. This always has interesting articles on cadet activities from home and abroad. Ask your Officers or Instructors to show you their copy.

Every Cadet Detachment should receive a copy of the Army Cadet Magazine sent direct to their Detachment.

At the end of every year ACFA produces an Annual Report setting out the different activities in which they have been involved and a report on the general "state" of the ACF throughout the UK.

Also listed are the various committees and the members who serve on them, illustrating the close liaison with the Ministry of Defence to give advice and guidance on the future role and policy for the continued success of the Army Cadet Force.

THE MINISTRY OF DEFENCE (MOD)

The MOD provides the military organisation, equipment and facilities for training and the finance via Reserve Forces & Cadet Associations (RF&CA) to run and administer the Army Cadet Force.

Perhaps one of the most important facility provided by MOD is the Cadet Training Centre, Frimley Park, Nr Camberley, Surrey. The majority of Officers and Adult Instructors will have attended courses at Frimley during their cadet careers.

As a senior Cadet NCO you could also have an opportunity to be a student at Frimley Park.

The MOD also provides the Annual Camp Locations for all the County Army Cadet Forces and the Combined Cadet Forces.

ORGANISATION

The ACF itself is organized on a County basis, other than in the greater London Area where it is divided into four Sectors. In every county the RF&CA (Reserve Forces & Cadet Association) has a County Cadet Committee which is responsible for all cadet business, working through the County Cadet Commandant and Secretary of RF&CA.

The Department of Education and Employment in England and Wales, the Scottish Department of Education and Employment and the Northern Ireland Department of Education also have an interest in the ACF.

The relevant Education Acts have placed on the Minister the general responsibility of seeing that help is given to all voluntary youth organizations.

THE ARMY CADET FORCE - PAST & PRESENT

In the ACF this means that the closest cooperation must exist between the Ministry and the ACF either directly or through the medium of the Standing Conference of Voluntary, Youth Organizations of which ACF is a member.

At County and district levels it means that the same cooperation should exist between County Youth Authority and the corresponding cadet authority. The encouragement, financial help and provision of equipment will, in the case of the ACF be mainly on the sport and citizenship training side.

The ACF is also indebted for help and encouragement to many other adult organizations.

The sporting associations have given solid backing, as have the St John's Ambulance, British Red Cross and the St Andrew's first aid societies, and especially those organizations which have come forward to assist in the development of the Duke of Edinburgh's Award Scheme.

Reserve Forces and Cadet Association (RF&CA)

The RF&CA's on behalf of the MOD look after most of the routine Administration and Logistics of the ARMY CADET FORCE within their Counties.

We are dependent on their help and the history of the Army Cadet Force shows that we were in the same position way back in the 19th century, when the cadets were a part of the Volunteer Battalions of the day, who were the ancestors of the present day Territorial Army.

The RF&CA's have a full time staff at their own County Headquarters. This usually comprises the Secretary who is a retired senior officer from the services, his deputy - also a retired officer, plus a small Administrative Office staff. Their work as far as the ACF is concerned is to look after the property provided for us, from the provision of new premises to the maintenance of existing cadet huts and vehicles used by the ACF.

This in no way means that we should not help to look after our property, as the money available for this is very carefully controlled through a system of grants.

They keep a "watching brief" on how the administration is carried out by the County ACF Headquarters, checking the different accounts where Public Money is being spent, the control of rations, cleaning and maintenance of uniform held in stock, general expenses and many other activities, so, you can see that they have a very important role to play in the smooth running of the administration of ACF in their County.

THE ARMY CADET FORCE - PAST & PRESENT

CADET TRAINING TEAMS

Regular Army provides Cadet Training Teams to "assist Division/
District/Brigade HQ's in the Training of the ACF" they are to:

1. Run courses for Officers and Adults Instructors.
2. Run Courses/Cadres for Senior Cadets.
3. To assist in the conduct of Adult Initial Training Courses and
   Senior Cadet Instructor Courses (4 Star).
4. To assist in the conduct of advanced training for Cadets,
   Adventure and Initiative training, NCO Cadres, Special to Arm.
   Infantry type training and similar activities.
5. To advise the County Cadet Commandant on training matters.
To provide assistance at Annual camps.

Many of the courses are carried out at Annual Camp, when a group
of Officers and Adult Instructors undergo a weeks training as a part
of their Initial Training Course run by the Cadet Training Teams
(CTTs).

Many of the teams members are ex-cadets and therefore have a good
understanding of how the Army Cadet Force functions.

THE COUNTY CADET COMMITTEE

To assist the RF &CA in 'cadet matters' there is a special County
Cadet Committee. The committee members are usually people who
have special interest in and experience of the Cadet Forces in general
within the County.

As an example, the members of the committee usually comprise of
some of the following:

The Secretary of RF&CA, the present County Cadet Commandant,
ex-Cadet Commandants of the County. Commanding Officers of TA
units who have cadets badged to them, the County Cadet Medical
Officer, serving ACF Area/ Battalion/commanders, County Padre,
representative of the County Youth Service, Police, Education:
Headmasters and Headmistresses Associations. Representatives of the
Sea Cadets and the Air Training Corps.

Others may be co-opted for special purposes or dealing with specifice
problems where professional help can be of benefit. Generally those
representing: Sport, Swimming, Shooting, WRVS, and many others all
of who can help in the support of Cadets in the County.

It will be appreciated that the 'spread' of representation will have a
wide influence on the direction of your County, preserving the
reputation of the Army Cadet Force and maintaining the spirit of all
those who serve in it.

THE ARMY CADET FORCE - PAST & PRESENT

ARMY CADET FORCE ASSOCIATION

In carrying out its responsibilities the MOD is assisted in its task by the advice and help of the Army Cadet Force Association. The functions exercised by the ACFA with the approval of the MOD and other Government Departments concerned.

ACFA is the representative body of the ACF membership and the Cadets. Amongst its many 'services' it carries out are the organising of Sports competitions, Shooting at Bisley and Pirbright, DofE Award, First Aid, Bands, The provision of the Army Cadet magazine. The financing of non military events, organising visits by overseas Cadet Forces and visits to forign countries.

ACFA organises the insurance cover for all cadet activities

It goes about its work without making any fuss, yet it has an important role in the promotion of the ACF in many Government Departments and other organisations.

RF&CA STAFF AT COUNTY HQ

In addition RF & CAs employ the full-time staff you will find at your own County Cadet HQ.

The Cadet Executive Officer (CEO) is the senior member of the staff and is accountable for the efficient and proper running of the administration within the county for the Cadet Commandant. This is a very important job and requires a great deal of experience in controlling and accounting for clothing, equipment, weapons, ammunition and on the financial side, for the pay and allowances, rations, Officers Mess and warrant officers and sergeants mess accounts. The CEO is assisted by a staff who take on the jobs of **County Quarter Master (QM)** and **Cadet Administrative Assistants.(CAA)** who visit detachments carrying out routine checks of equipment and security, delivering stores and uniforms.

In most county HQ there is a **Clerical Officer** who is responsible for the efficient running of the office, dealing with the requests for courses, orders, statistics and general office routine.

COUNTY (ACF) STAFF (Volunteers)
THE COUNTY CADET COMMANDANT

Like you the Commandant is a volunteer, and may be an officer who has had many years experience in the Cadet Force or is a retired senior officer from the Regular Army or TA.

They are appointed by the MOD on the recommendation of the County Cadet Committee normally serving for a three year term.

THE ARMY CADET FORCE - PAST & PRESENT

As the Chief Executive officer they are responsible for all matters relating to the ACF in the County

As the leader, they will be involved in the initial selection of potential Officers and Adult Instructors, and their training.

The Commandant will also be be watching the quality of training that the cadets are receiving and the results not only in APC passes, but how, as a result of the many activities the Detachment takes on in support of the community, encouraging the cadets to understand the importance of voluntary work as a part of turning them out as good citizens.

The Cadet Commandant's time is more directed at building an efficient and enthusiastic team of the right people, who put into practice the policies agreed by the County Cadet Committee.

In addition to his/her responsibility for Training and Discipline, which is a responsibility to MOD through the normal military channels, he/she is, of course, expressly nominated as the Commanding Officer of the ACF within his/her County.

THE DEPUTY COUNTY CADET COMMANDANT

Like the Commandant they are appointed by the MOD on the recommendation of the County Cadet Committee. They will 'stand in' on occasions when the Commandant is not available. Very often they take on special responsibilities for the Commandant, such as Discipline of the officers and instructors, planning Special Projects such as fund raising on a large scale, setting up audit boards, organizing `special event' days at Annual Camp and many more.

THE PADRE

The Padre's role is multifunctional. He/She has the obvious responsibility for the religious wellbeing of all cadets, adults and officers of the county/sector regardless of their religious denomination. If you need a 'listening ear' the Padre will provide it; they are there for you at any time - you do not have to go through the 'chain of command' to speak to them. They often help out when there is a shortage of officers or adults. Talk to your Padre whenever you get a chance - they know the right people!

THE COUNTY ADJUTANT

The role of Adjutant in the ACF county is in many instances multivarious. He or she answers directly to the County Commandant. They are usually experienced Cadet Officers who have the ability to forsee problems and take the necessary action to prevent it happening.

THE ARMY CADET FORCE - PAST & PRESENT

Their main occupation is the control and when required to discipline junior officers for 'minor acts of indiscipline'. Traditionally the giving of 'extra duties' is the form of punishment such as visiting the Guardroom in the small hours of the night! Invariably they are not popular, but it is worth keeping on their right side!. They act as the "eyes and ears " of the Commandant.

THE COUNTY TRAINING OFFICER

This job is normally taken on by a senior officer who has had a great deal of experience in training cadets at all levels. Working in close contact with the Commandant, the Training Officer is responsible for ensuring the Commandants Training Programme is met.
They will pay special attention to new Detachments, help new or inexperienced officers and instructors. They are often responsible for arranging adult training, Cadet NCO's Promotion Cadres, and monitoring the APC testing of cadets within the County.They play a large part in drawing up the Annual Camp plans under the guidance of the Cadet Commandant and work in liaison with the CADET TRAINING TEAM (CTT).

THE COUNTY SPORTS OFFICER

Every Detachment should practice some form of sporting activities. The competition between Detachments for the County Championship Cup and all other sporting activities would be the sort of job the County Sports Officer would be responsible for organising. If these competitions are not run then it makes it difficult for a County Teamto be picked from the best players.

DUKE OF EDINBURGH'S AWARD OFFICER

Appointed by the Cadet Commandant as the County D of E Officer. His/her role is to give assistance to Areas and Detachments who have cadets already enrolled in the scheme or helping those who wish to do so, and the training of Officers and Adult Instructors in how to run the scheme with their own cadets in the Detachment. Remember, that if you are a DofE Award holder at the Gold level it is a very valuable asset when you are going forward in your chosen career

COUNTY PUBLIC RELATIONS OFFICER

The County PRO is responsible for the promotion of the ACF in the County and is the main link with all types of media, newspapers, TV and local radio.

THE ARMY CADET FORCE - PAST & PRESENT

They make sure that all items of information are correct so as not to give the wrong message to the public. It is therefore important that any 'hot news' is sent direct to him/her and not communicated to any other sources. Every Detachment should have the telephone number of their PRO clearly shown on their Detachment Notice Board.

THE COUNTY RSM (Regimental Sergeant Major)

The RSM works closely with the Adjutant in maintaining the policies of the Cadet Commandant.

The job of RSM is always seen as setting the standards that make a good County ACF. He/she is the senior Rank amongst the Non Commissioned Officers and is held responsible for the conduct of the members and the running of the Sergeants Mess.

The standard of behaviour, dress and discipline set by the RSM is expected to be followed by all Adult Instructors and Cadets.

He /she does not like anyone wandering across his/her parade ground. If you must cross the parade ground - march smartly.

COUNTY SHOOTING OFFICER

He/she will ensure that ential 'good shots' have access to coaching and range days.

The Shooting Officer also ensures that Companies/Detachments are aware of the various shooting competitions and leads a team of 'coaches' to assist Cadets in the County Shooting Team to shoot in the National Competitions at Bisley and Pirbright.

COUNTY MEDICAL OFFICER

It is most likely that you will only see the Medical Officer whilst at Annual Camp. The MO arranges for his/her MI Room (Medical Inspection) to be set up in Camp. All personnel at Camp who wish to see the MO will attend the MI Room at the appointed times.

The MO is at times supported by members of the Reserve Forces (TA) as part of their Annual Training. You may have an MO who is a serving officer from a Medics Unit or more often the MO is a General Practitioner (GP) from your own County.

ARMY CADET LEAGUES

The Army Cadet Leagues are organised in some Counties across the UK. They have nothing at all to do with the control or direction of the ACF in their respective Counties.

The best way to explain their role is to call them a'Supporters Club' for the Cadets of their County similar to a Regimental Association.

THE ARMY CADET FORCE - PAST & PRESENT

Most Leagues are open to membership from any of those who are interested in supporting their Cadets, some are ex-members of the ACF who continue the friendships formed while in the ACF and many others are also members of the Army Cadet Force Association (ACFA). Any money they do raise is invested and goes into their funds. The interest the funds earn is then made available to provide Detachments with items that the Ministry of Defence do not. Such as sports equipment of all types, helping those Cadets who find it difficult to raise the funds to buy a pair of boots, or who cannot find their Annual Camp fees, etc.

They do not fund any requests to the full amount and expect you to raise half of the costs of whatever project is on hand.

If you have a Cadet League in your County and you can help support them with events they hold to raising funds, so much the better as some Cadet in need of help will benefit from your efforts.

THE ROYAL BRITISH LEGION

Many Cadet Detachments are officially affiliated to their local Branch of the Royal British Legion (RBL). It goes without saying that the important time of the year for the RBL is during the period leading up to Remberance weekend. This is when they raise the most money for their funds and the time they need the most help in collecting it.

Many Cadet Detachments are officially affiliated to their local RBL Branch, is your Detachment one of them?

No doubt you will have someone you know who is a member of RBL Branch in your area. It is a good idea if your Detachment is not Affiliated to RBL if you can invite one of their members to come down to your Detachment and tell you all about what they do for the ex-service men and women of the armed forces. Some of course will have very interesting stories to tell of their exploits when in the services. It will suprise you to know about the amount of support they give to their members in your own community.

There will be occasions when your help would be appreciated and if you are Affiliated to the local Branch this will be a natural request and of great benefit to you and the work of RBL.

Assuming you are taking part, your endeavours within the Duke of Edinburghs Award will be greatly helped by your participation and support for your local RBL Branch.

ACF Officers and Adult Instructors of Affiliated Detachments are invited to become members of the Royal British Legion Branch and have access to their Club facilities.

THE ARMY CADET FORCE - PAST & PRESENT

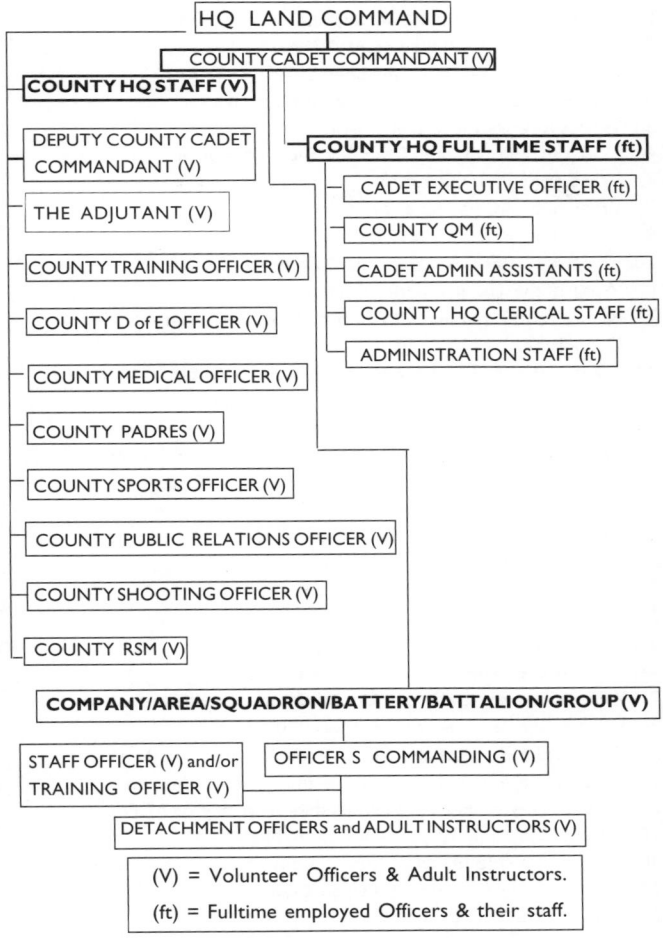

HQ LAND COMMAND

COUNTY CADET COMMANDANT (V)

COUNTY HQ STAFF (V)

DEPUTY COUNTY CADET COMMANDANT (V)

THE ADJUTANT (V)

COUNTY TRAINING OFFICER (V)

COUNTY D of E OFFICER (V)

COUNTY MEDICAL OFFICER (V)

COUNTY PADRES (V)

COUNTY SPORTS OFFICER (V)

COUNTY PUBLIC RELATIONS OFFICER (V)

COUNTY SHOOTING OFFICER (V)

COUNTY RSM (V)

COUNTY HQ FULLTIME STAFF (ft)

CADET EXECUTIVE OFFICER (ft)

COUNTY QM (ft)

CADET ADMIN ASSISTANTS (ft)

COUNTY HQ CLERICAL STAFF (ft)

ADMINISTRATION STAFF (ft)

COMPANY/AREA/SQUADRON/BATTERY/BATTALION/GROUP (V)

STAFF OFFICER (V) and/or TRAINING OFFICER (V)

OFFICER S COMMANDING (V)

DETACHMENT OFFICERS and ADULT INSTRUCTORS (V)

(V) = Volunteer Officers & Adult Instructors.

(ft) = Fulltime employed Officers & their staff.

SELF TEST QUESTIONS

1. What are the TWO supporting themes of the ACF.
2. What are the THREE roles of ACFA.
3. How can you become a member of ACFA.
4. How can you get the Army Cadet Magazine.
5. Who sponsors the Cadet Kit Shop
6. How can you get the Cadet Kit Shop Catalogue.
7. What does MOD stand for.
8. What does ACFA stand for.
9. What does RF&CA stand for.
10. What does RF&CA do for the ACF in the County.
11. What is the County Cadet Committee.
12. Name THREE people who might be on the County Cadet Committee.
13. What is the 'CEO' and who is it in your County.
14. What is the CEO responsible for in the County.
15. Who appoints the County Cadet Commandant.
16. How long is the Commandant's normal "Term of Service".
17. What is your County Commandant's rank and name.
18. What do you know about Frimley Park.
19. Who is your County DofE Officer.
20. What is the Cadet Training Team, what do they do.
21. Who is your County training officer.
22. What is the Email address of Military Pocket Books Ltd
23. Name the members of the Commandants County Staff.
24. What is the name of your County Padre.
25. What is the name of your County Shooting Officer.
26. What is the name of your County PRO.
27. What is the name of the CO of your Affiliated TA Regt/Corps.
28. What is the Army Cadet League, and what do they do.
29. Where will you find the Membership Secretary of ACFA
30. What is the name of your County RSM.
31. What is the role of an Adjutant, who does he/she answer to.
32. Where is your local British Legion Club.
33. Who are the members of the Royal British Legion.

Chapter 3

PERSONAL TURNOUT & DRILL

CLOTHING

Unlike many youth organisations, your uniform is issued to you free of charge. This costs a great deal of money to provide all Cadets with uniforms and carry stocks for exchanges. Please take care of it; keep it clean, pressed and in good repair. You will have been given instruction on its care in basic training.

"Sloppy Uniform, Sloppy Cadet"!

THE BRASSARD

The Brassard is worn in Jersey and Shirt Sleeve Orders only.

The Brassard is difficult to keep clean; it can be dry cleaned, but has to be treated with care. The ironing/pressing can be done in several ways, check with your Detachment Adults on the correct method for your County.

Badges of Achievement

The following badges and insignia may be sewn on. **Do not stick them on with glue.**

- Badges of rank and chevrons in white tape
- APC (ACF) Star badge at top right
- Not more than four Proficiency/Skill at Arms badges taking precedence from top left

Exchanges: You have ripped your combats on the weekend training exercise. There is a system for exchanging uniform, find out what to do about it.

Hints for Pressing Uniform

- Check the label; do not get your iron too hot.
- When ironing trousers or skirts, use an old tea towel (not terry toweling) as a pressing cloth. If using a steam iron, do not damp the cloth.
- Place the cloth on the item you are ironing, apply the iron.
- Don't be tempted to apply any substance to your trousers in order to have a 'permanent' knife-edge crease – it can go horribly wrong.

REMEMBER: DO NOT WEAR YOUR UNIFORM WITHOUT PERMISSION FROM YOUR DETACHMENT COMMANDER UNLESS YOU ARE ON CADET DUTIES

PERSONAL TURNOUT AND DRILL

THE BRASSARD

The brassard is a separate detachable sleeve shaped to the contours of the upper arm from the point of the shoulder to just above the elbow. It is secured at two points, at the point of the shoulder and at the lower end of the upper arm.

It is difficult to keep clean, it can be dry cleaned, but has to be treated with care. The ironing/pressing of the Brassard can be done in several ways according to the instructions that a County may give.
Brassard - Badges of Achievement.
The simplest method is to lay it out flat and carefully iron it with a WARM IRON, not to scorch it. It is worn in Jersey and Shirt Sleeve Orders only and the following badges and insignia may be sewn on to it.

Embroidered ACF shoulder titles County insignia or tartan patch Badges of rank, and chevrons in white tape.
Not more than 4 embroidered proficiency/Skill at Arms badges taking precedence from the top right, where the APC(ACF) star will be sewn, to top left to bottom right to bottom left.

THE BACK OUTSIDE COVER OF THIS BOOK ILLUS-TRATES THE BADGES OF ACHIEVEMENT YOU MAY EARN AS A MEMBER OF THE ARMY CADET FORCE

PERSONAL TURNOUT AND DRILL

EXTRA ESSENTIAL KIT

BOOTS

A pair of black regulation boots. Make sure they fit you correctly, too small; they will hurt and damage your feet too large; you will keep falling over.

Care and Cleaning of Boots

There are different ideas about how clean your boots should be. It is most likely that you will only have one pair and they will have to be worn for all your Cadet activities. It is almost impossible to wear them on exercise one day and have them fit for a Drill Competition the next! Most Counties have a common sense approach; they plan their activities to give the Cadets time to smarten their boots for a special parade.

What is most important is to make sure they fit you comfortably and are kept in good repair. The laces should be removed to thoroughly clean and polish your boots, make sure you lace them with the laces straight across the eyelet holes, not crossing over them. Should your boots get wet, do not dry them in front of a fire or over heat. It will make the leather hard and brittle, thus letting water in. It helps to stuff newspaper inside to absorb the wet/damp, replacing it after a couple of hours with dry paper. Always carry a spare pair of laces

Socks: Do not make the mistake of wearing 'normal' socks with your boots. You will soon find that they rub your feet, perhaps even cause blisters. Good thick wool or cotton mix boot socks will help cushion your feet and absorb moisture. It is suggested that you have a minimum of two pairs. If you are on exercise and space is limited, a pair of socks will last for two days (if they do not get wet), by turning them inside out for the second day.

DESIRABLE KIT

Although not essential, the following list could solve some Birthday present problems!

PERSONAL TURNOUT AND DRILL

Webbing: Most Detachment stores have supplies of '58 pattern webbing, the newer issue can be purchased through the many retail outlets, but it is quite expensive.

Rucksack: Ensure that it is comfortable to wear and is not too big for your height.

Knife, Fork and Spoon set: Useful to have, particularly if they all fit together

Mess Tins: Ensure that you mark them with your name or a distinguishing mark.

Sleeping Bag: As good a quality as you can afford. Make sure that it is washable.

Sleeping Bag Liner: Very useful particularly if you do not have your own sleeping bag.

Bungees elastic supports for bivies.

Compass: A Silva or Sunto Compass (degrees) and a Pathfinder Protractor/Romer

PERSONAL TURNOUT
MALES

* Face clean and shaved if necessary
* Hair not over the collar or ears, sideburns not below bottom of ears.
* Clothes clean, washed
* Personal hygiene, washing, clean nails, clean socks in good condition.

FEMALES

* **Hair:** If your hair is long enough to put up NEATLY, then do so. Try to keep your hair from 'falling' as it can be a problem on exercise or the ranges. Do not wear fancy hair slides, bobbles or fancy scrunchies.

* **Earrings:** ONE pair of plain studs. It is advisable to remove them whilst on exercise, to prevent loss.

General
Body Piercing

It is your personal choice whether you have body piercing. However, for your safety, these should be either removed whilst in uniform, or covered securely with a sticking plaster. There is a real danger of these piercings being caught or becoming infected whilst undertaking most cadet activities.

PERSONAL TURNOUT AND DRILL

Rings: One signet ring is acceptable, but 'Rings on every finger' does not look right when in uniform. There is also a possibility they may slip off during an exercise or getting caught when weapon cleaning.

Neck Chains and Bracelets: Should not be worn when in uniform, unless they are Medic Alert or similar.

PAYING COMPLIMENTS

Saluting – Origin and information

The salute with the hand, the present arms and salute with the sword were methods by which a person paying a compliment could show the person to whom the compliment was paid that no offence was meant. They were all gestures symbolic of loyalty and trust.

- You will be trained how to salute smartly and correctly
- It is discipline that you salute smartly when you meet an Officer
- If an Officer fails to return the salute, it is bad manners on their part.

THE QUEENS COMMISSION

All compliments derive their origin from the Sovereign, to whom the highest compliment, the Royal Salute, is paid. All Officers of the Army Cadet Force hold the Queens Commission, and when an Officer is saluted it is in recognition of the Queens Commission held in trust by that Officer.

Ask one of your Officers to bring their Commission Paper along for you to see. It is written on parchment paper, signed and sealed by Her Majesty The Queen.

When Compliments are paid:

THE NATIONAL ANTHEM

When on parade, stand to attention, **only** Officers and Warrant Officers salute, NCOs will if in charge of a party.

When **not** on parade, but in **uniform,** all ranks **will** salute. When not on parade, and in **plain clothes**, all ranks will stand to attention. If a hat is worn, it will be removed (**Females do not remove hats**).

STANDARDS GUIDONS AND COLOURS

As a squad on the march you will give an 'Eyes Left' or 'Right'.

As an individual, you halt; face passing Standards, Guidons or Colours.

PERSONAL TURNOUT AND DRILL

ARMY CADET FORCE BANNER

The Banner, presented by HRH The Duke of Edinburgh, is dedicated, but not consecrated; it does not rank as a Colour, Standard or Guidon. It will be accorded the respect of a Colour except that:
1. Individuals or parties of Cadets passing will not salute it.
2. When Banner passes, individual or parties stand to attention.
3. When taken over, individual taking it will salute first.

INTRODUCTION TO DRILL

Through history, British Army Drill has been the foundation upon which discipline; teamwork, pride and pageant have all taken equal part.

In the days of the 'Brown Bess' musket, when in battle, the infantry formed a square in their three ranks in order to give effective firepower.

This action was carried out as a drill, taught and practiced on the barrack square. The discipline required to 'hold the line' was the difference between defeat and victory. Drill parades were hard and rigorous, with harsh violence dished out by the instructors.

Times have changed, the Regular Army still rely on drill to build team spirit and to train the soldiers' mind to respond to orders given in the quickest possible time.

When you are first introduced to Drill Commands, you may find that your reactions are slow and mistakes easily made. Fortunately your initial lessons are all completed at the 'Halt' i.e. stood still. It is difficult enough to stand still, especially when there is a fly walking down your nose – no matter, stand still! Once you have mastered the initial movements and been taught how to march without your arms moving in the wrong order, you will suddenly find it all comes together, your squad starts to move as a team. It will probably feel even better when you take part in a Civic or Cadet Sunday Parade. You will be with the rest of your Detachment, smartly turned out and marching behind a band. It might sound odd to those of you who have not attended such Parades, but it gives you a real 'Buzz' and dare it be said, pride in your Detachment and the Army Cadet Force. (Particularly if your family and friends are watching!)

PERSONAL TURNOUT AND DRILL

PAYING COMPLIMENTS –
Saluting to the front: Common Faults.

1. Body and head not remaining erect, shoulders back.
2. Allowing the Right elbow to come forward.
3. Right hand not straight, not in the correct position, wrist not straight and thumb not straight.
4. Allowing the Left arm to creep forward.
5. Left fist not clenched with the thumb in front and in line with seam of trousers. Arm not tight in to the side.

As an aid to good saluting, remember your right hand – with the palm flat, thumb on top, travels the "Longest way up" and the "Shortest way down".

Having saluted, clench your fist, smartly cutting your arm down to your side, keeping the thumb to the front ready to align with the seam of your trousers.

THE UNION FLAG

PERSONAL TURNOUT AND DRILL

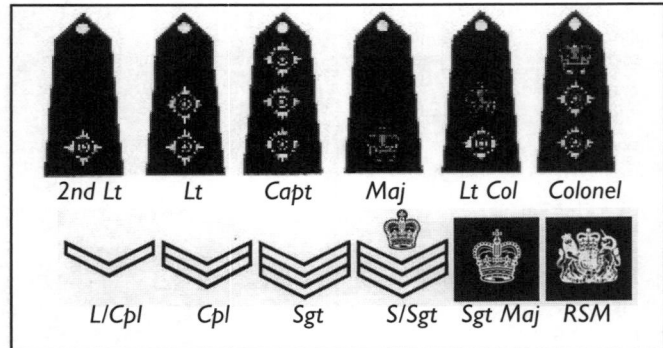

2nd Lt   Lt   Capt   Maj   Lt Col   Colonel

L/Cpl   Cpl   Sgt   S/Sgt   Sgt Maj   RSM

BADGES OF RANK
DRILL – INTRODUCTORY WORDS OF COMMAND

Used for Squad Drill Good instructors give INTRODUCTORY words of command giving warning of what the next word of command is to be.

Many instructors do not do this; the result is the squad turning in different directions at the same time!

Before moving a squad in any direction, the instructor indicates what direction they intend to move them by using an INTRODUCTORY word of command, before giving the actual command to execute the order. As a member of the squad, this does give you the time to work out the direction of your next move.

Look at the diagram. Turn it sideways as if you were standing in the center of the front rank of the 'squad', facing the same direction as the arrow pointing to 'ADVANCING'. The words of command you should be given to move the squad in any particular direction are as shown in the diagram. Suggest you enlarge this page by photocopy or scan and put it up on your bedroom wall - you will be ace at Drill.

PERSONAL TURNOUT AND DRILL

Timing of Words of Command
The table at the end of this chapter shows on what foot the executive word of command is given.

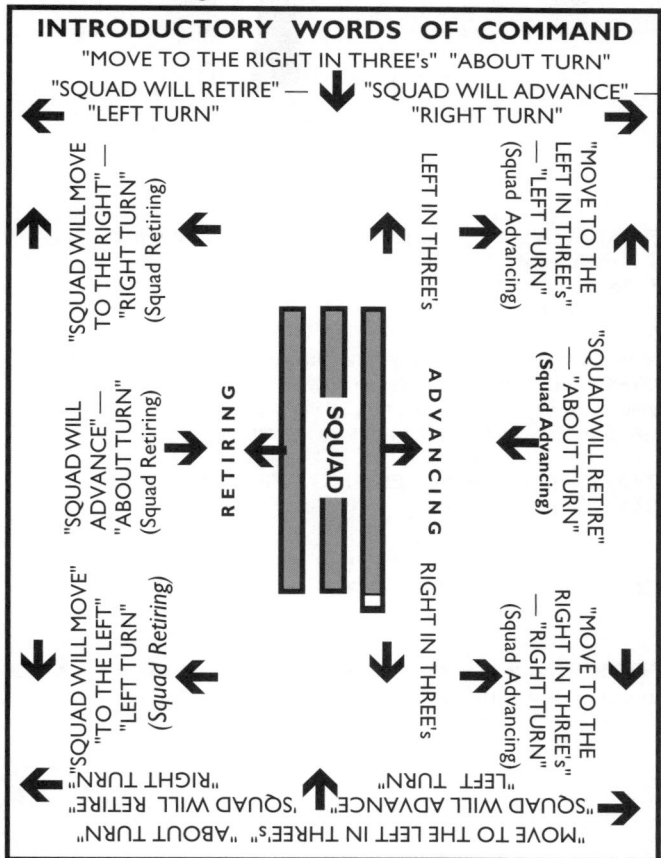

INTRODUCTORY WORDS OF COMMAND

"MOVE TO THE RIGHT IN THREE's"   "ABOUT TURN"

"SQUAD WILL RETIRE" —   "SQUAD WILL ADVANCE" —
"LEFT TURN"   "RIGHT TURN"

LEFT IN THREE's

"MOVE TO THE LEFT IN THREE's" — "LEFT TURN" (Squad Advancing)

"SQUAD WILL MOVE TO THE RIGHT" "RIGHT TURN" (Squad Retiring)

"SQUAD WILL RETIRE" — "ABOUT TURN" (Squad Advancing)

RETIRING   SQUAD   ADVANCING

"SQUAD WILL ADVANCE" — "ABOUT TURN" (Squad Retiring)

"MOVE TO THE RIGHT IN THREE's" — "RIGHT TURN" (Squad Advancing)

"SQUAD WILL MOVE TO THE LEFT" "LEFT TURN" (Squad Retiring)

RIGHT IN THREE's

"MOVE TO THE LEFT IN THREE's"   "ABOUT TURN"

"SQUAD WILL RETIRE"   "SQUAD WILL ADVANCE"
"RIGHT TURN"   "LEFT TURN"

PERSONAL TURNOUT AND DRILL

CHANGING DIRECTION - WHEELING ON THE MARCH

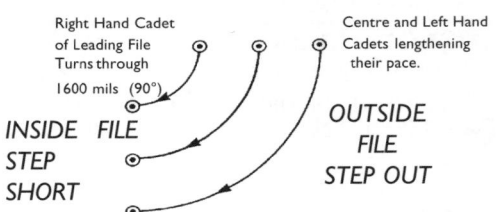

Right Hand Cadet of Leading File Turns through 1600 mils (90°)

Centre and Left Hand Cadets lengthening their pace.

INSIDE FILE STEP SHORT

OUTSIDE FILE STEP OUT

The term "Step Short" means reduce the length of your pace, "Step out" means slightly lengthen your pace.

By doing this while Wheeling you keep your Dressing in each file as it changes direction.

A common fault when giving the "Left or Right Wheel" is for the command to be given sharply, when in fact it should be drawn out - "WHEE-EEL", allowing the files to slowly change direction, keeping their dressing in three's. You must glance out of the corner of your eyes to check your dressing, not turning your head.

MARCHING AND DRESSING OFF

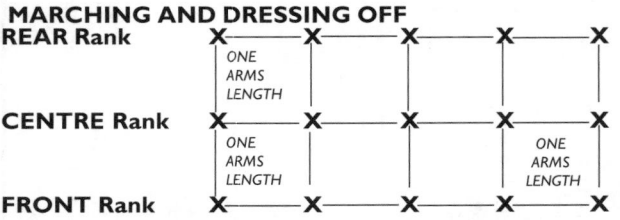

REAR Rank

CENTRE Rank

FRONT Rank

ONE ARMS LENGTH

ONE ARMS LENGTH

DIAGRAM OF A SQUAD IN CLOSE ORDER, CORRECTLY DRESSED AND COVERED OFF FROM LEFT TO RIGHT, AND FROM FRONT RANK - TO REAR.

PERSONAL TURNOUT AND DRILL

TEACHING DRILL

The aims of Drill are:

1. To produce a Cadet who has self respect, is alert and obedient
2. To provide the basis for teamwork

Drill is exacting and strict attention to detail must be observed. You will need the following qualities to become an excellent Drill Instructor.

1. PATIENCE. Never lose your temper.

2. ENTHUSIASM. You must fire your squad with a will to achieve.

3. CONSISTENCY. Set yourself and the squad a high standard and do not deviate from it.

4. HUMANITY. Understand the squad's problems; praise readily, do not become over familiar or humiliate individual members of your squad.

5. PERSONALITY. As a drill instructor you must impress your squad – always have them under control, lead by example:

When demonstrating, be accurate; never exaggerate a drill movement. If the movement is with a rifle use that article and nothing else. Never use bad language and sarcasm; it is the sign of a poor instructor. Ensure that your words of command are clear, DO NOT do as some drill instructors, create your own 'drill language', it is bad practice.

THE WORDS OF COMMAND

All words of command must be clear and powerful; the way in which they are given affects the reaction that they inspire. Words of command are divided into three parts:

1. INTRODUCTORY. This tells the squad what movement they are about to carry out, e.g. "MOVE TO THE RIGHT IN THREES".

2. CAUTIONARY. The drawn out and loud reminder to the squad, e.g. R –I – G – H – T.

3. EXECUTIVE. The high-pitched sharp command "TURN".

Sometimes there is no need for an *INTRODUCTORY* word of command, e.g. **"SQUAD – SHUN"**. Occasionally there is no *CAUTIONARY*, E.G. **"FORWARD"**.

The cautionary word of command should be consistently drawn out over about the equivalent of **Four paces** in quick time. There should be a pause between it and the executive word of command.

PERSONAL TURNOUT AND DRILL

There should be a pause between it and the executive word of command of:

1. At the Halt – the regulation pause.

2. In Quick Time – about four paces

3. In Slow Time – about three paces.

DEVELOP YOUR WORD OF COMMAND

The following information will help you develop good voice control. Practice whenever you can.

Explanation. Many drill instructors end up with sore throats after a prolonged drill practice. This may well be because they do not use their lungs correctly.

It is important to breathe in through your nose and take your breath 'right down to your stomach'. In other words, learn to breathe deeply. When giving a word of command, 'push' the air out.

Do not forget to stand to attention when giving commands. Standing with your feet apart or leaning backwards may result in straining your groin. KEEP YOUR WEIGHT FORWARD AND YOUR FEET TOGETHER.

Have your head up, looking directly at your squad; when giving the word of command AIM your voice straight over the squad.

Giving Words of Command.

Giving a Cautionary or preliminary word of Command you have to pitch your voice on the same note to ensure that it does not 'tail away' at the end. It must be short and sharp, "SQD". Then comes the Executive word of command, equally short and sharp, "SHUN".

It is most important to develop the correct method of delivering commands; nothing is worse than a poor drill instructor. If you really cannot do it properly, leave it to someone who can.

Words of Command.

They must be pronounced CLEARLY. It is not just a sound. A quick tightening of the stomach muscles so that the word comes out quick, short and higher in pitch than the Cautionary produces the Executive word of command. Ensure that there is a pause between the

PERSONAL TURNOUT AND DRILL

Cautionary and the Executive. Failure to do this may result in the squad anticipating the word of command, thus the whole purpose of drill is lost – and chaos will reign!

Note: Use your mouth; the wider open it is, the louder the sound!

To summarise:

Power: plenty of air into the lungs.

Pitch: Hold your head high and pitch the word of command high over the   Squad.

Punch: Given quickly by tightening the stomach muscles.

Pronunciation: Make your words CLEAR. LOUD and AS AN ORDER.

Communication Drill

1. First demonstrate to the squad all words of command at the halt, including rifle drill.

2. Then "conduct" the squad while they give elementary words of command; insisting on clarity and power from each cadet.

3. Divide the squad in to two ranks, place them about 25 metres apart, with 5 paces interval between each cadet.

4. Each cadet should now drill his/her opposite number 25 metres away without regard to those to the left or right of them.

5. After no more than ten minutes, change the ranks, so that the cadets in both ranks have a chance of controlling their opposite number.

Mutual Drill

Form the squad into three ranks and explain the introductory word of command and which is the DIRECTING FLANK.

Call out each member of the squad in turn to drill the squad and then call out another member of the squad to watch and be prepared to comment on his/her performance.

Note:

1. Be patient and make encouraging comments.

2. When correcting, be sure you address your remarks to the whole squad, they can all learn by one cadet's mistakes.

PERSONAL TURNOUT AND DRILL

AIDS TO BETTER DRILL

Calling out the time

All cadets in their early stages of training should call out the time of their Drill movements so that:

Every member of the squad has the regulation pause fixed in their head.

The squad learns to act together, building team spirit.

The squad should call out the words for a given movement.

They must learn to be still when calling out **"TWO THREE"** for the regulation pause.

When you can see your cadets improving, select individuals to call out the time for the whole squad. It helps to build the confidence of the more junior cadets.

TIMING AND PACE

All Instructors should know the rates of marching, measured in the number of paces taken in a minute, the length of the pace being taken, measured in inches/mm and the timings of both foot and arms drill. The recognised measurements are set out below.

However, it must be remembered that these are for grown adults NOT Cadets, therefore some allowance must be made as and when required.

RATES OF MARCHING

RATE	PACES TO MINUTE
1. Quick Time (normal)	116
2. Quick Time (Recruits)	up to 140
3. Quick Time (Light Infantry and Green Jackets Regt).	140
4. Slow Time (Normal)	65
5. Slow Time (Light Infantry and Green Jackets Regt).	70
6. Double Time	180

RATE OF MARCHING	LENGTHS OF PACE
1. Quick and Slow Time	30 inches (76 cm)
2. Stepping Out	33 inches (84cm)
3. Stepping Short	21 inches (54cm)
4. Double Time	40 inches (102cm)
5. Side Pace	12 inches (31cm)

PERSONAL TURNOUT AND DRILL

DEFINITIONS

Alignment – A straight line on which a body of Cadets is formed or is to form.

Covering - The act of placing yourself directly behind another body.

Depth - The space occupied by a body of Cadets from front to rear.

Distance - The space between Cadets or bodies from front to rear.

Dressing - The act of aligning oneself with and covering others within a body of Cadets.

File - (a) Either two or three Cadets of different ranks who are covering each other, or (b) A body of Cadets in two ranks facing a Flank.

Single File – Cadets one behind another on a frontage of one at normal marching distance.

Blank File - A file in which there is no center and rear Cadet, or no centre Cadet, due to the inequality of numbers within a body of Cadets.

Flank – Either side of a body of Cadets as opposed to its front or rear.

Directing Flank - The flank by which a body of Cadets takes its dressing.

Frontage - The extent of ground covered laterally by a body of Cadets, measured from flank to flank.

Interval – The lateral space measured between Cadets or bodies of Cadets on the same alignment.

Line – Cadets formed in the same alignment.

Markers – Cadets employed to mark points on which a movement is to be directed, or by which a formation or alignment is to be regulated.

Order (Close or Open) - The distance between ranks in line, which is either thirty inches or sixty inches depending on circumstances.

Rank – A line of Cadets side by side. (i.e. 'Front Rank').

Supernumerary Rank – the extra rank, fourth rank in three ranks, or third in two ranks, formed by the senior NCOs of a body of Cadets.

A Squad – Means a sub – unit formed for Drill and is used throughout to avoid explanations.

A REGULATION PAUSE. Refers to the short pause between two movements of drill, which is the equivalent of two marching paces in quick time, i.e. Forty movements to the minute.

SOME GUIDING PRINCIPALS FOR PARADES

A parade should always start with an inspection of all who are on it. Strict observance of rank should be shown; therefore an Officer, Adult

PERSONAL TURNOUT AND DRILL

Instructor or a Cadet, when they wish to either join or leave the parade, should report to the senior rank and ask permission to do so. Cadets should not walk across a parade ground when drill, in which they are not taking part, is taking place.

Those who are to command it should plan the form and purpose of a parade beforehand and ensure all participants are made aware of it.

At the end of a parade all ranks "Dismiss" to show respect to the senior rank present.

Having been dismissed from a parade, march smartly off the parade ground without stopping for a "Chat".

"Always be five minutes early rather than five minutes late"

PERSONAL TURNOUT AND DRILL

TABLE FOR TIMING WORDS OF COMMAND

WORD OF COMMAND	QUICK TIME (WHEN GIVEN)	SLOW TIME (WHEN GIVEN)	WHAT THE SQUAD CALL OUT	REMARK
"HALT!" (Marching)	On the Left foot	Left foot passes right.	"ONE, TWO"	
"QUICK (or SLOW) MARCH"	"QUICK!" and "SLOW!" both given on the left foot. "MARCH" both on the Right foot (ON SUCCESSIVE FEET)			
"RIGHT—TURN!" (incline)	As Left Heel Strikes ground	Right foot about to touch ground		"LEFT -TURN vice -versa
"ABOUT—TURN!"	As Right Heel strikes ground	Just before the Right foot reaches ground	Quick Time)"IN, LEFT, RIGHT, LEFT, FORWARD (Slow Time) "ONE STOP, TWO STOP, THREE STOP, FORWARD!"	
"MARK - TIME"	Over complete Left pace.	Over complete Right pace	(Quick Time) "IN"	
"HALT!" "FORWARD" (Marking Time)	Left knee fully raised	Right Knee fully raised		

3-17

PERSONAL TURNOUT AND DRILL

TABLE FOR TIMING WORDS OF COMMAND

WORD OF COMMAND	QUICK TIME (WHEN GIVEN)	SLOW TIME (WHEN GIVEN)	WHAT THE SQUAD CALLOUT	REMARKS
"CHANGE STEP!" (Marching and Marking Time)		"CHANGE!" on the left foot. "STEP!" on the right foot. (On successive feet)	(Marching) "LEFT, RIGHT LEFT!" (Marking time) "LEFT, LEFT, RIGHT!"	
"BREAK INTO QUICK TIME, QUICK - MARCH!"		"QUICK!" on the left foot. "MARCH!" on the right foot. (On successive feet)		
"BREAK INTO SLOW TIME, SLOW - MARCH !"	On right foot.			
"OPEN (CLOSE) ORDER!"	Over complete right pace.			
"SALUTING! EYES RIGHT" (Marching)	On LEFT foot	On RIGHT foot	(Quick time) " ONE, TWO, THREE, FOUR, FIVE, DOWN, SWING!"	
"SALUTING!" 1. To the front marching 2. As on sentry.	On the Left foot			

Note: For all movements of foot and arms drill at the halt in which there is more than one part the squad will call out "ONE! TWO, THREE, ONE!"   Moving only as they call "ONE!"

PERSONAL TURNOUT AND DRILL

SELF TEST QUESTIONS

1. What are the origins of paying compliments – Saluting?
2. How do you tell if a squad is advancing or retiring?
3. On what foot is the HALT given?
4. What does a DIRECTING FLANK mean?
5. Given the preliminary word of command, "Squad will retire", is the squad 'advancing' or 'retiring'?
6. When wheeling in a squad who 'steps short' and why?
7. What do you understand by a "INTRODUCTORY" word of command?
8. At "Close Order" what is the distance between ranks?
9. Marking time, the HALT is given when the knee is …..?
10. What six qualities are required of a good Drill Instructor?
11. What is meant by "Words of Action"?
12. What are the three stages in giving a Word of Command?
13. What is Communication Drill?
14. Cautionary Words of Command should be drawn out – Why?
15. What is Mutual Drill carried out for?
16. What are the reasons for calling out time in Drill?
17. What do you understand about "Dressing"?
18. What are Markers called out for?
19. What causes a "Blank File" in a squad?
20. What do you understand by a Regulation Pause?
21. Leaving or joining a parade, what should you do?
22. What is important about the position of your head when giving a command?
23. What have the Four "P"s to do with drill?
24. What does "Keeping your Dressing" mean?
25. What does it mean when you are given the order, "By the Left"?
26. How much does your uniform cost you when you join the ACF.
27. Which shoulder do you wear your brassard.
28. How are the badges fixed on the brasard.
29. How do you lace up a pair of boots - crossing over or straight across.
30. What is the best way to dry out very wet boots.

PERSONAL TURNOUT AND DRILL

31. What are the best type of socks to wear with your boots.
32. List the items of kit that are desirable to have.
33. Name the important points on Personal Turnout, male/female.
34. When are compliments paid and by whom.
35. When the National Anthem is played who salutes.
36. What is it relating to "the longest way up and shortest way down"
37. When saluting at the 'halt' what is the position of the left thumb.
38. When do you step short
39. What is the 'Aim' of drill.
40. Words of command are divided into three parts. What are they.
41. Why do some drill instructors finish up with sore throats.
42. In Quick Time what is the normal number of paces per minute.
43. What is the advantage of a Drill Squad calling out the time.
44. What is a 'Regulation Pause' and how long is it.
45. When' on parade' what will an inspecting officer be looking for.

Chapter 4

FIELDCRAFT

Introduction

Fieldcraft is the one subject that always gets you and your 'mates' to turn out in strength, especially if it says on the programme that it is an Escape and Evasion exercise, and if it's at night - so much the better. We are not suggesting that all cadets still like playing 'cowboys and Indians', but may be Field Craft could be described as organised cowboys and Indians!

If you live in a city/town you are at some disadvantage to see Field craft in action, however, if you are able to get into the countryside or live in or near it, you will be aware that the wild life 'get a living' off the land by being experts in the use of their skills of: stealth, patience, speed and fitness, stamina, planning and cunning and being natural experts at camouflage and concealment.

NATURAL SKILLS

Fieldcraft is their prime skill in catching their food and to be good at Fieldcraft you could do no better in many ways than to study wildlife at every opportunity.

Observe how a cat stalks its quarry, how the Sparrow Hawk hovers patiently, observing the right moment to drop in on the Field Mouse; the Fox who uses the hedgerows to move from one field to another, see how well a Rabbit is camouflaged against the ground, all of these examples are types of Individual Field Craft skills exercised for the purpose of either defence or attack.

In your case, having knowledge of Fieldcraft brings together and practices some of the skills required to achieve your APC 1 to 4 Star not only as an individual, but also as a member of a team or section. As Cadets you should normally work only at SECTION LEVEL, and for you to understand where a Section 'fits into' the organisation of an Infantry Battalion we set out on the next page a diagram showing the outline organisation of an Infantry Battalion and how the Section fits into it.

FIELDCRAFT

Outline Organisation of an Infantry Battalion

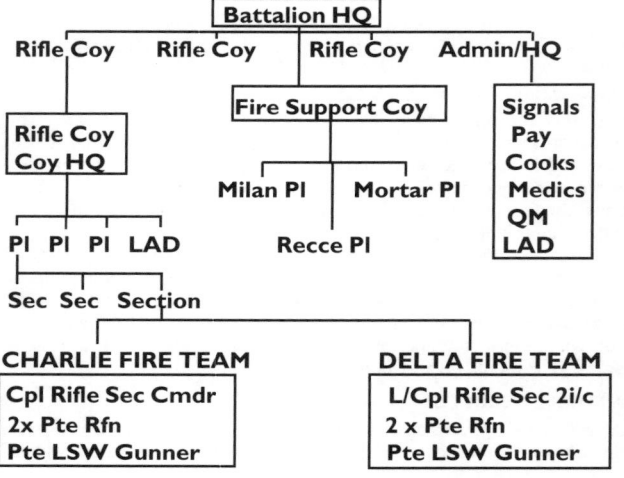

SECTION ORGANISATION

The normal fighting strength of a Section in the Regular Army is two NCO's and six men, but it can operate with one NCO and five men. The Rifle and the LSW are the main weapons of the Section. The Riflemen can be divided into smaller groups to provide better "fire and movement" capability.

The LSW provides support for the movement of the Section especially in the assault.

FIELDCRAFT

INDIVIDUAL FIELDCRAFT

Once you have an understanding of the need to imitate those skills that wild life practice to survive in the field, then you will be on the way to attaining an acceptable standard of Individual Fieldcraft. You need to be mentally alert, physically fit, and have a lot of practice and patience, to develop the natural ability to react instinctively to any given situation, both as an individual and as a member of a group.

As an NCO Fieldcraft gives you the opportunity to control and direct your section under field conditions, you must be expert at Individual Fieldcraft to command a Section.

METHODS OF JUDGING DISTANCE

WHY JUDGE DISTANCE: if you can judge distance you will know the approximate area in which to look when given an order. If your sights are not correctly adjusted, your shots will probably miss the target.

USE A UNIT OF MEASURE

100 metres is a good unit, The Range is marked out at 100 metre intervals.

A Full Size Football pitch is about 100 metres long.

DO NOT USE THE UNIT OF MEASURE METHOD OVER 400 METRES IF YOU CAN'T SEE ALL THE GROUND BETWEEN YOU AND THE TARGET.

REMEMBER

Things seem closer .. In bright light, if they are bigger than their surroundings, if there is dead ground between you and them, if they are higher up than you.

Further away ... With sun in your eyes, in bad light. When smaller than surroundings.

Looking across a valley, down a street or along a path in a wood, if you are lying down.

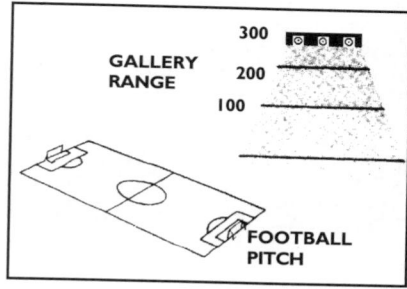

FIELDCRAFT

JUDGING DISTANCE

When you know what 100 metres looks like, practice fitting your Unit of Measure between you and your target.

AIDS TO JUDGING DISTANCE
APPEARANCE METHOD

By noting what a person looks like at a set distance, you can then use the Appearance Method

Common objects may also be used for this method.

FIELDCRAFT

Things seem closer

Further away

REMEMBER things seem closer .. in bright light, if they are bigger than their suroundings, if there is dead ground between you and them, if they are higher up than you.

Further away .. With sun in your eyes, in bad light,. When smaller than surroundings. Looking across a valley, down a street or along a path in a wood, if you are lying down.

AIDS TO JUDGING DISTANCE
If the range to one object is known, estimate the distance from it to the target.

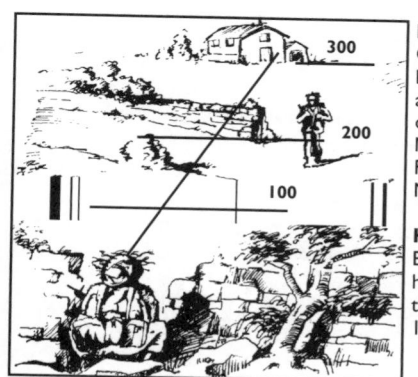

BRACKETING
Calculate mid-distance between nearest possible and furthest possible distance of target.
Nearest - 100
Farthest - 300.
Mid-distance - 200

HALVING
Estimate the distance halfway to the target then double it:
100 x 2 = 200

FIELDCRAFT

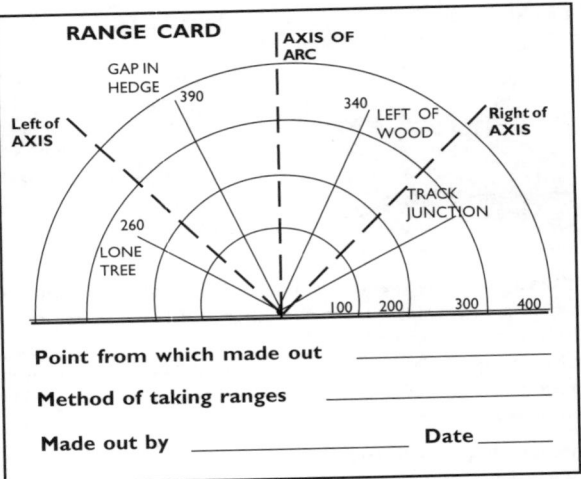

RANGE CARD

Point from which made out _____

Method of taking ranges _____

Made out by _____ Date _____

THE SMALL ARMS RANGE CARD

Range Cards are to be prepared whenever a position is occupied for more than 30 minutes or more.

Section and Platoon Commanders are responsible for ensuring the Range Card is made out accurately.

A Range Card must be made out for every position and should be passed on to the next occupant who must check its accuracy.

A printed Range Card is available on the 24 hour Ration Pack boxes, these should be retained and used when required.

When making out your Range Cards you will apply all the skills of Judging Distance and as a result improve your accuracy better than most.

.

FIELDCRAFT

PERSONAL CAMOUFLAGE AND CONCEALMENT

The enemy is looking for you so - don't make it easy.
Merge with your surroundings

| TOO MUCH | JUST RIGHT | TOO LITTLE |

LOSE YOUR SHAPE
Make sure nothing shines.
Blend in with your surroundings - if they vary, so must you.

AVOID SKYLINES

Stand back from windows - merge into the shadows - don't lean out you will be seen.

FIELDCRAFT

Don't use isolated cover - it stands out.

SOMETHING IS SEEN BECAUSE ITS:-

Shape
Shadow
Silhouette
} **FAMILIAR OR STANDS OUT**

Surface
Spacing
Movement
} **DIFFERENT FROM ITS SURROUNDINGS**

SEEING IS .... Noticing details.

EASY TO SEE   **DIFFICULT TO FIND**
SHAPE ...... Disguise your shape - including equipment
and weapons.

4 - 8

FIELDCRAFT

SHADOW .... Keep in the shadows

SILHOUETTE .... Don't skyline

SURFACE..... Don't differ from your surroundings.

FIELDCRAFT

SPACING... Keep spread out - but not equally spaced.

MOVEMENT .... Move carefully - slowly when concealed - sudden movement will attract attention.

**Look through cover - if possible - not round it .
You MUST SEE without being SEEN.**

TARGET RECOGNITION

The correct target must be located and fired at

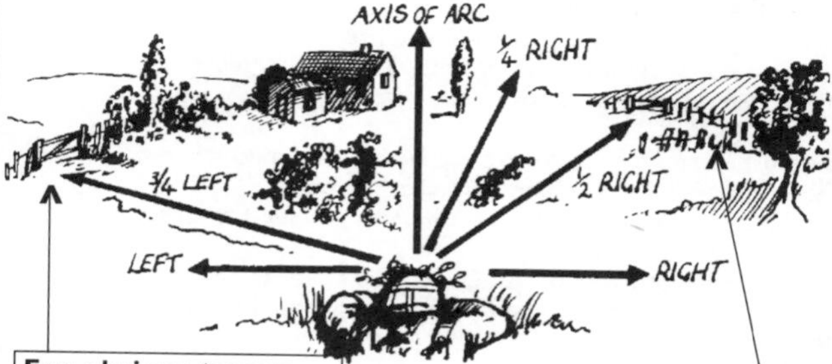
AXIS OF ARC
1/4 RIGHT
3/4 LEFT
1/2 RIGHT
LEFT
RIGHT

For obvious targets "400-3/4 left - gate"

For less obvious targets "450 - 1/2 right - gate slightly right - fence post"

For difficult targets use the Clock Ray Method

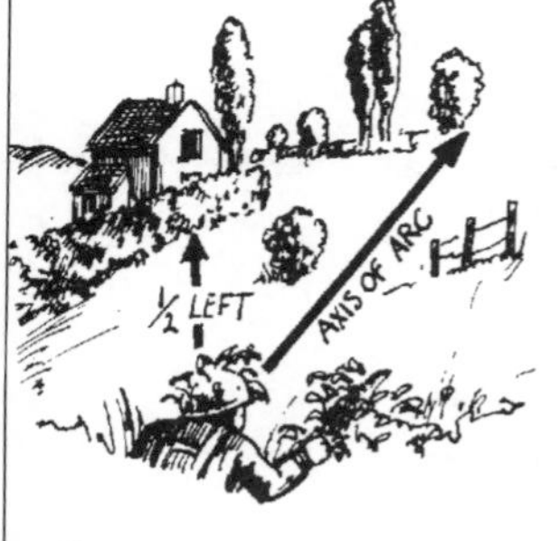
1/2 LEFT
AXIS OF ARC

"350 half left - house, right 3 o'clock - small bush"

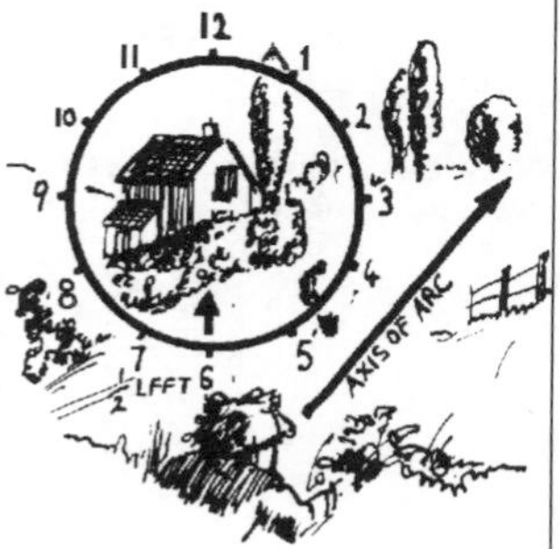
12
1
2
3
4
5
6
7
8
9
10
11
1/2 LEFT
AXIS OF ARC

"350 - half left - house, 8 o'clock hedge"

FIELDCRAFT

FIRE CONTROL ORDERS.
 When the Section comes under fire the Section Commander will give the order 'TAKE COVER'.
The drills for this are covered later, however there will come a time when the Section Commander will need to take control of the fire power of the Section to concentrate it on the target, this is achieved using a **Fire Control Order.**

You must learn how to do this instinctively so that you can:
   a. Re-act to the Fire Control Order correctly.
   b. Give an order yourself if no one else can see the target.

To give a correct Fire Control Order you have to follow tha set sequence, it will help you if you remember it by the "Key Word" **GRIT**, as follows:-

G =	WHICH **FIRE TEAM** IS TO FIRE ("*No 2 SECTION, DELTA*").
R =	**RANGE** IN METRES "450"
I =	**INDICATION** WHERE TO LOOK ("*HALF RIGHT GAP IN WALL*")
T =	**TYPE** OF FIRE ("RAPID FIRE")

When giving this type or order remember it is an **order** therefore to give it as an **order:** -

C =	Clearly
L =	Loudly
A =	As an order
P =	With Pauses

FIELDCRAFT

TYPES OF FIRE CONTROL ORDER

The details of the Fire Control Order you get depends on the Type of Target to be engaged.

BRIEF Orders -

"Sights down quarter right rapid fire".

FULL Orders - *"Delta - 450 left-house
doorway- bursts-fire".*

DELAYED Orders.

*"No 2 Section-300-quarter right-small wood -
when enemy appears - rapid -fire".*

INDIVIDUAL Orders

*"No I Section 300 - slightly left - small bushes -
enemy in that area - watch and shoot".*

MOVEMENT IN THE FIELD

When close to the enemy you do not want your movements to be seen- therefore use cover. Remember to - Use the hedges and walls for cover.

Leopard Crawl

Crawl on the inside of your knees and your elbows. Useful for moving behind

very low cover. Move by using alternate elbows and knees, rolling your body a little as you bend your knees. Keep your heels, head and body down, you must observe at all times.

LEOPARD CRAWL

FIELDCRAFT

Leopard Crawl — with a rifle.

Hold your Rifle with the right hand on the Pistol Grip and the left hand on the Hand Guard.

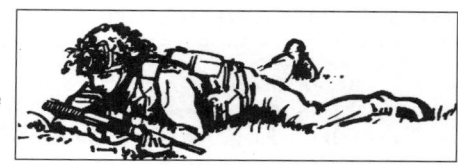

The Monkey Run

This is a normal "hands and knees" crawl. Useful to move behind cover about two feet high.

You can move quite fast, but it does make a noise.

Moving slower and to prevent twigs cracking as you move, put your knees on the spot where your hands have been.

Keep your "rear end" and head down, but continue to observe.

With a rifle hold it at the point of balance, make sure that no dirt gets into the muzzle.

The Walk

The Rifle is held in the ALERT position, ready for instant action. You must adopt a positive and alert attitude, observing in all directions.

Don't walk on the flat sole of your boots, use the edge so as to walk quietly. It helps to keep your balance if you slightly bend your knees as you move.

FIELDCRAFT

The Roll

The quickest way of getting off a skyline or crest of a hill.
Protect your Rifle, hold closely into your side. Keep feet together and your body straight.

MOVEMENT AT NIGHT

Always move quietly.
Movements used during daylight are not suitable at night- they have to be adapted.

The Ghost Walk

Lift legs high, sweeping them slowly outwards. Feel gently with toes for safe place for each foot, put weight down gently. Keep knees bent. Use the left hand to feel the air in front of you from head height down to the ground checking for obstructions, trip wires, booby traps or alarms etc .

The Cat Walk

Crawl on hands and knees. Search ground ahead for twigs, move knee to where hand has searched.

The Kitten Crawl

It is quiet-but slow. It is very tiring.
Lie on your front, search ahead for twigs, move them to one side.
Lift your body on your forearms and toes,

FIELDCRAFT

press forward and lower yourself on
to the ground.

NIGHT NOISES

At night you hear more than you see.
Stop and listen.
Keep close to the ground, turn your
head slowly and use a cupped hand
behind the ear.. Freeze if you hear a
noise.

MOVING AT NIGHT -
REMEMBER

Keep quiet .... have no loose equipment. Move carefully ... use the
ghost walk, cat walk or kitten crawl.
Clear your route ... dry vegetation will make a noise.
Use available cover ... flares, thermal imaging and night observation
devices will turn night into day.
Keep to the low ground ... you split your group at night at your peril.

LISTENING AT NIGHT

If the enemy is about - keep an
ear close to the ground.
The closer you are to the ground,
the more chance you have of
seeing the enemy on 'skyline'.

**USE ALL YOUR SENSES AT
NIGHT - ESPECIALLY
YOUR SENSE OF SMELL - A
'WHIFF' OF COOKING OR
SMOKE OR EVEN BODY
ODOUR CAN GIVE YOURS
OR THE ENEMY POSITION
AWAY.**

FIELDCRAFT

NIGHT VISION

We can see in the dark - but REMEMBER our eyes take 30 minutes to get used to the dark.

We see less than in daylight. We see shapes - not detail.

We see skylines and silhouettes. We may see movement.

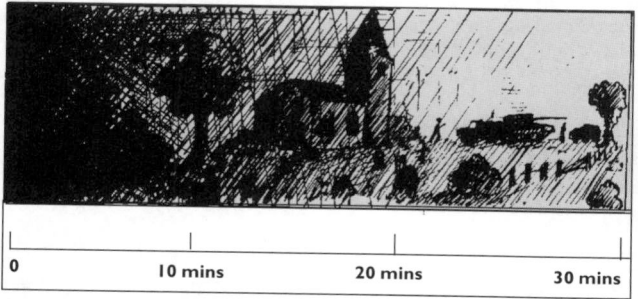

| 0 | 10 mins | 20 mins | 30 mins |

YOUR EYESIGHT

Your eyes have two sets of cells, one set for daylight (CONES) in the centre of your eyes, the other set for darkness (RODS), which are around the CONES.

The night cells work when the day cells are affected by falling darkness.

With constant practice night observation can be improved.

If you have a cold, headache or are tired it can reduce your night vision.

You will find that there is a limit to the time you can concentrate effectively on any given point or your vision becomes blurred.

Most Army unit use Thermal Imaging (night sights) that "turn darkness into daylight" in as much that they pick out an object giving out heat (body heat), The SUSAT sights on the SA80 Rifle/LSW (an optical sight) has advantages similar to that of binoculars for night observation.

FIELDCRAFT

BRIGHT LIGHT RUINS YOUR NIGHT VISION

If caught in the light of flares take cover at once in open ground.
If in a wood - **FREEZE.**
If you see a flare, quickly close one eye to protect your night vision, use the other eye to look about you taking advantage of the light, but do not move suddenly as this will give you away.

DUTIES OF A SENTRY

A sentry is the eyes and ears of the unit.
If the job is done well, the unit will be safe and secure.
When you are a Sentry make sure:-

That you know and understand your orders.

That you know what to do if your post is approached by a person or vehicle.

That you always ask questions if you do not understand anything

What ground to watch.

Direction of the enemy.

Signal for defensive fire.

Names of prominent landmarks.

Where neighbouring posts are.

About patrols that maybe in the area, or coming through your post.

FIELDCRAFT

SENTRIES AT NIGHT IN THE FIELD

At night sentries work in pairs.

Sentries must know:-

What to do if anyone approaches their post.

What ground to watch.

The Password.

Sentries close to the enemy must know :-

Direction of the enemy.
Name of land marks.

Where neighbouring posts are.

Signal for defensive fire.

About patrols that may come in or out through their post or near them.

FIELDCRAFT

HOW TO CHALLENGE.

When you see movements which you think may not be your own troops - alert your Section Commander.
Say 'HALT' HANDS UP.

'Advance one and be recognised'. "Halt".

Give the challenge half of the password - quietly, so that only the first man can hear it.

ACTION - Allow friendly troops through, **know how many and count them through - one at a time.** Section opens fire at enemy troops.

NOTE Be aware of a common trick which is for the enemy to approach a sentry, listen and learn the first half of a PASS WORD then fade away.

An inexperienced sentry may allow this to happen. The same enemy then approaches another sentry and challenges them before they can challenge them.

Again the inexperienced sentry might then give the reply then allow the enemy into the position.

So be careful and never allow anyone into your position unless you can positively identify them when in doubt call for help.

On a patrol or on duty as a sentry you will use your **EYES** and **EARS**, and your **TOUCH** when feeling your way through woods or difficult cover.

REMINDER - USE YOUR SENSES

What are your senses, how can they help in Fieldcraft? Your sense of **TASTE** may not be used, but your sense of **SMELL** — depending upon the SMELL — may remind you of taste. SMELL — Body smell or the smell of cooking, or anything else that drifts on the air and can give yours and the enemies presence away.

FIELDCRAFT

SECTION BATTLE DRILLS

These notes are for a Section organised as **FIRE TEAMS.**

DRILL No 1. BATTLE PREPARATION.

a. Personal camouflage.
b. Check weapons.
c. Check ammo.

Section Commanders Orders

a. Ground ref points.
b. Situation Enemy forces. Friendly forces. Pl formation and Task.
c. Mission - the section mission.
d. Execution Section formations Team for which Flank and Route to take.
e. Service support - Info passed down from Pl Commanders orders.
f. Command & Signals; any info passed down from Pl Commander.

REFERENCE POINTS & ANTICIPATORY ORDERS.

In the 'Advance to Contact' the Section Commander will look out for :
1. New reference points for fire orders.
2. Place where the Section can take cover if it comes under effective fire.

DRILL No 2 - REACTION TO EFFECTIVE FIRE.

The drill to be adopted is: On the order of the section commander -
"TAKE COVER", DASH - DOWN - CRAWL -OBSERVE -SIGHTS -
FIRE.

DRILLS No 3 - LOCATION OF THE ENEMY

Location of the enemy is usually difficult, failure means casualties and
section not be able to move and may lose the initiative as result.
Three stages in this drill:
a. Observation - look in area from which thump came from.
b. Fire - fire order to couple of riflemen to fire at likely target.
c. Movement - Section commander orders rifleman to move while
remainder of section observe.

DRILL No 4 WINNING THE FIRE FIGHT

As soon as the Section Commander knows the enemies position a fire
order must be given to bring sufficient weight of fire on the enemy to
neutralize them. (See Fire Control Orders)

FIELDCRAFT

SECTION BATTLE DRILL No 5
THE ATTACK BATTLE ORDERS

When a Section Commander reaches the forward enemy position they look for any defended positions. If they are any part of the objective they will issue snap orders so that they can carry out an assault. This is always divided into three stages;

The Approach - including Quick Battle Orders (QBO's)

The Fight Through

The Attack will always be one of the following depending on the number of stages in the attack. They will be as brief as possible.

Orders for a **one stage attack,** that is when the Assault Fire Team goes straight into the assault

1. Fire and Movement to close with en, L or R flanking.
2. Asslt Fire Team prep to move. *Fire Sup Team fires.*
3. *Assault Fire Team move.*

Orders for a **two stage attack,** that if when the fire support team move to another position before the assault fire team assaults.

1. Direction of assault, L or R flanking.
2. Fire Support Team moves first. *prepare to move*
3. Assault fire team fire. *Fire Support Team move*

Orders for a **three stage attack** in which the fire team moves first, then fire support team moves and finally the assault fire team assaults.

1. Direction of the assault, possibly L or R flanking.
2. Assault Fire Team moves first to ...Prep to move *Fire Support Team fires*
3. Fire Support Team move. *Assault Fire Team fires*
4. Assault Fire Team prep to assault. *Fire Support Team fire and switch.*
5. Assault Fire Team moves. *Fire Support Team fires*

Fire Suppoprt Team should fire or move automatically on the previous order to the Assult Fire Team.

The Assault and Fighting through the Objective

All movement by either fire team must be covered by fire from the other. An angle of 1600 mils between the two Fire Teams allows the most effective fire support for the assault. As the assult is made the Fire Suppoprt Team should fire across the objective for as long as possible, then switches it's fire across the objective onto enemy in depth positions.

FIELDCRAFT

Watch out for enemy interference from flanks. Section Cmdr make continuous appreciation during the fight through.

DRILL No 6 REORGANISATION

When objective cleared of enemy the Section Commander must regain close control over men and position, ready to beat off counter attack. Reorganisation must be swift and efficient, if not all that was gained will be lost.

The Section Commander will:

1 Allot fire tasks to each member of section.
2. Post sentries.
3. Check on casualties.
4. Check ammunition, arrange redistribution of ammo.
5. Supervise re-digging of shell scrapes.
6. Send prisoners and captured kit to rear.
7. Report to Pl Cmdr for orders.

The Fire Support Team will;

1. On prearranged signal, rejoin the Assault Fire Team once Section in in control of the objective.
2. Check SAW and redistribute ammo.

Riflemen should;

1. Check weapons and equipment.
2. Check ammunition and grenades.
3. Recharge all magazines.

NOTE: While the 'fight-through' is in progress the capture of the objective is the first priority. As soon as the position is cleared, then casualties take high priority.

FIELDCRAFT

SECTION AND PLATOON FIELD SIGNALS

Field Signal are a silent means of communication between members of the section and platoon.

They should be used whenever possible and be constantly practiced, even when going about normal duties it is as well to use them, so as they become second nature to everyone.

Very often there is a need to attract the attention of those who are to receive the signal, especially if the Section Commander wants to tell several members of his section at the same time.

Watch and Listen

This does not absolve you as a member of the section from watching out for signals, as there may be times when an audible signal is not practical for obvious reasons.

There are four recognised methods of attracting attention, they are:-

1. A **SINGLE** whistle blast - during fire contact only.
2. Snapping forefinger and thumb.
3. Knocking butt of weapon with knuckles.
4. Silent whistle.

Whistle BLASTS are often used to indicate situations, they are as follows:-

1. **SHORT BLASTS - ALARM** - air attack, NBC attack, etc.
2. **LONG BLASTS** indicate "STAND DOWN".

FIELD SIGNALS

The following pages set out the normal Field Signals used by the Infantry. We have not put the name of description of the signal with it, but have numbered them and listed the description etc — you will learn them better this way.

Key and Description of Field Signals

1. READY TO MOVE. Move hands as if cranking handle.
2. DEPLOY. Arm extended below shoulder level, waved slowly from side to side, hand open. If deployment to either flank is wanted, commander points to flank, after completing signal.
3. ADVANCE or FOLLOW ME. Arm swung from rear to front below shoulder.

FIELDCRAFT

4. HALT or REST. Arm raised until the hand is level with shoulder. Indicate length of halt by number of fingers. Point to 'rest area'.
5. GO BACK or TURN ABOUT. Hand circled at hip height.
6. CLOSE or JOIN ME. Hand placed on top of head, elbow square to the right or left, according to which hand is used. Point to RV area.
7. DOUBLE. Clenched hand moved up and down between thigh and shoulder.
8. SLOW DOWN (APC). Arm extended to the side below shoulder, palm downwards, moved slowly up and down, wrist loose.
9. LIE DOWN or DISMOUNT (APC). Two or three slight movements with the open hand towards the ground (palm downwards).
10. AS YOU WERE or SWITCH OFF (APC). Forearm extended downwards, hand open, waved across body parallel to ground.
11. ENEMY SEEN or SUSPECTED. Thumb pointed towards ground from clenched fist.
12. NO ENEMY IN SIGHT or ALL CLEAR. Thumb pointed upwards from clenched fist.
13. LSW. Clenched fist raised to shoulder height.
14. SCOUT GROUP. Clenched fist with forefinger upright.
15. RIFLEMEN. 'Victory' sign - fist and second finger extended and open in 'V' remainder of fist clenched.
16. LIGHT MORTAR. Weapon held vertical. Imitate loading mortar rounds.
17. LAW/MAW. Weapon placed on shoulder and held like a LAW/MAW.
18. SECTION CMDR. Two opened fingers held against arm to indicate Corporal's Stripes.
19. PLATOON CMDR. Two opened fingers held on shoulder to indicate a Lieutenant's stars.
20. GIVE COVERING FIRE. Weapon brought into aim.
21. OBSTACLES. CROSSING. TRACK JUNCTION. Arms crossed. For water obstacle make waves.
22. HOUSE or HUT. Hands folded in inverted 'V'; to indicate shape of roof.
23. RECONNAISSANCE. Hand held to eye, as though using eye glass.
24. ATTACK. A chopping movement with edge of hand in direction attack is required.
25. MOVE UP. Fingers spread, arms swung slowly in direction movement is required.

FIELDCRAFT

26. FORM AMBUSH. Hand placed over face, followed by pointing to place of ambush.
27. FREEZE AND LISTEN. Hand cupped to ear.
28. 'O' GROUP. Fingers together, moved in conjunction with thumb to indicate person talking.
29. RIGHT or LEFT FLANKING. A curved sweeping movement of the arm in direction concerned.
30. FIRE & MANOEUVRE. One hand used in a rolling forward action in front of the body.
31. SPACE OUT. Palm of hands held against weapon and moved away several times.
32. ARROW HEAD. Both arms forced backwards or forwards at an angle of 800 mils, depending whether arrow is backward or forward.
33. SINGLE FILE. One arm fully extended above head.
34. STAGGERED FILE. Both arms fully extended above head.
35. SPEARHEAD. As for arrowhead plus indicating Gun Group to move in at rear.
36. DIAMOND. Arms raised above the head with arms slightly bent so that hands touch to form diamond shape.
37. EXTENDED LINE. Arms raised to the side level with the ground, indicate which side group is to go.

FIELDCRAFT IS GREAT, YOU USE THE COMBINED SKILLS OF MAP READING, WEAPON TRAINING AND FIELDCRAFT, PLUS, YOU HAVE TO BE FIT. OBSERVE THE SAFETY RULES – THEN YOU WON'T HAVE TO USE YOUR FIRST AID SKILLS

FIELDCRAFT

FIELDCRAFT

THE ONLY WAY TO LEARN FIELD SIGNALS IS TO PRACTICE AND USE THEM ON EVERY POSSIBLE OCCASION

SECTION FORMATIONS

As a member of a Section you move as a part of your Fire Team within the Section.

How you move depends upon six factors

1. The type of ground you are moving across.
2. How far you can see.
3. The likely direction from which the enemy may fire on you.
4. How your Section Commander can best control the Section.
5. The need for the Section to produce the maximum fire with minimum delay.
6. Who controls the Air Space.

FORMATIONS

Section Formations are used to meet the above factors and are mostly decided upon by the Section Commander, who will change the formations as the Section moves over different types of ground during its advance.

Some of the formations are described on the following pages Good

FIELDCRAFT

SINGLE FILE

Good for moving along hedges or ditches or along the edge of woods. Good for control by the Section Commander especiallyat night. Bad formation to produce fire to front. Vunerable from frontal fire, especially downa ditch or sunken road/stream.Not good for observation or passing information to the members of the section.

FILE

Not good for observation or passing information to members of the section. A good formation for control and night movement. Can be used going down a track or either side of a hedge. Disadvantage — it makes a good target for the enemy.

ARROWHEAD

Best for moving across open country, produces effective fire against frontal attack. Easy to control, has good all round observation. Bad for exposing good target to enemy fire.
Formation used only when crossing open country at night.
Easy to control, has all round observation and protection, each person can see the next, the Section Commander can be at the front or in the middle.

FIELDCRAFT

DIAMOND

Formation used only when crossing open country at night. Easy to control, has all round observation and protection, each person can see the next and Section Commander can be at the front or in the middle

EXTENDED LINE

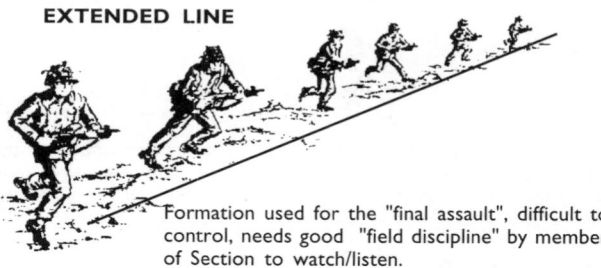

Formation used for the "final assault", difficult to control, needs good "field discipline" by members of Section to watch/listen.

REMEMBER

When moving in a Section Formation:-

1. Watch your Section Commander for hand signals.

2. Keep in contact with members of the Section on each side of you - but not too close.

3. Keep quiet and listen for commands and anticipatory orders.

4. Keep in correct position for formation.

5. Be observant.

6. Be ready to change to a new Section Formation.

FIELDCRAFT

CHOOSING A ROUTE

If you have to advance across country , check that you know exactly where you know to make for. Then decide on the best route to take.

REMEMBER

Routes must be planned ahead. You must move in bounds or stages from one observation point to another.

You must check your direction - are you keeping on course.

Always use a Compass.

Must not be seen but should beable to see the enemy.

If you have to take a chance, chose a route which offers the risks early in your approach rather than later on, since you will have less chance of being seen.

The best route will have places to observe the enemy - without being seen yourself.

Don't go blindly towards the enemy. Give good fire positions.

You must be able to fire if necessary. Give cover from enemy fire.

Lets you move without being seen.

Not to have impassable obstacles such as marsh land or open ground or ravines.

Establish and record reference points en route and their map references. bearings and time/distances to reach them.

FIELDCRAFT

PACING

Pacing is necessary because you must always know how exactly far you have gone when counting a number of your own 'paces'.

You should know your 'Pacing Scale', over different types of conditions, I.E tarmac roads, tracks, grasslands, woodlands etc.

To find your PACING SCALE, put two markers out 100m apart. Walk the distance between them as you would on a patrol, counting the paces as you go.

If it has taken you 120 paces to cover the 100m, then that is your PACING SCALE.

It follows, to use this scale if you were on a patrol and had to go a distance of 300m, you would have to count out 360 paces.

Under some conditions you can use a specific length of string, tying knots at every 120 paces.

Having used the length of string, un-tie the knots and repeat the process on the next 'leg' of your route.

It is always advisable to have a CHECK PACER, remembering to check that your PACING SCALE is the same by day and night.

AIDS TO KEEPING DIRECTION

Some of the aids to keeping direction are:-

a. The compass, map and air photographs.

b. A rough sketch copied from a map or air photograph.

c. Keeping two prominent objects in view.

d. Using a series of easily recognisable landmarks, each visible from the previous one.

e. The stars and also the sun and moon if their natural movement in the sky is understood.

f. Memorizing the route from a map or air photograph. Helpful details are the direction of streams, distances between recognisable features coupled with pacing, and the course of contours.

g. Trees in exposed country tend to grow away from the direction of the prevailing wind. Moss may grow on the leeward side of tree trunks.

h. Remembering the back view, patrols and others who may have to find their way back should look behind them from time to time and pick up landmarks to remember for the return journey.

j. Leaving directions marks on the outward journey, these may be pegs, small heaps of stones.

FIELDCRAFT

k. If the route is being walked by day by those who are to guide along it by night, they must take note of skylines and objects or features which they will be able to recognize in the dark.

NAVIGATION

This is the art of moving from one place to another and consists of three important stages that MUST be carried out if you are to be successful, they are as follows:-
1. PLANNING.
2. KEEPING DIRECTION.
3. GOOD PACING.

PLANNING -You must plan your route in advance, using maps, air photos, sketches and information from previous patrols or recces.

KEEPING DIRECTION - Always take several compasses and as many 'pacers'. Always get someone else to check your navigation, at both the planning stage and while you are executing the movement. It is often hard to keep direction, especially at night, in fog or in close country.

When it is necessary to make a detour to avoid an obstacle or seek cover, it is easy for leaders to miss the correct lines of advance.

ALWAYS CHECK YOUR 'ICE' (INDIVIDUAL COMPASS ERROR) WITH ALL COMPASS'S BEING USED AT THE SAME TIME AND FIND THE AVERAGE ERRORS.

SELECTING OF LINES OF ADVANCE

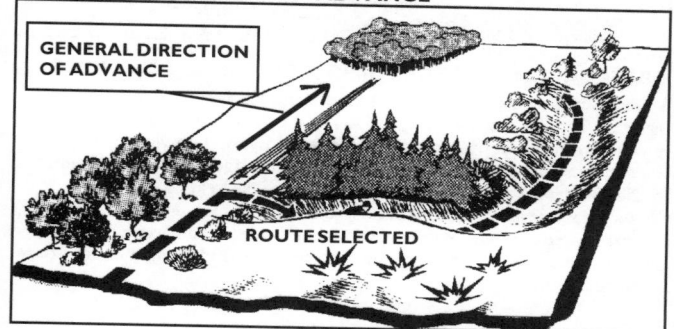

GENERAL DIRECTION OF ADVANCE

ROUTE SELECTED

FIELDCRAFT

SELECTING OF LINES OF ADVANCE.

Remember the keyword - **'G R O U N D'**

G	**G**round from the map. Open/close country, Rolling/flat.
R	**R**idges, water courses and watersheds (highest) mark on map or talc.
O	**O**bservation good view points.
U	**U**ndergrowth - study woods, scrub, trees, villages.
N	**N**on Passable obstacles, such as rivers, ravines, marsh land.
D	**D**efilade covered lines of advance and areas which offer cover can now be selected.

SEARCHING GROND

OBSERVATION — SEARCHING GROUND & SCANNING

The skill of searching ground is based upon learning to "scan" an area using an accepted system.

It will test your concentration and exercise your knowledge of "why things are seen" and the principles of Camouflage and Concealment.

In the diagram we have - for the purpose of illustrating to you — drawn lines across the landscape.

In practice you would choose prominent features, landmarks, roads etc., and draw your imaginary lines across the landscape through these reference points.

FIELDCRAFT

The landscape is divided into **FOREGROUND, MIDDLE DISTANCE** and **DISTANCE**. You can further divide this by indicating a centre line (again based on reference points), calling left of the line **"LEFT OF ARC"**, and right of the line **"RIGHT OF ARC"** as shown in the illustration on the previous page.

Having divided the landscape, the correct method is to scan each area horizontally (left to right or right to left).

View the area in short overlapping movements in a very precise manner, especially any features that are at an angle from your position.

SCANNING

While scanning you may see something move or that requires further investigation. There may be an area where you may come under observation from, it would be as well to check that out early.

Weather conditions can give you a clue when searching, frost on bushes, foot marks will show up clearly, if the weather is hot camouflaged positions can be given away when leaves or grass dry off changing colour.

Search across hedges and rows of trees , NOT along them. At all times consider WHY THINGS ARE SEEN.

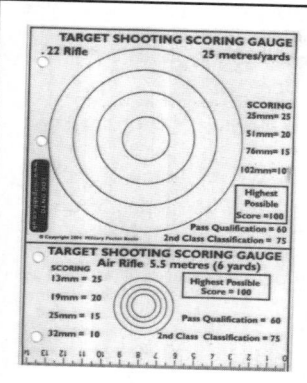

FIELDCRAFT

PATROLS

There are three reasons for patrolling:

1. To obtain up-to-date and accurate information.
2. To dominate the ground between a commanders own unit and that of the enemy.
3. To destroy and disrupt enemy forces.

Successful patrolling calls for a high standard of individual training, good team work, initiative and determination on the part of the patrol leader. Patrolling enables the defence to be conducted in an aggressive manner.

The foundation of successful patrolling is through preparation.

TYPES OF PATROL.

Reconnaissance Patrols

Patrols of minimum strength for task, usually I NCO and 3 men, who gain information by observation and operate by stealth.

They avoid combat except for self-protection or to take advantage of unusual opportunities.

The roles in which a reconnaissance patrol may be employed include:-

1. Collecting topographical information on features, tracks and state of ground.
2. Obtaining details of minefields and the extent of enemy positions.
3. Locating enemy machine gun and defensive fire (DF) areas, where fire is immediately directed on call in case of emergency.
4. Investigating noises made by the enemy, enemy habits and patrol routes.
5. Checking our wire and/or minefields at first or last light.
6. Acting as listening posts, to give early warning of enemy approach and with the ability to call down fire.

Standing Patrols

Minimum strength I NCO and 3 men, to gain information of enemy movement, to prevent or disrupt enemy infiltration.

They move into position quietly - try to remain hidden - gain information until required to withdraw or if discovered fight their way out.

Their main tasks are to:-

1. Watch and listen on likely enemy approaches.
2. Watch over dead ground in front of and between friendly areas.

FIELDCRAFT

3. Watch over mine fields and obstacles, for which they should have good communications, so that they can inform the main body.

Fighting Patrols

These are patrols organized for a particular task with sufficient strength and backup to achieve the mission. The strength can vary according to the task to be performed and the expected combat level:

1. Denying enemy patrols freedom of action in No Man's Land.
2. Driving in enemy protective patrols.
3. Interfering with enemy working parties.
4. Distracting enemy attention from other activities.
5. Carrying out raids.
6. Capturing prisoners for identification purposes.
7. Tank hunting.
8. Laying ambushes.
9. Protecting reconnaissance and working parties of other arms.
10. Escorting stretcher parties.

SEQUENCE OF ACTION TO MOUNT CARRY OUT AND DEBRIEF A PATROL.

The success of a patrol depends on good planning beforehand as well as good action during the actual patrol. Compliance with the following by the Patrol Commander ensures that nothing is forgotten.

PATROL COMMANDER

Issues a warning order to include brief outline of patrol task, members of patrol including second-in-command, time and place for briefing and any special administrative arrangements including weapons and equipment. Normally dress and equipment should be as light as possible but must include water and emergency rations in case the patrol is cut off and has to lie up for a period before returning to base. Studies, Air Photos, Maps, previous Patrol Reports and sketches. Selects observation posts for his recce.

FIELDCRAFT

RECCE

Carries out recce from OP's during which they look for:

a. Routes to and from objective (to be different).
b. Landmarks.
c. OP's.
d. Dead ground and covered approaches.
e. Obstacles.
f. Likely places for ambush - by us or by enemy.
g. Enemy positions, likely positions and DF areas.
h. CONSIDERS light and weather conditions, moon, etc.

Makes his Appreciation and Plan, keeping them as simple as possible.
DRAWS A FIELD SKETCH showing distances (in paces), bearings and
timings of bounds.
PREPARES MODEL of the area for briefing the patrol. PREPARES HIS
ORDERS. MEETS PATROL AT RV.

BRIEFS THE PATROL

By showing members the ground from an OP (individually if necessary)
and points out minefield lanes and gaps in wire etc.,
Gives out his orders:
With the aid of a cloth or sand model of ground, under the following
headings:-

1. GROUND.

Describes, incl. landmarks, obstacles, and "going". Use OP's, maps, air
photos, models, etc.

2. SITUATION

a. Enemy Forces. FEBA, ptl activity, routine, sentries, DF, FPF, minefields,
   wire, trip flares, fixed lines.
b. Friendly Forces. Own positions, other ptls, fire support available,
   minefields, wire, trip flares, fixed lines. DF, FPF, stand by ptl.

3. MISSION.

To Recce, Fighting - definite task.

FIELDCRAFT

4. **EXECUTION Phase 1**. General Outline.

a. Number of phases - route, action on objective, return.

b. Who taking part - appointments and position in the platoon.

c. Prep Moves - Drop Off Point. Time leaving rehearsal/base area. Method of move. Loading Plan. Route to and ref of DOP. Arcs of obsn/fire. Order of March (OOM).

d. Action if Ambushed. Action at DOP. Time out. Confirmation or orders/detail.

Phase 2. Route Out, to final RV (FRV).

Fmn. Obs drills/action on mines/trip wires/booby traps. Actions on: PW. Cas. If separated from ptl. If lost. Confirm FRV ref.

Phase 3. Action in final RV - on arrival

1. Occupation. Move in. Secure. Fmns, position of grps, sig for FRV.
2. Recce Group - Composition, Tasks. Route. OOM, fmns, arcs. Action on ambush, sig to open fire. Action if FRV gp loc by en.
3. Remainder - Composition, Tasks, Arcs, Actions - on en pre-seen or ambush, sig to open fire, if recce gp loc by en, on return of recce gp or if fails to return. Confirmation or orders/info.

Phase 4. Action on Objective

1. Cover/Fire Gp. Composition, Fmn, posn, routes, tasks, arcs, action if en act first, duration on SP's, Sigs for opening fire. Action if separated from group.
2. Recce/Assist/Snatch. Composition, fmn, task, posn, routes, action on recce/asslt/snatch, sigs for sp fire. Action if surprised, sig net, wire, illumination.

Phase 5. Withdrawal and action in final RV.

Sig to wdr. OOM sequence of gp wdr, arcs, fmns. Action and posns in FRV -pack kit etc. Head check and sig to move out. Actions: if in contact, PW's, if gp fails to return, if FRV gp has moved, if surprised in FRV. Pass on info sketches etc. Confirmation of orders/info.

From/To	Bearing	Distance	Fmn	Ground	RV
(1) Leg 1					
(2) Leg 2					
(3) Leg 3					

FIELDCRAFT

Phase 6. Route Back

Route. Fmns. RV's. Obs. Actions; en pre-seen, ambush, sig to open fire, cas, if lost, if separated. Action on arr at pick up point (PUP). Time in. Confirm orders/info.

Co-ordinating Instructions

Timings. Meals, rest, rehearsals (day/ni), weapons test, inspections, time in/out constraints. Debrief. Action on halts, lights. Fireplan. Rehearsals loc and details. Deception and security.

Summary of Execution.

1. Summary of Timings - Rehearsals, prep of eqpt, inspection, rest, meals test wpns, night rehearsals, final check time out, time in. RV's and refs.
2. Action on white Lts
3. Action on Halts - for obsn/protection.
4. Action to take on Meeting En if:-
   Pre-seen or Ambushed
   On the Route Out .... On the Route In ....
5. Action on Cas
   On Route Out........ On obj......... On the Route In........
6. Action on crossing Obs
7. Action with PW
8. Rehearsals
9. Lost procedure
10. Action on Mines
11. Distr on Ni Vis Aids

5. SERVICE SUPPORT

Ammo. Feeding. Dress and Eqpt. Special Eqpt - Toggle ropes, wire cutters, IWS/Suit, radio spares, etc. Wpns type and distribution. Rats, meals before during and after, water. Med, Fd dressings, stretcher, med pack, morphine, casevac method. PW handing on/after capture. Tpt to DOP/from PUP. Confirm orders/info.

6. COMMAND AND SIGNAL

Chain of command 1i/c, 2i/c and 3i/c and conditions for taking over cmd. Location of ptl comd. Sigs, radio, radio checks, other sigs. Password. Use of Radio and restrictions. De-briefing location, who doing. Patrol report. Special instrs on reporting Info.

FIELDCRAFT

Rehearsals

Carries out daylight or night rehearsals which must include:

a. Moving out and returning through own FEBAS.
   Patrol Commander goes forward to contact the sentry. Normal challenging procedure follows.

b. Formations and drill for changing formations.
   One or more of the three formations = single file, file or diamond - is adopted during a patrol depending on ground and visibility.

c. Use of Scouts. Move by bounds ahead and are followed by the Command Group (Patrol Commander, Radio Operator and his protector).

d. Movement. Every member is allotted his specific task, movement must be silent, frequent halts to observe and listen, when approaching the enemy position and also at night. When halted sink down to the ground level, avoiding a jerky movement, and make use of the skyline. Make use of the previously prepared signal to move - a silent "touch" signal - to ensure that no-one is left behind.

e. Action on objective. Nearby RV. This is an RV to which the patrol goes after completing the task, it must be easy to find and indicated to all members of the patrol during the approach to the objective.

f. Firm Base. If a patrol has to move a long way it may leave a party between its own and the enemy position, this forms a "firm base" from which remainder of patrol carries out main task and to return afterwards.

On arriving near the objective, the Patrol Commander will:-

1. Search the area, especially the RV or Firm Base for unexpected enemy.

2. Make a brief Recce, Appreciation and Plan, brief the patrol members concerned

g. **Action on Lights.** If time allows get away - otherwise, freeze, close one eye to preserve night vision. If a trip flare move from area quickly as possible, get down and observe.

h. **Encounter drill.** Action will depend on the task and circumstances. It may be desirable to avoid action and move away as quickly as possible. If this is impossible an immediate assault is the alternative. If ambushed, scatter and move individually to previously arranged RV.

FIELDCRAFT

j. Crossing Obstacles

1. On encountering an obstacle, Commander goes forward to recce it, decides whether to cross or go round.
2. Requirements of obstacle crossing drill are:-
   (a) Silent movement.
   (b) Posting a man to guide others over.
   (c) At all times at least one man ready to fire his weapon or throw a grenade if the patrol is surprised.

k. Casualty Evacuation

1. All casualties must be brought back.
2. Improvise a stretcher.
3. If on the way out, the patrol may have to pick up the casualty on its return or summon help.

Prisoners

1. If a fighting patrol takes a prisoner they must be brought back whether or not this was the task of the patrol. - prisoners are valuable sources of information.
2. If a prisoner cannot be taken with the patrol, they may be put under guard and collected later either by the sane patrol or by another one detailed or summoned by radio for this purpose.

Carries out Final Inspection

a. Dress and equipment light as possible, but include emergency rations and water.
b. Dress and equipment to be properly fitted and silent. Jumping up and down will show whether it is satisfactory.
c. No documents will be taken which can afford useful information to the enemy if captured.

LEADS PATROL OUT THROUGH FEBA.

a. Navigation. Previous study of air photos and maps etc. use of landmarks. By compass bearing and counting paces -especially at night. "Legs" to be measured to the nearest 50 paces from map. If the patrol becomes dispersed, RV at the end of the previous leg. Avoid prominent cover, e.g. edges of woods, tracks, hedges, defiles - likely places for enemy ambushes or standing patrols.
b. Fire Support. Pre arranged or called for by radio -
   (1) To distract enemy.
   (2) For support on objective.
   (3) To help the patrol extricate itself in emergency.

FIELDCRAFT

DE-BRIEFED ON RETURN.

Verbal report followed by a written report.

On the next page is shown the layout of a Patrol Report.

This is produced as guidelines for you to use when preparing a report, and includes many of the factors that should be taken into consideration.

This serves as a reminder of the vast amount of valuable information and activities that a Patrol Commander is expected to deal with.

This is a standard format use as a Patrol Report and you would be well advised to make a copy of it, study it in readiness for when you have to do a report.

POST EXERCISE ADMINISTRATION

On the completion of all exercises, stores have to be returned. Rotten chore, it is probably the last thing you wish to do, BUT - Kit must be cleaned, dried and checked then inspected for damage and deficiencies; any found must be reported to the Quarter Master. Thus ensuring that damaged equipment is not re-issued.

Note: it is always advisable to check kit when you draw it from the stores - especially if you are signing for it. If damaged, make sure that it is noted on your form 1033 before you leave the stores.

TIME SPENT IN RECONNAISSANCE IS SELDOM WASTED

The following pages deal with Patrols.

Patrols are perhaps the most enjoyed Fieldcraft activity that you will take part in.

The planning for mounting of a Patrol for a specific task can take some considerable time. The gathering of information, obtaining any special equipment, the planning and rehearsals involving other units - Armour-Signals-Engineers has to be carried out to the letter.

As a Cadet you will not be going into such depth, but is as well you appreciate that your Patrols are the initial training and introduction to this exciting aspect of Fieldcraft.

The gathering of Information, Intelligence from all Patrols is obtained through Patrol Reports made out by a Patrol Commander. Overpage is a specimen only of what a Patrol Report might contain.

FIELDCRAFT

PATROL REPORT

Date   Destination of Patrol

Aim

Maps

Size and composition of Patrol

Task

Time of Departure   Time of Return

Routes Out and Back

Terrain - (Description of the terrain - dry, swampy, jungle, thickly wooded, high brush, rocky, deepness of ravines, rivers/streams/ canals, width/ depth, condition of bridges as to type, size and strength, effect on armour and wheeled vehicles.)

Enemy - (Strength, disposition, condition of defences, equipment, weapons, attitude, morale, exact location, movements and any shift in dispositions. Time activity was observed, co-ordinates where activity occurred.

Conditions of Patrol -including disposition of any casualties)

Conclusions and Recommendations - (including to what extent the mission was accomplished and recommendations as to patrol equipment and tactics)

Date   _____   Time   _____   hrs

Signature of Patrol Commander   _____

ADDITIONAL REMARKS BY INTERROGATOR

Date   _____   Time _____ hrs

                                   Signature.

FIELDCRAFT

AMBUSHES

INTRODUCTION

Ambushes are usually carried out as a part of patrolling activity. It requires close team work, skill, intelligence, fitness, cunning and discipline. An ambush is a surprise attack, by a force lying in wait, upon a moving or temporarily halted enemy. It is usually a brief encounter, conducted at comparatively close quarters.

When well prepared and executed it can cause heavy causalities and serious loss of morale amongst the enemy; however poor planning, preparation and execution may result in failure, and serious losses to the ambush party.

TYPES OF AMBUSH

a.   DELIBERATE - with time to plan in advance.

b.   IMMEDIATE - In response to 'hot' information, to 'contact' the enemy, with no time for recce.

AMBUSH SITES

The best places for an ambush site include:-

a.   Known enemy routes.

b.   Known admin/supply/water points, food or ammo dumps, approaches to villages.

c.   Where the terrain changes - edge of woods or forest, where a valley has steep sides. Where a river crossing is shallow etc.

d.   Approaches to own bases or positions, also on route out of your own positions - if enemy follows you back.

PRINCIPLES OF AMBUSH

a.   Good intelligence to ensure contact and success.

b.   Thorough planning and preparation, planned Recce, ambush well rehearsed.

c.   Security - careful Recce - not to betray ambush site.

Be prepared for an attack on yourselves.

FIELDCRAFT

d. Concealment - good track discipline, no signs of your whereabouts, good camouflage and concealment.

e. Good control and communications - all know the plan in detail, signals, plan for springing ambush. Must be kept simple, and thoroughly rehearsed.

f. Discipline -ambush only successful if everyone alert, no noise, restricted movement, fast re-action to signals, weapons always ready to fire.

g. Safety - all weapons in "made safe" state while on the move. No firing at individuals - even when minimum distance of 50 metres between muzzle and the enemy.

THE DELIBERATE AMBUSH

The ambush parties are sub-divided into smaller groups, each with their own leaders. Normally the groups are as follows:-

a. **THE AMBUSH GROUP** - covers the chosen place for the ambush and springs the ambush. Group contains Ambush Commander and the LSW teams(s). Four men to ambush a section. A Section and Platoon HQ to ambush a Platoon.

b. **CUT-OFF/STOP GROUPS** - serve to give warning of enemy approach, cut off their lines of retreat or help to take care of a counter attack from a flank. For a section ambush the group would consist of two men. A platoon ambush would be a section strength.

PLANNING - prior to occupying an ambush position the following sequence of planning events must be carried out:-

Recce. Issue preliminary orders in the base camp. Preparation and rehearsals in the base camp.

Move to the ambush area.

Final Recce by Amb Cmdr and Cut Off Grp Cmdr's.

Amb Cmdr issues final orders if required.

Occupy ambush position.

RECCE - Amb Cmdr should - if possible - carry out recce of amb site before giving orders. He may be limited to air photographs, maps, patrol reports or sketches made.

Must try to put himself in enemy position/point of view, he must select/confirm:-

a. Ambush area, positions of the Ambush Group and cut off Groups, detailed siting of GUN GROUP(s), booby traps, trip flares etc.

b. Check positions for each group for: concealment, approach routes, good fields of view and fire and of the enemy approach route.

c. The withdrawal routes for all groups.

d. The final RV, and routes to and from it.

FIELDCRAFT

ORDERS, PREPARATION, REHEARSALS & MOVE OUT.

ORDERS - Like all Patrols the information given and the quality of the orders must be very thorough and detailed, using a model of the area and leaving sufficient time for preparation and rehearsals.

The orders for an ambush follow the same sequence and detail as Patrol Orders, but need to have extra details under the 'EXECUTION' phase, as follow:-

ACTION ON ARRIVAL AT FINAL RV/FIRM BASE

Entry order of march. Positions and arcs of fire - describe these, also cover in rehearsals. Sentries if necessary. Action if surprised. Action if recce party does not return within.... minutes. Confirmation of orders, timing, refs, RV's etc.

ACTION IN AMBUSH AREA

Order of march. Method of entry. Positions. Laying of communication cord. Arcs to be covered.

Sig for 'Ambush Set'. Time ambush to be set by ..... hrs.

ACTION ON APPROACH OF ENEMY -

Warning signal from Cut Off Groups. Signal to stop. Search party if required.

WITHDRAWAL TO RV/FIRM BASE - Signal for withdrawl.

Order of march. Action at final RV/Firm Base - reorg, check numbers, weapons, re-distribute ammo, prepare to move out.

Thorough preparation is essential for success and should include the following:-

Cleaning and testing of all weapons. Testing and checking special equipment, ropes, night viewing aids, boats or rafts, safety and medics. Radios and spare batteries. Camouflage of clothing and equipment.

REHEARSAL - If for a night ambush, then rehearsals should be held in the daytime and also at night.

They must:—

Show where each group and those who are within them are in relation to each other.

Test signals/communications.

Cover alerting, and springing of the ambush.

Practice withdrawal to Firm Base/Final RV.

FIELDCRAFT

MOVE TO AMBUSH AREA - Ambush party move to the Final RV/ Firm Base and take up defensive position and wait for the Amb Cmdr and the Cut Off Team Cmdrs to do their final recce.

FINAL ORDERS Only need for confirmation or last minute changes that need to be made as a result of the final recce. This could be more likely and important by night than day and could include:-

a. Description of the ambush area, enemy approaches and counter attack routes.

b. Individual tasks if they vary from rehearsals.

OCCUPATION SEQUENCE

Having completed his recce and returned from any Final Orders briefing, Ambush Cmdr will remain on the position, sending Cut Off Team Cmdrs back for remainder of party. If a platoon operation, sentries would be taken forward, posted and remain in position throughout the move to the ambush area.

Cut Off Team followed by Assault Group move into position, Ambush Cmdr places himself in central position for control and near to LSW Team.

SETTING UP AMBUSH - Once all groups in position, Cut Off Team start laying communications cord/cable to Ambush Cmdr. Set up trip flares, booby traps etc are set.

AMBUSH SET - When Ambush Cmdr receives signal from all groups that everyone in position, gives the 'Ambush Set' signal. After this signal no one leaves their position, Care to make no movement or noise. Get into a comfortable position for the time you are waiting for the ambush to be sprung.

SPRINGING THE AMBUSH - On sighting the enemy, Cut Off Team alerts Ambush Cmdr of their approach and direction using communication cord, alerts remainder of the force. All prepare for ambush, carefully moving into aim . Ambush Cmdr waits until as many of enemy are in ambush area. Gives signal for springing ambush. This signal usually a burst of fire from the LSW , a shot from commanders weapon or setting off a trip flare. It is NEVER the commander shouting 'FIRE'.

FIELDCRAFT

AFTER SPRINGING AMBUSH THE FIRE FIGHT - short and sharp. Cmdr gives 'STOP' or 'CEASE FIRE'. pause while all check for: movement of enemy. Enemy counter attack. Enemy moving back to collect casualties, thinking ambush has withdrawn.

WITHDRAWAL - On receiving withdrawal signal, all groups withdraw to Final RV, in order as rehearsed. Minimum time spent there, check all present, check no enemy follow up, re-call sentries and move off by return route.

PATROL HARBOUR

A patrol harbour is a position taken providing security when a patrol halts for a period. A form of advanced base from which it can service and send out Partrols Some of the reasons are:
1. To avoid detection.
2. To lie low while a recce is made prior to the formation of a plan and issue of orders.
3. A base from which operations can be mounted, e.g., attack, ambush, reconnaissance, or establishing OPs.
4. Provides an RV for small groups..
5. Provides secure base for admin halt after long periods on patrol

Triangular Harbour Drills

A patrol harbour is set up as a Triangular (three sided) defence position by a platoon or adopted by a smaller patrol.
The triangular harbour ensures the following:
1. All round defence, an LSW at each corner.
2. Mutual support ,in that an attack from any side is covered by two LSWs.
3. Ease of command /control with PL HQ in the centre.
4. Ease of administration simple, compact layout.

Stage I Selection harbour location

From map, air photographs, aerial reccce or on the ground. Site must be confirmed by recce, and area secured before occupied.

FIELDCRAFT

When selecting site you must consider:

1. Mission. The harbour must give the patrol best chance to achieve task.

2. Location. Choose site:

a. Which can be easily defended.

b. Dense vegetation, provide cover from air/ground.

c. Away from human habitation or areas or used by civilians.

d. With access to water.

e. With good routes in and out.

f. Where communications are good.

3. Avoid the following:

a. An obvious position.

b. Ridge lines or crests which may be used as routes.

c. Roads, tracks, etc.

d. Wet areas, steep slopes and small valleys.

Stage 2 - Occupation. Essential to have swift/efficient occupation of a harbour. A well practiced routine is essential. Carried out using hand signals without noise. Many different 'drills' can be used, an example is set out below:

a. Platoon stops just short of the chosen site. It should break track and set up an ambush on its previous route to engage any patrol following or tracking the platoon.

b. The platoon commander and reccee party (i/c sections, and a guide go forward to recce harbour in detail. The Pl Sgt stays in command

3. On the site of harbour, tasks are as;

a. Pl Cmdr selects Pl HQ and the location of the 6 and 12 o'clock positions.

b. The Pl Cmdr and Sec Cmdrs allocate the section areas, and the LSW positions.

c. The perimeter wire is laid setting out the triangle for the when the platoon occupies the harbour.

d. When recce finished, a Sec Cmdr and guide sent to up main body. Platoon led to the harbour site in single file.

e. Sections are met and each man is shown their position and arc to cover.

f. This ensure that an LSW is at each corner of the triangle, noise kept to a minimum the track plan is understood

g. When in position, each man removes their pack and adopts a fire position.

FIELDCRAFT

Section commanders should sites own positions centrally, having in view the platoon commander and own 2IC.

Pl Cmdr checks the perimeter to ensure liaison between sections Sec Cmdrs meet him at his corner LSW position; minor adjustments to layout of harbour made at this stage.

Stage 3 - Clearance Patrols.

1. On a signal from the platoon commander, each section sends out a clearance patrol to cover their own section's arc. The rest of the section remain 'stood to'.

2. The section commander or 2I/C and one or two men move out through the neighbouring section's LSW position. They go out to the limit of visibility and sound, then turn and move along their own section's frontage. This drill ensures that the section arc is fully covered. The clearance patrol then returns through their own section's LSW position. In this way all tracks into the position are covered by an LSW position.

3. Clearance patrols are to detect and report to Pl Cmdr:
   a. Signs of recent enemy activity.
   b. Possible approach routes enemy may take.
   c. Unexpected obstacles, (mines, contaminated ground and ravines).
   d. Streams and and dry river beds. High Ground.
   e. Possible ERV locations.

4. If initially thorough recce patrols have been carried out, on occasions it might not require Clearance Partols immediately after the occupation, easpecially at night.

   Also if there is not much time between occupation and last light, Pl Cmdrs may do without clearance patrols.

   However, if the patrol stays in its harbour during the next day, clearance patrols must go out at first light.

Stage 4 - Sentries. When clearance patrols finished, sentries to be posted.

Points to remember are:

a. Sentries should be posted beyond the limit of noise from the harbour (to avoid distraction and to alert the platoon before any enemy hear the harbour).

b. One sentry per section posted in depth will normally be enough.

c. The sentries to act as early warning of enemy approach.
   They should be armed with rifles but fire only in self defence. Their withdrawal route back to the harbour should be via the LSW

position and be clearly understood by all.

d. Communication between sentries and the LSW positions must be established. This should include use of communication cord.

e. Sentries are located outside the harbour only during work routine.

f. By night, sentries will normally consist of staggered double manning of the corner LSWS. The double manning provides continuity at the sentry position, allows one sentry to fetch the relief and reduces the chances of a sleeping sentry.

Stage 5 - Work Routine. Once sentries are posted, work begins to strengthen the harbour. Tasks include:

1. Preparation of stand-to positions and fields of fire, construction of shell scrapes and the positioning of warning devices (e.g, trip flares).

2. Preparation of a path to allow silent movement round the position. Shell scrapes should be on the outside edge of the path. Soldiers would live in and fight from their shell scrapes. Wire would be laid just inside the shell scrapes to mark the path and prevent accidental movement outside the harbour at night. This is lowered during daylight hours.

3. Laying of communications cord from sentries to LSW positions and/ or section commanders, and from section commanders to platoon commander.

4. Positioning of shelters. These are erected over shell scrapes at last light and taken down before first light. They may be erected in poor weather at the platoon commander's discretion.

5. Confirmatory orders by the platoon commander to establish an operational and administrative routine. The points are as for routine in defence and include:

a. Future operations (i.e., patrols).

b. Alarm and stand-to system (and its rehearsal).

c. Orders for opening fire and defence of the harbour Location of platoon ERV.

d. Sentry roster.

e. Re-supply.

f. Sleeping and feeding.

g. Track discipline.

h. Staggered cleaning of weapons.

j. Latrines these should be within the perimeter of the harbour or outside within the sentries arcs.

FIELDCRAFT

Security

The platoon commander must ensure:

a. Sentries are correctly posted and briefed.
b. Good communications with sentries to ensure early   warning of enemy approach.
c. All round defence is maintained.
d. Good battle discipline is maintained.
   Points to include:
1. Correct camouflage.
2. No lights, smells or unnecessary noise.
3. Webbing worn and weapons carried at all times. Kit not in use to be packed away.

STORES & EQUIPMENT

If you have the responsibility for drawing/collecting kit from the Stores you will have to sign for it on a form 1033. This means that you have taken on the responsibility of ensuring it is not misused, damaged, or goes missing. It is a good idea to check that the kit you draw is in good order /correct amount before you sign. When returning the stores they will be checked.

Once the check is complete, ensure that the stores copy of your form is either signed as 'stores returned' or destroyed in front of you.

The above applies for everything you sign for.

WARNING

SAFETY - FIRING BLANK AMMUNITION
With all field training when blank ammunition is in use.
NEVER aim directly at anyone.
DO NOT AIM AT ALL IF THEY ARE LESS THAN 50 METRES AWAY FROM YOU.

DO NOT FIRE BLINDLY IN THE DARK

THINK BEFORE YOU FIRE.

FIELDCRAFT

SELF TEST QUESTIONS

1. To be good at Fieldcraft you need to have what.
2. For what reason do you use: Unit of Measure. Key Ranges. Bracketing.
3. Who makes out a RANGE Card, what for and when.
4. When carrying out Personal Cam what do you have to remember.
5. What is "Isolated cover", would you use it.
6. Why are things seen, what must you remember about "smell".
7. What is important about Shape, Shadow, Silhouette.
8. How do you indicate a DIFFICULT target.
9. What is the "Key Word" for fire control orders and what does it mean, and how do you give an order.
10. How many types of Fire Control Orders are there and what are they.
11. Give a method of moving at night.
12. How long does it take for your eyes to get used to the dark.
13. When an illuminating FLARE 'goes up', what do you do.
14. When do sentries work in pairs.
15. Name the Duties of a Sentry.
16. What is the correct CHALLENGE a sentry should give, when and how should it be given.
17. How many members are there usually in an Infantry Section.
18. What is Fire Team within the Section.
19. How many Sections are there in a Platoon.
20. What helps you to listen at night.
21. What is the "drill" if you come under effective fire.
22. A Sentry close to the enemy must know — What.
23. What is the sequence and headings used by a Section Commander giving his orders
24. Give the three important points to consider when "choosing a route".
25. How do you work out your own PACING SCALE.
26. Give six methods to help you Keep your Direction when on a Patrol.
27. Give the meaning of the Key Word : G R O U N D and explain its use.
28. How do you split up an area you are going to SCAN and SEARCH.
29. Name two types of Patrols and the role that they play.

FIELDCRAFT

30. In daylight, you must not fire a blank at anyone less than, how many yards away, and at night what is the rule.

31. How should orders be given.

32. What should you remember by the letters C.L.A.P.

33. Where will you find the Cut Off Group.

34. Give three reasons for having Patrols.

35. Give the three important stages of Navigation.

36. What do you understand by a Three Stage Attack.

37. As a Sentry how loud do you shout to challenge anyone approaching your post.

38. Outline what you would expect the info a Patrol Report would give.

39. When would an interrogator be used.

40. How many types of Ambush are there and what are they called.

41. Setting up an Ambush site what would you look for.

42. What is a Patrol Harbour used for.

43. What is the role of a Clearance Patrol.

Chapter 5
MAP AND COMPASS

INTRODUCTION

We are fortunate to have excellent maps of this country produced
by the Ordnance Survey.
The Military Survey, a specialist branch of the Royal Engineers,
undertakes the provision of maps, charts, hydrographical, and other
geographical products for all three of the armed services. The ACF
use the maps made available by the MOD.

RELIABILITY OF MAPS

A map is literally a "Bird's eye view" of the ground drawn on paper.
It is accurate only at the time it was drawn. Today, maps are
produced from aerial photographs, which ensures their accuracy.
In just a few years, the shape of a landscape can change, villages may
disappear under a reservoir, new roads may appear, and whole
woods may disappear. For practical map reading purposes this will
not affect the accuracy as far as you will be concerned, any map
produced within the last few years may be relied upon unless
specifically stated otherwise.

CARE OF MAPS

Maps should be treated carefully or they soon become useless.
When using outdoors, it is advisable to fold the map to the area
required and place it in a map case or plastic bag to protect it.
When planning routes, place a transparent film over the map; writing
directly on to the map ruins it for further use. Ensure you learn
how to fold a new map correctly; it will prolong its useful life.

WHAT YOU WILL FIND ON MAPS

Marginal Information

On most maps you will find a part set aside for 'marginal
information', find this as soon as you unfold your map, it provides

MAP & COMPASS

useful information and guidance on how to interpret the detail on the map.

Until you have been map reading for some time, you will constantly refer to this section – until you have a good understanding of what all the symbols or CONVENTIONAL SIGNS mean.

The reference number and scale of the map is to be found at the top of the map.

The index giving adjoining sheet numbers is usually shown near the bottom right hand corner of the map. You will need this info if the route you are planning "Goes off the map".

Most maps now use metres as the "Unit of Elevation", this scale is to be found in the margin at the bottom of the map as "ELEVATION IN METRES".

THE GRID SYSTEM

The British National Grid System divides the whole country into large squares which are sub – divided and finish up as the GRID LINES printed on maps that you would normally use.

Grid Lines are used to 'pin point' a specific spot on the map by using the numbers of each line as shown in the margins around the outside of the map. Maps are printed with the North at the top of the sheet, one set of GRID LINES run up and down the map (North and South), the others run across the map (East and West). It is important that you are able to find a point on the map and then able to go out and find it on the ground. It is vital to be able to indicate on the map the exact place where you are standing on the ground.

To assist in the accurate use of the grid system it is advisable to obtain a Pathfinder Protractor/Romer, it provides two of the different scales of GRID SQUARES found on Ordnance Survey maps. The Romer is made of rigid plastic that you place on the GRID SQUARE of the map and read off the figures as described below, to the exact pinpoint position.

FOUR AND SIX FIGURE REFERENCES

When giving a reference there are a few simple rules to remember:

1. FIRST, count the figures along the BOTTOM of the map, from **left** (West), to **right** (East); these are called **"EASTINGS"**.
2. Next, count the figures up the side of the map from the bottom (South) to the top (North) these are called **"NORTHINGS"**

MAP & COMPASS

3. A reference must always contain an even number of figures.

4. GRID REFERENCES are

always given with the **"EASTINGS"** value first, followed by the **"NORTHINGS'** value. The example given in the diagram shows a black square that can be given the reference as square **8040 ('A four figure reference')**

This square could represent a whole square kilometre of ground, not exactly a 'pinpoint' location on a map or ground.

Should you use a four-figure reference you must add a feature such as a cross roads, a church or prominent physical feature to indicate exactly where you mean within the four-figure square.

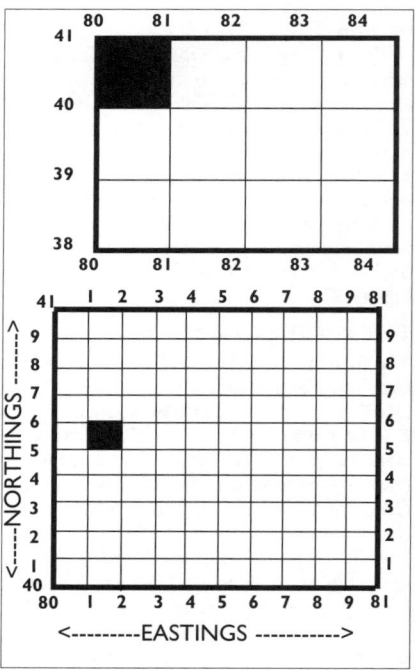

To get an exact position, the square can be further sub-divided into 10 squares in both directions. The bottom diagram illustrates this sub-division the black square is 'square 1- 5' these figures when added as explained below make up a *'six figure reference'*.

The first two figures of the EASTING value followed by the sub-divided square figure, then the two NORTHING value figures, followed again by the sub-divided figure to make up a six-figure reference of 801405

MAP & COMPASS

SETTING A MAP

The first and essential task on the ground with a map is to **'Set it'** or **'Orientating the map'**. It means aligning your map with the features on the ground. Until you have mastered this, you will not get the enjoyment out of map reading.

Setting your map using a Silva type Compass

Lay your map out flat, then find the MAGNETIC NORTH ARROW – usually in the margin of the map as shown at 'A' in the diagram.

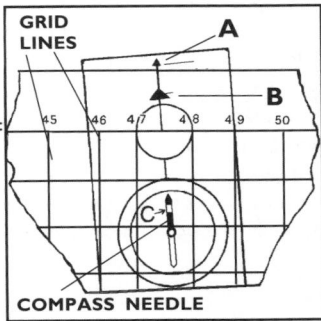

Lay the base of the compass on the map with the DIRECTION OF TRAVEL ARROW, ('B' in the diagram), in line with the MAGNETIC NORTH. (See diagram 'line-up').

Carefully turn the map and compass round – watching the compass needle swinging until the **RED MAGNETIC END** of the compass needle 'C' coincides with the DIRECTION OF TRAVEL ARROW 'B' and the MAGNETIC NORTH ARROW 'A' on the map. Your map is now **'Set' or 'Orientated'** in relation to the ground.

MAP & COMPASS

SETTING A MAP WITHOUT A COMPASS
BY CAREFUL OBSERVATION

This can be easy, once you have identified exactly where you are on the map, and if you are standing on a straight road, line up the road on your map with the road you are standing on.

Make certain that the map is pointing in the right direction, i.e the right way round.

If not on a road, you will need to find other objects on the ground such as a road/track junction, church, prominent hill top or farm buildings.

You must also find the same objects on your map, using them as shown in the diagram by turning your map to set or orientate it in relation to the ground

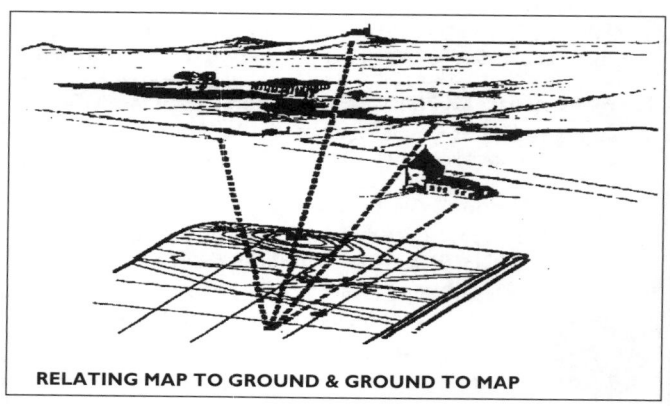

RELATING MAP TO GROUND & GROUND TO MAP

MAP & COMPASS

THE SILVA COMPASS

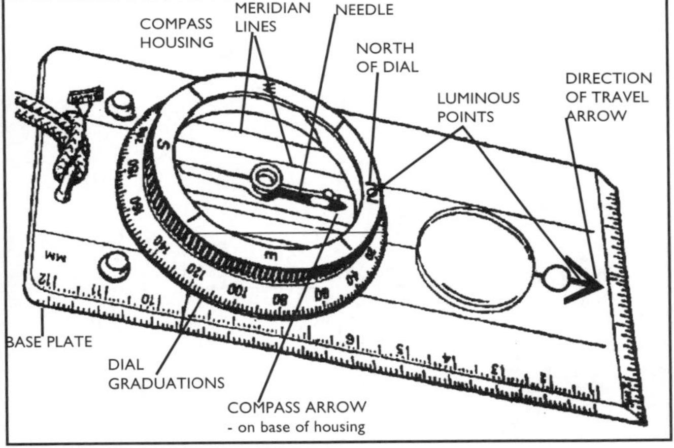

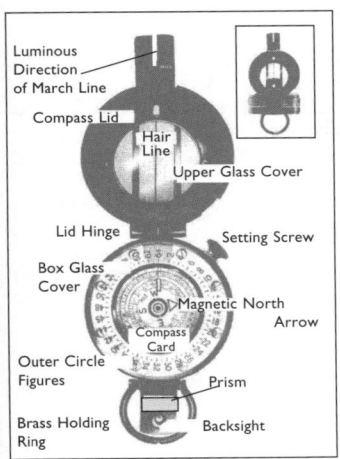

COMPASS HOUSING
MERIDIAN LINES
MAGNETIC NEEDLE
NORTH OF DIAL
LUMINOUS POINTS
DIRECTION OF TRAVEL ARROW
BASE PLATE
DIAL GRADUATIONS
COMPASS ARROW
- on base of housing

Luminous Direction of March Line
Compass Lid
Hair Line
Upper Glass Cover
Lid Hinge
Setting Screw
Box Glass Cover
Magnetic North Arrow
Compass Card
Outer Circle Figures
Prism
Brass Holding Ring
Backsight

THE PRISMATIC COMPASS

This is the compass that the Army uses. It is a very accurate instrument and therefore costly to make.
Not issued to cadets, but we include it for interest only.

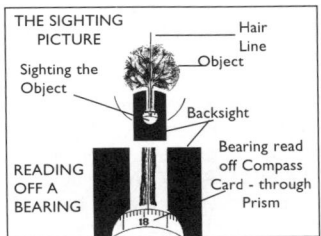

THE SIGHTING PICTURE
Hair Line
Object
Sighting the Object
Backsight
READING OFF A BEARING
Bearing read off Compass Card - through Prism

MAP & COMPASS

CARDINAL POINTS of the compass.

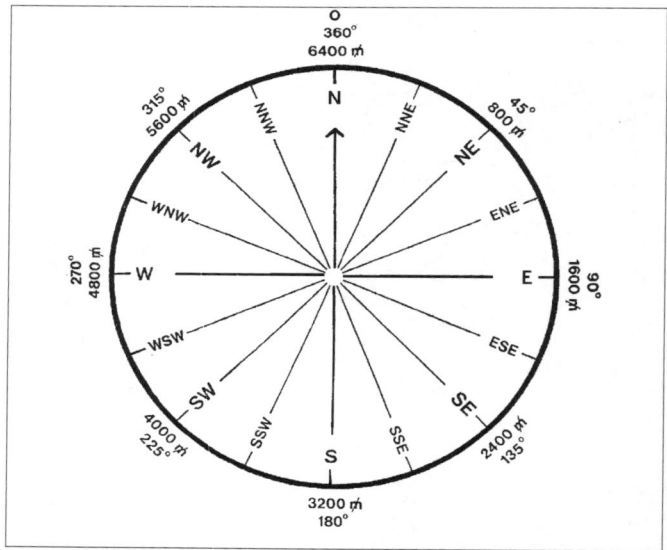

CARDINAL POINTS of the compass.

There are 32 points of the compass, but only 16 of them are normally used in map reading for the description of direction. These 16 are the four Cardinal Points and 12 intermediate points as shown in the diagram above.

The **INTERMEDIATE POINTS** are combined with the Cardinal points, e.g. **SE** is **SOUTH EAST**, **NNW** is **NORTH NORTH WEST** etc.

These points describe direction only to within one sixteenth of the full circle. For more accurate indication of direction it is necessary to use sub-divisions of the circle using **'mils'** or **'degrees'**.

The **MILS SYSTEM** divides the circle of the compass into 6400 MILS, the zero being the North Point. The **Degrees system** divides the circle into 360° degrees.

MAP & COMPASS

The MILS system is used by the Army to give greater accuracy than degrees. Cadet Forces work in Degrees - 360 degrees in a circle. The four quadrants or quarters of the circle are each 90^0, and so the East, South and West points fall at 180^0, 270^0, 360^0 degrees respectively, as illustrated on the previous page.
The symbol normally used for Degrees is the ^{0} as shown above.

NORTH POINTS

There are THREE NORTH POINTS

1. **TRUE NORTH** – the actual direction of the geographical North Pole
2. **GRID NORTH** - the direction of the vertical GRID LINES on a map. For all practical purposes, TRUE and GRID are the same.
3. **MAGNETIC NORTH** – the direction towards which the compass needle is attracted is the **MAGNETIC NORTH POLE** – see the diagram.

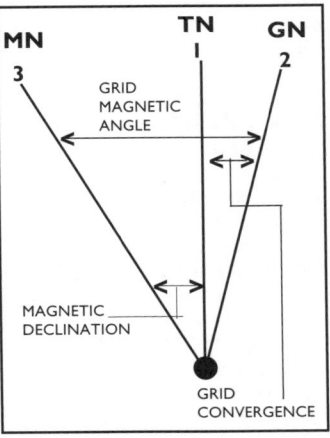

ANGLES BETWEEN NORTH POINTS (GMA)
Grid Magnetic Angles

This is sometimes called the **magnetic variation**; it is the angle between GRID NORTH and MAGNETIC NORTH; it depends on two factors:

1. TIME: as the position of the Magnetic North Pole moves slightly eastwards, so the GMA (Grid Magnetic Angle) changes. This is called the **ANNUAL MAGNETIC CHANGE** and must be taken into account when converting MAGNETIC BEARINGS to GRID BEARINGS and vice versa.

2. PLACE: The GMA **(Grid Magnetic Angle)** also varies from one part of the country to another. These two factors are included in the marginal information on a map.

MAP & COMPASS

MAGNETIC DELINATION

This is the angle between MAGNETIC and TRUE NORTH as shown on the diagram on the previous page.

GRID CONVERGENCE

This is the angle between GRID NORTH and TRUE NORTH which can in practice, be ignored since for practical map reading purposes TRUE NORTH and MAGNETIC NORTH are the same.

BEARINGS – TYPES OF BEARINGS

There are three kinds of bearings according to the North point from which they have been measured:

1. **A MAGNETIC BEARING** is one taken with a compass (an accurate compass needle always points towards MAGNETIC NORTH)
2. **A GRID BEARING** is one measured on a map with the Silva compass used as a protractor or using your Pathfinder Protractor/ Romer.
3. **A TRUE BEARING** cannot be measured direct, it must be calculated from the other two. However this can be ignored for practical map reading purposes.

NOTE: INDIVIDUAL COMPASS ERROR (ICE)

The accuracy of each compass is subject to error, it is important that you should check your own compass to establish the INDIVIDUAL COMPASS ERROR by checking it against other compasses. Having done so, make a note of the ICE on a small sticky label stuck on to the base of your compass. **Don't forget to allow for it!**

TO TAKE A MAGNETIC BEARING

1. Point the compass direction of march arrow at the object.
2. Turn the compass housing until the red arrow is under the needle.
3. Read off the MAGNETIC BEARING on the compass housing.

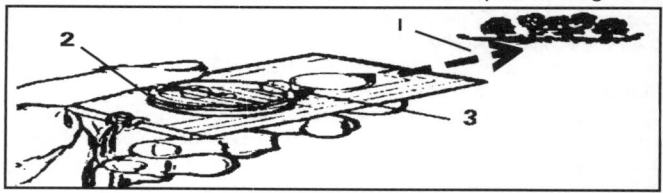

MAP & COMPASS

To use your Silva compass for a **BACK BEARING,** keep the compass on the bearing you have taken (as '**X**' to '**Y**' in the diagram), rotate the **COMPASS HOUSING** through 180⁰ (180 degrees) The compass is now **SET** to march on the **BACK BEARING** (in the direction of **'Y'** as shown in the diagram) of your original **FORWARD BEARING.**

To retrace your route – (from **'Y'** to **'X'**) march on the bearing given as your **BACK BEARING.**

This is a very important skill, easily learned with your Silva Compass.

Using Forward and Back bearings is one of the best methods of preventing yourself from getting hopelessly lost; **remember practice makes pefect**

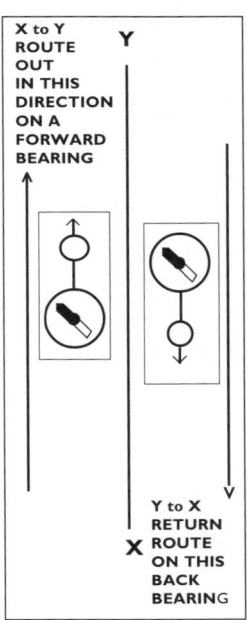

MAP & COMPASS

FIND YOUR POSITION BY COMPASS - RESECTION

There may be times when you need to find your exact position both on the map and on the ground. This could be as a result of being "dropped-off" on an exercise or if you were unfortunate enough to crash land in wild country. You could find your position by using a compass and following the instructions set out below.

You will need to refer to the diagram on this page.

1. Set/orientate your map. Select TWO prominent objects or features which you can be sure of identifying on the map. These objects/ features need to be a good distance away, more than 1000 metres and also be separated by an angle of approximately 10 o'clock to 2 o'clock - see diagram opposite.

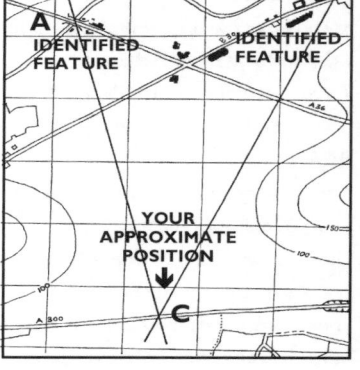

2. On the "plastic" cover of your map, mark the objects/ feature at **"A"** and **"B"**. From the position at which you are standing, (call it **"C"**) take a bearing on to each of the objects/features in turn, writing down the bearings.

   As this has to be accurate, don't move from your position and take a further two bearings on both of the objects/ features. Add together the three bearings to each object/feature and divide by three to get the average bearing to each. It is important to do this as accuracy is essential.

3. These are COMPASS Bearings, therefore they are MAGNETIC Bearings.

   As you are to use them to 'plot on a map', they have to be converted from MAGNETIC to GRID Bearings.

MAP & COMPASS

NOTE: You will always be best advised to draw a small diagram - until you become familiar with working with bearings - showing the NORTH POINTS as shown on page 5.14, this will remind you to make an allowance for the GMA (Grid Magnetic Angle).

The current GMA is approximately 100 mils (6^0) This is the figure that you would subtract from the MAGNETIC BEARING.

REMEMBER: "MAG TO GRID - GET RID"

4. Check the resulting bearing and adjust it to the nearest 25 mils. Remember the settings or divisions on the compass card of a Silva or Light Weight Compass are 25 mils.

5. Now set up the GRID BEARING on your compass for bearing **"A"**. Use a wax pencil with a fine point , put the point on **"A"** . Hold it in a vertical position, place the long edge of the compass against the pencil with the DIRECTION OF TRAVEL ARROW pointing in the direction of **"A"**, and the NORTH ARROW pointing approximately to the top of the map.

6. Using the pencil still in a vertical position, pivot the compass about the pencil point until the NORTH ARROW points exactly towards the top of the map, with the edge of the compass or any of the red setting lines on the compass base parallel to the nearest GRID LINES on the map.

7. Hold the compass firmly in this position while you draw a line along the side of the compass.

   Repeat the same procedure from point **"B"**.

   Where the two lines you have drawn from **"A"** and **"B"** cross each other is your calculated position on the map/ground. Now work out your exact six figure GRID reference of your location.

> ## "ONLY WITH CONSTANT USE AND PRACTICE WILL YOU LEARN TO TRUST YOUR COMPASS"

MAP & COMPASS

IDENTIFYING A FEATURE

Set/orientate your map, use the edge of your protractor or a pencil, place it on the map with the edge running through your position, swing it across the map until it lines up with the feature you can identify on the ground.

The feature should be easy to pick out, provided it is not too far away and that it is on your map!.

This like so many Map Reading skills need constant practice until you carry it out as a "drill" and second nature.

After a while you will be able to locate and identify features by just looking across the map.

In setting your map, no matter what method you use, it is the constant relating and comparison of the map and ground which will build a good foundation for your navigational skills.

We remind you that this skill above all will go a long way to prevent you getting lost on your DofE Expedition.

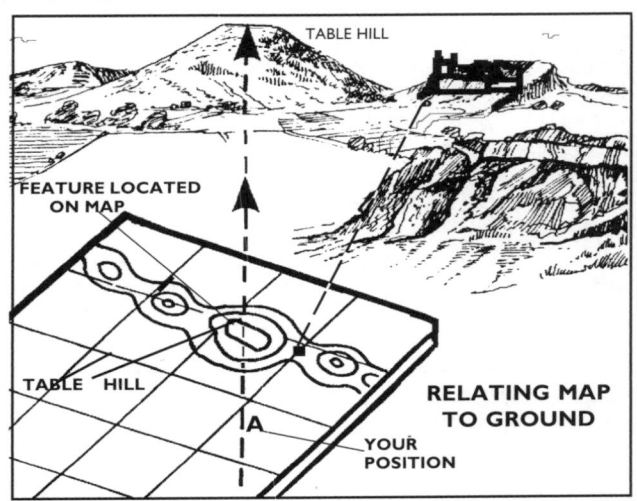

TABLE HILL

FEATURE LOCATED
ON MAP

TABLE HILL

**RELATING MAP
TO GROUND**

A

YOUR
POSITION

MAP & COMPASS

GRID MAGNETIC ANGLE

(GMA) in UK is as follows:

GMA = 2° 42"or 43 mils West in 2008* (*approx.)

GMA changes yearly and you can get an accurate GMA reading from:

http://www.geomag.bgs.ac.uk/cgi-bin/gma_calc

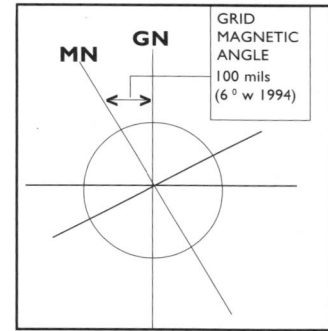

REMEMBER
"Grid to Mag - ADD"
"Mag to Grid get RID"

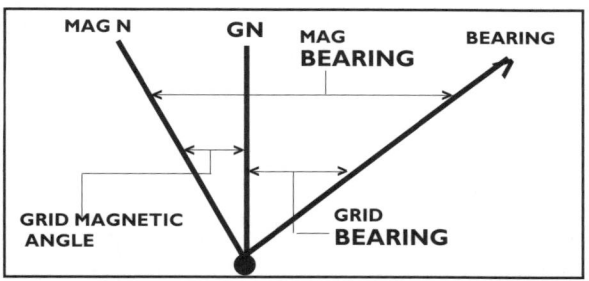

Remember all bearings are measured in a clockwise direction from the NORTH point. A MAG bearing will always be GREATER than the GRID bearing taken, by the amount of the GRID MAGNETIC ANGLE.

Therefore to convert GRID to MAG ADD the GRID MAGNETIC ANGLE.

To convert a MAG bearing to a GRID, SUBTRACT the GRID MAGNETIC ANGLE.

MAP & COMPASS

TO MARCH ON A BEARING

Having converted your GRID BEARING to a MAGNETIC BEARING, set the graduated circle on you compass to read the MAGNETIC BEARING at the DIRECTION OF TRAVEL line.

Then turn the whole COMPASS until the NORTH end of the NEEDLE coincides with the NORTH ARROW and is par allel to the MERIDIAN LINES on the COMPASS HOUSING, holding the COMPASS in front of you march in the direction indicated by the LINE OF TAVEL ARROW.

So long as the compass needle and the NORTH ARROW are kept together, the DIRECTION OF TRAVEL ARROW will remain on the required bearing.

BACK BEARINGS with a SILVA COMPASS

When marching on a bearing - especially at night - over some distance you may often have a doubt in your mind that you may go wandering off course and finish up being lost.

NORTH END OF COMPASS NEEDLE OVER TOP OF NORTH ARROW

The ability to use your compass and to **trust it** by taking a back bearing on to the point from which you started, will prevent you getting into difficulties.

The simplicity of the Silva compass makes the use of back bearings an easy navigational aid.

MAP & COMPASS

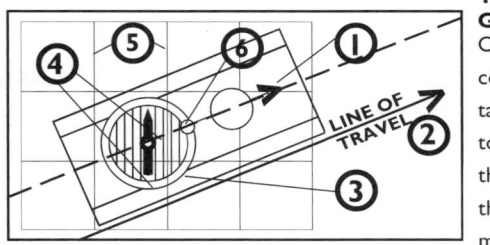

TO TAKE A GRID BEARING

One of the most common uses of taking bearings is to take one from the map to find the bearing to march on.

With your SILVA compass or your protractor it is quite simple to do.

Note: IGNORE THE COMPASS NEEDLE

1. Place the long edge of the compass along the desired line of travel, making sure that the DIRECTION OF TRAVEL ARROW on the compass *POINTS IN THE DIRECTION YOU WISH TO GO.* ①

2. Turn ③ COMPASS NEEDLE HOUSING so that NORTH on the housing rim points to NORTH on the map. You will notice that the MERIDIAN LINES on the COMPASS are parallel to the GRID LINES ④ on the map – *or they should be!* ⑤

3. Read the number of mils/degrees against the DIRECTION OF TRAVEL LINE; this is the GRID BEARING. ⑥ Having taken a GRID BEARING from the map, you must take into account and make allowances for the GRID MAGNETIC ANGLE (GMA).

HILLS AND VALLEYS

The method of showing how the ground is shaped in terms of hills and valleys (termed as **RELIEF**), appear as thin brown lines on the map and are called **CONTOUR LINES.** They are described as "An imaginary line joining all points of equal height above sea level". You must check the information at the bottom of the map near the scale diagram to find the **"Contour Interval",** that is the height between each contour.

5-16

MAP & COMPASS

The following information will give you a better understanding of how contour lines can give a three dimensional view of the area covered by the map.

UNDERSTANDING AND INTERPRETING CONTOURS

Firstly, you must understand that contour lines follow the same height round hills. They do not immediately provide a picture of the shape of the land, but with practice you will begin to interpret the shape of the land in your mind.

SPURS AND RE-ENTRANTS

A **SPUR** projects out from the landmass, a **RE-ENTRANT** is exactly the opposite, a shallow valley running up into the mass. It is not always possible to tell which is the top of the slope and which is the bottom without being able to find the contour figures. When the contour figures can be read with both the map and the figures the correct way up you will be able to tell if the ground is rising or falling.

A general idea of which way the slopes run can be obtained by looking at other features; particularly lakes, ponds, rivers, streams and railway lines. A stream running near a set of contours indicates at once which is the bottom of the slope.

Features such as railways, villages and large woods are more likely to be found at the bottom of a hill than at the top.

CONVEX AND CONCAVE SLOPES

A **CONVEX** slope is one that 'bulges' outwards, a **CONCAVE** slope is one that curves inwards. Standing at the top of a CONVEX slope you would not be able to see all the way down to the bottom, because the outward slope would obscure your view. It is important to recognise that this is 'dead ground', and as such can hide obstacles.

When standing on the top of a CONCAVE slope There will be a clear view down to the bottom (unless it is heavily wooded).

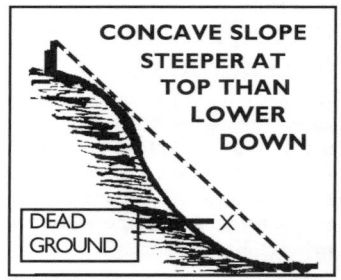

CONCAVE SLOPE STEEPER AT TOP THAN LOWER DOWN

DEAD GROUND —X

MAP & COMPASS

CONTOUR VALUES

If you had several paths around a hill, each one keeping at the same level, and were walking round one of them, you would find that where the paths were near to each other the ground would be steep between the paths.

Where the paths are some distance apart, the ground will slope gently; the further they were apart, the less the slope would be.

CONVEX SLOPE
BULGES OUT
AT TOP

STEEPER
AT THE
LOWER
END

MORE ABOUT CONTOURS

On gentle slopes the CONTOURS are far apart, on steep slopes the CONTOURS are close together. If the ground is broken and rugged there will be many **SPURS** and **RE-ENTRANTS**, a path would be constantly turning in and out. Irregular, sharply turning contours shows broken and rugged country. Where the slopes are smooth, the path will curve gently, bending out as it follows the line of a SPUR and swinging in at a RE-ENTRANT. On gentle slopes the contours appear as smooth flowing curves. Contours may appear to wander about all over, but if you follow them they naturally come back to where they started from; the only exception is when you find a cliff face with a sheer drop, then all the contour lines are so close together they appear to be one.

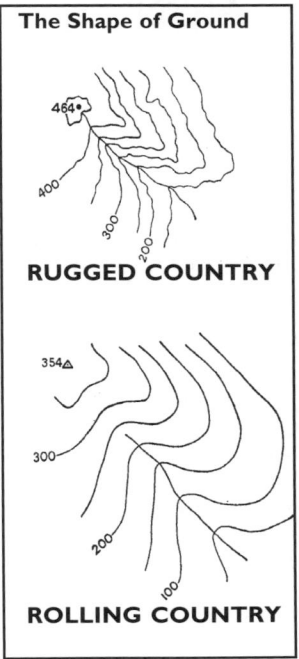

The Shape of Ground

RUGGED COUNTRY

ROLLING COUNTRY

MAP & COMPASS

UNDERSTANDING VERTICAL INTERVAL (V.I.)

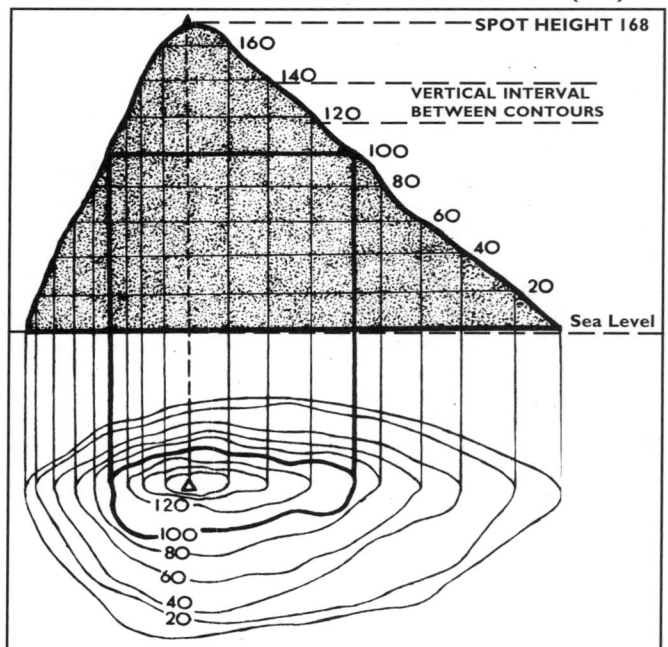

SPOT HEIGHTS

Apart from contours, height is shown by **SPOT HEIGHTS** which is marked on a map by a dot and number ● 168. This is the exact height in metres or feet above sea level.

You will also find **TRIG POINTS**, shown on the map as a small blue triangle with a number next to it ◿ 576, this again is the exact height above sea level.

MAP & COMPASS

Every curve or bend in a contour indicates a SPUR or a valley, a rise or fall in the ground, just as it does on the side of a hill. Remember - the distance apart the contours are still indicates the steepness or flatness of the ground.

Each contour is drawn at a specific height above sea level and each one is the same vertical height above the one below. The difference in height between the contours is called the **VERTICAL INTERVAL (V.I.) See illustration on previous page.**

These heights are written into the contour lines at intervals along their length. On Ordnance Survey maps figures showing the height of contours are always printed so that they read facing up the hill. It is useful to remember this so that you may quickly find out which direction the ground is sloping.

Check the information in the margins of the map to find out if the VI (Vertical Interval) is in Feet or Metres.

Whenever you are 'out and about' look at the ground in the area and draw imaginary contour lines around the hills and valleys. Make a rough sketch and then get a map of the area and see how accurately you have interpreted the ground.

Practice as much as you can, interpreting contours correctly is important when you are planning the route of an expedition, or trying to find a different route out of a difficult area.

MAP & COMPASS

Contours and the shape of ground

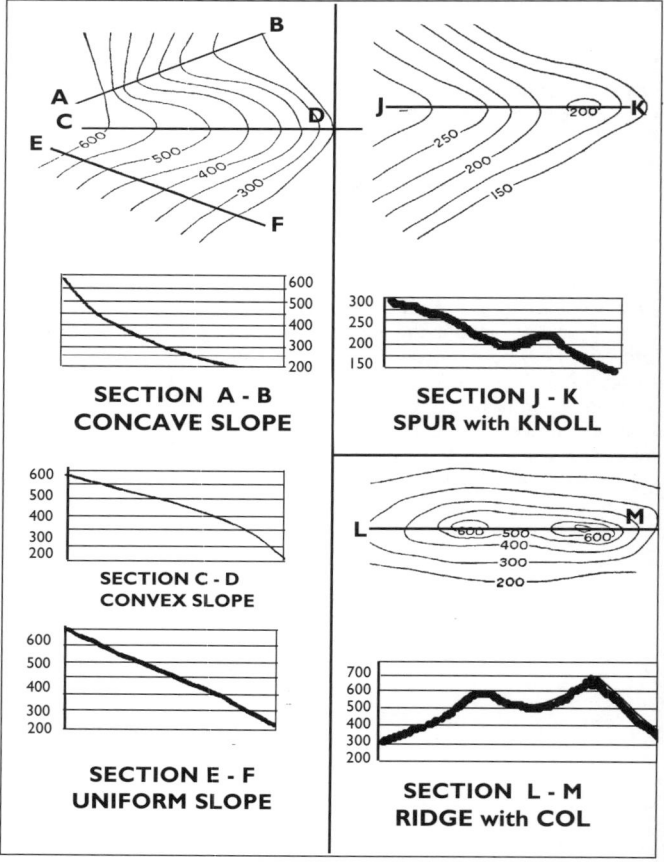

SECTION A - B
CONCAVE SLOPE

SECTION J - K
SPUR with KNOLL

SECTION C - D
CONVEX SLOPE

SECTION E - F
UNIFORM SLOPE

SECTION L - M
RIDGE with COL

MAP & COMPASS

KNOW YOUR CONTOUR PATTERNS

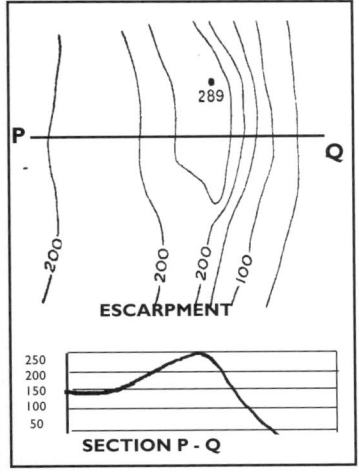

ESCARPMENT

SECTION P - Q

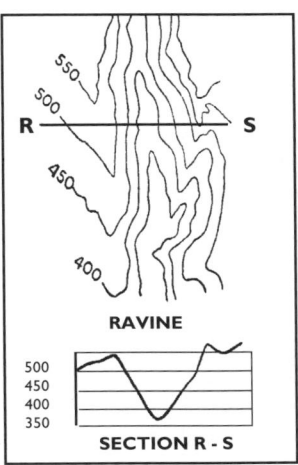

RAVINE

SECTION R - S

1. Contours close together mean steep slopes.
2. Contours far apart mean gentle slopes.
3. When contours are evenly spaced the slope is uniform, thes slopes have small undulations and pockets of dead ground.
4. When the spacing of the contours, reading from high ground to low, decreases, the slope is convex. Convex slopes mean short visibility; dead ground becomes very close.
5. When spacing of contours, reading from high to low, increases, the slope is concave.
   Concave slopes mean good visibility and little dead ground.
6. Wandering contours at various distances apart and never close, mean undulating ground. Important to note the general direction of the fall in the ground.
7. Gently curving contours indicate an area of country of rounded slopes. As the ground becomes steeper the contours come closer together; as it becomes more rugged the curves disappear and the contours take on 'jagged' shapes.

MAP & COMPASS

SCALES AND MEASURING DISTANCE

The scale of a map is the relationship between the actual distance measured from one point to another on the ground and the distance between the same two points on a map. The way that the 'scale' of a map is expressed is by the **Representative Fraction.** It used to be expressed in words, "one inch to a mile" or "four miles to one inch".

The **Representative Fraction (RF)** is the standard method used on all continental maps and wherever the metric system is used. Most British maps are now expressed in metric. It is simple to use if you remember that the RF is 1/X, one unit of distance on the map represents X units of distance on the ground. For example, a scale of 1/50,000 means that one inch/centimetre/metre on the map represents 50,000 inches/centimetres/metre on the ground.

The essential connection is that the SAME unit of measurement applies both to the map and to the ground measurement. A distance of 2cms on a 1/50,000 map therefore represents 2 x 50,000 cm on the ground = 100,000cm = 1000 metres.

All maps are printed with graphic linear scales, usually in the centre of the bottom margin, from which any horizontal distance may be measured on the map in kilometres and metres, or in miles and yards. A linear map scale is always shown in the form of a diagram, you will notice that the zero mark is set from the left of the scale by one major division, which is then subdivided into ten (or other suitable) sub-divisions usually not longer than about 4mm each.

SCALE   1 : 50 000

2 Centimetres to 1 Kilometres (one grid square)

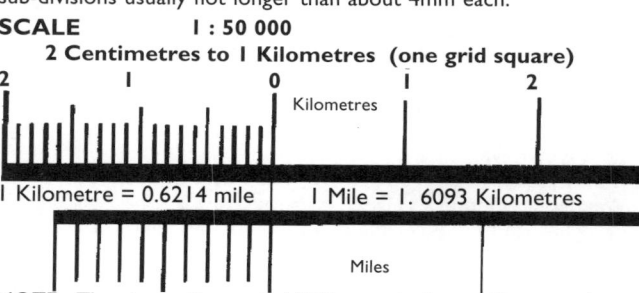

NOTE: The above diagram is NOT to scale, but to illustrate the scale found on a 1: 50 000 map. Any measurements falling between these sub-divisions must be estimated.

MAP & COMPASS

PACING

Pacing is necessary because you must always know how exactly far you have gone when counting a number of your own 'paces'. You should know your 'Pacing Scale', over different types of conditions, I.E tarmac roads, tracks, grasslands, woodlands etc. To find your PACING SCALE, put two markers out 100m apart. Walk the distance between them as you would on a patrol, counting the paces as you go.

If it has taken you 120 paces to cover the 100m, then that is your

PACING SCALE.

It follows, to use this scale if you were on a patrol and had to go a distance of 300m, you would have to count out 360 paces. Under some conditions you can use a specific length of string, tying knots at every 120 paces. Having used the length of string, un-tie the knots and repeat the process on the next 'leg' of your route. It is always advisable to have a CHECK PACER, remembering to check that your PACING SCALE is the same by day and night. You will have to make adjustments according to the terrain, weayher, wind, temperature, rain etc.

MAP & COMPASS

LINEAR MAP SCALE

How To Measure Distance

Make a mark on the straight edge of a piece of paper, put the mark on the point you wish to measure from and make successive marks along the edge of the paper as y you follow the route from your starting point to the final point.

This is easy if you just wish to measure along a straight road, but if it means going round corners you will have to pivot the paper and make several marks as you progress.

The total distance is recorded along the edge of the paper.

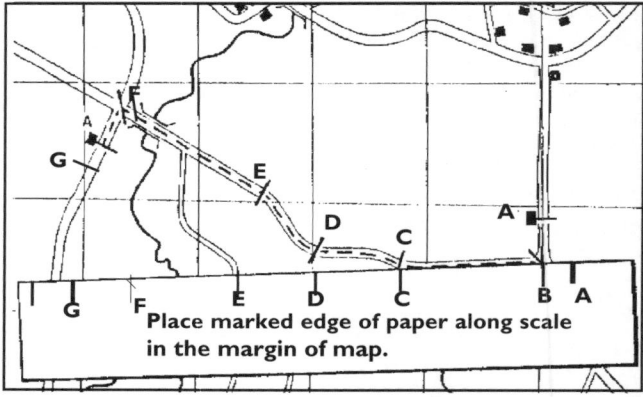

Place marked edge of paper along scale in the margin of map.

Lay the paper along the scale on the map, with the right hand, tick against one of the major divisions, so that the left hand tick lies against the sub-divisions to the left of the zero mark. The total distance is then the number of major divisions plus the distance to the left of the zero.

With practice this is quite an accurate method of measuring distances.

MAP & COMPASS

MOVING ROUND OBSTACLES

Obstacles are often found on a route and in order to keep a really
accurate direction you should go round them by plotting a series of
right angles and measuring by paces as illustrated in the diagram, **200 x
500 x 200**

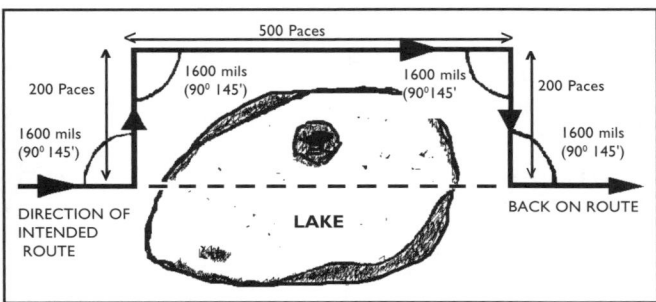

FINDING TRUE NORTH FROM THE SUN USING A WATCH

When you do not have a map or
are map reading without a
compass, it can help if you are
able to find the rough direction
of TRUE NORTH or SOUTH.
The method explained will give
you an approximate direction –
not accurate enough for reading
bearings or other measurements.

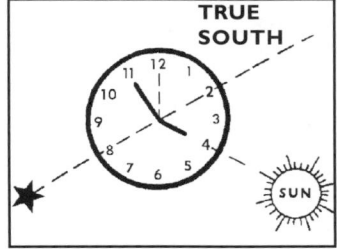

INFORMATION – as the sun rises in the EAST, and moves (in the
Northern Hemisphere) through the Southern sky, setting in the
WEST, the position of the Sun, when visible, is always a rough guide to
the direction of NORTH.

MAP & COMPASS

A watch, when set to Greenwich Mean Time (GMT) for UK (or to local time for other areas some distance EAST or WEST of Greenwich may be used.

If summertime or other artificial time is in local use, your watch should be adjusted to Greenwich Mean Time (GMT) or to the local standard time.

METHOD – lay your watch flat, with the HOUR HAND pointing to the Sun.

In the NORTHERN Hemisphere, TRUE SOUTH will then be midway between the hour hand and twelve o'clock on the watch – see the diagram.

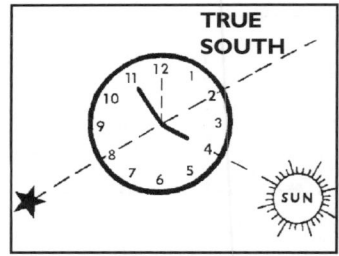

In the SOUTHERN Hemisphere, lay your watch with twelve o'clock pointing to the Sun.

TRUE NORTH then lies midway between the hour hand and twelve o'clock.

When the Sun is high up in the sky, this method cannot be used with any success. In any case the result is unlikely to be accurate to better than five degrees.

FINDING TRUE NORTH – by the stars (Northern Latitude)
In latitudes less than 60^0 the **POLE STAR** is never more than about 40 miles away from the **TRUE NORTH**.

The position of the **POLE STAR** is indicated by the "pointers" of **The Great Bear or Plough – see diagram.**

All stars revolve round the POLE STAR and the Plough may be either below it low down near the horizon and "right way up" or above it in the sky and "upside down" or in any position between.

If the Plough is obscured or below the horizon, **Cassiopeia** which is shaped like a **'W'** and is on the opposite side of the POLE STAR from the Plough, may be visible; the POLE STAR is the nearest bright star within the arms of the 'W'.

Above 60^0 the POLE STAR is too high in the sky to be a good guide to NORTH.

At the NORTH POLE it is vertically overhead.

MAP & COMPASS

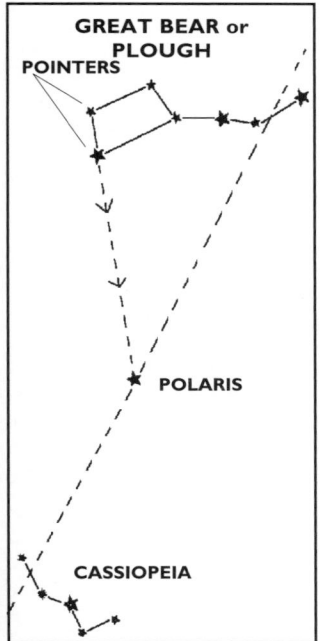

GREAT BEAR or PLOUGH

POINTERS

POLARIS

CASSIOPEIA

The only way to learn night navigation is to get out in the dark, identify the constellations shown in the diagram on the left and practice moving in different directions by using stars and then checking with your compass. As with all map reading and compass work – *PRACTICE MAKES PERFECT*

MAP & COMPASS

ROUTE CARDS

The purpose of a ROUTE CARD is to ensure that you plan the route you are taking and from the start become aware of the distances you are proposing to travel, the obstacles that you will encounter, either overcoming them or taking action to find a route round them. RV's and the locations for your campsites, approximate timings. Always ensure that you give a copy of your Route Card to a responsible person to ensure that if there is an emergency the rescuers know where to start looking.

The illustration of the route card on the next page is self-explanatory; you need plenty of space in each column to write your information. Never be short on detail, it is better to have more information than you need rather than not enough. List mobile phone numbers and names

If you are in a group, ensure that each member of the group has a good copy of the route card, again we stress that it is important to ensure that you leave a copy with someone you will be in contact with during your expedition.

Remember, always include your CHECK POINTS and the **expected TIMES** that you will be there on your Route Card.

	ROUTE CARD						

Date_____

Produced by_____ Start Point Grid Ref _____ ETD _____
Date finish_____ Finishing Point GridRef_____ ETA _____

	From		To		Bearings			Remarks Landmarks Hazards
Leg	Location	Grid Ref	Location	Grid Ref	Grid	Mag	Distance	
		Example of headings and layout of a Route Card - reduced in size.					

MAP & COMPASS

The hands on the diagram of a clock face are pointing to a quarter past eight.

If it was in the morning (Ante Meridian - **AM** - before noon), you would call it 0815 hours.

If it was in the evening, (Post Meridian – **PM** - after noon), you would call it 2015 hours.

The importance of using the 24 hour clock system cannot be ignored as it avoids any confusion over timings and is explicit in its meaning. The Armed Services use what is know as the date/time group, which includes the date as two figures in front of the time.

Examples: 122200 June would be 2200hrs on the 12th of June, i.e. 10pm in the evening of the 12th of June.

This system is used when timings cover several days,
e.g. START Exercise 170600 END Exercise 201000
The Exercise will begin at 6am on the 17th and end at 10am on the 20th.
As with any new skill, make use of the 24 hour clock when giving the time - practice makes perfect!

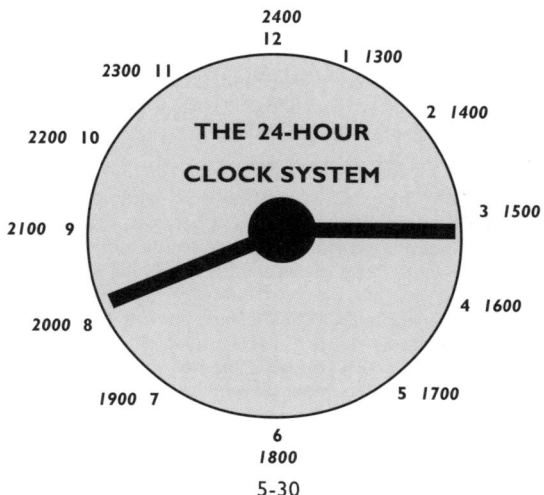

MAP & COMPASS
ORIENTEERING

Orienteering is like a car rally on foot, and as a sport has become well established in the UK. It can be over a mile or two or made to cover a vast area. It can be a morning's fun, last a day or several days. "Tough" orienteering can include crossing mountains, or be "improved" by including rafting or even canoes. It can take the form of a 'Treasure Hunt', or finding 'escaped prisoners'.
It will depend upon the imagination of your instructors to make it fun.

It is a highly competitive sport testing your map reading skills and your ability to think quickly on your feet. You need to be physically fit and have determination to safely navigate around a set course laid out by the organisers. The 'event' is judged by the shortest time it takes competitors to navigate and complete the course with the most correct points scored. Your progress is recorded on a Control Card that contains spaces for the individual checkpoint marks.

HOW IT IS ORGANISED
A **MASTER MAP** of the area in which the orienteering is to take place will be set up for all competitors to see. Normally you will be given a list of **MAP REFERENCES** that are the **CONTROL POINTS.** You will be issued with your own map in a plastic cover or case. You are given time to plot the CONTROL references on your map from the Master Map, and then when it is time for you to begin, set out for your first CONTROL.

CHECK POINTS OR CONTROLS

The CHECK POINTS or CONTROLS, which make up the route, are usually marked in some way to distinguish between them. In some Forestry Commission areas these markers are diamond shape painted red and white, fixed to posts each one being separately numbered.
In competitions moveable CONTROLS are put out before the competition. This allows the organisers to use different areas and different courses. To prove you have been to the CONTROL you have to make a note of the number or symbol carved into the top of each post or use a special punch called a Swedish marker punch on your event card. These will be checked on your return, time penalties

MAP & COMPASS

are added for incorrect CONTROL marks.

The Controls are not easy to find, more often than not they can only be seen from a close distance, usually less than 30m, therefore accurate map reading is essential if you are to find them.

It is a good idea to chose an easily identified point like a track junction near to the CONTROL (this is called an ATTACK POINT) and then pace the distance on a bearing to the CONTROL.

EQUIPMENT

To Orienteer safely you normally require: Map and Map Case (or plastic cover), Compass (Silva type), Pen/Pencil, and Whistle.

CLOTHING

The type of clothing you wear depends on the time of year, the location of the course, the type of country and how long the event is to last. Check with the organisers, some will refuse entry to competitors inadequately dressed for the area. If you really enjoy the sport and wish to make it a hobby you may wish to buy special kit. Remember, experienced Orienteerers take only what they need.
The following list may be useful.

Wool or cotton shirt or vest

A lightweight waterproof cagoule

Long trousers/track suit bottoms to protect legs against thorns, nettles bracken, etc.

Cotton or wool socks

Strong walking/running shoes (spare laces)

A towel for when you return to base

A change of clothing and shoes, (you may be very wet and dirty).

KEEPING DIRECTION

To Orienteer successfully you must be able to keep going in the correct direction. This can be achieved in two ways:

1. USING A COMPASS. This will always tell you where NORTH is and by SETTING the compass you can find the direction in which you want to go. This is only useful in open country like moor land.

2. USING THE MAP. This is perhaps the best method since it is hard to get lost if you use your map correctly. The compass is only used to orientate the map, (point the map North). Once the map is orientated always use known features to get you to your destination.

MAP & COMPASS

This involves planning your route in advance and in a number of short, easily navigated "legs". If there is a leg with no easily identified features, trust your compass.

GETTING LOST

Even the best navigators can sometimes get lost, however this is not usually the disaster it may seem, since it is not too difficult to find yourself again.

If you do get lost, ***STOP AND THINK IT THROUGH.***

1. Don't panic – a cool head is needed.
2. Use the compass and orientate your map, try and trace your route.
3. Try to identify the ground around you and match it to the map. If you succeed, then you are no longer lost, plan your route onward.
4. If you cannot identify the ground, then try and re-trace your route to the previous Checkpoint.
5. If this also fails, set your compass and walk toward a road or other easily identifiable line on the ground then stay there until found.

MAP & COMPASS

THE ORIENTEERING MAP

The map is usually a large scale, (1:10000 or 1:15000 scale) representation of the land, the information around the margin of the map will tell you what the colours and symbols mean. Study your map and identify everything.

Colours on the SPECIAL ORIENTEERING MAPS are used to indicate the speed at which you can MOVE, not the TYPE OF GROUND, for instance an area shaded dark green might indicate ground which would be very difficult to move through, usually known as "FIGHT" because you would have to fight your way through it, whereas a light green area could indicate close woodland or very rough ground through which you would walk.

White may indicate where you could run, perhaps grassland or very mature woodland where the trees are well spaced.

Because of it's scale, the orienteering map shows great detail and will accurately position depressions in the ground, holes and mounds, earth walls and embankments which would normally not be shown. Learn these new symbols as soon as you can, identifying them on the ground could be the difference between being lost and finishing the course. You must know exactly where you are at all times, you will only achieve this by checking your map and always keeping it orientated.

NAVIGATION TECHNIQUES, CHOOSING A ROUTE

When you chose your route try and find the best way of getting to the first CONTROL by selecting a good, easily identifiable **ATTACK POINT** like a track junction and then plan your route to this **ATTACK POINT**

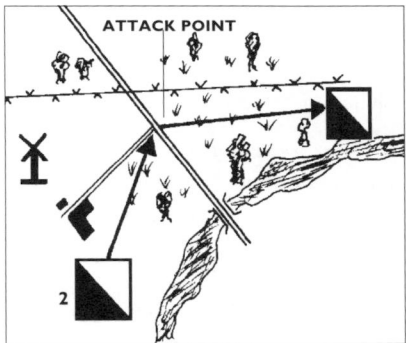

MAP & COMPASS

using easily followed features like tracks, fence lines, forest edges and streams. These features are known as **COLLECTION POINTS** because as you move around the course you can 'collect them'. Attempting to go directly to a **CONTROL** is not a good idea since they are easily missed.

Continue to plan your route round the course in the way described, chose a route that has as many **COLLECTION POINTS** on it as possible. Remember to periodically check your route with your compass.

Try to avoid bogs, dense forest and very steep hills, as these will either slow you down or prove to be impassable. It will often be better to go round an obstacle, even if the distance covered is greater, it may well be easier and faster. To help you decide, remember the following:

The Short Hard Route versus The Long Easy Route; swim across a lake or go around it: climb up and over a mountain or go round the valley. Remember to periodically check your route with your compass.

A good runner will typically take the following amounts of time to complete 400 metres over differing terrain:

a. Path – 2 mins.
b. Heath land – 4 mins
c. Open Forest – 6 mins
d. Thick Firs - 10 mins or more.

The Steep Short Route versus The Long Flat Route

When orienteering in hilly country you will often find that the course has a number of **CONTROLS** at opposite sides of a steep hill or valley. You must then make the decision whether or not it will be quicker to go over the top or to 'contour' round. To help you make your choice, a 25-metre height gain will be the equivalent to 100 metres on the flat.

AIMING OFF

Sometimes the **CONTROL** you are aiming for is on a linear feature such as a track or stream at right angles to your line of approach. This will mean that the **CONTROL** may be difficult to find if you aim straight for it since if you miss it, you will not know for sure whether it is North or South, for example.

Simply AIMING OFF to one side o the **CONTROL** can overcome

MAP & COMPASS

this problem, let us say the North, then when you reach the stream/track you will know that the **CONTROL** is to the South. This will cut down time spent searching for the **CONTROL.**

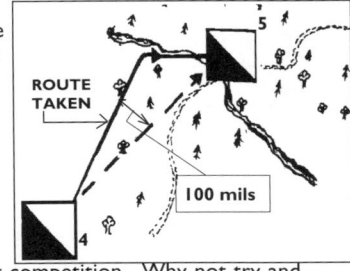

Many ACF Counties run their own competitions, some Districts organise 'finals'. The Regular Army organise the cadet forces annual orienteering competition. Why not try and arrange a 'challenge' at your Detachment, Cadets v. Adult Instructors. You may even win!

ON MAPS

The majority of maps in your Detachment will be Ordnance Survey 1:50000 scale.

Most Military Maps used onAnnual Camps, and at weekends on military land will be produced as1:25000 scale (some are 1:50000 so do check them)

You will find that the actual sheet size of some maps are large and difficult to handle. They require careful folding to leave exposed the area you are working on. Keep them in a plastic cover or a proper Map Case to keep them clean and dry.

Points to note

1. The marginal information is usually at the bottom of the map, and the information includes extra items, such as "No Go' and 'Out of Bounds' areas.

2. "No Go" areas are subject to frequent change in some areas, so ensure that your map is the latest issue before you start planning routes.

3. Remember that contour lines that appear to be further apart are NOT, it is a larger scale map than the 1:25000; don't be caught out and find you have a steep climb instead of a gentle slope.

4. Because of the larger scale, there will be far more information given; this may be rather confusing for a while.

Remember as always "practice makes perfect"

MAP & COMPASS
TERMS USED IN MAP READING

BEARING: The angle, measured clockwise, that a line makes with a fixed zero line. It may be a True Bearing, measured from True North - a Magnetic Bearing measured with a compass from Magnetic North, or a Grid Bearing measured from Grid North.

COL (SADDLE): The low land or ridge, connecting two hilltops.

CONTOUR: An imaginary line on the surface of theground at the same height above mean sea level throughout its length. Contour line are drawn a map to show the shape of the ground.

CREST: The highest part of a hill or range of hills.

DETAIL: All the topographical information on a map.

ESCARPMENT: The steep hillside formed by a drop in land level, usually at the edge of a plateau.

GRADIENT: A slope described by a percentage, mostly used on roads to indicate a steep hill.

GRID: Lines drawn on the map forming squares as a basis for a system of map references.

LEFT or RIGHT BANK: The appropriate bank of a stream or river when facing DOWN stream.

LOCAL MAGNETIC ATTRACTION: Attraction of the compass needle due to presence of metal or magnetic iron ore. NOT to be confused with Magnetic Variation.

MAGNETIC VARIATION or DECLINATION: The angle between True North and Magnetic North.

MAGNETIC NORTH: The point in far north of Canada, to which a compass needle points.

MERIDIAN: A true north and south line.

ORIENTATING A MAP: Placing it so that its True North line points

MAP & COMPASS

True North (or Magnetic or Grid North line points to Magnetic or Grid North), also called "Setting the Map".

PLATEAU: A raised plain, usually quite flat, above a level of the land

PLOTTING: Transferring to a map bearings and other measurements.

RAY: A line drawn from the position of an observer to fix the direction of an object.

RE-ENTRANT: A shallow valley running into a hill, usually between two spurs, found where a stream runs off a hillside.

RE-SECTION: The process of finding a position by taking bearings on two identifiable points and plotting them on a map, also by fixing a position by observation of at least two previously fixed points.

SPOT HEIGHT: A point on a map whose height has been found by survey methods, identified on a map by a dot with figure against it.

SLOPES: (Concave and Convex): Convex "bulges out", Concave "caves in".

SPUR: A hill feature or low ridge, running out from a hill or high ground, often found between two re-entrants.

TRIG POINT: A concrete pillar with a brass mounting used by Ordnance Survey for their survey work. The correct name is a Triangulation Point. Marked on a map by a small triangle with the height above sea level shown next to it.

TRUE NORTH: The direction of the North pole from that point.

VERTICAL INTERVAL (V.I.): The difference in height between two adjacent contours.

WATERSHED: The line, usually mountain range where waters divide to flow in different directions.

Deception using a large scale maps
A tip to remember when using large scale maps, contour lines close together indicate steep sloping ground, but due to the scale you may be misled as to the severity of the slope on the ground

---

MAP & COMPASS

GLOBAL POSITIONING SYSTEM

GPS is a simple concept involving a complex system of ground stations, satellites and receivers. The first GPS satellite was launched by the Americans for military use by the in 1989.

For the civilian user, GPS accuracy has improved greatly over the years. Refinements in technology and removal of selective availability by the US government mean that the average user can now pinpoint their position to within 20 yards. However, GPS is still only a navigational aid; it does not work indoors because a clear view of the sky is needed.

Now, 24 satellites (soon to be 30), orbit the earth every 12 hours from a distance of 11,000 miles, sending signals to a GPS receiver to compute velocity, time and position. The receiver must lock on to four of the satellite signals to compute a 3-D position fix for accurate reading.

A typical GPS device consists of a 12 channel parallel receiver, an antenna, internal memory, and a LCD screen. Many sizes and configurations are available. GPS planning programs contain so much information that is has become virtually impossible to get lost, with over a million waypoints (latitude/longitude coordinates) that translate into markers on a GPS unit. There are web – enabled packages that provide up to date weather and construction warnings along your route, hiking trails, hospitals and much more. Some of the more sophisticated programs include spoken and voice – activated commands for use with multimedia laptops and PDAs.

GPS technology is similar to the internet in that both were created by the United States Government for government use. In the near future, GPS will be part of our everyday life; un – manned vehicle navigation may be closer than we think!

If you are planning to buy a GPS, do some research before you buy; consumer GPS units are produced by several manufacturers, PC software manufacturers are integrating GPS support into many of their trip – planning and mapping programs.

MAP & COMPASS
PATHFINDER PROTRACTOR/ROMER
IMPROVE YOUR MAP READING TRAINING & SKILLS

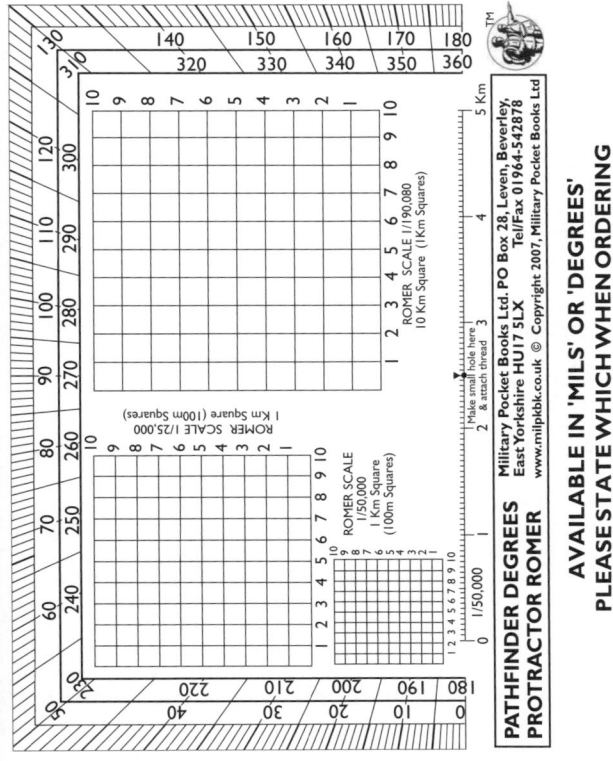

PATHFINDER DEGREES
PROTRACTOR ROMER

Military Pocket Books Ltd. PO Box 28, Leven, Beverley,
East Yorkshire HU17 5LX   Tel/Fax 01964-542878
www.milpkbk.co.uk © Copyright 2007, Military Pocket Books Ltd

AVAILABLE IN 'MILS' OR 'DEGREES'
PLEASE STATE WHICH WHEN ORDERING

ROMER SCALE 1/190,080
10 Km Square (1Km Squares)

ROMER SCALE 1/25,000
1 Km Square (100m Squares)

ROMER SCALE
1/50,000
1 Km Square
(100m Squares)

1/50,000

Buy yours Protractro Romer Direct
Military Pocket Books Web Shop
www.milpkbk.co.uk

MAP & COMPASS

SELF TEST QUESTIONS.

1. Who produces maps for the Army.
2. Where will you find the Map Sheet number.
3. What is the Grid System used for.
4. Do you normally use a four or six figure reference to pin point a item.
5. On a map sheet where is North.
6. What is a Romer used for.
7. What is to Orientate a map for.
8. Where do you find Meridian lines on a Silva compass.
9. How can you set a map without a compass.
10. Name eight Cardinal Points.
11. How many North's are there.
12. What do you understand by the GMA.
13. What is Grid Convergence.
14. How many types of Bearings are there, and what are they called.
15. What is I.C.E, and what do you do about it.
16. Taking a bearing, which two arrows on a compass do you "line-up".
17. Taking a Grid bearing, what do you do with the compass needle.
18. Complete the sentence: "Grid to Mag Add, _ _ _ _ _".
19. What is the reverse of a forward bearing.
20. What use has a contour line, give a definition.
21. Concave and Convex slopes, which "bulges" out, which has good visibility.
22. Where are you most likely to find a re-entrant.
23. What type of ground will you find if contours are close together.
24. What is the name given to the height between contours.
25. It says; "one unit of measure on the map, equals X on the ground". Explain what is this about.
26. When finding North with a watch (that has hands) which hand is pointed to the sun.
27. Without a compass, how would you find North on a clear night.
28. You are to make out a Route Card, give the headings required to do so.
29. When do you use a Master Map.
30. When Orienteering, why do you "Aim Off
31. What is the scale of most MILITARY maps you will be given to use on military training areas,.

FIRST AID, HEALTH & SAFETY

Chapter 6

Bearer Company of the
1st. Cadet Battalion King's Royal Rifle Corps 1907
The lessons of the South African War led to wholesale changes in the way in which the regular army was trained. This was reflected in the new training manuals prepared for cadets and resulting programmes were both lively and varied. Ironically, the tactics of manoeuvre on which training was based in no way prepared for the trench war that was to come.

Standards were high, matching up to a system in which units were inspected annually and the efficiency of each cadet tested. In the larger units, specialist sections or companies were the order of the day. They included bands, signallers, pioneers, ambulance sections and cyclist sections. This was indeed a golden age and few modern cadet units could match either the variety of activities or the high standards set.

We illustrate members of the Bearer Company of the 1st. Cadet

Bearer Company. 1st. Cadet.Bn.
King's Royal Rifle Corps. 1907.

Battalion King's Royal Rifle Corps.

These were fully trained cadets who had gone on to qualify in ambulance work.

As with shooting, there was active competition in this field. In 1906 this particular unit won the Challenge Shield of the Volunteer Medical Association.

The cadets wear the rifle green uniform of the K.R.R.C. with the interesting addition of matching slouch hats with green plumes. For a number of years following the South African War slouch hats remained in fashion for field training

FIRST AID, HEALTH & SAFETY

Introduction

First Aid is the immediate help given to someone who is ill or injured. Think for a moment, if you were ill or injured wouldn't you want someone to stop help and you? First aid skills are easy to learn and with regular practice and knowledge it can be of benefit through-out your whole life, to you, your family members and friends. Please note that first aid is not an exact science and often casualties do not respond in a way you hope they will and of course the outcomes of a casualty are not always successful, so don't be afraid to talk things through with someone if you have been affected by giving first aid treatment. As a junior cadet, you have access to gaining the nationally recognised Youth First Aid qualification which is valid for three years, approved by ACFA, a special centre of St John Ambulance. A senior cadet aged over 14 can undertake the adult first aid qualification Activity First Aid, progressing from aged 16 years to the Health & Safety Executive recognised First Aid at Work certificate. Remember DO NO HARM.

Assessing the Situation (AMEGR)

As a first aider when you come across a situation you must act quickly, but calmly to
Assess the situation. After finding out what happened you must remove any hazards or dangers to
Make the Area Safe, ensure you do not become a casualty. Then approach the casualty to see if they are conscious and decide to give the appropriate
Emergency Aid treatment. Once you have got the facts,
Get Help, lastly
Report what has happened to your detachment staff, they may be able to help you. You may need to *clear up* the area, *stock up* your first aid kit, then *brew up* after all your hard work and efforts!

Telephoning for Help

After assessing the situation and casualty/ies you can dial 999 or 112 for the emergency services. State which service you require; police, fire, ambulance, mine, mountain, cave and fell rescue (via the police).
If you are unsure of your location, do not panic, your call can be traced. Stay on the line until the control officer clears the line. You will need to tell the emergency services:

FIRST AID, HEALTH & SAFETY

1. Your telephone number
2. The exact location of the incident
3. Type of incident eg. Traffic accident, two cars, three people.
4. The number, gender and approximate age of the casualties and any other information you may know about their condition such as "Man, late fifties, suspected heart attack"

Details of any hazards such as gas, toxic substances, relevant weather conditions such as ice or fog.

If you have to leave a casualty alone minimise the risk to the casualty by carrying out *Emergency Aid*. If you have a helper, ask them to do this and tell them to come back and tell you help is on its way.

The Primary Survey (DRAB)

Remembering this sequence is really important to enable you to look for life-threatening conditions quickly.
It can be used on casualties over the age of 1.

D – DANGER

Are there any risks to you, the casualty or by-standers. If so, remove it if safe to do so or you may need to enlist help to move the casualty. Top tip – never move a casualty unnecessarily.

R – RESPONSE

Check the casualty, are they visibly conscious? Does the casualty respond to your voice or gently stimulation, if yes, check for other conditions and treat as necessary. If no, carry on with the primary survey. **Summon help if needed by shouting.**

A – AIRWAY

Open the casualty's airway by gently tilting the head back and lifting the chin.

B – BREATHING

Check for breathing by placing your ear by their mouth and nose to listen, look and feel for no more than 10 seconds. What kind of breathing is it? Noisy, easy or difficult. Are they breathing normally? If they are breathing you will need to place the unconscious casualty into the recovery position.
Are you alone or do you have a helper? Either go or send for help at this point. You must have carried out your DRAB checks before sending for help – the emergency services will need to know this information. Any casualty unconscious for more than 3 minutes will need to go to hospital, urgently.

FIRST AID, HEALTH & SAFETY

In an unconscious casualty, the greatest danger is that food, vomit, blood, water, other substance or the tongue may block the **AIRWAY** and prevent the casualty from breathing.
OPEN THE AIRWAY, LIFT THE CHIN UPWARDS WITH THE INDEX FINGER AND MIDDLE FINGERS OF ONE HAND, WHILST PRESSING THE FOREHEAD BACK WITH THE PALM OF THE OTHER HAND.

How to place in Recovery Position (from laid on their back).

1. Kneel beside the casualty. Remove bulky objects such as phones, keys, spectacles.
2. Ensure the casualty has straight legs.
3. Place arm at right angles, palm facing upwards.
4. Bring arm farthest away across the chest, holding the back of the hand against the side of the cheek nearest to you.
5. With your other hand grasp the far leg, on the far side just under the knee and pull it up, keeping the foot flat on the floor.
6. Keep the hand against the cheek, pull on the far leg towards you and onto their side.
7. Adjust the bent leg nearest to you at right angles. Tilt the head back gently to keep the airway open. If left in the recovery position for longer than 30 minutes, then turn onto the other side.
8. If you suspect spinal injury, try to keep the spine straight, inline with the head.

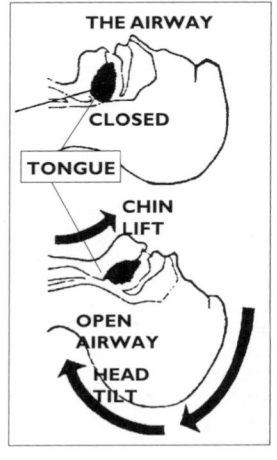

THE AIRWAY

CLOSED

TONGUE

CHIN LIFT

OPEN AIRWAY

HEAD TILT

FIRST AID, HEALTH & SAFETY

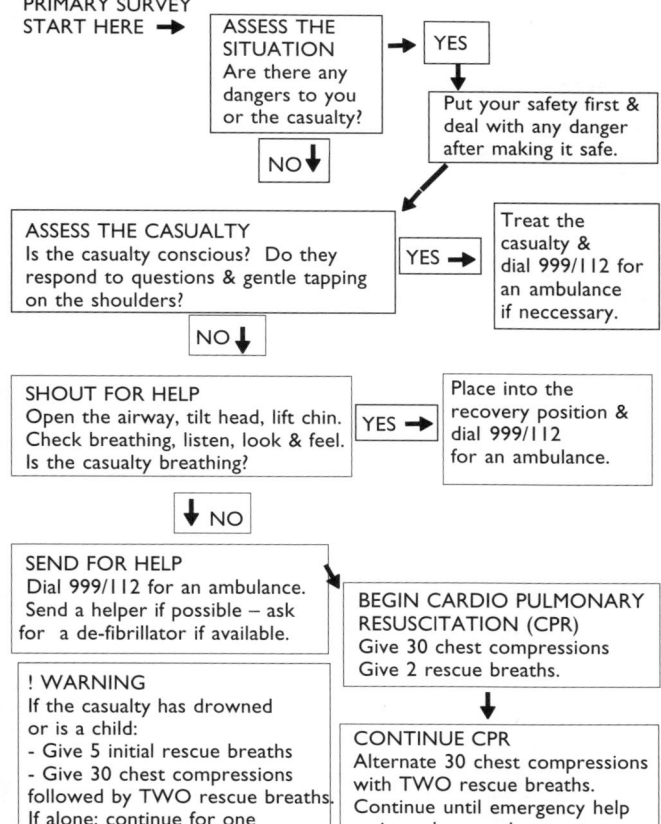

PRIMARY SURVEY
START HERE ➡

ASSESS THE SITUATION
Are there any dangers to you or the casualty?

➡ YES

Put your safety first & deal with any danger after making it safe.

NO ⬇

ASSESS THE CASUALTY
Is the casualty conscious? Do they respond to questions & gentle tapping on the shoulders?

YES ➡

Treat the casualty & dial 999/112 for an ambulance if neccessary.

NO ⬇

SHOUT FOR HELP
Open the airway, tilt head, lift chin. Check breathing, listen, look & feel. Is the casualty breathing?

YES ➡

Place into the recovery position & dial 999/112 for an ambulance.

⬇ NO

SEND FOR HELP
Dial 999/112 for an ambulance. Send a helper if possible – ask for a de-fibrillator if available.

BEGIN CARDIO PULMONARY RESUSCITATION (CPR)
Give 30 chest compressions
Give 2 rescue breaths.

⬇

! WARNING
If the casualty has drowned or is a child:
- Give 5 initial rescue breaths
- Give 30 chest compressions followed by TWO rescue breaths.
If alone: continue for one minute, then call an ambulance.
Then - CONTINUE CPR ➡

CONTINUE CPR
Alternate 30 chest compressions with TWO rescue breaths. Continue until emergency help arrives, the casualty starts breathing normally, or you are too exhausted to continue.

CHAIN OF SURVIVAL

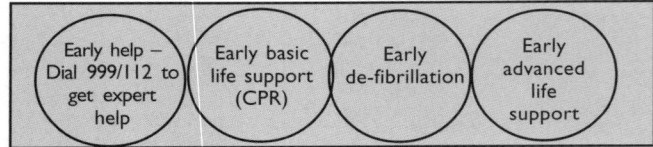

Early help – Dial 999/112 to get expert help

Early basic life support (CPR)

Early de-fibrillation

Early advanced life support

A Secondary Survey (Head to Toe)

Once you have provided the initial treatment for the casualty, you will need to look for other clues to find out what is wrong with the person. It involves taking a history and physically examining a casualty and scene around them. Do they have any medication on them? Do you know if they have any allergies? When did they last eat? To carry out a head-to-toe survey you will need both hands to examine the casualty, to compare and contrast opposite sides of the body and limbs. Look carefully at the situation they are in and at the casualty. Ask the casualty and on-lookers questions and listen carefully to their answers. Your senses may prove helpful in looking for clues, such as unusual smells. Communication is key and you will need to inform your casualty about what you are doing and also gaining their permission. Some casualties may be very sensitive about you touching them. Do things that only the casualty will let you. DO NO HARM.

Head to Toe (Secondary) Survey

1. Start at the head, run your hands over the scalp & look for bleeding, swelling or indentation. In all cases, try not to move the head or neck.
2. Check both ears for fluid.
3. Check eyes, the pupils should be equal in size.
4. Check the nose for any fluid such as blood.
5. Check the rate & depth of breathing, note any unusual odour.
6. Check the mouth. DO NOT remove dentures unless they are causing an obstruction. Look for wounds.
7. Look at the face for wounds, any irregularity or symmetry.
8. Note the colour and temperature of the skin.
9. Loosen tight clothing at neck; look for swelling or wounds.
10. Look for a medic alert or talisman, worn at the neck or wrist.
11. Feeling down the chest for swelling, irregularities or wounds. If they are conscious ask them to take a breath to assess for equal movements and to listen for any lung sounds.

12. Check the collar bones for deformities.
13. Check each arm in turn for irregularities, wounds, needle marks etc. Ask them to bend and straighten fingers and elbows.
14. Check both hands & fingers for injury.
15. If there is a problem with movement or loss of feeling in the arms do not examine the spine, otherwise place your hands under the hollow of the back to check for swelling, tenderness or irregularity.
16. Look at the abdomen for bruising, wounds, tenderness or rigidity.
17. Place your hands on either side of the hips & gently rock the pelvis, noting any differences in motion. Make a note of any incontinence or bleeding from the private areas.
18. Check and examine each leg in turn for wounds, swelling or stiffness at the joints. Ask the casualty to bend & straighten in turn.
19. Examine each foot and ankle for swelling, irregularity and movement.

Following a secondary survey, treat any problems you find, and note down any abnormalities you may have found to pass on to the emergency services.

Cardio Pulmonary Resuscitation (CPR)

The circulatory system pumps blood around the body. When the heart stops we can artificially pump blood around the body by performing chest compressions. Combining chest compressions with rescue breaths is known as CPR. It is important firstly to ensure professional medical help is on its way to ensure the best outcomes of the casualty and then carry out CPR to buy time until help arrives. After carrying out the *Primary Survey* and checking for normal breathing, you may find agonal breathing – which is described as short irregular gasps, sometimes referred to as the death rattle (the last breath of the casualty). This is not normal and this casualty requires CPR.

Adult Procedure

1. Kneel beside the casualty.
2. Aim for the centre of the chest and place the heel of one hand on the chest. Now place the other hand on top of this and inter lock your fingers and keep them off the casualty's ribs.
3. Keep your arms straight and directly over your wrists, do not bend your elbows.
4. Press straight down 5-6cm (two to two and half inches), keeping your elbows straight. Release the pressure fully but don't take your hands off the chest.

FIRST AID, HEALTH & SAFETY

5. Give 30 chest compressions at a rate of 100 - 120 compressions per minute (about two per second).
6. Give 2 rescue breaths.
7. Continue giving 30 chest compressions and 2 rescue breaths until:
   - Professional help takes over
   - The casualty shows signes of consciousness, such as coughing, open their eyes, speaking or moving purposefully is breathing nomrally
   - You become exhausted

Rescue Breaths Adult Procedure

1. Ensure the airway is open by gently tilting the head back and lifting the chin.
2. Keep supporting the casualty's chin with the index and middle fingertips of one hand.
3. With your other hand, pinch the nostrils with your thumb and forefinger.
4. Take a breath and place your mouth over the casualty's making a good seal (you can use a face shield if you have one).
5. Breathe steadily into the casualty's mouth for about one second whilst looking out of the corner of your eye, watching the chest rise.
6. Keep your hands in position, remove your mouth from theirs, let their chest fall.
7. Make no more than two attempts to achieve two effective rescue breaths, before repeating chest compressions.

- If you are unable to give rescue breaths or unwilling then give chest compressions only.
- If it is a drowning casualty give five initial rescue breaths before you start chest compressions. If alone, call an ambulance after one minute of CPR.
- If breathing is absent or agonal, call 999 or 112 – if there is a bystander, ask them to do this for you. Get a de-fibrillator if there is one available.
- If there is another rescuer present change over every one to two minutes with minimum disruption.
- CPR is an important part in the chain of survival for a casualty whose heart has stopped.

FIRST AID, HEALTH & SAFETY

BLEEDING

First aid priorities
- Assess the casualty's condition
- Reassure and comfort the casualty.
- Think about hygiene – wear disposable non-latex gloves if possible.
- Control blood loss by applying pressure and elevating the injured part (or if it's a minor wound, clean with water first)
- Minimise shock
- Get medical help if necessary

To control severe bleeding - remember EXPEL

*E*xpose the site of injury

e*X*amine the injured part for any foreign particles or objects

*P*ressure upon the wound (get the casualty to do it if possible)

*E*levate injured limb (above the level of the heart will reduce blood loss)

*L*ay the casualty down in the most appropriate position (unless it's bleeding in the head – raise the head, if it's bleeding in the chest sitting is best)

"If the face is pale – raise the tail". (Generally).

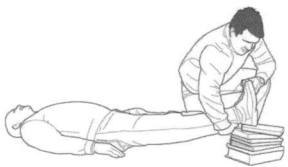

APPLYING A DRESSING

- Wear disposable gloves
- Place pad over area to be dressed, retain hold of short end of bandage
- Wind remainder and secure
- If blood comes through that first dressing you will need to put another on top
- If blood comes through both dressings – remove them, start again, applying a bit firmer pressure
- Check for circulation beyond the bandage (feel warmth of skin, check circulation at ends of fingers, press nail bed briefly until pale

FIRST AID, HEALTH & SAFETY

then release the pressure – if the colour doesn't return, the bandage may be too tight – remember to ask the casualty if it is too tight!)

If an object is embedded
- Wear disposable gloves
- **Do not remove the object**
- Press on either side of the embedded object
- Build up padding on either side of the object and secure
- Support the injured part in an elevated position

Whilst waiting for help. carrying out your secondary survey, in all casualties you will need to monitor the vital signs and record them if possible. These are **B**reathing, levels of **R**esponse and **P**ulse.
Remember BRP!

BURNS AND SCALDS
First Aid Priorities
- To stop the burning and relieve pain
- To maintain an open airway
- To treat associated injuries
- To minimise the risk of infection
- Get urgent removal to hospital

The priorities are to quickly cool the burn or scald and treat the casualty for shock, the casualty will need hospital treatment.
Remember to:

STOP (the casualty from panicking),

DROP (the casualty onto the ground),

WRAP (in a blanket or jacket) and

ROLL the casualty to extinguish any flame.

To assess the severity of burns use the following as a guide:

Size of burn (1% is classed as the size of the casualty's palm)

Cause (flame, chemical, steam, hot liquids, electrical, sunburn, friction etc)

Age of casualty (the very young and old are more vunerable)

Location on the body (some areas are more sensitive than others)

Depth (there are three depths; superficial, partial-thickness & full-thickness)

FIRST AID, HEALTH & SAFETY

Recognition (dependent on cause)   Pain, blistering,
reddened skin, signs of shock, intense stinging pain, tenderness, skin pale
and waxy, peeling skin, charred skin, singed hair etc.

Treatment (Burns and Scalds)

1. Do not touch the burned area
2. Apply cold running water for at least 10 minutes (20 for a chemical)
3. Remove any jewellery or other constrictions
4. Cover with a sterile dressing – cling film or a polythene bag make
   good temporary dressings
5. Treat for shock (lay casualty down, maintain normal body
   temperature, reassure)
6. Get medical help if necessary

Bone, Muscle and Joint Injuries

These are caused by sudden impact. The type of injury is determined
often by the mechanism or mechanics of injury (how something has
happened, the forces applied). It can be difficult sometimes to
determine exactly what the injury is, if in doubt – ship them out.
When you are in any doubt always treat as a suspected fracture.

Fractures – Recognition

A history or fall or recent blow, snapping sound, difficulty in moving
limb, severe pain, tenderness, distortion or swelling, bruising, signs of
shock if injury is severe.

Treatment

1. Tell the casualty to keep still & not to move

2. Wear gloves if possible

3. Cover any wounds and secure

4. Steady and support the injured limb and stabilise with any props or
   materials you have handy

5. Get medical help

If you are in a remote situation and help is a long time in arriving you
will need to use plenty of bandages (if available) to immobilise the limb.
Use padding between joints for comfort. Tie off bandages on the
uninjured side.

FIRST AID, HEALTH & SAFETY

A. Closed Fracture. Skin not broken.

B. Open Fracture. Bone has broken surface of skin.
Dangerous; external loss of blood and serious risk of infection.

C. Complicated Fracture.
When internal nerve or organ is also injured and when fracture is connected with a dislocated joint.

D. Symptoms and Signs.
Casualty heard it break.
Pain at site of injury.
Swelling, bruising later.
Deformity, bone grating and shock.

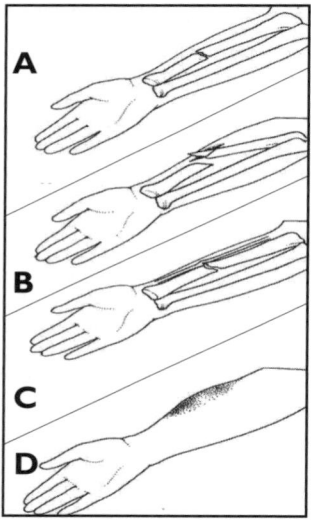

Sprains and Strains – Recognition
Pain, tenderness, difficulty in moving the limb, swelling or distortion, bruising.
Treatment
1. Any doubt, treat as a fracture
2. Use the RICE procedure (as explained below)

RICE Procedure
Rest the injured area

Ice – apply ice wrapped in material or cold compress to the area for 10 minutes.

Compression – apply soft even pressure with a stretchy bandage

FIRST AID, HEALTH & SAFETY

Elevate – the limb (check the bandage every 10 minutes that it is not too tight)

Shock

Disruption to the circulatory system caused by illness or injury which prevent blood being pumped to the vital organs such as the brain, heart, lungs and kidneys can cause a potentially fatal medical condition known as shock.

Recognition

Pale, ashen, cold clammy skin, rapid pulse, becoming weaker as time progresses. As the casualty becomes worse you may see; rapid shallow breathing, nausea, vomiting, casualty feels weak or giddy, dizzy, restlessness. The casualty may be aggressive due to the brain being short of oxygen – in this case they are literally fighting for their life. You may see yawning or gasping for air, again due to low blood oxygen in the body's tissues. Decreasing consciousness.

Treatment

1. Treat any cause
2. If injuries allow, lay them down, keep the head low (no pillows) and raise the legs gently (this improves blood flow to the brain)
3. Give plenty of reassurance, loosen tight clothing (if appropriate) at waist and neck
4. If appropriate insulate underneath the casualty by using a blanket, cover them also. Remember to maintain normal body temperature.
5. Dial 999 or 112 for an ambulance – if you have had to treat someone in this position, they will need to be transported in this position
6. Monitor the vital signs BRP (breathing, levels of response and pulse)
7. If the casualty goes unconscious, carry out your DRAB then place into the recovery position

DO NOT – move a casualty unnecessarily, leave them alone unless to get help, give a sweet drink, allow them to smoke or eat. If the casualty complains of thirst, moisten their lips.

Head Injuries

These should be taken as serious conditions. Medical advice should always be sought. There are three main types of head injury:

1. Concussion – where a temporary loss of consciousness is followed by complete recovery after a blow to the head.

FIRST AID, HEALTH & SAFETY

2. Compression – a build up of pressure on the brain, which is usually corrected by surgery. This can develop up-to several days after the impact.

3. Skull-fracture – where impact is strong enough to fracture (break) one of the bones of the skull. Your role is simple: Maintain an airway, monitor levels of consciousness, get medical help.

Extremes of Temperature

Hypo-thermia

This develops when the body temperature falls below 35 degrees celsius (95 degrees Fahrenheit). This can be caused by prolonged exposure to cold temperatures out-doors. Made worse with a wet casualty. Moving air will have a greater cooling effect so a high "wind-chill factor" can increase the risk of a person developing hypo-thermia (see page 8-26 Wind Chill Factor).

Recognition

Shivering, pale, dry cold skin, apathy, disorientated, or irrational behaviour, lethargy or impaired consciousness. Slow and shallow breathing, slow weakening pulse.

Treatment

First Aid Priorities

- To prevent the casualty from losing more body heat
- To re-warm the casualty slowly
- To obtain medical help if necessary   **Action**
1. Quickly replace any wet clothes, with warm, dry garments
2. If a warm bath is available then do this, the water should be   warm but not too hot – about 40 degrees Celsius
3. Put casualty to bed, give warm drinks, soup or high energy chocolate to help re-warm them
4. Cover the head for additional warmth
5. Stay with the casualty until colour and warmth return

FROSTBITE

Recognition

Initially pins and needles, paleness (pallor) followed by numbness, hardening or stiffening of skin, colour change to the skin of the affected area.

FIRST AID, HEALTH & SAFETY

Treatment
1. Move the casualty to a warm place
2. Warm the affected area (usually the extremities) in your lap or the casualty's armpits, AVOID rubbing
3. Place affected area in warm water, apply a light dressing
4. Raise or support the affected limb and take the casualty to hospital

Effects of Heat
You may come across sunburn, prickly heat, heat exhaustion and heat stroke.

Sunburn – over exposure to the sun or sunlamp, made worse at high altitude or where water or snow is present. This is often superficial, in severe cases can appear lobster-red and blistered and the casualty may also from heat stroke. Treatment – move the casualty out of the sun, relive pain and discomfort. Cool with cold water, use calamine or after-sun preparation.

Prickly heat
This can be a highly irritating, prickly red rash, tiny red spots or blisters occurring in hot weather. Due to sweat glands being blocked by bacteria and dead skin cells. Sweat is trapped and cannot evaporate. Treatment – move the casualty to a cool area, cool the skin by sponging with cold water.

Heat Exhaustion
Caused by loss of salt and water from the body through excessive sweating. The casualty sweats profusely, due to prolonged activity, dehydration develops leading to heat exhaustion. There may be headache, dizziness and confusion, loss of appetite and nausea, sweating with pale, clammy skin, cramps in the arms, legs or abdominal area, rapid, weakening pulse and breathing.
Treatment – move to a cool place, lay casualty down, raise the legs, give plenty of water to drink (with a weak salt solution – I tea spoon per litre), even if they recover quickly, ensure they get urgent medical help.

Heatstroke
Caused by the "thermostat" in the brain not working properly. The body becomes dangerously overheated often due to a high fever or prolonged exposure to heat. This condition can develop quickly, often

FIRST AID, HEALTH & SAFETY

with no warning. It may also follow heat exhaustion. There may be headache, dizziness, and discomfort, restlessness and confusion, hot, flushed and dry skin, rapid deterioration in the levels of response, a full bounding pulse and the body temperature may be over 40 degrees celsius.

Treatment –

Lower the casualty's temperature after removing outer clothes by wrapping them in a cold, wet sheet and keep the sheet wet until their temperature falls to 38 degrees. You can fan the casualty or sponge them alternatively. Once the body temperature is back to normal, replace the wet sheet with a dry one or dry clothes.

Remember – if it's a medical problem – get medical help.

As a first aider generally all you can do is apply a plaster or dressing, put a casualty in an appropriate casualty recovery position, keep a casualty comfortable, care for someone until professional help arrives. We don't administer anything or move anyone unless they are in immediate danger – and never put ourselves at any unnecessary risk. Nothing can substitute attending a first aid course and maintaining your skills by regular training of practical scenarios which will equip you with simple, effective life-saving skills for the benefit of your friends, family members or strangers in the street.

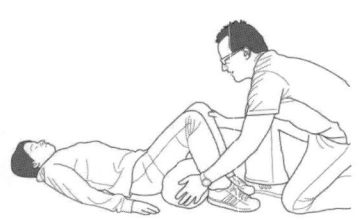

CASUALTY POSITIONS

*This position with the casualty **laid down and the knees raised** slightly is suggested for fractured pelvis and abdominal wounds.*

*This is referred to as the **half-sitting position, sat up,** supported against something stable, knees raised, useful for chest injuries, conscious heart attack casualty, breathing problems, massive allergic reaction (anaphylaxis). If it's in the chest – sitting is best.*

FIRST AID, HEALTH & SAFETY

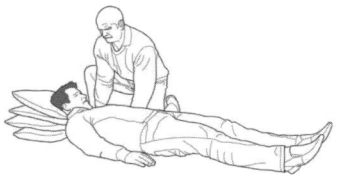

Laid down with head raised, used for head injuries (unless Spinal injury is suspected) or eye injuries. If it's in the head - raise the head.

Sat leaning forward, good for nose bleeds, fractured jaw, airway problems, some breathing problems such as asthma

ACKNOWLEGEMENT

The First Aid element of this chapter have been written for Military Pocket Books Ltd by:

Michelle Summer

Serving Sister of the Most Venerable
Order of St John of Jersualem,
15 (NE) Brigade First Aid Advisor,
County Duke of Edinburgh Award officer,
North & West Yorkshire Army Cadet Force.

FIRST AID, HEALTH & SAFETY

HEALTH & WELL BEING

Under this heading we are going to look at some of your actions that can affect your personal Health and Safety and contribute to wellbeing and quality of life in general.

This all sounds rather serious, yes it is. Some of you will be well aware of the information given and act accordingly, while others may not have given it a moments thought. So now is the time to consider how you can be better at taking care of your Health and Safety.

A BALANCED DIET

Means eating food from differents types of food groups. If you eat a lot of different food you will get the balance right for you to exercise to the best of your ability, to be alert, fit and feel healthy.

Types of food related 'families'

- Bread, rice, pasta, cerals, potatoes.
- Fruit & Vegetables: oranges, bananas, apples, brocoli, sweetcorn, carrots.
- Meat: Beef, lamb,pork, chicken,turkey,
- Fish: Cod, salmon, tuna, (not Fish & Chips)!
- Milk and Dairy foods,:Cheese, yoghurt.
- Food containing fat, foods and drinks that contain sugar: Chocolate, crisps, fizzy drinks.

All foods should be eaten in moderation.

CARBOHYDRATES

Provide ENERGY to your muscles, so the following should be part of your diet:-

Breakfast -cerals, whote grain cereals, bran, porridge, wholemeal bread, baked beans, fresh and dried fruits.

Lunch: - potatoes - mashed, boiled, jacket, bread, pasta, noodles, lasagne, rice.

Night time: breakfast cereals, toast, sandwiches, fruit juice. low fat yoghurt, fresh and dried fruit.

FIRST AID, HEALTH & SAFETY

PROTEIN

Your body needs Protein to grow and repair muscles after any active exercise.

You should include in your diet many different proteins such as lean meats, fish (fresh, frozen or canned). Poultry (chicken, duck, pheasant, pigeon), Milk. eggs, cheese, beans, lentils, nuts.

FAT

You do need some fat in your diet - not a lot. Fat is concealed in many foods especially takeaway foods. Fat can lead to serious health problems later in your life.

- The fat that is good for you is from oily fish - salmon, mackeral, herring, fresh tuna and nuts.
- The fat that NOT good for you called 'saturated fat' is from fried food, chips, burgers, pastry.   CHIPS WITH EVERYTHING - NO NO NO!!!

FIBRE

- Eating enough fibre helps with digestion, keeps the stomach healthy and prevents constipaton.
- So include in your diet an increased amount of wholemeal and granary breads.
- High fibre cerals, shredded wheat. whole-wheat pasta, increase vegetables all fresh fruit.

VITAMINS & MINERALS

IRON

Some vitamins are added to breakfast cerals and bread.

The UK Department of Healh are doing their best to get us to eat more vitamins through their slogan 'EAT FIVE A DAY' that is fruit and vegetables.

- Iron an important mineral found in lean red meat, green leafy vegetables- runner beans, spinach brccoli. Liver and kidney.
- Pulses - peas, lentils, baked beans, red kidney beans, dried fruit.
- Oily fish - fresh tuna, salmon, mackerel, sardines, trout, herring,
- Wholemeal bread, eggs, fortified with iron breakfast cerals

CALCIUM

Calcium strengthens your bones and can help in preventing stress fractures occuring. It is important that you understand the need for calcium to be part through lack of calcium in the diet to prevent bones from becoming thin and brittle. In later life it can lead to a condition called osteoporosis in the part through lack of calcium in the the diet.

The best source for calcium is milk in all its various forms, drink it as often as you can. Generally all other ingredients already mentioned help towards building a strong bone structure in your body.

SALT

Eating too much salt can increase your blood pressure which in turn can affect the condition of your heart.
Foods to avoid as their salt content is more than is good for you are:-

- Processed ready meals, bacon, crisps, salted & roasted nuts, sweet & savoury biscuits, chips with added salt, smoked and cured meat and fish, cooking sauces, soy sauce and ketchup, olives in brine, soup, stck cubes, some breakfast cerals.
- To cut down on your salt intake;-
- Avoid the foods mentioned above.
- Don't add salt to your meal before tasting it.
- Don't add salt during cooking.

FLUID INTAKE REQUIRED

How much fluid should you drink a day? It is important that you know how much you need and the way to find out is to do the URINE TEST. Your needs will change depending upon the amount of exercise you do.

- The minimum amount of liquid a day is not less than 1.2 litres to avoid dehydratin.
- You will need more than this if you are sweating.
- You will be DEHYDRATED and become a casualty.
- DEHYDRATION causes a complete collapse of your physical ability.

SEVERE DEHYDRATION CAN BE FATAL

URINE TEST

Check your urine colour: a good indicator of dehydration volume
- If you are well hydrated, your urine will be light in colour and there will be lots of it.
- If you are dehydrated, your urine will be darker in colour, and there will be less of it.

SUBSTANCE MISUSE

In First Aid, you learn that a poison is any substance that taken in sufficient quantity can cause temporary or permanent damage to your health. Believe it or not, it is quite possible to poison yourself with water. The pharmaceutical industry has invested countless billions of pounds to 'invent' drugs to assist our Doctors and Specialists in the prevention and control of medical and psychological conditions. Many of these 'drugs' have side affects; at some time you have probably taken medication that has made you feel sleepy, dizzy or worse! Taken in controlled conditions these side affects can be monitored and the dosage or drug altered. When these 'drugs' are misused, there is a real danger doing damage to your body.

The first paragraph mentions 'any substance'; this section will cover the majority of substances that people 'misuse', what it is, how to take it and the probable side affects.

TOBACCO

Tobacco is one of the most widely used addictive substances in this country.
What is does to you: when smoking, you take tar, nicotine and carbon monoxide into your body. Its not just smokers who inhale - of course - its those around themtoo. The more you smoke, the more likelyyou are to suffer from heart disease, blood clots, cancer, strokes bronchitis, bad circulation and ulcers.
Pregnant women who smoke a lot tend to have smaller babies and they run a greater risk of losing their child before or after birth.

ACID

ACID, is a man made substance; minute quantities are impregnated into small squares of blotting paper, which are then allowed to dissolve on the tongue. The squares often have colourful designs on them.
Note: sometimes squares sold as LSD contain none at all.
What it does to you: A trip begins about one hour after taking, and fades gradually in about twelve hours, depending on the dose. Effects depend on the user's mood, where they are, whom they are with and the strength of the dose. Trips often include distortion of vision and hearing, or a feeling of being outside the body. Bad trips can lead to

depression, dizziness, even panic. Bad trips are more likely is the user is anxious or in unfamiliar surroundings. Anyone driving whilst under the influence of LSD will endanger themselves and others.

CANNABIS

Street names: DOPE, BLOW, WACKY BACKY, SKUNK, SPLIF, GRASS, WEED, WACKY BACKY,
Cannabis comes from a plant know as Cannabis Sativa. **Hash** is the commonest form in this country, is resin blocks made from the sap of the plant. Herbal cannabis or marijuana is generally mixed with tobacco, rolled into a cigarette and smoked.
What it does to you: Cannabis makes people feel more relaxed and talkative. It can also reduce the ability to carry out complicated tasks; which would make it dangerous to operate machinery or drive whilst under the effects of the substance. Inexperienced people using high doses, or taking it when depressed, may sometimes experience panic attacks. *Cannabis takes effect very quickly. It can be mixed with food or drink and it is difficult to assess how much has been taken. This can be distressing for the user, particularly if un –knowingly taken, or alcohol is taken at the same time.* Cannabis is not addictive, but users come to rely on it as a method of relaxing.

COCAINE two types - Powder Cocaine and Crack.

Street names: COCAINE: BADROCK, BEAM, BEAT, BIG C, CANDY, CAINE, NOSE CANDY. CRACK: CRACK, CUBES, COOKIES,
Cocaine is obtained from the leaves of the COCA plant, it is refined and mixed with other substances to form white powder. Crack Cocaine a chemical mix and turne into chunks about the small of a pea. is take by sniffing through the nose or direct injecting a
What it does to you: using this drug in either form will create a dependency on the drug and user becomes highly addictive to it. Cocaine causes: *loudness, excitable, nervous, anxiety, irritability, paranoia, insomnia, tremors, musclue twitches increase heart rate, violent behavior, loss of self control.* There are many more effect these drugs have on the individual. The longer terms of addiction to the drug are **Neurological:** *seizures, coma, convlustions,* **Heart Diesease**: *altered heart rhythm, chest pain, very high or very low blood pressure, stroke and sudden death,* **Lung Damage and Disease:** *difficulty breathing, ruptured lung, collapsed lung, respiratory failure.*
The effects of this drug can cause long term heath problems and death if talem to an excess where an overdoes is taken.

FIRST AID, HEALTH & SAFETY

SOLVENTS

Solvents are found in products like glue, lighter fuel, paint, aerosols and petrol. When the vapours from these substances are inhaled, they produce a similar affect to alcohol. Some users increase the effect by inhaling inside a plastic bag placed over the head.

What is does to you: The effects are similar to being drunk (including the hangover). Vapours are absorbed through the lungs and quickly reach the brain. Repeated inhaling can cause loss of control.

A NASTY WAY TO DIE! *A number of users have died as a result of the miss use because they have squirted aerosol gases directly into their mouths, thus freezing their air passages.* Sniffers can be accidentally injured when they are 'high' because they are in an unsafe place – on a roof or by a railway line; perceptions of danger are non – existent.

Sniffers can suffocate I they inhale the solvents by putting plastic bags over their heads. The mouth and nose areas of users are often reddened and blistered. There is a real danger of Sniffers becoming unconscious and choking on their own vomit. Heavy solvent abuse can result in lasting damage to the brain, kidneys and liver.

BARBITURATES

Street names: BARBS, BLUES, REDS, SEKKIES

Barbiturates - DOWNERS, are used medically to calm people down (as sedatives) and as sleeping pills (hypnotics). Most come in powdered form and are sold in coloured capsules. Users will swallow them, occasionally with alcohol, or inject. *Injecting Barbiturates is one of the most dangerous forms of drug misuse.*

What they do to you: Users of this drug tend to develop a tolerance to them and then a physical as well as mental dependence. Sudden withdrawal can even kill. The effects can include irritability, nervousness, faintness, sleeplessness, sickness, twitching, delirium and convulsions.

TRANQUILLISERS

Street names: TRANX, BENZOS, EGGS, JELLIES

Doctors prescribe tranquillisers to control anxiety and tension, or to help people sleep. Although they are supposed to be taken in pill form, users sometimes inject them in to the body.

What they do to you: they lessen alertness and affect skills where concentration is required. They can also release aggression by lowering inhibitions. Mixed with alcohol they can even cause death. Dependence is fairly common among long-term users. Once people stop taking the drug, they can feel confused, irritable, anxious and unable to carry on with their normal routines.

FIRST AID, HEALTH & SAFETY

HEROIN

Street names: SMACK, JUNK, 'H', SKAG

Heroin along with other opiates is made from the opium poppy. In its purest form, it is a white powder. Heroin is sometimes sniffed like cocaine, sometimes smoked, sometimes injected.

What it does to you: Heroin depresses brain activity, widens the blood vessels (giving a feeling of warmth) and causes severe constipation. Opiates create a feeling of total relaxation and detachment from pain or anxiety. They make people warm, drowsy, content, and it appears to relieve stress and discomfort. But this is where the bad news starts. Once physical dependence has established itself simply the relief of getting hold of the drug replaces this pleasure. Users find that they need more and more of the drug to get the same feeling of well being.

As the intake increases, as it inevitably must, the user feels the effects, even between doses. These include aches, tremors, sweating, chills, and sneezing, yawning and muscular spasms.

Overdosing or using a bad fix results in unconsciousness and coma: often if the user is not discovered in time, death from breathing failure. The chances of dying are even greater if other drugs such as alcohol are used at the same time. First time users often feel sick and vomit, especially if they have injected. Damage to the body is common with users. It is usually caused by repeated injections with dirty needles and by the substances mixed with the heroin by the suppliers to make more money from the batch they are selling. By this time, the user lives for the next 'fix', spending their time trying to raise the money by whatever means they can.

General Note: Users who share needles place themselves at risk of at the least, infection, at the worst, Hepatitis or contracting HIV the virus that can lead to AIDS. Most large towns and cities have chemists who have the facility of providing users with clean hypodermics and needles.

DRUG AND OTHER ABUSE POISONING

You will be well aware of the use of drugs, which is the "broad heading" given to Painkillers, Tranquillisers, Stimulants, amphetamines and LSD, Cocaine, Narcotics, Solvents and in addition Alcohol Poisoning.

It will be necessary for you to keep strictly to the Primary Survey DRAB of First Aid when dealing with them.

We set out on the following pages a chart showing the "cause" and "effect" of drug poisoning which vary depending on the drug taken and the method by which it has been taken.

FIRST AID, HEALTH & SAFETY

DRUG	EFFECT
Painkillers Aspirin (commonly swallowed)	Upper abdominal pain, nausea, and vomiting (possibly blood stained) Ringing in the ears. "Sighing" breathing. Confusion or delirium.
Paracetamol (commonly swallowed)	Little effect at first. Later, features of liver damage, upper abdominal pain and tenderness, nausea, and vomiting.
Nervous system depressants barbiturates and tranquillisers (commonly swallowed)	Lethargy and sleepiness, leading to unconsciousness. "Shallow" breathing. A weak irregular, or abnormally slow or fast pulse.
Stimulants and hallucinogens - amphetamines and LSD. (commonly swallowed) cocaine (commonly inhaled)	Excitable, hyperactive behaviour, wildness and frenzy. Sweating. Tremor of the hands. Hallucinations, casualty may be "hearing" voices, and/or "seeing" things.

FIRST AID, HEALTH & SAFETY

DRUG	EFFECT
Narcotics - morphine,heroin (commonly injected)	Constricted pupils. Sluggishness and confusion, possibly leading to unconsciousness. Slow, shallow breathing, which may cease. Needle marks may be infected, or infection may be introduced by <u>dirty</u> needles.
Solvents (commonly inhaled) - glue, lighter fuel	Nausea, vomiting and headaches. Hallucinations. Possibly unconsciousness. Rarely, cardiac arrest

TREATMENT
YOUR AIMS ARE: To maintain AIRWAY, BREATHING &
CIRCULATION.   To arrange urgent removal to hospital.
CARRY OUT THE ABC of FIRST AID.
        DO NOT ATTEMPT TO INDUCE VOMITING.

ALCOHOL POISONING
        Early Stage
        Smell, flushed face, deep noisy breathing, full bounding
        pulse.
        Later
        Swollen face, shallow breathing, weak, rapid pulse.
DANGER The unconscious casualty may well choke on their
        vomit.
        Hypothermia may develop *if* casualty is not kept warm.

BE AWARE - Alcohol may conceal other serious injury.

**TREATMENT Carry out DRAB the Primary Survey of First
Aid. *if* casualty is unconscious - place in Recovery Position.**
        URGENT REMOVAL TO HOSPITAL.

FIRST AID, HEALTH & SAFETY

SELF TEST QUESTIONS

1. Name the three types of fracture.
2. Name two signs of a possible fracture.
3. When do you carry out a Head to Toe survey?
4. What causes Shock?
5. What is the treatment for Shock?
6. What must a casualty not do if suffering from Shock?
7. How do you tell if a casualty is breathing?
8. In what position do you place an Unconscious, Breathing casualty
9. What is the treatment for a burn or scald?
10. What size burn or scald requires medical attention?
11. In Casualty Management, which casualty must have priority?
12. Name the three key points in the treatment of severe bleeding.
13. What is the treatment for Heat Exhaustion?
14. What is the cause of Heat Stroke?
15. What is your action when you are on your own, and have a
    casualty who is not breathing and shows NO sign of physical
    injury or drowning?
16. How long should you check to see if a casualty is breathing?
17. Where do you find the Carotid pulse?
18. When doing Cardio Pulmonary Resuscitation, do you stop and
    check that there is no heart beat?
19. What is the ratio of rescue breaths to compression for C.P.R?
20. What three things do you do to check the level of consciousness?
21. Treating a casualty for shock, what are the four things you do
    NOT do.
22. Treating Heat Stroke,what keeps temperature down.
23. Free circulation of air near skin, prevents what.
24. What may cause a patient to have dilated pupils.
25. Give the four effects it has on a brain when its oxygen supply is
    weakened.
26. Who are the principal First Aid Providers in the UK
27. Explain what the initials D.R.A.B. mean and how they are applied.
28. When do you especially SHOUT HELP,
29. What are the AIMS of First Aid.

FIRST AID, HEALTH & SAFETY

30. What factors are considered when Assessing the Emergency.
31. Diagnosis, three "key words", what are they and explain the meaning of each one.
32. You can save a life by maintaining a casualties vital needs, what are they.
33. What could cause "noisy, bubbling, gasping breathing".
34. How can you tell if the casualty is breathing.
35. In an emergency what do you dial to call the emergency services.
36. Where is the Carotid artery.
37. How do you carry out Chest Compression and when is it done.
38. When is the recovery position used.
39. If the casualty has severe bleeding their vital organs are deprived of what.
40. How do you control severe bleeding.
41. A casualty with severe burns or scalds will lose what, and as a result what condition will occur.
42. What do you understand by anything constrictive in the injured area.
43. What MUST NOT be used on a burn or scald.
44. Name three types of fracture.
45. How do you immobilise an injured arm.
46. How do you immobilise an injured leg.
47. What are the symptoms of a casualty with SHOCK
48. What must you NEVER DO with an unconscious casualty.
49. Explain what DILATED PUPILS look like.
50. What affects the "CORE" temperature in the body.
51. What is HEAT EXHAUSTION, its cause and treatment.
52. What is HEATSTROKE, its cause and treatment.
53. List the contents your Detachment First Aid Box. and where is it kept in the Detachment.

Chapter 7

THE DUKE OF EDINBURGH'S AWARD

INTRODUCTION.

The Army Cadet Force was one of the organisations that took part in the Pilot Scheme for this award. Perhaps not surprising as the Duke of Edinburgh was then and still is the Colonel-in-Chief of the Army Cadet Force.

To gain the award is a personal achievement that takes self discipline. The Duke of Edinburgh said that anyone who was determined to gain the award would have to have 'STICKABILITY' to see it through all the way. It is an excellent programme; many thousands of young people throughout the Commonwealth take part.

THE MAIN PRINCIPLES
1. THE AWARD IS ENTIRELY VOLUNTARY.
2. THE AGES ARE FROM 14 TO 25 YEARS OLD.
3. THE AWARD HAS FOUR SECTIONS COMMON TO ALL LEVELS

VOLUNTEERING- EXPEDITION - SKILLS - PHYSICAL and RESIDENTIAL AT THE GOLD LEVEL ONLY

There are three levels of the Award:

BRONZE	SILVER	GOLD

4. The minimum time for completing each level is

Bronze	Silver	Gold
6 MONTHS	12 MONTH (6 MONTHS via Bronze)	18 MONTHS (12 MONTHS via Silver)

THE CHALLENGE
Taking part in the Award it is entirely voluntary at each level. It is an individual effort on your part; your Detachment does not enter a "team", nor are you expected to follow exactly the same elements as other Cadets. You choose what you would like to do and then go for it.

THE DUKE OF EDINBURGH'S AWARD

YOUR CONTACT

Find out who is your Detachment or Area/Company Duke of Edinburgh's Award Officer and make contact to enrol in the DofE. There will also be a County D of E Award Officer.

You will have to buy your **Entrance Pack** which will include your Record Book. This is your first commitment to the Award - your personal stake in it.

Help will be given to you along the way, but **it has to be your effort.** As you progress, you will be expected to choose, design and develop your own programme from the many options available.

ADVANTAGES

The D of E adds an extra dimension, excitement and purpose to your Cadet career and beyond to your 25th birthday.

The Award will bring you into close contact with many other young people and you will no doubt develop lasting friendships.

The self confidence, awareness, determination and enthusiasm displayed by successful participants has given Award holders holders a deserved good reputation, giving you a distinct advantage when embarking on you career. Potential employers recognise the D of E and its objectives and see it as evidence that you have **STICKABILITY.**

YOUR OPPORTUNITY

As a cadet you have the advantage to take part in the DofE, whilst continuing with your cadet career.

This has been made possible by many of the subjects within the APC Syllabus fitting in with the requirements of the Award.

Once you have completed your ONE STAR training and are 14 years old, if you decide to enrol in the Award you can, with some extra effort, gain your BRONZE by completing for example APC 2 Star First Aid, Expedition Training, Shooting/Skill at Arms and Physical Recreation

It must be stressed, that it is not compulsory or mandatory for you to only count ACF related activities towards your DofE award, nor is the list of activities mentioned in the chart the only ones accepted, there are a great many more that your Award Leader will be able to tell you about.

However, any aspect of ACF activity can, with some help and imagination on the part of your instructors, working with the Award

THE DUKE OF EDINBURGH'S AWARD

Leader, be brought into a DofE Award programme; this is most likely to be the case in respect of the Expedition option in the Silver and Gold Awards.

Your Award Leader will have several leaflets and books that you will be able to read. It is advisable that you do just that before making up your mind to take up the challenge.

All that we can tell you, is that if you do join the Award, and see it through all the way, you will never regret it.

HOW ACF TRAINING MIGHT COUNT TOWARDS THE DUKE OF EDINBURGH'S AWARD
BRONZE AWARD
(normally about APC 2 Star level)

TIME SCALES OF INVOLVEMENT

Volunteering 3 months	Skills 3 months	Physical 3 months	Expeditions Plan, train for and undertake a 2 day expedition
An additional 3 months must be undertaken in any one of these sections			

VOLUNTEERING SECTION

Suggestion:

Pass 2 Star First Aid and give practical service for the remaining period. Older Cadets commencing Bronze while undertaking 3 star or higher level, may use Service to the ACF

EXPEDITION SECTION

Suggestion:

To have been trained and passed APC TWO STAR Expedition Training (but see note below). You must have been on at least one practice expedition.

To have learned Map and Compass (Including Route Cards).

The expedition must have an aim and you will be required to produce a report (oral or written) in some detail of a venture that you have taken part in. This will include sketches, Route Cards, diagrams and how you coped with the challenge.

Note: A Qualifying Venture complying with all the conditions of the Bronze Expedition, will automatically count as passing Expedition Training at 2 star.

THE DUKE OF EDINBURGH'S AWARD

SKILLS SECTION
Suggestion:
This requires you to take up an approved activity from the Duke of Edinburgh's Award Handbook.

You will need to talk to your Award Leader, to help you decide what you are to do. You will be required to take a keen interest in this and study it in some depth, during which time you will become quite an expert in your own right.

Note: Should you wish to take up a skill not listed, then it can be submitted by your DofE Officer through the proper channels for approval. You must wait for approval before proceeding. This applies to all levels of the Award.

As examples, some of the Military activities are: Skill at Arms & Shooting, Ceremonial Drill, Military and Brass Bands, Forces Insignia, Marksmanship, Signalling, Model Soldiers etc.

An assessor, who will be a recognised expert in the activity will be appointed to see you through the skill. You will be given an "ideas list" of things you could do to progress in the activity, and you will agree with your assessor how far you can progress in the time allowed (3 or 6 months depending on choice). If you are new to the Skill you will probably start at the beginning.

If you have already had some experience in the Skill, you will start from a point where you will be extending your knowledge. At the end of the period you will be assessed on how well you have done.

PHYSICAL
Suggestion:
To choose an activity from the list in the Duke of Edinburgh's Award Handbook and participate for a minimum period. Again you will discuss this with your Award Leader. If there are standards set by the governing body of the activity, you will be expected to try for these.

Note: The Award requires regular participation over 3 or 6 months, which significantly exceeds the minimum period required by the APC. You will need to consider this when choosing your Physical Recreation.

RESIDENTIAL
No requirement at Bronze

THE DUKE OF EDINBURGH'S AWARD

SILVER AWARD
(normally about APC 4 Star level)

TIME SCALES FOR INVOLVEMENT

Volentering	Skills Physical	Expeditions
6 months	One Section for 6 months & the other section for 3 months	Plan, train and undertake a 3 day, 2 night Expedition
Direct Entrants must undertake an extra 6 months in either the Volunterig or the the longer of the Physical Skills section		

VOLUNTEERING SECTION
Suggestion:

You may use your 'Service' in the ACF to qualify for the Silver Award. It is suggested that you work through the following list. If you are opting to spend 12 months on Volunteering (direct entrants), or if you have already completed some of the items, you may need to undertake additional activities from the ideas list.

1. Attend and perform satisfactorily at a Junior Cadet Instructors Cadre
2. Successfully complete the THREE STAR syllabus for the Cadet and the Community
3. Know the history of the ACF, and its organisation in your own detachment, area and county, plus the history of the Regiment/ Corps to which you are badged. This must be to a higher standard than required by APC at 2 Star.
4. The total period of involvement in these activities must be at least 6 months and may be 12 months

ALTERNATIVE OPTIONS

1. To gain a recognised adult First Aid qualification from a Voluntary Aid Society, (3 and 4 star First Aid), and give practical service e.g. first aid cover on Detachment Training evenings or camps, training for first aid competitions etc.
2. The Cadet and Community syllabus at 3 and/or 4 star could also be used to count towards Service provided the time scales for the Award are adhered to.
3. Obtain the Community Sports Leaders Award (CSLA) -which also counts for 4 star Cadet and the Community.

THE DUKE OF EDINBURGH'S AWARD

EXPEDITION SECTION
Requirement:
4 Star Expedition standard is required at this level (Two nights out and three days, each with 7 hours of planned activity. Your expedition can be on foot, by canoe, boat, bicycle (or horse). APC 3 star expedition training could be used as a practice for the Silver expedition.

SKILLS SECTION
Requirement:
As for the Bronze Award you must participate in your chosen Skill for a minimum of 3 or 6 months depending on choice
It you are starting the Award for the first time at Silver, then you may opt to follow your Skill for 12 months.
The conditions are the same as for Bronze, but if you are following the same Skill, you will be expected to work further through the ideas list, taking up where you left off. You may, of course, choose a different Skill. Once again you will agree your goals with your assessor.

PHYSICAL SECTION
Requirement:
Choose an activity from the Duke of Edinburgh's Award Handbook as at Bronze. It may be the same activity or a different one. It is up to you. Remember that 3, 6 or possibly 12 months will have to be spent on the activity, and you will be expected to try for standards if appropriate.

RESIDENTIAL
No requirement at Silver.

THE DUKE OF EDINBURGH'S AWARD

GOLD AWARD
(normally post APC level)

Volunteering	Skills Physical	Expeditions
12 months	One Section for 12 months and the other Section for 6 months	Plan, train for and undertake a 4 day, 3 nights experdition
Residential Undertake a shared activity in a residential setting away from home for 5 days and 4 nights		
Direct Entrants must undertake an additional 6 months in either the Volunteering or the longer of the Physical or Skills section.		

VOLUNTEERING SECTION
Suggestion:
You are able to use your cadet 'service' as a qualification at this level, by working through the list. If you have not yet completed items from the list shown for Silver, you should do those first.

1. Attend and perform satisfactorily at the Senior Cadet Instructors' Cadre
2. Carry out tasks of special responsibility or give some specific service to your detachment, e.g. making training aids, organising fund raising events, be responsible for training a specific group of cadets.
3. Hold at least the rank of Corporal for not less than 12 months or if as a Cadet where there is no NCO vacancy, be a 3 Star cadet
4. The period of training and practical service will be at least 12 months, and may be 18 months (direct entrants)

ALTERNATIVE OPTIONS (If not taken up at Silver)

1. To gain a recognised adult First Aid qualification from a Voluntary Aid Society, (4 star First Aid), and give practical service.
2. The Cadet and Community syllabus at 3 and/or 4 star.
3. Obtain the Community Sports Leaders Award (CSLA)

EXPEDITION SECTION
Requirement:
Expeditions at this level are only permitted to take place in specified areas of the country providing suitable "wild country".
The Gold Expedition lasts three nights and four days each with 8 hours of planned activity, at least half of which must be journeying

THE DUKE OF EDINBURGH'S AWARD

At Gold level only there is the option of "Adventurous Projects" when the venture you want to undertake departs from the normal conditions for an expedition or exploration.

A great deal of preparation is required to ensure correct training is carried out and equipment checked and you have had some practical experience, including at least one practice journey.

The expedition is very much a **team effort,** practising Leadership, Map Reading, Campcraft and First Aid Skills.

SKILLS SECTION - Requirement:

As for the other Awards, you will choose a Skill and agree goals with your assessor, using the ideas list and participate for 6, 12 or 18 months depending on choice. If you have followed the same Skill at Bronze and Silver you may find difficulty in progressing much further. If this is the case you should consider trying a new Skill.

PHYSICAL SECTION - Requirement:

Choose an activity from the Duke of Edinburgh's Award Handbook as at Bronze and Silver. Remember that 6, 12 or possibly 18 months will have to be spent on the activity, and be expected to try for standards where necessary.

RESIDENTIAL - Requirement:

The intention is for you to undertake a project with a group, most of whom will not be your usual companions. The project should be carried out over a 5 day and four night period. Attendance at many of the normal cadet activities can qualify you for this as long as you are spending time mainly with people you would not normally spend time with.

Annual Camp of 5 days or more, *provided you are separated from your Detachment friends, including during "off-duty" times.*
The Cadet Leadership Course at Frimley and elsewhere. Any of the various Canadian Challenge Courses. MoD Courses or attachments, TA Camps or courses.

In very special circumstances you may be able to carry out your Residental over a series of weekends, if you are unable to have a week off. Your Award leader will advise you.

THE DUKE OF EDINBURGH'S AWARD

CHART SHOWING HOW ACF ACTIVITIES CAN COUNT TOWARDS YOUR DofE AWARD

VOLUNTEERING	EXPEDITION (ON FOOT)	SKILL	PHYSICAL	RESIDENTIAL
BRONZE APC 2 Star First Aid	2 star Expedition Training using DofE Bronze conditions	ACF Activities	Choose from:	No requirement
SILVER Service to the ACF or APC 3 &/or 4 Star Cadet and the community or APC 3 and 4 Star First Aid, plus practical First Aid or CSAL	3 star Expedition Training (may be used as a Practice Expedition for Silver) and 4 star Expedition Training	Ceremonial Drill Drumming Bugling Signals Shooting Marksman Military Band Piping Map Making Lecturing/Public Speaking Model Soldiers War Games Model Construction	Individual Sports Physical Achievement and Fitness Training Other Activities as listed in the Handbook	No requirement
GOLD Service to the ACF or APC 3 and/or 4 star Cadet & Community, or APC 3 and 4 star First Aid (if not used at Silver), or CLSA (if not used at Silver)	Post 4 star training NOTE: Expeditions can also be by other means, e.g. horseback, sailing, etc	Goals to be negotiated with assessor.	Period of involvement in accordance with individual choice.	Attendance at: Cadet Leadership Courses. Senior Cadet Instructors Course. Master Cadet and MOD Courses. TA Attachments Annual Camp

7-9

THE DUKE OF EDINBURGH'S AWARD
THE PROCESS TO BE FOLLOWED FOR THE SECTIONS OF THE AWARD
VOLUNTEERING SECTION

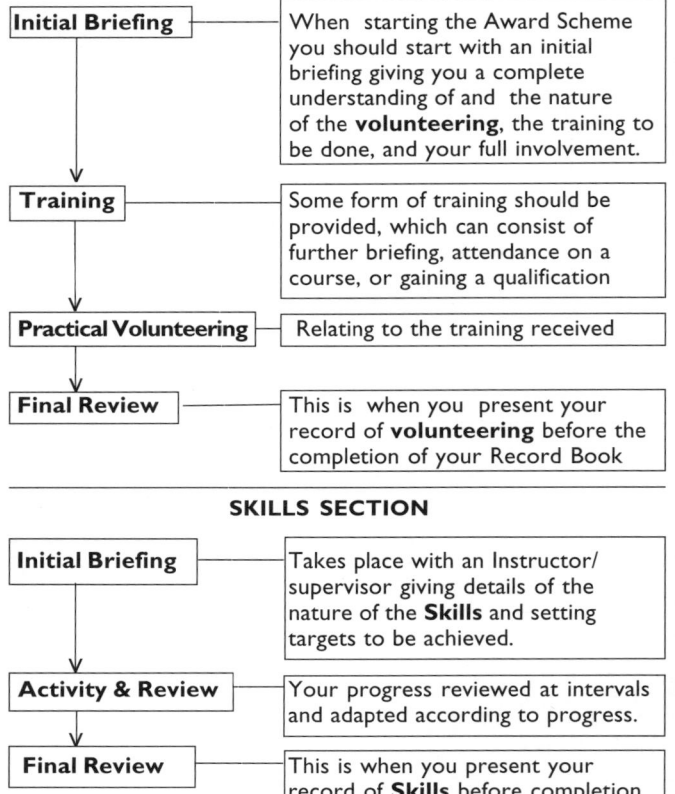

Initial Briefing → When starting the Award Scheme you should start with an initial briefing giving you a complete understanding of and the nature of the **volunteering**, the training to be done, and your full involvement.

Training → Some form of training should be provided, which can consist of further briefing, attendance on a course, or gaining a qualification

Practical Volunteering → Relating to the training received

Final Review → This is when you present your record of **volunteering** before the completion of your Record Book

SKILLS SECTION

Initial Briefing → Takes place with an Instructor/supervisor giving details of the nature of the **Skills** and setting targets to be achieved.

Activity & Review → Your progress reviewed at intervals and adapted according to progress.

Final Review → This is when you present your record of **Skills** before completion of your Record Book

THE DUKE OF EDINBURGH'S AWARD

EXPEDITION SECTION

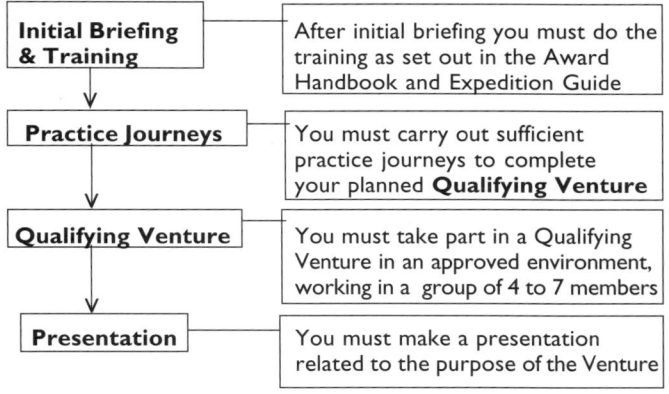

Initial Briefing & Training	After initial briefing you must do the training as set out in the Award Handbook and Expedition Guide
Practice Journeys	You must carry out sufficient practice journeys to complete your planned **Qualifying Venture**
Qualifying Venture	You must take part in a Qualifying Venture in an approved environment, working in a group of 4 to 7 members
Presentation	You must make a presentation related to the purpose of the Venture

PHYSICAL SECTION

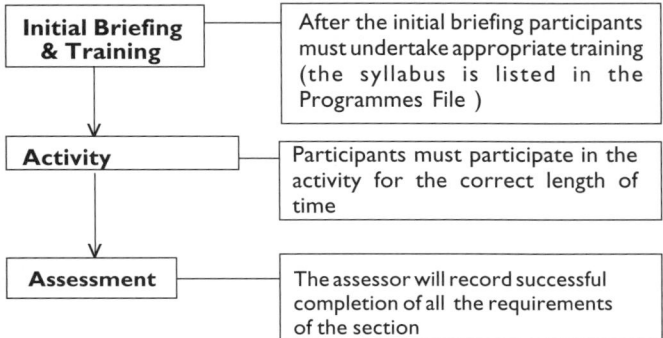

Initial Briefing & Training	After the initial briefing participants must undertake appropriate training (the syllabus is listed in the Programmes File)
Activity	Participants must participate in the activity for the correct length of time
Assessment	The assessor will record successful completion of all the requirements of the section

PHYSICAL FITNESS

SPORTS AND PHYSICAL FITNESS

As a Cadet and young person it is important to be as physically fit as you can. It will assist you in your Cadet career, keep you mentally alert and increase your stamina.

Sport and fitness is part of your training, give it as much effort as any other training you do. Participate in Detachment, Company and County sporting events it is part of your commitment to the Cadets. You may not attain a winner's medal, but any Cadet who is prepared to try is a winner.

TEAM SPIRIT

Individual sports', swimming for example, requires encouragement, self-discipline and constant practice. An individual swimmer relies on team spirit to succeed; the coach, fellow swimmers, family support are all involved in the success of an individual.

Taking part in sport or physical training as part of a team is the same. Sometimes a team has to help an individual to shine in order to win the game – TEAM SPIRIT!

THE SPORTS PERSON

A SPORTSPERSON IS ONE WHO:-
PLAYS THE GAME FOR THE GAMES SAKE.

PLAYS FOR THE TEAM AND NOT FOR THEM SELVES.

IS A GOOD WINNER AND GOODLOSER;
I.E; MODEST IN VICTORY AND GENEROUS IN DEFEAT.

ACCEPTS ALL DECISIONS IN A PROPER SPIRIT.

IS CHIVALROUS TOWARDS A DEFEATED OPPONENT.

IS UNSELFISH AND ALWAYS READY TO HELP OTHERS TO BECOME PROFICIENT.

AS A SPECTATOR APPLAUDS GOOD PLAY ON BOTH SIDES.

NEVER CHALLENGES UMPIRES, JUDGES OR REFEREES - NO MATTER WHAT THE DECISION

PHYSICAL FITNESS

ALWAYS LOOK FOR OPPORTUNITIES TO PLAY ENERGETIC GAMES - ESPECIALLY AT CAMP

If you work hard at your exercises - play games hard and enter into sport with a will and the right spirit — you will not have any fitness problems.

The Army Sports Control Board governs all sporting activities in the Army. Over 50 years ago they drew up their definition of a **SportsPerson**. (See the previous page)

It is just as relevant today, and as difficult to follow, but keep it in mind whenever taking part in sports.

YOUR HEALTH

Unless you are fit and have the stamina to carry out the different types of training throughout your Cadet career, your Instructors will have to make a decision NOT to allow you to take part in some of the activities or exercises because of the risk of you becoming a casualty through being unfit.

Food

Many of us are 'Food Junkies', eating too much sugar, fat and starch - or just eating too much! If you decide to increase your stamina and get your muscles working for you rather than against you, it may well be that your desire to 'binge' disappears!

Medical

Those of you with medical conditions should always check with their Doctor to ensure that they can take part in sports and physical activities. It is perhaps even more important for you to keep fit. As a passing note, some of our top athletes have Diabetes and look what they have attained.

N.B. Make sure that your Adult Instructors and Officers are aware of your medical condition.

PHYSICAL FITNESS

EXERCISE DISCIPLINE

You do not need to join a Health Club or build a 'Home Gym' in your bedroom, just practice some of the simple exercises you know already – DAILY. Sit – Ups, Press Ups, Running on the Spot, Arm Swinging etc. Do not forget the two-mile speed walk or run twice a week.
Use the Duke of Edinburgh's Award Fitness Tests as the measure of your ability.

The Fitness Feeling

Once you have attained a good level of fitness you will feel great! Alert and ready to take part in other activities. All you need now is the SELF DISCIPLINE to keep it up.

A WORD OF CAUTION

Remember that you are ONLY INSURED WHEN TAKING PART IN OFFICIALLY RECOGNISED CADET EVENTS AND ACTIVITIES, SUPERVISED BY QUALIFIED COACHES AND/OR INSTRUCTORS.

For example, if you have challenged another Detachment to a game of football, get it made 'official', that way if anyone is injured or property damaged, it will be covered by insurance.

THE DUKE OF EDINBURGH'S AWARD

PHYSICAL ACHIEVEMENT TESTS

These may be used to qualify in the Physical Section of the DofE Award.

Points required to qualify for your APC Star Grades

Basic - 12 points	One Star - 18 points.
Two Star - 24 points.	Three Star - 30 points.

NOTE: For the Award you are required to undertake all SEVEN events and select SIX to count. A reasonable rest is allowed between each event. Tests may be spread over TWO days.

SCORING FOR MALE CADETS					
Points Scored					
Events	1	2	3	4	5
Speed Test Time (secs)	28	26	25	24	23
Ball Speed Bounce Catches 30secs	30	35	40	45	50
Trunk Curl Test - Number in minute	20	28	34	40	45
Bailey Bridge - Number in 30 secs	12	17	19	21	22
Push-Up hand/foot version No in 1min	15	23	27	34	50
or Push-Up hand/knee moderated version. Number in minute	25	37	44	58	68
Single Leg Squat Thrust. No in 30 secs	40	60	70	76	82
Run Time (mins & secs)	4.20	4.00	3.40	3.20	3.10

NOTE: Score may be counted for either Push-Ups hand/foot version, or Push-ups hand/knee moderated version but not both.

THE DUKE OF EDINBURGH'S AWARD

SCORING FOR FEMALE CADETS

Events	Points Scored				
	1	2	3	4	5
Speed Test Time (secs)	32	28	27	26	25
Ball Speed Bounce. Catches in 30 secs	20	26	32	36	38
Trunk Curl Test. Number in 1 minute	10	20	28	32	36
Bailey Bridge Number in 30 secs	12	16	18	20	22
Push-Ups hand/foot version. No in 1 min	8	14	18	24	30
or Push-Up hand/knee moderated version. Number in 1 minute	14	24	28	40	45
Single Leg Squat Thrust. No in 30 secs	35	50	65	72	80
Run Time (minutes and seconds)	4.50	4.30	4.10	3.50	3.40

Note: Scores may be counted for either Push-ups hand/foot version or Push-Up hand knee moderated version, **but not both.**

Physical Achievement Programme

Points required for Star Awards.

The MINIMUM number of points for you to qualify at each level of this subject are set out in the chart below.

Training Level	Participation	Performance	Additional Pts	Pass Qual
Basic Training	6	3	3	12
One Star	10	4	4	18
Two Star	12	6	6	24
Three Star	12	6	12	30

Note: Points are awarded for *participation* on a basis of 1 point for each half-hour of training. No more than two participation points may be gained in any one week.

Additional points may be gained by either further participation or by improved performance

THE DUKE OF EDINBURGH'S AWARD

DESCRIPTION AND CONDITIONS OF TESTS

Speed Test: Cross **TEN** times between two lines marked on ground or floor NINE metres apart. Each line crossed or touched by one foot.

Stamina Run

Twenty laps of a regular circuit 12 metres by 8 metres, each corner marked by a small object. The score is determined by the time in which this exercise is completed.

Ball Speed Bounce

Using a Netball or a size 5 Football, stand behind a line 2 metres from a wall. Hold the ball with two hands against the chest. Ball must be thrown with two hands so as to rebound from the wall into the hands behind the restraining line.

Count each successfully caught ball in 30 seconds. It is recommended that a brick or similar solid surface is used for this event to ensure a satisfactory rebound.

Push-Ups

Hand/Foot version: Lie face down on the floor, hands under shoulders, palms flat on the floor.

Straighten arms without locking, to lift body, leaving only palms and toes on floor.

Bend elbows until nose only touches the floor or return to starting position. **Repeat push-ups.** Scoring ceases if body sags. The score is the number of push-ups completed in one minute. or alternatively:-

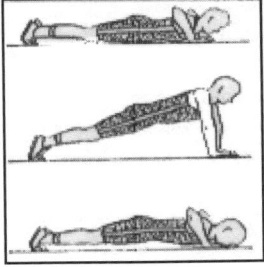

Hand/knee moderated version:

Lie face down on the floor, hands under shoulders, palms flat on the floor with lower legs bent upwards from the knees.

THE DUKE OF EDINBURGH'S AWARD

Straighten arms, without locking, to lift body, leaving only the palms and knees on floor, so that knees, hips and shoulders are in a straight line.

This straight line should be maintained and the hands should not be allowed to move back towards the knees. Bend elbows until nose touches the floor or return to starting position.

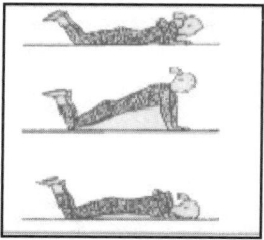

Repeat push-up. The score is the number of push-ups completed in one minute. Girls may find it easier to lie face down on the floor, hands under shoulders, palms flat on the floor with legs bent upwards from the knees on the floor.

Bailey Bridge

Start in the front support position (body in a straight line supported by hands and toes only) with shoulders near to and facing a chair, stool or box on which is placed a small object, bean bag, keys, a stone etc.,.

The seat of the chair should be 45cm from the floor.

Take the object from the chair seat with one hand, place it on the floor, pick up the object with the other hand and replace it on the chair seat.

Continue the cycle, using alternate hands. Count the number of times the object is successfully placed on the chair in 30 seconds

THE DUKE OF EDINBURGH'S AWARD

SINGLE LEG SQUAT THRUST
Starting Position:
Set up two lines 50cm apart. Crouch with both hands placed flat on the floor and with the toes touching the front line.

Take one leg back so that the foot is on the floor behind the rear line.

The test:
Change legs so that each foot is alternately thrust over the rear line, with the hips remaining high.

The score is the number of single leg squat thrusts, ie when each foot crosses the line, completed in the thirty seconds.

TRUNK CURL TEST

(To be performed on a towel, mat or suitable equivalent).

Lie on the back with legs bent. A 90 degree angle should be maintained between the upper and lower legs. Place hands on cheeks. Ankles should not be held. Sit, curling trunk and head until both elbows touch upper legs and then return to the starting position. Although the feet may leave the floor, the right angle between the upper and lower legs must be maintained. The score is the number of curls completed in one minute.

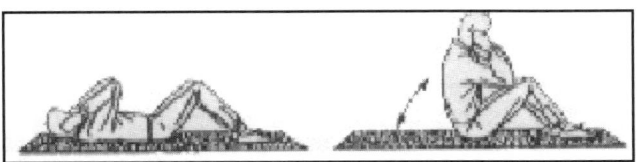

THE DUKE OF EDINBURGH'S AWARD

SELF TEST QUESTIONS

1. What four sections are common to all Awards.
2. What is the age you can enter the Bronze, Silver and Gold Awards?
3. At what Star level of your APC training are you most likely to qualify for the Bronze Award.
4. Give two examples of where a Senior Cadet Instructors Cadre might fit into an Award.
5. What is the upper age limit for gaining an Award.
6. How many kilometres are suggested for Bronze, Silver and Gold Expeditions on foot.
7. Before going on an Expedition what do you leave behind.
8. What is the minimum period of time you must undertake for a particular Skill at Silver level?
9. In the Physical Recreation section what is the minimum period of time you must take to qualify?
10. What is the important proviso which enables you to count Annual Camp as your Residential Project (apart from the time requirement)?
11. During Expeditions the minimum recommended calorie intake per day is 1000, 2000, 3000 or 4000?
12. Can Drill be taken as a Skill in the Award?
13. What do you have to buy to start your Award.
14. Do you all enter as a team in your unit for the Award?
15. Who is the Award Officer in your County?
16. Are you permitted to do an expedition other than on foot?
17. Can Skill at Arms be counted as a Skill towards the Award?
18. How many in the team doing a Qualifying Venture?
19. Who sets the targets to be achieved in Physical Recreation?
20. Who completes an account of the Expedition?
21. Name fourteen recognised 'skills'.
22. At what level of the Award do you do a Residential Project?
23. Name two alternative types of Expedition you can undertake over the age of 16?

Chapter 8
EXPEDITION TRAINING

Expedition training can be the most exciting and fun subject of your cadet training. It is also the most important, bringing other skills you have been taught in to practical use. The skills and knowledge you gain in expedition and adventurous training will benefit you throughout your life. Not forgetting that it is an important part of the Duke of Edinburgh's Award Scheme.

THE COUNTRY CODE

Expeditions may take you over Military Training Areas, privately owned property, or land where the public has rights of access. The Country Code applies wherever you are. You have a personal responsibility to ensure that you protect the natural beauty of the countryside and the wildlife living there. The message is, **abuse it and lose it.**

THE PRAYER OF THE TREE

You who pass by and would raise your hand against me, hearken ere you harm me.

I am the heat of your camp fire on a cold night, the friendly shade screening you from the summer sun.

My fruits are refreshing draughts quenching your thirst as you journey on.

I am the beam that holds your house, the board of your table, the bed on which you lie, the timber that builds your boat.

I am the handle of your hoe, the door of your homestead, the wood of your cradle, the shell of your last resting place.

I am the gift of God and the friend of man.

You who pass by, listen to my prayer, harm me not.

Anon

EXPEDITION TRAINING

The COUNTRY CODE is a series of ten reminders based on common sense – and common failings. Thoughtless disposal of litter is perhaps the most unsightly and costly problem our countryside faces. For instance, did you know that cows love shiny ring pulls from drink cans; they eat them along with the grass and they can perforate their stomachs. Next time you are in the country, have a look at the rubbish others leave behind – pretty isn't it?

"LEAVE NOTHING BUT YOUR FOOTPRINTS"

RESPECT THE PEOPLE AND LIFE OF THE COUNTRYSIDE

PROTECT ALL WILD LIFE

GO CAREFULLY ON COUNTRY ROADS

SECURELY FASTEN ALL GATES

EXPEDITION TRAINING

THE COUNTRY CODE

GUARD AGAINST RISK OF FIRE

USE GATES AND STILES

KEEP DOGS UNDER PROPER CONTROL

LEAVE NO LITTER

KEEP TO THE FOOTPATHS

SAFEGUARD WATER SUPPLIES

EXPEDITION TRAINING

DISCIPLINES OF PERSONAL HEALTH AND HYGIENE

HOW TO WALK – BOOTS AND FEET

You are issued with one pair of feet, with some of the most delicate bones in your body; so it makes sense to try and look after them! Some of you may already have problems with your feet through wearing badly fitting shoes.

BOOTS

It is most important to make sure that your boots are comfortable, giving your ankles the support and protection they require. They are expensive, and even if you can afford two pairs – one polished up for parades, the other kept for 'heavy work', unfortunately your feet will grow and trying to walk in boots at the age of 16 bought when you where 14, is a very painful experience and will do untold damage to your feet.

Good quality, well fitting boots or shoes are an investment, not only will they look after your feet, preventing problems later on, they SHOULD last longer.

FITTING BOOTS

1. When you go to buy new boots, take a thick pair of socks or two pairs of normal socks to wear when trying on your boots.
2. Make sure you can move your toes and that when standing still your toes do not touch the toe of the boot.
3. A method of testing the fitting is to be able to get a finger down between your heel and the back of the boot. If you can do this and your toes just touch the toe of the boot, they should fit you comfortably.
4. Fully lace up the boots to check that the uppers have enough room for your foot and that they are comfortable.

CARE OF BOOTS

1. Keep your boots 'well fed', leather will dry and crack if you do not put polish on them regularly.
2. If your boots get wet, do not dry them too close to heat, they will go hard and crack. Stuff them with newspaper; changing it often, this draws out the damp.
3. Always clean mud off your boots, it dries the polish out of the leather causing cracking and lack of water resistance.

EXPEDITION TRAINING

CARE OF YOUR FEET
SOCKS
To give you and your feet the best chance of comfort, it is important to have natural fibre socks. Make sure that you have at least two pairs of thick Wool, Cotton or a mix of the two is ideal. Natural fibre lets your feet 'breathe'. Keep your socks in good repair; 'holey' socks cause blisters. If you use the terry 'tube' socks, they are better worn inside out as there is less chance of friction.

FEET
When walking with a backpack, the extra weight you carry on your back is equivalent to more than three times the same weight on each foot. Your balance is more critcal and you will adjust to a different 'gait'
When walking the weight of your body is transferred to the ball of your foot rather than the heel. Your normal "civilian pedestrian" feet will need some extra help to cope.
Make sure your boots are "broken in"before expedition work.
Wear thick 'boot socks'
Prepare your feet – if you have corns etc. see a chiropodist - if you don't wish to be a casualty
Keep your feet clean, dust them every morning (or more often if necessary) with a foot powder. Do not use too much powder, it will 'clump' and be uncomfortable.
Wash your feet regularly, rub them dry and check that your toe nails are not sharp.
Change your socks from one foot to the other, (stops the sock from forming too closely to your foot).
NEVER SOAK YOUR FEET WHEN ON THE MARCH, a quick dip, quick dry and then walk on IS beneficial.

TREATMENT OF BLISTERS
Prevention is better than cure, if when you check your feet you find a reddened patch of skin, this is a blister waiting to happen. To prevent further pressure, apply a plaster or a strip of hypoallergenic tape to the affected area.

EXPEDITION TRAINING

If you already have a blister and wish to open it, either use a sterile lance or sterilize a needle by holding it in the flame of a match and letting it cool before use.

To lance the blister, prick the skin at the side then gently press the liquid out until the blister is flat. Apply a plaster or a sterile dressing secured by two strips of plaster applied like a cross. It is important to keep the area clean to guard against infection.

WET FEET

Should you get your feet wet, if at all possible dry them and your boots, putting on fresh socks. "Walking to dry them" will make your skin tender and you will end up a casualty.

CRAMP

If you have been walking for a long period, or perhaps your boots are laced up too tightly, you may get a sudden very painful spasm in your

are YOUR FEET always happy ?

leg muscles. Loosening off your boots and massaging the affected area is the best treatment. The cramp should go in a few minutes.

APART FROM YOUR FEET....

THIRST

After the first few hours of walking, particularly in hot weather, you may find that you develop a great thirst, not necessarily because your body has need of fluid, but by your mouth feeling dry. An alternative to drinking large quantities of water is to chew a blade of grass or suck a prune. A further alternative is to carry a piece of raw onion in your

EXPEDITION TRAINING

mouth; it also helps prevent your lips from cracking. (Petroleum jelly does the same job for your lips).

When on an organised Cadet or Duke of Edinburgh's Award expedition, care is always taken to ensure that there is an adequate supply of water available. Remember you should drink 3/4 litres of water each day. However, should you have been without water for a long period, sip slowly to prevent your stomach going into cramps. Never swallow snow or ice, let it melt first, preferably by boiling it. Do not assume that spring water is fit to drink, who knows what is in the water further upstream? Remember to sterilise your water bottle before you use it, by using a sterilising tablet.

ALCOHOL

As a Cadet you are not supposed to drink alcohol. Alcohol slows reaction, impairs thinking and in cold weather can make you more susceptible to hypothermia. Alcohol slows down the heart rate, and therefore slows the 'heating system' to the body.

PERSONAL MEDICATION

If you have a medical condition that requires you to take medication, **ENSURE THAT YOU HAVE ENOUGH WITH YOU, MAKE SURE YOU PACK IT WHERE YOU CAN FIND IT!**

PERSONAL HYGIENE

This might be seen as a low priority when you are on expedition or camping, yet the reverse is true. Sweat stays on the skin surface and if not removed can lose you friends and cause sores particularly between the legs, under the arms, around the waist and feet. It takes self-discipline to keep clean, particularly so if there is only cold water to wash in.

Clean your teeth regularly; a build up of old food and drink makes your mouth feel dry.

Weather and time permitting, wash out dirty socks and underwear, this will prevent them festering in your kit.

Wash Kit

Keep your soap in a soapbox; it prevents it from going soggy and becoming un-usable.

EXPEDITION TRAINING

Try and dry your towel out, it will stop it smelling - hang it out in the fresh air.

Keep all your wash kit in a plastic bag to keep it clean and dry.

CLOTHING AND EQUIPMENT

You are never certain what sort of weather you may be faced with in the UK, in less than an hour it can change from bright warm sun to cold, damp or rain. This makes it difficult to be dressed in the right gear. You need to remember that whatever you chose to wear needs to:

Keep water out – keep your body heat in"

JACKET/ANORAK

If your jacket lets water in, your clothing underneath will get damp or wet. Wet clothing will not insulate your body; in fact it will cool you quicker, increasing your chances of becoming a casualty through hypothermia.

Cheaper waterproofs are effective - they keep water out. The down side is that because the fabric cannot 'breathe' your body heat cannot escape and you may get very hot and damp from the inside.

Modern 'breathable' waterproofs are available. They are lightweight, keep you dry and are expensive! It is suggested that if you really enjoy walking or expeditions and plan to continue after you have completed your APC and/or Duke of Edinburgh's Award, then save up for one of these jackets.

A less expensive alternative is to have a decent warm jacket (non – waterproof), and buy a waterproof CAGOULE. Most have a ventilated yoke at the back and they pack neatly to sit on the top of your kit for easy access.

SHIRTS AND UNDERWEAR

Many experienced walkers wear woolen vests and tops because it has the best insulating and breathing properties. Some people find that wool next to the skin is most uncomfortable. Whatever you wear, apply the 'ONION SKIN PRINCIPLE'. This means wearing several thin layers of clothing (two minimum), to trap the warmth in. It is better to wear two thin layers rather than two thick – it holds more air in. Always keep an extra 'layer' in your kit, as you may well need it.

EXPEDITION TRAINING

HATS

If the sun is blazing down, wear a hat; it will protect you from uncomfortable sunburn and prevent possible sunstroke.

If the weather is cold and damp, wear a hat; it will prevent you losing valuable body heat. BALACLAVAS are a good choice as they can be pulled down over your ears and face if it is very cold or windy.

PERSONAL KIT LIST

Expeditions are either in uniform or civvies. Whatever the kit, wear your jacket. (Your County may well have cagoules to loan out for expedition work).

The following lists are an example of what you will need to carry with you.

To be carried on you:

Map, compass, Pathfinder Protractor/Romer, Whistle on lanyard. Matches in a waterproof container. Plasters, Pencil and notebook. Unless told otherwise a mobile phone in working order.

To be carried in your backpack:

Personal cleaning kit, towel, spare underclothes and socks, Mess tins with knife fork and spoon, pan scrub for cleaning your mess tins, reserve food such as Kendal mint cake, chocolate, raisins.

Remember – you carry what you take so think about weight.

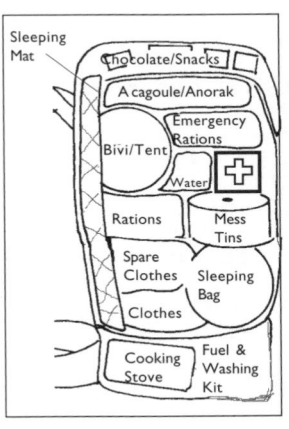

Mug – metal preferred as you can heat it up, but plastic will do. A water bottle with a secure top. Groundsheet and a good length of strong string. A small torch, sleeping bag liner and a survival bag or blanket.

The following can be put into a kit bag to be delivered to camp site – if that is how the expedition is being organised, otherwise you will have to carry them yourself.

Sleeping bag, spare change of clothing, spare boots or shoes if available. Trainers, wool pullover. *NOT TO FORGET YOUR BUNGEES*

EXPEDITION TRAINING

PACKING YOUR BACKPACK

The type and capacity of backpack you are able to use can make all
the difference to the way it is packed. If it does not have a frame, you
will need to be careful not to overload it as you may end up with hard
and odd shaped items sticking into your back whilst carrying it.

The emphasis is packing INTO the backpack, not hanging boots or
other items on the outside until you look like a Christmas tree on the
move. Look carefully at the **LOAD CARRYING** and the
DISTRIBUTION of the load as illustrated in the diagrams. Stove fuel
should be packed in a well-sealed polythene bag stored well away from
your rations. All clothing and your sleeping bag should also be kept in
polythene bags. It is a good idea to use a strong polythene bag as a
liner for your kit bag; it will keep the contents dry.

It is worthwhile taking some time to practice packing your backpack
correctly and then wear/carry it to ensure that it is comfortable.

As a rough 'rule of thumb' you should not carry more than one quarter
of your body weight.

LOAD CARRYING — The RIGHT and Wrong methods

RIGHT	WRONG
LOAD CARRIED CORRECTLY	LOAD CARRIED INCORRECTLY
WEIGHT APPLIED VERTICALLY	HANGING OUT FROM SHOULDERS
	LOOSE ITEMS OF KIT HANGING

Carry not more than a quarter of your body weight

EXPEDITION TRAINING

LAYOUT OF A CAMP SITE

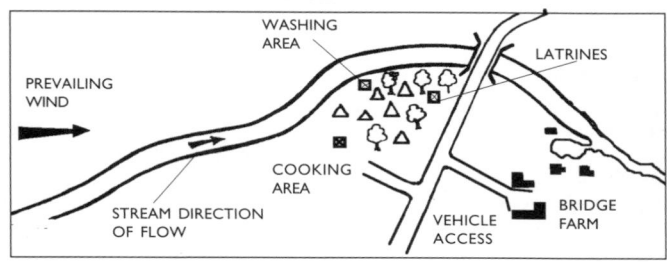

Your Officer or Adult Instructor will have gained permission for you to camp on the land and for you to have the training time. If you are camping out with some friends for a few days, remember it is very important to gain permission from the landowners first.

The ideal campsite is one offering shelter from the prevailing wind, on well-drained fairly level area, facing East to hopefully catch the early morning sun. It should be as far away as possible from any houses, be close to a clean water supply and be in the open.

IS IT SAFE?

1. Is the site below the level of a river, lake, dam or reservoir, whose banks could burst or overflow in the event of a severe storm, or in a dried-up stream which 'comes to raging life' in a storm.
2. Is the site under overhanging rocks or cliffs, or any other form of danger, for example under a bridge or viaduct.
3. Ensure that the ground does not slope down from the bivi area to where the cooking area is set out, and that the tents are not close enough to be a fire risk.

CAMP LAYOUT

1. Can the tents/bivi's be correctly pitched in the area and sheltered from the wind and not under trees
2. If a platoon or section camp, a COOKING AREA sited where there is no risk of causing fire, properly set out for the purpose to be conveniently close to the bivis, but again, not too close in case of fire.

EXPEDITION TRAINING

3. Toilet/washing area defined, sited down wind and away from the tent site and cooking area. Latrines must be given some privacy.
4. Some access for a vehicle.

LATRINES

One of our normal everyday occurrences is the use of a toilet. Normally you sit in solitary comfort, door shut and perhaps a magazine to read. You will not find it quite so civilized in the field! There are a few important things to remember.

Hygiene: In spite of being "in the field" you have to take more care about using the toilet facilities and cleaning your hands. There is a greater possibility of infection: to have digestive problems in the field is no picnic.

CONSTRUCTION OF A FIELD LATRINE

On military land it is normal to see portable toilet units servicing frequently used camp areas. Some Counties have chemical toilets for field use. However, should these items not be available, knowing how to construct a field latrine is a useful skill. It will need a spade or shovel as digging a hole in the ground is essential as any exposed excrement attracts flies. Try to lift any grass over the chosen site carefully; it can be replaced before leaving .

You will need to dig a hole not less than 44cm (one foot six inches) deep and 22cm (nine inches) wide. The earth taken from the hole should be piled up ready to be used by each individual to cover excrement and finally to fill the hole before leaving the site. If time permits, a 'seat' can be made for the latrine, see diagram.

Before leaving, the ground used for the toilet must be clearly marked with a sign stating that it is 'soiled ground'.

Privacy when using a latrine is an important factor, therefore some sort of screen or concealment is desirable. Your Instructors will no doubt introduce some sort of control.

EXPEDITION TRAINING

One method is to provide a container for the toilet paper that is left in a prominent position. Each user must remember **to return it after use.** The message – when the toilet is "engaged" the container is **not there**. Simple, but effective.

Note: it is important to put the toilet roll in a plastic bag to keep it dry.

PREPARING FOOD IN THE FIELD

Your experience of cooking may be limited to zapping a pre-prepared meal in the microwave, cooking in the field is a little different.

Traditionally, one of the first tasks on reaching a campsite is to "brew-up" for the whole group.

During cold weather, particularly if you have been physically active or walking, it is important to have hot drinks regularly, and when you do have a meal, to ensure that it is hot, to sustain you.

COOKERS

You may use butane gas cookers, or 'hexi cookers' that use small blocks of solid fuel in a folding tin container. The most effective way of using a hexi cooker is to scrape a hole in the ground deep enough to shield your mess tins when they are on the cooker. This prevents any wind blowing your fuel out and keeps the food from chilling.

Important note: Make sure that you never use your hexi/butane/other cooker where it could cause a fire, for instance on dry leaf mould in wooded areas.

MESS TIN COOKING

Mess tin cooking is usually carried out with two of you "teaming up" as a cooker is efficient enough to produce hot food for two.

If you are issued with tinned rations, there are two important points for you to remember.

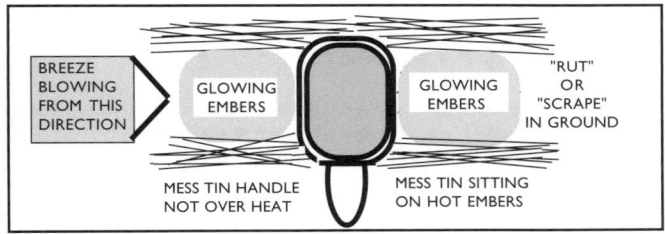

BREEZE BLOWING FROM THIS DIRECTION

GLOWING EMBERS

GLOWING EMBERS

"RUT" OR "SCRAPE" IN GROUND

MESS TIN HANDLE NOT OVER HEAT

MESS TIN SITTING ON HOT EMBERS

EXPEDITION TRAINING

1. Make sure there are two holes made in the top of the tin before you heat it, otherwise the tin could 'blow' and scald you badly.
2. If you have aluminum mess tins, do not use the water your tins have 'cooked in' to make a hot drink. It can be used for washing yourself or your tins.

Solid fuel cookers make a sticky black mess on the bottom of your mess tins, an easy way to remove most of it is to rub it hard along grass, then use a pan scrub to remove the rest. Remember to clean the inside, wipe out with grass, and then wash out.

FOOD RATIONS

A balanced diet becomes more important as the distance you travel or activity increases. If a journey is to take several days you will need to plan your menus carefully. The amount of food required each day depends on the country you are moving over. If it is mountainous then your body will use more energy and require more food. (Carbohydrates, sugar and starches).

Food has to be carried, too much is unnecessary weight, too little and you will go hungry. Dried potatoes weigh less than a bag of potatoes. Rice or pasta weighs little when uncooked. Dehydrated foods are excellent but expensive, plus the need to carry extra water. All in stews are a good standby; they only need one mess tin.

Whatever you decide to take, make sure that it is simple to cook and most important, you like it.

Ensure that you have sufficient to drink, avoid fizzy drinks; they do not quench your thirst.

FOOD HYGIENE

When on an expedition or exercise the very last thing you will think about will be food hygiene.

Food Poisoning - through using dirty mess tins or using fresh rations that have not ben properly cooked can really spoil your fun - and everyone elses!

1. While you are eating your hot food put a mess tin of water on to boil.
2. Ensure you clean Mess Tins and KFS **properly** use very hot water.
3. Carefully wrap cooked food if you intend to eat it later.
4. NEVER EVER RE-HEAT RICE.
5. Take all your rubbish, tins, plastic with you - **leave nothing but your footprints**

EXPEDITION TRAINING

COMPOSITE RATIONS

As a Cadet you may have Service issue Composite Rations (**COMPO**) issued on field training. These rations have been developed over many years to give the soldier a high quality balanced diet.

CONTENT OF COMPO RATIONS

Compo is issued in a 24 hour Ration Pack ('rat pack'), which is produced in different menu selections. Compo rations are slowly being replaced by a pouched system. Pouched rations can be eaten hot or cold. If heating, follow the instructions on the pack ensure the food is hot. If a pouch is punctured and food is visible it should not be eaten.

BOIL IN THE BAG

Ensure that you carry extra water - or have access to extra water for these meals as they require more to cook correctly.
Cook your food in your mess tin to ensure it is thoroughly heated, thus preventing possible food poisoning

TO HEAT CANS

You can cook compo rations 'in the can' by piercing **TWO** holes in the lid of the can, stand the can in your mess tin and fill with water until the can is half submerged. Bring to the boil and boil for TEN minutes. Handle carefully when opening a hot can. This is a quick and easy method of cooking the food, but it does not taste quite as good as when heated out of the tin.

WATER PURIFICATION TABLETS

These are part of your ration pack and it is important that you know how to use them. Normally, drinking water is provided on Cadet organised training, but there may be an occasion where this does not happen. For Drinking Water, add one tablet to a litre of water, leave for TEN MINUTES before use. Leave for at least **THIRTY MINUTES** if using to make up your Lemon or Orange drinks. You must remember your **liquid intake** must be 3 to 4 litres per day. Once you are thirsty, it is too late.

WINDPROOF/WATERPROOF MATCHES

These matches MUST be kept for lighting your Hexamine blocks in bad weather conditions. Don't use them for any other reason or you will be in difficulty if rain or bad weather sets it and you have:

EXPEDITION TRAINING

NO WINDPROOF/WATERPROOF MATCHES ......
NO HOT FOOD – NO HOT DRINK – NO WARMTH

Don't forget you will be assessed on you outdoor cooking for your APC

USEFUL MEASURE TO NOTE

If you fill your small mess tin to the bottom rivet that holds the handle hinge, you will have HALF a PINT of water in the tin.

HILL WALKING SKILLS

Any walk over a reasonable period of time requires you to have a rhythm in the way you walk. This is especially so when HILL WALKING and carrying a loaded backpack. It is best to start out at a steady pace, one that you feel capable of keeping up for a few hours.

If you are finding it difficult to talk or sing whilst walking, you are walking too fast – slow down. A slow plodding pace will get you to your next stop point as quickly as walking fast and having to take regular breaks. The other bonus is that you will not feel hot, sticky and overheated. Wise walkers conserve their energy and enjoy their walk.

WRONG   RIGHT

CLIMBING A HILL

Climbing directly up a hill puts strain on your calf muscles and Achilles tendons. Walking in a "zigzag" fashion across the slope your feet will be in full contact with the ground, with less chance of slipping. It may be slightly further to walk, but far less tiring.

GOING DOWN HILL

Descending a slope safely carrying a full backpack requires some skill. Running or attempting to slide down is not recommended. Your balance plays a great part, the main thing is to bend both knees and lean forward.

EXPEDITION TRAINING

By adopting this stance your legs act as springs and absorb the shaking up your body would have had. Descend by traversing across the slope, keep your hand on the uphill side and near to the ground for support should you slip. Keep off any slopes with loose stones or scree. The golden rule is if a slope frightens you too much – find another way down.

KEEPING YOUR BALANCE

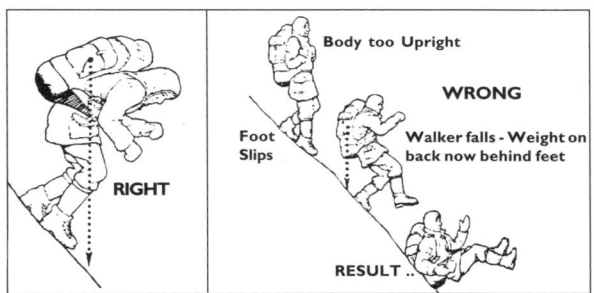

CROSSING RIVERS or STREAMS

In the first place never attempt to coss a river on your own.
Such hazards are best avoided unless there is no safer alternative. When crossing a stream or shallow river an Instructor must always be present. Never attempt to cross a river or stream in full flood. Water is a powerful element and it is easy to underestimate its force. There may also be hidden dangers such as stones, weed etc. that will cause you to fall. Remember, you will end up with wet boots and probably wet feet. The best plan is to find a good crossing point, a bridge or ford. Do not attempt to build a raft unless one of your qualified instructors are with you and checks it for safety before use.

STOPPING FOR A REST

On any walk taking several hours you must stop and rest at regular intervals. The time between each stop will depend on the 'going' – difficult or easy. When resting lay down and raise your feet higher

EXPEDITION TRAINING

than your head. Don't halt for more than five minutes or your muscles will stiffen up.

CARE OF THE ENVIRONMENT

Trees are a valuable natural resource, which take many years to mature. Many of the wild animals, birds and insects rely on trees for their food and protection.

In Britain we cannot grow sufficient trees to meet our needs and import many million pounds worth of timber each year.

We must take care in preserving what we have, follow the Country Code. Do not break branches off trees, or carve in to the trunks. Remember the Prayer of the Tree at the beginning of this Chapter.

IMPROVISED SHELTER

There will be occasions when you do not have a tent to shelter in. The British soldier has the reputation of being able to improvise, "Any fool can rough it, but a good soldier will make himself comfortable under any conditions". As a Cadet, you should try and follow their lead. The following illustrations give a few ideas on how to put up improvised shelters.

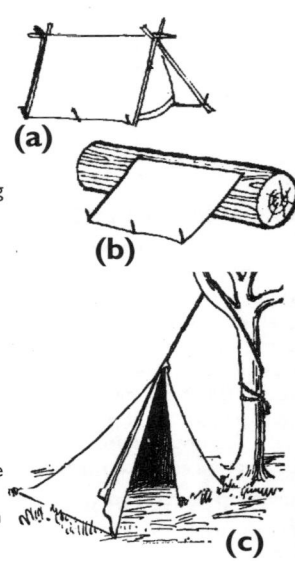

(a) A shelter with two ponchos constructed on the same principle as a BIVI for two.

(b) A poncho shelter made against a fallen tree trunk for one person. The groundsheet must be on the side of the trunk away from the prevailing wind.

(c) Another example of a poncho type of shelter for one person. The rope must be strong enough and the open side of the poncho away from the prevailing wind.

EXPEDITION TRAINING

IMPROVISED TENT

Using a string/rope between two
supports, (perhaps suitable trees),tie
poncho over the string, peggingthe
bottom edges to the ground. This
type of "tent" can also be put up
against a fence or wall using one half
of the tent as shown in the picture
as the triangle A – B – C.

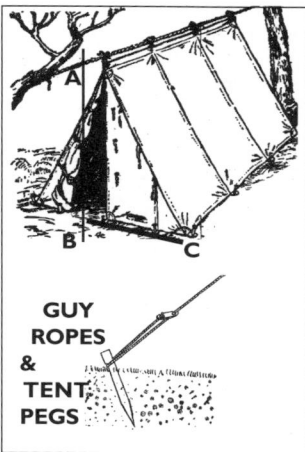

To make a Basha for two you need
two ponchos string or bungees (at
least 6), meat skewers or tent pegs
are useful (8 or 12 are needed). A
length of strong string is always
useful to have in your kit. Tent pegs
must not be driven into the ground
with the head of an axe, use the
proper mallet. The pegs should be
driven in to the ground at an angle
(see diagram) and not so far in the ground that they cannot be seen.

ADVENTUROUS TRAINING & PHYSICAL ACTIVITIES

Having a responsible attitude towards all activities you take part in
goes a long way to ensuring your safety and the safety of others. This
means careful planning and preparation. The Rescue teams often
report that "The party was totally unprepared for the expedition", or
"They had not been trained in map reading", even worse, the Coroner
at an Inquest reported "They had no idea that the deceased was
suffering from Hypothermia".

Your Officers and Adult Instructors have the responsibility of ensuring
that all adventurous training and physical activities are correctly
planned; this includes suitably qualified persons to instruct or guide
you through. Part of the planning is briefing you the Cadet in all
aspects of the activity. This will include the kit you require, who will be
in charge of the training/activity, who the designated First Aid Person
is, where they will be sited.

You may also be given 'no go' areas, make sure you know where they
are.

EXPEDITION TRAINING

Your responsibility to yourself is to make sure you take the correct kit and follow instructions given.

Your responsibility to all the other Cadets is to be alert. Watch out for others, if you are working in hot weather, heat exhaustion can occur quickly. In cold or wet and windy weather, hypothermia can happen to the best of us. Your Instructors will be watching out, but it is almost impossible to see everything.

If you see another Cadet about to do something that will put him/herself or others at risk, don't be slow in trying to stop them. It is not 'sneaky' it is being responsible.

Perhaps most important of all, enjoy the experience – give it your best.

THE ACTIVITIES THAT ARE CONSIDERED AS ADVENTUROUS & PHYSICAL ARE AS FOLLOWS:

Mountaineering – including Hill Walking, Rock Climbing, Abseiling, Skiing, Caving, Canoeing, Off Shore Sailing, Rafting, Swimming, Gliding or Hang Gliding, Paracending, Sub – Aqua Diving and all activities involving the hazard of water.

OFFICIAL PERMISSION

On no account should you organise activities without the knowledge and assistance of your Officers or Instructors.

For your safety's sake,
REMEMBER – SHOULD THERE BE AN ACCIDENT YOU ARE ONLY COVERED BY INSURANCE IF THE ACTIVITY IS OFFICIALLY PLANNED AND ORGANISED.

EXPEDITION TRAINING

PREVENTION OF ACCIDENTS ON OUTDOOR ACTIVITIES - PLANNING

Your Instructors will expect you to work through and be involved withthe planning process as part of your training.

Plan your route beforehand, ensure all members of the group are fully briefed and all have copies of the Route Card, map refs and check points and RVs, campsites and your Estimated Time of Arrival all supported by **accurate map references.**

If you are walking in areas where there are rescue posts or mountain rescue posts, know their locations and procedures including the map references of telephone boxes. Decide on a **Lost Drill** e.g. "Go West till you strike the main road" or "Keep walking down – stream".

BEFORE YOU GO

1. As an individual, always carry a map, compass, protractor, pencil, whistle, small first aid kit and a torch in your jacket or in pockets
2. Have emergency rations such as chocolate, glucose tablets, dried fruit etc. DON'T eat them unless in an emergency.
3. Always carry warm clothing, but reduce non – essentials like two sweaters when one will do.

BEFORE YOU SET OUT

1. Don't overdress, leave off the pullover – carry it on top of your pack until the harder part of the walk is over.
2. Report to the local Rescue Post giving them a copy of your Route Card and expected time back.
3. Check the weather conditions and the forecasts for the duration of your walk

OUT ON THE HILLS

1. Always stay together; unless there is an injured person, in which case half of the party should stay with the casualty, while the other half goes for help.
2. Walk at the pace of the slowest person.
3. If you go out as a group, never travel in groups of less than five.
4. Remember to observe the Country Code.
5. Carry at least one polythene survival sack or sleeping bag per two persons.

EXPEDITION TRAINING

6. Stick to the route agreed.
7. Make one decision among the group on the direction to take. If a compass bearing is used, have others check it, then trust your compass.
8. Do not assume that your mobile phone will work.

If the weather deteriorates – **DON'T PRESS ON; TURN BACK.**

9. If fog descends, **carefully** find a sheltered place, ensure you keep as warm and dry as possible, have a hot drink. Use your whistle to make the distress call if necessary.
10. Don't throw stones; these can dislodge bigger ones and could cause an accident.

IF YOU DO GET LOST:

1. **DO NOT SPLIT UP**

2. **DO NOT PANIC**

3. **DO NOT FORGET TO USE YOUR MAP, COMPASS AND COMMON SENSE**

4. **REMEMBER THE INTERNATIONAL DISTRESS CALL – SIX BLASTS ON YOUR WHISTLE OR SIX TORCH FLASHES PER MINUTE.**

SAFETY ON THE HIGHWAYS

By day or night, when moving as an individual on foot you must:

1. Use a footpath; if there is not one, walk on the side of the road facing the nearest traffic (normally the right hand side), keep as close to the side as possible.
2. Cross motorways by bridges or underpasses, railways by bridges or level crossings.
3. When dark, keep an extra sharp lookout and wear a high visibility jacket/tabard or if not available, light coloured clothing which will show up in the lights of a vehicle.

Note: Walking on the highways at any time as a group should be organised and led by an Instructor.

EXPEDITION TRAINING

EMERGENCY PROCEDURES
Emergency Messages
The Police are responsible for calling out the rescue services. The information they will require is as follows:

A. The exact location of the injured person(s) with a six-figure grid reference and a description/landmarks of the area for a helicopter pilot to identify.

B. The number of injured persons and their names.

C. The nature of their injuries.

D. The time of the accident.

E. Mobile Phone number(s) held by members of the group.

Those going for help must remember the area and landscape with any particular reference point to help find the site on return with a rescue party. (Write the information down).

Waiting for help to arrive
1. Those looking after the injured should set up shelters and carry out emergency first aid with particular reference to the prevention of hypothermia/exposure.
2. It will be necessary to mark the site with light coloured clothing or bandages on sticks where they can easily attract attention.
3. There are International **Ground to Air Signals** that can be used to communicate with rescue aircraft; these are shown on the next page.
4. In addition to these signals, **A RED FLARE, A RED SQUARE OF CLOTH** or a **FIRE** are also recognised **International Alarm Signals.**
5. Setting out clothing or items of kit, or a person lying down taking up the shape of the letter can make the shape of each signal. Get help any way you can.
6. Be alert; watch out for the rescue party to guide them in by the quickest route.
7. Make yourselves as comfortable as possible; 'brew up', eat HOT food, keep together, keep warm, keep up the morale.

EXPEDITION TRAINING

GROUND TO AIR SIGNALS

letter	signal	
V		REQUEST ASSISTANCE
↑		WE ARE PROCEEDING IN THIS DIRECTION
X		MEDICAL ASSISTANCE REQUIRED
N		NO WE DO NOT NEED ANYTHING

GO FLY - A SURVIVAL KITE

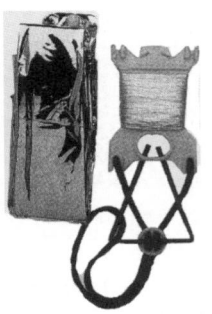

A Pocket Sized piece of kit to rescue those lost on an expedition or lost as darkness falls, may, if kitted out with a Survival Kite be brought to safety sooner.

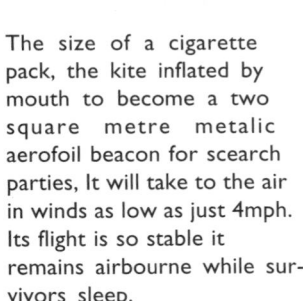

The size of a cigarette pack, the kite inflated by mouth to become a two square metre metalic aerofoil beacon for scearch parties, It will take to the air in winds as low as just 4mph. Its flight is so stable it remains airbourne while survivors sleep.

Kite reflects radar signals and its visability can be further enhanced by adding a small "light stick", the brightly glowing chemical indicator.

Other uses, it can be worn as a vest under outer garments directing heat back to the body or wrapped around a broken limb and then inflated, used as a splint.

EXPEDITION TRAINING

WIND CHILL FACTOR

Insufficient attention is paid to the combined effect of air temperature and wind speed has on the human body. This combined effect is the **Wind Chill Factor.** The air temperature may be quite warm, but it only needs a wind blowing at 24 k.p.h. (15 m.p.h.) to cause body cooling, particularly to the head, face and hands.

Wind speeds above 24 k.p.h. cool the body slower, but can cause the body to burn up more energy; there is also the hazard of being blown over whilst walking. The following diagram is reproduced from the book Mountain craft and Leadership by Alec Langmuir and illustrates graphically how important it is to be aware of the Wind Chill Factor. As an example it shows:

The air temperature at +5 degrees C, at a wind speed of 50 k.p.h. (31 m.p.h.) it crosses the Wind Chill Line at "Very Cold".

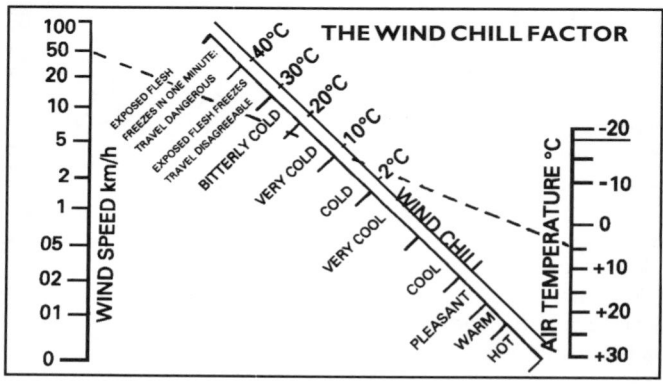

EXPEDITION TRAINING

PRECAUTIONS & ADVICE

Before setting out on a hill walk or expedition, you would be well advised to check out the wind speeds and ensure that you take adequate steps to prevent rapid chilling.

Try and keep warm and dry, wet clothing combined with Wind Chill can cause Hypothermia

Wear a hat and gloves

Eat the right food, keep energy levels high

Do not get too tired

Never underestimate or ignore the Wind Chill Factor.

Check First Aid Chapter for the treatment of Extremes of Temperature (heat and cold).

SUMMARY

Accidents don't just happen; they are CAUSED.

Most accidents occurring on outdoor adventurous activities no matter where they take place are due to one or more of the following reasons:

1. Not involving senior more experienced members of your unit and not gaining permission to carry out the activity.
2. Insufficient detailed preparation, planning and training. RECCE not done properly, no rehearsals. Menu not planned for the activity or area to be traveled.
3. Not having the right clothing, e.g. wearing jeans and unsuitable footwear for hill walking.
4. Carelessness or casual attitude by those taking part.
5. Overestimation of the strength and stamina of those taking part.
6. Not enough practical experience – especially in map reading and camp craft.
7. Not paying sufficient attention to detail, failing to notice the signs of deteriorating weather conditions.
8. Not turning back when common sense says 'turn back'.

EXPEDITION TRAINING

KNOTS AND THEIR USES

A lot depends on knowing how to tie just the right knot or hitch for a particular job.

While learning to tie knots it is no use using a thin string or twine made up of loose strands. You need a piece of rope or cord not less than a quarter of an inch thick and several feet long.

An important point to remember is that it is not a good idea to ever cut a rope just to shorten it, as you will find that no sooner had you cut it, than you needed a longer rope for some other purpose.

As mentioned in the Expedition Training, it is always useful to have a length of string or rope with you, but there is not much point in having a rope if you don't know how to tie a useful knot in it.

Like most skills it is only through practice that you will become proficient, this is especially so with knots.

The occasion you need to use a knot will more than likely be in an emergency situation, you must realise that this will mean instant re-action with no time to think of what to do. This is when your ability to tie the — "right knot at the right time" — could prevent a disaster.

A ROPE

The main part of a rope is called the "standing part" - see illustration. When the end is bent back toward the standing part, the loop formed is called a "bight", regardless of whether it crosses the rope or only lies parallel with it.

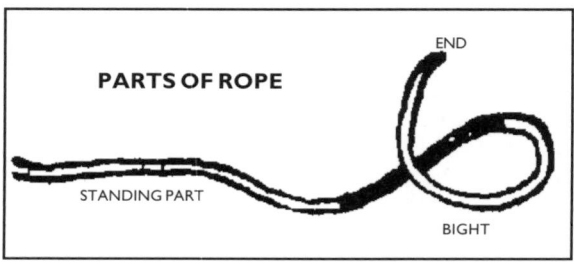

PARTS OF ROPE

END

STANDING PART

BIGHT

EXPEDITION TRAINING

KNOTS AND THEIR USES.

THUMB KNOT and FIGURE OF EIGHT KNOT
Both used to make a 'stop' on a rope: to prevent a rope from fraying at the end.

REEF KNOT.
For joining two dry ropes of the same size. The most generally useful knot. Always used in First Aid

SINGLE SHEET BEND.
For joining two ropes of different size.

DOUBLE SHEET BEND.
For joining two wet ropes of different size.

HAWSER BEND.
For joining larger ropes or cables.

DRAW HITCH.
For fastening a 'head rope' (e.g., a boat's painter) so that it can be quickly released.

EXPEDITION TRAINING

CLOVE HITCH
This is the most useful knot that you will ever learn. It can be made under strain, will not slip on itself nor along a pole, and can easily be cast loose.

TIMBER HITCH
is useful for hauling, the more it is pulled the firmer it holds.

TWO HALF HITCHES.
Two turns of a rope, which, when drawn together, holds securely. It is the quickest and simplest way to make a rope fast to a post.

ROUND TURN and TWO HALF HITCHES.
The quickest way to make a rope fast under strain. One of the most useful and easily made knots.

FISHERMANS BEND.
For fastening ends of ropes to spars, poles, etc., or to other ropes.

BOWLINE ON THE BIGHT
To form a loop that will not slip. One loop is made larger than the other. This is the sling for lowering a person from a building.
It enables the person to be supported, with the longer loop under the knees and the short loop under the armpits.

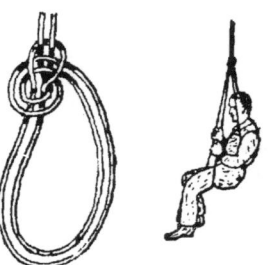

8-30

EXPEDITION TRAINING

THE SPANISH WINDLASS

This is not a knot, but is closely related to them. You may come across a situation where knowing how to use a Spanish Windlass could be helpful.

The windlass as you will see from the diagram, gives you great pulling power on a rope, by means of a lever using it to wind the rope round a post or stake, one end of which is in the ground.

The rope is wound round the post and a bar or piece of wood with the rope hitched over it.

The power given could be used to haul a boat out of the river or to move a vehicle, one end of the rope is fastened to the object to be moved, and the other is made fast on to a tree or some other suitable anchor. The stake or post must be strong and sound, likewise the material used for the lever as there is considerable pressure on both when in use.

Check your rope for any damage and be sure it is strong enough for the job.

Arrange your rope as in the diagram, pulling the lever round the stake.

The stake needs to be held firmly by driving it into the ground making the hole big enough for it to turn. It may be necessary to "overhaul" your windlass as too much rope may be wound round it, it will depend upon the size of the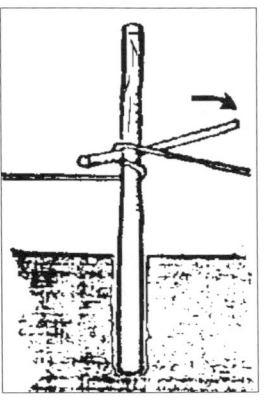

stake used for the windlass and the distance you have to haul the object.

Warning - it can be dangerous if you do not use strong enough material, or if it snaps or if you let go of the lever.

Check your rope and Windlass frequently, secure the load you are pulling with other rope to prevent it running away in the event of an accident.

EXPEDITION TRAINING

LASHINGS

Lashings are used for fastening poles or spars together they should be finished with a reef knot when both ends of the rope or yarn are available, or with a clove hitch if only one end is available.

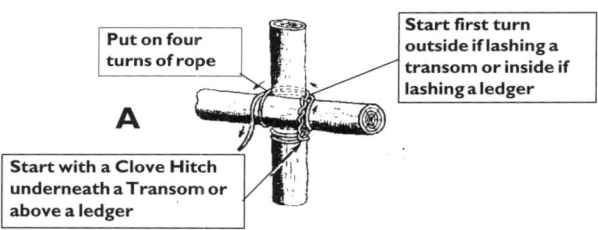

Put on four turns of rope

Start first turn outside if lashing a transom or inside if lashing a ledger

A

Start with a Clove Hitch underneath a Transom or above a ledger

(A) Straight lashing to spars.

For lengthening a spar or for repairing a broken spar. The lashing is made fast to the spar with a clove hitch, and is then passed round and round the spars; the end is made fast by another clove hitch or by passing the end under the last few turns and then tightening them up.

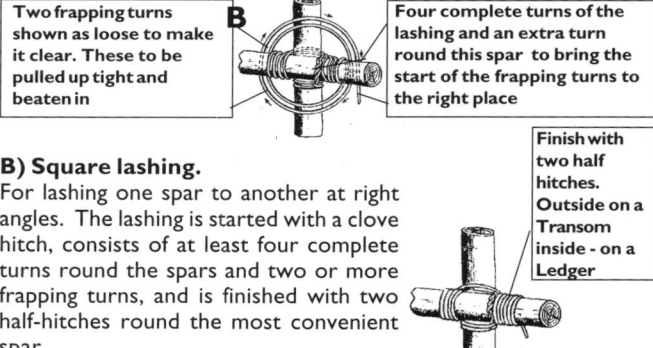

Two frapping turns shown as loose to make it clear. These to be pulled up tight and beaten in

B

Four complete turns of the lashing and an extra turn round this spar to bring the start of the frapping turns to the right place

Finish with two half hitches. Outside on a Transom inside - on a Ledger

B) Square lashing.

For lashing one spar to another at right angles. The lashing is started with a clove hitch, consists of at least four complete turns round the spars and two or more frapping turns, and is finished with two half-hitches round the most convenient spar.

SHEAR LEGS LASHING

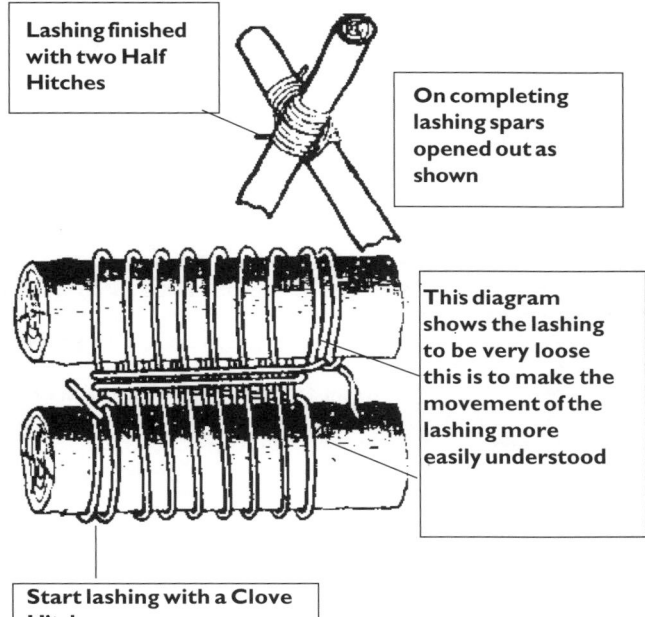

Lashing finished with two Half Hitches

On completing lashing spars opened out as shown

This diagram shows the lashing to be very loose this is to make the movement of the lashing more easily understood

Start lashing with a Clove Hitch

Shear legs lashing

For lashing spars at adjustable angles. The spars are placed side by side; a clove hitch is made round one spar and the rope is taken loosely six or eight times round both spars above the clove hitch without riding.

Two frapping turns are made round the lashing, and the end of the rope is made fast to the other spar by two half hitches just above the lashing.

EXPEDITION TRAINING

SPLICING

Diagram 'A' shows strands ready for splicing. Diagram 'B' shows the splice after each of the 6 strands have been passed through twice. From here, the strands are reduced in diameter by half and worked through once, then by half again, and through once to finish. Work from right to left, 'over and under'.

Splices are permanent and strong, and do not increase the thickness of the rope by much.

a. Short splice.   **For joining two ropes.**
b. Back splice.   **For ending off a rope permanently.**

WHIPPING

Whipping is used to prevent the end of a rope unravelling and is best done with sail twine; it is less permanent than the backsplice but does not greatly increase the thickness of the rope.

Rope 'Whipped' at end to prevent fraying

**KNOWING HOW TO TIE THE RIGHT KNOT, IS
A SKILL YOU WILL USE THROUGHOUT YOUR LIFE.
PRACTICE AND MORE PRACTICE MAKES PERFECT**

EXPEDITION TRAINING
SELF TEST QUESTIONS

1. What are the ten Country Code Rules.
2. What sort of socks should you wear on an expedition
3. The weight you carry on your back is equal to ....times the weight on your feet.
4. What do you dust your feet with.
5. How do you open a blister and what with.
6. If you are very thirsty, should you eat snow.
7. What do you carry on the outside of your ruck sack.
8. When looking for a camp site, what do you have to have from the owners.
9. What do you check out for safety when choosing a camp site
10. Is it a good idea to put up a tent under trees.
11. If you have to use water from a stream, what do you first do with it.
12. Where would you site the latrine and washing area, and why.
13. In a camp for several days you construct a latrine, how is it done and what are the important sizes.
14. When sighting a latrine what do you do about providing privacy, and how important is it.
15. How is privacy maintained for those using a Portaloo or field toilet.
16. What is the advantage of digging a small hole to put your cooker into.
17. What should you always leave behind at a camp site.
18. Why can't you go off on your own expedition as a Cadet,
19. Five of you are on an expedition, one is injured, how many would normally go for help.
20. When planning a route what must you produce and give someone a copy of .
21. The weather is getting bad on an expedition, do you go on or turn back.
22. What is the distress call/signal with: a. Whistle. b. Torch, and the Emergency Ground to Air Signals.
23. What do you understand by the Wind Chill Factor.
24. What added danger is there if you get wet on a cold and windy day.
25. You use ONE Water Purification Tablet to how much water.
26. Before heating tins in a mess tin of boiling water, what must you do.
27. Describe three types of improvised shelters.
28. How would you sterilize a water bottle.
29. How do you 'end-off' a rope.
30. What happens if you walk for some distance with boots full of water.

EXPEDITION TRAINING

31. How can you test a pair of boots are about the right size.
32. In cold weather without anything covering your head, how much body heat can you lose.
33. With pouched rations what is the best way to ensure you get a hot cooked meal.
34. What do you always take away from your camp site.

FINALLY -

When you draw a tent from the stores to use on exped, what state do you expect it to be in ?

Answer: dry, clean, good repair and complete with guy ropes, pegs and mallet all properly packed.

How do you ensure that your tent is as described above?

Answer: **POST EXPEDITION ADMIN!STRATION** or in other words, ensure that all stores returned are clean, dry and complete as issued. Report defects/damage to the Quarter Master.

Your ability to carry out the Post Expedition Administration efficiently when you are tired and required to check that all is correct takes a great deal of self discipline - don't forget it is all a part of your test.

Chapter 9

SIGNALS TRAINING

INTRODUCTION

Communications are an essential part of modern day armed forces. It enables a commander to exercise his command and speak to all parts of his force. Efficient comms (communication) ensures the smooth flow of vital information up the chain to the Commanders (who plan) and down the chain to the front line forces (who carry out that plan). So its in everyone's best interests that the information is accurate/ timely.

There are many types of radio covering a wide range of military applications, too many to list here, however it is worth understanding the broad categories of radio frequencies which dictates there application.

Extremely Low Frequency Super Low Frequency Ultra Low Frequency Very long range	ELF SLF ULF VLF	very Low Frequency submerged submarine comms
Low Frequency	LF	aircraft beacons and amateur 2 way radio
High frequency	HF	long range military radio for voice and data
Very High Frequency	VHF	tactical voice and data radios typically less than 50Kms
Ultra High Frequency	UHF	mobile phones, GPS, satellite communications
Super High Frequency	SHF	satellite TV & WLAN and search radars
Extremely High Frequency	EHF	microwave radio relays, targeting radars, direct energy weapons

SIGNALS TRAINING

VOICE PROCEDURE (VP)
Voice procedure is the method used to speak on a military radio, the language armed forces use, it is designed to provide the fastest, most accurate, uncomplicated method of speech transmission. You may well find yourself using it on the phone, phrases such as "Say again" do exactly what they say on the radio net.

It is not a "dark art" and people shy away from practicing, but take every opportunity to practice to get better at it, make your mistakes in training not on operations.

GENERAL POINTS ON THE NET
The radio network you'll be talking on is referred to as "the net", there may be multiple users, so be brief, accurate, before you press the talk button, don't talk over/interrupt others, wait your turn, take a few seconds to rehearse what you're going to say. Speak clearly, if you can't get through, try and move or rebroadcast through another callsign, don't say "please" "thank you" or "sorry". You're not on the phone, you're on the NET.

> *"No radio transmission, wherever it is made, can be regarded as safe from interception"*

And you don't need a radio to practice VP, you can do it over a cuppa with a mate, at the end of the session or record yourself on your mobile or tablet, to become really good at something you have to practice.

SIGNALS TRAINING

A - ALPHA	N - NOVEMBER
B - BRAVO	O - OCTOBER
C - CHARLIE	P - PAPA
D - DELTA	Q - QUEBEC
E - ECHO	R - ROMEO
F - FOXTROT	S - SIERRA
G - GOLF	T - TANGO
H - HOTEL	U - UNIFORM
I - INDIA	V - VICTOR
J - JULIET	W - WHISKEY
K - KILO	X - XRAY
L - LIMA	Y - YANKEE
M - MIKE	Z - ZULU

PHONETIC ALPHABET

saying the letter K on the net, might sound like A or J, leading to confusion, there are other letters in the alphabet that may sound similar, B could be confused with E or G and so on....
To avoid this, VP makes extensive use of the phonetic alphabet. You can get your head round these with practice.

In the car for example you can practice calling out the VRN (vehicle registration number) of passing vehicles.
OE52 MKG would read *"Oscar Echo Five Two Mike Kilo Golf"*. And the same goes for figures, if its a difficult net 2359 hrs would read *"Figures two, three, five, nine hours"*.

"YORK, i spell Yankee, Oscar, Romeo, Kilo"

SIGNALS TRAINING

And it's not just on a military net, if you're dealing with the Police, Ambulance, Fire Service using the phonetic alphabet can help. I came across a crashed glider in a field a few years ago, the pilot had a broken back, I checked he was alive/ relatively comfortable and called 999 giving them a grid and the best approach route. They got to him quickly and I got a mention on the news that night for helping them.

"Hello 0 this is B30 over"

CALLSIGNS (C/S)

Callsigns are collections of letters and numbers that designate each individual user on the radio net.

As such they hide the real identity of the user and are an aid to security. In the British Army callsigns are made up of letters and numbers, which are said phonetically, for example: BRAVO TWO FOUR CHARLIE (written B24C).

To illustrate this, lets look at a typical Inf section, the section might have the call sign B24, the section commander would be identified on the net as B24A *"Bravo Two Four Alpha"* and his Section 2ic (second in command) would be *"Bravo Two Four Bravo"*

CODE WORDS

A code word is a single word with a prearranged meaning, which will be covered in the orders, and given over the net. They can be used for

"0 this is B30, we have a visual on Trojan over"

an alert, or to initiate a plan or operation, there may be a number of code words to indicate the progress of a section onto a target or route.

They may also be used to identify specific individuals, locations or equipment. Most are designed to be used only once and can therefore be sent in clear over an insecure net. However their meaning is always classified.

RADIO APPOINTMENT TITLES

Radio appointment titles are not codewords and are often used when working with other services and other coalition nations. The only appointment title the British Army use routinely on single service radio nets is SUNRAY, which is to denote the Commander at any level, be that Regiment, Battalion, Company, Platoon, or Squadron, Troop or Section qualified by 'MY' or 'YOUR', etc.

SECURITY

The enemy will try to get the following information from intercepting and analysing our transmissions:

C Combat Effectiveness - vehicle and personnel casualties
O Order of Battle - unit identities, command structure and function of the radio net.
I Intentions - future plans and orders, timings.
L Locations - locations of HQs, operational areas and boundaries.

No radio transmission, wherever it is made, can be regarded as safe from interception. It is important to remember that intercept receivers are designed to receive weaker signals at greater distances than standard receivers. Since the only sure way to know you have not been intercepted is to not transmit the best defence is to:

C Change frequency - unpredictable times can be effective however most model radios will be able to automatically change frequency. This is called frequency hopping.

DEFENCE AGAINST INTERCEPTION
Change frequency
Avoid all unnecessary transmissions

A Avoid all unnecessary transmissions - essential addressees only.

K Keep transmissions short - less than 20 secs. and end with OUT.

U Use other means to communicate - particularly for routine admin messages.

Most modern tactical radios incorporate some form of encryption allowing the user to pass sensitive information over the radio securely.

This will prevent the enemy from discovering what you have said but much intelligence can still be gained by analysis of the amount of radio traffic on a net and the numbers of stations, so you must still aim to keep transmissions short.

Radios carried at the very lowest levels such as Personal Role Radios (PRR) are not encrypted but employ the defense of using much lower power so that they are less likely to be intercepted by the enemy.

"Do it nice, or do it twice"

AIDS TO ACCURACY

We have mentioned the phonetic alphabet, and how useful it is, and in a few pages will cover common pro-words (ways of saying specific things) but let's look at a few more aids to accuracy.

SIGNALS TRAINING

All messages should be pre-planned, logically constructed & brief.
In exactly the same way that you'd phone up to order a take away,
you know what you want and how to ask for it quickly, you've
rehearsed it in your head.

Whenever possible write down the message: even brief notes
will reduce the risk of error. If it's not practical to write it down,
take a few seconds to think through the whole message before
transmitting, if you get it wrong you'll only be asked to repeat it, so
"Do it nice, or do it twice"

When you're about to talk, think about the pneumonic **RSVP:**
R Rhythm. Use short sentences in a natural rhythm.
S Speed. Slightly slower than for normal conversation. Where
conditions are difficult increase pauses between phrases rather
than between each word which can be difficult to understand.
V Volume. Speak as in normal conversation, do not shout.
P Pitch. Slightly higher than for normal

DISCIPLINE
On bigger nets discipline may imposed on the net by a control
station. This station always has the callsign ZERO (0) and has
the authority of the commander. There are 5 simple rules to
maintaining discipline on the net and 6 things you should never do:
1. All users must maintain a constant listening watch and answer
   calls to them promptly and in the correct order.

2. Users should answer in strict alpha numeric order. Eg. B31
   answers before C10 who in turn answers before J11.

3. Always listen to the net before speaking to ensure you do not
   talk over the top of another message and cause confusion.

SIGNALS TRAINING

4. Use the correct frequency.

5. Release the push-to-talk (or pressel) switch promptly and make sure the radio returns to receive.

Never:
1. Violate radio silence.
2. Compromise classified information.
3. Make unnecessary transmissions.
4. Identify yourself, your unit or any others.
5. Speak too fast for the user in the worst conditions to receive and understand.
6. Swear or loss your temper.

TYPES OF CALL

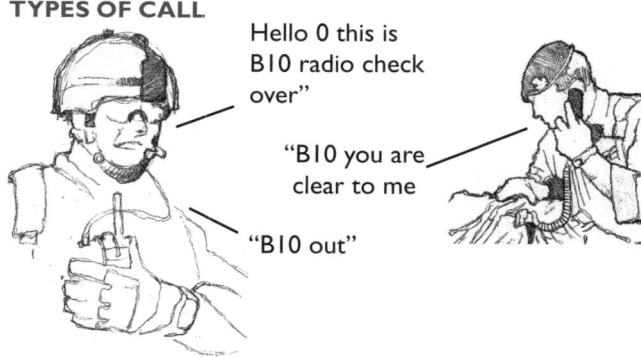

Hello 0 this is B10 radio check over"

"B10 you are clear to me

"B10 out"

SIGNALS TRAINING

There are three types of call on the radio, single, multiple or collective call.

A **single call** is from one user to one other.

A **multiple call** is from one user to many other users where each recipient has to answer in turn. This can add considerable time to the call and if you call all the users on the net then this can be very useful to the enemy.

"Hello B20 and B30 this is B10 0A is on route to your location over"

"B20 Roger out"

"B30 Roger out"

A **collective call** (CC) is to a pre-designated group of users under a particular pre-arranged group callsign known as a CHARLIE CHARLIE callsign. The CC callsigns are usually give numbers so that you can cover different groups of users in this way.

These CC callsigns disguise who and how many users are in the group which increases security and allows for one recipient to answer on behalf of all the users in the group thereby speeding up the process.

"Hello CHARLIE CHARLIE 2 this is 0, move now, G30A acknowledge over"

"G30A roger out"

SIGNALS TRAINING

SENDING A MESSAGE

All messages start in the same way, this is known as the initial call. It is the first part of the transmission. It sets up the call by establishing who is speaking and to whom the caller wishes to speak. It always follows the same format:

"HELLO" - This alerts the net. "CALLSIGN/S" - This is the user or users you wish to speak to. "THIS IS CALLSIGN" - This is the user making the call. For example...

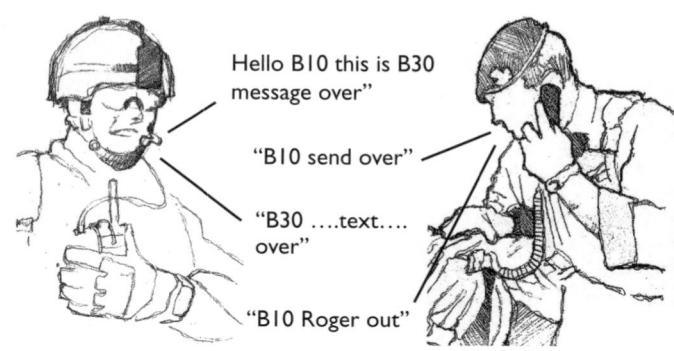

Hello B10 this is B30 message over"

"B10 send over"

"B30 ....text.... over"

"B10 Roger out"

OFFERS

If you have a long or complex message, that you think the station you are calling will need to write down, it is best practice to offer the message. This will allow time for them to prepare to receive your message but is unnecessary and wastes time for short simple messages.

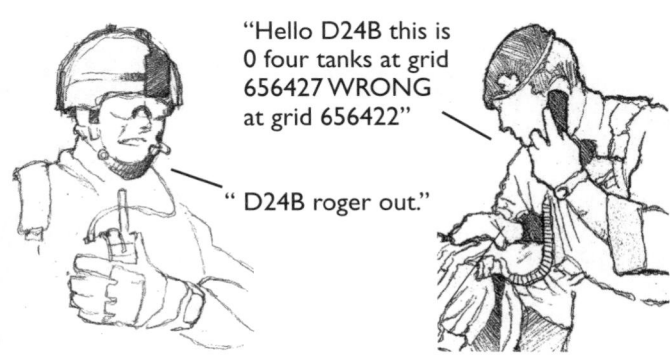

"Hello D24B this is 0 four tanks at grid 656427 WRONG at grid 656422"

" D24B roger out."

SIGNALS TRAINING

CORRECTIONS AND REPETITIONS

A sender may make a mistake during a transmission and have to correct it. This is done by using the proword WRONG then going back to the last correct word sent.

If you need to emphasise a particularly important part of a message you could use the proword I SAY AGAIN. Alternately if the receiving station missed the message completely they may ask for you to SAY AGAIN.

"Hello B20 this is B10 approach my location form the west I SAY AGAIN approach my location from the west."

"Hello F33 this is 0 say again WORD AFTER/BEFORE, ALL AFTER/BEFORE, FROM ....TO.... over"

"F33 I SAY AGAIN ...... over"

"0 roger out"

This should only be used sparingly as it uses more time on the net. If the receiving user misses only part of a message it is always better to ask for just that part than get the sender to SAY AGAIN the whole message. To do this the receiving user must identify the section of the message that was heard or understood and the first part of the next heard or understood section. He can then request the sending station to say again the section between these two, saving a lot of time on the net.

SIGNALS TRAINING

PROWORDS
Specific prowords are used on the radio to aid accuracy and speed up communications. Common prowords and their means are included below:

I SPELL . . . . Stand by for me to spell a word.

FIGURES . . . . Stand by for figures following this.

SEND . . . . I am ready to receive your message.

MESSAGE . . . . Stand by for a message you may need to write down.

CANCEL . . . . Disregard my last message.

ACKNOWLEDGE . . Confirm you have received my message.

MINIMISE . . . . Reduce traffic to essential messages only.

CONTACT . . . . The enemy has been met.

RELAY . . . . Pass messages through me and I will pass them on.

VERIFY . . . . Check again your information is correct.

WRONG . . . . What I have just said is incorrect.

I SAY AGAIN . . . . . . Repeat the last sent message

FETCH . . . . Get the person asked for on to the radio net.

REPEAT . . . . Artillery is to fire again on a target.

SUNRAY . . . . Radio proword for the commander of a unit.

ROGER . . . . Message received and understood.

ROGET SO FAR . . . . Message received and understood up to this point.

OUT . . . . My transmission ends, I do not expect an answer.

OVER . . . . My transmission ends, I expect a response.

OVER TO YOU . . . . . My transmission ends, but I have further messages for other users.

WAIT OUT . . . . I am unable to answer you right now and will get back to you.

NOTHING HEARD . No reply has been heard to a radio check.

DIFFICULT . . . . The quality of communication is poor.

SIGNALS TRAINING

A RADIO NET

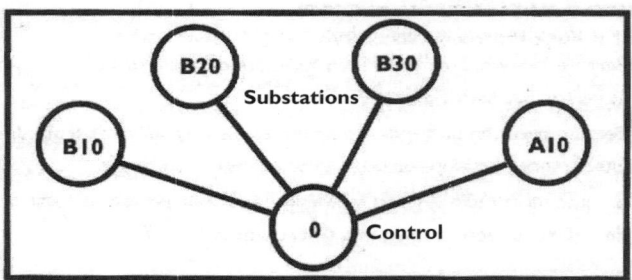

This can be defined as a group of stations working together for the purpose of communication with each other. There are two types of station.

a. Control
b. Substation

Note: Control has callsign 0 and the substations are callsign B10, B20, B30 and A10,

SIGNALS TRAINING

PRC 343 PRR
The PRC 343 more commonly know as Personal Role Radio (PRR) is used at Section level It has a range of 500 meters in open terrain or through 3 floors of a building. It has a total of 256 possible channels.

SET-UP
1. Check PRR is switched off.
2. Connect the headset.
3. Insert 2x AA batteries.
4. Set the channel selector to the correct channel.
5. Switch and set the volume.

Tones
Volume and channel changes, I beep per step change.
Power ON
Power OFF
Battery low
CNR Call waiting
Wireless PTT affiliation/de-affiliation taking place. Repeated if successful.
Unsuccessful affiliation/de-affiliation of the wireless PTT.

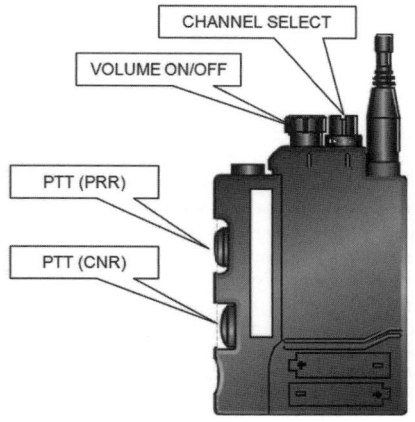

SIGNALS TRAINING

Signal Section. Imperial Cadet Yeomanry 1912

In 1910 the War Office set up the Territorial Cadet Force, an
organisation which was to include all cadet units giving military
training, other than those school corps which in 1908 had elected
to become part of the Officers Training Corps. Powers to recognise
and administer cadet units were delegated to the Territorial Force
Association of each county. Behind the new move was a feeling that
cadet units had an important part to play in providing recruits for
the Territorial Force.

Most cadet units were now affiliated to a Territorial Force unit.
Here we see members of a signal section receiving instruction. They
form part of the Yorkshire Squadron, Imperial Cadet Yeomanry,
affiliated to the Yorkshire Hussars. Another squadron of the Imperial
Cadet Yeomanry was based in City of London. It should be pointed
out that no mounted instruction was undertaken, all cadet units had
to follow a programme of infantry training.

Increasing numbers of cadet units now wore khaki service dress,
though more colourful uniforms still persisted. The speed of change
was governed by cost, uniforms were still paid for either by the
individual cadet or locally raised funds.

Chapter 10

BANDS IN THE ARMY CADET FORCE

INTRODUCTION
If you joined a Cadet Band in the past, not only did you have band practice, you had to keep up with ALL the APC training as well.

BAND UNITS/DETACHMENTS
Many Counties have Detachments or Units where all the Cadets are members of the Band. This does not mean that it is to the exclusion of other training, you will have to pass your One Star training alongside your Band training. The syllabus then changes from Two Star onwards, and is directly related to improving standards and ability with the instrument(s) you have chosen to play. Many 'Band Cadets' chose to continue with their APC training, often to assist them in completing their Duke of Edinburgh's Award work. It is worth noting that a Band Cadet who chooses to continue with their APC and Band training has far more to learn than a non – band Cadet. The Cadet who has some distance to travel to his/her Band Unit rather than attend the local Cadet Detachment also shows considerable commitment.

This is before all the extra nights down at the Detachment practicing for a special parade, the cleaning and maintenance of instruments, special uniforms and equipment – that's DEDICATION!

DRUM AND BUGLE BANDS
Many Cadet Detachments have their own bands, the majority of which are Drum and Bugle. Although there may only be a few in a Detachment who play, they normally join together with other Detachment Bands for practices and parades, especially at Annual Camp.

OTHER SKILLS REQUIRED
As a Bands person you not only have to play your instrument well, you have to be proficient at foot drill and do both together, not as easy as it may appear. It is also expected that your Turnout must be immaculate at all times.

BANDS IN THE ARMY CADET FORCE

BANDS IN THE ACF

The reason for this is twofold, firstly, you. Why spoil all your hard work by not looking and sounding the best? Secondly, the public frequently sees your Band; you are representing your County and the ACF each time you are on parade. Feel good about it!

QUALIFICATIONS AND EQUIPMENT

Qualifications: this is dependent on whether you are either able to take lessons through your school or the level of musical instruction your Instructors in the Band can take you to. However, if you are keen enough to continue, being able to play a musical instrument well is a much envied and rewarding talent. Parents are usually very supportive (and proud!) when they see you doing something so worthwhile.

If you have the opportunity to play in a Full Military Band, Corps of Drums or Pipes and Drums you will be tested in accordance with band syllabus as laid down by Headquarters Land Policy. Your OC Band will have details of this or contact Major Tex Carlton on 01743-262223

DRUM AND PIPE BANDS

As with the Full Military Band testing, appropriate levels of attainment are set out for the Bagpipes the Band Instructors will advise you. Instruments: some Bands have a pool of instruments for Cadets to use, but the majority expects Cadets to buy their own instrument. These can be costly, especially if bought new. Second hand instruments are often advertised in the press, specialist music magazines or on the Internet; shop around you may find a bargain. Another resource could be family or friends; they may have just what you are looking for tucked away in the loft

For further information on Pipes & Drums contact Captain Jim Stout
  Tel 0131-310-5235   email acfpdeo@btconnect.com

FINANCE AND SUPPORT

Bands in the Cadet Force are NOT supported financially by the Ministry of Defence or issued with instruments, uniforms or other equipment. Travel to engagements is often difficult; many parents, Band Officers and Instructors will use their own transport to ensure Cadets get to the engagement. However, Cadet Bands do get encouragement and support from their County and Band helpers to raise funds. They also receive donations or a fee when they attend a function.

BANDS IN THE ARMY CADET FORCE

MUSIC IN THE ACF

Since 2005 the the Cadet Vocational Qualification Organisation (CVQO) have offered Cadets over 16 years old the opportunity to earn the vocational qualification that is equivalent to four GCSEs at A* to C grade or four Scottish Standard Grades.

Music is an integral part of Cadet organisations and through the ACF it gives you the chance to direct your musical interests and ability by being involved in attaining your CVQO diploma in music.

This wiil continue to improve your musical proficiency as well as learning the many practical skills needed for a career in the music industry.

Cadets taking part in the programme will be given training in all aspects of music including how to plan and promote events, budget forecasting, rehearsal management and performance appraisal.

Now Cadets with musical skills

No longer are Cadets *in the band* seen to be marching up and down again, making a noise playing the same out of tune blasts on a Sunday morning.

Now make no mistake about it, it is for real, a step in the right direction Cadet Music has arrived

ACFA has recognised the fact and established band courses and has encouraged annual Band concentrations during the Easter holiday period and other school half term holidays.

How to contact CVQO Music

Should you want to make any enqury regarding CVQO qualifications, contact the Music Department on 01276 - 601709

THINKING OF FORMING A BAND?

For information and support in forming, outfitting and training your band or Corps of Drums please contact:-

Major Tex Calton   Email: hqadmin@cadetforcemusic.com
HQ Cadet Force Music
Bligny House   Tel: 07974 879950
Copthorne Barracks
Shrewsbury
SY3 8 LZ

BANDS IN THE ARMY CADET FORCE

BEARDMORE CADET CORPS 1918

The 1914-18 war saw a massive expansion of the Cadet Force, once initial losses of adults to the regular forces had been overcome. Existing units increased in size and many new ones were formed. In spite of a small War Office capitation grant, the movement had to remain largely self-sufficient and uniforms had to be purchased. Few weapons remained available and most units trained with dummy rifles or obsolete carbines. Our illustration on the next page shows a bugler of the Beardmore Cadet Corps, Glasgow.

This was a unit recruited from employees of the Beardmore Engineering Company and was affiliated to the 7th. Battalion Highland Light Infantry. By now, khaki was in general use for cadet units, but Scottish units could present a more colourful picture.

A rifle green glengarry is being worn, carrying the regimental badge.

The khaki tunic is of the pattern peculiar to Scottish regiments, the bottom edge being rounded and cut away at the front.

On the shoulder straps a bugle is worn over the word BEARDMORE.

Though affiliated to a lowland regiment, a kilt is worn in the Mackenzie tartan. Trews are confined to officers of the unit.

The sporran has a black top which carries a regimental badge, the hair is in black with three tassels in white. Red and white hose tops together with white spats complete the uniform.

BANDS IN THE ARMY CADET FORCE

Unlike many units, the Beardmore Cadets continued to operate during the post-war years and by 1929 could still muster 120 cadets. With the temporary withdrawal of official recognition in 1930, the unit became Beardmore Company of Scottish Cadets' and the cap badge of the Corps of Scottish Cadets was worn.

Though the Beardmore works is no more, the unit continues in-existence.

Today it is affiliated to the Royal Highland Fusiliers, the regiment formed by the amalgamation of the Highland Light Infantry and the Royal Scots Fusiliers. The background of the picture depicts the Toll Booth Glasgow.

BEARDMORE CADET BUGLER 1929

BANDS IN THE ARMY CADET FORCE

SELF TEST QUESTIONS

1. How could you get a copy of the Band Training Syllabus.
2. What personal contribution do you have to make to be a member of the band.
3. What is important about turnout and drill
4. Playing in the Band when do you experience the *feel good factor*
5. How do public appearances help with band funds.
6. What does CVQO stand for.
7. When was CVQO Music qualifications started
8. Where could you get information on ACF Drum & Pipe Bands,
9. Band instruments are expensive, do you have a Band Members Instruments Saving Fund.
10. Who could give you advice on setting up a Band
11. Who are the Band Helpers in your Band.
12. How can you get a Diploma in music.
13. What is a 'band concentration' for.
14. Where is the HQ Cadet Force Music based.
15. At what time of the year are band training courses held.
16. Where and what was the Beardmore Cadets
17. The illustration of the Beardmore Cadet what tartan was his kilt.
18. What Regiment are the Beardmore cadets affiliated too today.

Chapter 11

METHODS OF INSTRUCTION

The 'Golden Rule' of successful instruction:

THE SIX P'S

PRIOR PREPARATION AND PRACTICE PREVENTS POOR PERFORMANCE

INTRODUCTION

Methods of Instruction, (MOI) follows the system used by the Army. Providing you apply the well tried and practiced framework called a **Lesson Plan** you will find that instructing becomes simplified and there is less chance of you 'losing your way' in a class.

As a Senior Cadet, the skills you acquire following this system will improve your confidence; it is a skill that you may be able to put to good use in your career.

QUALITIES REQUIRED

The main qualities you need as an instructor are:

1. Enthusiasm – boredom is infectious
2. Self confidence – through following the 6 P's
3. Good knowledge of your subject. Your class soon picks up on 'Surface knowledge'.
4. Look the part – be smart
5. Good manner and bearing - look up whilst you speak, your voice will travel further.
6. Vary the pitch/strength of your voice to stress a particular point and keep the class alert.
7. Be firm but fair - encourage your class to join in – to a point!
8. Never be satisfied with your standard of instruction, always look for ways to improve your presentation skills
9. The ability to instruct **clearly, completely, patiently, giving information at a suitable pace, one stage at a time.**

METHOD OF INSTRUCTION

AVOID

The following are the **"DO NOT's"**

1. Use sarcasm to get a laugh
2. Make a fool of one of the cadets in front of the class
3. Use remarks that have a double meaning or that may offend one of the class
4. Pick on one cadet to answer questions too often
5. Do not 'cut corners' by omitting important information or assuming knowledge
6. Overload your lesson with too many aids, e.g. a projector, flip chart, overhead projector video recorder, camera and computer for one lesson will detract from subject matter. Keep it simple but effective.
7. Watch yourself for distracting mannerisms such as saying 'OK' or 'RIGHT' after each statement, scratching your nose etc. You know how it is when you are the student and your teacher/ instructor's mannerisms become more interesting than the lesson.

PREPARE AND PLAN

1. What is the objective?
2. Which is the best method – lecture, lesson, discussion, exercise or demonstration.
3. Where is the instruction to take place – a small room may rule out some of the activities you may wish to use.
4. What is the size of the class?
5. What time is available?
6. What equipment and training aids are available?
7. Are the aids suitable, simple enough, large enough or even necessary?
8. What handout notes should be produced?
9. What is the present standard of the class's knowledge?
10. Prepare your list of questions and answers for this lesson and have your questions and answers ready from the previous lesson if appropriate.

METHOD OF INSTRUCTION

SKILLS LESSONS – (Drill, Skill at Arms, etc.)

Remember and use the sequence: (EDIP)

EXPLANATION – DEMONSTRATION – IMITATION - PRACTICE

STAGE	KEY POINT
BREAK DOWN THE LESSON TO AS MANY STAGES AS YOU LIKE	IMPORTANT POINTS NOT TO BE MISSED
1	STRESS SAFETY, ANYTHING THAT CAN CAUSE DAMAGE
2	"MEMORY TICKLER" FOR SIZES, MEASUREMENTS REFERENCES, COLOURS ETC

A SIMPLE LESSON PLAN

Rule up sheets of paper using the sample as a guide, setting out the **STAGES** or **BLOCKS** of information as headings on the subject, and the **KEY POINTS** which are the important points to be made, such as safety, figures, codes, references and the correct training aid to use at this particular point, use this section as a prompt, drawing as many lines as you require. Don't forget to write large enough and clearly as you may be using your plan when standing up - **NOT** held in your hand, reading from it!

The plan is divided in to three stages:

STAGE ONE – BEGINNING

Subject: Class/Squad: Time: Location:

Dress: Stores required and Training Aids:

Time allowed:

METHOD OF INSTRUCTION

'Prelims': Roll Call: Safety Precautions: Class Formation: Seating Plan: Comfort of the Class: Lighting Levels: Standard of Visual Aids. Training aids make sure they all work and you have sufficient for the class; spare bulbs for OHP

Introduction: Make sure the class know your name.

Objective: must be clearly stated and understood, attainable in the time allowed.

Reason Why: give a realistic reason, incentive to achieve

Results: Benefits to be gained from the lesson.

Revision: Check the classes' knowledge/skills in the subject previously taught. Cadets soon forget.

STAGE TWO – THE MIDDLE

The main instruction to be taught. Time allowed – divide the subject in to several **STAGES**, select from each stage the **KEY POINTS** that you must bring out in your instruction, for example, SAFETY to ensure a complete understanding of the lesson.

CONFIRMATION

At the end of each **STAGE** of the instruction, confirm that the key points have been understood. It is important to ensure that all the class are 'kept on their toes' you must therefore **pose the question to the whole squad,** wait for a few moments for them **ALL** to think of the answer, then **select or nominate one of them to answer.**

Note: if a cadet is unable to answer the question, give a little time, then re-nominate. Correct any errors as they occur. Do not keep nominating the same cadet – even if they give the correct answers!

ASK - PAUSE – NOMINATE

METHOD OF INSTRUCTION

STAGE THREE – THE END

Invite questions from the class; if you are asked a question and do not know the answer, do not try and bluff your way out, ADMIT IT, but find out and let them know – **MAKE SURE THAT Y OU DO!**

Use your prepared questions to confirm that the class has achieved the objective of the lesson. In the case of skills based instruction you will confirm by practical assessment.

Summary: – bring out and stress the achievement of the objective. Once you have taken the time to plan and produce a Lesson Plan - stick to it - it is so much easier than getting lost for words!

Look forward: state when the next lesson will be/what the next lesson will be.

KEEP ALL YOUR LESSON PLANS – CAREFULLY FILE THEM FOR EASY REFERENCE. THE NEXT TIME YOU TAKE THAT LESSON – HALF YOUR WORK WILL HAVE ALREADY BEEN DONE.

TRAINING AIDS

There are various methods of presentation available today such as OHP, Power Point, Videos, etc all of which have their advantages and disadvantages.

Whatever medium you decide to use always be prpared for a 'system failure' or lack or equiment. Have a 'back up' and be prepared to improvise.

You will have to allow plenty of time to set up equipment and ensure it is all working. Likewise check that any handouts are available and set out in the order they are required. Rehearse any demonstration and check that those who may be assisting do know what and when to perform.

IMPROVISED TRAINING AIDS

Many Detachments will have a box in their stores of 'training aids' which amongst other item will have an old blanket used as a 'cloth model' for tactical training or perhaps a lump of plasticene for teaching contours and relief for map reading. What appears to be a blood stained trophy is in fact an improvised wound for a compound fracture. If your Detachment does not have improvised Training Aids now is the time to make some. It makes a good competition as to who can produce the best and most useful aids.

METHOD OF INSTRUCTION

SELF TEST QUESTIONS

1. What is the "Framework" used for good instruction.
2. When preparing a lesson what do you have to take to do it correctly.
3. What are the qualities required of a good instructor.
4. What should you do about habits.
5. Look up when you speak, — why.
6. What do you understand by "looking the part".
7. Complete the following sentence; "Instruct, Clearly, completely one_ _ _ _ _ at a _ _ _ _
8. As an instructor how can you check your own performance.
9. What are the six "Basic Points of Instruction.
10. Name six of the ten things to do before you Prepare and Plan a lesson.
11. How do you use the "Questioning Technique".
12. If instructing a SKILL, what is the "Sequence of Instruction".
13. What do you understand by a. "A STAGE. b. "A KEY POINT".
14. A COMPLETE lesson is broken into how many parts or stages, what is the name of each one.
15. What are you doing if you are carrying out the "PRELIMS".
16. What do you do about Training Aids before a lesson.
17. If asked a valid question and you don't know the answer, what do you do about it.
18. Name three methods to confirm that all your class members have learned the lesson given.
19. Why and how should you keep the lesson plan that you have just used.
20. What is the last thing you tell a class before finishing.
21. If the lesson is on any Skill at Arms subject, (including Shooting), what is the FIRST and most important action to carry out and who takes part in it.

Chapter 12
THE CADET NCO & OPPORTUNITIES AFTER TWO STAR

County ACFs have different methods of NCO selection and training. The following are intended as general comments.

Every Cadet has the opportunity to earn promotion. The skills and abilities you require can only be developed by training and practice.

To a great extent your opportunity for promotion is entirely in your hands. From your first Parade night your attitude towards your mates, how you respond to being given instructions and how well you carry them out. Some of the essential qualities are:

Loyalty and pride in the Regiment or Corps to which you are badged, your County and Detachment and the Army Cadet Force.

Enthusiasm in all that you do, encouraging other Cadets to imitate you.

Sense of humour: especially when things go wrong. Do not laugh AT others; laugh with them.

Initiative to anticipate what will be required of you.

Knowledge of your subjects – giving others confidence in your ability

Instructional ability, watch and learn from good instructors

Self discipline in the way you behave

Reliability is important, if you say that you will do something, DO IT

Good manners are never forgotten

PROMOTION IS NEVER AUTOMATIC

Promotion is related to your qualifications as well as your ability. You will need to achieve the standards set out below and be recommended for consideration as a candidate for promotion by your Officers and Instructors.

Lance Corporal	Not before passing **One Star**
Corporal	Not before passing **Two Star**
Sergeant	Not before passing **Three Star**
Master Cadet	having attained your Four Star, completed the Master Cadet Course at Frimley Park, and subsequently been recommended by your County Cadet Commandant.

THE CADET N.C.O. & OPPORTUNITIES AFTER 2 STAR

Under Officer having passed your Four Star and also been recommended by your County Cadet Commandant.
Changes to these rules will only be permissible in exceptional circumstances and with the approval of your County Cadet Commandant.

PROMOTION CADRES

Most County Cadet Forces take the promoting of their Cadets very seriously. They have a system of promotion courses similar to the Army system; these courses are called NCO's Cadres.
The Cadres are usually organised over a weekend or perhaps at Annual Camp, when potential NCOs are brought together and given the opportunity of showing how the have developed, not only in their APC skills, but to see how they behave when with their fellow candidates. The Cadre usually follows the form of planning and taking lessons, command exercises, lecturettes, initiative tests, games and other activities.
Cadets who have taken part usually say that it is great fun and a good method of finding out their strengths and weaknesses, to see how you behave under different circumstances and conditions. All the Officers and Instructors make an assessment before final recommendations are made concerning your suitability as an NCO.

CADET NCOs

Duties and Responsibilities
Junior N.C.O.

You will learn how to instruct the basic APC subjects and also how to take command of a squad.
With the other NCOs in the Detachment, you are responsible to your Detachment Commander to assist with the organisation and smooth running of your Detachment at the level of your rank.
When you earn your first stripe, it is easy to start "throwing your weight around". The first to know about it are the mates who were happy to have a laugh with you before, but now avoid you. It could be that they respect your promotion, now you have to prove to them and yourself that you are worthy of it. This is a good time to consider some of the actions and failings of bad **Cadet NCOs.**

THE CADET N.C.O. & OPPORTUNITIES AFTER 2 STAR

FAILINGS

1. Intimidate individuals by shouting at them, particularly when standing close up to them.
2. Making personal contact (touch) when addressing them.
3. Use foul language, make offensive personal remarks about an individuals background, height etc, or make threats of what might become of them.
4. Make an example of an individual by punishing without due reason, or belittling them in front of others.
5. Keep picking on an individual in front of others. If they are persistent offenders, not reporting individual for OC to deal with.
6. Borrowing money or asking favours of Cadets.
7. Not sharing duties or "chores" fairly, not having a duty roster displayed.
8. Being late with orders/information, not allowing time for all to respond.
9. Asking Cadets to clean, press etc. your personal kit or equipment.
10. Not reading Orders, being un-informed of duties, events.
11. Fail to check untidy Cadets and/or their rooms.
12. Always late for parades and duties.
13. Puts off dealing with complaints and problems reported to them.
14. Does not praise or give encouragement for good work.
15. Passes on responsibilities to others, lacks personal discipline; does not bother to prepare lesson plans.
16. Using first names when "On Parade" – difficult, but surnames should be used.
17. Failing to report serious breaches in discipline, theft, illegal substance taking, Cadets out of bounds.
18. Sets a bad example by being untidy in uniform and civilian clothes.
19. Annoying mannerisms such as saying "OK" or "Right" after every sentence etc.
20. Throwing their weight about, always going to the front of the queue in the Naafi or Dining Hall.
21. Behaviour either as an individual or a member of a group that may harm the reputation of the ACF and the Detachment.

No doubt you can think of many more, make sure you are not guilty of them!

Don't forget that:
WITH AUTHORITY GOES _RESPONSIBILITY_

THE CADET N.C.O. & OPPORTUNITIES AFTER 2 STAR

Senior N.C.O.

As a Senior Cadet NCO in your Detachment, you have responsibilities at all times; on or off Parade. In any activity where Cadets are involved or it is known that you are a member of the Army Cadet Force.

You will be directly responsible to your Detachment Commander for the Cadets in your Detachment.

Delegation of Responsibility

The Detachment Commander and Instructors in your Detachment 'share' some of their authority in running the Detachment with you. This means that they must be seen to give you the backing or authority to carry out tasks within the Detachment leaving you to probably make mistakes. This is all part of the learning curve; providing you do learn from your mistakes.

In return your Detachment Commander and Instructors will expect you to measure up to the trust they have in you.

DEVELOPING YOUR ABILITY AS AN NCO
RESPECT AND DISCIPLINE

"Respect is not a right, it has to be earned"

Respect and discipline are together; one cannot exist without the other. How can you gain respect? There are two ways firstly through fear, by proving you are bigger, stronger, can hit harder and swear better. To put it briefly, by being a bully.

Secondly, by gaining the Cadets trust and through that their respect and wish to do as you ask.

In America in 1940, they needed one million managers to run their war effort. They were aware of the need for good relations in the work place, resulting in the introduction of the **"Foundation For Good Relations"**. They have been converted into "Cadet speak" as follows:

1. Let your Cadets know in advance of things that affect them; what's on, date, time, place and the reason why it is being done.
2. If someone does well – give him or her the credit for it when it is due – at the time, NOT afterwards.
3. NEVER criticize or check other NCO's or Cadets in front of assembled Cadets.

4. Always take the individual "out of earshot" of others if you are to reprimand them.
5. Recognise the ability of other Cadets and NCO's, give them every opportunity to show and use their talents.

If Cadets know that you will ensure they are kept informed, trust, respect and good teamwork will follow. Listen to those who supervise you both now and throughout your career. You will know immediately those who value Good Relations and the importance they place upon it.

Following the **Foundation For Good Relations"** requires the same control as remembering not to swear, shout and dish out punishments for every minor offence; self-discipline. You will get far more out of your squad wheresoever you are, **"Speaking softly, but carrying a big stick"**. In other words, use the trust and respect you have earned to control your Cadets; not shouting or using discipline unnessarily.

WORKING WITH SUBORDINATES

Unlike your counterparts in the Regular or Territorial Army, you have no power to order any form of punishment. Physical punishment such as 'push ups' or making the Cadet look small in front of other Cadets is not allowed. NEVER touch, i.e. *personal contact,* strike, push trip up or in any other way deliberately touch a subordinate Cadet, it could result in legal action being taken, and it is a form of bullying.

When a Cadet's uniform needs adjusting, let them do it themselves, that way they learn by their mistakes.

DISCIPLINING A CADET

When disciplining a Cadet, ensure that the reprimand is not made in the hearing or presence of others and that it is done at the time or immediately after the incident. Where possible, use constructive criticism, for example, a Cadet is fooling about in a lesson, when you speak to him/her you could say; "You have been doing so well at (whatever subject they are good at), I am disappointed that you are not making the same effort in (whatever subject the lesson is), I expected better of you". It takes practice to get constructive criticism right, but it really does work well if your Cadets have respect for you as an NCO.

BULLYING

Bullying comes in many forms, and most of us have been victims, perhaps without realising it.

Earlier on in this Chapter there is a list of some of the actions of a bad NCO, many of these are recognised as bullying. As an NCO you must guard against appearing to "pick" on a particular Cadet, it gives them bad feelings about the Cadet Force and it **IS** bullying. Issuing threats and promises is another common form of bullying and an easy trap to fall in to. As a senior Cadet NCO, watch newly appointed junior NCOs to ensure they get it right from the start and follow the **Foundation For Good Relations.**

Bullying destroys a person's self esteem; it makes them withdraw from the 'team', lose interest in activities, and stops them attending Detachment Parades. If you recognise the signs in a Cadet, watch, listen and when you have **proof**, report it.

As an NCO you will perhaps find a junior Cadet "Disclosing". This is the term used for a child or young person admitting to physical or mental abuse against them. If this occurs, you must tell the Cadet concerned that you have to inform your Officer in Charge. DO NOT try to deal with the problem yourself, or talk to anyone other than the people in charge, it is a serious matter and requires official action.

WHEN YOU MAKE MISTAKES

The more inexperienced you are, the more likely you are to be reprimanded by your superiors. At times you may feel a rebuke was not warranted and unfair. It is not so much what you may have done, but the way you take being 'torn off a strip'. Never sulk, or feel someone has a 'down on you', accept that the rebuke was carried out in good faith. However, if the matter is serious and you genuinely were not at fault, do not complain to everyone within earshot, it does not help your image. Accept the rebuke, then gather your facts together, ask for an interview with the Officer or Instructor concerned **- in private** and present your facts.

ATTITUDE TO ORDERS

There are times when you will be required to carry out an order given by a superior which you know will be unpopular with the Cadets. This order should be given as 'your order', never apologise for it, just carry it out to the letter. If it is an order or instruction that you disagree with, carry it out, gather your facts and evidence in logical sequence and present them to the Officer or Instructor concerned. Use the procedure described in 'when you make mistakes'.

Should you be given an order or instruction which through the individual's lack of specific knowledge or experience is illegal, dangerous or in contravention of safety rules, then in spite of the individual being of superior rank, it would be important to point out the facts to them. Try and do this away from other people if possible, but safety is paramount, you cannot be ordered to break safety rules.

COURTESY TO SUPERIORS

At times you may find it difficult to give the respect due to certain Officers and Instructors in your County. It helps to remember that you are giving respect to their rank not the individual. Question yourself about why you feel the way you do, what is it about the individual's behaviour/attitude; ensure that you do not make the same mistakes and continue to give the rank the respect it requires.

THE PARADE GROUND

In some Regular Army units you may find that the square is the 'personal property' of the RSM and is only used for drill parades and should NEVER be walked across in a casual way. It perhaps would be as well to assume this when visiting a Regular Army base and ensure that all Cadets are encouraged to follow your example.

OFFICER'S, WARRANT OFFICERS & SERGEANT'S MESS

Many Counties arrange for the more senior Cadets (3 and 4 Star) to visit the Mess on the afternoon prior to their formal Mess Dinner. Your guide is usually a senior member of the Mess, who will explain the history of the Mess silver, procedures and etiquette that is expected from Mess Members when attending a Mess Dinner. These dinners are usually formal, and follow the Regular Army in format.

THE CADET N.C.O. & OPPORTUNITIES AFTER 2 STAR

1. The Mess Steward will allocate your duties, you may be given a section of table to care for, or you may be given specific items to serve.

2. You will be taken in to the Dining Room to familiarise yourself with the layout, where items are to be found and how your duties will be carried out.

3. You may well assist in the placing of the cutlery and glasses, a sample layout of a "Dinner cover" or "Place setting" is shown further on in this section along with an explanation of how to 'navigate' the setting should you be invited to a formal dinner.

4. **The evening commences:** it is common practice for the diners to congregate at the Mess approximately 30 minutes before the Dinner is to commence. You will perhaps be asked to serve sherry to Mess Members and their guests. You will notice that no one is late for this 'gathering', it is seen as an insult to the Mess.

5. The Mess Steward will gain the attention of the Mess Members, (usually by a gong, and shouting out "Ladies and Gentlemen, Dinner is served"). The Senior Officers and Guests are allowed to enter the Dining Room first, followed by others in order of rank. The reason for this is clear when you study the Seating Plan, the more senior ranking Officers are nearest the 'top table' .it is therefore common sense as well as courtesy that they should enter the room first.

6. All remain standing until Grace is said, then when the top table is seated, all others take their seat. A note here, if there are female Mess Members or Guests, it is still seen as 'good manners' to pull her chair back and assist her to the seat. In some Messes, it is a 'Waiter' who performs this task, in others it is expected of a male diner seated next to her.

7. **The Meal:** The Mess Steward will 'give the nod' for you to begin serving food. You will be shown how to serve food; it is not as easy as it looks! No plates are cleared from any table until all the diners have completed the course.

8. Keep a sharp eye out for signals from diners, they may have dropped a knife or fork, spilt some wine etc. it is part of your duties to provide clean cutlery or a cloth for mopping should it be required.

9. **Wine:** If you experience problems with a Mess Member concerning the amount of wine he/she is demanding, be polite and quickly advise the Mess Steward who will take the appropriate action. Some Cadets take the opportunity to 'refresh' themselves with the nearly empty bottles of wine. **TAKE CARE!** You have probably been training in the morning, working in the Mess in the afternoon and will not get to bed until after midnight. Wine will

cloud your judgment of distance, and make you sleepy. Keep alert, save the wine until the work is finished.

10. **The Loyal Toast: Port** is served to the Mess Members, watch for those who do not wish to have Port, they will require water in their glass in order to drink to the toasts called.

11. **Leaving the Table:** When the Senior Officers present and their guests stand to leave their tables, one of two things may occur, firstly, all other diners remain seated, or secondly, all other diners stand until the parties have left the Dining Room and moved to the Ante-room.

Hors d'Oeuvre: is a dish served as a relish at the beginning of a meal. If you are offered a selection, choose three or four; don't aim to sample them all! They are eaten with both a fish knife and fork or with a tea spoon depending on the item, for melon, a dessert spoon and knife or fruit fork and knife are used.

Soup: taken with a round-bowled soup spoon. Drink your soup from the **side** of the spoon

- Tip the soup bowl **away** from you to finish the last of the soup
- The bread bun should be **broken not cut**
- Do not put the bread in your soup or use it to clean the soup bowl
- If you wish to use butter, butter a small bite sized piece of bread at a time.

Fish: use a fish knife and fork, if you have used your fish knife and fork for the Hors d'Oeuvre, and you have not been provided with 'new', ask the waiter for them.

- If the fish is on the bone, do not turn it over; you will never get the bones out!
- If you are unlucky enough to get a fishbone in your mouth, it is the **only time** you can remove it from your mouth with your fingers (unobtrusively behind your napkin).

Entrée: this is a dish served between the fish course and the main course, eaten with a knife and fork.

Main Course: self-explanatory, usually meat or poultry. If you find gristle or bone in your mouth, remove with your fork and place on the side of your plate.

THE CADET N.C.O. & OPPORTUNITIES AFTER 2 STAR

Pudding: usually eaten with a spoon and fork. The fork may be used alone, but not the spoon unless a special spoon is provided for ice cream or fruit salad.

Dessert: are items such as petit fours (marzipan sweetmeats).

Fruit: eaten with a dessert knife and fork, normally cut up (or peeled), before eating. Use the finger bowl if provided, to clean sticky fingers, just dip them in the water and dry on your napkin.

Cheese board: usually with a selection of cheeses and biscuits. Take small quantities of three or four cheeses.

General Notes:

1. **Salt, Pepper and Mustard:** salt should be placed on the side of your plate, not scattered over the meal, as pepper is. Mustard should also be placed on the side of the plate, do not tap the spoon on the plate to dislodge the mustard.

2. **Mess Silver:** when dining in an Officer's or Warrant Officer's Mess, do not touch the Mess Silver. In some messes this can mean a fine.

3. **Other diners:** always be mindful of their needs, ask if they require the salt, etc.

4. **Ask:** do not reach far across the table for an item; ask for it to be passed to you, or request the waiter/steward to get it for you.

5. **Dropped cutlery:** do not dive under the table, ask the waiter to provide clean.

6. **Talk to your neighbours:** at either side and directly across the table, do not attempt to talk to a person where it means either shouting, or leaning in front of someone. This does **NOT** include catapulting peas or pieces of paper at them; it will earn you a severe telling off from the PMC. (President, Mess Committee).

7. **Napkins:** at the end of the meal, rough fold it and leave on the table.

8. **General Behaviour:** in some Messes, it is the custom that once the senior mess members and guests have departed, the junior mess members 'Let off steam'. This often includes finishing the port, playing forfeits etc.

Dancing on the table and playing football with the mess silver is not a recommended course of action - let others make that mistake! Excuse yourself and disappear.

THE CADET N.C.O. & OPPORTUNITIES AFTER 2 STAR

The diagram below shows a typical "Cover" or "Place setting" for a four-course meal. The following section is for those of you who wish to know how to 'navigate' the array of knives and forks, and check that they have the basic good table manners they will perhaps need for the future, when dining with the Managing Director of their company, or indeed if they decide to enter the Armed Forces (particularly as an Officer).

A Dinner usually consists of at least four courses; the cutlery is laid out in accordance with the menu and is used from the outside towards the centre. The napkin should **not** be tucked into your shirt neck!

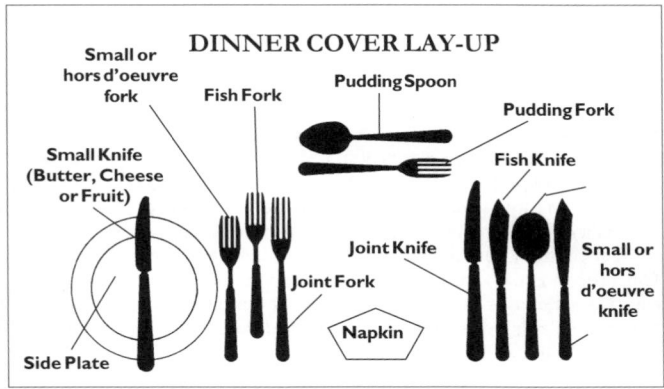

DINNER COVER LAY-UP

Small or hors d'oeuvre fork

Fish Fork

Pudding Spoon

Pudding Fork

Small Knife (Butter, Cheese or Fruit)

Fish Knife

Joint Knife

Small or hors d'oeuvre knife

Joint Fork

Napkin

Side Plate

The diagram above of a *cover lay-up* or a *place setting* is related to the Menu. On studying any menu you can relate the items of knives, forks and spoons to be used with each course on the menu.

Start by using each pair of *KFS* from the extreme left and right of the place setting.

The knife on the side plate is for spreading butter on pieces of a Roll or toast, NOT for cutting either.

Repeat - you always break a roll on your side plate using both hands, and if you wish to butter the Roll use 'bite-size' pieces and butter each piece as you eat them.

THE CADET N.C.O. & OPPORTUNITIES AFTER 2 STAR

Some of the more senior Cadets will be invited to 'wait on table' for Mess Dinners, and may receive some training in what and how things should be done.

OPPORTUNITIES AFTER 2 STAR

INTRODUCTION

A Cadet with APC 2 Star has "One foot on the lower rung of the ladder" giving access to a whole variety of exciting and challenging opportunities. APC training can at times be difficult and demanding, but it is also rewarding especially now it is linked to the Duke of Edinburgh's Award Scheme, although not part of the APC Syllabus or testing. This offers you better opportunities than many other national youth organisations, read about it in the chapter about the Award Scheme.

Outside the APC Syllabus there are courses organised by the Ministry of Defence for 3 Star Training Cadets and above. They are a bonus for you as a Cadet, introducing you to the practical and technical skills and trades within the Army. These courses are normally run during the Easter and summer holiday period but depend entirely on the availability of personnel and facilities. It should be appreciated that the number of these courses are limited and subject to change.
The information given is purely a guide to encourage you to talk to your Detachment Commander about what is available. Course places are limited; 'bids' have to be made in good time for you to stand a chance of gaining a place.

The Army puts what time and resources it has into the planning and organising of these **Special To Arm** courses. The best way to show your appreciation is to make sure that all the places are taken up – *if you are lucky enough to be selected,* **you should make sure you attend.** If for some reason it is impossible, make sure that you let your Detachment Commander know straight away so that another Cadet can take your place and to save the good name of your County.

When attending one of these courses, you will be required to pay a Daily Ration Fee, similar to your weekend camp ration money. Remember to ensure that this is paid either through your Detachment

Commander or by taking the money with you; either way, always get a receipt and keep it safe.

Special To Arm courses all take place at Army establishments. Be smart, behave, be keen, be ready to learn all you can and ENJOY yourself. That is all the Army will require of you.

The following are examples of the variety of courses. A reminder that these courses are subject to change, new courses established, others withdrawn, please check with your Officers and Adult Instructors.

THE ROYAL ARTILLERY

Courses are held at the Royal School of Artillery, for a five-day period.
Qualifications: for Cadets badged to the Royal Artillery
Object of the course: To introduce you to field gunnery.

ROYAL SIGNALS

CLASSIFIED SIGNALLERS COURSE

Courses are held at the Royal School of Signals for a five-day period.
Qualifications: You must have a thorough knowledge of Voice and Operating Procedures and must have passed your Cadet Signals Classification Test.
Object of the course: As a classified signaler to give you an insight into Army Signaling. To demonstrate and give practice in handling signaling equipment used within an Infantry Battalion.

ADVANCED SIGNALLERS COURSE

Courses are held at the Royal School of Signals for a five-day period.
Qualifications: Passed GCSE Math's and Physics Grade A, B or C, if not passed, should actually be studying these subjects at this level in the year you are nominated for the course. You must have a thorough knowledge of Voice and Operating Procedures and passed your Cadet Signal Classification Test.
The aim of the course: The Advanced Signaling Course is one form of post classification training for the senior Cadet.

THE CADET N.C.O. & OPPORTUNITIES AFTER 2 STAR

Object of the course: Is to train selected Cadets in more advanced signaling and to widen your technical interest in the Royal Signals.

ROYAL ELECTRICAL & MECHANICAL ENGINEERS MECHANICAL AND AUTOMOTIVE ENGINEERING COURSE

Object of the course: To give you an elementary knowledge of general engineering, including bench fitting, welding and automotive engineering which will assist you either in the Services or Industry.

ELECTRONICS APPRECIATION COURSE

Object of the course: To introduce you to Electronics and electronic equipment currently in use in the Army.

PHYSICAL TRAINING CADET PT INSTRUCTORS COURSE

Object of the course: Is to teach you the principles and organisation of Physical and Recreational Training as required by the APC Syllabus.

OUTWARD BOUND COURSE

UK LAND CADET LEADERSHIP COURSE

Courses held at various venues, duration eight to nine days.
Qualifications: You must be over sixteen and under seventeen and a half on the 1st April. You are required to have passed your APC 3 Star, or be considered sufficiently knowledgeable to manage the instruction given. Be a Cadet NCO, physically fit, capable of marching twelve miles in boots. Able to take part in obstacle and confidence courses. Rations: you will be expected to pay Ration costs similar to Annual Camp Messing fees.

You must have applied to your Cadet Commandant, who in turn will have to recommend you to take part in the course.

Object of the course: To develop the more senior Cadet's ability as a leader.

Special Note: Full instructions and kit list will be provided prior to the course. Your Parent/Guardian will be asked to sign a form consent for you to undergo surgery in an emergency.

THE CADET N.C.O. & OPPORTUNITIES AFTER 2 STAR

CADET TRAINING CENTRE LEADERSHIP COURSE

Courses are held at the Cadet Training Centre, Frimley Park, the course lasts one week.

Qualifications: It is open to Cadets of the CCF (all three service sections), The Air Training Corps, The Sea Cadets and Army Cadets. Those nominated to attend should be Cadet NCOs who have obtained APC (CCF) Advanced, or APC (ACF) 3 Star or hold an equivalent qualification in the Sea Cadets and Air Cadets. You are expected to have at least one year or more to serve in the cadet force. You must be fit, over sixteen and not over 18 at the time of attending the course. Ensure that you are physically fit to 'stay the course'.

Object of the course:

To develop your initiative and self-reliance. You will carry out exercises involving problems of practical leadership.

CANADIAN ARMY CADET LEADERSHIP AND CHALLENGE COURSE

Courses are held at Banff, Western Canada and last for six weeks

Qualifications: Open to those who are already 4 Star Cadets and over sixteen years of age. You need to be fit as strict fitness requirements are laid down:

Run 1.5 miles	(male) 11.15 min	(female) 13.45 in min.
Sit Ups	(male) 42 in min.	(female) 36 in min.
Push Ups	(male) 29 in min.	(female) 25 in min.
Chin Ups	(male) 5	(female) 3

You must be able to hike a distance of 20km. You must be able to hike a distance of 15km carrying a load of 15kg within 240 minutes. Note: There is a cost for this course; some Cadets fund raise to pay their way.

THE LORD LIEUTENANT'S CADET

Background:

There is a Lord Lieutenant appointed by Her Majesty the Queen for every County in Britain. It is an honorary appointment; the role is that of a personal representative of Her Majesty. In recognition of the appointment, the Lord Lieutenant is treated with due respect and courtesy. The Lord Lieutenant performs duties on behalf of the Queen, from attending events such as the annual Remembrance

THE CADET N.C.O. & OPPORTUNITIES AFTER 2 STAR

Parade, Military parades, functions, and open days, formally opening public buildings, hospitals etc. and supporting large scale public celebrations.

INTEREST IN THE CADET FORCES

As a mark of the Lord Lieutenant's interest in the Cadet movements, many County Cadet Forces (Sea, Army and Air) are required to annually appoint a Lord Lieutenant's Cadet. In the majority of counties, the Lord Lieutenants keep their Cadets very busy, accompanying them on many of their official engagements, acting as escort and carrying out minor duties on their behalf.

TOP JOB

This is a job for the 'Top Cadet' in the County. To be seen in public at the side of the Queens Representative requires an individual with special qualities; being a good Cadet can attain these. It is a particular honour to be selected as the **Lord Lieutenant's Cadet** and carries with it the responsibility of representing all the members of the ACF in the County.

SELECTION

Most Counties have a nomination system followed by a selection board often held at Annual Camp. Cadets who wish to be nominated will probably have passed their APC 3 Star, be 16 years old, of particularly smart appearance, keen and at ease when talking to their seniors. They will require an out-going personality and will probably have attained the rank of Cadet Sergeant. They may well be taking part in the Duke of Edinburgh's Award Scheme.

Some Counties have different requirements, but if you ask your Officers/Instructors they will give you information as the Cadet Commandant usually publishes the 'rules'.

Working towards being nominated for Lord Lieutenant's Cadet is not a short-term project. You will need to ensure you are known for entering into your Cadet life with:

- Determination
- Enthusiasm that encourages other Cadets
- Firm but fair with your juniors
- Enjoyment
- Being a good listener
- Confident enough to speak up when necessary

THE CADET N.C.O. & OPPORTUNITIES AFTER 2 STAR

- Look the part; be smart, well pressed and clean even in your civvies.
- Remember your good manners

The points made on the previous page are not in any particular order, but as mentioned before, being a good Cadet goes a long way towards attaining a nomination for Lord Lieutenant's Cadet. If you are successful, it will remain one of the most unforgettable 'milestone' in your Cadet career.

CONDITIONS CHART

The chart on the next page shows the different 'routes' you might take on your 'cadet career'. You will notice that some of the boxes on the chart have messages in them. The **'notes'** referred to are set out on following page 13-20.

CONDITIONS CHART NOTE "A"

It is a requirement to have successfully completed the 4 STAR to become eligible for consideration and subsequent appointment as an Under Officer.

This is **NOT AUTOMATIC;** you will have to prove over a period of time that by performance and aptitude as a responsible senior cadet you have the qualities that are considered essential for further progress.

A good report on the **MASTER CADETS COURSE** will help. Your dedication to the Cadets in your unit, your manners and behavior on and off parade, your reputation within the County and the recommendation of your Officers will all be taken into consideration before you are recommended as a potential Under Officer. You will have to attend selection interviews within your County Cadet Force. It must be mentioned that in some County ACFs' as a policy they not to appoint Cadet Under Officers.

CONDITIONS CHART NOTE "B"

Having been recommended by your Officers and instructors to be appointed as an Adult Sergeant Instructor, and approved by the County Cadet Commandant, you will become a member of the Warrant Officers and Sergeants Mess.

THE CADET N.C.O. & OPPORTUNITIES AFTER 2 STAR

Your Regimental Sergeant Major will without doubt, take a special interest in you as a member of the Mess. He will expect you to observe the rules of the Mess, be a supportive Member of all Mess activities and become a member of the County team of senior ranks. Your progress will be watched, you will be expected to attain a high standard in all you do. Further opportunities will be made available to you as your service and experience progresses.

CONDITIONS CHART NOTE "C"

If it becomes apparent that your interest in the ACF and your performance as an adult member of the County is outstanding in every respect, then you may well be considered as a potential officer.
As a potential officer you will be involved in the selection process, which will be fully explained to you. If you are appointed to a commission it will be for a probationary period of two years, during which time you will be expected to fulfill certain training obligations.

They are as follows:
1. During your first year you will complete your Initial Training Course, which is usually within your own County.
2. During your second year you will be expected to attend the Cadet Training Centre, Frimley Park to do your Instructors Course. It will also be expected of you to attend at least one Annual Camp during the two years.

On completion of this period, and having carried out the obligations required, earned a satisfactory report on your performance and suitability as an officer, your commission may be confirmed – subject to your Cadet Commandant's recommendation.

In the Army Cadet Force promotion is not automatic.
All officers attend the Cadet Training Centre for courses to qualify for promotion to Captain, Major and Lt Colonel/Colonel.
Each County Cadet Force has what is known as and establishment' of officers and instructors. This controls the number of officers or instructors in each rank that may be appointed; therefore promotion is often subject to a vacancy being available in a particular rank.

THE CADET N.C.O. & OPPORTUNITIES AFTER 2 STAR

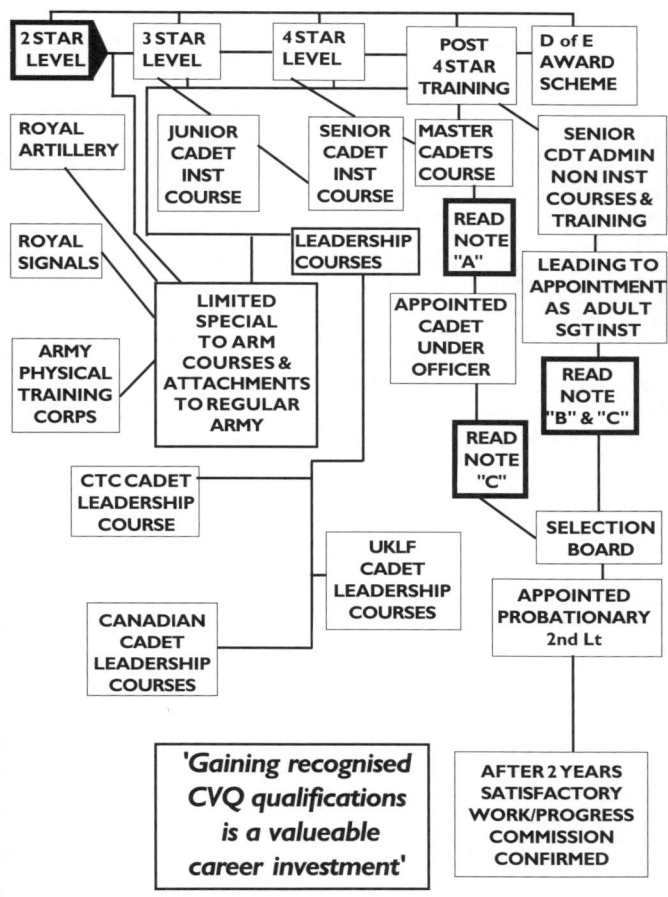

'Gaining recognised CVQ qualifications is a valueable career investment'

SEE PAGES 13-16 &13-17 REFERENCE CHART NOTES "A", "B" & "C"

Cadet Vocational Qualification Office (CVQO)

Based at the Cadet Training Centre in Camberley, Surrey, CVQO is a registered Charity responsible for managing vocational qualifications for members of the Combined Cadet Forces, Sea Cadet Corps, Army Cadet Force and Air Training Corps.

The qualifications on offer have been carefully selected to show employers and educators the wide range of skills that young people and adults learn in the Cadet Forces. These skills include leadership, teambuilding, problem-solving, communication, health and physical fitness.

By offering qualifications designed to develop and improve these important practical skills, CVQO aims to provide members of the Cadet Forces with greater opportunities in both the classroom and the workplace.

"By providing a trusted standard of excellence, CVQO encourages and rewards achievement in both vocational and academic education."
Lieutenant Colonel Edward Woods, Director, CVQO

CVQO is accredited by Edexcel, City & Guilds and the Institute of Leadership and Management (ILM) to deliver a wide range of qualifications including the BTEC First Diploma in Public Services and the BTEC First Diploma in Music for Cadets, and up to level 5 Graduateship Awards for Adult Instructors.

BTEC First Diploma in Public Service

This internationally respected qualification is equivalent to 4 GCSEs at A*-C level (4 Standard Grades at levels 1-3 in Scotland). The course mixes theory and practical elements with an emphasis on leadership, teamwork, communications, problem solving and fitness.

The syllabus has been designed to improve valuable life skills including CV preparation, interviewing techniques, communication, first aid, adventure training, health and nutrition.

Cadets must be at least 16 years old to enrol.

In addition to existing Cadet activities, Cadets are required to complete the course syllabus which includes supervised adventure training activities and occasional weekend training.

The BTEC Award is accredited by Edexcel.

The BTEC Programme is FREE for Cadets.

To enrol, contact your local Cadet headquarters.

THE CADET N.C.O. & OPPORTUNITIES AFTER 2 STAR

"When I applied to university, the admission's tutors were very interested in the fact that I had earned a qualification completely in my own time outside of school and I feel it helped set me apart from the other applicants." Joanna Woods, former Cadet RSM from Sussex ACF

BTEC First Diploma in Music

"The qualifications offered by CVQO focus on communication, leadership and teamwork; all important skills that Universities look for in potential students."
Dr. Alan Pearson, Principal of St Hild and St Bede, Durham University

Since September 2005, Cadets over 16 with an interest in music are able to earn a vocational qualification equivalent to 4 GCSEs at A*-C level (4 standard grades at levels 1-3 in Scotland).

The BTEC First Diploma in Music curriculum has been designed to develop a basic understanding of the music industry and combines technical skills with theory and practical elements. The BTEC Award is accredited by Edexcel.

Upon successful completion, Cadets will have demonstrated an understanding of all aspects of the music business including music selection, composition, performance, marketing, legal issues and budget forecasting. Cadets are expected to be able to play a musical instrument prior to enrolling on the course.

The BTEC Programme is FREE for Army Cadets.
To enrol, ask to your Detachment Commander or contact your local Cadet Headquarters or log onto www.vqaward.org

Duke of Westminster Award
The Duke of Westminster Award is an annual prize which has been created by CVQO to recognise outstanding Cadet.
To be considered for the Duke of Westminster Award, Cadets must possess a wide range of skills and have demonstrated these attributes through a consistently high level of commitment and ac throughout his/her Cadet career.
Cadets are nominated by their unit headquarters and must be enrolled in CVQO's BTEC Program to be considered for the award.

NVQ ADULT QUALIFICATIONS

Once nominated, Cadets must write a letter to CVQO explaining why they should be considerec From these letters, a short list is produced and the finalists are interviewed by members of CVQO management team.

Nominees are judged on academic achievement, contribution to society, communication skills, and contribution to Cadets.

The winning Cadet is presented with a certificate along with a cash prize to be used towards further training.

Adult Qualifications

For those of you who stay on in the ACF as adults there is the added advantage of continuing your vocational training. Whether you are teaching nutrition in the classroom or survival skills in the forest, Adult Instructors are inspiring today's youth to become tomorrow's leaders.

It is the aim of CVQO to reward the efforts of those individuals, by providing them with the opportunity to earn a respected vocational qualification that recognises their achievements within the Cadet Forces and will also be beneficial in their civilian career

With a wide range of awards on offer, CVQO has the ideal qualifications to help Adult Instructors get ahead both personally and professionally.

No funding is available at this time for Adult Qualifications and participating adults are responsible for all costs. For more information on each qualification please visit_ **www.vgaward.org**

'Gaining recognised CVQ qualifications is a valueable career investment'

NVQ ADULT QUALIFICATIONS

Qualifications on Offer

Qualifications	NVQ	Awarding Body
Learning and Development		
L10 & L11 - Enables Teaching Through Instruction,	Part Level 3	Edexcel
Presentation and Demonstration		
A1 - Assessment Using a Range of Methods	Level 3	Edexcel
A2 - Assessmentl through Observation	Level 3	Edexcel
V1 - Verification Award. Demonstrates Ability to	Level 4	Edexcel
Conduct Quality Assurance of Assessment Process		
First Line Management		
Introductory Certificate in First Line Management	Level 3	ILM
Licentiateship		
Licentiateship in Youth Leadership & Training	Level 4	City & Guilds
Graduateship		
Graduateship in Youth Management & Training	Level 5	City & Guilds

MAKE YOUR FUTURE COUNT

CVQO

YOUR OPPORTUNITY TO STEP FORWARD AND STAND OUT

THE CADET N.C.O. & OPPORTUNITIES AFTER 2 STAR

SELF TEST QUESTIONS

1. What are the nine essential qualities a Cadet NCO should have.
2. What is required of you to be promoted to a Corporal.
3. What qualifications are required to be a Master Cadet,
4. When can you be promoted to be an Under Officer.
5. Why would you be selected to go on a Cadre.
6. As an NCO in a Detachment what is your main purpose.
7. You will know many of the weaknesses of a Cadet NCO, how many of them can you list.
8. As an NCO it is said that with Authority goes _____?
9. Finish this quotation "*Respect is not a right it ___ __ __ _____.*
10. What are the '*foundation for good relations*'
11. As an NCO if you have to reprimand a Cadet how/when do you do it.
12. As an NCO you are aware of a Cadet being bullied, what do you do.
13. If you are subject to being 'torn off a strip' and it is not a valid reason what can you do about it.
14. If you are given an order by a superior that you know is illegal, dangerous, in contravention of safety rules, what do you do.
15. If the RSM sees you strolling across the square, what will he say.
16. Explain a formal Dinner is organised and conducted in a Mess.
17. Which way do you tip a Soup Bowl.
18. When are Hors d'Oeuvre served at dinner.
19. What might be the penalty if you touch any of the silver on the mess table.
20. When the cheese board with a selection of cheeses come to you, how much do you take.
21. When don't you dive under the table.
22. What is meant by 'special to arm' courses
23. What grades/subjects do you need to go on the Advanced Signallers course.
24. What qualifications do you require to go on the Cadet Training Centre Leadership Course.
25. What is the role of the Lord Lieutenants Cadets in the County.

Chapter 13

LIFE AFTER CADETS

The world of work becomes more competitive each year; there is also a growing industry in new technology presenting challenges and many opportunities.

As a member of the Cadet Force you will have learned some useful skills, knowledge and experience. Now is the time to think of taking it a stage further by joining in the CVQ scheme leading to BTEC Diplomas and later in your Career as an adult.

Information on CVQ is explained in Chapter12 page 21 to 24.

FURTHER EDUCATION

You may have left school without many useful qualifications, or need further qualifications to follow your chosen career. Colleges of Further Education offer career studies and leisure courses in formats to fit in with most people's lives. Many thousands of people of all ages study through the Open University, an excellent way to take your own time in gaining qualifications, perhaps even a degree.

THE FACTS OF LIFE

Contributing a percentage of your wages to pay for housekeeping should not include all washing, ironing, cleaning and cooking. Take the opportunity to learn how to do all these strange things - you may need them when you set up on your own.

LEAVING HOME

During your Cadet career, you were away from home on weekends and Annual Camps. Although this may give you an advantage over those who have never been away without their parents, it is still a very emotional time. You may be only too pleased to leave 'home' and feel a sense of relief at finally escaping, but If you have been fortunate in having a caring home environment, where despite disagreements you share common interests and count your parent(s) or those who have guided you through childhood as friends, it is more difficult to leave without real heartache and bouts of homesickness.

Write, phone, text, email, visit - let your family and friends know your safe, share in your successes and support you when things are not so good.

LIFE AFTER CADETS

HOBBIES AND INTERESTS

Perhaps you already have a hobby that gives you hours of pleasure, it may even be the foundation of your future career, for example you may make your own clothes and go on to become a designer or perhaps you were introduced to woodworking by a member of your family, enjoyed it so much you decide to become a carpenter/joiner. Many people do not have a formal hobby; they use their time within the community, working with people with disabilities, fund raising for the local Hospice, teaching people with literacy problems to read, or helping one of the many charities, the list is endless. For those of you that have not yet found a hobby keep looking.

DECISION MAKING
JOIN THE S.W.O.T. TEAM

S.W.O.T. means Strengths, Weaknesses, Opportunities, Threats. Doing a SWOT list is an excellent aid to decision-making, particularly career choices. It is simple to create the form but more difficult to complete, as you must be honest with yourself.

Take a sheet of paper and draw four columns. Place the headings along the top of the page along with the subject of your SWOT list. You may well find that one of the difficulties in completing the form is that your Threats can also be seen as Opportunities; your Weaknesses, Threats or Opportunities. That is the idea of this list, to make you think where you need to improve and to highlight your Strengths. When you have completed your lists, number each point in order of importance to you and make your decisions using all the information you have on your form.

THE WORLD OF WORK

When you have made your choice, whether it is further education or the workplace, you will still need to complete application forms and write letters to prospective employers.

From the moment you apply for the application form your aim is to convince the employer that you are the person for the job. The following list is provided as a prompt.

1. Photocopy your application form, or use sheets of paper to draft out what you want to say.

2. When you have completed your application form - take a photocopy to remind you of what you have written, very useful if you are fortunate enough to gain an interview. It may also be useful for completing other application forms.

LIFE AFTER CADETS

3. Some advertisements ask for applications "in your own writing". This may be because the vacancy requires some written work.
4. Put a covering letter with your application saying what job you are applying for.
5. Where an advertisement states "Letter of application and CV" use the Specimen Letter provided in this section as a guide.
7. Make sure that the completed letter is neat, well set out and with no spelling mistakes. Use good quality paper, and where appropriate, matching envelope. Keep a photocopy for your records.
8. You can, if you would like a job at a particular firm/business, write and enquire about possible vacancies. Address your letter to the appropriate person and ensure you have their correct name, initials, job title and address.
9. CURRICULUM VITAE means the course of your life' is normally abbreviated to CV. when writing be honest about experience and qualifications. Remember to update it regularly your Careers Advisor will have given/can give you useful formats for this document.
10. Keep your CV short, factual and a maximum of two A4 pages, if possible.
11. Personal References and Testimonials: Chose someone who knows you well, your cadet Company Commander, any adult outside the family circle. You will be asked for the name of your previous employer if applicable. Do not forget to ask these people before you give their names.

YOU HAVE AN INTERVIEW

Congratulations! All your hard work has had the desired result. Now, prepare properly for the final stage - your interview.

THE AIM OF AN INTERVIEW

The prospective employer has sifted through all the application forms and short-listed several suitable candidates. Obviously, they will need to meet you, ask questions, and expand on the information you have given them.

WHAT YOU NEED TO KNOW ABOUT EMPLOYERS

1. What sort of training will they give you, is it formal and part of your contract of Employment?
2. Do they allow time off for block release or Further Education as part of your training, and encourage staff to attend?

LIFE AFTER CADETS

3. How easy or difficult is it going to be to get to and from work, how long does it take, how much will it cost.
4. If you are a member of the Territorial Army, or Cadet Force, will they grant you leave for Annual Camp or courses.
5. Are there any outside activities, sports etc. that the company encourages?
6. How do they promote people - is it internal or internal and external applications
7. Make clear notes of what questions you want answered at the interview; remember to take the notes with you.

YOUR IMAGE

If you want the job, you have got to make the right impression on the person(s) interviewing you.

*   Ensure your appearance is smart but comfortable.

*   Be on time, five minutes before due time if possible.

*   Take your Cadet Log Book, Certificates etc. and put them in a folder.

*   On entering the interview room, make eye contact, shake hands with the Interviewers and make a greeting (good morning/ afternoon etc.).

*   Sit comfortably, and do not slouch.

*   Think through your answer, and then speak. Always try and answer as fully as possible, don't 'woffle'.

*   Make eye contact with your interviewer(s) when answering their questions

*   If you do not understand the question, say so.

*   If you are asked if you have any questions, those that have arisen from the interview should come first, then produce your question list, and ask!

Questions that you might be asked at an Interview

I.   Tell me/us about yourself
2.   Why do you want to work for this company
3.   What makes you think you would be suitable for this job
4.   What personal qualities do you have to offer us

LIFE AFTER CADETS

5.   Where do you see yourself in 5 years from now

6.   What subject did you enjoy most and why (taken from your CV)

7.   Have you had any experience of work

8.   Why did you leave your last employment

9.   Would you be interested in attending training courses.

10. Would you be prepared to go to day release

11. Would working overtime be any problem for you.

12. Would you be prepared/like to move between departments

13. Are you prepared to move from the area if necessary

14. Can you work on your own

15. Do you play any sports if so who for.

16. What other hobbies and interests do you have

17. Do you use a computer at home

18. Would you like to ask any questions

AFTER INTERVIEW

If you were successful, congratulations, if not, wait a few days then, phone the company and ask for feedback. They may give you some constructive criticism to help you with your next interview - if it is for the same company, you will be remembered positively.

YOUR JOB

Being a member of the Cadet Force will help you fit in with their disciplines of working life. Apply the principles of being a good Cadet to being a good employee, and remember, all experience is useful even if it does not appear so at the time.

It often said that only with time can you gain experience, the problem is that you cannot buy time,

LIFE AFTER CADETS

Mr J.M.Jones (Initials & name of the person)   *Your home*
The Job Title. Director. Manager. Partner etc.   *address*
The Name of the Firm.   *here on the right*
Number & Name of Street,   Telephone/ Email
Name of Town/City.   to contact you
County & Post Code.   Day/Date/Month/Year

Dear Sir/Madam or the persons surname Mr/Mrs if you already know them.

The first sentence saying what job it is you are applying for.

Details of your age, school attended, say what subjects you have studied and to what standard.

Any part-time jobs you have had, training schemes taken part in.

A paragraph about yourself, school duties, clubs or organisations you belong to and any responsibilities you have had.

Your hobbies or interests, sports activities.or involvement in the ACF, Duke of Edinburgh Award or any other achievements that would be of interest to a potential employer.

Tell them that you would like to work for them and that you would like to be considered for an interview.

A sentence at the end saying when you would be available to attend for an interview if you were chosen as a potential employee.

You finish it off

Yours faithfully,

Sign your name - then under it

PRINT YOUR NAME - NEATLY - IN BLOCK CAPITAL LETTERS.

LIFE AFTER CADETS
SELF TEST QUESTIONS

1. Where in this pocket book can you find information on CVQO.
2. How and where could you study to obtain a degree
3. If living at home how much should you contribute to housekeeping.
4. Have you ever experienced being 'homesick'
5. When away from home what must you do for the family.
6. Outside the Cadet Force what other Hobbies or interests have you.
7. Explain what the SWOT Team is about and how you could used it..
8, Having completed a Job Application form what next do you do with it.
9. Will you have to apply for a job in your own hand writing.
10, Do you have a CV written as an example - you may need it for real.
11.When writing your CV what do you have to give/say about yourself.
11.You have an appointment for an interview. How do you prepare for it
12. What is the aim of someone interviewing you.
13. Who would you ask to give you a Personal Reference and why.
14. If you are to give the name of someone to give you a reference,
      what should you do before.
15. Make a list of the important questions you will ask an employer.
16. Name the important things *you* muat do to make the right
      impression at your interview.
17. If you don't understand a question - what do you do.
18. Name/explain ten of interviewers most often asked questions.
19. Having written a letter applying for a job vacancy what must you
      do before sending it.
20. On leaving an interwiew what is the last thing you say to the
      interviewer(s)

CAREER OPPORTUNITIES

Chapter 14

INTRODUCTION

This introduction to Welbeck Defence Sixth Form College should be useful in gaining an insight into the unique role it plays in providing a first-class education for young men and women making a head start to careers in the Armed Services and the Ministry of Defence Civil Service. Welbeck's continued success has enabled the Ministry of Defence to invest in a brand new purpose-built site for the College at Woodhouse near Loughborough in Leicestershire. which was first opened on 7th Sept 2005

In 2004 the College became a quad-Service institution, admitting students with a career ambition to join The Royal Navy, The Army, The Royal Air Force or to become Ministry of Defence Civil Service engineers.

Students entering Welbeck will join a state-of-the-art college with the highest quality residential and teaching facilities, benefiting from the latest educational and technological advances.

The College offers a unique programme of personal, physical and intellectual development which will provide students with a rounded education specifically designed to meet the needs of today's modern technical Armed Services.

The programme does not end after a two-year A-level programme: the four Services continue to monitor and support students through university and on to professional training with their respective Armed Service or within the Ministry of Defence Civil Service.

When you join as a student, you gain the experience of a lifetime. At Welbeck you will face a variety of intellectual and physical challenges that will test your abilities and stretch your mind.

You will pursue sports, travel overseas and experience adventurous activities that build your self-confidence and develop your leadership potential.

CAREER OPPORTUNITIES

The College team of trained and experienced staff - both civilian and military - is always available to assist, encourage and support you, providing every chance to make the best of the wonderful opportunities Welbeck offers.

The Welbeck Experience

Young men and women from a variety of backgrounds, all looking for something that exceeds the average sixth form experience. Alongside academic study, you will learn how to develop loyalty and teamwork, as well as how to communicate as a leader.

The programme of extra-curricular activities includes a heavy emphasis on sport and fitness including outward-bound 'activities such as rock climbing, dinghy sailing and navigation. In addition, all Welbeck students are members of the College Combined Cadet Force and take part in regular military training activities, including a range of adventurous training pursuits.

Study at Welbeck and you will leave the College a more confident and responsible individual, fully equipped to read for a degree that will in turn be the gateway to a truly rewarding career:

2 years' sixth form study at Welbeck
Lower sixth: 4 AS-levels
- Upper sixth: 3 A-levels
3- or 4-year degree at a leading UK University
- Usually Newcastle, Southampton, Aston (Birmingham), Northumbria, Loughborough, or exceptionally Cambridge or Oxford

Initial Officer/Professional Development Training

- At Britannia Royal Naval College Dartmouth,

- The Royal Military Academy Sandhurst or RAF College Cranwell

- Ministry of Defence Civil Service candidates will undertake up to 2 years' Initial Professional Development

- Gain a commission in one of the Armed Services leading to a career as an Officer, or join the Ministry of Defence Civil Service as a graduate engineer.

in the other, as well as a C grade or better in English Language.

CAREER OPPORTUNITIES

Further, candidates must score at least 40 points (38 in Scotland) for their best seven subjects (which must include both Mathematics and Science) on the basis of

ACADEMIC SCORING SYSTEM

GCSE GRADES	POINTS	SCE STANDARDS GRADES
A*	8	
A	7	1
B	6	2
C	5	3

Your school or college must supply a reference showing that you are expected to achieve the minimum entry requirements. Candidates must also be capable of taking Mathematics and Physics and two other subjects for the first year of their sixth form, as well as an ECDL (European Computer Driving Licence) course.

Contact Details:

WELBECK - THE DEFENCE SIXTH FORM COLLEGE
Forest Road,
Woodhouse,
Loughborough,
Leicestershire
LE12 8WD
Telephone: 01509 891700 - College hours only
Email: helpdesk@dsfc.ac.uk
www.dsfc.ac.uk

CAREER OPPORTUNITIES

BRITISH ARMY ORGANISATION

When you wish to find out about the great many opportunities the Army has to offer, the jobs and skills that an Army career can give you.

To help you focus on the overall picture this part of your Pocket Books sets out whereabouts in the Army you would be working, and what roles and duties the relevant regiments and corps perform.

The role of the Army can be divided into the titles of the paragraphs that follow:

COMBAT

One weapon is more important to the Army than any other: the Mark 1, never-bettered British combat soldier. Whether keeping the peace in war-torn areas or delivering aid, the life of a combat soldier is varied and exciting.

ENGINEERING

The Army uses all kinds of equipment, vehicles and electronic systems to get the job done. Building, maintaining and fixing it all is the responsibility of Army engineers - highly trained specialists in their fields.

LOGISTICS & SUPPORT

Keeping troops fed, fuelled and supplied involves the movement of over 750,000 items of equipment. The Army's logistics and support specialists get the job done, in all conditions, wherever they are in the world.

INTELLIGENCE, IT & COMMUNICATIONS

State-of-the-art weapon systems are useless if messages can't get to the front line. Gathering information and passing it on quickly and securely is the job of the Army's intelligence and communications experts.

HR & FINANCE

The Army has its own Human Resources (HR), finance and IT specialists to ensure it runs effectively, and to support its soldiers. Duties include managing database systems and a wide range of personnel issues.

CAREER OPPORTUNITIES

A LIFE LESS ORDINARY ..... THE REGULAR ARMY

Army life and professional, practical qualifications are an unbeatable combination. The Army will help you get into shape physically and mentally. You will be having so much fun you won't even notice that you are developing your natural abilities in a practical way.

The Army lets you share your world with people your own age, working together under pressure, facing physical and mental problems and finding the solutions.

If you choose to make the Army your career, there are several routes of entry. If you are under 18, there are four junior entry schemes you may like to consider.

The Army has four colleges.

The Army Foundation College (Harrogate) offers a 42 week course for school leavers who want to become combat soldiers.

Army Development Centre (Winchester) is for those who want to learn a trade – an intensive 28 week course combining basic military training with technical education leading to Key Skills and NVQs.

Army Development Centre (Bassingbourn) trains soldiers for all branches of the Army (except the Paras, Royal Artillery and Royal Armoured Corps) and offers two courses for sixteen year olds.

Finally, there's **Welbeck TheDefence Sixth Form College**, that has been explained in previous pages.

Attending one of the colleges means that you commit to the Army for a certain period of time, but if things don't work out there is an opportunity to leave the scheme. All four colleges offer potential students the opportunity to visit, along with their families, to help you decide which one is for you.

All four schemes offer the chance to train as a soldier plus the opportunity to gain practical skills and qualifications which are recognised and welcomed both in the Army and Industry.

Apart from those who attend Welbeck College, you will be paid from the start and there will be lots of action, sport and adventure.

CAREER OPPORTUNITIES

Army Foundation College, Harrogate

Two Course are offered, **49 weeks f**or those joing the Royal Artillery, Royal Logistics Corp and the Royal Armoured Corp/Household Cavalry. **23 weeks** for the Royal Electrical and Mechanical Engineers, Royal Engineers, Royal Signals, Royal Army Medical Corps, Army Air Corps and some Royal Logistic Corps

To join you need to be between 16 and 17 years and one month when the course starts and you'll need to have passed the Army entrance tests.

The skills learnt on this course are Skill at Arms, Fitness Training, Qualities of a Soldier, Military Knowledge, Battlefield Casualty Drills, individual Health and Education.

The Army Training Regiment Winchester

Royal Signals – Using every kind of technology from hand held radios to satellite to ensure accurate and secure transmission of information

Royal Logistic Corps – Sustaining the Army anywhere in the world, from front line to storehouse.

Royal Electrical and Mechanical Engineers – Vehicle Mechanic, Vehicle Electrician, Armourer, Metal smith, or Recovery Mechanic ensuring all equipment is ready at a moment's notice

Royal Engineers – As a Combat Engineer building bridges, navigating rivers or crossing minefields; not an office job!

Royal Army Medical Corp - As a Combat Medic you will be supporting all arms of the Army and attached to a unit or field hospital.

Intelligenc Corps - As an Intelligence gather you will be provide crucial information for the units on the ground.

Conditions of Entry

A 14-week training course (known as the Common Military Syllabus) which is completed by all adult 17+ recruits when they join the Army. The course is designed to develop the individual and team skills in a progressive manner, preparing recruits for their Phase 2 training, where they learn the specific skills for their chosen Army trade.

The skills learnt on this course are Skill at Arms, Fitness Training, Qualities of a Soldier, Military Knowledge, Battlefield Casualty Drills, individual Health and Education.

CAREER OPPORTUNITIES

Army Training Center, Pirbright
14-week training course (known as the Common Military Syllabus) which is completed by all adult 17+ recruits when they join the Army. The purpose is to coaching and mentoring to help recruits complete the course and move on to Phase 2 training where they learn the specific skills for their chosen trade.

The skills learnt on this course are Skill at Arms, Fitness Training, Qualities of a Soldier, Military Knowledge, Battlefield Casualty Drills, individual Health and Education.

Infantry Training Centre Catterick (ITC Catterick)
All Infantrymen joining the British Army and produces some of the best Infantry soldiers in the world.

Recruits joining any of the Infantry Regiments, including The Footguards, The Parachute Regiment and The Brigade of Gurkhas undertake all their initial training at ITC Catterick.
They complete the relevant Combat Infantryman's Course, which represents their combined Phase 1 and 2 training.

Junior entry Infantry soldiers (aged 16-17) receive Phase 1 training at the Army Foundation College Harrogate. They then come to ITC Catterick to complete their Phase 2 training.

There are 4 version of Combat Infantryman's course
Line Infantry, Foot Guards, PARA, Gurkha Training (for Guarkha Soldiers only).

What is a Bursary?
Find out how you could be eligible for a £2000 Bursary, one-on-one career advice and a guaranteed job after college
Imagine being able to make money, study, learn a trade and get set up for a great job - all at the same time.
Can't be done? Under the new **Army Further Education Bursary** Scheme (FEBS), that's exactly what's happening in colleges across the UK right now.

CAREER OPPORTUNITIES

People just like you are being financially rewarded for their college achievements, learning vital job skills - and getting one-on-one career support and guidance from the Army while they're doing it.

Bursary? What's that? It's money that's given in exchange for a commitment from the person receiving it.

How much money, and when?

An Army Bursary is worth £2000. You get £1000 while you're at college, and you'll get another £1000 at the end of the course when you join the Army (assuming you complete your Phase 1 training).

"If you're on the Bursary Scheme you're a person who's worth investing in"

The commitment you make in return is to spend a minimum of four years in the Army.

Why should I do it?

Lots of reasons. For a start there's the cash, but an Army Bursary gives you a lot more than just money. It marks you out as someone special-someone who's been recognised by the world's most professional fighting force as a person worth investing in.

It is also the way into a fantastic new learning experience that will literally set you up with a career for life.

Who can apply?

Anyone aged **between 16 and 32 and who is going into Further Education** in September can apply to be part of the Army FE Bursary Scheme.

CAREER OPPORTUNITIES

ARMY EDUCATION GRANTS & 'GOLDEN HELLOS'

These offer financial support to those who:

- wish to study a vocational subject, prior to enlisting as a soldier
- have studied a specified vocational subject to a set level
- or wish to enter one of the technically demanding trades at the basic level.

Who can apply for an Army Grant?

The scheme is open to any British applicant at school or college in the UK, Channel Isles, the Isle of Man or at an Army school overseas Candidates should be in year 11 or S4 and considering going on to Sixth Form College or further education in year 13 or S5 – 6 and considering going on to higher education.

In principle, the Army is looking for A levels or National Qualifications (Scotland) or vocational awards equivalent to A level. This would include the advanced level (AVCE) or BTEC at National Diploma Level in the following broad range of vocations:

Construction and Built Environment

Engineering

Health and Social Care

Hospitality and Catering

Information and Communication Technology

Science

You will be aware that a single AVCE is equivalent to 1 A Level Your commitment to the Army is a standard minimum engagement of 4 years from date of entry.

Where would you be employed in the Army?

Royal Engineers -

Clerk of Works.ME (Military Engineer) Fitter (all)

Royal Logistic Corps:

Ammunition Technician. Chef. Movement Controller Petroleum Operator.

Royal Electrical and Mechanical Engineers :

Vehicle Mechanic

Intelligence Corps:

Operator Military Intelligence (Language)

Army Medical Services

Student Nurse. Biomedical Scientist. Pharmacy Technician.

CAREER OPPORTUNITIES

The 'Golden Hello' may be paid to those who are already qualified – providing they are eligible.

There are no retrospective payments on this scheme, however, if you have a full Academic year to complete, you may be considered for a bursary, or advised to apply for a 'Golden Hello".

THE UNDERGRADUATE BURSARY

If you are thinking about completing a degree and pursuing a future in the Army, you should consider applying for an Army Undergraduate Bursary.

The Army recognizes that may young people prefer to study for a degree before beginning a career. The Undergraduate Bursary offer financial support and the chance to broaden your mind, intelligence and experiences.

You remain a civilian throughout your university course, receive financial support, and gain the opportunity to take advantage of paid training whilst at university.

On graduation, your immediate future is assured. You will begin training at Sandhurst with a further monetary grant.

Your minimum commitment thereafter is for three years commissioned service, with the opportunity of progressing to a full career.

Financial Sponsorship at University

Army sponsorship gives you financial security while you study for your degree. It allows you to make the most of all the opportunities that university has to offer whilst guaranteeing you excellent training at the Royal Military Academy Sandhurst (RMAS) after graduation. This will not only stand you in good stead for a challenging and rewarding career as an officer but will prove invaluable should you eventually wish to move on to a career outside the Army.

The Army Undergraduate Bursary

The Army grants more than 150 Bursaries a year, typically with a value of £6,000 each - this comprises £1,000 per annum at university and £3,000 on arrival at RMAS (Based on 3 years at University with a bursary throughout: students on a 4-year degree course, with a bursary throughout, will receive £7,000 in total). The Bursary is exempt from income tax.

CAREER OPPORTUNITIES

There are two Bursary Boards each academic year. The first is in September and the second the following February (for a retrospective award). Provided applicants have passed the Regular Commissions Board (RCB) with a suitable recommendation, by the first of the preceding month, they will be considered by the Bursary Board.

graduation which is to be before your 29'~ birthday. (There are separate rules for vets, nurses, doctors and dentists).

Who Can Apply?

You can apply if:

You have applied to the Regular Commissions Board (RCB) for selection as an Army Officer, or if you have already passed the RCB. You have a confirmed place for a recognised first degree at a UK university or college of higher education. Those with a conditional acceptance may apply but the award depends on confirmation of acceptance.

Conditions of the Bursary are:

* That you serve a minimum of 3 years on a Short Service Commission (SSC) after the 44 week Commissioning Course at RMAS (unless you join The Army Air Corps, when you must serve for 6 years due to the investment in your pilot training). Those who join as Army Officers without financial sponsorship also serve for a minimum of 3 years. However, the vast majority of officers enjoy the Army so much that they choose to serve for longer.

* That you join the University Officer Training Corps (UOTC) and agree the amount of training you will do with the Commanding Officer. You will be paid for the training you do (even adventurous training) at the appropriate TA rates and you can qualify for an annual bounty of up to £180, in addition. You will also be paid extra for any holiday attachments

* You agree to enter RMAS on the first Commissioning Course after graduation which is to be before your 29th birthday. (There are separate rules for vets, nurses, doctors and dentists).

CAREER OPPORTUNITIES

Who Can Apply?

You can apply if
You have applied to the Regular Commissions Board (RCB) for selection as an Army Officer, or if you have already passed the RCB.

- You have a confirmed place for a recognised first degree at a UK university or college of higher education. Those with a conditional acceptance may apply but the award depends on confirmation of acceptance.

You are already reading a degree and have passed RCB before 1 January in the final year of study.

- You satisfy the nationality and residency rules.

- You meet the required medical standards.

How to apply - contact your local Army Careers Adviser to make application for a Commision in the British Army and obtain other information.

Postgraduate Studies

Awards are normally for first degree courses. However if you did not receive Army sponsorship for your first degree, you may be considered for financial sponsorship for a second degree.
Additionally, if you are reading for a Postgraduate Certificate of Education or a Diploma in Education you may also be entitled to an award for this year, on top of your first degree award, as long as you intend to join the Educational and Training Services Branch of the Adjutant General's Corps (AGC(ETS)).

Veterinary Bursaries

The Army grants bursaries to selected veterinary students, who have passed RCB and apply before their final year at university. This consists of £1,000 a year at university for a maximum of 5 years and £3,000 on completion of the Army Medical Services Entry Officers Course.
Return of service is 4 years, inclusive of the Entry Officers Course.

CAREER OPPORTUNITIES

Nursing Officer Bursaries

A number of nursing officer bursaries are awarded each year with a maximum value of £6000. This is based on 2 or 3 years at university and comprises £1000 in the year of the award of the bursary, £1000 in each subsequent year and £3000 on joining RMAS.

Providing applicants have commenced a Nursing Degree or Diploma in Adult Health, have passed the bursary filter board and are selected at RCB as suitable for officer training, they will be awarded an officer bursary. The return of service is 3 years on completion of military training.

Medical Cadetships

The Army grants around 60 Medical Cadetships a year. Medical Cadetships, awarded for a maximum of the last 3 years of degree training, are currently worth approximately £50,000 each which includes salary and tuition fees. Closing dates for applications are the first of July, September, February and May. Return of service is 6 years from full GMC (General Medical Council) registration.

Dental Cadetships

The Army grants up to 8 Dental Cadetships a year. Dental Cadetships, awarded for the last 3 years of degree training are worth approximately £50,000 each. Closing dates for these applications are 6 months prior to the start of the applicant's 3rd to 5th year at university. Return of service is 6 years (after vocational dental practitioner training).

Every effort has been made to ensure that this information is correct at the time of publication. However, it may not reflect late changes of policy. and/or conditions. If in doubt please askstaff at your local recruiting centre to check details.

British Army Equal Opportunities Statement

The Army welcomes people from all backgrounds. Whatever your race, ethnic origin, gender, religion or belief, there is a role for you in our team. No account is taken of sexual orientation, social background or partnership status; we have a strict code of conduct that ensures a zero tolerance for bullying, harassment, discrimination and victimisation on any grounds.

CAREER OPPORTUNITIES

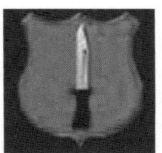

Infantry

If you want to be at the heart of all soldiering, join the Infantry, part of Combat Arms. You'll be trained to fight and survive on the front line and seize enemy territory, whether you get there on foot, by vehicle or air.

Household Cavalry & Royal Armoured Corps

Along with the combat element of the Household Cavalry, the RAC performs reconnaissance and armoured attack duties using the Scimitar and Striker vehicles plus the formidable Challenger 2 main battle tank.

Royal artillery

To get trained to use some of the most powerful and sophisticated weapons around, including missile systems for heavy bombardment, become a gunner in the Royal Artillery.

Army Air Corps

Supporting, manning and piloting the Army's aircraft, you'll be working with cutting-edge technology whether you pursue a career on the ground or in the air.

CAREER OPPORTUNITIES

Royal Signals

The Army relies on reliable and secure communication networks, and it's the job of the Royal Signals to set up and maintain those systems, as well as conducting various hi-tech electronic warfare operations.

Royal Logistic Corps

To be effective on operations, every branch of the Army needs a reliable supply of equipment, ammunition, fuel, food and clothing. The RLC achieves this by providing a self-sufficient transport and distribution network.

Royal Electrical and Mechanical Engineers

The Army has a vast range ofweapons and equipment, and needs an expert team of specialists to ensure it all works - whether it's mechanical or electrical, on the front line or back at base.

Royal Engineers

The RE has the largest range of career options in the entire Army. Also known as Sappers, they build and maintain essential structures for all three Armed Forces, as well as civilian areas affected by disaster or war.

CAREER OPPORTUNITIES

Royal Army Medical Corps
Formed in 1898, the RAMC keeps all Army personnel fit and healthy by providing a range of care from first aid on the front line to hospital-based treatment in a range of medical facilities all over the world.

Adjutant General's Corps
The AGC provides essential administrative and financial support to Army units deployed around the world, and is available 24 hours a day to provide HR and personnel support to soldiers, officers and their dependants.

Military Police

Human Resources & Finance

Judge Advocate General (Legal Dept)

Royal Army Veterinary Corps
The RAVC relies on a range of specialists trained to look after the health and wellbeing of all the Army's animals. This includes dogs used for security purposes and horses used by mounted regiments.

Royal Army Dental Corps
The RADC is dedicated to ensuring the Army's personnel always have healthy teeth, through both preventative measures and treatment. Its staff generally work in dental centres but might deploy to field units when needed.

CAREER OPPORTUNITIES

Queen Alexandra's Royal Army Nursing Corps

QARANC has been in existence for over a century, and today provides all parts of the Army Medical Services with highly trained nursing staff dedicated to giving a wide range of care to Army personnel.

Intelligence Corps

One of the most specialised parts of the British Army, the Intelligence Corps has a range of analysts and linguists trained to be experts in anticipating threats to our country and knowing how to counter them.

Corps of Army Music

It might be the newest corps in the Army (it was formed in 1994), but the Corps oftlrmy Music is one of the largest musical organisations in the world, providing the Army's renowned military bands with their musicians.

Royal Army Chaplains' Department

The RAChD consists of 150 Chaplains, and it is their job to provide support for soldiers and their families wherever they are posted. Chaplains, known as 'padres', often work on the front line.

CAREER OPPORTUNITIES

SELF TEST QUESTIONS

1. Where is Welbec Defence Sixth Form Colllege located
2. When was Welbec opened in its present location.
3. What is meant by Welbec being a tri-service college.
4. When does the College year start.
5. What is the age you can apply for a place at Welbec.
6. The organisation of the Army is divided into five areas of different roles. What are they.
7. How long is the course at Army Foundation College Harrowgate.
8. What training is carried out at Army Train Centre at Pirbright.
9. At Harrogate Army Foundation College how many Course are there?
10. How is trained at ITC Cattrick.
11. What do you understand by a Bursary.
12. Who can apply for a Bursary and what is the age range.
13. Army Education Grants and 'Golden Hellos' are available to support those who A............................ B........................C...............................
14. Who can apply for an Army Grant.
15. How long would you serve as part of the Army Grant conditions.
16. When and why would you consider applying for a Undergraduate Bursary.
17. For Army Undergraduate Bursaries, How many bursaries does the Army grant each year.
18. Students on a four year course would receive a total bursary of how much £ ....
19. Does a student have to pay tax on a bursary.
20. Who can apply for an Army Undergraduate Bursary.
21. A condition of having a bursary is that you serve a minimum of .... years.
22. Give four of the Cadetships and/or Bursaries that the Army award for specialist university courses.
23. If you are a student reading for a Postgraduate Certificate of Education or a Diploma in Education, in what branch of the Army would you serve.
24. Who makes up the Adjutant General Corps,

ABBREVIATIONS

ACF	Army Cadet Force	DOP	Dropping Off Point
ACFA	Army Cadet Force Assoc	DS	Directing Staff
AI	Adult Instructor	DP	Drill Purposes
APC	Army Proficiency Certificate	DTG	Date Time Group
ACIO	Army Careers Information Office	DZ	Dropping Zone
		ECC	External Chest Compression
Adj	Adjutant		
AM	Ante Meridian	ES	Extreme Spread
ATO	Ammunition Technical Officer	ESA	Expected Scoring Area
		ETA	Estimated Time of Arrival
AWOL	Absent Without Leave	ETD	Estimated Time of Departure
BAOR	British Army of the Rhine		
BC	Battery Commander	En	Enemy
Bn	Battalion	Engr	Engineer
Brig	Brigadier	Eqpt	Equipment
BRCS	British Red Cross Society	Fmn	Formation
CAA	Cadet Administrative Assistant	FEBA	Forward Edge of Battle Area
Capt	Captain	Fup	Forming Up Place
cam	camouflage	FPF	Final Protective Fire
CCRS	Council for Cadet Rifle Shooting	FFI	Free From Infection
		freq	Frequency
CP	Command Post	F&M	Fire and Movement
CPOA	Corrected Point Of Aim	FRV	First Rendezvous
CTC	Cadet Training Centre	Gen	General
CCF	Combined Cadet Force	GN	Grid North
CTT	Cadet Training Team	GMA	Grid Magnetic Angle
Cdt	Cadet	GP	General Purpose
CEO	Cadet Executive Officer	GPMG	General Purpose Machine Gun
CO	Commanding Officer		
C of E	Church of England	GRID	Grid Reference
Col	Colonel	HE	High Explosive
Coy	Company	HQ	Headquarters
Cpl	Corporal	HQ Land	Headquarters Land Command
CSM	Company Sergeant Major		
CQMS	Company Quarter Master Sergeant	IA	Immediate Action
		i/c	In Command
CWS	Common Weapon Sight	ICE	Individual Compass Error
CZP	Correct Zeroing Position	II	Image Intensification
D of E	Duke of Edinburgh's Award	ISCRM	Inter Services Cadet Rifle Meeting
Dets	Detachments	JCIC	Junior Cadet Instructors Course
DF	Defensive Fire		
Dvr	Driver	Km	Kilometre

ABBREVIATIONS

Km/h	Kilometres Per Hour	RSM	Regimental Sergeant Major
L/Cpl	Lance Corporal	RC	Roman Catholic
LAW	Light Anti-Tank Weapon	RF & CA	Res Forces & Cadet Assn
LMG	Light Machine Gun	RV	Rendezvous
Lts	Lights	SAA	Small Arms Ammunition
Lt/Lieut	Lieutenant	SCIC	Senior Cadet Instructors Course
Lt Col	Lieutenant Colonel		
Maj	Major	Sgt	Sergeant
Mt	Motor Transport	SI	Sergeant Instructor
MTO	Motor Transport Officer	S/Sgt	Staff Sergeant
MO	Medical Officer	Sig	Signaler
MP	Military Police	SITREP	Situation Report
MPI	Mean Point of Impact	SLO	Schools Liaison Officer
MN	Magnetic North	SOP	Standing Operating Procedure
MOD	Ministry Of Defence		
MR	Map Reference	SSI	School Staff Instructor
MTM	Mouth To Mouth	SUSAT	Sight Unit Small Arms Trilux
NBC	Nuclear Biological Chemical		
		Tech	Technical
NSP	Normal Safety Precautions	TI	Thermal Imaging
NCO	Non Commissioned Officer	Tk	Tank
		TO	Training Officer
NRA	National Rifle Association	TEWC	Tactical Exercise Without Cadets
Ni	Night		
NVQ	National Vocational Qualification	TMH	Trigger Mechanism Housing
OC	Officer Commanding	Trilux	Lamp in SUSAT Sight
OIC	Officer In Charge (pl.tp,patrol etc)	Wdr	Withdraw
		WO I	Warrant Officer 1st Class
offr	Officer	WO II	Warrant Officer 2nd Class
'O' Gp	Orders Group	Wpns	Weapons
OP	Observation Post	U/S	Unserviceable
Ops	Operations	USOP	Unit Standing Operating Procedure
OS	Ordnance Survey		
Pl	Platoon	VCP	Vehicle Check Point
Psn	Position	veh	Vehicle
PM	Post Meridian	Wng O	Warning Order
POA	Point Of Aim	wpn	Weapon
Ptls	Patrols		
PUP	Pick Up Point		
PV	Permissible Variation		
QM	Quartermaster		
RO	Retired Officer		

PERSONAL INFORMATION

Name	
Address	
Post Code	Tel No	Email
Name	
Address	
Post Code	Tel No	Email
Name	
Address	
Post Code	Tel No	Email
Name	
Address	
Post Code	Tel No	Email
Name	
Address	
Post Code	Tel No	Email

IMPORTANT DATES

Date	Subject/Reason

Sophie
ou
la fin des combats

HENRI TROYAT

Henri Troyat
de l'Académie française

La lumière des justes
★★★★★

Sophie
ou
la fin des combats

Éditions J'ai lu

PREMIÈRE PARTIE

1

La porte s'ouvrit devant Sophie et elle franchit le seuil, en vacillant, chassée par la bourrasque. Le vent et la neige s'engouffrèrent dans le vestibule avec une force telle, que Nathalie Fonvizine dut s'arc-bouter pour refermer le battant. Un peignoir de flanelle jaune enveloppait son corps aux formes rebondies. L'effort rougissait son visage mafflu. Pendant qu'elle poussait le verrou, Sophie s'adossa au mur et pressa ses deux mains sur sa poitrine. Elle était hors d'haleine et penchait la tête sous sa lourde toque de renard. Au bout d'un moment, elle se redressa, fixa sur Nathalie un regard étonné et dit :

— Comment, vous n'êtes pas encore prête ?

— Je ne pensais pas que vous viendriez avec cette tempête de neige ! soupira Nathalie.

— Habillez-vous vite ! Il faut partir !

— Par un temps pareil ? Ce serait de la folie ! Nous irons demain !

— Demain, il sera trop tard ! N'avez-vous pas envoyé Matriona au centre de triage ?

— Si ! Elle doit déjà y être, avec les provisions. Mais cela ne fait rien. Si elle ne nous voit pas venir, elle comprendra et retournera à la maison...

Tant de mollesse irrita Sophie. Quand elle avait pris une décision, elle ne pouvait y renoncer sans une véritable douleur physique.

— Eh bien ! J'irai seule, dit-elle en se dirigeant vers la porte.

— Oh ! non ! s'écria Nathalie. Attendez-moi ! J'en ai pour cinq minutes !

Et elle se précipita dans sa chambre. Sophie l'aida à s'habiller. Elles ressortirent ensemble, bras dessus bras dessous, courbées en deux pour lutter contre l'ouragan.

Une neige aux grains durs volait dans l'air et leur piquait les joues comme de la mitraille. Leurs yeux brouillés par la danse des flocons ne distinguaient rien à dix pas devant elles. Mais elles connaissaient trop le chemin pour risquer de se perdre. Elles y étaient allées si souvent, à ce centre de triage ! Dès qu'un convoi de prisonniers en route pour le bagne s'arrêtait à Tobolsk, les femmes des décembristes qui se trouvaient en résidence surveillée dans cette ville s'ingéniaient à faire parvenir aux forçats un peu d'argent et de nourriture. La police tolérait ces pratiques charitables parce qu'elles s'adressaient à des criminels de droit commun. Aujourd'hui, pour la première fois, il s'agissait de criminels politiques : un groupe de jeunes fous, qui, l'année dernière, un quart de siècle après les décembristes, avaient osé conspirer contre le tsar. Leur chef, Michel Pétrachevsky, était, disait-on, un socialiste, un fouriériste. Dénoncés par un espion, les malheureux avaient été jetés, comme leurs prédécesseurs, dans les cachots de la forteresse Saint-Pierre et Saint-Paul, et, après huit mois de prison, condamnés à mort. Mais, par une sinistre comédie, sur la place de l'exécution capitale, on leur avait annoncé que leur peine était commuée en travaux forcés. Cette aventure lamentable avait ému les survivants de l'insurrection du 14 décembre 1825. A peine avaient-ils appris l'arrivée des prisonniers à Tobolsk, qu'ils s'étaient enquis du moyen d'entrer en contact avec eux. Comme Matriona, l'ancienne nourrice des enfants Fonvizine, était du dernier bien avec un sous-officier de garde au centre de triage, Nathalie l'avait chargée d'obtenir, pour elle et pour Sophie, une entrevue avec ceux que déjà on surnommait les « pétrachevtsy ». Si elle échouait, on s'adresserait à quelqu'un de plus haut placé.

Nathalie buta contre une motte gelée et mit un genou à terre.

— Courage ! Nous sommes presque arrivées ! dit Sophie en l'aidant à se relever.

— Vous verrez que ce sera pour rien !

— Auriez-vous peur ?

Nathalie se cambra sous l'insulte, raffermit son chapeau sur sa tête et dit :

— Allons !

Elles repartirent avec obstination, dans le vent glacial qui leur coupait la figure. Déjà, les maisons s'espaçaient, écrasées sous des toits volumineux et blancs. Un long mur de briques se déroula dans le tourbillonnement de la neige : la citadelle, la prison... Sophie sentit les battements de son

7

cœur se précipiter. Elle s'étonnait d'être encore capable d'enthousiasme après tant d'épreuves. Depuis dix-sept ans que Nicolas était mort, elle subissait l'existence plus qu'elle n'y participait vraiment. Mais, par une sorte de discipline intérieure, chaque fois qu'elle était sur le point de sombrer dans le découragement, elle avait un sursaut, jetait les yeux autour d'elle et s'évertuait à découvrir une nouvelle raison de vivre. Constater que quelqu'un avait besoin d'elle était sa meilleure défense contre l'engourdissement de la solitude. Ce qui l'attirait, en cette minute, vers les condamnés politiques de passage à Tobolsk ce n'étaient pas leurs idées (il y avait longtemps qu'elle était revenue de ces extravagances libérales !) mais la pensée des souffrances qui les attendaient au bagne. En les plaignant, elle oubliait son propre chagrin. Du reste, elle était obligée de convenir que les autorités lui avaient marqué beaucoup de mansuétude. Certes, elle n'avait jamais pu obtenir le droit de retourner en Russie, malgré toutes les lettres qu'elle avait adressées à l'empereur. Mais, par égard pour son deuil, on lui avait permis de quitter le hameau perdu de Mertvy Koultouk et de s'installer d'abord à Tourinsk. De Tourinsk, elle avait été transférée, cinq ans plus tard, à Kourgane. De Kourgane, dix ans plus tard, à Tobolsk. Là, elle avait retrouvé, avec une joie profonde, quelques anciens compagnons de captivité et leurs femmes : Ivan et Pauline Annenkoff, Michel et Nathalie Fonvizine, Svistounoff, Séménoff, Youri Almazoff, le Dr Wolff... On se réunissait entre amis, tantôt chez l'un tantôt chez l'autre, on évoquait les souvenirs de Tchita, de Pétrovsk, on se communiquait les lettres de décembristes disséminés sur l'immense territoire de la Sibérie.

Tous avaient fini leur temps de bagne et vieillissaient maintenant, à demi libres, à demi heureux, sous la surveillance de la police. Quelle grisaille après les flammes de la passion et du désespoir ! Il semblait à Sophie qu'il n'y avait pas de caractère, si impétueux fût-il, qui résistât au prodigieux pouvoir d'absorption de ce pays. Elle pensait à une éponge, promenée sur une aquarelle, dont les teintes, une à une, pâlissent. N'était-elle pas un exemple de cette mystérieuse décoloration des âmes ?

— J'ai l'impression qu'ils ont doublé les sentinelles ! dit Nathalie en s'arrêtant.

— Toujours, quand il y a un nouvel arrivage, dit Sophie en la reprenant par le bras.

Elles franchirent le porche et pénétrèrent dans le poste de garde, qui était sombre et sentait le chou. Près du poêle, siégeait un sous-officier rubicond, dont les moustaches en accolade soutenaient les bajoues. La nounou, Matriona, se dandinait devant lui, robuste et rose, en douillette bordée de fourrure. Elle portait un panier à chaque bras. Les soldats la regardaient avec envie. Mais, visiblement, c'était le sous-officier qui avait ses faveurs.

— Voilà justement ces dames ! s'écria-t-elle en faisant un large salut. Elles vous diront comme moi qu'elles ne viennent que par charité.

— La charité, la charité, grommela le sous-officier, qu'est-ce que ça signifie ? Vous me demanderiez de voir des droits communs, comme d'habitude, je ne dirais pas non. Mais là, avec des politiques, je suis obligé de me montrer sévère !

— Nous ne voulons rien d'autre que leur don-

9

ner un peu de nourriture et le livre des Evangiles, dit Sophie.

— Vous ne leur parlerez pas en français ? demanda le sous-officier rendu soupçonneux par l'accent de la visiteuse.

— Je vous le promets, dit-elle.

— Parce que le français ! *Oh ! là, là, mademoiselle !...*

Il rit à pleine gorge. Puis son rire se figea, son visage prit une expression rêveuse, la bouche entrouverte, l'œil au plafond. C'était le moment : Sophie posa un billet de dix roubles, plié en quatre, sur la table. Le sous-officier fit semblant de ne pas le voir et se tourna vers Matriona, qui minaudait en tortillant à deux mains un coin de son tablier brodé :

— Alors, Nicéphore Martynitch, que décidez-vous ? Nous sommes à votre merci, faibles femmes !

— Bon, dit-il. Mais pas plus de dix minutes. Un de mes hommes vous accompagnera.

Tout en parlant, il avait empoché l'argent avec dextérité.

Un gardien partit pour ouvrir les portes. Les trois femmes lui emboîtèrent le pas. Il leur fit traverser une cour, les précéda dans un couloir, tira des verrous et, soudain, elles se trouvèrent dans une salle basse, peu éclairée et pleine de monde. Dans la pâle lumière qui tombait d'une fenêtre aux barreaux de fer, grouillait une foule d'hommes de tous âges, exsangues, loqueteux et barbus. Saisie à la gorge par une odeur de ménagerie, Sophie laissait courir ses yeux sur les visages qui se pressaient devant elle. Chaque fois qu'elle voyait des forçats, elle éprouvait le même malaise fait de honte et de pitié. Les condamnés

10

à vie avaient la moitié du crâne rasé « en longueur », du front à la nuque ; les condamnés à
temps, le devant de la tête rasé « en travers »
d'une oreille à l'autre ; tous portaient sur la face
une marque au fer rouge indiquant qu'ils étaient
des criminels de droit commun. En vain Sophie
cherchait-elle une figure intelligente parmi ces
masques de bêtise, de vice et de misère. Les « politiques » devaient être parqués ailleurs. Au bourdonnement des voix, se mêlait le cliquetis des
chaînes, traînant sur le sol. A entendre ce bruit
familier, Sophie sentait tout son passé lui remonter en mémoire. Les premières années du bagne...
Nicolas debout devant elle, les fers aux pieds...
Il bougeait et les anneaux tintaient faiblement entre ses jambes... Un souvenir plus précis la visita
et elle en fut incommodée, comme par une bouffée de chaleur.

Assis sous la fenêtre, devant un grand registre,
un scribe cochait des noms sur une liste. Lui-même était un ancien forçat, avec des lettres ta-
touées sur le front. Le gardien lui parla à l'oreille.
Ils rirent avec un bruit de tuyauterie engorgée.
Puis le scribe demanda :

— Qui voulez-vous voir ?

— Pétrachevsky, dit Sophie.

— Il est à l'infirmerie.

Sophie eut une seconde d'affolement. Aucun
autre nom ne lui venait en tête. Du regard, elle
appela Nathalie à la rescousse. Celle-ci hésita,
rougit et dit d'une voix défaillante :

— Alors... alors, Douroff !

— Qui ?

— Douroff ! répéta Nathalie.

Et, pour donner plus de poids à sa demande,
elle ajouta précipitamment :

— C'est un de mes parents !

« Comme elle ment mal ! » pensa Sophie avec tendresse.

— Douroff ! Douroff ! dit le scribe en faisant glisser son gros doigt crasseux dans la colonne de gauche du registre. Ah ! voilà ! Cellule numéro 2 !

Il paraissait étonné lui-même de l'ordre qui régnait dans ses paperasses.

— Tout est là-dedans ! reprit-il en appliquant une claque sur son livre. Tout ! Donnez-moi mille aiguilles, je les classerai, je les inscrirai, il ne s'en perdra pas une seule !

Le gardien se dressa, face à la foule des bagnards, et cria :

— Eh ! vous autres ; rangez-vous !

Dociles, les forçats s'écartèrent devant les visiteuses. Elles passèrent, baissant la tête, entre deux haies de mendiants enchaînés. Sophie devinait tous ces regards d'hommes attachés à elle, et qui s'étiraient, comme si, en se déplaçant, elle eût distendu le filet où elle était prise. Leur odeur, l'odeur de la pauvreté, de la prison, l'odeur du peuple russe... Reconnaissable entre mille ! Un murmure de malédiction ou de prière. Rapidement, elle fouilla dans son réticule et distribua un peu de monnaie, au hasard. Elle évitait de lever les yeux sur ceux à qui elle faisait l'aumône.

Le gardien s'arrêta devant une porte, l'ouvrit à l'aide de deux clefs différentes.

— Douroff ! hurla-t-il. On demande Douroff !

Et il invita les dames à entrer. Elles franchirent le seuil avec circonspection. Le cachot était plongé dans la pénombre. Contre le mur, des hommes reposaient sur des grabats. L'un d'eux se leva et s'avança en traînant ses chaînes.

12

— Nous venons vous faire une visite d'amitié, dit Sophie. Vous êtes bien M. Douroff ?

— Oui, balbutia-t-il.

On ne lui avait pas rasé la tête. Il était grand et maigre, le regard fiévreux. Un air de fatigue et de résignation était répandu sur son visage.

— Et vous, Mesdames, puis-je vous demander qui vous êtes ? dit-il. Pourquoi vous intéressez-vous à moi ?

Sophie se nomma et nomma Nathalie.

— Comment avez-vous dit ? s'écria-t-il. Ozareff, Fonvizine ? Vous existez donc réellement ? A force d'entendre parler des décembristes et de leurs admirables compagnes, j'avais fini par les considérer comme des personnages de légende ! Si vous saviez comme on vous vénère en Russie ! Et vous êtes là ! Après vingt-cinq ans de martyre, vous venez au secours de ceux qui ont pris votre relève ! Merci ! Merci !

Les larmes l'étouffaient. Il baisa les mains des deux femmes. La gorge contractée, Sophie se disait : « Mon Dieu ! comme il est jeune ! » Elle s'était figuré en venant qu'elle allait rencontrer des hommes de son âge et découvrait des garçons qui auraient pu être ses fils. « Nicolas n'était guère plus vieux à l'époque de son arrestation », pensa-t-elle encore. Et toutes les fibres de son corps se mirent à trembler. Attirés par les exclamations de Douroff, quatre de ses camarades s'approchèrent ; le cinquième resta couché.

— Je vous présente Spéchneff, Lvoff, Grigorieff, Toll, dit Douroff. Nous avons tous été arrêtés et jugés ensemble. Mais nous n'aurons pas, comme vos maris, la chance de faire notre temps de bagne parmi des condamnés politiques. Nous ne sommes pas assez nombreux pour cela. On nous enverra dans quelque forteresse, avec des assassins et des voleurs !

Des tics nerveux secouaient sa figure.

— Nous voudrions vous aider, dit Nathalie. Que pouvons-nous faire pour vous ?

— Rien, rien !... Vous êtes venues, c'est déjà extraordinaire !... Avez-vous su, ici, ce qu'a été notre condamnation, notre simulacre d'exécution, le 22 décembre dernier ? Les troupes disposées en carré sur la place. Pétrachevsky, Mombelli, Grigorieff attachés aux poteaux d'infamie, un capuchon sur les yeux. Les soldats qui les mettent en joue. Et, tout à coup, le contrordre : on ne tire pas ? L'auditeur lit la nouvelle sentence impériale. Au lieu de la mort, la Sibérie...

— Oui, nous sommes au courant, dit Sophie. Des amis nous ont écrit pour nous raconter cela.

— Déjà ?

— Les nouvelles vont vite en Sibérie, à condition qu'on ne les confie pas à la poste !

— Lorsqu'on m'a détaché, j'ai cru devenir fou, dit Grigorieff. Je riais, je pleurais...

— Moi, dit Spéchneff, je regrette de n'avoir pas été fusillé sur place.

— Comment peux-tu dire cela ? s'écria l'homme qui était resté allongé sur son grabat. C'est bête et c'est lâche ! La vie, quelle qu'elle soit, est admirable. La vie est partout la vie. La vie est en nous et non dans le monde qui nous entoure !

Sophie regarda l'inconnu à la dérobée et lui trouva un visage maladif et disgracieux. Des cheveux blonds hirsutes, un nez informe, une maigre moustache. Tout en parlant, il s'était laissé glisser à bas de sa couchette. Il s'approcha du groupe en soutenant ses chaînes d'une main, à hauteur des genoux.

14

— Je vous présente mon camarade Fédor Mikhaïlovitch Dostoïevsky, dit Douroff. Une brillante carrière littéraire lui était promise. Vous avez peut-être lu son livre, *les Pauvres Gens* ?

— Non, dit Sophie. Je regrette...

— Mesdames, dit le gardien, dépêchez-vous. Il ne faudrait pas que l'inspecteur vous trouve ici.

Nathalie fit signe à Matriona qui ouvrit ses deux paniers. L'un contenait du saucisson et des biscuits. L'autre les livres des Evangiles.

— Je n'en ai que cinq exemplaires, dit-elle, et vous êtes six !

— Rassurez-vous, je me passerai très bien de cette lecture ! dit Spéchneff avec un sourire. Je suis athée.

Les autres acceptèrent avec reconnaissance. Dostoïevsky pressa le livre saint contre sa poitrine. Il avait un regard d'une force et d'une luminosité presque insupportables.

— Il y a un billet de dix roubles caché dans une fente de la couverture, chuchota Nathalie.

Comme le gardien s'impatientait, les prisonniers eux-mêmes prièrent les femmes de se retirer pour éviter un esclandre.

Elles se retrouvèrent dehors, trop émues pour parler. Chacune ruminait ses propres impressions en marchant. La bourrasque s'était apaisée. Il neigeait, à petites plumes sages, sur la ville grise et blanche. Çà et là, brillait, au loin, l'or voilé d'une coupole. Tout à coup, Sophie s'arrêta et dit :

— Que pensez-vous de notre visite ?

— Vous aviez raison ! s'écria Nathalie. Mille fois raison ! Je suis transportée ! Je ne sens plus ma fatigue !

— Il faut que nous nous arrangions pour les

revoir plus tranquillement. Si nous en parlions à Macha ?

Macha, de son vrai nom Marie Frantzeff, était la fille du procureur du gouvernement à Tobolsk. Elle avait beaucoup d'amitié pour les décembristes et les soutenait toujours dans leurs entreprises charitables.

— Mais oui ! dit Nathalie. Comment n'y avons-nous pas songé plus tôt ? Elle interviendra auprès de son père. Et, si son père veut bien dire un mot à l'inspecteur de la prison...

Elles se regardèrent, radieuses, et se remirent en route avec un regain d'énergie. Matriona marchait derrière elles, ses paniers vides au bras. Marie Frantzeff habitait en bordure du jardin public.

★

Le lendemain, sur l'avis favorable du procureur, l'inspecteur de la prison invita Mmes Fonvizine et Ozareff à rencontrer les condamnés politiques dans son propre appartement. L'entrevue eut lieu sous la surveillance discrète d'un officier, qui feignait de lorgner par la fenêtre. Il y avait quelque chose d'insolite dans ces forçats en guenilles assis au milieu du salon. Leurs chaînes reposaient entre les pieds galbés des fauteuils. Ils parlaient avec des voix timides, enrouées. Puis l'officier se retira et ils s'enhardirent. Sophie les interrogea sur leurs opinions politiques. Leurs réponses la troublèrent beaucoup. Ils n'avaient pas de la révolution la même conception que les insurgés du 14 décembre 1825. Pour eux, il ne s'agissait plus simplement de libérer les serfs et d'imposer un régime

16

constitutionnel en Russie, comme le souhaitaient jadis les décembristes, mais d'abolir la propriété individuelle, d'instituer une communauté où chacun travaillerait pour tous et où tous travailleraient pour chacun, de permettre au peuple de se gouverner lui-même... C'était surtout Pétrachevsky — barbe noire et regard de feu — qui soutenait ces idées. Il était sorti de l'infirmerie et semblait en bonne santé. A tout propos, il citait Charles Fourier, Proudhon, Saint-Simon, Herzen, Bakounine... Ses compagnons l'approuvaient par de petits hochements de tête. « Ils sont encore plus fous que nous ne l'étions ! » songea Sophie. L'officier revint et, prudemment, on parla d'autre chose. A quatre heures, la femme de l'inspecteur fit servir le thé. L'apparition du samovar sur la table bouleversa ces hommes qui, depuis longtemps, avaient oublié les douceurs de la vie familiale. Douroff réprima un sanglot. Dostoïevsky détourna la tête. Spéchneff dit entre ses dents :

— Oh ! il ne fallait pas !...

Nathalie Fonvizine et Sophie remplirent les verres, passèrent les gâteaux secs.

— Vous êtes très mal servi, Fédor Mikhaïlovitch. Encore un peu de biscuit...

Gelés, affamés, les bagnards s'efforçaient de garder de bonnes manières. Ils s'appliquaient à boire lentement, à manger peu. Leur dignité dans la misère excitait la pitié de Sophie. Elle pensait qu'en aucun autre pays du monde une scène pareille n'eût été possible.

De tous les prisonniers, c'était Douroff qui lui paraissait le plus sympathique, à cause de ses traits réguliers et de son regard tendre. Détail curieux, il n'y avait pas un noble parmi eux, pas un fils de grande famille. L'esprit d'émancipation était descendu d'un étage dans la hiérarchie sociale. Un jour, peut-être, les idées libérales, venues d'en haut, creuseraient leur chemin plus loin encore, jusqu'aux basses couches de l'humanité. Alors le peuple, enfin éclairé, ne s'en remettrait plus à d'autres du soin de faire la révolution. Fallait-il l'espérer ou le craindre ? Nathalie Fonvizine offrit du thé à l'officier de garde, qui en avala deux verres coup sur coup. Ensuite, pour remercier les dames de leur attention, il quitta de nouveau la pièce. A peine eût-il refermé la porte derrière lui, que Pétrachevsky se remit à parler de la vie heureuse que les hommes de demain pourraient mener dans les phalanstères, le travail s'y transformant en joie et l'obéissance en liberté. Ces propos passionnés amusaient Sophie et elle regrettait de n'en être pas dupe. Son manque de crédulité lui rappelait son âge. Qu'était-elle pour ces garçons ? Une vieille dame, qui avait cru jadis en la révolution, mais dont vingt-trois années de Sibérie avaient usé l'enthousiasme. Ils devaient la trouver aussi démodée dans ses idées que dans ses vêtements. La liberté ne se portait plus ainsi chez les jeunes.

L'officier reparut, au bout de dix minutes. Cette fois, il venait chercher les prisonniers pour les reconduire dans leur cachot. Ils se levèrent, dociles. Les dames leur fourrèrent encore des biscuits et des bonbons dans les poches :

— Que Dieu vous garde ! Nous vous écrirons !

Le bruit des chaînes s'éloigna dans le corridor. Sophie et Nathalie restèrent seules, tête basse, devant la table vide. La femme de l'inspecteur de la prison vint leur demander, un sourire mondain aux lèvres, si tout s'était bien passé. Elles la remercièrent de son hospitalité et se hâtèrent

18

de partir à leur tour. On les attendait, pour le compte rendu, chez les Annenkoff.

★

En arrivant dans l'antichambre, le premier regard de Sophie fut pour le portemanteau. Au milieu de quelques pardessus insignifiants, pendus côte à côte aux patères, elle reconnut la pelisse du Dr Wolff et se réjouit. L'amitié tendre qu'il lui témoignait depuis qu'elle s'était installée à Tobolsk mettait un peu de chaleur dans sa vie. Nathalie la pressait d'entrer dans le salon, mais elle prit le temps de vérifier sa tenue devant une glace. La figure qui lui apparut ne fut pas tout à fait de son goût : le creux des joues marqué par la fatigue, le regard fort et sombre entre des paupières fanées, la bouche qui souriait tristement et, débordant la toque de fourrure, des bandeaux de cheveux bruns à peine striés d'argent. Heureusement, sa taille était restée mince et son port de tête n'avait pas fléchi. A cinquante-sept ans, elle en paraissait quarante-cinq. Elle dressa le cou, dégagea les épaules, alluma ses yeux dans le désir inconscient de plaire et passa le seuil en donnant le bras à Nathalie. Aussitôt, elles furent entourées par des visages de connaissance. Tous les décembristes en exil à Tobolsk se trouvaient là. Pauline Annenkoff conduisit les nouvelles venues vers une table servie. On se rassit autour d'elles dans un grand bruit de chaises. Elles protestèrent qu'elles avaient déjà pris le thé. Mais leurs paroles se perdirent dans le flot des questions :

— Alors ? Comment sont-ils ? Que vous ont-ils dit ?...

Elles racontèrent, l'une coupant l'autre, l'entre-

19

vue qu'elles venaient d'avoir avec les « pétrachevtsy ». Pendant tout le récit, Sophie ne cessa
d'observer le Dr Wolff. Son visage au teint basané
était barré d'une grosse moustache grise, mais
ses sourcils étaient restés noirs. Derrière ses lunettes rondes, ses yeux avaient un regard intelligent et doux. A plusieurs reprises, Sophie per-
çut entre elle et lui un contact de pensées aussi
rapide, aussi précis, que le jaillissement d'une
étincelle. Lorsqu'elle évoqua les opinions politiques de Pétrachevsky, les hommes redoublèrent
d'attention. Sans doute certains mots avaient-ils
gardé le don de les émouvoir. Ils écoutaient les
échos des batailles de leur jeunesse. Tout à coup,
ils parurent très vieux à Sophie. Même le Dr Wolff.
Elle ne les avait jamais vus ainsi. Ivan Annenkoff était un gros monsieur désœuvré, paresseux,
taciturne ; Youri Almazoff inclinait une face tri-
angulaire de momie sous un crâne à demi chauve ;
Pierre Svistounoff avait perdu ses dents de devant et sa bouche se creusait en entonnoir entre
son menton proéminent et son nez pointu. Comment eût été Nicolas, s'il n'était pas mort a
trente-neuf ans ? se demanda Sophie. Peut-être,
pour leur amour à tous deux, valait-il mieux
qu'elle ne l'ait pas vu vieillir, qu'il ne l'ait pas vue
vieillir ? Surprise par cette idée, elle se retira de
la conversation et laissa Nathalie parler à sa
place. Le ton montait.

— Les théories de ces malheureux relèvent du
socialisme le plus utopique ! grogna Ivan Annenkoff en engloutissant une cuillerée de confiture.

— Parfaitement, renchérit Svistounoff, nous
étions tout de même plus proches de la réalité
russe !

— La réalité russe, observa Youri Almazoff,

c'est un pouvoir fort au-dessus d'un peuple faible. La structure géographique de notre pays le commande. Il n'y a pas à sortir de là !

— Vous êtes donc d'avis qu'il ne faudrait rien changer ? demanda le Dr Wolff avec un sourire ironique.

— Peut-être ! Nous nous sommes trompés ! Et les « pétrachevtsy » se sont trompés ! Tout à fait entre nous, je ne vois pas pourquoi nous leur dirions merci. Leur complot n'a servi qu'à renforcer la méfiance du tsar envers tout ce qui est libéral. S'il nous restait un vague espoir de retourner un jour en Russie, nous pouvons en faire notre deuil !

— Qu'est-ce que tu racontes ? cria Michel Fonvizine. Serais-tu devenu un suppôt de l'autocratie ?

— Messieurs, Messieurs, je réclame la parole ! vociféra Sémenoff en tapant le bord de la table avec une cuillère.

Soudain, avec une précision extraordinaire, Sophie imagina Nicolas prenant part au débat, le visage animé, les dents blanches. Puis tout s'éteignit autour d'elle. Youri Almazoff avait raison : déjà, la révolution de 48 en France, les soulèvements populaires dans les états allemands, la folle entreprise des Hongrois prétendant s'affranchir du joug autrichien avaient convaincu le tsar que le poison des théories nouvelles risquait de gagner la Russie. La découverte, à Saint-Pétersbourg, d'une deuxième société secrète ne pouvait que le rendre plus intransigeant envers les survivants de la première. « Je finirai mes jours en Sibérie », pensa Sophie. Après des années de rébellion, elle s'était habituée insensiblement à cette conclusion mélancolique. Le parfum du thé et

des confitures emplit sa tête, l'écœura doucement. Pauline Annenkoff voulut remplir sa tasse.

— Non, merci, chuchota Sophie.

Elle reporta ses yeux sur le Dr Wolff. Mais leurs
regards ne se croisèrent pas. Il écoutait Michel
Fonvizine, qui disait avec chaleur, en froissant
sa serviette :

— Ce qui me console dans tout cela, c'est la
pensée que notre sacrifice n'a pas été complètement inutile ! Les gens de la nouvelle génération
ont peut-être des idées plus avancées que nous,
ils sont socialistes, communistes, fouriéristes,
mais ils ne seraient rien du tout si, le 14 décembre 1825, nous ne nous étions rassemblés sur la
place du Sénat, face aux canons du grand-duc Nicolas Pavlovitch !

— Oui, dit Youri amèrement, nous leur avons
rendu le service de préparer pour eux le chemin
de la Sibérie.

— D'autres reprendront le flambeau, dit Ivan
Annenkoff dans un bâillement.

— Les pauvres ! soupira Pauline.

Elle avait beaucoup engraissé avec l'âge. Dans
l'épaisse pâtisserie de son visage, ses petits yeux
étaient coincés comme deux raisins secs. Svistounoff éclata de rire :

— Vous avez l'air de considérer que les révolutionnaires seront toujours à plaindre, en Russie !

— Mais oui... N'ai-je pas raison ?...

— « Point n'est besoin d'espérer pour entreprendre ni de réussir pour persévérer ! » dit le
Dr Wolff sentencieusement.

— Que c'est beau ! s'écria Nathalie.

— La formule n'est pas de moi !

— Et de qui ?

— De Guillaume d'Orange, à ce que je crois.

22

— Il a réussi ?

— Oui, à se faire beaucoup d'ennemis et à mourir assassiné.

— Vous êtes toujours terriblement caustique, Docteur ! dit Pauline en le menaçant du doigt.

Le Dr Wolff parut flatté d'avoir conservé cette réputation malgré les années. A regarder vivre ses amis, Sophie avait l'impression que tous, ici, jouaient le rôle de leur jeunesse, bien qu'ils n'eussent plus ni le physique ni le caractère de l'emploi. Mais, de même que les habitués d'un théâtre ne remarquent pas les rides des acteurs, qui, depuis un quart de siècle, incarnent pour eux les amoureux du répertoire, de même, à force de se rencontrer et d'évoquer ensemble leurs souvenirs, les décembristes de Tobolsk se prenaient les uns les autres pour ce qu'ils n'étaient plus. Au milieu de cette illusion collective, Sophie souffrait de sa propre lucidité. Elle dut se remettre dans le ton de son entourage. Nathalie Fonvizine envisageait maintenant la possibilité d'écrire aux « pétrachevtsy » et de leur servir de marraine :

— Partout où ils passeront, il faudra qu'ils trouvent des décembristes pour les aider. Nous devrions créer une chaîne de bienfaisance...

— Vous êtes une sainte ! murmura Svistounoff.

Un crépuscule bleu gagnait la pièce. Les visages perdaient leurs contours. Seules brillaient dans la pénombre les dorures d'une icône et la panse du samovar. Une servante entra pour allumer les lampes. Les messieurs regardèrent leurs montres. Comme il se faisait tard, le Dr Wolff offrit à Sophie de la raccompagner chez elle.

Une demi-heure après avoir quitté Tobolsk, le traîneau s'arrêta en rase campagne. Il n'y avait pas de vent, mais le froid était vif. Pelotonnées l'une contre l'autre sous les couvertures, Sophie et Nathalie tournèrent les yeux vers la chaussée blanche, qui se perdait, au loin, dans le brouillard. D'après les renseignements qu'elles avaient pu recueillir la veille, au centre de triage, un premier convoi de condamnés politiques devait partir, ce matin, à huit heures, pour la forteresse d'Omsk. Les gendarmes d'escorte, attendris par un bon pourboire, avaient promis de ne pas s'opposer à une dernière entrevue, au bord de la route, entre les dames et les prisonniers. Sophie ne savait au juste pourquoi elle tenait tant à revoir ces jeunes gens avant le grand voyage qui allait, pour des années, les retrancher du monde. Il lui semblait, confusément, qu'elle avait une dette envers eux. Comme si elle eût été responsable indirectement de leur rêve politique et de ses conséquences. Les épreuves qu'elle avait subies avec Nicolas l'avaient rendue à jamais solidaire de tous ceux qui souffraient en Russie. Seule la mort la débarrasserait, pensait-elle, de cette encombrante, de cette dévorante pitié. Ses yeux se fatiguaient à scruter la nudité du paysage. Le cocher faisait le gros dos pour résister au froid. Des deux chevaux de l'attelage, l'un restait calme, l'autre renâclait, secouait la tête et soufflait de la vapeur par les naseaux. Des paillettes d'argent brillaient dans l'air immobile. Sophie sentit que son visage se désagrégeait lentement. Elle se frotta le nez, les oreilles, pour les ranimer.

— Ils sont en retard ! gémit Nathalie. Nous ne pouvons les attendre ainsi pendant des heures !...

— Ecoutez ! s'écria Sophie. Les clochettes !...

En effet, au fond du silence, il y eut comme un entrechoquement de glaçons. A peine perceptible d'abord, le son monta, se divisa, éclata, en même temps que, de l'abîme nébuleux, surgissaient deux troïkas échevelées. Arrivés à hauteur des dames, les traîneaux s'arrêtèrent. Chacun contenait un prisonnier et un gendarme. Sophie et Nathalie sautèrent dans la neige molle et s'approchèrent des voyageurs. Ils descendirent à leur tour, en tenant leurs chaînes. C'étaient Douroff et Dostoïevsky. Ils étaient vêtus de courtes houppelandes pénitentiaires et coiffés de bonnets de fourrure à oreillettes. La barbe de Douroff était blanche de givre. Le nez de Dostoïevsky pointait, bleu, dans une face blême. Ils baisèrent les mains qui se tendaient vers eux.

— Et vos compagnons, où sont-ils ? demanda Nathalie.

— Les départs s'échelonneront sur plusieurs jours, dit Douroff. Tâchez de les voir, eux aussi. Malheureusement, nous nous sommes renseignés, vous n'aurez pas le droit de nous écrire...

26

— Au début, sans doute, dit Sophie. Mais, peu à peu, la discipline se relâchera...

Nathalie appela l'un des gendarmes et lui glissa une lettre pour le prince Gortchakoff, gouverneur de la Sibérie occidentale, à Omsk. Elle était en relations amicales avec ce haut personnage et ne doutait pas qu'il témoignerait de la bienveillance aux jeunes gens qu'elle lui recommandait. Le gendarme jura que la missive serait remise en mains propres à son destinataire, mais supplia les dames d'abréger leurs adieux.

— Que le Seigneur vous bénisse ! dit Nathalie en faisant un signe de croix devant Douroff et Dostoïevsky.

Ils courbèrent la tête.

— Merci, merci pour tout, dit Douroff d'une voix enrouée.

Les deux hommes remontèrent chacun dans son traîneau. Un cri s'échappa des lèvres de Sophie :

— Ayez confiance ! Nous nous reverrons peut-être !...

Sa voix se brisait. Elle ne savait plus où elle en était de sa vie. N'étaient-ce pas des décembristes qui repartaient pour le bagne ? Les chevaux, éveillés par un coup de fouet, s'élancèrent en balançant leurs grandes têtes sombres. La neige volait autour de leurs sabots. Hors des caisses peintes en bleu, deux visages se penchaient pour regarder en arrière. Sophie et Nathalie agitèrent longtemps la main, puis, fatiguées de saluer le vide, retournèrent tristement à leur traîneau.

— On rentre en ville ? demanda le cocher.

— Oui, dit Nathalie. Vite ! Je suis gelée !...

L'équipage reboussa chemin. Après dix minutes de course éperdue, il parut tout à coup à Sophie qu'une lumière éclairait son cerveau. L'évi-

27

dence, qu'elle avait longtemps niée, s'imposait à elle sans effort, sans douleur, avec la calme plénitude des levers de soleil sur la neige. Jusqu'à présent, elle avait considéré que son installation à Tobolsk était provisoire. Sans croire à proprement parler qu'elle serait bientôt rappelée de l'exil, elle se contentait d'une isba misérable aux confins de la cité européenne. Elle trouvait presque réconfortant d'y être campée, comme si, en refusant de prendre ses aises, elle eût conjuré le sort qui cherchait à la maintenir en ces lieux. Il avait fallu l'arrivée des « pétrachevtsy » dans la ville pour la tirer de ses illusions. Ses conversations avec eux lui avaient ôté non seulement l'espoir de retourner en Russie, mais encore l'envie de regarder de ce côté-là. Pour la première fois depuis le début de sa relégation, elle choisissait la Sibérie. Elle se dit même, avec une pointe d'orgueil, qu'elle la choisissait *librement*. Il y avait une maison à vendre, près du jardin public. Le prix en était certes exorbitant. Mais en l'achetant elle se rapprocherait de ses amis, qui, tous, habitaient ce quartier. Avoir un intérieur agréable. Ne plus vivre comme quelqu'un qui, d'une minute à l'autre, s'apprête à boucler ses malles ! Elle eut un élan de tendresse vers les malheureux qui, en partant pour le bagne, l'aidaient à retrouver son équilibre. Douroff, Dostoïevsky... Elle se souviendrait de ces noms.

A chaque cahot, sa tête ballait contre les capitons du dossier. Elle calcula qu'elle serait rentrée juste à temps pour donner sa leçon de français à la fille du directeur des Postes. Son succès comme professeur était si grand, qu'elle devait refuser des élèves. Elle avait commencé à enseigner par désœuvrement, alors qu'elle se trouvait encore à Kourgane. Là-bas aussi, il y avait des décembristes en exil. Leur affolement à tous, lorsqu'au début du mois de juin 1837 ils avaient appris l'arrivée prochaine du tsarévitch Alexandre Nicolaïevitch ! Bercée par les mouvements du traîneau, Sophie revoyait la cohue endimanchée qui, au crépuscule, s'était avancée sur la route pour accueillir le grand-duc héritier. Des marchands ambulants vendaient des lampions, des chandelles. Bientôt, mille petites lumières s'étaient mises à palpiter dans la campagne, comme pour la nuit de Pâques. C'était la première fois, disait-on, qu'un membre de la famille impériale se rendait en Sibérie. Sa venue était attendue par les petites gens comme un événement surnaturel. Les heures passaient sans entamer la ferveur de la foule. Peu après minuit, un hurlement avait retenti au loin : « Hourra ! » Deux courriers de cabinet étaient passés, ventre à terre, et, derrière eux, des calèches, des dormeuses roulant à grand fracas. Dans l'une d'elles se trouvait l'héritier du trône. Il n'avait vu personne et personne ne l'avait vu. On avait éteint les chandelles, les lampions, et on était rentré en ville pour apprendre que Son Altesse impériale, épuisée par le voyage, avait sauté de sa voiture dans le lit préparé à son intention chez le gouverneur. Le lendemain, les décembristes avaient fait remettre au tsarévitch des suppliques pour leur retour en Russie. Le poète Joukovsky, de la suite du grand-duc, s'était entretenu longuement avec eux et leur avait promis d'appuyer leur requête. Une messe solennelle avait été célébrée le soir, à six heures. Sur l'ordre de Son Altesse impériale, tous les délégués pour crime politique assistaient à la cérémonie. Etrange tableau, une foule de fonctionnaires chamarrés ; dans un

29

coin, les révoltés du 14 décembre ; et, debout, seul, devant l'autel, le fils de Nicolas Ier. Il avait dix-neuf ans, à l'époque. Grand, mince, l'air doux et las. Sophie le voyait bien, dans le créneau formé par les épaules de deux chambellans. Lorsque le prêtre avait prononcé la belle prière pour le salut « des malades, des malheureux et des prisonniers... », il s'était retourné vers les décembristes et s'était signé avec lenteur en les regardant. Il était reparti le soir même, laissant derrière lui un immense espoir. Sophie, comme tous les autres, avait cru que le tsar se laisserait toucher par le rapport du grand-duc et autoriserait le rapatriement des condamnés politiques en Russie. La réponse de l'empereur ne s'était pas fait attendre : « En ce qui concerne ces messieurs, la route pour la Russie passe par le Caucase. » Par application de cette sentence, Lorer, Narychkine, Nazimoff, Likhareff, Rosen, et bien d'autres avaient été incorporés comme simples soldats dans l'armée. La plupart d'entre eux devaient être tués au combat ou mourir du typhus. Malgré cette désillusion, Sophie avait encore adressé des lettres à l'empereur, à l'impératrice, à Benkendorff, à Orloff. Une par an, à peu près. Toujours pour rien. Maintenant, elle n'écrirait plus. C'était décidé. Elle se pencha vers Nathalie et dit :

— Vous savez, j'ai pris une grande résolution ! Je vais déménager pour me rapprocher de vous !

— Ah ! comme je suis heureuse ! s'écria Nathalie. Il faut que nous resserrions le cercle ! Nous sommes de moins en moins nombreuses à avoir connu certaines choses...

La pensée des morts traversa l'esprit de Sophie : Alexandrine Mouravieff, Camille Le Dentu, Ivacheff, Vadkovsky, Iouchnevsky, Kuhelbecker, les frères Borissoff, le général Léparsky... Le commandant du bagne s'était éteint au mois de mai 1837 et les derniers prisonniers encore détenus à Pétrovsk avaient suivi son enterrement comme celui d'un ami. Avec le recul du temps, Sophie appréciait mieux encore la naïveté et la générosité de ce vieux serviteur du régime impérial. Il lui avait écrit, après la disparition de Nicolas, une lettre si affectueuse !... Elle en chercha les termes dans sa mémoire, mais le mouvement de l'air sur son visage, la blancheur de la plaine dans ses yeux, l'empêchaient de réfléchir comme elle l'aurait voulu. Au loin, sur la hauteur qui surplombait l'Irtych, se montraient les toits de la ville, couverts de neige et dominés par les tours et les clochers de l'ancienne forteresse.

Nathalie reconduisit Sophie en traîneau jusqu'à sa maison. Douniacha, la servante, se tenait sur le pas de la porte.

— Dépêchez-vous, barynia ! cria-t-elle. On vous attend !

Ayant embrassé Nathalie à la volée, Sophie se précipita dans le vestibule et tomba sur la petite Tatiana, la fille du directeur des Postes, debout, ses cahiers sous le bras. Elle avait treize ans, un visage rond semé de taches de rousseur et des yeux bleus, très pâles.

— Asseyez-vous, mon enfant, dit Sophie en la faisant entrer dans l'unique pièce confortable de l'isba. Nous allons commencer tout de suite. Que vous avais-je donné à apprendre ?

Tatiana se recueillit, leva son regard au plafond et récita d'une voix monocorde :

Un pauvre bûcheron, tout couvert de ramée...

Elle prononçait les mots français avec un accent russe si âpre et si chantant à la fois, que

31

Sophie se retenait de sourire. L'application de son élève l'attendrissait, comme un hommage maladroit rendu à la France. Il lui semblait admirable qu'au fond de la Sibérie le moindre fonctionnaire voulût élever ses enfants dans la langue de La Fontaine. A vivre en exil, depuis tant d'années, elle avait acquis une sensibilité maladive envers tout ce qui lui rappelait sa patrie. Si elle avait souri autrefois de quelques émigrés maniaques, collectionneurs de souvenirs, elle en arrivait elle-même, maintenant, à rassembler des bibelots, à découper des images dans des revues, pour reconstituer autour d'elle l'atmosphère d'un pays où elle ne reviendrait jamais plus. Les murs de la pièce s'ornaient de lithographies représentant les vieux métiers de Paris. Sur la table à ouvrage reposaient quelques numéros du *Petit Courrier des Dames*. La pendule était un coq de bronze perché sur un tambour, avec cette devise gravée dans le socle de marbre : « Son cri réveillera le monde. » Et, sur un lutrin, s'étalait une partition illustrée : *Le Val d'Orléans*, « grande valse vendue au profit des Inondés de la Loire ». Chacune de ces acquisitions avait coûté à Sophie beaucoup de ruse et de persévérance. Certes, elle eût aimé avoir quelques estampes relatives à la révolution de février 1848, mais il était vain d'espérer trouver des documents de ce genre en Russie. Elle devait se contenter des comptes rendus édulcorés des journaux. En vérité, cette Seconde République, née d'un généreux sursaut populaire, lui semblait étrange, à distance. Elle ne comprenait pas qu'après avoir renversé la monarchie, ses compatriotes eussent élu comme chef de l'Etat un neveu de Napoléon, le prince Louis-Napoléon Bonaparte. Drapeau tricolore,

Marseillaise, discours vibrants à l'Assemblée législative, tout cela était bel et bon, mais pourquoi n'avoir pas fait appel plutôt, pour diriger le pays, à des hommes d'un esprit libéral au-dessus de tout soupçon, tels que Ledru-Rollin ou Lamartine ? Décidément, il était impossible de porter un jugement là-dessus si on vivait loin de Paris. Il fallait se plonger dans ce bouillonnement de passions contradictoires pour y voir clair. Les chroniques des journaux vite lues et vite oubliées, les succès et les scandales de la Comédie-Française, les caricatures méchantes, les élégances tapageuses, les professions de foi, les bons mots, les attelages dans l'allée des Acacias, le bruit du marteau tapant sur l'enclume, du rabot sifflant dans les faubourgs, les chansons des rues, le cri du marchand d'eau, la musique des revues militaires, le fracas des voitures omnibus et, par-dessus ce remue-ménage quotidien, l'extraordinaire sentiment que toutes les opinions sont permises et qu'un éclat de rire suffit à renverser une statue, c'était cela que Sophie avait perdu en quittant la France. Elle y pensa tristement, tandis que, devant elle, la fille du directeur des Postes de Tobolsk ânonnait en dodelinant de la tête :

Le trépas vient tout guérir ;
Mais ne bougeons d'où nous sommes ;
Plutôt souffrir que mourir,
C'est la devise des hommes.

— Très bien ! murmura Sophie.

Et on passa aux explications de mots. Tatiana n'était point sotte. Après avoir donné la définition de « ramée », de « faix », de « chau-

33

mine », de « fagot », elle voulut savoir s'il était vrai, comme le prétendait La Fontaine, que les hommes préféraient la souffrance à la mort.

— Pas tous ! dit Sophie avec un demi sourire. Elle songeait à ceux qui avaient risqué leur vie à Paris, sur les barricades, à Saint-Pétersbourg, sur la place du Sénat. Fuir la Sibérie, retourner en France... Elle en avait formé le projet autrefois. Mais il était impossible de transgresser la volonté de l'empereur. Sans passeport, elle serait arrêtée au premier relais. D'ailleurs, n'avait-elle pas pris, un instant plus tôt, la résolution de s'installer dans une maison plus agréable, près de Fonvizine et des Annenkoff ?

— Oui, dit la fillette. Par exemple, les soldats aiment mieux périr dans la bataille que d'être vaincus !

— Certains soldats.

— Les héros !

— C'est cela.

— Je déteste les héros.

— Pourquoi ?

— Je ne sais pas. Ils empêchent les autres de vivre tranquilles. Moi, ce qui me plaît, c'est la maison, la famille, la couture, les bébés. Est-ce que vous avez connu des héros ?

— Oui.

— Lesquels ?

Sophie se troubla, ouvrit un livre sur la table et dit brièvement :

— Nous allons faire une dictée. C'est un texte de La Bruyère... Vous y êtes ?... « Ménalque descend son escalier, ouvre sa porte pour sortir, il la referme... »

Tout en parlant avec lenteur, elle revint à son

34

projet de déménagement. Des chiffres s'addition-
naient dans sa tête. La dépense ne l'inquiétait pas.
Elle ne manquait de rien, grâce aux revenus de la
propriété de Kachtanovka. Le maréchal de la noblesse de Pskov lui envoyait régulièrement sa
part, tous les trois mois. Mais jamais elle n'avait
reçu la moindre lettre de son neveu. A croire que
Serge ignorait son existence ! Il ne lui avait même pas écrit à la mort de Nicolas. Certainement,
son père le tenait sous sa coupe. « Quel âge a-t-il
maintenant ? Vingt-trois ans... Non ! Plus ! Vingt-
cinq ! » Elle s'effraya et resta une seconde, bouche bée. Comme le silence se prolongeait, Tatiana
leva les yeux de son cahier. Son visage exprimait
une curiosité affectueuse. Visiblement, Sophie l'intriguait. On racontait tant de choses, en ville, sur
les décembristes ! Sans savoir au juste ce qu'on
leur reprochait, les enfants devaient les considérer
comme des êtres à part, plus instruits et plus
malheureux que les autres, des réprouvés investis
du don des langues, de l'arithmétique et de l'or-
thographe.

— « ... il voit que son épée est mise du côté
droit, que ses bas sont rabattus sur ses talons, et
que sa chemise est par-dessus ses chausses... », reprit Sophie.

— Qu'est-ce que c'est que des chausses, Madame ?

— Une espèce de culotte qui descend jusqu'aux
genoux.

La plume se remit à glisser sur le papier. Sophie songea que, dans la plupart des bourgades
sibériennes, il y avait maintenant un décembriste
qui enseignait les rejetons des notables locaux.
Certains même avaient créé des écoles. Cependant, par une singulière injustice, si les condam-

nés politiques se transformaient en éducateurs, leurs enfants étaient encore, dans bien des cas, considérés comme des serfs de la Couronne. En 1842, l'empereur s'était déclaré prêt à admettre les fils et les filles de ses anciens ennemis dans les établissements scolaires de l'Etat, à condition qu'ils y fussent inscrits non point sous leur nom de famille — Troubetzkoï, Volkonsky, Davydoff, Annenkoff — mais sous le prénom de leur père, comme des moujiks ! Les parents avaient été unanimes à refuser cette grâce insultante et les enfants avaient poursuivi leurs études à la maison, sous la surveillance de leurs proches, mieux qu'ils ne l'eussent fait ailleurs. Enfin, en 1845, après la mort de Benkendorff, son successeur, le comte Alexis Orloff, avait obtenu de Nicolas Ier que les mesures draconiennes visant « la jeune génération » fussent rapportées. Par voie de conséquence, Alexandra et Lise Troubetzkoï, puis Nelly Volkonsky avaient reçu le droit d'entrer à l'Institut des Jeunes Filles d'Irkoutsk, tandis que Michel Volkonsky et les fils des Annenkoff étaient admis comme internes au gymnase de la même ville. Mais, comme toujours en Russie, cet acte de clémence était accompagné de restrictions mesquines. Ainsi, Pauline Annenkoff, qui souffrait d'être séparée de ses enfants, n'avait jamais pu arracher aux autorités de Tobolsk un sauf-conduit pour aller les voir. Le moindre déplacement nécessitait des cachets et des signatures. Les lettres étaient ouvertes et retenues, parfois pendant une semaine à la poste. Il arrivait que, sur une dénonciation anonyme, un policier se présentât au domicile d'un décembriste, posât quelques questions oiseuses et se retirât avec un sourire menaçant. Défense d'avoir un fusil de chasse, défense d'envoyer des

36

daguerréotypes en Russie, défense d'apprendre l'escrime aux enfants... Soudain, Sophie se demanda si le directeur des Postes n'interrogeait pas Tatiana, quand elle rentrait à la maison, sur ce qu'elle avait vu et entendu chez son professeur de français. Elle croyait recevoir des élèves et c'étaient de petits espions qui s'asseyaient à sa table et écrivaient sous sa dictée.

— « On l'a vu une fois heurter du front contre celui d'un aveugle, s'embarrasser dans ses jambes, et tomber avec lui, chacun de son côté à la renverse... »

Tatiana eut un éclat de rire si clair, si franc, que Sophie en fut rassurée. Dans ce monde affreux d'ennui et de délation, il fallait qu'elle résistât au penchant de déceler des ennemis partout.

— Que c'est drôle, Madame ! s'écria la fillette. Est-ce qu'il vit encore, La Bruyère ?

— Non, il est mort depuis plus de cent cinquante ans.

— Je ne pensais pas qu'on pouvait être drôle si longtemps après sa mort !

Sophie relut le texte, corrigea les fautes. Tatiana, debout derrière elle, se penchait en avant pour mieux voir et respirait dans sa nuque. Un parfum de gamine émue flottait autour de Sophie. Elle éprouva, une fois de plus, le regret de n'avoir pas d'enfant et d'en être réduite à élever ceux des autres.

— Sept fautes, dit-elle. Ce n'est pas brillant !

Tatiana baissa la tête. La leçon était finie. Déjà, dans l'antichambre, piétinaient les deux fils de Soumatokhoff, le plus gros cultivateur de la région. Sophie reconduisit Tatiana à la porte et fit entrer les garçons. Dix et douze ans ; de bonnes petites trognes de moujiks, aux joues rouges de froid ; ils abordaient juste l'étude du français ; tout en peinant sur la conjugaison du verbe être, ils jouaient à remuer des osselets dans leur poche ; Sophie dut les leur confisquer. Ensuite, ce fut le tour de la femme du curateur des établissements charitables, toute en frisettes et en froufrous, qui venait uniquement pour apprendre à placer quelques mots français dans la conversation. Elle exaspéra Sophie par ses mines, ses roucoulades et ses rires.

A midi et demi, enfin, il se fit un grand calme dans la maison. Sur la table, débarrassée des livres et des cahiers, Douniacha apporta un plat de viande froide garnie de choux aigres. Habituée de longue date à ces repas solitaires, Sophie ne souffrait même plus du vide et du silence qui l'environnaient. Elle dînait rapidement, sans penser à la nourriture, et s'amusait parfois, en levant les yeux, de voir des fantômes de passants flotter derrière la vitre aux arborescences de givre. Sa cuillère attaquait une fade gelée de fruits arrosée de lait, quand il lui sembla reconnaître une silhouette d'homme, au col dressé et au large manteau. Trois coups frappés à la porte : elle ne s'était pas trompée ! Une joie tumultueuse l'envahit.

— Va ouvrir, Douniacha, murmura-t-elle en se penchant vers une glace.

Elle releva une mèche de cheveux sur sa tempe, tira sa blouse dans sa ceinture et se tourna, souriante, vers le Dr Wolff qui entrait. Il avait un visage rayonnant de bonheur.

— Je viens de voir Pauline ! s'écria-t-il. Elle m'a dit que vous vouliez acheter la petite maison, près de chez elle ! Est-ce vrai ?

— Oui, répondit Sophie. Je crois que ce serait

38

plus raisonnable. Je suis tellement mal installée ici !...

— Vous êtes surtout trop loin de nous ! Ne laissez pas cette occasion. Achetez ! Déménagez ! Vite !...

Elle sentit comme le poids d'une main sur son épaule et sa gêne augmenta.

— Avez-vous dîné ? demanda-t-elle.

— Bien sûr ! Entre deux rendez-vous, selon mon habitude.

— Vous prendrez bien un verre d'eau-de-vie de frambroise ?

Il voulut refuser. Sophie insista. Elle avait l'impression qu'il était très important pour elle que le Dr Wolff goûtât cet alcool. Mais où était la bouteille ? Depuis le temps qu'elle n'y avait plus touché !... Elle ouvrit le buffet, souleva le couvercle du coffre en bois, courut à la cuisine... Rien ! Le Dr Wolff riait :

— Ne vous donnez pas tant de mal !

Elle enrageait : « Il va croire que je suis désordonnée, que je ne sais même pas ce que j'ai à la maison ! » Ce désagrément prenait dans sa tête des proportions dramatiques. Elle gourmanda Douniacha qui avait sûrement jeté la bouteille par mégarde. La fille éclata en sanglots.

— Aide-moi au lieu de pleurnicher ! dit Sophie.

Et le Dr Wolff qui entendait tout ! C'était ridicule ! Enfin, en déplaçant des fagots derrière le poêle, Douniacha découvrit le précieux flacon. Sophie l'apporta triomphalement sur la table. Le Dr Wolff dut se résigner. A la première gorgée, il décréta :

— Un vrai velours !

Elle le regardait siroter son eau-de-vie et se laissait aller à une secrète gratitude. Un homme dans sa maison, carré au creux d'un fauteuil, le verre à la main — ce spectacle contentait en elle un besoin féminin, vieux comme la terre, de se dévouer à de petites tâches matérielles et de créer le bien-être autour du mâle fatigué par son travail. Elle l'obligea à se resservir.

— Quand déménagez-vous ? demanda-t-il.

— Que vous êtes pressé ! dit-elle en riant. Je ne suis pas encore tout à fait décidée. J'aimerais revisiter les lieux...

— Voulez-vous que nous y allions ensemble maintenant ?

La voix était jeune, joyeuse, sans rapport avec l'homme grisonnant qui se tenait assis devant Sophie. Elle eut conscience de ce dédoublement et il lui sembla qu'elle-même avait une âme qui courait et un corps qui ne pouvait suivre.

— Le propriétaire, Polzoukhine, est un de mes clients, reprit-il. Vous obtiendrez de lui ce que vous voudrez ! Mais peut-être n'êtes-vous pas libre tout de suite ?

— Si, dit-elle en dressant la tête. Justement, je n'ai pas de leçon avant cinq heures...

Et elle se sentit pareille à une de ses élèves devant la promesse d'une récréation.

La maisonnette se composait de trois petites pièces délabrées au rez-de-chaussée et d'une grande pièce, à usage de billard, au premier étage. Par les fenêtres, on apercevait une rue large, bordée de façades en bois, peintes de couleurs vives. C'était le quartier européen, officiel, le quartier des fonc-

40

tionnaires. Le propriétaire ne manqua pas de le faire observer à Sophie, pour se justifier de vendre si cher des locaux en si mauvais état. Il était cassé en deux, le teint cadavérique, la respiration sifflante. En parlant, il lorgnait d'un œil inquiet le Dr Wolff, qui, évidemment, tenait en laisse la meute des maladies et pouvait les lâcher sur lui à tout instant. Quand le médecin lui reprocha son âpreté au gain, il balbutia qu'il ne demandait qu'à discuter, qu'une diminution était toujours possible. Et, de concession en concession, pour ne pas s'aliéner la faveur d'un homme dont dépendaient sa santé et peut-être sa vie, il en vint à accepter le prix très raisonnable de mille deux cents roubles. Le Dr Wolff lui fit immédiatement signer un papier, afin d'être sûr qu'il ne se dédirait pas. Le bonhomme se retira en grognant, à la fois rassuré et furieux, comme s'il avait sauvé sa peau mais laissé sa bourse dans une mauvaise rencontre.

Restée seule avec le Dr Wolff, Sophie le remercia de son intervention et s'occupa d'imaginer sur place tous les aménagements praticables. Elle allait et venait avec décision, pivotait sur elle-même, ordonnait à un mur de reculer, à une fenêtre de se draper de rideaux, au plancher de reluire.

— Ici, je placerai la table et le gros buffet... Devant la croisée, mes deux fauteuils... Ma chambre, je la vois là !...

— Méfiez-vous, dit le Dr Wolff, cette pièce est orientée vers le nord.

— Vous avez raison. Mais celle d'à côté est trop petite. A moins d'abattre ce mur...

Le Dr Wolff tapota le mur, l'ausculta d'un air médical, et conclut :

— Vous pouvez y aller ! Ce n'est qu'une cloison !

Puis, tirant un crayon et un carnet de sa poche, il proposa à Sophie de tracer tout de suite un plan de l'ensemble. Elle mesura la dimension des pièces, en faisant de grands pas. Il portait sur son dessin les chiffres qu'elle lui annonçait. Cette collaboration affectueuse la gênait et la charmait dans le même temps. Elle se rendait compte qu'en associant cet homme à ses soucis d'installation future elle le traitait comme s'il eût réellement partagé sa vie. Eût-elle visité la maison avec son mari, que leur conversation n'eût pas été différente. Il dépendait d'elle de faire cesser le jeu. Mais elle n'en eut pas le courage.

— C'est parfaitement clair ! dit-elle en regardant le croquis. Vous avez un talent de dessinateur que je ne soupçonnais pas !

Ils passèrent dans la pièce voisine. De nouveau, elle marcha devant lui, en comptant :

— Longueur, six pas. Vous y êtes ?

Il la regardait si intensément, qu'elle devina qu'il était très loin de l'architecture.

— Et en largeur ? dit-il d'une voix sourde.

Cette fois, elle dut se contraindre pour mettre un pied devant l'autre. Ses mouvements les plus simples manquaient de naturel. Elle pensait à l'impression qu'elle produisait sur lui en arpentant la chambre.

— Quatre pas et demi, murmura-t-elle en arrivant à l'angle opposé.

Soudain, elle se dit que cette maison était trop grande pour une femme seule. Le Dr Wolff, lui, louait une chambre dans l'appartement d'un colonel en retraite, au bout de la rue. Là, il dormait, mangeait, recevait ses malades. Jamais il ne s'était plaint d'être logé à l'étroit. Pourquoi ne lui céderait-elle pas le premier étage ? Il en ferait un laboratoire, un dispensaire... Cette idée la réjouit, puis l'inquiéta. Elle n'avait pas le droit d'introduire un homme chez elle. Par égard pour le souvenir de Nicolas. Non qu'elle doutât d'elle-même, mais elle ne voulait pas donner prétexte aux gens de salir son passé par leurs clabaudages.

— Vous serez vraiment très bien ici, dit-il en la suivant dans l'antichambre.

Ils gravirent l'escalier et débouchèrent dans une salle aux tentures fanées, aux lambris décollés et au plancher gris de poussière. En plein milieu : un vieux billard, bas sur pattes, dont le drap était déchiré et maculé de cire.

— Magnifique ! s'écria le Dr Wolff. Avec votre permission, je viendrai, de temps en temps, faire quelques carambolages pour me délasser.

Sophie éprouva une émotion inattendue, démesurée, et balbutia :

— Mais oui ! Venez aussi souvent qu'il vous plaira ! Cette pièce... cette pièce sera un peu la vôtre !...

Si le Dr Wolff avait répondu deux mots aimables, n'importe quoi, elle se fût ressaisie. Mais il ne disait rien et la considérait fixement, avec tendresse. Sous ce regard pénétrant, tout ce qui aurait pu se calmer en elle tournait à l'extravagance. Elle le vit jouant au billard, sous une lampe à l'abat-jour vert, descendant l'escalier, allumant un cigare, appelant Douniacha, ouvrant la porte de la chambre comme s'il eût été chez lui. Sur le point de s'avouer qu'elle était troublée, elle préféra, par une esquive, négliger ses propres sentiments pour s'intéresser à ceux de l'autre. « Comme il me regarde ! Sûrement, il est amoureux de moi ! Il va me le dire ! Et s'il me demandait en mariage ? » Elle tâcha de changer le cours de ses réflexions et en fut incapable. Trois ans après la mort de Nicolas, Youri Almazoff lui avait offert de l'épouser. Elle avait refusé sans hésitation. Pour un peu, elle eût éclaté de rire au nez du brave garçon, qui se croyait investi, par son amitié envers un compagnon de bagne, du droit et du devoir de le remplacer auprès de sa veuve. Aujourd'hui, le problème était différent. Le Dr Wolff n'était pas un quelconque Youri Almazoff. Calme, doux, intelligent, courageux, il avait toujours agi selon la conception que Sophie se formait d'un homme de cœur. Elle l'admirait. Elle ne voulait pas lui causer de peine. La seule pensée d'avoir à lui dire non la glaçait. Et pourtant, il le faudrait, sans doute. Elle ne pouvait appartenir à un autre après Nicolas. Même si cet autre était de la grande famille des décembristes. D'ailleurs, elle était âgée, fanée. Cette union serait ridicule. Elle eut la perception d'un petit poids de chair molle sous son menton et tendit le cou. « Evidemment, je pourrais l'aider dans son métier, je pourrais m'occuper de ses malades, je pourrais, je pourrais... » Sa vie se meubla soudain, s'éclaira, prit une dimension et un sens extraordinaire. Un besoin maternel d'organisation et de sauvetage la possédait. Elle beurrait des tartines et faisait de la charpie. Surtout, elle était aimée ! Elle sortit de ce tourbillon, la tête rompue, le regard vague. Le voyage n'avait pas duré trois secondes. En face d'elle, le Dr Wolff l'observait toujours avec une gravité affectueuse. Allait-il se décider ? Elle l'espéra, elle le redouta. Il hocha la tête et dit :

— Savez-vous à quoi je pense ?

Elle eut de grands battements de cœur.

— Vous devriez transformer cette pièce en bibliothèque, reprit-il. Vous laisserez le billard où

44

il se trouve et vous placeriez des volumes joliment reliés tout autour.

Elle cacha sa déception derrière un sourire :

— Ce serait une bonne idée ! Mais je n'ai pas assez de livres !

— Je vous apporterais les miens. Je ne sais où les mettre !

— Et si vous en aviez besoin ?

— Je viendrais les lire chez vous !

Elle fut reprise par l'agréable sensation d'oublier son âge, de quitter la terre. Le petit poids de chair neutre, sous son menton, s'effaça. La fatigue glissa de ses épaules. « Pourquoi serait-il interdit à des êtres comme nous d'unir leurs vies ? Il a aimé jadis la pauvre Alexandrine Mouravieff, j'ai aimé Nicolas. Tous deux sont morts. Nous ne renierons pas notre passé en essayant de créer ensemble un nouveau bonheur. » Il lui prit la main et la porta à ses lèvres :

— Chère Sophie, comme il est bon de vous voir ainsi, tout exaltée par la perspective de votre prochain emménagement ! Pour que vous soyez heureuse, il faut que vous ayez quelque chose à construire !

— Oui, dit-elle, la voix étranglée.

Et elle remarqua, avec surprise, qu'il faisait plus clair dans la pièce. Le soleil d'hiver émergeait de la brume. Des poussières d'or dansaient dans un rayon. Le drap vert du billard avait des reflets d'herbe tendre. Elle eut envie de rire, de respirer à pleins poumons, de marcher dans la neige.

— Si nous sortions ? dit-elle. Le beau temps est revenu !

Il la regarda interloqué, comme si, l'ayant perdue dans une galerie, il l'eût retrouvée entre deux colonnes, à un endroit où il ne l'attendait pas. Elle comprit qu'elle l'amusait, qu'elle l'intriguait et décela, au fond d'elle-même, maladroite, inemployée, la coquetterie de sa jeunesse.

Ils descendirent l'escalier et sortirent dans la rue, qui brillait, toute blanche, avec des ombres bleues au pied des maisons. Le sol était glissant. Le Dr Wolff arrondit son bras et Sophie s'appuya dessus, aussi légèrement que possible.

— Où allons-nous ? demanda-t-il.

Elle avança le menton :

— Par là...

Il n'y avait guère d'autre but de promenade à Tobolsk que la partie haute de la ville et la citadelle. L'enceinte crénelée, surmontée de tours, enfermait la cathédrale, l'église, le monastère, l'évêché, le palais du gouverneur, des casernes, la prison centrale. Ils errèrent quelques minutes entre de vieux bâtiments de brique et de maçonnerie. Le froid sec et le soleil clair conféraient à cette architecture un air de gaieté.

— Nous devrions saluer la cloche, proposa le Dr Wolff.

Sophie acquiesça de la tête en souriant. Ils pénétrèrent dans la cour de l'évêché, où se trouvait la fameuse cloche d'Ouglitch, qui, en 1591, avait donné le signal d'une insurrection. Le tsar Boris Godounoff, après s'être emparé des principaux émeutiers, les avait envoyés en Sibérie et avait expédié là-bas, en même temps, la cloche coupable de lèse-majesté. Pour que le châtiment fût complet, elle avait été privée de son battant et fouettée en place publique. Les décembristes l'appelaient « la doyenne des exilés ».

Sophie et le Dr Wolff s'arrêtèrent devant la lourde forme de bronze. Une toux se fit entendre derrière eux. Un policier sorti de l'ombre les observait. Chaque fois que les décembristes s'aventuraient dans cette cour, un représentant de l'ordre s'attachait à leurs pas. Craignait-on, en haut lieu, que la cloche d'Ouglitch ne devînt un objet de culte pour les condamnés politiques ? A tout autre moment, Sophie se fût amusée à exaspérer le surveillant par des réflexions à double sens. Mais, cette fois-ci, elle avait surtout envie de se retrouver seule avec le Dr Wolff et d'oublier qu'ils étaient des réprouvés.

— Venez, murmura-t-elle. Cette cloche ne nous dira rien. On lui a arraché la langue !

Ils s'éloignèrent. Le policier les suivit, les mains derrière le dos, pendant quelques pas. Puis ils ne sentirent plus sa présence. En passant par les anciens remparts, ils découvrirent, tout en bas, le quartier pauvre avec ses maisonnettes bancales, ses bazars, et la steppe blanche, sans limite, coupée par le Tobol et l'Irtych, pris sous la glace. A côté de la forteresse, s'étendait le jardin public, semblable à tous ceux qui égayaient les villes de province en Russie. Un maigre bois de bouleaux, avec, au centre, un kiosque-restaurant fermé pendant l'hiver. Sur la terrasse qui dominait la route, s'élevait un obélisque de marbre, à la mémoire du cosaque Yermak, conquérant de la Sibérie : « 1581-1584 ». Des gamins tournaient autour du monument et se battaient à coups de boules de neige.

Sophie avisa un banc, au soleil. Le Dr Wolff le débarrassa de sa couche de givre, étala dessus, en guise de coussin, une écharpe de laine tricotée, et ils s'assirent côte à côte, face au paysage brumeux et scintillant. Le vent était tombé. Sophie ne sentait plus le froid sur sa figure. « Dans quatre mois, la fonte des neiges, la débâcle, le printemps ! pensait-elle. Alors, tout s'animera dans les bas quartiers de la ville ; une forêt de mâts bougera dans le port libéré des glaces ; la steppe fleurira à perte de vue ; les dames sortiront leurs chapeaux de paille ; un orchestre militaire jouera dans le kiosque ; le théâtre de Tobolsk affichera *Iphigénie en Aulide* ou quelque chose de ce genre ; je serai installée dans ma nouvelle maison ; seule, ou mariée peut-être... » Elle dut respirer profondément pour recouvrer son calme. Personne n'appelait Wolff par son prénom : Ferdinand. Ce n'était pas un prénom russe. Elle murmura :

— Ferdinand Bogdanovitch, je vous retiens, sans doute. Vous devez avoir des rendez-vous...

— Le rendez-vous que j'ai en ce moment est le plus important de tous, dit-il.

Sophie eut peur de cet engagement rapide et détourna la tête. Il fallait trouver un autre sujet de conversation. Elle se rappela les deux malheureux qui glissaient en traîneaux, de relais en relais, à travers la plaine blanche, vers le bagne. Son bonheur présent les lui avait fait oublier. Quel égoïsme affreux dans l'âme la mieux disposée à la compassion ! Elle balbutia, comme parlant en rêve :

— Où sont-ils maintenant ?

— Qui ? dit le Dr Wolff.

— Douroff et Dostoïevsky.

— C'est vrai, je ne vous ai pas demandé de leurs nouvelles. Les avez-vous vus, ce matin ?

— Oui. Ils étaient calmes, courageux... Plus courageux que moi qui les regardais partir ! Combien d'hommes devront encore perdre la liberté pour qu'un jour tous les hommes soient libres ?

— Tous les hommes ne seront jamais libres, dit le Dr Wolff. D'ailleurs, ils n'en ont pas tellement

envie ! Ceux qui éprouvent réellement l'amour de
la liberté sont rares. La majorité préfère res-
sembler au voisin, penser comme le voisin et même ne pas penser du tout !

— Vous êtes cynique !

— Cynique, non. Désabusé, peut-être. Plus je
réfléchis, plus je me persuade qu'en exigeant pour
nos semblables le droit d'agir à leur guise, nous
sommes en contradiction avec la nature de l'homme qui est de s'agglomérer en troupeau. Si nous
arrachons le pouvoir au tsar pour le donner au
peuple, le peuple s'empressera de l'offrir à quelqu'un d'autre. Le peuple a mieux à faire qu'à se
gouverner. Il a à travailler, à manger, à dormir, à
s'amuser, à aimer, à procréer...

— Vous parlez du peuple russe !

— C'est le seul que je connaisse. Mais je suppose que le peuple français, lui aussi...

Sophie secoua la tête :

— Détrompez-vous. La notion de masse est slave, ou plutôt asiatique. Ici, on ressent la puissan-
ce écrasante des grands courants humains. En
France, au contraire, chacun se prend pour le seul
détenteur de la vérité. C'est le champ clos où s'af-
frontent toutes les opinions possibles, la patrie
des dissonances folles, la réserve où grouillent les
idées de demain...

— J'aime vous entendre parler de la France, dit
le Dr Wolff en plissant les yeux. Vos joues deviennent toutes roses. Vos narines battent...

Elle crut qu'il se moquait d'elle, tant ces compliments convenaient peu à une femme de son
âge. Mais il la couvait d'un regard si naïf qu'elle
dut se rendre à l'évidence. Il ne voyait d'elle que
ce qu'il voulait voir. Vite, elle effaça les deux petits sillons verticaux que l'attention creusait entre

ses sourcils. Le soleil l'aveuglait. Elle baissa légèrement le front. Le Dr Wolff dit :

— Viendra-t-il un jour où vous ne regretterez plus votre pays ?

— Certainement pas, répondit-elle. Mais je me suis profondément attachée à la Russie. Je dirais, presque, à la Sibérie...

— Merci, dit-il d'une voix enrouée. Vous venez de me procurer une grande joie.

Elle frissonna et remonta son col d'une main tremblante.

— Vous avez froid ! s'écria-t-il. C'est ma faute. Nous n'aurions pas dû nous asseoir sur ce banc !

Elle posa une main sur son poignet large et osseux :

— Mais non, je suis très bien. Seulement, il est tard. Mes élèves m'attendent. Partons, voulez-vous ?

Ils se levèrent. Des moineaux, qui picoraient autour de l'obélisque, s'envolèrent en pépiant. Sophie savait que le Dr Wolff ne lui dirait plus rien de décisif. Il avait laissé passer le moment... Elle en était soulagée, après avoir souhaité qu'il se déclarât. « J'ignore moi-même ce que je veux », pensa-t-elle avec mélancolie. Ils sortirent du jardin. Dans la rue, ils croisèrent plusieurs personnes de leur connaissance. Sophie répondit gracieusement à leur salut. Elle était fière d'être vue au bras du Dr Wolff.

3

Surpris par l'arrivée de Sophie, les ouvriers, qui bavardaient en grignotant des graines de tournesol, se remirent précipitamment au travail.

— Que vous avais-je dit ? murmura-t-elle en se penchant vers Nathalie et Pauline qui l'accompagnaient. Dès que j'ai le dos tourné, ils se croisent les bras !

Depuis un mois et demi que les réparations étaient en train, les menuisiers avaient à peine raboté le plancher et redressé les portes ; quant aux maçons, ils en étaient encore à enduire de plâtre le lattis du plafond. Ce n'étaient pas des gens de métier, mais d'anciens criminels de droit commun. Chaque lundi arrivait en ville un petit groupe de relégués. Aussitôt, les habitants de Tobolsk allaient dans la cour de la prison embaucher les hommes dont ils avaient besoin. Tarif : dix roubles par mois. Les laissés pour compte étaient expédiés dans les villages voisins. Sophie inspecta son monde avec accablement. Un énorme gaillard, barbu et ventru, maniait mollement la truelle. A côté de lui, un bossu plantait des clous dans une planche, sans conviction.

— Jamais cette maison ne sera prête pour Pâques ! gémit Sophie.

— Mais si, barynia ! dit le gros barbu. Vous verrez, tout ira très bien ! D'ailleurs, le docteur a promis de nous envoyer encore deux hommes, demain, pour nous aider !

— Vous avez vu le docteur ?

— Il est venu ce matin, jeter un coup d'œil.

Elle rougit. L'intérêt que Ferdinand Wolff portait à son installation lui semblait une déclaration de tendresse déguisée. Nathalie et Pauline l'observaient avec malice. Avaient-elles deviné le penchant qu'elle éprouvait pour le médecin ? Pourtant, ils ne s'étaient jamais avoué leur amour. Ce mot, du reste, ne convenait pas au sentiment calme et fort qui les liait l'un à l'autre.

— Et si j'emménageais avant la fin des travaux ? dit-elle. Je pourrais camper au rez-de-chaussée, pendant que les ouvriers termineraient le premier étage...

— Ce serait intenable ! s'écria Pauline. Le bruit, la poussière ! Soyez sage ! Le vrai bonheur est toujours le fruit d'une longue patience !

Sophie entrevit une intention ironique dans cette phrase. Depuis quelque temps, toutes les conversations lui paraissaient pleines de sous-entendus. Elle était à la fois flattée et confuse de cette fausse atmosphère de fiançailles.

— J'ai tout de même l'impression, dit-elle, que si je me trouvais sur place du matin au soir, les travaux avanceraient plus vite.

— Et vos élèves ? dit Pauline. Comment les recevriez-vous ? Non, à mon avis...

Elle se tut, la langue coupée par la surprise.

Dans l'encadrement de la porte venait de surgir un gendarme.

— Mme Ozareff ? demanda-t-il en saluant militairement.

Il était grand et fort, le visage rouge, bosselé comme un chaudron.

— C'est moi, dit Sophie.

— Veuillez me suivre chez le gouverneur.

Elle fut saisie d'une crainte froide :

— Chez le gouverneur ? Pourquoi ?

L'absurdité de cette question était si manifeste que, sans attendre la réponse, elle ajouta :

— Très bien. Retournez dans l'antichambre. Je viens tout de suite.

Le gendarme claqua des talons et disparut.

— Ah ! mon Dieu, que vous veut-on encore ? s'écria Nathalie en levant les yeux au plafond.

— C'est sûrement à cause de vos rencontres avec les gens de Pétrachevsky ! décréta Pauline.

— Si c'était cela, on n'aurait pas attendu près de deux mois pour me rappeler à l'ordre ! dit Sophie.

— Vous avez raison, dit Nathalie, je pense plutôt qu'on va vous reprocher les textes que vous faites apprendre aux enfants !

— Les fables de La Fontaine ?

— Certaines sont très subversives !

— On verra bien ! dit Sophie avec un sourire résigné.

Nathalie et Pauline l'accompagnèrent jusqu'à la citadelle. Chemin faisant, elles lui chuchotaient des encouragements. On ne la laisserait pas se débattre seule, on préviendrait tous les amis, on alerterait le procureur par l'intermédiaire de Marie Frantzeff... Derrière les trois femmes qui trottaient dans la neige, marchait le grand gendarme

53

à la prunelle vide et aux bras ballants. Devant le palais du gouverneur, il fallut se séparer. Nathalie, les larmes aux yeux, bénit Sophie d'un signe de croix :

— Que Dieu vous assiste, ma colombe !

Sophie se retrouva dans une antichambre nue et glaciale. Cinq minutes plus tard, le gouverneur Engelke la recevait dans son bureau. Un feu brûlait dans une cheminée de marbre. Sur les murs, vert bouteille, se détachaient des cadres d'or. Mais on ne voyait pas ce que représentaient les tableaux dont les couleurs s'étaient enfumées. Engelke était petit, gras, avec des lunettes d'argent et un ventre en tonnelet, porté par des jambes torses.

— Dans les ingrates fonctions que j'exerce, il est des minutes lumineuses, parmi lesquelles je compterai celle-ci, dit-il.

Sophie crut à un compliment et fit un sourire crispé. Elle était assise au bord de son fauteuil, le dos roide, et regardait fixement le gouverneur, en se demandant quel coup il se préparait à lui assener.

— Vous êtes, reprit-il, la vivante preuve que, dans un monde chrétien, il ne faut jamais s'abandonner au désespoir. Alors que tout semble perdu, brusquement les nuages se dispersent, le soleil luit, le bonheur est là !

— Que dois-je comprendre, Excellence ? demanda Sophie.

— Vous ne devinez pas ? dit Engelke en plissant un œil.

— Non, je vous assure...

— Quelque chose qui vous tient à cœur depuis très longtemps, quelque chose que vous réclamez à l'empereur dans toutes vos lettres...

54

Un vide se creusa dans la poitrine de Sophie. Elle eut peur de la question qu'elle allait poser. Enfin, elle balbutia :

— Mon retour en Russie ?

— Bien sûr ! s'écria Engelke. Votre retour en Russie ! Vous n'y croyiez plus, avouez-le !...

— Non, dit-elle, la voix blanche.

Il se gonfla de solennité joyeuse, brilla de l'œil, des dents, du menton, et dit, en pesant ses mots :

— Je vous annonce que Sa Majesté, ayant pris connaissance de votre dernière requête, en date du 13 octobre 1849, a décidé, eu égard au fait que vous êtes française et que votre mari est mort depuis dix-sept ans, de vous autoriser à rentrer en Russie.

Sophie resta un moment interdite, comme si, à force d'espérer cet événement, elle avait perdu la faculté de s'en réjouir. Le gouverneur lui montra une feuille de papier frappée de l'aigle impériale. Machinalement, elle lut son nom au milieu du document. Cette grande page calligraphiée pour elle toute seule ! Elle marmonna :

— C'est incroyable !... Pourquoi maintenant ?... Pourquoi si tard ?...

— Il n'est jamais trop tard pour bien faire, comme on dit en France ! Je suppose que le remplacement de feu le comte Benkendorff par le comte Alexis Orloff vous a été favorable. Toutefois, je dois vous signaler que vous n'aurez pas le droit d'habiter à Saint-Pétersbourg ni à Moscou. Vous vous fixerez dans votre propriété de Kachtanovka et ne pourrez vous déplacer que dans un rayon de quinze verstes.

A mesure qu'il parlait, Sophie sentait monter en elle une tristesse incoercible. L'idée de la maison qu'elle venait d'acheter acheva de lui ôter tout courage. Elle voyait ses plus chers projets réduits à néant. Et parmi ces ruines, Ferdinand Wolff, debout, étonné, les mains vides. Pourquoi avait-elle écrit toutes ces lettres à l'empereur ? Qu'espérait-elle trouver en Russie, à son retour ? Un neveu qui ne la connaissait que de nom, un domaine où personne n'avait besoin d'elle. En allant là-bas, elle s'exilerait pour la deuxième fois. Son pays, maintenant, c'était la Sibérie ; sa famille, les quelques décembristes dont elle avait partagé les souffrances depuis vingt-trois ans ; son avenir — l'un d'entre eux, peut-être... Au fond, si elle avait poursuivi ces démarches, c'était parce qu'elle était sûre du refus des autorités. Et voici qu'on la prenait au mot. Voici qu'on la punissait en l'exauçant. Elle eut conscience que le gouverneur attendait d'elle des paroles de gratitude. Mais son visage demeurait empesé. Elle murmura :

— Je vous remercie... Je suis très touchée...

Heureusement, Engelke prit son embarras pour un excès d'émotion.

— Et moi, je vous félicite, Madame, dit-il. Vous êtes la première personne à recevoir une pareille faveur de Sa Majesté. J'espère que vous saurez vous en montrer digne. Quand comptez-vous partir ?

— Je ne sais pas encore, dit Sophie. Tout cela est si nouveau pour moi ! Laissez-moi le temps de me ressaisir...

— Mais bien sûr ! Rien ne presse !...

Il la reconduisit jusqu'à la porte avec tous les égards dus à une femme de qualité. Sur le seuil, elle eut encore l'énergie de sourire. Mais, une fois dehors, ses pensées la reprirent si violemment, qu'elle ne vit plus rien autour d'elle. Les décisions du tsar jouaient à contretemps avec les prières qui lui étaient adressées. Il savait très bien qu'il accablait Sophie en lui octroyant la liberté à cinquante-sept ans. Oblige-t-on quelqu'un à boire un verre d'eau dont il n'a pas envie, sous prétexte qu'il l'a réclamé jadis, quand il mourait de soif dans le désert ? Cependant elle pouvait refuser cette grâce. Elle la refuserait ! Au risque de passer pour une ingrate. Le scandale ne l'effrayait pas. « Je resterai. Je m'installerai dans ma nouvelle maison. Ferdinand Wolff viendra chez moi jouer au billard, lire, méditer, se reposer... » Elle sortit de la citadelle, portée par l'espoir et la colère. Sa première idée fut d'aller chez les Fonvizine pour leur rendre compte de son entrevue avec le gouverneur.

Elle était attendue : Nathalie, son mari, Pauline et Ivan Annenkoff, Pierre Svistounoff, Youri Almazoff. Mais Ferdinand Wolff n'était pas là. Il avait été appelé d'urgence pour soigner un malade dans quelque lointain village. Tant mieux ! Ainsi, elle serait plus à l'aise pour expliquer sa déception. Dans le salon provincial, aux gros meubles d'acajou noirci et aux murs violet tendre, l'atmosphère était à l'angoisse. Par habitude, chacun se préparait à une mauvaise nouvelle. Quand Sophie annonça la grâce dont elle était l'objet, une commotion joyeuse bouleversa tous les visages.

— Ma chérie, s'écria Pauline, c'est inespéré !

Ce fut le signal d'une grande démonstration d'allégresse. Etourdie par des exclamations discordantes, Sophie essaya d'affirmer qu'elle n'était pas satisfaite de cette solution. On ne l'écoutait pas, on la congratulait, on l'embrassait, on pleurait sur son épaule.

— La bonne messagère ! La colombe de l'ar-

che ! Vous êtes la colombe de l'arche ! chevrotait
Nathalie en se tamponnant les yeux avec un mouchoir.

A cet instant, il y eut un décrochement dans
l'esprit de Sophie. Elle se vit engagée dans un malentendu affreux. Elle ne pouvait décevoir tous
ces braves gens. Comme elle, ils avaient sollicité
l'autorisation de rentrer en Russie. En acceptant
la faveur impériale, elle créait un précédent dont,
plus tard, ils se réclameraient. En la refusant,
elle risquait de vexer le tsar et de lui ôter pour
toujours le désir de leur être agréable. De quel
poids étaient ses petites préférences de femme solitaire devant l'espoir de toutes ces grandes familles russes éloignées de la terre de leurs ancêtres, de tous ces fils, de toutes ces filles, nés en
exil et qui ne pouvaient même plus prétendre au
nom de leurs parents ?

— Vous êtes heureuse ? demanda Pauline.

— Mais oui ! murmura Sophie.

Elle se contraignait à sourire et ses joues flam-
baient, une boule se formait dans sa gorge.

— Ah ! que je vous envie ! s'exclama Nathalie
en joignant les mains. Vous allez reparaître dans
le monde libre comme une ressuscitée ! Vous donnerez de nos nouvelles à tous nos amis ! Pour la
première fois, quelqu'un des nôtres pourra raconter ce que fut réellement notre vie !

— Tant de mensonges circulent sur notre
compte ! soupira Pauline.

Sans doute ne pouvait-elle oublier cet abominable roman d'Alexandre Dumas, *Le Maître d'Armes,* publié jadis à Paris et dont des exemplaires
étaient parvenus jusqu'à Tobolsk. Son aventure
avec Ivan Annenkoff y était relatée de façon scan-
daleuse. Renseigné par on ne savait qui, l'écrivain

58

la représentait comme une grisette française, éprise d'un professeur d'escrime et vendant ses faveurs à un jeune noble russe dépravé. L'auteur eût mérité une leçon. Mais il vivait à l'autre bout du monde. Comment écrire de Sibérie en France ?

— Vous redresserez l'opinion des gens mal informés, reprit Pauline. Vous préparerez les esprits à l'idée de notre retour à tous !

— Croyez-vous vraiment que, nous aussi, nous pourrons revenir ? demanda Youri Almazoff avec une expression d'avidité pitoyable sur sa figure de vieux jeune homme pommadé.

— Je ne le croyais pas avant cette minute ! Mais puisque le tsar a décidé de rappeler notre amie, tous les espoirs sont permis ! Elle ouvre la voie au rapatriement des autres !...

Chaque parole augmentait la sujétion de Sophie. « Et voilà, pensa-t-elle, maintenant il m'est tout à fait impossible de reculer. Ils me poussent ensemble dans le dos. Plus de petite maison, plus de salle de billard... Je dois partir et paraître contente. Contente de leur joie. Car, moi, je n'en ai aucune. Pas plus que je n'ai de liberté à l'instant où le tsar me l'accorde. »

— Qui sait si, dans deux ou trois ans, nous ne nous retrouverons pas tous en Russie ? dit Ivan Annenkoff rêveusement.

— Taisez-vous, Ivan Alexandrovitch ! s'écria Nathalie en se signant. Ce serait trop beau ! J'ai peur, si j'y pense, de lasser la bienveillance de Dieu ! Une femme qui part pour la Russie ! Montrez-moi comment c'est fait !

Elle saisit la main de Sophie et la pressa contre sa joue :

— Je voudrais être dans votre tête, chérie ! Savoir ce qui s'y passe !...

— Vous seriez très déçue ! dit Sophie en se dégageant avec douceur.

— Moi, grommela Youri Almazoff, je suis heureux que vous ayez obtenu le droit de rentrer en Russie et malheureux que vous nous quittiez ! Tobolsk sans vous sera sinistre !

— Mais puisque nous nous en irons tous bientôt ! dit Pierre Svistounoff.

Evidemment, ils voulaient s'en persuader les uns et les autres, pour atténuer la tristesse de la séparation. Sophie ressentit, comme une insuffisance d'air et de lumière, l'absence de Ferdinand Wolff. La porte qui séparait le salon de la salle à manger s'ouvrit à deux battants. Une table servie apparut, avec un samovar au milieu. Cette vue ranima les courages. Nathalie prit Sophie par le bras pour l'obliger à la suivre. Les dames burent du thé, les messieurs du vin de Madère. On se souriait, les yeux humides, comme dans un banquet de funérailles. A six heures, Sophie, épuisée d'émotion, invoqua une leçon pour rentrer chez elle.

★

Le lendemain matin, elle se leva très tôt, sans presque avoir dormi, s'habilla, huma une tasse de thé brûlant et s'assit, désœuvrée, devant la fenêtre claire. Elle écoutait Douniacha fourgonner dans la cuisine et, le regard perdu, pensait à son prochain voyage. Puisque cette solution était inévitable, elle s'excitait à y prendre goût. Elle n'avait jamais pu revenir sur la tombe de son

60

mari, à Mertvy Koultouk. Encore moins obtenir qu'il fût transporté ailleurs. Il resterait donc au bord du lac Baïkal, pour toujours. Mais, à Kachtanovka, elle retrouverait mieux qu'une croix sur un bourrelet de terre : l'âme de Nicolas, éparse dans l'air de la maison et de la campagne. Et puis, il y aurait Serge, là-bas, Serge qu'elle ne connaissait pas et dont la rencontre ouvrirait peut-être une ère de joie dans sa vie monotone. Serge qui ne pouvait être quelqu'un d'indifférent, puisqu'il était du sang de Nicolas. Serge qu'elle avait, tout enfant, aimé comme son fils !... Pour se persuader de sa chance, elle se rappelait la vieille maison avec ses colonnes blanches, l'allée de sapins noirs, un banc rustique, un étang, les pauvres villages des alentours. Que de morts mêlés à ces feuillages, à ces labours, à ces miroirs d'eau ! On respirait en ce lieu la douce amertume des bonheurs enfuis. Oui, elle y serait bien, parmi les souvenirs de Nicolas, de Marie et même de Michel Borissovitch. Elle renouerait le fil de son destin, après la tragique coupure de la Sibérie. Des cahiers d'élèves attendaient, sur la table. Elle feuilleta le premier, s'engagea dans un défilé de phrases puériles et, tout à coup, s'arrêta, l'esprit cabré. Ferdinand Wolff devait savoir qu'elle avait reçu l'autorisation de partir. S'il n'était pas venu lui en parler ce matin, c'était, sans doute, qu'il était pris par ses malades. Elle décida de passer chez lui. Souvent, elle lui avait rendu visite, pour discuter de choses moins importantes. Dix minutes de conversation entre deux rendez-vous : cela suffisait à éclairer leurs journées. Et sa leçon d'onze heures ? Tant pis, elle enverrait Douniacha pour décommander Tatiana et les fils Soumatokhoff. En un tournemain, elle fut habillée, coiffée et chaussée de bottillons de feutre. Il habitait à l'autre extrémité de la ville européenne. Sophie pressa le pas, poussée par la crainte d'arriver trop tard. Quand elle atteignit la porte du docteur, elle n'avait plus de jambes et son cœur lui battait dans la bouche.

Une servante, enveloppée de tant de fichus, de blouses et de jupes qu'elle ressemblait à une boule de chiffons, la fit entrer dans une pièce exiguë où cinq personnes étaient assises, en rang d'oignon, sur des chaises. Rien que des paysans laids et tristes, qui souffraient en silence. Ils avaient dans les yeux l'humble résignation des bêtes domestiques. Derrière la porte, Ferdinand Wolff parlait, en détachant chaque mot, de façon à être compris par quelqu'un de très simple. Cette voix sans visage émut Sophie, comme si, en l'écoutant, elle eût surpris un secret. Soudain, la porte s'ouvrit et Ferdinand Wolff parut, raccompagnant une vieille qui serrait une bourse dans sa patte jaune et sèche de volaille. En apercevant Sophie, il sourit et chuchota en français :

— Oh ! vous êtes venue !... Justement, je comptais aller vous voir après avoir examiné mes malades !... Entrez vite !...

Elle pénétra dans un petit bureau, encombré de livres et de fioles. Une odeur de phénol la prit à la gorge ; l'encrier était un crâne de plâtre ; dans une corbeille, traînait de la charpie maculée de sang brun ; le papier des murs se décollait ; un paravent dissimulait à demi le lit de camp ; il faisait froid ; on se serait cru dans la chambre d'un vieil étudiant, sans goût, sans argent, sans femme.

Pendant que Sophie s'asseyait sur la chaise réservée aux malades, Ferdinand Wolff retroussa

62

ses manches, versa de l'eau dans une cuvette et
se lava les mains.

— Pauline m'a appris la grande nouvelle, dit-il.
Vous devez être très contente !

Son visage lourd, aux rides tristes, au regard
fatigué, démentait l'entrain de ses paroles. Il s'essuya avec une serviette à franges rouges. Sophie
se sentit gênée, tout à coup, d'être là, devant lui,
en visiteuse. Qu'allait-il se figurer ? Elle se contraignit au calme et dit :

— Bien sûr que je suis contente ! Contente
et triste à la fois ! J'aurai du chagrin de quitter
Tobolsk, notre groupe si gentil, si fraternel ! Mais
on ne peut refuser la liberté !

— Oui, oui, grommela-t-il.

Et ils s'enfoncèrent, face à face, dans le silence.
Au bout d'un moment, il reprit d'une voix plus
ferme :

— D'ailleurs, si vous repoussiez la faveur impériale, on ne vous laisserait tout de même pas
à Tobolsk. Le tsar n'a pas l'habitude d'essuyer des
camouflets de ce genre sans riposter aussitôt.
Pour vous châtier d'avoir mal répondu à sa mansuétude, il vous assignerait un autre lieu de résidence, quelque village perdu, au-delà du lac Baïkal !...

Elle n'y avait pas pensé. Un motif de plus pour
partir. Tout se liguait contre elle. Ferdinand Wolff
jeta la serviette chiffonnée dans un coin et s'assit
derrière la table.

— C'est mieux ainsi, ajouta-t-il. Si vous étiez
restée, je n'aurais pas eu le courage de continuer
à me taire. Et ce que je vous aurais dit aurait
tout gâché entre nous...

— Je ne vous comprends pas, Ferdinand Bogdanovitch, balbutia-t-elle.

En vérité, elle le comprenait si bien que la respiration lui manquait.

— Mais oui, Sophie, dit-il. Ayons le courage de considérer les choses en face. Vous auriez refusé. Et j'aurais été très malheureux... Tandis que maintenant, voyez, rien n'est changé, nous sommes des amis, de grands amis, comme autrefois...

Elle acquiesça d'un battement de paupières. Des secondes passèrent avec lenteur. Ils se regardaient intensément, chacun puisant dans les yeux de l'autre une raison d'aimer et de souffrir. Enfin, elle murmura :

— Quand je songe à la maison que j'ai achetée, où j'étais si impatiente de m'installer !...

— Vous n'aurez pas de peine à la revendre, dit-il.

— Je ne la revendrai pas. J'y ai mis trop de moi-même pour la laisser à des inconnus. D'ailleurs, je n'ai pas besoin d'argent. J'ai pensé...

Elle hésita, puis dit légèrement :

— J'ai pensé qu'il n'y avait pas de dispensaire à Tobolsk et que, peut-être, cette maison vous serait très utile pour recevoir vos malades...

Il eut un mouvement de surprise et l'observa plus attentivement par-dessus ses lunettes. Cette attitude le vieillissait.

— Si c'est pour mes malades, j'accepte, dit-il. Vous êtes très bonne...

Elle baissa le front. Ce n'était pas de la bonté. Elle ne songeait pas aux malades en offrant sa maison à Ferdinand Wolff. Simplement, il lui était agréable de savoir, que, d'une façon ou d'une autre, il vivrait chez elle, qu'elle pourrait l'imaginer de loin.

Il jouait avec une plume d'oie. Ses phalanges étaient tachées par les acides. Un bouton manquait à son habit. Tout à l'heure, il mangerait vite, n'importe quoi, servi par la vieille domestique, sur un coin de table, entre la tête de mort et les bouquins.

Quelqu'un toussa derrière la porte. Sophie se rappela les malades qui attendaient. Elle n'avait plus rien à dire. Elle se leva.

— Serez-vous ce soir chez les Annenkoff ? demanda-t-il.

— Mais oui.

Tandis qu'il se penchait pour lui baiser la main, elle aperçut la peau de son crâne entre ses cheveux clairsemés. Ce signe d'usure physique la bouleversa et, en même temps, la confirma dans l'idée qu'un mariage entre eux, au déclin de leur vie, eût été ridicule et navrant. Un voile de larmes l'aveugla. Elle sortit rapidement, sans tourner la tête.

Les routes étant peu praticables pendant la fonte des neiges, Sophie décida de retarder son départ jusqu'à la fin du mois de mai. Ainsi, du moins, put-elle passer les fêtes de Pâques à Tobolsk, avec ses amis. Comme chaque année, dédaignant les pompes liturgiques de la cathédrale, ils écoutèrent la messe de minuit dans la petite église de la prison. La nef était pleine de bagnards enchaînés. Au moment des génuflexions, un cliquetis se mêlait au chant grave du chœur. Quand le prêtre annonça la résurrection du Christ, le bruit des fers s'enfla brusquement et toutes les têtes hideuses, aux crânes rasés, se balancèrent, de gauche à droite, pour l'accolade fraternelle. Assassins, voleurs, faussaires, s'embrassaient dans la lueur des cierges et la fumée de l'encens. L'enfer célébrait l'espérance.

Dehors, Sophie et ses compagnons défilèrent entre deux rangées de prisonniers, qui tenaient des œufs coloriés dans leurs mains. Ils vendaient aux amateurs ces petits cadeaux de l'administration.

Un souper était préparé chez les Fonvizine.

Champagne et vodkas diverses arrosaient les hors-
d'œuvre et le traditionnel cochon de lait au raifort. Six domestiques servaient deux tables, celle
des grandes personnes et celle des enfants, qui
étaient tous réunis à Tobolsk pour les vacances de
Pâques. Sages et endimanchés, ceux que leurs
camarades de classe traitaient de « fils de forçats » se racontaient à voix basse des histoires
d'école avec autant de passion que leurs parents
discutaient de politique européenne. Au dessert.
il y eut des chansons et des toasts. Sophie regardait, de l'autre côté de la table, Ferdinand Wolff
qui souriait tristement en levant son verre. On
but à l'heureux voyage de Sophie. Elle répondit
qu'elle n'était pas pressée de partir. La soirée
s'acheva à quatre heures du matin.

Le lendemain, le gouverneur Engelke convo-
qua Sophie dans son bureau et lui dit :

— J'ai appris, à mon grand étonnement, qu'au
cours d'un souper chez les Fonvizine vous avez
affirmé ne pouvoir fixer la date de votre départ.

Sophie blêmit. Qui avait rapporté ce propos au
gouverneur ? Un domestique, sans doute.

— C'est exact, dit-elle.

— Voilà qui est regrettable ! Si vous tardez encore, Sa Majesté pourrait prendre ombrage de
votre peu d'empressement à profiter de la grâce
qu'Elle vous a faite. Puisque vous hésitez, je vais
décider à votre place. Vous quitterez Tobolsk le
12 mai prochain.

Une vague de froid toucha le cœur de Sophie.
Elle balbutia :

— Ce... ce n'est pas possible !

— Pourquoi ?

— Je ne serai jamais prête !

— Mais si ! Vous aurez largement le temps de

68

régler vos affaires et de préparer vos bagages. Un gendarme vous accompagnera.

Elle eut un haut-le-corps :

— Pourquoi un gendarme ? Je ne suis pas une criminelle !

— Nul n'en est plus persuadé que moi, Madame. Mais le règlement est formel. Vous ne pouvez voyager seule, puisque vous êtes rappelée d'exil à la condition de vous fixer dans votre propriété de Kachtanovka. Le gendarme d'escorte devra vous conduire d'ici au lieu de votre nouvelle résidence et obtenir une décharge du gouverneur général de la province de Pskov à qui incombera dans l'avenir le soin de vous surveiller.

— C'est une étrange liberté qui m'est offerte là !

— Pour la liberté comme pour toute chose, il faut un apprentissage, dit Engelke en souriant de biais. Nous guidons vos premiers pas avant de vous laisser courir à votre guise. Quoi de plus naturel ? Je fais établir votre passeport et votre feuille de route. Ils seront à votre disposition dès demain.

Elle le quitta, outrée, malheureuse, comme si, en quelques mots, il eût rapproché d'elle une échéance qu'elle voyait lointaine.

Le dimanche suivant, les Annenkoff donnèrent un bal pour la jeunesse. Leur fille aînée, Olga, était très belle. Un ingénieur des mines et un lieutenant de cavalerie la faisaient danser à tour de rôle. Les dames, en les regardant, hasardaient des pronostics de fiançailles. L'orchestre était composé d'anciens forçats. Le gouverneur Engelke avait condescendu à accepter l'invitation, ce qui était un succès pour les décembristes. Il se tenait près du buffet, avec les maîtres de maison. Ferdinand

Wolff, lui, n'avait pu venir, appelé au dernier moment pour soigner un malade dans le quartier tartare. Sophie se sentait très seule. Les éclats de la musique l'assourdissaient. Elle s'étonnait du plaisir que prenaient les jeunes filles à tourner jusqu'au vertige dans les bras de leurs cavaliers. Son regard errant sur la foule accrochait au passage une robe rose ou bleue, des yeux brillants de gaieté, un ruban dans des cheveux blonds, une main gantée, un médaillon sur une chair de lait. Et tout cela lui semblait appartenir à un monde absurde et heureux, dont les raisons de vivre étaient différentes des siennes. A minuit, comme elle s'apprêtait à partir, Ferdinand Wolff apparut. Il jetait les yeux autour de lui avec inquiétude. Elle comprit qu'il la cherchait et en fut réconfortée. Dès qu'il l'aperçut, il se transfigura et se dirigea vers elle, en évitant les importuns qui tâchaient de le retenir. Il ne lui avait jamais reparlé de ses sentiments, depuis la conversation qu'ils avaient eue dans son bureau. Mais Sophie avait l'impression qu'en s'interdisant toute allusion à ce qui aurait pu être, ils aggravaient l'un et l'autre un trouble qu'ils eussent voulu étouffer.

Arrivé devant elle, il commença par l'entretenir de mille riens. Puis, naturellement, ils en vinrent à discuter des travaux qui se poursuivaient dans la petite maison. La salle du premier étage avait déjà été transformée en dortoir et allait recevoir six lits. Sophie le regrettait un peu. Elle eût aimé pouvoir imaginer Ferdinand Wolff jouant au billard avec des amis, le soir, après ses visites. Pour le reste, elle était enchantée de sa décision. Chaque jour, elle se rendait au chantier, comme si elle eût été personnellement intéressée à la réussite de l'ouvrage. Tout devait être terminé le 15 juin. Elle ne serait pas là pour l'inauguration du dispensaire.

— C'est trop injuste ! dit Ferdinand Wolff. Il faut que j'en parle au gouverneur. Je suis sûr que, si je lui explique nos raisons, il nous accordera un sursis d'un mois !

Et, malgré les protestations de Sophie, il alla chercher Engelke, qui fumait le cigare, entouré de messieurs déférents. Le gouverneur se laissa amener, trottant sur ses petites jambes, le bedon en avant, le sourire aux lèvres, mais, en présence de Sophie il se montra aussi intraitable que par le passé.

— Fiez-vous à ma vieille expérience, dit-il. Quand une résolution est prise, en retarder l'application c'est multiplier les chances d'en souffrir. D'ailleurs, je ne peux plus rien changer. J'ai transmis les dates à Saint-Pétersbourg. Vous êtes attendue en Russie, Madame !

Il s'inclina et tourna les talons, laissant Sophie et Ferdinand Wolff face à face. L'orchestre jouait une valse. Des couples virevoltèrent, insouciants, sous le lustre aux petites flammes inégales. Un courant d'air venait d'une porte-fenêtre entrouverte. Sophie et Ferdinand Wolff sortirent sur le perron. La fraîcheur d'une nuit de printemps les enveloppa.

— Plus que huit jours ! dit Sophie.

— Engelke a raison, grommela Ferdinand Wolff avec une rage soudaine. Il vaudrait mieux que ce fût demain !

Des rires passèrent en farandole derrière leur dos. Les yeux levés vers le ciel semé d'étoiles, Sophie avait la sensation de tomber dans le vide. Pauline vint chercher le docteur parce qu'une jeune fille s'était foulé le pied en dansant.

Le 12 mai, à l'aube, un gendarme se présenta au domicile de Sophie. Trente ans au plus, grand et fort, le visage hâlé, la moustache noire hérissée comme un écouvillon, il déclara se nommer Dobroliouboff et avoir ordre d'accompagner la femme Ozareff jusqu'au terme de son voyage. Par égard pour elle, le gouverneur avait commandé deux tarantass : elle monta seule dans le premier, le second étant réservé à son garde du corps. L'itinéraire fixé par les autorités prévoyait un trajet d'un millier de verstes, par voie de terre, de Tobolsk à Perm. Là, Sophie et son compagnon devaient embarquer sur un bateau, qui, en suivant le cours de la Kama, puis en remontant la Volga, les amènerait en une semaine à Nijni-Novgorod. Il n'y aurait plus ensuite qu'à reprendre la route pour aller, de relais en relais, à Saint-Pétersbourg et à Kachtanovka dans la province de Pskov. En tout, près d'un mois de pérégrinations ! Sophie en avait fait plus pour rejoindre Nicolas à Tchita. Mais, à cette époque-là, elle était jeune, un espoir exaltant la guidait, elle se dévouait à une cause.

Aujourd'hui, elle partait sans entrain, à la rencontre d'elle ne savait quoi. Ce qu'elle laissait ici comptait tellement plus que ce qu'elle pourrait trouver là-bas ! Elle fit ses adieux à Douniacha, qui sanglotait, à quelques voisins, et s'étonna qu'aucun de ses amis ne fût venu l'embrasser avant son départ. Il y avait bien eu, la veille, une soirée en son honneur, chez les Fonvizine ; on avait bu, pleuré, chanté ; mais elle avait cru qu'elle reverrait les décembristes ce matin encore. Leur désaffection la peina. En arrivant au hameau de Pod-Tchouvachy, elle eut l'explication du mystère : ils étaient tous réunis au bord de l'eau, près du bac qu'elle devait prendre pour traverser l'Irtych. Même deux de ses élèves s'étaient dérangés : la petite Tatiana et l'un des fils Soumatokhoff. Le gendarme, bon prince, consentit à un dernier échange de recommandations et de baisers. Ferdinand Wolff n'était pas venu. Mais sa vieille servante était là. Elle remit à Sophie un papier plié en quatre et cacheté de cire noire. Sophie le glissa dans sa manche. Un ciel bleu tendre, strié de nuages blancs, dominait, au loin, les toits de la ville. Le fleuve charriait de minces glaçons. Sur les berges spongieuses, la nouvelle herbe se dressait par touffes.

— Madame Ozareff, je vous en prie, le passeur attend ! dit le gendarme.

— Une minute, une minute encore ! balbutia Sophie.

Nathalie se jeta sur elle, comme une assoiffée, l'étreignit, la palpa, la barbouilla de larmes, la couvrit de signes de croix. Puis Sophie passa aux mains de Pauline, de Macha Frantzeff, d'Olga Annenkoff, et chacune lui chuchota quelque douceur à l'oreille. Les hommes se montrèrent, avec

elle, aussi émus, mais moins bavards. Youri Almazoff, qui se prétendait « toujours amoureux et
toujours meurtri », l'aida à remonter en voiture
et lui baisa les deux mains en marmonnant :

— Ma jeunesse, ma jeunesse qui s'en va !

Elle avait hâte d'être loin pour lire la lettre
de Ferdinand Wolff. Enfin, le bac, portant les deux
tarantass, s'écarta de la rive. Sous les regards de
Sophie, la déchirure entre le passé et le présent
s'agrandit. Attachés au sol de l'exil, ses compagnons d'autrefois n'étaient déjà plus que des souvenirs. Elle agita son mouchoir, jusqu'au moment où les deux tarantass eurent retrouvé la
terre ferme. Les chevaux, longtemps contenus,
s'élancèrent sur la route. Sophie décacheta le pli
de Ferdinand Wolff et lut, malgré les cahots :

« Ma chère et tendre amie,

« Jamais je n'oublierai ce que vous avez été
pour moi. Si je continue à travailler, à vivre, ce
sera pour me montrer digne de votre confiance.
Excusez-moi de n'être pas venu, ce matin : je
n'aurais pas supporté la curiosité compatissante de nos amis. Que va-t-il vous arriver, loin
de moi ? Dieu vous garde, Sophie ! Je prierai pour
vous. Je suis très malheureux. Il y a un grand vide
soudain dans mon existence ! Adieu, adieu, Sophie ! »

« FERDINAND WOLFF ».

Elle fléchit la tête. La tristesse montait en elle
rapidement, la submergeait, l'étouffait. Puis, par
une bizarre alchimie, un peu de bonheur se mêla
à son désespoir. Elle s'abandonna à ce sentiment
doux amer, à cette paix mélancolique, comme en
donne parfois la contemplation d'un grand espace
dénudé.

★

Parcourant en sens inverse la route qu'elle avait suivie vingt-trois ans plus tôt, Sophie reconnaissait avec émotion certaines étapes de son premier voyage. Mais alors, son compagnon était Nikita, dont la jeunesse éclairait le monde, et non ce pesant et inutile gendarme, sanglé dans un uniforme bleu. Dobroliouboff était peu loquace, mais avait un grand appétit. Il s'empiffrait aux relais et digérait en voiture. Cela ne l'empêchait pas de surveiller, d'un petit œil porcin, les moindres mouvements de Sophie pendant qu'on changeait de chevaux, à la maison de poste. Craignait-il de la voir s'enfuir à pied dans la steppe ou se glisser dans la voiture d'un autre voyageur ? Elle lui avait reproché un jour de la traiter en prisonnière, bien qu'elle fût redevenue une femme libre. Il avait répondu, sans se démonter :

— Vous n'êtes ni libre ni prisonnière ; vous êtes prisonnière-libre.

Cette formule avait paru à Sophie le juste reflet de la réalité russe. Dobroliouboff lui avait expliqué aussi que sa carrière dans la gendarmerie dépendait de l'exactitude avec laquelle il s'acquitterait de sa mission :

— Vous me considérez comme un gardien, mais c'est moi qui suis à votre merci, Madame. Qu'il vous arrive quelque chose, et mes chefs ne me le pardonneront pas. C'est pourquoi je vous prie de m'aider dans cette affaire. Si tout se passe bien, nous en aurons, vous et moi, beaucoup de satisfaction...

— Est-ce votre premier voyage à Saint-Pétersbourg ? demanda-t-elle.

— Le dix-septième.

— Toujours comme convoyeur ?

— Non, les autres fois je portais des plis offi-

76

ciels, dit-il en se gonflant de suffisance. Des dépêches pour des ministres. C'est moins agréable, parce qu'on n'a pas de compagnie !

A mesure qu'ils approchaient de l'Oural, le gendarme se dégelait et affectait même une certaine galanterie. Sophie le trouvait bien jeune pour être son gardien. Par manque de chevaux, ils durent passer la nuit à Ekaterinbourg, sur les banquettes de la maison de poste. Le matin, en prenant son thé dans la salle commune, Dobroliouboff marmonna d'un air embarrassé :

— Je me demande pourquoi nous voyageons dans deux tarantass !

Elle ne comprit pas tout de suite où il voulait en venir.

— C'est très bien ainsi, dit-elle.

— C'est très bien, mais ça coûte cher !

Elle s'indigna :

— Est-ce vous qui payez ?

— Non, bien sûr, c'est l'Etat ! J'ai sur moi la somme nécessaire pour régler tous les frais. Mais, si je puis faire des économies, ce sera autant de gagné pour moi. Notre solde est très maigre. J'ai de vieux parents, une sœur infirme. Cela vous gênerait vraiment si je montais dans votre voiture ? Nous ne sommes plus tellement loin de Perm !

Elle demeura interloquée, puis haussa les épaules :

— Si vous voulez !

— Je vous remercie, dit-il avec sentiment.

Et, aussitôt, il commanda du jambon, des œufs durs et un quatrième verre de thé.

Le tarantass de Sophie était assez spacieux pour qu'on pût y tenir à deux avec les bagages. Dobroliouboff s'assit en face d'elle, sur des sacs de paille, inclina la tête et se mit à ronfler. Des souvenirs de nourriture devaient lui parfumer la bouche. Sa moustache frémissait de plaisir. Sophie le regardait dormir et pensait aux amis qu'elle avait quittés et qu'elle ne reverrait jamais plus. Le destin des décembristes lui apparaissait encore plus étrange à distance. Dans leur jeunesse, ils avaient cru que leur mission était de combattre jusqu'à la mort pour leurs convictions politiques ; dans leur âge mûr, ils avaient abdiqué tout héroïsme pour se consacrer au défrichement des terres et des esprits. Grâce à eux, les rudes habitants de la Sibérie avaient vu, pour la première fois, avec stupeur, des gens qui aimaient lire des livres et écrire des lettres, des gens qui se passionnaient davantage pour les idées que pour l'argent, des gens qui n'avaient plus ni fortune ni situation, et dont cependant il était impossible de nier l'ascendant sur leur entourage. Quel que fût le village pourri où l'administration reléguait un de ces insurgés, on pouvait être sûr qu'il se rendrait utile, fonderait une bibliothèque, instruirait des enfants. Sophie se rappela avec amusement la réflexion d'un arpenteur de Kourgane : « Dommage qu'il n'y ait pas eu plus de décembristes arrêtés en 1825 ! Encore quelques centaines de forçats dans leur genre, et la Sibérie serait à la tête des pays civilisés ! » Elle sourit et se dit que, peut-être, pour les générations futures, la vraie gloire des décembristes ne serait pas de s'être révoltés, un jour, contre le tsar, mais d'avoir voué le reste de leur vie à la lutte contre l'apathie et l'ignorance de leurs semblables. Un homme comme Ferdinand Wolff, par exemple, était un piètre révolutionnaire, mais tous ceux qui l'avaient approché lui étaient redevables d'un enrichissement moral. Et Poushine, Lounine, Poggio... Les seuls qui se fussent abaissés étaient ceux qui avaient épousé des femmes au-dessous de leur condition. Tel était le cas de Bassarguine, d'Obolensky, de Kuhelbecker, qui par fatigue, par faiblesse, par horreur de la solitude, s'étaient mariés avec des paysannes ou des bonnes d'enfants. Il y en avait aussi qui avaient sombré dans l'alcoolisme et la misère. Mais ils étaient peu nombreux. Dans l'ensemble, presque tous avaient dignement surmonté l'épreuve de la relégation. En regagnant la Russie, Sophie avait l'impression de laisser derrière elle le pays des âmes nobles pour se rapprocher du pays des mensonges, des jalousies et des lâchetés devant le pouvoir. Saurait-elle respirer dans cet air confiné après avoir connu l'atmosphère salubre de la Sibérie ? Il est vrai qu'elle s'arrêterait peu de temps à Saint-Pétersbourg et qu'à Kachtanovka elle serait loin de toutes les intrigues !

La route coupait un pays non point montagneux mais ondulé, parsemé d'étangs et de petits lacs. Puis la pente se raidit à l'entrée d'une épaisse forêt. Le gendarme se réveilla, jeta un regard autour de lui et dit :

— Nous traversons la propriété des Démidoff.

Une heure plus tard, on changea de chevaux, on prit une collation, on repartit au son des clochettes et, avant de se rendormir, Dobroliouboff marmonna :

— Toujours la propriété des Démidoff !

Sophie se revit, enfant, penchée sur un livre d'images : le Chat Botté présentait les immenses domaines du marquis de Carabas. Toute une province aux mains d'un seul homme. Ce qui semblait incroyable en France était normal en Russie. Encore des verstes et des verstes de route bosselée, dans la poussière, le craquement des roues et l'odeur du cuir chaud. Les membres endoloris, la tête creuse et sonore, Sophie attendait avec impatience la prochaine halte. Le gendarme rota discrètement et ouvrit les yeux. Son estomac était réglé comme une horloge : il s'éveillait toujours dix minutes avant le relais. Le ciel s'assombrissait au-dessus des cimes noires et inégales des mélèzes. Soudain, la maison de poste surgit, grande, massive, toute en rondins, pareille à une montagne de bûches superposées.

— Ici, dit le gendarme, j'ai mangé autrefois d'extraordinaires gélinottes.

Le tarantass s'engouffra dans la cour. Des valets d'écurie sautèrent à la tête des chevaux et se laissèrent traîner par eux jusqu'à l'arrêt de la voiture.

★

Arrivés à Perm, Sophie et le gendarme apprirent que le bateau pour Nijni-Novgorod ne partirait que dans vingt-quatre heures. Vite, il fallait chercher une chambre pour la nuit. Ils en trouvèrent une à l'Hôtel du Club. Un lit, mais pas d'oreiller, pas de traversins, pas de draps. Sophie se coucha toute habillée sur un matelas suspect, Dobroliouboff dormant dans la salle commune. Le lendemain, elle voulut visiter la ville. Son convoyeur lui fit observer qu'il était obligé de la suivre dans tous ses déplacements. Elle sortit donc, flanquée du gendarme qui cambrait la taille, troussait sa moustache et roulait des yeux.

Il n'y avait rien d'intéressant à voir dans ce grand bourg provincial. De larges rues rectilignes aux trottoirs en planches, des palissades enfermant un carré d'herbe et quelques bouleaux, de petites maisons de bois, toutes semblables, avec un perron, des rideaux de tulle et des pots de fleurs derrière les doubles fenêtres. C'était dimanche et tous les passants se hâtaient vers le jardin public, au bord de la Kama. Là, des allées de tilleuls, d'ormes et de frênes canalisaient le flot des promeneurs : musulmans aux longs caftans, jeunes filles tartares à la taille souple, officiers en uniforme vert, bourgeois en redingote noire et chapeau rond, dames russes habillées à la mode de Paris... Sophie et Dobroliouboff suivirent le mouvement, mitraillés de tous côtés par des regards curieux. Ils descendirent ainsi jusqu'au port. Un bateau à vapeur manœuvrait pour accoster. Sa haute cheminée fumait. Ses roues à aubes brassaient l'eau avec violence. Sophie n'avait jamais rien vu de pareil. Elle en était restée à l'époque de la marine à voile. Cette constatation lui donna la mesure du temps qu'elle avait passé en exil. Ne disait-on pas aussi qu'on pourrait se rendre bientôt par le chemin de fer de Moscou à Saint-Pétersbourg ? Les progrès de la science étaient vertigineux. A ce rythme-là, les hommes deviendraient fous d'orgueil. Le bateau remorquait une énorme barcasse, aux flancs percés de fenêtres grillagées. Derrière les barreaux, se pressait un salmigondis de visages blafards. Encore des forçats ! La prison flottante se rangea le long du quai. Sur le pont, des soldats s'affairaient, des officiers hurlaient des ordres, des marins ouvraient les écoutilles. Comme un ver sort d'un fruit, une procession de bagnards émergea lentement à l'air libre. Ils pouvaient être deux ou trois cents. Leurs faces hâves, barbues, disaient la fatigue d'un long voyage. Traînant leurs chaînes, ils descendirent la passerelle et s'assemblèrent en colonne par quatre.

Ils étaient vêtus de capotes grises et certains portaient un losange de drap jaune cousu dans le dos.

— Ce sont bien des condamnés de droit commun ? demanda Sophie.

— Oui, dit Dobroliouboff. Rassurez-vous : il n'y a pas un politique dans le tas !

— Où va-t-on les mener ?

— A la maison d'arrêt, en attendant de les diriger sur Ekaterinbourg.

— Y a-t-il souvent des arrivages de bagnards, à Perm ?

— Deux fois par semaine, pendant la belle saison.

En effet, ce spectacle devait être habituel aux badauds, car ils contemplaient le débarquement avec indifférence. Des soldats, baïonnette au canon, encadrèrent les forçats. Un officier à cheval prit la tête du détachement. Le convoi se mit en marche, dans le tintement des chaînes balancées. Le public se dispersa pour aller vers le kiosque à musique, d'où s'échappaient les accords sautillants d'une polka. Dobroliouboff, qui observait Sophie du coin de l'œil, lui proposa, pour la distraire, de visiter, à l'autre bout du quai, le bateau sur lequel ils embarqueraient demain.

★

Il n'y avait que trois cabines particulières sur le bateau et toutes les trois étaient occupées. Sophie dut se contenter de réserver sa place, pour la nuit, sur l'un des canapés de la salle commune, qui servait à la fois de restaurant, de dortoir et de fumoir. Dans l'entrepont, s'entassaient les passagers guenilleux et odorants de la troisième classe.

82

Au-dessus, s'élevait une plate-forme, à laquelle n'accédaient que les possesseurs d'un billet de première ou de seconde. Un kiosque, haut perché, permettait de contempler le paysage en se tenant à l'abri du soleil. Ce fut là que Sophie s'installa après avoir rangé ses bagages. Elle eût aimé être seule. Mais Dobroliouboff, qui la suivait comme son ombre, vint s'asseoir à côté d'elle, sur le banc. La rivière coulait entre des berges verdoyantes et boisées. A travers le grondement monotone des machines et le sourd clapotis de l'eau ruisselant sur les pales des roues, on percevait, au loin, des chants d'oiseaux. Le navire étant chauffé au bois, la fumée, que le vent rabattait sur le pont, avait un parfum agréable. Un bercement imperceptible agitait la coque. Sophie se laissait aller à une rêverie sinueuse. Soudain, elle remarqua que le gendarme, affalé contre son épaule, donnait des signes de malaise. Il s'épongeait le front, déboutonnait son col et déglutissait fortement sa salive. Son teint coloré virait au gris de cendre.

— Vous ne vous sentez pas bien ? demanda-t-elle.

— Pas très, marmonna Dobroliouboff. A chaque voyage, c'est la même chose. Je ne supporte pas le bateau.

— Pourtant, il ne tangue presque pas.

— Cela me suffit, soupira Dobroliouboff. Peut-être que si je mangeais un peu...

Il se leva sur des jambes molles et descendit dans la salle commune. Comme il était midi, Sophie décida de le suivre. Il n'y avait pas de table d'hôte à bord. Chacun pouvait se faire servir une collation à l'heure qui lui plaisait. Ayant mangé et bu, Dobroliouboff parut plus malade encore et se précipita dehors pour se soulager. Sophie le retrouva dans le kiosque, étendu de tout son long sur la banquette. Elle lui donna des sels à respirer et lui posa un mouchoir imbibé d'eau fraîche sur le front. C'était une situation très humiliante pour un gendarme. A plusieurs reprises, il murmura :

— Je suis déshonoré !

Puis, peu à peu, il s'habitua au mouvement du bateau, reboutonna son col et s'assit, l'œil brouillé et la bouche pâteuse. Quelques passagers, ayant assisté de loin à la scène, se détournèrent, par crainte qu'il ne leur reprochât leur indiscrétion. L'uniforme leur en imposait plus que le personnage.

Les rives de la Kama se bombaient en douces collines, se couronnaient de villages charmants. Au milieu d'un pré, apparaissait une plaque de neige entourée de fleurs. Le feuillage naissant des bouleaux et des trembles suspendait un pointillé vert tendre dans l'air bleu. De loin en loin, surgissait la barque à voile d'un pêcheur ou un énorme radeau de forestier, qui descendait le courant avec sa cargaison de planches et de rondins. Sur tout ce bois de construction et de chauffage, solidement assemblé, se dressait une isba, habitée par les mariniers et leur famille. Quand le steamer les dépassait, une grande vague soulevait le radeau et des enfants en chemises rouges agitaient la main et criaient avec des voix acides.

Vers six heures du soir, le navire accosta le long d'une jetée, pour renouveler sa provision de combustible. C'étaient des femmes qui s'occupaient du chargement. Jeunes ou vieilles, le teint cuit, un foulard de cotonnade noué sous le menton, elles allaient et venaient de la rive au bateau, transportant des piles de bûches sur des brancards. Parvenues au-dessus de la trappe centrale, elles y déversaient leur fardeau, qui s'écroulait dans la cale avec un fracas d'avalanche. Tous les habitants du village voisin étaient rassemblés sur la berge. Les hommes regardaient travailler leurs épouses ou leurs filles, mais ne les aidaient pas. Debout, pieds nus dans la poussière, des marchands offraient sur des caisses de bois, du kwass, du lait, du poisson séché et de grossières pâtisseries. Quelques passagers de troisième classe descendirent à terre pour se ravitailler.

A huit heures du soir, le ciel était encore clair. Une lumière mauve indéfinissable irradiait des eaux lustrées de la Kama. Des insectes bourdonnaient autour d'un fanal. Dans les buissons du rivage, des rossignols se mirent à chanter. Jamais Sophie n'en avait entendu un si grand nombre. Une passagère revint à bord, les bras chargés de muguet fleuri.

— Ai-je le temps d'aller en chercher, moi aussi ? demanda Sophie.

— Avec votre permission, c'est moi qui irai ! s'écria Dobroliouboff.

Il se précipita à terre, disparut dans le crépuscule et resta si longtemps absent, que Sophie crut qu'il ne reviendrait pas. Elle se demandait avec inquiétude ce qui se passerait si le bateau partait sans lui. Il avait tous les papiers : elle n'existait pas, administrativement, sans son passeport et sa feuille de route. Déjà, les femmes de peine, ayant fini leur chargement, s'alignaient sur la jetée pour se faire payer par le capitaine. Les machines se mettaient en marche et une vibration mécanique montait à travers le pont dans les jambes des voyageurs. Affolée, Sophie scrutait le rivage nocturne et priait de toutes ses forces pour qu'on lui rendît son gendarme. La cloche du bord retentit au-dessus de sa tête. Alors qu'elle se désespérait, comme une épouse délaissée, Dobroliouboff surgit, courant à pas menus sur l'étroite passerelle. Il rapportait quatre brins de muguet : tout ce qu'il avait pu trouver ! Elle le remercia, soulagée. Le navire s'éloigna de la berge en battant l'eau légèrement. Puis il prit de la vitesse et s'entoura d'une collerette d'écume phosphorescente. La cheminée fumait très fort. L'inconvénient du chauffage au bois, c'était la quantité de flammèches qui s'échappaient vers le ciel et retombaient sur le pont. Dans la nuit calme, un véritable feu d'artifice dominait le bateau. De temps à autre, une femme poussait un petit cri et éteignait d'une tape l'escarbille qui s'était posée sur sa robe. On ne voyait plus les rives. Des lampes à pétrole s'allumèrent sur le navire. Dobroliouboff se plaignit d'avoir une faim de loup. Guéri de ses nausées il rêvait d'un repas copieux « à la sibérienne ».

Sophie le rejoignit dans la salle commune et se contenta de commander du thé, avec du pain et des confitures. Lui, en revanche, avala une soupe rafraîchissante, à base de fines herbes, de raifort, de choux et de kwass, où nageaient des morceaux de poisson fumé et de gros glaçons. Ensuite, vinrent un *sterlet* de la Volga, entouré de carottes et de câpres, de la viande en sauce et une gelée de framboise, si compacte, que la cuillère restait plantée dedans à la verticale. Ayant arrosé le tout d'une bière de Kazan rousse et mousseuse, le gendarme se renversa sur le dossier de sa chaise avec un visage radieux. Sophie comprit que, s'il avait économisé l'argent du voyage en tarantass, ce n'était point tant pour secourir sa famille indigente, que pour se payer de bons repas. Peut-être même cette famille n'existait-elle que dans son imagination. Elle l'admira dans sa ronde simplicité de goinfre. Comme la plupart des passagers s'étaient réunis pour souper à la même heure, il y avait beaucoup de monde autour de la grande table qui occupait le milieu de la salle. On se serrait les coudes et on mangeait, côte à côte, sans se connaître. Des serveurs tartares, en frac noir et tablier blanc, s'affairaient dans le dos des convives. Les conversations entrecroisées maintenaient, sous le plafond bas, un brouhaha de kermesse. Aux riches fumets de la nourriture se mêlait l'odeur des lampes à pétrole dont les mèches filaient. Pas un souffle d'air n'entrait par les fenêtres ouvertes. Sophie, incommodée, remonta sur le pont avec Dobroliouboff.

La nuit était si sombre, que l'eau et le ciel se confondaient. Dans tout ce noir, les roues, en tournant, soulevaient des dentelles d'écume et la cheminée crachait des étincelles d'or. Le gendarme soupira profondément et dit :

— A Nijni-Novgorod, on pourra se reposer un jour ou deux, si vous voulez. Il y a là-bas de très bonnes auberges. La ville est gaie. Mais peut-être êtes-vous pressée d'arriver ?

— Oh ! non, dit Sophie.

— Personne ne vous attend ?

— Personne.

— Alors, c'est un triste voyage ?

Elle ne répondit pas. Fallait-il qu'elle fût pitoyable pour qu'un gendarme s'avisât de la plaindre ! La lettre de Ferdinand Wolff lui revint en mémoire : « Que va-t-il vous arriver, loin de moi ? » Elle eut peur de l'avenir.

— Il est tard, dit-elle. Je vais descendre.

Dobroliouboff lui emboîta le pas. De nombreux passagers s'étaient déjà étendus, tout habillés, sur les couchettes de la salle commune. D'autres continuaient à boire du thé et à jouer aux cartes. Il n'y avait plus qu'une lampe sur deux d'allumée. Sophie s'allongea sur une banquette de cuir, les jambes enveloppées dans un plaid, son sac de voyage glissé sous la nuque en guise d'oreiller. Dobroliouboff se recroquevilla, en chien de fusil, sur la banquette d'en face. A peine eut-il fermé les yeux, qu'il se mit à ronfler. Sophie envia ce repos de brute rassasiée. Elle avait beau se tourner dans tous les sens, le sommeil fuyait ses paupières. Les gens assis à la grande table parlaient haut, riaient, sans se soucier de ceux qui voulaient dormir. Quatre gros marchands fêtaient, en buvant du champagne, la conclusion d'une affaire. Puis ils se mirent à chanter. Personne ne protesta. La fumée des pipes et des cigares flottait en écharpe entre les grêles colonnes qui soutenaient le plafond.

À deux heures du matin, il ne restait plus qu'une dizaine de joueurs qui claquaient des cartes sur la table en poussant des jurons. Enfin, eux aussi se couchèrent. Un marin éteignit les lampes. Seules brillèrent les veilleuses bleues et rouges, suspendues dans le coin des icônes. Pour détendre ses nerfs, Sophie essaya de calculer dans combien de temps elle arriverait à Kachtanovka. Encore six jours de bateau, plus huit jours de voiture, plus... Elle s'embrouilla dans ses comptes et se désintéressa du résultat. La figure inclinée vers la cloison, elle sentait sa raison s'engourdir et ses membres se dénouer. Bientôt, le silence ne fut plus troublé autour d'elle que par les respirations rauques des passagers, le bruit sourd des machines et un ruissellement de cascade qui provenait des roues à aubes tournant sans relâche dans l'eau.

★

Sophie et son convoyeur débarquèrent à Nijni-Novgorod le 1er juin, à midi, par un violent orage. Pendant qu'elle s'installait dans une chambre d'hôtel, petite mais propre, avec un vrai lit et de vrais draps, Dobroliouboff se rendit au bureau de gouverneur pour faire viser la feuille de route. A toutes les haltes importantes, il devait signaler son passage pour permettre aux autorités de vérifier que le voyage se déroulait selon l'itinéraire et dans les délais prévus. Ensuite, il irait commander un tarantass et des chevaux afin de repartir le lendemain, par la route, en direction de Moscou. Après s'être lavée des pieds à la tête dans un baquet d'eau chaude et avoir changé de vêtements, Sophie s'assit à la fenêtre. La pluie coulait sur la vitre et le paysage se déformait dans ce déluge lourd et gris. Subitement, les nuages se déchirèrent, l'averse s'arrêta et les toits brillèrent dans le soleil. Sophie voulut profiter de l'éclaircie pour visiter la ville. Il y avait tant de choses à voir à Nijni-Novgorod : l'emplacement de la foire, le Kremlin, la cathédrale, le couvent Pétchersky !... Elle se préparait à sortir, lorsqu'on frappa à la porte de sa chambre. C'était Dobroliouboff. Elle lui trouva l'air important et préoccupé.

— Votre visite au gouverneur s'est bien passée ? demanda-t-elle.

Il fronça les sourcils :

— Oui et non. J'ai une mauvaise nouvelle pour vous. Un de vos parents est mort. Un nommé Sédoff.

Elle pensa immédiatement à Serge, perdit le souffle et balbutia :

— Mon neveu ?... Serge... Serge Vladimirovitch Sédoff ?...

— Non, dit-il. Le père : Vladimir Karpovitch.

L'angoisse de Sophie tomba d'un seul coup. Une apathie lui succéda. La disparition de cet homme ne contentait même plus le besoin de vengeance qui l'avait si longtemps et fortement tourmentée.

— Comment est-il mort ? demanda-t-elle.

Dobroliouboff grimaça du nez et de la moustache :

— Une sale histoire ! Il a été, paraît-il, assassiné par ses moujiks, le mois dernier. Le gouverneur vient de l'apprendre par une dépêche officielle. Il m'a dit de vous prévenir doucement. Il voudrait vous voir.

— Je vais y aller, dit-elle, je vais y aller tout de suite...

Mais elle ne bougeait pas. Ce meurtre, il lui semblait qu'elle l'avait déjà vécu dans une autre vie. C'était un dénouement connu. Une redite. Vladimir Karpovitch Sédoff ne pouvait finir autrement. Elle goûta, le temps d'un éclair, l'impression d'entrer en contact avec l'envers du monde. Son voyage prit une signification dont elle ne s'était pas avisée plus tôt. Serge orphelin. La route libre. Un élan d'espoir la souleva. « Mon Dieu ! que m'arrive-t-il ? Je suis heureuse ! » songea-t-elle avec un tremblement. Le gendarme, surpris, la regardait sourire dans le vide.

DEUXIÈME PARTIE

1

Un écriteau à demi effacé accrocha le regard de Sophie. Elle lut : Kachtanovka. Il se fit, dans tout son corps, un silence de préparation. Déjà, deux rangées de vieux sapins sombres et haillonneux s'écartaient devant elle, comme le jour où, pour la première fois, elle avait suivi cette allée. Elle arrivait de France avec un jeune mari qui devait la présenter à son père. Leur calèche dansait dans les ornières inégales. Elle portait une witchoura garnie de petit-gris. Nicolas lui serrait le bras, avec tendresse, avec inquiétude. Elle le regarda et vit à sa place un gendarme, à la rude moustache noire dans un visage luisant de sueur. Dobroliouboff dit :

— C'est un très beau domaine. Combien d'âmes ?

— Je ne sais pas, murmura-t-elle.

Le présent et le passé entrechoquaient leurs images dans sa tête, en un mouvement de ressac. Elle reconnaissait un carrefour, un rocher couvert de mousse, le toit de la cabane de bains, et chaque détail suscitait tant de réminiscences, que l'air en était épaissi. Comment allait-elle retrouver Serge ? Elle avait beau essayer de se le figurer en homme, elle le revoyait toujours au berceau. Le pauvre garçon devait être très affecté par la mort de son père. Elle lui avait écrit pour lui exprimer ses condoléances et le prévenir de son arrivée. Et, en passant pas Pskov, elle s'était présentée avec le gendarme chez le gouverneur. Tout était en règle. De grands cahots la secouèrent. La route avait toujours été défoncée à cet endroit. Un chien sortit des fourrés, puis un autre, et ils se mirent à courir en aboyant à côté de l'attelage. Des paysans se montrèrent au débouché d'un sentier. Ils ôtèrent leur chapeau devant la visiteuse. C'étaient, peut-être, les fils de ceux qu'elle avait soignés autrefois. Enfin, dans une trouée de lumière, surgit la maison. Cette façade au crépi rose écaillé, au toit vert et aux colonnes blanches, appelait Sophie, de toutes ses fenêtres, comme un visage. Malade d'émotion, elle fouilla des yeux le groupe qui se tenait devant le perron. Rien que des domestiques. Serge était-il absent ? Le tarantass s'arrêta en grinçant et Dobroliouboff sauta à terre. Des serviteurs se précipitèrent sur les bagages. Sophie descendit à son tour, et, tout à coup, ses jambes faiblirent, son cœur s'arrêta de battre. La double porte donnant sur le perron venait de s'ouvrir et Nicolas s'avançait vers elle. Nicolas à vingt-cinq ans, grand, mince, les épaules larges, le visage noble et régulier sous un casque de cheveux blonds. Il portait une redingote noire à col de velours, une cravate noire, des souliers noirs. Elle le reconnaissait et il ne la reconnaissait pas. Avait-elle tant vieilli ? Elle fut prise de vertige en face de ce revenant impassible. Puis, brisée, elle balbutia :

— Serge !... Ah ! mon Dieu, comme tu lui ressembles !...

Il lui baisa la main et l'invita à entrer, ainsi que le gendarme. Elle revit, comme à travers une brume, les trophées de chasse, les fusils, les couteaux qui décoraient le vestibule ; puis elle pénétra dans le bureau de son beau-père. Les mêmes rideaux vert épinard encadraient la fenêtre et, sur la table de travail, brillait le même presse-papier en malachite. Il était impossible de regarder cet objet sans imaginer les vieux doigts noueux de Michel Borissovitch qui le caressaient jadis machinalement. Sophie se laissa descendre dans un fauteuil. Aucun des êtres qu'elle avait connus à Kachtanovka n'était là pour la recevoir : Nicolas, Marie, Michel Borissovitch... morts, morts, morts !...

— Le voyage vous a fatiguée, ma tante ! dit Serge en français.

Elle tressaillit : la voix de Nicolas, en plus métallique peut-être. Mais Serge parlait le français moins bien que son oncle et avec un fort accent russe. Elle lui sut gré d'avoir appris cette langue, comme s'il l'eût fait par égard pour elle.

— Oui, marmonna-t-elle. Surtout la dernière étape...

En disant cela, elle l'observait intensément et essayait de déchiffrer sa figure. Il n'avait rien de sa mère. Rien de son père, non plus. Si, ces prunelles petites, sombres et fixes, ce pli dédaigneux de chaque côté de la bouche. Le reste, tout le reste, était de Nicolas. Elle se surprit à penser que cette manie des comparaisons était un défaut de vieille dame. Le gendarme toussota pour rappeler sa présence. Il se tenait sur le seuil, gêné, les bras ballants. Elle voulut lui faire servir une collation, mais il refusa : il devait repartir immédiatement pour Pskov.

— Eh bien ! adieu, dit-elle. Vous avez été pour moi un fort agréable compagnon de voyage.

Le gendarme rougit de plaisir. Elle lui glissa vingt roubles en assignats. Ils se séparèrent comme de vieux amis. Lorsqu'il eut refermé la porte, Sophie se tourna vers Serge. D'instinct, elle l'avait tutoyé en le voyant. Elle n'osa continuer.

— J'attendais d'être seule avec vous pour vous parler à cœur ouvert, dit-elle. Vous devez être si malheureux, Serge ! Ce qui s'est passé ici est abominable !

Il s'était adossé à la bibliothèque, les mains dans les poches, et regardait la pointe de ses souliers. Sur son visage, un air de dignité et de froideur. Cette retenue plaisait à Sophie.

— Comment est-ce arrivé ? reprit-elle. Le gouverneur de Pskov m'a simplement dit que les moujiks avaient attiré votre père dans un guet-apens...

— Oui, près de la cabane de bains, soi-disant pour lui montrer le plancher sur pilotis qu'ils devaient réparer... Là, ils l'ont assommé, étranglé... Ils étaient trois...

Il parlait lentement, sans intonation, en homme qui refuse de se laisser emporter.

— Et vous avez pu les identifier ? demanda Sophie.

— Très facilement. La commission d'enquête s'est transportée sur les lieux et a interrogé tous les paysans, tous les domestiques, tous les familiers. Les coupables ont été vite confondus. Ils

94

sont en prison, à Pskov. On les jugera, je pense, le mois prochain...

Il y eut un silence. Serge fronça les sourcils et reprit son souffle. Par crainte de le tourmenter dans son chagrin, Sophie hésita un instant à poursuivre la conversation. Il y revint lui-même.

— Des crapules ! dit-il entre ses dents. Des bêtes féroces !

Ses yeux s'agrandirent, comme s'il eût contemplé un affreux spectacle, tout proche, et pourtant visible de lui seul.

— Pourquoi ont-ils tué votre père ? dit Sophie.

— Il était dur avec les moujiks. Dur, mais juste. Souvent, je lui avais conseillé de se méfier : il ne m'écoutait pas. C'était lui qui dirigeait le domaine, depuis la mort de mon grand-père. Arrivé à ma majorité, je l'ai aidé de mon mieux. Nous nous entendions bien. Très bien, même. Quel homme remarquable ! Son intelligence, sa vivacité, son autorité en imposaient à tout le monde ! Depuis qu'il n'est plus là, je constate chaque jour davantage combien sa présence m'était utile...

Cet hommage rendu à Sédoff par son fils embarrassa Sophie. Elle aurait dû s'y attendre et, cependant, elle s'en irrita. D'autant plus qu'elle n'avait pas le droit de tirer Serge de son aveuglement. Soudain, elle se dit qu'il ne la connaissait que par les récits de son père. Quelles horreurs Sédoff lui avait-il racontées sur elle et sur Nicolas ? Il était étonnant que ce garçon la reçût avec courtoisie après le portrait que, sans doute, on lui avait tracé d'elle. Il était bien élevé. Que souhaiter de plus, pour l'heure ? Ce n'était pas la première fois qu'elle était accueillie avec hostilité à Kachtanovka. Mais, quand elle tenait tête à Michel Borissovitch, elle était jeune, ardente, indomptable, amoureuse. Aujourd'hui, elle se sentait la chair lourde, les os douloureux devant cet adolescent plein de superbe indifférence.

— Je vous ai fait préparer votre chambre, dit-il en s'inclinant légèrement devant elle.

Sophie le remercia. Allons ! tout serait plus facile qu'elle ne le supposait. Elle le suivit ; il lui montrait le chemin, avec prévenance, ainsi qu'à une étrangère :

— Par ici, ma tante.

Dans l'escalier, il dit encore : « Attention ! les marches sont un peu hautes ! » comme si elle ne l'avait pas su avant lui.

Quand il ouvrit la porte de la chambre qu'elle avait occupée jadis avec Nicolas, un malaise la saisit. Les meubles avaient changé de place. Les tentures s'étaient fanées. Tout paraissait plus petit, plus vieillot, plus délabré que dans sa mémoire. Elle regarda le lit, la table de nuit, l'icône, un chandelier de cuivre ; des souvenirs la remuèrent ; elle se mordit les lèvres pour ne pas pleurer.

— N'avez-vous besoin de rien ? dit Serge.

Elle fit signe que non. Il se retira discrètement, comme pour la laisser en conversation avec quelqu'un.

★

Le soir, Sophie et Serge se retrouvèrent en tête à tête, pour le souper, chacun à un bout de la grande table. Des domestiques inconnus faisaient le service. La chère était copieuse, lourde, épicée, comme du temps de Michel Borissovitch. Brusquement, Sophie eut l'impression qu'elle n'était plus seule avec son neveu, que le repas avait attiré d'autres convives autour d'elle, son beau-père, Nicolas, Marie, que tous étaient contents de la revoir, et elle eut un moment de bonheur insensé. Puis elle demanda :

— Qu'est devenu M. Lesur ?

— Il est mort un an après mon grand-père, dit Serge.

— Et Vassilissa ? La nounou Vassilissa ?

— Morte.

— Et Antipe ?

— Il vit encore, au village. Mais il est très vieux. Il n'a plus sa raison.

— Et le père Joseph ?

— Mort aussi, l'année du choléra.

Sophie cita encore quelques noms, se rendit compte qu'elle tisonnait un tas de cendres et revint à Michel Borissovitch. Elle voulut savoir quelle image Serge avait conservée de son grand-père.

— J'avais cinq ou six ans à peine, dit-il, quand il est mort. Je revois très vaguement un homme voûté, avec d'épais favoris blancs, de grosses lunettes. Il me permettait de jouer avec ses plumes d'oie, avec sa tabatière, avec les pièces de son échiquier. C'est tout...

Elle pensa à la somme d'attention, d'orgueil, de tendresse que Michel Borissovitch avait dû dépenser autour de son petit-fils et au peu de souvenir que celui-ci avait gardé de cette dévotion. Cruauté inconsciente de la jeunesse, qui ne s'élève qu'en oubliant ceux qui l'ont précédée. Le repas tirait à sa fin et Sophie se sentait de plus en plus seule, comme si tous les gens de son âge eussent disparu de la terre.

Après le souper, elle accepta le bras de Serge

pour se rendre au bureau. Un serviteur alluma les lampes, car la nuit venait. Il faisait chaud. Des papillons fous entraient par la fenêtre ouverte. Sur un réchaud brûlaient des charbons odorants dont les émanations écartaient les moustiques. Serge demanda la permission de fumer une pipe. Sophie le regarda battre le briquet, tirer à pleines joues sur le tuyau de buis et songea au bébé qu'elle avait apporté dans ses bras, par une nuit de vent et de pluie, à la maison. Que savait-il de sa mère ? Lui avait-on seulement dit qu'elle s'était pendue ?

— Vous aviez quelques mois lorsque je vous ai quitté, murmura-t-elle. Votre enfance n'a pas dû être douce. C'est la vieille Vassilissa qui vous a élevé ?

— Non. Mon père.

— Je veux dire... comme nourrice ?

— Oui. Elle et bien d'autres ! Mais je ne me rappelle pas leur nom.

Sophie se pelotonna dans un fauteuil, dont le cuir frais collait à ses épaules.

— J'ai beaucoup aimé votre mère, dit-elle. Avant de mourir, elle m'avait chargé de veiller sur vous comme sur mon propre fils. Je n'ai pu lui tenir parole, parce que j'ai dû suivre mon mari en Sibérie. C'était une femme d'une sensibilité exceptionnelle, tendre et brûlante à la fois...

Les lèvres de Serge se plissèrent dans un sourire.

— Oui, marmonna-t-il, je crois qu'elle n'était pas très équilibrée.

L'indignation frappa Sophie.

— Pourquoi dites-vous cela ? balbutia-t-elle.

— Je ne fais que répéter ce que tout le monde raconte.

98

— Tout le monde ? C'est-à-dire votre père ?

— Entre autres, oui. Ma mère s'est tout de même tuée à cause d'une histoire absurde. Ce n'est pas parce que mon père a été obligé de vendre quelques paysans pour payer ses dettes qu'elle devait se désespérer ainsi ! Elle prenait tout trop à cœur ! Vingt fois déjà elle avait tenté de se suicider !

Sophie écoutait se dérouler cette suite de mensonges qui, pour Serge, avaient force de vérité et elle souffrait de ne pouvoir le contredire immédiatement avec quelque chance d'être crue. Plus tard, elle essaierait de le convaincre. Pauvre Marie qui avait tout manqué, même sa mort, et dont le suprême châtiment était, peut-être, le dédain dont son fils entourait sa mémoire !

— On ne peut juger les êtres si on ne les a pas directement connus, dit Sophie.

— Quand il m'est impossible de me former une opinion par moi-même, j'adopte celle des gens qui ont ma confiance.

— Et vous ne craignez jamais de vous tromper ?

— Il existe des témoignages irréfutables, des témoignages qui sont étayés par des faits !

— Voilà qui est fort inquiétant pour moi ! soupira Sophie.

— Je ne comprends pas pourquoi, ma tante ?

— Si vous acceptez sans discussion ce que vous entendez dire par votre entourage, il est probable que vous n'éprouvez aucune sympathie envers ceux qu'il est convenu d'appeler les décembristes.

Les traits de Serge se tendirent brusquement, son regard se durcit.

— En effet, dit-il, je ne vous cacherai pas que je me sens très loin de ces messieurs.

— Sans partager leurs idées, vous pourriez compatir à leur sort !

Il redressa la taille :

— Excusez-moi, ma tante, mais je me refuse à plaindre des gens qui ont voulu mettre la Russie à feu et à sang pour satisfaire leurs ambitions personnelles. Je suis un ami de l'ordre. Il est normal que le gouvernement éloigne les individus qui risquent de troubler la vie de la société.

Elle le considéra avec une surprise attristée. Etait-ce bien le neveu de Nicolas qui parlait ainsi ? Michel Borissovitch lui-même n'eût pas tenu des propos plus réactionnaires. Si tous les jeunes Russes étaient comme ce garçon !... Elle se ressaisit en pensant que Nicolas, lorsqu'elle l'avait connu à Paris, avait, lui aussi, des opinions antilibérales. Pour changer de conversation, elle demanda :

— Quelle est votre vie à Kachtanovka ? Voyez-vous beaucoup de voisins ?

— Le moins possible ! dit Serge. Ils ne sont guère intéressants !

— Je crois me rappeler pourtant qu'il y avait parmi eux des gens de bonne compagnie. Votre oncle était très lié autrefois avec Vassia Volkoff.

— Cela ne m'étonne pas, dit Serge. Volkoff passe dans le pays pour un républicain. Il a même été inquiété, paraît-il, au moment du procès des décembristes. Mais on ne l'a pas arrêté.

— Et sa mère ?

— Elle vit avec lui. Les sœurs se sont mariées à Moscou. Toutes des folles !

Sans se démonter, Sophie demanda à Serge des nouvelles de quelques autres connaissances. Chaque fois, il lui répondit d'un ton tranchant et avec méchanceté. A trente verstes à la ronde, il n'y avait pas un être humain qui trouvât grâce devant lui.

Elle mit cette intransigeance sur le compte de la jeunesse et de la fatuité. Il voulait, à tout prix, passer auprès d'elle pour un homme de caractère. Un peu de fraîcheur entra par la fenêtre, avec le murmure des feuillages remués par le vent.

— Je ne puis croire que je suis revenue à Kachtanovka, dit Sophie. Malgré moi, il me semble que, derrière ces murs, c'est encore la Sibérie. J'y ai laissé de si bons amis !

— Vous regrettez d'avoir quitté Tobolsk ? demanda-t-il d'un air sarcastique.

— Il y avait de la grandeur d'âme, là-bas ! dit-elle en le regardant droit dans les yeux.

— La grandeur d'âme est le luxe de ceux qui n'ont rien à faire !

— Est-ce parce que vous aviez beaucoup à faire que vous n'avez jamais répondu à mes lettres ?

— Je ne vous connaissais pas.

— Ce n'est pas une raison, Serge !

Il s'inclina dans un salut moqueur :

— Pour moi, si, ma tante. Maintenant que je vous ai vue, c'est différent : si nous devons encore nous séparer, je ne manquerai pas de vous écrire. Mais nous ne nous séparerons plus ! D'abord, parce que vous n'avez pas le droit de bouger de Kachtanovka. Ensuite, parce que nous avons, ici, des intérêts communs. Ce domaine vous appartient autant qu'à moi. J'ai des comptes à vous rendre !

Il était si odieux, que Sophie en arrivait à le trouver amusant.

— C'est vrai, dit-elle. Mais nous avons bien le temps de nous plonger dans les calculs.

— Non, non, j'insiste... Je veux que vous constatiez, dès à présent, le soin avec lequel nous avons tenu les livres...

Il ouvrit un registre sur une petite table devant Sophie. Elle vit des chiffres alignés : « Dépenses, recettes... Coupes de bois... »

Penché sur son épaule, Serge lui expliquait la marche du domaine. Elle ne l'écoutait pas et regardait l'écriture : sèche, pointue, avec, par endroits, de grosses barres d'encre qui écorchaient le papier.

— Est-ce votre père qui a écrit cela ?

— Non, c'est moi. Si vous voulez vérifier...

— Demain, dit-elle en refermant le registre.

— Pourquoi ?

— Quelle paix dehors ! Je ne voudrais pas gâcher cet instant !

Il rangea le livre. Elle prêta l'oreille aux bruits de la maison. Tintement lointain de la vaisselle, craquement d'un meuble taraudé par les vers, battement régulier de l'horloge. L'envoûtement du passé agissait sur elle. Levant les yeux, elle aperçut Serge derrière le bureau et lui trouva un air anachronique. Il s'était trompé d'époque. Il n'avait rien à faire là. Puis elle comprit que c'était elle qui n'était pas à sa place. Les morceaux du puzzle ne s'ajustaient pas bien. Elle fit un effort pour se remettre tout entière dans le présent. Serge souriait en silence. L'expression méchante avait disparu de sa figure. Quand on ne le provoquait pas dans ses opinions, il redevenait aimable. Sans doute n'était-il pas assez sûr de lui pour supporter la contradiction. Sa brusquerie était une défense de gamin. Cependant, il avait du courage, de la franchise. Elle appuya sa nuque au dossier du fauteuil, ferma les yeux, essaya de ne penser à rien. Une chouette ululait dans un arbre proche. Quelqu'un marchait dans la pièce en faisant grincer le parquet sous son pas. Ce pourrait être Nico-

102

las, ou M. Lesur, ou Michel Borissovitch... Non, elle savait que c'était Serge. Elle le savait et n'en éprouvait aucun déplaisir. Il était entré dans sa vie, celui-là aussi, avec tous ses défauts. Elle avait de nouveau une famille. Un étrange contentement se développa en elle.

— Il est tard ! dit-elle. Je vais monter me coucher.

Serge voulut l'aider à se lever de son fauteuil. Elle l'écarta de la main et se dressa, toute seule, avec vivacité, par crainte qu'il ne la prît pour une vieille dame.

Après le dîner, tandis que Serge se retirait dans
son bureau avec les registres du domaine, Sophie
monta dans sa chambre. Elle ne pouvait attendre
plus longtemps pour écrire à Ferdinand Wolff. Le
début de la lettre l'embarrassa. Puis, soudain, elle
retrouva le ton de leurs conversations et sa plume
courut sur le papier. Elle raconta la fin de son
voyage, son arrivée à Kachtanovka, ses premières
impressions... Il était devant elle, sérieux et triste ; il l'écoutait. Elle lui demanda de ses nouvelles. En vérité, elle devait se surveiller pour ne
pas mettre trop de tendresse dans ses questions.
À la relecture, sa lettre lui sembla un peu réservée.
C'était mieux ainsi. Elle écrivit aussi à Pauline
Annenkoff, à Nathalie Fonvizine, à Marie Frantz-
zeff. Demain, le cocher porterait le courrier à la
poste de Pskov. Quand recevrait-elle une réponse ?
Dans cet ordre d'idées, la sagesse était de ne rien
espérer.

Elle alla se promener dans le parc, refit connaissance avec la tonnelle, un petit bois de bouleaux, une famille de châtaigniers centenaires, et

revint, chargée de réminiscences nostalgiques, vers le bâtiment des communs. Les domestiques qu'elle vit là lui parurent nouveaux. La plupart étaient jeunes et de bonne figure. On avait dû renvoyer les vieux dans leurs villages. Si Sophie ignorait encore le nom de tous les serviteurs, eux savaient déjà qui elle était et lui témoignaient de la déférence. Serge lui avait réservé comme soubrette une paysanne blonde, plantureuse et souriante, qui s'appelait Zoé et était la femme du cocher David.

Il faisait si beau que Sophie eut envie de faire immédiatement le tour des villages dépendant de la propriété. Elle ordonna à David d'atteler une calèche. Replacée dans le décor de sa jeunesse, elle retrouvait d'instinct le ton du commandement. Il lui semblait naturel de voir s'affairer autour d'elle une valetaille désœuvrée et obséquieuse. Elle monta dans la voiture et, quand les chevaux s'ébranlèrent au pas dans l'allée, elle se retourna et aperçut, à une fenêtre du bureau, Serge qui la regardait partir.

Passés les derniers arbres du parc, la route s'étirait dans une campagne à peine vallonnée. Des champs de blé, de seigle, de maïs, couraient à droite et à gauche, tachetés de légers boqueteaux. Ensuite vint un champ de pommes de terre et Sophie se rappela que jadis, il avait fallu menacer les paysans des verges pour les obliger à planter cette « herbe du diable », importée de l'étranger. Dans l'ensemble, il y avait plus de terres cultivées que du temps de Michel Borissovitch. L'administration des deux Sédoff, père et fils, avait été bienfaisante. Bercée par les ressorts de la calèche, Sophie ne se lassait pas d'admirer le domaine. Cette richesse, l'apparente liberté de sa promenade, le pouvoir dont elle dis-

posait avec son neveu sur quelque deux mille
paysans serfs, contrastaient avec l'interdiction
qui lui était faite par le gouvernement de s'éloigner à plus de quinze verstes de Kachtanovka.
La réflexion du gendarme lui revint en mémoire.
« Vous êtes une prisonnière-libre ! » Elle s'amusa de cette situation ambiguë. Des bouleaux au
feuillage mince dansèrent devant ses yeux ; une
rivière brilla dans une dépression de terrain ; les
isbas de Chatkovo apparurent entre des bouquets
de tournesols. Surprises par l'arrivée de la voiture, quelques paysannes, qui parlaient au milieu
de la rue, rentrèrent chez elle précipitamment.
Autrefois, quand Sophie visitait le village, les habitants s'assemblaient autour d'elle avec amitié.
Elle s'étonna de cette débandade et demanda au
cocher :

— Pourquoi s'en vont-elles ?

— Eh ! elles ont peur, grommela-t-il.

— De quoi ?

— Est-ce qu'on sait ? Les femmes, chez nous,
c'est craintif, c'est bête !...

D'un bout à l'autre de la rue, les portes se fer-
maient, comme si Sophie eût apporté la mort dans
les plis de sa robe. Elle descendit de calèche, marcha vers la première maison, poussa le battant
avec autorité et se trouva devant une famille
tremblante. Deux femmes, une très vieille, l'autre
un peu moins, et, autour d'elles, une marmaille en
loques, d'où s'élevaient des regards d'une déchi-
rante candeur. Couché en travers du four, assoupi
dans la broussaille de sa barbe, le grand-père. Sur
tout cela, l'ombre, la saleté et l'odeur d'une taniè-
re trop peuplée. Pendant une seconde, on n'entendit que le bourdonnement des mouches, ivres de
bonheur. Sophie dit qui elle était, d'où elle venait,

et les deux femmes fondirent en larmes. Le grand-père glissa du four, se prosterna et alla chercher les voisins. Bientôt, il y eut un rassemblement autour de la maison et Sophie dut sortir pour se montrer. Tous les hommes et les femmes valides travaillaient dans les champs, mais les vieillards, les impotents étaient nombreux. Sophie reconnaissait, çà et là, un visage, à travers un réseau de rides. Ces faces flétries étaient comme des pièces de monnaie dont on devine la valeur malgré l'usure du métal. Un nom, puis un autre, lui montaient aux lèvres :

— Ah ! mon Dieu, mais c'est Agaphon !... C'est Marthe !... C'est Arsène !...

Chaque fois, celui ou celle qu'elle avait appelé s'exclamait, se signait, reniflait de gratitude.

— C'est Maximytch !

— Non, barynia, je suis son fils ! J'avais dix ans quand vous êtes partie !

— Et là, qui est-ce ? Je te connais, toi !... Nicanor !... Non ?

— Lui-même ! Que Dieu vous bénisse, barynia ! Vous n'avez pas changé !

Un chœur respectueux approuva en sourdine :

— Non, non, elle n'a pas changé !

— Toujours aussi belle ! Aussi bonne !

Une femme sanglota :

— Et ce pauvre Nicolas Mikhaïlovitch !

Le chœur reprit la plainte en l'amplifiant :

— Dieu ait son âme ! C'était un barine comme on n'en rencontrera plus ! Il a souffert pour nous, en Sibérie ! Et vous aussi, vous avez souffert, barynia ! Vous êtes des saints, tous les deux !

Sophie était émue de voir que les moujiks ne l'avaient pas oubliée. Pourtant, elle avait fait bien peu pour leur bonheur. Ils étaient si privés de ten-

108

dresse, que les soins qu'elle leur avait prodigués autrefois avaient dû prendre dans leur souvenir une proportion démesurée. Elle remarqua des regards extatiques dirigés sur elle et sentit qu'en son absence une légende était née, contre laquelle elle ne pouvait rien. Plus on est pauvre, plus on a besoin de croire aux anges. Elle sourit, gênée, tendit les deux bras. Des baisers s'abattirent sur ses mains.

— Que de morts ! Que de morts ! soupira-t-elle.

— Le choléra en a pris beaucoup par ici ! dit Marthe. A commencer par notre petit père Michel Borissovitch ! Le royaume des cieux pour lui ! Il s'y trouve maintenant, entre sa fille et son fils !

Devant tous ces gens qui se signaient, en bénissant le nom de son beau-père, Sophie songea que les paysans avaient vite pardonné la dureté de leur maître. Encouragée par leur sympathie, elle voulut leur parler du meurtre de Vladimir Karpovitch Sédoff. Aussitôt, toute expression s'effaça des visages. Les uns se détournaient, d'autres plantaient leur regard en terre. On eût dit que Sophie les interrogeait sur quelqu'un qu'ils ne connaissaient pas. Enfin, le vieux Maximytch, qui était devenu maigre et noueux, comme un paquet de cordes, eut le courage de rompre le silence.

— C'est un grand malheur ! dit-il.

Et il cracha entre ses pieds.

— Les assassins sont de votre village ? demanda Sophie.

— Oui, répondit Maximytch.

— Je les connais ?

— Non. Ce sont des jeunes. Ossip le roux, Fédka, Marc...

— Pourquoi ont-ils fait ça !

— Dieu seul le sait. Ou le diable !

— Ils ont des parents parmi vous, une famille ?

— La femme d'Ossip le roux est aux champs... Ça, ce sont les vieux de Fédka et de Marc...

Sophie vit une paysanne qui essayait de se cacher derrière les autres et un grand moujik borgne, grêlé, qui baissait la tête. Elle s'approcha de lui et dit à mi-voix :

— Tes fils ont-ils eu d'autres histoires avant ?...

— Non, barynia, jamais !

— Qu'ont-ils dit quand on les a arrêtés ?

— Je ne sais pas... Il ne fait pas bon parler de ces choses, barynia... Excusez-nous...

Déjà, quelques femmes s'éloignaient du groupe avec des mines inquiètes. Sophie comprit qu'en insistant elle chasserait tout le monde.

— Je ne vois pas Antipe, dit-elle. Il habite bien ici ?

— Oui, mais il est allé ramasser du bois, dit Agaphon. Va le chercher, Mitka !

Un gamin partit en courant si fort, que ses talons nus lui battaient les fesses. Reprenant ses habitudes, Sophie passa d'une maison à l'autre, réconforta un vieillard malade, admira des bébés dans leurs berceaux suspendus et rendit visite au père Hilarion, qui avait remplacé le père Joseph.

Le nouveau pope était jeune, triste, malingre, avec une petite barbe noire et pointue, comme trempée dans de la poix ; son épouse avait de la santé pour deux ; autour d'elle, les meubles luisaient de cire, des canaris jaunes chantaient dans une cage et une profusion de napperons tricotés, disposées sur toutes les surfaces planes, témoignaient de l'industrieux passe-temps de la maîtresse de maison. Le père Hilarion accueillit Sophie avec une politesse réservée et douceâtre. Visiblement, il se méfiait de cette Française dévouée au

pape et qui, de surcroît, revenait des bagnes sibériens. Quand, après lui avoir parlé de sa paroisse,
elle évoqua la mort violente de Vladimir Karpovitch Sédoff, il échangea avec sa femme un regard
épouvanté. Sophie ne put leur tirer un mot sur la
façon dont s'était déroulé le drame ni sur les motifs qui avaient inspiré les assassins.

— Que Dieu ne se détourne pas de notre humble
village après cette abomination, c'est tout ce que
je demande ! dit le père Hilarion.

Et il reconduisit Sophie, en la poussant même
un peu, pour qu'elle sortît plus vite. Justement, par-
derrière l'église, arrivait Antipe, trottinant à côté
du gamin qui était parti à sa recherche. Un Antipe
rabougri, racorni, et dont la tignasse et la barbe
rousses étaient maintenant d'un blanc pisseux. A
la vue de Sophie, toutes ses rides se contractè-
rent ; sa bouche riait et ses yeux pleuraient ; il
tomba à genoux devant elle et baisa le bas de sa
robe. Elle le releva et le pria de la conduire chez
lui : elle voulait lui parler seule à seul.

Il habitait au bout du village, dans une isba plus
petite et plus sale que les autres. Pour que Sophie
pût s'asseoir, il essuya le banc avec sa manche et
chassa une poule qui picorait sous la table. Il était
trop ému pour prononcer un mot. Debout devant
sa maîtresse, il remuait les lèvres et hoquetait faiblement.

— Et bien ! mon pauvre Antipe, dit-elle, nous
voici réunis de nouveau, tous les deux ! Je ne sup-
posais pas que je te reverrais un jour !

— Moi non plus, barynia ! gémit-il. Vous avez
vieilli, et moi aussi j'ai vieilli ! Mais ce n'est pas
la vieillesse qui est lourde à porter, c'est le malheur ! Je ne peux pas vous regarder sans penser
à notre cher Nicolas Mikhaïlovitch, à notre clair

111

soleil ! Qu'est-ce que la vie pour le chien, quand son maître est sous terre ? Il n'y a pas de second maître pour le chien ! Le chien se couche devant la tombe et attend que ses jours finissent !

Les larmes coulaient sur ses joues sales et y traçaient des sillons rosâtres.

— Quand on a su que Nicolas Mikhaïlovitch n'était plus, tout le village s'est saoulé pendant deux jours ! reprit-il avec fierté entre deux sanglots.

— Comment Vladimir Karpovitch Sédoff vous a-t-il annoncé la nouvelle ? demanda Sophie.

Antipe cessa instantanément de pleurer et ses petits yeux, encore humides, brillèrent de hargne :

— Pensez-vous qu'il allait se déranger pour nous annoncer quelque chose, celui-là ! Nous l'avons appris par les domestiques de la maison. De bouche à oreille. C'est plus sûr...

Soudain, il se donna un coup de poing sur le front et poursuivit avec emphase :

— Imbécile ! Tu t'étais juré de protéger le jeune barine toute sa vie, tu l'as soigné dans les bivouacs, tu l'as escorté sur les champs de bataille, tu l'as suivi jusque dans la France perverse (excusez, barynia !) et maintenant, il repose sous une croix, quelque part, au bout du monde, pendant que tu chauffes ta vilaine carcasse de serf au soleil ! Où est la justice ? Si vous m'aviez laissé vous accompagner en Sibérie, barynia, les choses se seraient passées autrement !

— Mais... c'est toi qui n'as pas voulu m'accompagner, Antipe ! dit Sophie en souriant. Rappelle-toi ! Tu suppliais Michel Borissovitch de ne pas t'envoyer chez les bagnards !

La fougue d'Antipe tomba et il se gratta la tête.

— Vraiment ? grommela-t-il. C'est drôle ! Dans ma caboche, tout était différent ! J'oublie, j'oublie !... C'est l'âge... En tout cas, vous auriez dû me forcer à y aller, barynia !... Je vous aurais rendu plus de services que ce pauvre Nikita, Dieu ait son âme !

— Tu es au courant, pour lui aussi ? murmura Sophie.

— Bien sûr ! Comme il était de Chatkovo, il a fallu le rayer sur le registre de la paroisse. C'est le barine qui lit les lettres et c'est le moujik qui sait tout avant lui !

— Et les parents de Nikita ? demanda-t-elle.

Antipe fit le simulacre de chasser une mouche avec la main et dit simplement :

— Le choléra.

— Les deux ?

— Oui.. Son père et sa belle-mère... Oh ! ils n'étaient plus jeunes...

Il soupira, comme font les gens du peuple chaque fois qu'ils évoquent un mort. Sophie se dit qu'il n'avait jamais été plus lucide.

— Tu ne travailles plus à Kachtanovka ? demanda-t-elle.

— Non, dit-il avec un regard malin. La tête, la tête est fêlée. On ne peut pas compter sur moi comme domestique. On m'a renvoyé au village. Ici, je suis bien !

— Et les autres ?

— Quoi, les autres ?

— Les autres moujiks, sont-ils contents ?

— Vous avez déjà vu un moujik content, barynia ?

— Les terres ont l'air mieux cultivées qu'autrefois.

— Pour ça, oui. Mais qui en profite ?

Un chant monta dans la campagne et se rapprocha, clamé par une troupe en mouvement.

— Ce sont les nôtres qui rentrent, dit Antipe.

Sophie se leva, entrouvrit la porte et vit venir, par la route, des paysans qui marchaient en rangs, comme des soldats, avec des pelles, des râteaux, des haches sur l'épaule. Derrière, s'avançaient les femmes, en fichu, poussant des brouettes. Tous les visages étaient luisants de sueur, tirés de fatigue, une expression hébétée dans le regard. Quatre hommes, armés de gourdins, encadraient le groupe.

— Qui sont ceux-là ? demanda Sophie.

— On les appelle les « conducteurs ». C'est le barine qui les choisit en dehors du village. Il les paye pour nous garder. Avec eux sur notre dos, pas de danger que le travail traîne !...

— Qu'est-ce que tu racontes ? Jamais. autrefois...

— Eh non, barynia ! Autrefois, c'était le bon temps. Le vieux barine criait, menaçait du knout, donnait une paire de gifles et, l'orage terminé, personne ne s'en portait plus mal. Aujourd'hui, avec les nouveaux messieurs, il n'y a plus de colère. Tout se passe froidement. Les « conducteurs » sont là pour appliquer la règle. Travaille ou on va te chatouiller les côtes !...

Sophie hésitait à croire Antipe. Il avait toujours eu la réputation d'un menteur.

— Est-ce parce que Vladimir Karpovitch était cruel avec ses paysans qu'ils l'ont tué ? demanda-t-elle.

— Peut-être bien ! Nous autres, nous ne sommes pas sur terre pour juger mais pour subir !

Dans les poils blancs de sa barbe, sa bouche riait, rouge et mouillée. Ses yeux se plissaient sur un fourmillement d'étincelles. Il secoua le front, comme s'il eût porté un bonnet à grelots :

— Aïe, ma tête ! ma petite tête !

Sophie le quitta en lui promettant de revenir bientôt, échangea quelques mots, dans la rue, avec les travailleurs au retour des champs et remonta en calèche. Les « conducteurs » — une demi-douzaine — étaient assis sur le talus, à l'entrée du village, et bavardaient en grignotant des graines de tournesol. Ils saluèrent la barynia. Des bourreaux, pensa-t-elle, ne lui auraient pas marqué tant de politesse.

Serge l'attendait pour passer à table. Il portait une redingote noire, avec un gilet violet sombre à boutons d'améthyste. Une cravate de deuil, à trois tours, lui soutenait le menton. Son visage était lisse et agréablement coloré.

— Avez-vous fait une bonne promenade, ma tante ? demanda-t-il en s'asseyant devant elle dans la salle à manger aux fenêtres ouvertes sur le jardin.

— Excellente ! dit-elle.

Des serviteurs glissaient derrière son dos. Elle prit un peu de poisson en gelée dans son assiette. Ce n'était pas elle qui avait composé le menu. A l'avenir, il faudrait qu'elle revendiquât cette prérogative. Elle avait beau se répéter qu'elle était chez elle dans cette maison, à tout moment, sous le regard de son neveu, elle se sentait une invitée, une intruse. Ils mangèrent en silence, chacun enfermé dans ses propres réflexions, puis, pendant un changement de plats, Serge dit en français :

— Comment avez-vous trouvé le domaine ?

— Je n'ai pas encore eu le temps de me former une opinion, répondit-elle, mais il me semble que les terres sont bien exploitées.

115

— En cinq ans, nous avons doublé la production de blé, de maïs et de sarrasin, dit-il avec fierté, triplé la production de pommes de terre ! Nos concombres, nos betteraves, nos fèves sont les meilleurs de la région ! Nos fruits...

Elle l'interrompit avec douceur :

— Et nos moujiks ?

— Ils prolifèrent comme des lapins ! Deux mille âmes du temps de mon grand-père ! Deux mille sept cent cinquante aujourd'hui ! C'est un beau résultat !

— Sans doute, mais je les ai trouvés fatigués, soucieux... Qui sont ces « conducteurs » installés par vous dans les villages ? Ils me rappellent les gardes-chiourme sibériens !

— Vous leur faites trop d'honneur ! Ce ne sont que des surveillants.

— Armés de gourdins !

— Simple mesure d'intimidation. Le moujik est paresseux de nature. Si vous ne le menacez pas, il invente mille excuses pour ne pas travailler.

— Est-ce une idée de votre père ?

— Non, de moi. Mais mon père s'y était rallié avec enthousiasme. Je suppose que les moujiks vous ont présenté leurs doléances à ce sujet ?

— Pas du tout, dit-elle précipitamment.

— Ils le feront un jour ou l'autre. Ne les écoutez pas. Je vous soupçonne d'avoir l'âme trop sensible. Cela ne vaut rien, quand on dirige un vaste domaine. L'idéal serait d'avoir le cœur sec et l'esprit équitable.

— Est-ce votre cas ?

— Je le crois, oui, dit-il avec une gravité soudaine.

Un serviteur apporta une compote de fruits, un autre alluma les bougies de deux candélabres. La

116

nuit était chaude, immobile et moite. Les vêtements de Sophie pesaient à ses épaules.

— Il faudra, dit Serge, que nous organisions notre vie. Je ne pense pas que vous teniez beaucoup à vous occuper de l'exploitation du domaine...

— De son exploitation, non ; de la condition des serfs, oui, dit-elle.

Il se rembrunit :

— Nos serfs ne manquent de rien, je vous assure !

— Peut-être d'un peu de charité...

— Ils prendront votre charité pour de la faiblesse. Non, non ma tante, laissez de côté ces rêves humanitaires ! Je vous vois beaucoup mieux dirigeant la maison. Vous êtes une femme, les questions domestiques sont plus de votre ressort que les questions agricoles...

Elle préféra ne pas le contrarier tout de suite.

— Rien ne presse, dit-elle. Nous verrons plus tard quelles seront les attributions de chacun.

— Comme vous voulez, ma tante.

Elle remonta une mèche de cheveux sur sa tempe. Aussitôt, Serge claqua des doigts, et une servante, jaillie de l'ombre, agita un éventail devant le visage de Sophie pour la rafraîchir. L'éventail était parfumé au jasmin. Cette odeur douceâtre écœura Sophie qui fit la grimace.

— Vous n'aimez pas ? demanda-t-il.

— Non, je l'avoue...

Alors, il cria, en russe :

— Arrête, idiote !

La fille partit en courant. « Il est surtout mal élevé », pensa Sophie.

3

Il semblait à Sophie qu'elle ne se fatiguerait jamais de redécouvrir le charme de Kachtanovka. Les journées s'écoulaient si vite que, chaque soir, elle s'étonnait de n'avoir presque rien fait et de se sentir pourtant apaisée et heureuse. Elle dirigeait les domestiques, régnait sur les réserves de nourriture et les coffres de linge, commandait les repas, vérifiait les comptes de la vieille Zénaïde, qui avait succédé à Vassilissa dans les fonctions d' « économe », mais, le plus clair de son temps, elle le passait en promenades dans les champs et en visites aux villages. L'été avançait, dans le soleil, l'odeur de la terre craquelée et le bourdonnement des moucherons. Jamais, aux dires des anciens, le blé et le sarrasin n'avaient poussé si dru. La douce fourrure de l'avoine tremblait en longues moires au souffle du vent. Dans les grandes prairies proches de la rivière, l'herbe était haute, il fallait la faucher. Les paysans se mirent à l'ouvrage. Sophie faisait arrêter sa calèche au bord de la route pour les voir travailler. Ils progressaient en ligne oblique, et l'éclair de leurs faux couchait devant eux des vagues de verdure. A la fin, le paysage, tondu court, fut méconnaissable, rajeuni, ahuri. Par chance, il n'y eut qu'une pluie légère, les jours suivants. Des femmes en fichus multicolores aidèrent les hommes à empiler le fourrage en meules. Les charrettes commencèrent leur va-et-vient des champs aux hangars. Puis arriva le temps de la moisson. Tous les villages y participèrent. Des gerbes de blé doré s'alignèrent à perte de vue. Serge surveillait personnellement les opérations. Les conducteurs avaient des faces de gendarmes. La récolte fut si bonne, que le maître promit une distribution d'eau-de-vie après les fêtes de l'Assomption. Il demanda à Sophie de l'accompagner à l'église de Chatkovo, ce jour-là. Elle assista avec lui à la messe. Debout au premier rang des femmes, elle avait le sentiment de servir de bouclier à mille vies orthodoxes, laborieuses et obscures. Quand, après l'office, elle sortit avec son neveu sur le parvis, toutes les têtes s'inclinèrent devant eux. Tant de déférence la gênait, mais elle ne pouvait changer les mœurs de ces gens habitués, depuis des siècles, à la servilité. Serge l'aida à monter en voiture, s'assit à côté d'elle et murmura :

— Au fait, vous ai-je dit que je devais m'absenter demain ? Je vais à Pskov, témoigner au procès des assassins de mon père.

Sophie tressaillit. Depuis le temps que les trois moujiks croupissaient en prison, elle avait fini par admettre, inconsciemment, que leur affaire était réglée.

— Est-ce demain qu'on les juge ? balbutia-t-elle.

— Eh ! oui. Ce n'est pas trop tôt ! J'espère que la sentence sera impitoyable ! Malheureusement,

120

la peine de mort n'existe pas dans notre pays pour les crimes de droit commun !

— Les débats auront lieu à huis clos, n'est-ce pas ?

— Bien sûr ! Nous ne sommes pas en France où les procès sont devenus des spectacles publics !

— Dommage ! dit-elle. J'aurais aimé assister au jugement.

La calèche partit, au son des clochettes.

★

Les trois moujiks, convaincus d'avoir assassiné leur maître, furent condamnés aux travaux forcés à perpétuité. Serge annonça le verdict à Sophie, le soir même, à table, avec une gravité qui ressemblait à de la tristesse. Elle crut que la pitié chrétienne l'emportait enfin chez lui, sur le désir de vengeance, mais il poursuivit en déchiquetant une aile de poulet dans son assiette :

— Je vous avais dit, hier soir, que je souhaitais un châtiment exemplaire, eh bien ! je me trompais. Perdre trois serfs à la fois c'est trop pénible ! Si encore il s'agissait de vieux !... Mais des gaillards comme ceux-là — jeunes, solides — je ne les remplacerai jamais ! Ossip le rouquin vous taillait n'importe quel meuble en trois coups de hache, Fédka n'avait pas son pareil pour construire un tarantass !... Si j'avais su !...

— Quoi ? dit-elle. Vous ne les auriez pas dénoncés ?

Serge haussa les épaules :

— Si, bien sûr !... Il le fallait... Pour l'exemple !... Et puis... enfin... pour contenter la justice !... Mais tout de même, quand on les a emmenés après la sentence, j'ai senti qu'on m'arrachait quelque chose du ventre !...

— Que voilà une charité étrangement inspirée ! dit-elle.

— Je suis ainsi, ma tante ! J'ai l'instinct de propriété très développé. Tenez, je comprends fort
bien le plaisir que vous éprouvez à vous promener en calèche dans le domaine. Moi aussi, quand
je parcours les routes à cheval, quand je regarde
les champs, les villages, les arbres, la rivière, les
serfs, et que je me dis que tout cela m'appartient
— nous appartient — il me vient une ivresse dans
l'âme. Je me sens maître après Dieu. Existe-t-il
une plus haute volupté pour l'homme que l'exercice conscient de la toute-puissance ?

La froideur moqueuse qu'il affectait d'ordinaire
fondait au feu d'une passion qu'il ne savait ni ne
voulait dominer. Les serviteurs apportèrent une
tarte aux abricots — un de ses desserts préférés
que Sophie avait commandé exprès, la veille — et
il ne le remarqua même pas, tant il était exalté
par la violence de son propos :

— Prendre une motte de terre dans sa main, la
pétrir, et se dire qu'elle est le prolongement de
vous-même ! Ordonner que les serfs fassent ceci
ou cela, et ils le font, comme vos jambes vous
obéissent quand vous leur commandez de marcher ! C'est le vrai bonheur ! La ville, les sorties,
les amitiés extérieures ne m'intéressent pas...

Il pérora longtemps ainsi, devant son assiette
pleine. Puis il engloutit la tarte en deux bouchées
et se leva pour suivre Sophie dans le bureau. Elle
prit une tapisserie dans la boîte à ouvrage et s'installa sous la lampe. Le dessin représentait une
corbeille débordant de fleurs, dans le style de Redouté. Elle tirait les laines multicolores à travers
le canevas. Du train dont elle allait, elle n'en aurait pas fini avant deux ans.

— N'avez-vous jamais songé à vous marier ? demanda-t-elle.

Il partit d'un rire sonore :

— Jamais ! Excusez-moi, ma tante, mais j'estime idiot de se mettre la corde au cou, quand on peut goûter les mêmes plaisirs en restant libre !

Elle avait déjà remarqué qu'une ou deux fois par semaine il s'habillait et allait passer la soirée en ville. Sans doute avait-il, là-bas, quelque liaison. A moins que, plus simplement, il ne voletât d'une fille à l'autre. Les prostituées ne manquaient pas à Pskov.

— Mais vous avez bien des amis ? dit-elle.

— Pas un.

— A votre âge, pourtant...

— A mon âge, comme aux autres, il faut vivre pour soi et brouter autour de son piquet. Que voulez-vous ? j'aime mon carré d'herbe ! Je l'aime passionnément !

Un air de gourmandise enflammait son visage. Il reprit sa respiration et continua :

— Il y a de quoi s'amuser sans sortir du domaine !... J'ai des projets extraordinaires !... Faire peindre toutes les isbas en blanc... A l'intérieur, on verrait, pendu au mur, dans un cadre, l'inventaire des ustensiles de ménage... Les paysans seraient tous habillés de la même façon... Quelque chose de propre, de joli, de commode... Il y aurait un emploi du temps, le même pour tous, que les conducteurs seraient chargés de faire respecter... On obligerait toutes les filles, toutes les veuves, à se marier... Une amende serait infligée à celles qui n'auraient pas d'enfants dans un délai donné... Ces enfants, dès l'âge de huit ans, seraient retirés à leur famille et élevés par des instructeurs spécialisés, pour devenir de parfaits travailleurs...

Elle l'interrompit :

— Ce que vous décrivez là me rappelle fort les colonies militaires que prônait Araktchéïeff. Vous savez comment les choses se sont terminées ?...

— Si les paysans se sont révoltés dans les colonies militaires, c'est que la règle leur a été appliquée stupidement, par des fonctionnaires qui n'étaient pas directement intéressés au résultat. Moi, je serai pour mes serfs comme un père. Je ne les laisserai jamais mourir de faim, mais les verges seront conservées dans le sel, pour que les coups soient plus cuisants !

Sophie était partagée entre l'envie de rire et celle de s'effrayer devant cette naïveté énorme. Elle croyait entendre un enfant, la cervelle tournée par des rêves absurdes. Mais cet enfant avait le pouvoir de mettre toutes ses idées à exécution. Deux mille sept cent cinquante êtres vivants étaient soumis à son bon plaisir. Elle dit :

— Je ne vous conseille pas de tenter cette expérience.

— Pourquoi ?

— Parce que je m'y opposerai.

— Mais puisque ce sera pour le bien de nos paysans !

— Ce bien-là sera pire que le mal !

Serge se renfrogna. Sophie lut, sur sa figure, la contrariété du gamin dérangé dans son jeu. Il devait trouver qu'elle faisait exprès de ne pas le comprendre. Elle reprit sa tapisserie et murmura :

— Dites-vous bien, Serge, qu'un jour ou l'autre le tsar sera forcé d'émanciper les serfs. On en parle déjà. Des commissions ont été nommées, paraît-il, pour s'occuper de l'affaire.

— Jamais, s'écria-t-il, jamais notre empereur ne commettra cette folie ! Ce serait la ruine du pays, l'effondrement de toute la structure sociale russe, le chaos, l'injustice, parfaitement, l'injustice !

Il se tut, haletant, les oreilles rouges. Puis, peu à peu, son visage revint au calme. Il alluma une pipe, en tira deux bouffées, soupira, regarda la nuit par la fenêtre.

— Quand les envoie-t-on aux travaux forcés ? demanda Sophie.

— Demain, sans doute...

L'aiguille en suspens, elle pensa à ces hommes qui allaient partir, enchaînés, pour la Sibérie. Bien qu'ils fussent des assassins, elle ne pouvait s'empêcher de les plaindre. Ah ! la grisaille des visages fatigués, le cliquetis des fers, l'odeur des vêtements imprégnés de sueur et de crasse... Elle avait vu tant de forçats sur les routes, aux relais, aux centres de triage, qu'ils se confondaient dans sa tête comme les vagues de la mer

4

L'été s'acheva par des pluies torrentielles. Mais toutes les récoltes, même celle de pommes de terre, furent rentrées à temps. Pendant plusieurs jours, Kachtanovka flotta comme une arche dans le déluge. Les routes étaient inondées, un pont de bois fut emporté. Serge enrageait de ne pouvoir aller négocier la vente de son blé en ville. Pourtant, au début du mois d'octobre, le soleil reparut, l'automne s'installa, brumeux et doux. Dès que les chemins furent de nouveau praticables, Serge partit pour Pskov. Il revint, le soir, crotté jusqu'aux yeux, mais fier d'avoir conclu l'affaire dans de bonnes conditions. Il rapportait un paquet de lettres qui, à cause du mauvais temps, étaient restées en souffrance à la poste. Avec un sourire éminemment ironique, il tendit à Sophie un pli marqué du cachet de Tobolsk. Elle faillit pleurer d'émotion en reconnaissant l'écriture de Pauline Annenkoff.

C'était la première fois que lui parvenaient des nouvelles de Sibérie. Elle monta dans sa chambre et se jeta sur ces pages couvertes d'une écriture serrée. D'après Pauline, ni elle, ni le Dr Wolff, ni aucun de leurs amis n'avaient reçu la moindre lettre de Sophie. De leur côté, ils lui avaient tous écrit. à plusieurs reprises et s'inquiétaient qu'elle ne leur eût pas encore répondu. Sophie se désola, s'indigna : la poste russe était une institution abominable, dirigée par des espions ! Inutile de compter sur des lettres de Sibérie lorsqu'on en revenait soi-même !

« Peut-être aurai-je plus de chance avec cette missive qu'avec les précédentes, écrivait Pauline. Nous aimerions tant savoir ce que vous êtes devenue ! Ne nous oubliez pas, pour l'amour du ciel ! Ici, la vie n'a pas changé. Tout le monde est en bonne santé. Les enfants grandissent, le Dr Wolff a ouvert son dispensaire et ne sait où donner de la tête, car le nombre de ses malades augmente chaque jour. Nous parlons souvent de vous, avec lui. Vous ne pourriez pas lui faire de plus vif plaisir qu'en lui envoyant quelques lignes de votre main... »

Un flot de tendresse déferla sur Sophie, la ramollit, l'affaiblit, tandis que des idées simples la visitaient : « Il réussit... il est très occupé... C'est bien ! » Après s'être reprise, elle décida d'écrire, séance tenante, à Ferdinand Wolff. Mais la pensée que sa lettre n'arriverait sans doute pas à destination lui gâcha son entrain. Quand elle eut cacheté le pli, il lui sembla qu'elle n'avait su ni raconter sa vie ni exprimer ses sentiments.

Pendant le souper, Serge lui demanda, d'un ton négligent, si tout allait bien chez ses amis « de l'autre côté de l'Oural ». Elle n'eut garde de relever l'insolence de sa question. Visiblement, il cherchait une petite querelle pour corser la soirée. Maintenant qu'elle le connaissait mieux, elle le jugeait comme un garçon égoïste, infatué, coléreux, mais avec qui, somme toute, il était possible de s'entendre, à condition de ne jamais lui parler de bonheur du peuple et de la forme idéale du gouvernement. On eût dit que certains mots du vocabulaire politique provoquaient, par commotion, un rétrécissement de son cerveau. Soudain, il se butait, son visage se fermait, devenait méchant et bête. Elle dévia la conversation en l'interrogeant sur la façon dont il avait mené les pourparlers avec les acheteurs de Pskov. Et, pendant qu'il se racontait, avec un plaisir évident, elle retourna, en songe, parmi sa vraie famille, composée de gens qui la comprenaient, qui l'aimaient, qui avaient subi les mêmes épreuves qu'elle et que, sans doute, elle ne reverrait plus.

Les jours suivants, elle attendit d'autres lettres. Quand le cocher revenait de la poste de Pskov, elle se précipitait sur le perron afin de savoir, vite, s'il ne rapportait rien pour elle dans sa sacoche. Il prit l'habitude, du plus loin qu'il la voyait, de secouer la tête négativement. Les déceptions s'ajoutaient l'une à l'autre et cependant elle s'obstinait dans l'espoir. L'heure du courrier passée, elle traînait, dolente, désœuvrée, dans le parc de Kachtanovka. Les allées étaient jonchées de feuilles mortes. De tous côtés, des arbres, à demi dépouillés par le vent, dressaient leurs fortes charpentes couronnées d'un frémissement de pourpre et de rouille. Dans ce flamboiement végétal, les sapins, sombres et coniques, faisaient figure de gigantesques éteignoirs. Au cours d'une de ses promenades, Sophie déboucha dans une clairière où elle était déjà venue souvent dans le passé. C'était le petit cimetière des maîtres. Derrière une grille, de simples croix de pierre, surmontées

d'un toit en accent circonflexe : les ancêtres de
Michel Borissovitch, des oncles, des tantes, Michel
Borissovitch lui-même, sa femme, sa fille, enfin
Vladimir Karpovitch Sédoff. Celui-là n'avait rien
à faire dans la réunion ! Une fois de plus, Sophie
regretta que les autorités eussent refusé le trans-
fert du corps de Nicolas. Elle eût aimé pouvoir lui
parler ici, seule à seul, à travers la terre. Chaque
année, elle avait plus de mal à l'imaginer vivant.
Quand elle pensait à lui, elle voyait le grand lac
lumineux auprès duquel il reposait, dans le murmure des vagues renouvelées. Ou bien encore, il
se présentait à elle en noir et blanc, comme l'image
d'un livre. Toujours immobile, irréel, sans épais-
seur et sans chaleur. Une paysanne balayait les
feuilles mortes autour des tombes. Sophie reprit,
tête basse, le chemin de la maison.

Ce soir-là, par une coïncidence insolite, Serge
lui annonça qu'il ferait dire, le 15 novembre prochain, à l'église de Chatkovo, une messe pour le
repos de l'âme de son père, mort depuis juste six
mois. En dépit des sentiments que lui inspirait
Vladimir Karpovitch Sédoff, elle ne put refuser
d'assister à l'office. D'autant que, par la même occasion, le prêtre appellerait la bénédiction de Dieu
sur tous les défunts de la famille.

A l'aube du 15 novembre, le vent se leva avec
force, poussant de lourds nuages gris au ras de
l'horizon. Pendant que Serge et Sophie se rendaient
en voiture à l'église, la pluie se mit à tomber. Malgré le mauvais temps, tous les paysans de Chatkovo et des villages voisins s'étaient rassemblés
dans la nef. Des « conducteurs » les y avaient
amenés comme du bétail. Serrés coude à coude,
les hommes d'un côté, les femmes de l'autre, ils
formaient une masse compacte, mais qui s'ouvrit

en chuchotant pour laisser les maîtres s'avancer jusqu'à l'iconostase. Le père Hilarion était vêtu de noir, l'air tragique, l'étole croisée sur le dos. Un petit diacre rouquin tenait l'encensoir, d'où s'échappait une fumée bleuâtre au parfum oriental. Par les fenêtres haut perchées tombait la lumière livide de l'orage. Dès le début de la messe, un roulement de tonnerre courut au loin. Quand le prêtre psalmodia l'oraison de pénitence : « Seigneur, maître de ma vie... » une houle agita les fidèles et ils s'agenouillèrent, écrasés par la conscience de leur indignité.

« Seigneur, ouvre mes yeux de pécheur ! » poursuivit le prêtre d'une voix caverneuse.

Et le ciel se déchira avec fracas. Dans la lueur de l'éclair, les ors de l'iconostase flamboyèrent, puis tout s'éteignit. Le père Hilarion leva des yeux inquiets vers la voûte. Un second coup de tonnerre, plus violent et plus proche, fit trembler les vitres. Sophie observa Serge à la dérobée. Un genou en terre, le front incliné, il méditait, imperturbable. Alors, elle regarda en arrière : le peuple ne priait plus. Une épouvante sacrée était sur tous les visages. Figés sur place, les moujiks, les femmes, leurs enfants semblaient attendre la fin du monde. Ce fut dans ce bruit d'avalanche, que se déroula toute la seconde moitié de l'office. Lorsque le prêtre en vint à parler du défunt et prononça le nom du « serviteur de Dieu Vladimir », un gémissement unanime lui répondit. Serge se signa. Les fidèles répétèrent son geste et, prosternés, frappèrent le sol de leur front. Enfin, le tonnerre s'éloigna, le ciel rengaina ses épées de feu.

En sortant de l'église, Sophie découvrit un village reverni par l'averse. Il ne pleuvait plus. L'air était pur, silencieux. Des nuages paisibles se retlétaient dans les flaques. Au moment de remonter en calèche avec Serge, elle se ravisa et dit :

— Tout compte fait, je préfère vous laisser rentrer seul : j'ai quelques familles de moujiks à visiter ici. Pourrez-vous me renvoyer la voiture ?

Surpris par la soudaineté de cette décision, il ne sut que murmurer :

— Certainement, ma tante.

Mais ses yeux brillaient de rancune. Il bondit dans la calèche, dont les ressorts grincèrent, frappa du poing le dos du cocher et hurla :

— Va ! Va ! Triple imbécile !

Le départ fut si brutal, que Sophie dut se reculer pour n'être pas éclaboussée. Déjà, autour d'elle, les moujiks se dispersaient, comme s'ils eussent craint qu'elle ne leur adressât la parole. La frayeur qu'ils avaient ressentie à l'église paraissait les obséder encore. Même le prêtre décampa sans un mot, même le staroste. En quelques minutes, Sophie se retrouva seule au milieu du village. Intriguée, elle essaya de relancer les paysans chez eux. Partout, on la reçut avec méfiance. Elle avait beau savoir le rôle de la superstition chez ces êtres arriérés, elle ne pouvait supposer qu'un simple orage les eût impressionnés à ce point. Il y avait autre chose qu'ils ne voulaient pas lui dire. En désespoir de cause, elle se rendit chez Antipe.

— Ah ! barynia ! s'écria-t-il en joignant les mains. Pourquoi êtes-vous venue ?

— Toi seul peux me renseigner, Antipe. Que se passe-t-il ? Tout le village a l'air terrorisé !

— Il y a de quoi, barynia ! Vous avez entendu le tonnerre à l'église ? L'homme a dépassé la mesure ! Il a commis le sacrilège !

Il se signait et jetait autour de lui des regards traqués.

132

— Quel sacrilège ? demanda Sophie.

— Cette messe, barynia, il n'avait pas le droit de la faire dire !

— N'est-ce pas une tradition ?...

— Pour suivre la tradition, il faut avoir la conscience tranquille ! Neuf jours après la mort de Vladimir Karpovitch, il y a eu un office funèbre et tout s'est bien passé. Quarante jours après, il y a eu un nouvel office funèbre et, cette fois encore, tout s'est bien passé. Mais aujourd'hui enfin, Dieu a donné sa réponse. Pendant que le fils indigne osait prier pour le repos du père, le ciel a protesté et tous les chrétiens l'ont compris. Ce qui m'étonne c'est qu'il ne soit pas tombé foudroyé au milieu de l'église.

— Pourquoi le détestes-tu ? dit Sophie.

— Parce qu'il a fait condamner des innocents !

— Ce ne sont pas les trois moujiks qui ont tué Vladimir Karpovitch ?

— Non, barynia ! Ils l'ont trouvé mort, étranglé, dans la cabane de bains, un matin qu'ils allaient travailler là-bas ! Ils ont couru prévenir le jeune barine ! Et le jeune barine leur a dit : « C'est vous les coupables ! »

Etonnée par cette révélation, Sophie mit quelques secondes à rassembler ses esprits. Malgré le peu de confiance que lui inspirait son neveu, elle refusait de partager les vues d'Antipe.

— S'ils n'étaient pas coupables, ils n'avaient qu'à nier, dit-elle.

— Ils ont nié !

— Et puis ?

— Et puis, ils se sont laissé faire.

— Pourquoi ?

— Ce ne sont que des moujiks ! Un moujik, à la fin, doit toujours dire oui !

— On ne force pas un homme à avouer un crime qu'il n'a pas commis ?

— Même en le menaçant de quatre cents coups de knout ?

— Qui les a menacés ?

— Bien malin qui pourrait le dire ! C'est une supposition...

— Et qui, d'après toi, est l'assassin ?

— Je n'en sais pas plus que vous !...

— En somme, tes soupçons ne reposent sur rien.

Il éclata d'un rire faux et servile :

— Sur rien, barynia ! Sur rien du tout !...

— Tout à l'heure, pourtant, tu disais...

Il fit un salut profond en ouvrant les bras et en avançant une jambe, le talon à terre, la pointe du pied levée :

— Tout à l'heure, j'étais fou ! Maintenant, je suis raisonnable ! Si vous croyez que les trois moujiks ont tué, c'est qu'ils ont tué réellement et qu'on a bien fait de les envoyer au bagne !

— Ils étaient peut-être en état de légitime défense, concéda-t-elle.

— Qu'est-ce que ça veut dire ?

— Si leur maître les avait frappés le premier...

— Ce doit être ça ! Il les a frappés le premier ! Et eux, couic, ils lui ont tordu le cou ! Paraît qu'il n'était pas beau à voir ! Tout bleu ! La langue sortie !...

Antipe se frottait les mains en parlant. Son visage avait une expression de férocité craintive.

— Si seulement il pouvait arriver au fils la même chose qu'au père ! dit-il encore.

— Tais-toi ! gronda Sophie.

Elle traversait un terrain louche, marécageux,

134

qui fuyait sous ses pas. Ce qui l'agaçait le plus, c'était l'impossibilité d'interroger Serge sur les véritables circonstances du meurtre, sans qu'il la soupçonnât de s'être renseignée auprès des paysans. Comme s'il eût deviné les hésitations de sa maîtresse, Antipe proféra d'une voix chevrotante :

— Ne répétez à personne ce que je vous ai dit, barynia ! Ce sont des mensonges ! De sales mensonges de serf ! Même l'orage, il ne faut plus y penser ! Il a éclaté, comme ça, par hasard ! La vérité, c'est que notre bon maître a été étouffé par de méchants moujiks et que les méchants moujiks n'auront pas assez de toute leur vie pour expier ce crime !

Elle le quitta, plus troublée qu'elle ne l'aurait voulu. Entre-temps, la calèche était revenue au village. Il faisait sombre, froid, humide. Le cocher, David, aida Sophie à monter en voiture et lui enveloppa les jambes dans un plaid. Tout au long de la route, les chevaux pataugèrent dans la boue. Enfin, entre les branches nues, apparurent les fenêtres éclairées de la maison.

Pendant le souper, Serge garda le silence. Son visage était sévère, ses gestes compassés. Ce fut seulement lorsque Sophie et lui se retrouvèrent dans le bureau, qu'il laissa percer son mécontentement.

— Etait-il si important que vous restiez au village ? demanda-t-il.

— Je vous ai dit que j'avais à faire là-bas, répondit-elle en prenant son ouvrage.

— Avec les moujiks ? Vous vous intéressez trop à eux, ma tante ! Dieu sait ce qu'ils vous ont encore raconté après l'orage ! Le tonnerre, les éclairs, en pleine messe funèbre ! Bêtes comme ils sont, ils ont dû trouver là leur compte de malédictions !...

— Oh ! laissez-les... Ce sont des gens simples !...

Serge marchait de long en large devant elle. Il s'arrêta et dit rudement :

— Ne cherchez pas à les excuser ! Je sais qu'ils me haïssent, comme ils haïssaient mon père et mon grand-père, comme ils haïront toujours celui qui les condamnera ! Plus on se montre doux avec ces animaux-là, plus ils deviennent exigeants, remuants !...

— Je me suis beaucoup occupé d'eux autrefois et je n'ai pas l'impression d'avoir jeté le désordre dans leurs esprits !

— Ce n'est pas ce qu'on m'a raconté ! Il paraît que vous prêchiez aux paysans les délices de la liberté et de l'égalité républicaines !

— Je ne sais qui vous a rapporté ces sottises, mais, du moins, à l'époque de Michel Borissovitch, il n'y a pas eu parmi les moujiks une seule révolte comme celle qui a coûté la vie à votre père !

Il dressa le menton. Ses narines se pincèrent, blanchirent.

— Mon père n'a pas succombé à une révolte, il a été assassiné lâchement, par des gredins !

— Ne les avait-il pas provoqués par des exactions ?

— Je vous prie de ne pas insulter sa mémoire !

— Vous m'avez dit vous-même qu'il était souvent très dur avec les moujiks !

Il la considéra, égaré de colère, et, ne trouvant rien de sensé à répondre, grommela :

— Je n'ai de comptes à rendre à personne !

— Moi non plus, Serge, dit-elle froidement. Et pourtant, vous m'en demandez.

136

Il ricana :

— Je me garde bien d'oublier que ce domaine vous appartient autant qu'à moi, ma tante. D'après les étranges dispositions testamentaires de mon grand-père, je ne peux même pas vous racheter votre part. Nous devons rester dans l'indivision jusqu'à la mort de l'un de nous deux. Si je disparais le premier, vous hériterez de tout. Si c'est vous qui...

— Où voulez-vous en venir ? trancha-t-elle.

— A ceci, qui est fort important : vous avez beau être à égalité de droits avec moi dans cette affaire, vous n'êtes qu'une reléguée. Le gouverneur de Pskov m'a chargé de votre surveillance. Vous devez donc vous soumettre à ma volonté. Je puis vous interdire tout agissement qui me paraîtrait suspect. Or, il me déplaît de penser que vous courez de village en village sous des prétextes charitables. Le paysan russe n'a que faire de la politique française. Les malheurs que vous avez déjà suscités en propageant vos théories révolutionnaires devraient vous inciter à plus de modestie. Restez à la maison, cela vaudra mieux pour tout le monde !

Elle faillit s'emporter, mais se maîtrisa et dit avec une terrible douceur :

— Serge, vous excédez les bornes, vous oubliez qui je suis, d'où je viens !

— Vous venez de Sibérie, où vous avez vécu parmi des condamnés politiques, ce qui est une mauvaise recommandation pour moi ! Vos idées, je ne veux à aucun prix qu'elles contaminent les gens de Kachtanovka ! Malgré tout le respect que je vous dois, ma tante, j'ai décidé de diriger le domaine à ma façon. Contentez-vous, comme je vous l'ai déjà dit, de vous occuper des questions domestiques, et nous resterons bons amis...

La violence de cette sortie la stupéfia. Jamais encore Serge ne lui avait parlé avec tant d'insolence. Pourquoi, aujourd'hui, cette mise au point comminatoire, ce brusque sursaut d'autorité ? On eût dit qu'il voulait la réduire une fois pour toutes à l'impuissance, comme s'il eût craint, en la laissant libre, de perdre tout pouvoir sur elle et sur les moujiks. Elle l'observait avec un intérêt passionné. Avait-elle réellement trouvé un jour qu'il ressemblait à Nicolas ? Il n'y avait rien de commun entre ces deux êtres, rien, sinon le modelé du visage et la couleur des cheveux. Serge avait volé le masque de son oncle pour s'en couvrir la face, mais ses yeux bruns et vifs le trahissaient. Sophie lisait en eux toute la méchanceté, toute la duplicité qu'elle avait décelées jadis chez Vladimir Karpovitch Sédoff. Renforcée dans son désir de lui tenir tête, elle dit d'un ton sec :

— Apprenez, Serge, qu'il n'est pas dans mes habitudes de plier devant la menace. Surtout lorsque celui qui prétend m'en imposer est un gamin de vingt-cinq ans, mon propre neveu. Je suis ici chez moi. J'agirai comme bon me semble !

Il y eut un silence. Elle reprit sa respiration et poursuivit avec un sourire moqueur :

— Si cela vous contrarie, vous pourrez toujours vous plaindre au gouverneur. Qui sait, peut-être, désespérant de me faire entendre raison, me renverra-t-il, sur votre demande, en Sibérie ? Je vous préviens tout de suite qu'une telle perspective n'est pas pour m'effrayer !

Quand elle se tut, il resta un moment sans réaction, puis son visage se détendit, son regard s'alluma, il dit d'une voix aimable :

— Ne vous fâchez pas, ma tante. Condamnés à vivre ensemble, sous ce toit, nous finirons bien par nous entendre. Je vous prie simplement de me prévenir lorsque vous voudrez aller vous promener dans les villages d'alentour.

Elle secoua le front :

— Je ne vous préviendrai pas, Serge. J'irai quand il me plaira, où il me plaira, dans un rayon de quinze verstes, puisque telle est la limite qui m'a été imposée par le gouvernement...

Serge s'assit sur le bras d'un fauteuil et baissa la tête. Il paraissait vaincu et, cependant, elle avait conscience qu'il ne se repliait sur lui-même que pour mieux l'attaquer ensuite. Après une longue pause, il bâilla, s'étira, fit craquer les phalanges de ses mains unies et marmonna :

— Vous ai-je dit que je partais demain matin pour Pskov ?

Elle se retint de sourire. Sans doute allait-il là-bas pour ses pauvres fredaines hebdomadaires. Il rentrerait assagi.

— Si vous avez quelques emplettes à faire, je suis à votre disposition, reprit-il.

— Je vous remercie, dit Sophie. Je compte me rendre moi-même en ville un de ces prochains jours.

Il lui lança un regard en dessous, se leva, grogna : « Bonsoir ! » et sortit.

Serge partit à cheval, tôt le matin, pour la ville.
Quand il eut disparu au bout de l'allée, Sophie
éprouva un sentiment de délivrance. Elle refusait
de croire que les façons tranchantes de son neveu
l'eussent impressionnée et, cependant, elle devait
reconnaître que, lui absent, elle respirait mieux.
Chaque fois qu'il s'en allait, la maison semblait
s'éveiller d'une contrainte. Les portes claquaient ;
on entendait rire aux éclats du côté des communs ;
des enfants serfs se poursuivaient en courant autour de la grande pelouse... Après s'être habillée
avec l'aide de Zoé, Sophie décida de se rendre non
plus à Chatkovo, mais dans les autres villages
qu'elle avait un peu négligés, ces derniers temps.
Elle ouvrit la fenêtre et cria à un domestique qui
passait de faire préparer sa calèche.

Une demi-heure plus tard, quand elle entra dans
l'écurie, elle constata que rien n'était prêt. David,
le cocher, n'était même pas en tenue. Elle se fâcha :

— On ne t'a pas prévenu que je voulais sortir ?
David eut un mouvement de recul et une expres-

141

sion de frayeur bouleversa son gros visage barbu.

— Si, barynia, bredouilla-t-il.

— Alors, qu'attends-tu pour faire atteler ?

Deux valets d'écurie, qui fourchaient du foin, se plaquèrent peureusement contre le mur, un autre se cacha derrière la croupe du cheval qu'il était en train de panser.

— C'est impossible, barynia ! dit David.

— Pourquoi ?

— Le jeune barine nous l'a défendu.

Sophie fut désarçonnée par cette réponse, puis elle se révolta :

— Quand je donne un ordre, il n'a pas à me contredire ! s'écria-t-elle. Je suis votre maîtresse !

— Certainement, barynia.

— Vous m'avez obéi jusqu'à ce jour ?

— Oui, barynia.

— Eh bien ! Alors ? Qu'y a-t-il de changé ? Je vous somme d'atteler cette calèche ! Vite ! Vite !

David poussa un long soupir, qui parut lui arracher les poumons, regarda les valets d'écurie à la dérobée et baissa le nez. Sa barbe se plia sur sa poitrine.

— Tu entends ce que je te dis ? demanda Sophie d'une voix forte.

Pas de réponse. Il se figeait, il s'alourdissait, on avait coulé du plomb dans sa tête. Sophie comprit qu'elle n'obtiendrait rien de ces hommes terrorisés.

— C'est bien, dit-elle, je me passerai de vous.

Elle décrocha un harnais pendu au mur, le posa sur le premier cheval venu, fixa les courroies comme elle l'avait vu faire, poussa la bête dans les brancards d'une calèche, serra la sous-ventrière, ajusta les traits, pendant que le cocher et les palefreniers, immobiles, perclus de crainte, suivaient

ses gestes avec des yeux ronds. Quand elle monta
sur le siège du conducteur, David gémit :

— Pardonnez-nous, barynia !

Elle fit claquer le fouet ; le cheval partit au pas
dans l'allée et accéléra son allure ; Sophie, rudement secouée, dut réunir ses guides dans une main
et retenir de l'autre son grand chapeau de paille à
rubans qui menaçait de s'envoler. La route était
un cloaque. Des giclures de boue jaune sautaient
de chaque côté des roues. Dans les champs ramol-
lis, se déplaçaient des silhouettes brumeuses de
moujiks. Que pouvaient-ils bien faire par si mauvais temps ? Sophie visita successivement Tcherniakovo, Krapinovo, Bolotnoïé et jusqu'aux plus
petits hameaux du domaine. Partout, elle retrouva
la même atmosphère de tristesse dans l'ordre,
d'anxiété dans le bien-être. Serge pouvait être fier
de sa réussite : la discipline qu'il avait instaurée
était si efficace, que tous ses paysans, déjà, se
ressemblaient... D'isba en isba, Sophie oublia
l'heure du dîner ; au début de l'après-midi, elle
décida de pousser jusqu'à Pskov pour acheter
quelques médicaments dont elle aurait probablement besoin cet hiver, quand les routes seraient
coupées par les neiges.

Conduisant sa calèche, elle arriva en ville vers
trois heures. Une bruine crépusculaire pesait sur
les toits mouillés. La rue principale n'était qu'une
traînée de vase noirâtre, sur laquelle on avait jeté
des bottes de paille. Dans la boutique de l'apothi-
caire brûlaient deux lampes à huile, dont les reflets se multipliaient au flanc des bocaux. Pendant que le préparateur servait Sophie, elle entendit la porte s'ouvrir derrière elle, se retourna
et vit une forte femme, au chapeau emplumé et au
manteau bleu barbeau à galons noirs, qui fran-

chissait le seuil avec majesté. Après une seconde
d'indécision, elle éprouva un sentiment désagréa-
ble et reconnut Daria Philippovna. Comme elle
avait vieilli et engraissé ! Ses yeux étaient coincés
entre deux bourrelets de chair molle. La pâte de
ses joues pendait de part et d'autre d'une bouche
en cerise. Elle respirait péniblement, le ventre cor-
seté, le poitrail en cuirasse. Même en se forçant,
Sophie ne pouvait croire que Nicolas eût été
l'amant de cette corpulente créature. Que faire ?
Impossible d'éviter la rencontre. Le mieux était de
s'en tenir à un petit salut sec... Elle se demandait
encore quelle attitude prendre, lorsque Daria Philippovna, l'apercevant, s'épanouit dans un sourire
et lui tendit les deux mains. Sophie se raidit et
tenta, elle aussi, de sourire. L'aisance de cette
femme la surprenait. Une seule explication : Daria
Philippovna se figurait que Sophie avait toujours
ignoré l'infidélité de son mari. La détromper ? A
quoi bon ? Tant d'années avaient passé sur cette
lamentable aventure !

— Chère, chère Madame ! s'écria Daria Philippovna. Quelle émotion de vous revoir ! Je savais
que vous étiez revenue ! Justement je voulais vous
écrire pour vous inviter à la maison ! Maintenant
que je vous tiens, je ne vous lâche plus ! Vous
êtes à Pskov pour faire des courses ? Moi aussi !
Nous irons donc ensemble !...

Cette bruyante amabilité eut raison des réti-
cences de Sophie. A contrecœur elle se laissa accompagner d'un magasin à l'autre. Parfois, elle
croyait reconnaître, au loin, la silhouette de Serge
et se demandait ce qu'il penserait en la voyant
avec cette jacasse emplumée. Mais il était peu
probable qu'il traînât dans les rues : il ne venait
pas à Pskov pour flâner.

Les deux femmes échouèrent enfin dans l'atelier d'une couturière, Tamara Ivanovna, qui était un peu bossue, un peu bigle, mais avait des doigts de fée. Daria Philippovna essaya une robe en pou de soie amarante, qu'elle avait choisie, Dieu sait pourquoi, puisque, de son propre aveu, elle ne sortait jamais. Sophie promit de revenir pour commander quelque chose elle-même. Après l'essayage, Tamara Ivanovna proposa aux deux dames de passer dans l'arrière-salle où un samovar chauffait en permanence à l'intention des visiteuses altérées. Sophie, qui était fatiguée par sa longue promenade, accepta avec plaisir de prendre une tasse de thé. Ayant servi ses deux clientes, la couturière les laissa seules, car elle avait du travail en retard.

Il faisait déjà sombre dehors. Une lampe à huile bien astiquée et coiffée d'un abat-jour vert à franges éclairait la petite pièce où flottait une odeur d'empois. Le samovar chantait sous la théière pansue. Aux murs s'alignaient des images découpées dans des journaux de mode français. Les sièges étaient recouverts de housses. Daria Philippovna lapait son thé avec des soupirs de contentement et, entre deux gorgées, posait à Sophie des questions qui prouvaient qu'elle s'intéressait aux épreuves des décembristes. Elle était bête mais bonne, indiscutablement. A tout propos, elle s'indignait, se désolait, gémissait : « Ah ! mon Dieu ! Quel calvaire a été le vôtre ! » Elle voulut savoir comment Nicolas était mort et pleura en écoutant le récit très simple de Sophie.

— Le pauvre ! Lui si gai, si insouciant, si courageux ! Je ne peux pas le croire ! Excusez-moi, je ne peux pas le croire !...

Elle se moucha. Son menton duveteux tremblait au-dessus de sa collerette. Deux femmes en deuil du même homme, devant un samovar. Et, des deux, c'était l'épouse légitime qui avait les yeux secs. Le ridicule de la situation apparut à Sophie et, pendant un moment, elle fut irritée de cette affliction qui s'étalait. Comme si elle eût craint de trahir son secret en se lamentant davantage, Daria Philippovna se versa une autre tasse de thé et dit :

— J'imagine avec quelle émotion vous avez retrouvé Kachtanovka ! Certes, bien des êtres manquent en ces lieux où vous avez été si heureuse ! Mais le décor, du moins, n'a pas changé et, à notre âge, il n'est pas de plus grand réconfort que la promenade quotidienne parmi les souvenirs !

L'expression « à notre âge » amusa Sophie, qui savait avoir dix ans de moins que son interlocutrice.

— Vous avez dû être surprise de tomber sur ce grand neveu ! reprit Daria Philippovna. Vous ne le connaissiez pour ainsi dire pas !

— Serge avait quelques mois lorsque je suis partie.

— Il est très bien de sa personne. Mais si sauvage ! On le voit rarement en ville. Moi, je trouve qu'il ressemble beaucoup à Nicolas !

— Physiquement, oui.

Daria Philippovna battit des paupières et exhala son regret :

— Pour le moral, bien sûr, c'est autre chose ! Vous entendez-vous bien avec lui ?

— Ni bien ni mal, répondit Sophie avec prudence.

— Je vous dis cela parce qu'il a été élevé dans des idées qui, évidemment, ne sont pas les vôtres !

— Je m'en suis déjà rendu compte, dit Sophie. Mais je ne suis pas une sectaire !

— Lui, si !

— C'est de son âge ! Il ne fait que répéter ce qu'il a entendu. Il aimait beaucoup son père...

— Je ne le crois pas, dit Daria Philippovna en hochant la tête. Ils se disputaient souvent.

Sophie s'étonna :

— A quel sujet ?

Cet aveu d'ignorance enflamma Daria Philippovna. La joie de renseigner quelqu'un parut sur son visage. Elle murmura :

— Comment, vous ne savez pas ? Toujours la même chose ! A cause de Kachtanovka ! Vous me comprenez ?...

— Non. J'ai trouvé que le domaine était très bien tenu, très bien exploité. Mieux que du temps de mon beau-père...

— Bien sûr ! Mais c'est grâce à votre neveu ! Uniquement grâce à lui !... D'ailleurs, cela tombe sous le sens !... Vous connaissiez Vladimir Karpovitch !... Il aurait vendu la propriété, s'il avait pu, pour satisfaire ses caprices de joueur. Tant qu'il a été le tuteur de l'enfant, il en a profité (d'après ce qu'on m'a dit) pour se défaire de quelques paysans en cachette, écouler des moissons sur pied à bas prix, emprunter à un taux exorbitant. Quand Serge Vladimirovitch a eu atteint sa majorité, il a exigé des comptes. C'était fatal ! Il en est résulté des discussions très vives. On raconte que les éclats de voix s'entendaient des communs ! Moi, en toute conscience, je donne raison au fils. Savez-vous qu'il a la passion de la terre ? Le mois dernier, il a encore voulu m'acheter trois villages qui jouxtent votre propriété. J'ai dit non, parce que, moi aussi, ce que j'ai c'est sacré, je le garde ! J'ai dit non, mais j'ai pensé : bravo !... Si seulement mon Vassia était comme lui !... Mais il se désintéresse complètement de notre chère Slavianka... Il vit chez moi comme à l'hôtel, en vieux célibataire, parmi ses livres... C'est consternant !... Heureusement, mès filles me donnent toutes les satisfactions que mon fils me refuse... Elles habitent Moscou... L'une est mariée à...

Elle partit dans des considérations familiales et Sophie, indifférente, s'isola comme sur un caillou au milieu d'un flot de paroles. De temps à autre, elle entendait : « Mon autre fille... Mon gendre... Mes petits-enfants... » et pensait : « Elle a toute une famille, nombreuse, chaude, grouillante. Comme une vraie femme, qui a fait son métier de donneuse de vie. Moi je n'ai personne, hormis Serge. Mais qui est Serge ?... » Elle s'interrogeait et s'inquiétait. Daria Philippovna lui toucha la main :

— Mon fils serait si heureux de vous voir !

— Moi aussi j'aimerais le voir, dit Sophie évasivement.

Les yeux bleus de Daria Philippovna pétillèrent :

— Il faut absolument que vous veniez prendre le thé à la maison, un de ces jours ! Jeudi prochain, cela vous conviendrait ?

D'abord Sophie voulut refuser. Elle ne pouvait oublier que Nicolas s'était battu en duel autrefois contre Vassia Volkoff. Bien que les deux hommes se fussent plus ou moins réconciliés par la suite, le souvenir de cette dispute était encore lourd à supporter pour elle. Cependant, une curiosité la poussait. Elle s'entendit murmurer :

— Jeudi prochain ? Oui... Je vous remercie.

— Il n'y aura que mon fils et moi, je vous le

promets ! Avez-vous déjà revu quelques connaissances ?

— Personne. Je ne suis pas pressée.

— Vous avez bien raison ! Laissez-les se languir ! Vous n'avez pas changé ! Il me semble que vous nous avez quittés hier ! Ce n'est pas comme moi ! Quand je me regarde dans ma glace, je crois voir ma pauvre maman !

Elle vida sa tasse de thé et tira de son sac un mouchoir en dentelle pour se tamponner les lèvres. Sophie jeta un regard vers la fenêtre et s'étonna de voir les vitres toutes noires. Il devait être plus de six heures. Elle aurait une longue route à faire, dans la nuit. Daria Philippovna la gronda d'être venue seule, sans cocher. Par fierté, Sophie répondit qu'elle aimait mieux conduire elle-même !

— Ce n'est guère prudent, dit Daria Philippovna. Voulez-vous que je demande à mes gens de vous raccompagner ?

Elle refusa. Les deux femmes se séparèrent dans la rue. Daria Philippovna avait quelques visites à faire. Sophie monta bravement dans sa calèche et partit. Après les dernières maisons de la ville, les ténèbres s'épaissirent. La campagne exhalait une odeur de champignon et de bois brûlé. Il n'y avait pas de lanterne à la voiture. Mais le cheval, connaissant la route, trottait au jugé. Les yeux écarquillés sur l'ombre dansante, Sophie récapitulait un à un les événements de la journée et laissait croître sa colère contre Serge, qui avait interdit à David de lui obéir.

En descendant de voiture, devant le perron, elle sentit sa fatigue. Un gamin saisit le cheval au mors pour le ramener à l'écurie. Autour de la maison, régnait un calme insolite. Les fenêtres du bureau

149

étaient éteintes. Personne dans le vestibule. Mais le chapeau et le manteau de Serge étaient accrochés à une patère : il était déjà revenu de Pskov. Elle allait pouvoir lui dire son indignation. Auparavant, elle voulait se rafraîchir, se rajuster. Elle monta dans sa chambre et appela Zoé, qui accourut pour l'aider à changer de robe. La fille avait les yeux rouges, la respiration entrecoupée.

— Qu'as-tu ? demanda Sophie. Tu as pleuré ?

— Oh ! non, barynia ! gémit Zoé.

Mais son menton, arrondi comme un œuf, continuait de bouger spasmodiquement.

— Je vois bien que si, dit Sophie. Tu peux tout me dire, à moi. C'est à cause de ton mari ?

— Oui, renifla Zoé.

— David a été méchant avec toi ? Il t'a battue ?

— C'est lui qu'on a battu !

— Qui l'a battu ?

— Les hommes du barine, tout à l'heure... Avant que vous n'arriviez... Cinquante coups de verges... Il a le dos en sang... Il est couché...

Sophie fronça les sourcils. La fureur lui remontait à la tête après une accalmie.

— Pourquoi l'a-t-on battu ? dit-elle d'une voix sourde.

Zoé détourna les yeux :

— A cause de vous, barynia.

De surprise, Sophie resta la bouche ouverte.

— A cause de moi ? murmura-t-elle enfin. C'est impossible !

— Si, barynia. Il devait vous empêcher de partir. Il n'a pas su. Alors, le jeune barine l'a fait fouetter au milieu de la cour...

Dans le silence qui suivit, Sophie fut sur le point de perdre le contrôle d'elle-même. Ses idées

150

se soulevaient avec violence. Elle entendait battre son sang.

— Il a fait fouetter aussi les valets d'écurie, reprit Zoé. Mais je vous en supplie, ne lui dites pas que je me suis plainte à vous ! Il serait furieux, il se vengerait ! Après tout, ce n'est pas grave ! David guérira bientôt ! Il est solide, malgré son âge !

— Non, non, cette fois, c'en est trop ! bredouilla Sophie, se parlant à elle-même.

Elle boutonna nerveusement son corsage et se précipita hors de la chambre. L'escalier trembla sous ses pieds. Persuadée que Serge était dans le bureau, elle y entra en coup de vent, s'arrêta, déconcertée, au milieu de la pièce sombre et vide, ressortit, jetant les yeux autour d'elle. Un domestique, qui traînait dans le vestibule, lui dit :

— Si vous cherchez le barine, il est dans sa chambre.

Sophie remonta l'escalier, suivit le couloir en sens inverse et frappa à la porte de Serge.

— Entrez, dit une voix affable.

Il était assis devant un petit bureau et compulsait des papiers. Une robe de chambre en brocart mordoré l'enveloppait jusqu'aux chevilles. Il se leva, resserra sa cordelière et son visage exprima la surprise que lui causait cette visite intempestive. Encore essoufflée d'avoir gravi les marches, Sophie dit avec colère :

— Pourquoi avez-vous fait battre David ?

Les sourcils de Serge se haussèrent sur son front :

— Je lui avais donné des ordres, ma tante.

— Ne les a-t-il pas exécutés ?

Il eut un imperceptible sourire. Sans doute avait-il prévu cette scène et goûtait-il un secret plaisir à conserver son calme devant cette femme exaspérée.

— Vous avez pu partir malgré tout, dit-il. Donc, David est coupable. Rassurez-vous, une bonne raclée n'a jamais fait de mal à un moujik. Cela active la circulation de son sang, qu'il a naturellement assez lourd. Evidemment, il ne faudrait pas abuser de cette discipline. Il dépend de vous seule que les choses en restent là ! Si vous voulez bien vous conformer à mes prescriptions, le cocher et les palefreniers ne seront plus inquiétés. En revanche, si vous recommencez votre escapade, je me verrai dans l'obligation de les faire passer par les verges. Je tiens à ce que tout soit en ordre chez moi. Chaque chose à sa place et chaque être à son rang. Puisque vous aimez tant les serfs, vous pouvez bien leur sacrifier un peu de votre indépendance. Charitable comme vous êtes, il vous en coûtera moins de demeurer à la maison que de penser qu'à cause de vous ces malheureux se font écorcher l'échine !...

Sophie l'écoutait avec horreur. Aucune des excuses qu'elle lui avait trouvées naguère ne tenait devant l'affirmation tranquille de cette méchanceté. Elle fixa sur lui un regard méprisant et dit en détachant chaque mot :

— Je vous jure, Serge, que, quoi qu'il arrive, vous ne toucherez plus à un cheveu de vos moujiks.

— Que vous me connaissez mal, ma tante !

— C'est vous qui me connaissez mal ! Je ne me laisserai pas intimider par votre chantage Si vous faites ce que vous avez dit, je remuerai ciel et terre, j'irai jusqu'au gouverneur !

— A pied ? demanda-t-il avec insolence.

— A pied, oui, s'il le faut ! Quelques verstes ne

sont pas pour me faire peur. Je révélerai aux autorités la façon dont vous traitez vos serfs !...

Elle disait n'importe quoi, emportée par l'indignation, et, soudain, elle remarqua un vacillement dans les prunelles de Serge. Comme si, sans le savoir, elle l'eût touché à un point vulnérable. Ce désarroi fut si rapide, qu'au moment où elle s'en avisait il s'était déjà ressaisi.

— Et vous vous imaginez que le gouverneur vous écoutera ? dit-il en ricanant.

— Je me suis déjà fait entendre de gens plus importants que lui, répliqua-t-elle.

— Au bagne ?

— Et à Saint-Pétersbourg ! Le seul fait que je sois revenue de Sibérie vous prouve à quel point je suis opiniâtre ! Je n'hésiterai pas à me servir de toutes mes relations pour que mes droits soient respectés dans cette maison !

— Nul ne songe à contester vos droits, dit-il, subitement apaisé.

— Si ! Vous osez interdire à mes gens d'obéir à mes ordres ! Vous leur infligez la torture pour obtenir leur soumission ! Vous vous servez d'eux pour me séquestrer ! Kachtanovka est à moi autant qu'à vous ! Ce qui se passe ici me déplaît, me révolte ! La police en sera avertie !...

Quand elle s'arrêta, hors d'haleine, à bout d'imprécations, Serge était un peu plus pâle que d'habitude. Les commissures de ses lèvres étaient infléchies vers le bas. Il eut un regard fuyant et murmura :

— A force de vivre parmi des bagnards, ma tante, vous avez perdu la notion de la distance qui doit séparer un serf de son maître !

Trop fatiguée pour continuer la dispute, elle le toisa, sortit rapidement et claqua la porte.

Dans sa chambre, elle retrouva Zoé en larmes.

— Sois tranquille, lui dit-elle. Désormais, vous êtes tous sous ma protection. Il ne peut rien vous arriver de fâcheux.

Elle affectait une confiance radieuse, mais, en réalité, elle n'était pas sûre de pouvoir défendre ses gens contre les violences de Serge. Si demain elle repartait seule, en calèche, pour une promenade, il était capable, par orgueil, par bravade grossière, de mettre sa menace à exécution. Et, en dépit de ce qu'elle avait dit, elle ne se voyait pas courant à Pskov pour se plaindre à un gouverneur qui refuserait, sans doute, de la recevoir. Elle était trop nouvelle dans le pays, trop mal notée ! Il fallait attendre une meilleure occasion pour engager l'épreuve de force. Dans sa jeunesse, elle eût dédaigné un pareil calcul ; elle se fût lancée, tête baissée, dans l'aventure. Maintenant, elle devait compter avec la fatigue de son corps et les remontrances de sa raison. Feindre de renoncer à la lutte pour mieux se préparer à bondir. L'adversaire était de taille. Un monstre, un second Sédoff, plus horrible que le premier, parce qu'il dissimulait sa sécheresse de cœur derrière un beau visage. Elle s'assit devant sa coiffeuse et se regarda dans la glace. Ses traits étaient creusés, un cerne bistre entourait ses yeux. N'avait-elle pas eu tort d'accepter l'invitation de Daria Philippovna ? Non ! Dans sa situation, elle ne pouvait se permettre de décourager une personne si bien intentionnée. Plus que jamais elle avait besoin d'aide ! Elle dénoua ses cheveux. Ses idées partirent à la dérive. Zoé prit un peigne et une brosse sur la table.

— C'est étrange, dit Sophie, tu es mariée avec David, mais il a au moins vingt ans de plus que toi !

— Vingt-sept, dit Zoé.

— Depuis quand es-tu sa femme ?

— Il y a trois ans que le barine défunt m'a obligée à l'épouser.

— Comment ça, obligée ?

— Oui, j'en aimais un autre... Pétia, le forgeron... Ça n'a pas plu à Vladimir Karpovitch... Il l'a marié à une vieille toute tordue, toute édentée, et moi, il m'a donnée à David... J'ai pleuré, pleuré, sur le moment !... Et puis je me suis habituée... Ce n'est pas un mauvais homme... Il ne boit pas, il n'a pas la main lourde... Quelquefois, seulement, quand le soir vient et qu'il fait chaud, j'ai l'âme qui voudrait s'envoler !...

Elle poussa un soupir et se mit à coiffer Sophie avec des gestes lents.

★

Le soir, Sophie prit une grande résolution et descendit, très habillée et très calme, pour le souper. Elle ne voulait pas avoir l'air de céder, si peu que ce fût, aux intimidations de son neveu. Il sembla priser en connaisseur cette façon de le braver. Lui aussi s'était habillé avec soin, comme pour effacer par son élégance le souvenir des propos discourtois qu'il avait tenus. Assis de part et d'autre de la longue table, dans la lumière des candélabres et l'étincellement des cristaux, ils paraissaient fêter ensemble la guerre qu'ils s'étaient déclarée. Durant tout le repas, solennel et sinistre, Sophie demeura silencieuse, gourmée, mangeant à peine et ne regardant pas son vis-à-vis.

En sortant de table, ils passèrent dans le bureau et Sophie prit son ouvrage de tapisserie. Elle était décidée à ne monter se coucher qu'après être restée en bas un temps raisonnable. Paisiblement installée dans un fauteuil, elle tirait son aiguille et dessinait, point à point, sur le canevas, le pourtour d'une feuille verte. Serge, assis devant elle, lisait un journal illustré. Le poêle en faïence chauffait, craquait. Les chiens de garde aboyaient dans le parc obscur. « Il est le seul être au monde à qui je n'aie rien à dire ! » pensa Sophie avec tristesse. Le silence, à la longue, était si gênant, que Serge grommela :

— Vous plairait-il d'avoir quelques nouvelles de France ? Un de vos écrivains, M. Honoré de Balzac, est mort le 18 du mois dernier... Le prince-président a quitté Paris pour visiter les départements de l'Ouest... On reparle d'une loi que votre Assemblée législative a votée sur la déportation... Y aurait-il des bagnes ailleurs qu'en Russie ?

Elle ne répondit pas. Il marqua une pause et reprit :

— Vous voyez, je reçois des journaux français. Les mêmes que du temps de mon père. Il s'intéressait beaucoup à la France ! En quels termes étiez-vous avec lui ?

Elle crut qu'il se moquait d'elle et répliqua promptement :

— Vous devez le savoir mieux que moi !

— Il m'a toujours parlé de vous avec beaucoup de considération, dit Serge.

Il posa son journal, croisa les jambes, inclina la tête et dit encore :

— Je trouve qu'en dépit des apparences nous avons, vous et moi, un point commun.

Elle leva les yeux de son ouvrage avec étonnement. Content de l'effet qu'il avait produit sur elle, il poursuivit d'un ton plus animé :

— Oui, ce domaine, vous l'aimez autant que

156

moi ! Comme moi, vous êtes prête à tout sacrifier pour lui !

— Tout ? Non ! dit-elle. Je me passionne pour les êtres, non pour les choses. Ce qui m'attache à Kachtanovka, ce sont les gens qui l'habitent !

— Ils ne font qu'un avec la terre !

— Quand il s'agit de les vendre, peut-être !

Serge fronça les sourcils.

— Je n'en vendrai jamais un seul ! dit-il avec force. A cet égard, je ne suis pas du tout comme mon père !...

Ils se turent. La maison les entoura de sa rumeur. Une ondée fouetta les vitres. Puis Serge marmonna négligemment :

— Des amis m'ont dit vous avoir aperçue cet après-midi, en ville, avec Mme Volkoff.

— En effet, dit Sophie.

— Drôle de relation ! Comptez-vous la revoir ?

— Oui.

— Quand ?

— Cela ne vous regarde pas !

— J'ai besoin de le savoir.

— Pourquoi ?

— Pour donner des ordres au cocher !

— Ce n'est pas vous qui lui donnerez des ordres, mais moi ! Rappelez-vous ce que je vous ai dit tout à l'heure !

Les dents de Serge étincelèrent dans un éclat de rire :

— Eh bien ! ma tante, nous n'allons pas nous étriper pour des histoires d'écurie !... S'il vous plaît de courir à Slavianka pour y rencontrer cette vieille colporteuse de mensonges et le fils abruti qu'elle tient sous son talon, je mets à votre disposition toutes les voitures et tous les chevaux de la propriété ! David sera prévenu qu'il doit

157

vous obéir comme à moi-même. Ordonnez et vous serez servie !

Il s'inclina dans un salut comique. Sophie se demanda pourquoi il cédait si facilement. L'avait-elle impressionné par son ton résolu ou préparait-il une riposte qu'elle ne soupçonnait pas ? En vérité, elle était plus inquiète de le voir conciliant que s'il s'était montré intraitable. Un domestique apporta une carafe de liqueur et des verres sur un plateau. C'était le moment qu'avait fixé Sophie pour remonter dans sa chambre. Elle se leva et dit :

— Bonsoir, Serge.

Il allait se pencher pour lui baiser la main, mais elle ne lui en laissa pas le temps et se dirigea vivement vers la porte. En franchissant le seuil, elle se retourna et le vit qui se versait un verre d'alcool, le humait, l'avalait d'un trait en basculant la tête. Une réminiscence la troubla. Quelque chose de très lointain et de très doux, qu'elle ne savait pas définir, se déroulait dans sa mémoire. Elle y pensa sans arrêt, avec impatience, en se déshabillant. Une fois dans son lit, enfin, elle se rappela le jour où elle avait offert à Ferdinand Wolff de l'eau-de-vie de framboise. Elle s'endormit, attendrie par ce souvenir.

Dans la calèche qui l'emportait vers Slavianka, Sophie essayait de se convaincre qu'elle avait eu raison d'accepter l'invitation de Daria Philippovna. Mais ça gêne persistait. Il lui semblait qu'elle allait se replonger dans la boue en rendant visite à ces deux êtres qui avaient été si intimement mêlés à l'histoire de sa disgrâce. En même temps, elle se sentait irrésistiblement attirée par eux, comme s'ils eussent été ses meilleurs alliés contre la solitude. Devant elle, le dos de David oscillait à chaque cahot. Il avait mis ses beaux habits pour la conduire. Cette fois, il n'avait pas peur : le barine avait confirmé les ordres de la barynia.

Par comparaison avec Kachtanovka, le domaine de Slavianka paraissait à demi abandonné. Beaucoup de champs restaient en friche, la route, à peine entretenue, était creusée de fondrières, les villages dressaient au bord de la chaussée des isbas sales, croulantes, des jardinets envahis d'orties. Il ne pleuvait pas, bien que les nuages fussent bas et sombres. Un vent glacé sifflait dans les branches. Le parc de la propriété, vaste, paisible et inculte, avait le charme mélancolique d'une forêt. A travers une déchirure de feuillages jaunes, Sophie aperçut la maison de maître, toute en bois, longue, enfumée, avec de petites fenêtres aux volets de couleur.

La calèche s'arrêta devant le perron et Daria Philippovna, engoncée dans une robe gris perle à volants, dévala les marches et se précipita vers son invitée. Etourdie par ses exclamations de bienvenue, Sophie se laissa conduire dans la salle à manger, où, sur une table ovale, dominée par un samovar rutilant, s'alignaient des pots de confiture et des pyramides de petits pains. A peine assise, elle vit arriver un homme qui avait l'air d'un chanteur italien sur le retour, ventripotent, grisonnant, avec de grands yeux noirs dans un masque adipeux. Il était vêtu avec négligence d'une veste de velours marron et d'un pantalon beige aux sous-pieds distendus. Avec un pincement au cœur, elle reconnut le beau, l'élégant Vassia Volkoff. Sa mère bêtifia, comme s'adressant à un jeune garçon :

— Eh bien ! La voici ! Elle est venue ! Tu avais tellement envie de la voir !

— Je t'en prie, maman ! dit-il d'un ton morne.

Il baisa la main de Sophie, s'assit, se laissa servir un verre de thé, écouta un moment, avec ennui, le bavardage des deux femmes, puis, profitant d'un silence, murmura, sans lever les yeux :

— Ma mère m'a raconté, au sujet de Nicolas... C'est affreux !... Je voulais vous dire que j'ai beaucoup pensé à lui, pendant les longues années qu'il a passées en exil... A lui et à tous ceux qui ont eu le courage de souffrir pour leurs opinions politiques... Vous savez que moi, par un étrange concours de circonstances, je ne me trouvais pas à

160

Saint-Pétersbourg le jour de l'émeute... Des affaires de famille m'avaient appelé à Pskov...

— De très graves affaires de famille ! souligna Daria Philippovna.

— Ainsi, par miracle, j'ai échappé au châtiment. On m'a convoqué, interrogé, relâché. Mais, bien que n'ayant pas été condamné, je me suis toujours senti solidaire de ceux qui sont partis pour la Sibérie. J'ai... j'ai pleuré pour eux... avec eux... J'ai conservé le culte de mes camarades... Encore aujourd'hui, il ne se passe pas de jour que je ne prie pour eux, vivants ou morts... Et mes idées... mes idées n'ont pas changé !...

Sophie suivait avec étonnement ce plaidoyer lamentable. Sans doute Vassia était-il honteux d'avoir abandonné les décembristes, à la dernière minute, sous un prétexte auquel lui-même ne croyait plus. Il cherchait, avec maladresse, à se justifier, comme si celle qui l'écoutait eût représenté à elle seule tous les hommes, toutes les femmes qui étaient restés en Sibérie. Pourtant, les années de vie paisible, à la campagne, auraient dû atténuer son remords. Tandis qu'il parlait, sa mère l'observait avec inquiétude.

— Tu as tort de t'échauffer, dit-elle enfin. Notre grande amie sait tout cela. Dans chaque catastrophe, il y a des victimes et des survivants ; a-t-on jamais vu les survivants rougir de n'être pas des victimes ?

— Tais-toi, maman, dit-il avec humeur.

Et, tourné vers Sophie, il demanda :

— Avez-vous eu l'occasion de parler de moi, là-bas, avec nos amis ?

— Mais, oui, affirma-t-elle. Très souvent...

En vérité, elle avait l'impression que personne, parmi les décembristes, ne s'était jamais intéressé à Vassia Volkoff, pour l'absoudre ou pour le condamner.

— Que vous ont-ils dit de moi, Madame ?

Elle mentit, par charité :

— Ils vous ont gardé leur confiance.

— Le fait que je n'aie pas été pris avec eux sur la place du Sénat ?...

— Nul n'a songé à vous en tenir rigueur.

— Tu vois ! triompha Daria Philippovna. Je vous remercie, chère Madame. Vous ne pouvez savoir le bien que vous nous faites. Vassia se rend malade avec ces histoires. Il s'imagine...

— Je ne m'imagine rien, dit Vassia avec fureur. De quoi te mêles-tu ?

Daria Philippovna rentra la tête dans les épaules et glissa à Sophie un regard d'humble connivence.

— Et Nicolas ? reprit Vassia. Nicolas ?... Il n'a pas été déçu ?...

— Par quoi ?

— Mais par... enfin, par mon absence à ses côtés, le 14 décembre ?...

— Il vous a envie d'être resté libre, c'est tout, dit Sophie. L'expérience du bagne restitue à chaque chose sa vraie valeur. Tout à coup, on comprend que le plus important dans la vie ce n'est pas une doctrine, si généreuse soit-elle, mais la santé, la liberté d'aller et de venir, des notions toutes simples...

Vassia l'écoutait avec avidité, le visage tendu.

— On ne parlait donc pas de politique, là-bas ? demanda-t-il.

— Si, bien sûr ! Mais plutôt par habitude que par conviction sincère. En fait, la plupart de vos amis avaient reconnu l'impossibilité d'instaurer un

162

régime constitutionnel en Russie avant de nombreuses années...

— Vassia, lui, est plus enragé que jamais ! dit Daria Philippovna dans un élan de fausse joie. Il lit, il lit !... Rien que des livres français subversifs !... Et, chaque fois que des gens viennent ici, il tient des propos républicains !... Il est d'une imprudence !... Un de ces jours, il se fera donner sur les doigts !...

— Pourquoi dis-tu cela, maman ? grommela Vassia. Tu sais bien que ce n'est pas vrai !

— Comment ce n'est pas vrai ? s'écria-t-elle. Rappelle-toi quand le directeur des Postes et sa femme ont déjeuné à la maison. Tu leur as parlé avec enthousiasme de ce prêtre français qui était plus près du peuple que du pape... Un certain Lamonnaie... ou Lamennais...

Vassia poussa un soupir et jeta sa figure dans ses mains, vieil enfant accablé par une mère autoritaire et bavarde. Aussitôt, Daria Philippovna se calma comme si elle eût redouté, en insistant, de le précipiter dans une crise. Inclinée vers Sophie, elle lui confia entre haut et bas :

— Il ne veut pas que ce soit dit, mais allez dans sa chambre, vous verrez sa bibliothèque ! Notre ami commun Troussoff, le maréchal de la noblesse de Pskov, m'a affirmé : « C'est de la poudre de guerre ! »

Vassia releva la tête et un sourire triste effleura son visage :

— Oui, je me console du désœuvrement par la lecture. Plus on réfléchit, moins on a envie d'agir. Au lieu d'interdire les livres politiques en Russie, le gouvernement devrait en encourager la publication. Nous nous transformerions tous en rêveurs. Nous deviendrions inoffensifs...

163

Il tournait sa cuillère dans son verre à support d'argent.

— Bois, dit Daria Philippovna. C'est déjà tout froid !

Il obéit machinalement.

— Le plus pénible, reprit-elle, c'est qu'il n'a personne avec qui échanger des idées ! Moi, n'est-ce pas ? je ne connais pas grand-chose à ces questions... Nos amis sont plutôt d'un autre bord... Alors, il reste seul... Il rumine des heures entières dans sa chambre... Ce n'est pas sain !... Ah ! si Nicolas Mikhaïlovitch était encore de ce monde !...

Elle se moucha. Vassia lui décocha un regard de colère. Il y eut un silence, pendant lequel Sophie sentit s'appesantir sur elle les habitudes de cette mère et de ce fils, leur animosité maniaque, leur entente secrète dans la paresse, la négligence et la gourmandise. On respirait auprès d'eux comme un fumet de vieux ménage aigri et indissoluble. Vassia roulait des boulettes de pain entre ses doigts, nerveusement. Sophie se demanda, en l'observant, si l'échec de l'émeute du 14 décembre 1825, l'emprisonnement de ses amis et sa propre impunité n'avaient pas détraqué son caractère.

— Il faudra que vous veniez me voir à Kachtanovka avec votre mère, dit-elle.

Il sursauta. Son visage aux traits fins, noyés dans la graisse, eut une contraction peureuse, puis se raffermit.

— Je m'excuse, dit-il, c'est impossible !...

— Pourquoi ?

— A cause de votre neveu, Serge Vladimirovitch. Je ne puis supporter la façon dont il traite ses gens. Alors que la majorité des propriétaires fonciers, même les plus vieux, même les plus rétrogrades, sentent qu'on ne peut plus exploiter les serfs comme autrefois, que l'idée de l'émancipation est dans l'air, qu'il faut s'y préparer et y préparer le peuple, lui continue à se conduire en tyranneau de province. Il prend un plaisir sadique à aller jusqu'au bout des pouvoirs que la loi lui accorde. Il se croirait déshonoré de renoncer à une parcelle de son droit seigneurial. Regardez nos moujiks, ou ceux de nos voisins, les Guédéonoff, les Massloff... Quelle différence y a-t-il entre eux et des cultivateurs libres, à première vue ? Ils se figurent même que la terre est à eux. « Nous sommes à toi, barine, me disent-ils, mais la terre est à nous ! » Pensez-vous que les paysans de Kachtanovka parleraient ainsi à Serge Vladimirovitch ? Ils sont terrorisés, ils courbent le dos, ils se laissent frapper et tondre ! Des bêtes, il a fait d'eux des bêtes !...

Il haussait le ton. Un tremblement agitait ses mains.

— Quand je songe, reprit-il, que tant d'hommes éminents ont été envoyés en Sibérie pour avoir rêvé de libérer les serfs et que, vingt-cinq ans plus tard, le neveu d'un de ces hommes fait condamner des moujiks aux travaux forcés pour sauver sa peau, je doute que ces deux événements aient pu se dérouler dans le même pays !

D'abord, Sophie ne comprit pas le sens de cette protestation. Daria Philippovna s'agita :

— Tu exagères, Vassia ! Tu n'as aucune preuve !

— Tout le monde le sait et personne n'ose le dire ! s'écria-t-il en repoussant son assiette.

— Qu'est-ce que tout le monde sait ? demanda Sophie.

Il la considéra d'un air égaré et répondit tout d'un coup :

165

— C'est votre neveu qui a tué !

L'univers, autour de Sophie, perdit la couleur et le tranchant de la réalité. Un moment, elle flotta dans le vide. Enfin, rassemblant ses idées, elle balbutia :

— Ce n'est pas possible !... Son propre père ?...

— Il le détestait ! dit Vassia.

Sophie se tourna vers Daria Philippovna, qui acquiesça de la tête :

— Oui, je ne vous l'ai pas dit l'autre jour... J'hésitais à vous troubler davantage... Tu as peut-être tort de parler de cela, Vassia !

— Pourquoi ? Il faut mettre Mme Ozareff au courant de tout !

— Vous-même, qui vous a mis au courant ? interrogea Sophie.

— Vos domestiques l'ont dit à notre intendant. La veille de l'assassinat, il y a eu une scène horrible à Kachtanovka. Vladimir Karpovitch avait, paraît-il, signé une reconnaissance de dettes ou commis quelque autre folie... Son fils s'est enfermé avec lui dans le bureau, l'a insulté, l'a giflé. Toute la valetaille écoutait, épouvantée, dans le couloir. Puis le père et le fils, fatigués de se crier des injures, se sont calmés et ont bu ensemble...

— Ce ne sont, peut-être, que des racontars d'office, murmura Sophie.

— Il n'y a pas de fumée sans feu, Madame ! Le lendemain, Vladimir Karpovitch était trouvé mort, étranglé, dans la cabane de bains.

— Et s'il s'agissait d'une simple coïncidence ? Il n'existe pas d'indices matériels permettant d'accuser mon neveu ! D'ailleurs, les moujiks ont avoué...

Vassia eut un rire haineux :

— On sait ce que valent les aveux des moujiks

166

sous la menace du knout ! Quant aux indices matériels, la commission d'enquête n'a même pas cherché à en réunir ! Pour la tranquillité des consciences et le maintien de l'ordre, il valait mieux condamner trois serfs innocents qu'un barine coupable !... Un fait est certain : dans le pays, cette mort n'a étonné personne. On s'y attendait depuis longtemps. Cela ne pouvait pas finir autrement !...

Pendant qu'il parlait, Sophie songeait aux révélations d'Antipe. Lui aussi avait prétendu, entre deux grimaces, que les moujiks n'avaient pas massacré leur maître. Dans le silence intérieur que crée une extrême attention, elle sentit ses soupçons tourner à la certitude. Pourtant, elle ne voulait pas céder à la panique. Elle cherchait des arguments pour s'opposer à l'horreur qui l'envahissait. Daria Philippovna engloutit une cuillerée de confiture et soupira :

— C'est abominable ! Mais on n'y peut rien !

— Comment, on n'y peut rien ? s'écria Vassia. Il doit y avoir un moyen de faire éclater la vérité ! Si j'étais sur place...

— Moi, je suis sur place, dit Sophie, mais les moujiks se méfient de ceux qui leur veulent du bien. Impossible de savoir ce qu'ils pensent. Ils ont trop peur des représailles !

— Patience ! dit Vassia. Les langues se délieront ! Ne trouvez-vous pas intolérable que des malheureux, qui n'ont rien fait et dont on n'a même pas écouté les protestations, soient partis enchaînés pour la Sibérie ?

Cette phrase répondait si bien au trouble de Sophie qu'elle crut l'avoir prononcée elle-même. De tous les crimes dont une société était capable, l'erreur judiciaire volontairement commise lui semblait le plus odieux. Elle ne respirerait pas à l'aise, pensait-elle, tant qu'un doute subsisterait dans son esprit sur la culpabilité des trois serfs. Mais que faire ? Auprès de qui se renseigner ? Et comment, ensuite, obtenir la révision du jugement ? La notion de son impuissance l'accabla. Brusquement, elle comprit qu'elle ne pourrait pas rester dix minutes de plus à cette table. Elle avait besoin de retourner à Kachtanovka, de revoir Serge, de scruter son visage, de percer le mystère de ses sentiments. Quand elle annonça qu'elle était obligée de partir, Daria Philippovna se désola :

— Déjà ! Moi qui m'étais mis en tête de vous montrer le parc, la rivière, le moulin...

— N'insiste pas, maman ! intervint Vassia. Mme Ozareff n'a certainement pas l'esprit à se promener, en ce moment !

— J'avoue, murmura Sophie, que je suis encore sous le coup de ce que vous m'avez dit.

Il se pencha vers elle :

— Si vous apprenez du nouveau, faites-le moi savoir, je vous en prie.

Daria Philippovna eut un sourire de mère comblée : enfin, son fils s'intéressait à quelque chose, manifestait de la sympathie envers quelqu'un !

— Bravo ! dit-elle. Il faut revenir nous voir très vite, chère amie !

— Oui, oui ! s'écria Vassia. Il le faut absolument !

Ses gros yeux noirs s'emplirent de larmes. Il ressembla à une vieille femme émotive. Sophie se leva. On voulut la retenir encore. Elle dut suivre Daria Philippovna dans le salon, admirer les portraits au daguerréotype des trois filles et de leurs maris, s'intéresser à une dentelle grossière qui se tricotait dans un village du domaine. Enfin la mère et le fils raccompagnèrent leur invitée jusqu'à sa calèche. Après un brillant accès de colère, Vassia était retombé dans l'apathie. On eût dit qu'il avait oublié jusqu'à la cause de son indignation. Il courbait les épaules dans son veston froissé et ne levait pas les pieds en marchant. A deux reprises, Daria Philippovna voulut lui arranger son col. Il la repoussa :

— Laisse... Laisse donc !

Le trajet du retour parut interminable à Sophie. Une fois dans sa chambre, elle se reprit à souffrir d'impatience. Peu avant l'heure du souper, elle descendit dans le bureau, où Serge l'attendait pour passer à table. En le voyant, elle reçut un choc. Un visage aussi calme ne pouvait être celui d'un assassin. Il était impossible d'imaginer ce garçon, au maintien dégagé, aux traits aimables, serrant à pleins doigts le cou de son père jusqu'à l'asphyxie. Vassia était un fou et sa mère une imbécile ! Pourquoi les avait-elle écoutés ?

— Votre visite à Daria Philippovna a-t-elle été agréable ? demanda-t-il.

— Très agréable, dit Sophie, l'esprit ailleurs.

— Vous êtes rentrée bien tôt !

— J'étais un peu lasse. Je voulais me reposer.

— Ne préférez-vous pas souper dans votre chambre ?

— Mais non, pourquoi ?

Le valet de pied ouvrit la porte à deux battants. La table apparut, trop grande, avec ses flambeaux d'argent. La vue de ce décor familier acheva de rassurer Sophie.

— Ne me demandez pas ça, barynia ! soupira Antipe. Si je réponds, le toit s'écroulera sur ma tête !

Il leva un regard inquiet vers le plafond de son isba et se signa la poitrine. Sophie répéta la question :

— Puisque ce ne sont pas les moujiks qui ont tué Vladimir Karpovitch, qui est-ce ?

— Je vous assure que je ne le sais pas !

— Moi, je vais te le dire !

— Non ! Non ! bredouilla-t-il en arrondissant des prunelles épouvantées.

— C'est son fils.

Antipe tomba à genoux :

— Sainte Mère de Dieu ! Peut-on, sans pécher, prononcer de telles paroles devant les icônes ?

— Assez de grimaces ! J'ai besoin de savoir la vérité ! C'est lui, n'est-ce pas ?

— Oui, dit Antipe.

Et il promena les yeux autour de lui, comme pour vérifier que personne d'autre que Sophie ne l'avait entendu.

La porte et la fenêtre fermées maintenaient dans la pièce une pénombre odorante. Sur la table, il y avait une tranche de pain noir et du sel dans un morceau de journal.

— Comment peux-tu en être sûr ? demanda-t-elle.

— Je n'en suis pas tout à fait sûr !

— Mais presque ?

— Oui.

— Pourquoi ?

Il se releva en geignant et secoua sa grosse tête ridée et hirsute à la démancher.

— Quand on est vieux et qu'on n'a rien à faire toute la journée, on réfléchit, dit-il. C'est le 15 mai, au petit jour, que les trois moujiks ont soi-disant tué Vladimir Karpovitch dans la cabane de bains. Mais pourquoi sont-ils allés dans la cabane de bains ?

— Pour réparer le plancher, dit Sophie.

— Et qui leur a dit de réparer le plancher ?

— Je ne sais pas... Vladimir Karpovitch lui-même, sans doute...

— Non, barynia ! Son fils ! Serge Vladimirovitch est arrivé au village, à pied, le 14 mai, tard dans la soirée. Il avait l'air bizarre, les vêtements poussiéreux, une égratignure sur la joue. Il a ordonné à Ossip le roux, à Marc et à Fédka d'aller sans faute, le lendemain, avec leurs outils, au bord de la rivière, pour réparer le plancher de la cabane de bains. D'habitude, dans ces cas-là, un conducteur accompagne nos gars pour surveiller leur travail. C'est le règlement et Serge Vladimirovitch y tient beaucoup, vu que c'est lui qui l'a inventé. Eh bien ! ce soir du 14 mai, le voilà qui dit aux moujiks : « Pas besoin de conducteur, demain ! Allez-y entre vous ! Ce sera plus simple !... »

172

— Qu'y a-t-il de surprenant à cela ?

— Eh ! barynia, s'ils y étaient allés avec un conducteur, celui-ci n'aurait pas pu jurer, ensuite, sur l'Evangile, qu'il les avait vus étrangler leur maître. Mais ils se sont amenés là-bas tout seuls, naïfs comme des poussins. Ils sont tombés sur le cadavre. Effrayés, ils ont couru prévenir le jeune barine. Et lui, il n'attendait que ça. Il les a accusés d'avoir fait le coup. Mais le coup, c'est lui qui l'avait fait, la veille. Toute la maisonnée l'a entendu se disputer avec son père, dans le bureau. Après, ils se sont réconciliés, ils ont vidé une bouteille et ils sont partis ensemble, bras dessus bras dessous, vers la cabane de bains. Qu'est-ce qu'ils allaient faire là-bas ? Peut-être se baigner, malgré le froid ! Quand on a bu, on a de ces idées !... C'était quasiment la nuit. Des domestiques les ont vus sortir de la maison, personne ne les a vus rentrer. Est-ce que vous comprenez, maintenant ?

Ce qui troublait le plus Sophie, c'était que Serge fût intervenu personnellement, la veille du meurtre, pour empêcher qu'un conducteur n'escortât les moujiks jusqu'à la cabane. Une telle manœuvre entraînait incontestablement une présomption de culpabilité contre celui qui l'avait ordonnée. Encore fallait-il que tout cela n'eût pas été inventé par Antipe ! Depuis qu'elle était arrivée à Kachtanovka, elle avait l'impression de tourner en rond dans le brouillard. Ici, le mensonge n'était qu'une des formes de la vérité. On ne pouvait compter sur personne, car chacun trichait pour sauver sa carcasse, perdre le voisin ou se donner de l'importance. Antipe ayant lâché son paquet, tenait une main devant sa bouche, comme si la révélation qu'il avait faite lui eût cassé les dents au passage. Sophie alla vers la porte.

— Vous ne pouvez pas partir comme ça, barynia ! s'écria-t-il en lui barrant la route.

Il lui avait remis une bombe et elle allait la lancer n'importe où.

— Barynia, barynia ! reprit-il. Que voulez-vous faire ?

Elle ne répondit pas, l'écarta et sortit. Il courut derrière elle en boitillant. La calèche attendait au milieu du village. Comme Sophie montait en voiture, elle avisa un cheval de selle attaché à un piquet, devant l'église. Il n'y était pas lorsqu'elle était arrivée à Chatkovo. Elle reconnut la monture de Serge. Antipe suivit la direction de son regard et changea de visage.

— Notre barine ! chuchota-t-il. Aïe ! Aïe ! Aie ! Qu'est-ce qu'on va lui raconter ?

— Mais rien ! Que crains-tu ? dit Sophie.

Au même instant, la porte du presbytère s'ouvrit et Serge parut sur le seuil, raccompagné par le prêtre et sa femme. Il prit congé d'eux et se dirigea vers Sophie, la démarche balancée, un sourire narquois aux lèvres :

— Quelle agréable rencontre ! Vous rendiez visite à cet aimable fou ?

Aussitôt, Antipe se ratatina, battit des paupières et passa un bout de langue entre ses dents. Il branlait de la tête et bafouillait :

— Barine, notre beau soleil ! Que les grâces du ciel te couronnent ! Tu devrais venir me voir, toi aussi ! Je te donnerais une puce ! Elle joue de l'harmonica ! Là où elle s'assied, tu creuses et tu trouves de l'or ! Qui n'a besoin d'or ? Même le tsar, dans son palais, en demande ! Et moi, je sais où il y en a ! A cause de ma puce...

Il fit le simulacre de saisir une puce entre deux

174

doigts, sur sa manche, cligna de l'œil et poursuivit :

— Tu veux la voir ?

Serge le repoussa d'une bourrade :

— Va-t-en, imbécile !

— Oh ! ma puce ! Où est-elle tombée ?

L'air consterné, il s'assit à croupetons et chercha par terre. Sophie se demanda s'il n'avait pas
réellement perdu la raison sous le choc de la surprise. Mais un regard intelligent qu'il lui lança de
bas en haut lui prouva qu'il feignait la folie pour
avoir la paix.

— On devrait pouvoir supprimer des individus
pareils ! grommela Serge. Ils ne servent à rien. Ils
sont d'un mauvais exemple pour les autres...

— Nul n'a le droit de décider si un être est
utile ou non, dit Sophie en le considérant, les yeux
dans les yeux.

Il rit :

— Vous avez raison ! Ne nous substituons pas
à Dieu ! Cela finirait par nous attirer des ennuis.
Je dois me rendre à Krapinovo ! Irez-vous aussi de
ce côté-là ? Nous pourrions faire la route ensemble...

— Non merci. Je préfère rentrer à la maison.

— Eh bien ! bonne promenade !

Il la salua, marcha vers son cheval, se mit en
selle avec légèreté et partit, d'un trot vif, par le
chemin boueux.

— Ouf ! dit Antipe en se redressant.

Mais il remarqua que le cocher le lorgnait par-
dessus son épaule et, de méfiance, ravala sa langue.

— Surtout ne t'inquiète de rien ! lui dit Sophie.
On ne te fera pas de mal ! En route, David !

Antipe esquissa des signes de croix devant les
chevaux jusqu'au moment où la calèche s'ébranla.

A la sortie du village, Sophie cria au cocher :

— Pas si vite ! Je vais t'arrêter bientôt !

En allant à Chatkovo, elle avait vu une équipe de paysans qui désouchaient les abords d'un boqueteau. Elle se fit amener au plus près de cet endroit en voiture, et coupa à pied, par les champs, pour rejoindre les travailleurs. Ils l'accueillirent, chapeau bas. Un conducteur les surveillait, grand et fort, botté, barbu, la face cuite, le nez bleu et poreux. Elle le prit à part et lui demanda, tout à trac, si c'était bien sur l'ordre du jeune barine que, le 15 mai dernier, les moujiks s'étaient rendus à la cabane de bains sans être convoyés.

— Bien sûr ! dit-il. Autrement, vous pensez bien qu'on les aurait accompagnés, comme c'est la règle ! Mais pourquoi que vous me demandez ça ?

— Parce que, si ces hommes avaient décidé eux-mêmes de se passer de vous pour aller à la cabane de bains, ils auraient été doublement coupables !

— Ça, c'est vrai ! reconnut le conducteur, l'œil stupide.

— Vous l'avez dit à la commission d'enquête ?

— Quoi ?

— Que le jeune barine vous avait donné certaines instructions la veille du crime ?

— On ne nous l'a pas demandé.

— Cela pouvait être important !

— Oh ! non, les messieurs de la justice ont très vite compris ce qui s'était passé. En dix minutes, les coupables n'ont plus su que dire. Ils ont avoué, sur l'Evangile. Alors, on a tout mis par écrit, les noms, les prénoms, les dates, avec des cachets et des signatures. C'est devenu officiel. Il n'y a plus à revenir là-dessus !

Pendant qu'il discourait, les paysans avaient relâché leur effort.

— Eh ! vous travaillez ou vous dormez, vous autres ? hurla-t-il sans méchanceté, en faisant des moulinets avec son gourdin.

Sophie revint sur ses pas. Son angoisse prenait des proportions telles qu'elle dut s'arrêter, incommodée par les battements de son cœur. David l'aida à remonter en voiture. Depuis que Serge lui avait ordonné d'obéir à Sophie, il était plein de prévenances pour elle.

— Vous êtes fatiguée, barynia, dit-il. Nous rentrons ?

— Non. Conduis-moi à la cabane de bains.

Il la dévisagea avec une frayeur superstitieuse :

— C'est un lieu maudit, barynia ! Il ne faut pas y aller !

Elle lui donna une tape sur l'épaule ; il se signa, siffla et fit partir les chevaux.

La cabane de bains était nichée dans la partie la plus sauvage du parc de Kachtanovka, au bas d'un sentier, entre deux saules pleureurs aux troncs inclinés et tordus. Une bicoque en rondins servait de vestiaire. Devant, s'étendait un plancher sur pilotis. Une échelle de bois permettait d'entrer dans l'eau sans s'accrocher aux herbes du bord. A un pieu était attachée une barque plate, aux rames vermoulues. Sophie n'était presque jamais venue dans ce coin perdu, où il y avait, l'été, beaucoup de moustiques. Mais Nicolas, autrefois, y pêchait, s'y baignait, par les grandes chaleurs. Elle s'assit sur un tabouret et respira l'odeur de la vase. Il faisait froid et humide. Des reflets ronds comme des soucoupes dansaient au milieu du courant. Une collerette d'écume se formait autour d'un caillou. Le murmure continu de l'eau entraînait à la rêverie.

Sophie ne savait à quelle impulsion elle avait

obéi en s'arrêtant ici. Le regard perdu dans le lointain, elle ne cherchait pas un indice, mais une inspiration. Il lui semblait qu'elle comprendrait mieux les circonstances du crime en y réfléchissant sur les lieux mêmes où il avait été commis. Deux mains de fer serrées autour d'un cou décharné, où la vie, bat, gronde, s'essouffle ; des prunelles qui se révulsent ; la chute maladroite d'un corps sur le ponton. Elle abaissa les yeux. Le plancher, à ses pieds, s'étalait, nu et gris, mouillé, raboteux, d'une banalité fascinante. Quelques lattes étaient pourries : celles que les moujiks auraient dû remplacer. Personne n'y avait touché depuis le drame. Par les interstices, on apercevait l'eau qui filait. Sophie avait beau interroger ces choses qui avaient tout vu, tout entendu, elle n'en recevait pas de réponse. Un engourdissement montait de ses membres à son cerveau. Tout à coup, dans la fente d'une vieille planche, un objet minuscule et brillant attira son attention. Elle le ramassa : c'était un bouton d'améthyste. Où donc avait-elle vu les mêmes ? Sur un gilet de Serge... Cette constatation ne la troubla pas d'abord ; puis il y eut dans son être une secousse qui ne dura que le temps d'un battement de cœur, mais la laissa affaiblie et glacée. Si ce bouton d'améthyste se trouvait là, c'était que Serge l'avait perdu en luttant avec son père. Le doute n'était plus possible. Il fallait avertir la police. Verser cette pièce à conviction au dossier. Exiger la révision de la sentence. Mais ne lui répondrait-on pas que Serge avait pu perdre ce bouton n'importe quel jour, avant le crime, en se déshabillant pour se baigner dans la rivière ? Arrêtée en plein élan, elle mesura avec surprise jusqu'où son exaltation l'avait emportée. Comment ne s'était-elle pas rendu compte qu'elle construisait toute une fable sur rien ? Dans le creux de sa main, la petite pierre violette étincelait. Elle voulut la jeter à l'eau, se ravisa et la glissa dans un sac pendu à sa ceinture, comme elle eût fait d'un talisman. Même si la découverte de ce bouton d'améthyste n'était d'aucune importance, l'ordre que Serge avait donné aux conducteurs, la veille du crime, eût suffi à fonder une nouvelle accusation. En un clin d'œil, elle fut reprise par son agitation justicière. Ses idées bouillonnaient. Elle souffrait de n'avoir personne à qui confier ses soupçons. Ah ! comme il lui manquait aujourd'hui, son grand ami de Sibérie ! Lui l'eût calmée, réconfortée, conseillée... Elle eût supporté n'importe quoi, si seulement elle avait pu correspondre avec lui ! Mais il était clair maintenant que les lettres qu'ils écrivaient ne parviendraient jamais à destination. Pauline elle-même se taisait, s'éloignait... A regret, Sophie se leva et remonta le sentier qui conduisait à la route. David la regardait venir avec crainte, du haut de son siège. Les chevaux hennirent.

— Tout le temps que vous étiez là-bas, ils ont bougé leurs oreilles, barynia, dit-il. C'est signe qu'il y a un fantôme qui rôde. Allons-nous-en, vite !...

Elle s'assit sur la banquette, ferma les yeux et regretta de n'être qu'une femme solitaire, impuissante, devant un problème qui la dépassait.

★

Le vent hurla pendant les premières heures de la nuit, puis il se fit un grand silence. Le matin, en s'approchant de la fenêtre, Sophie découvrit un monde uniformément blanc. De gros flocons descendaient du ciel invisible. Derrière ce lent tis-

179

sage, les lointains s'estompaient, les sapins s'effilaient en fumée, la route nivelée se confondait avec la pelouse. Il semblait à Sophie que le paysage se travestissait devant elle pour égarer ses soupçons. La neige accumulée effaçait les traces du crime. Tout, subitement, devenait pur, irréel, innocent.

Vassia Volkoff traversa le grand vestibule dallé, échangea quelques mots avec l'huissier qui se tenait près de la porte et revint s'asseoir à côté de Sophie en chuchotant :

— Il paraît que ce ne sera plus très long !

Elle le remercia. Sans lui, elle n'aurait pas osé demander cette audience. Dire qu'elle avait hésité trois semaines avant de retourner le voir à Slavianka ! En apprenant ce que lui avait raconté Antipe, il avait immédiatement décidé d'aller avec elle chez le gouverneur. Il était en parenté avec ce haut personnage et ne doutait pas de le persuader qu'il fallait réviser le procès pour « fait nouveau ». Autant il était mal fagoté chez lui, autant, pour cette sortie en ville, il s'était habillé et coiffé avec soin. Sa veulerie habituelle avait fait place à un air de mâle résolution. Piqué, roide, au bord de sa chaise, la pelisse largement ouverte sur un plastron blanc, il dardait dans le vide un regard inquisiteur. Pourtant, cette fière attitude ne suffisait pas à rassurer Sophie. A mesure que le temps passait, elle appréhendait davantage l'entrevue qu'elle allait avoir avec le conseiller d'Etat actuel Tcherkassoff, dont l'autorité s'étendait sur tout le gouvernement de Pskov. Une sonnette retentit, l'huissier disparut, revint et pria les visiteurs de le suivre.

Sophie pénétra dans un vaste bureau, orné de sièges à médaillons en velours cramoisi. Elle connaissait le gouverneur pour s'être présentée à lui, en arrivant à Pskov, au retour de la Sibérie. C'était un vieillard maigre et digne, dont les cheveux d'argent retombaient en crinière sur les épaules. Derrière lui, une grande glace au cadre doré, penchée en avant, reflétait le parquet au point de Hongrie. Il fit asseoir Sophie et Vassia dans deux fauteuils incommodes, se rassit lui-même à sa table de travail, distilla quelques propos aimables pour lier la conversation, puis, poussant un soupir, demanda ce qui lui valait l'honneur de cette visite. Au moment de lancer l'accusation, la tête de Sophie se vida, ses mains se refroidirent. Comme son hésitation se prolongeait, Vassia Volkoff lui adressa un regard d'encouragement. Soudain, sans l'avoir voulu, elle remua les lèvres :

— C'est au sujet du meurtre de Vladimir Karpovitch Sédoff...

Le visage du gouverneur devint si attentif, qu'il ressembla à un cadavre.

— J'ai des révélations... des révélations capitales à faire, reprit-elle avec plus de force.

— Je vous écoute, Madame.

— La veille du crime, mon neveu s'est rendu au village de Chatkovo...

Maintenant, elle parlait avec une facilité déconcertante, sans avoir peur et sans chercher ses mots. Son récit se déroulait comme un ruban qu'on tire. Quand elle se tut, Tcherkassoff demeura impassible, au point qu'elle se demanda si elle n'avait pas tenu tout ce discours en rêve. Inquiet de ce long silence, Vassia Volkoff intervint :

— Ces faits m'ont paru si importants, Votre Excellence, que j'ai insisté auprès de Mme Ozareff pour qu'elle vous en informe. Connaissant votre passion de la justice, je n'ai pas douté une seconde que vous seriez bouleversé !...

— Je le serais peut-être si les coupables n'avaient pas reconnu leur forfait, marmonna le gouverneur avec un sourire.

— Ils savaient ce qui les attendait s'ils continuaient à protester de leur innocence ! dit Sophie.

Le gouverneur haussa le buste en prenant appui des deux mains sur le bord de la table. Ses sourcils poivre et sel se froncèrent.

— Madame, proféra-t-il sévèrement, vous avez une singulière conception de la justice russe. Le procès des assassins de Vladimir Karpovitch Sédoff a été entouré de toutes les garanties nécessaires. La sentence prononcée par le juge est irrévocable. Quant à l'accusation de parricide que vous portez contre votre neveu, je ne sais si vous en mesurez la gravité...

— J'ai bien réfléchi avant de me décider à vous en parler, Excellence....

— Vous n'avez pas encore assez réfléchi, Madame. Sinon, vous vous seriez rendu compte que Serge Vladimirovitch jouit dans ce pays d'une réputation irréprochable, qu'il n'a jamais eu maille à partir avec les autorités et que la mort de son père l'a affecté profondément ! J'ajoute que vous devriez être la dernière personne à déposer contre lui !

— Parce qu'il est mon neveu ? demanda-t-elle.

— Parce que vous revenez de Sibérie, Madame. Permettez-moi de vous dire que, dans votre situation, vous avez intérêt à vous montrer très discrète. Plus on vous oubliera, mieux cela vaudra pour vous. Il en va de même pour M. Volkoff, qui a cru habile d'appuyer votre démarche. Lui aussi ne doit sa tranquillité actuelle qu'à la bienveillance du tsar.

Vassia Volkoff baissa la tête, comme un élève réprimandé. Toute sa morgue avait disparu. Sophie ne put contenir son indignation. Elle s'écria :

— Ainsi, le fait d'avoir des idées libérales nous enlève, à l'un et à l'autre, le droit de porter plainte contre qui que ce soit !

— Il vous enlève le droit de porter plainte contre des personnes qui, contrairement à vous, sont au-dessus de tout reproche !

— Vous introduisez de fausses notions de politique dans la justice !

— C'est moins grave que d'introduire de fausses notions de justice dans la politique, à la façon de vos amis les conspirateurs ! Je devrais considérer votre intervention dans cette affaire comme une entreprise diffamatoire et vous en demander raison au nom de celui que vous attaquez. Mais je ne tiens pas à soulever un nouveau scandale dans le district. J'oublierai ce que vous m'avez dit. C'est tout ce que je puis vous promettre.

Pendant une seconde, le conseiller d'Etat actuel Tcherkassoff apparut à Sophie comme un personnage grotesque et mesquin, qui se perdait dans des soucis de procédure, alors que trois innocents étaient envoyés au bagne.

— Excellence, vous ne pouvez refuser de véri-

fier l'exactitude des faits que je vous rapporte !
balbutia-t-elle. La seule idée qu'une erreur judiciaire ait pu être commise devrait vous inciter à
ordonner une contre-enquête. Je vous en supplie,
an nom des malheureux qui...

— En voilà assez, Madame ! trancha le gouverneur. Gardez votre charité pour de meilleures causes !

Il se leva. L'âge semblait avoir vidé ce grand
corps de tout son sang, ne laissant qu'une enveloppe de parchemin, qui se plissait au creux des
joues. Il agita une sonnette entre ses doigts sque-
lettiques. La porte s'ouvrit. Vassia susurra à
l'oreille de Sophie :

— Il n'y a plus rien à faire. Partons...

Elle le suivit. Le traîneau de Vassia les attendait devant le palais du gouvernement. Sophie
avait laissé son propre équipage à Slavianka. Il valait mieux, pensait-elle, que David, qui avait la
langue bien pendue, ignorât qu'elle s'était rendue
à Pskov ce jour-là. Vassia la fit asseoir à côté de
lui dans la caisse, l'emmitoufla d'une couverture
d'ours et prit les guides en mains. Le cheval secoua la tête sous son arc de bois colorié et partit,
d'un pas moelleux, dans la neige. La barrière fran-
chie, il accéléra son allure. Sous le ciel gris, la plaine s'étendait, blanche, terne, avec, çà et là, quelques grêles bouleaux dépouillés. Des corbeaux sur-
volaient ce vide froid en croassant avec colère.

— Je vous demande pardon de vous avoir en-
traînée dans cette aventure, dit Vassia. Mais pou-
vais-je prévoir qu'on nous recevrait si mal ? Ah !
la Russie est un pays bien décourageant ! J'espère,
en tout cas, que notre démarche ne nous attirera
pas d'ennuis !...

— Quels ennuis pourrait-elle nous attirer ? demanda Sophie.

— Si votre neveu l'apprenait ?...

— Cela l'inciterait peut-être à me respecter davantage !

— Ou à mieux vous haïr !

— Il ne peut rien contre moi !

— Il ne pouvait rien, non plus, contre son père ! Voyez comme il s'est débarrassé de lui ! Méfiez-vous, Madame ! C'est un homme capable de tout ! Vous devriez solliciter du gouverneur un changement de résidence.

— Où irais-je ? Kachtanovka est le seul lieu au monde où je sois chez moi !

— N'avez-vous pas songé à retourner en France ?

— Si, bien sûr ! Mais c'est impossible ! Il a fallu dix-sept ans pour qu'on m'autorise à passer de Sibérie en Russie. Combien en faudrait-il pour qu'on m'autorisât maintenant à passer de Russie en France ? D'ailleurs, ce serait lâche ! Ma place est ici, parmi les paysans. Je peux beaucoup pour eux...

— Vous venez de constater le contraire !

— Je suis arrivée trop tard pour ceux-ci, j'aurai plus de chance avec d'autres.

Vassia remit son cheval au pas. Le froid parut moins vif à Sophie. Sans doute son compagnon n'était-il pas pressé de regagner Slavianka.

— Si vous étiez allée seule chez le gouverneur, peut-être vous aurait-il mieux reçue ! dit-il.

— Je croyais que vous étiez en excellents termes avec lui !

— Je le croyais aussi ! Mon père et lui étaient vaguement cousins. Admirez le résultat !... La vérité, c'est que je ne suis bon à rien ! Je porte la guigne à ceux que je veux secourir ! Cela date du 14 décembre 1825 ! Est-ce qu'il vous arrive de rêver aux pendus ?

— A quels pendus ?

— Aux chefs des décembristes : Ryléïeff, Pestel, Mouravieff-Apostol, Bestoujeff-Rioumine, Kakhovsky...

— J'avoue que non, dit-elle.

— Moi, souvent je les vois, la nuit. Ils me tirent la langue du haut de leur potence. Ils m'injurient. Maintenant, en plus des cinq pendus, il y aura les trois moujiks innocents de Kachtanovka qui vont me tourmenter... Ce qui m'étonne le plus dans le monde, c'est que toutes les injustices, finalement, se digèrent. Des êtres qu'on croyait irremplaçables tombent, et les rangs se reforment, la vie continue...

Il clappa de la langue. Le cheval repartit au trot. Sophie se reposa dans le tintement des clochettes. Les lamentations de Vassia l'avaient agacée. Elle se remettait difficilement de son insuccès devant le gouverneur. L'idée qu'il lui faudrait accepter l'état de fait et vivre aux côtés d'un assassin que tout le monde considérait comme un honnête homme, la rebutait au point qu'elle imaginait mal son retour à la maison. Elle reconnut les deux collines qui annonçaient l'approche de Slavianka. Un sourire fade reparut sur le visage de Vassia.

— Maman nous attend pour prendre le thé, dit-il.

D'abord, Sophie se déroba :

— C'est très aimable de sa part, mais je ne pourrai pas rester...

— Oh ! pourquoi ? Ne partez pas encore ! A

moins que vous ne craigniez de mécontenter Serge Vladimirovitch en rentrant trop tard !...

Cette phrase suffit à retourner Sophie.

— J'ai tout mon temps, dit-elle.

— Eh bien ! alors ?...

Elle accepta l'invitation comme elle eût relevé un défi.

Jour après jour, Sophie s'enfonçait plus avant dans une situation fausse qu'elle exécrait et à laquelle elle n'imaginait pas d'issue. Elle ne pouvait ni dire à son neveu qu'elle avait voulu le dénoncer comme assassin ni jouer l'ignorance. Dès qu'elle l'apercevait, elle éprouvait un malaise fait de dégoût et de colère. Elle le regardait, affable, souriant, et voyait des mains de tueur au bout de ses manchettes blanches. Incapable de supporter ce défi permanent à la justice, elle s'ingéniait à éviter les occasions de le rencontrer. Mais, comme la neige bloquait les routes, Serge restait la plupart du temps à la maison. Alors, elle s'enfermait dans sa chambre. Parfois même, elle y prenait ses repas en prétextant une migraine. Il ne pouvait être dupe de ses excuses, mais feignait de les accepter, soit qu'il y trouvât son avantage, soit qu'il redoutât un esclandre. Ainsi, sans se concerter, en arrivèrent-ils à mener sous le même toit des existences parallèles. Cette paix haineuse épuisait Sophie. Pour se réconforter, elle se disait qu'elle n'avait pas encore joué toutes ses cartes, qu'elle finirait bien par démasquer le coupable.

Les fêtes de Noël passèrent, puis celles du Nouvel an, et elle dut se montrer avec Serge pour recevoir les vœux des domestiques. Le 5 janvier au soir, juste avant le souper, comme elle allait chercher un livre dans le bureau, il entra derrière elle et referma la porte. Elle se retourna, furieuse. Il dit :

— Pardonnez-moi de vous déranger, ma tante. Mais, ces dernières semaines, vous êtes insaisissable. Il m'a donc fallu vous aborder par surprise. Vous savez que, demain, c'est l'Epiphanie...

Sophie voyait déjà où il voulait en venir. De tout temps, les maîtres de Kachtanovka avaient assisté à la cérémonie de la bénédiction des eaux. Après les prières, des moujiks se baignaient dans un trou de glace. Elle se rappela Nikita émergeant de la rivière et prenant pied sur la neige, la face marbrée de froid, les yeux avivés de fierté juvénile, une croix de baptême sur sa poitrine imberbe...

— Je compte sur vous pour m'accompagner à Chatkovo où se déroulera l'office religieux en plein air, reprit Serge. Nous partirons à huit heures du matin, si vous n'y voyez pas d'inconvénient...

Le ton était aimable et le regard impérieux. Sophie sentit toute sa rancœur qui refluait dans sa tête.

— Non, dit-elle. Je n'irai pas !

— Comment, ma tante ? C'est un si grand jour ! Il faut que nos paysans vous voient à mes côtés pendant la cérémonie !

— Pour leur prouver qu'en dépit des apparences nous sommes d'accord sur tout ?

— Pour leur donner l'impression que, quoique catholique, vous ne dédaignez pas leur croyance.

— Ils n'ont pas besoin de me voir en prière pour savoir que je pense à eux !

— Soit, grommela-t-il. Je ne vais pas vous traîner là-bas de force. Mais laissez-moi vous dire que je vous trouve bien arrogante ! Votre conversation avec le gouverneur aurait pourtant dû vous donner à réfléchir !

Il souriait, les yeux mi-clos, la tête penchée sur l'épaule. Dans la minute qui suivit, Sophie éprouva une profonde angoisse. Puis un soulagement s'opéra en elle. Plus besoin de feindre. Elle allait pouvoir affronter l'ennemi à visage découvert. Qui avait renseigné Serge ? Le gouverneur lui-même, sans doute. Elle entendait un battement sourd dans les artères de son cou.

— Eh bien ! oui, prononça-t-elle d'une voix atone. J'ai vu le gouverneur. Je lui ai dit ce que je pensais du crime...

— Et il ne vous a pas convaincue de mon innocence ?

Elle le provoqua du regard et serra les dents. Il s'assit sur un coin de table, croisa ses jambes et imprima un faible balancement à son pied droit.

— Evidemment, murmura-t-il, vous êtes très difficile à persuader. Quand vous enfourchez une idée, bonne ou mauvaise, vous la cravachez et galopez d'une traite jusqu'au but, c'est-à-dire, la plupart du temps, jusqu'au fossé. Voyons les choses de près. Je ne tiens pas tant à me disculper qu'à vous démontrer qu'avec un peu de réflexion vous auriez pu vous éviter le ridicule d'une accusation contre nature...

— Ce qui est contre nature, s'écria-t-elle, c'est

la façon dont vous avez laissé condamner ces trois paysans, alors que !...

— Alors que c'était moi le coupable ? dit-il. Séduisante théorie ! Pourtant, les sentiments que je portais à mon père, et qui sont connus de tous, devraient suffire à me justifier...

— N'avez-vous pas eu une grave altercation avec lui, la veille du meurtre ?

— Si. Mais qu'est-ce que cela signifie ? Nous nous sommes disputés pour des questions d'argent...

— Vous avez échangé des coups !

— N'exagérons pas !

— On vous a entendus !

— Nous avions bu l'un et l'autre. Après nous être expliqués — un peu bruyamment, je l'avoue — nous sommes allés nous promener du côté de la cabane de bains. Là, j'ai remarqué quelques lattes pourries et, laissant mon père rentrer seul à la maison, je me suis rendu à Chatkovo.

— A pied ? C'est impossible !...

— Pour vous, peut-être. Pas pour moi. J'aime marcher ! A Chatkovo, j'ai désigné trois moujiks pour réparer le plancher de la cabane, le lendemain matin.

— Vous avez pris soin de les envoyer là-bas sans la moindre escorte !

— Mes trois gaillards étaient d'excellents charpentiers. Ils n'avaient pas besoin de surveillance, alors que j'avais à peine assez de conducteurs pour suivre le travail des autres moujiks, dans les champs.

Cette explication toute simple déconcerta Sophie. Ses idées se mirent à flotter. Effrayée de la déroute qui gagnait son esprit, elle réagit avec force :

192

— Ceux qui vous ont vu, ce soir-là, sont tous d'accord pour dire que vous aviez l'air désemparé, que vos vêtements étaient froissés, que vous portiez une égratignure à la joue !

— N'ai-je pas reconnu que j'avais eu une querelle avec mon père ? dit Serge.

— Et puis, que s'est-il passé ? Vous êtes retourné à Kachtanovka et vous avez soupé avec votre père ?

— Non, il était déjà couché. Je lui ai souhaité une bonne nuit dans sa chambre.

— Personne ne l'a vu rentrer à la maison ! C'est étrange !

— Ce sont des choses qui arrivent.

— Et personne, non plus, ne l'a vu ressortir, le lendemain matin, pour aller à la cabane de bains !

— Les domestiques n'étaient pas encore levés.

— Quelle heure était-il donc ?

— Cinq heures du matin, je pense...

— Qu'allait-il faire si tôt au bord de la rivière ?

— Comment le saurais-je ? C'était un original ! Peut-être avait-il rendez-vous avec une fille serve ? Arrivé là-bas, il est tombé sur les moujiks qui se mettaient au travail ! Il les a insultés parce qu'ils le dérangeaient. Il leur a tapé dessus. L'un d'eux, en se défendant, lui a porté un mauvais coup. Ensuite, craignant qu'il ne les dénonçât, ils l'ont achevé en l'étranglant et sont venus me raconter qu'ils avaient découvert son cadavre...

Il avait réponse à tout. Présentés par lui, les événements les plus suspects s'enchaînaient logiquement. Sophie ne trouvait plus d'arguments à lui opposer, mais, le cerveau vide, refusait encore de s'avouer vaincue. Pendant un long moment, il la laissa se débattre dans le silence, puis, toujours

193

assis au bord de la table et balançant son pied, il dit avec un sourire sarcastique :

— Et maintenant, qu'allons-nous faire ?

Elle ne répondit pas.

— Vous avez comploté derrière mon dos, reprit-il. Vous avez alerté les autorités contre moi. Vous vous êtes déclarée mon ennemie, alors que je vous avais accueillie avec toute la bienveillance possible ! Il ne peut être question d'une réconciliation entre nous !

— Non, dit-elle.

— Certes, le gouvernement vous a assigné Kachtanovka comme résidence. Je dois donc accepter votre présence à la maison. Mais cette situation devient de plus en plus intolérable. Je ne vois qu'une solution au problème : votre départ. Il faut que vous sollicitiez l'autorisation d'habiter ailleurs. A Saint-Pétersbourg, à Moscou, à Paris, à Pékin... Où vous voulez ! Mais pas ici !...

Elle sentait qu'il avait raison et, pourtant, une force incoercible lui fit répliquer :

— Cela vous arrangerait que je parte ? Eh bien ! n'y comptez pas ! Je resterai ici, même s'il m'en coûte ! Ce domaine est à moi autant qu'à vous !

— Aussi continuerez-vous à toucher la moitié des revenus, où que vous soyez.

— Je ne pense pas à l'argent en disant cela ! Je pense aux gens... aux pauvres gens qui vivent sur cette terre... Tant que je serai parmi eux, je pourrai prendre leur défense contre vous !

— Contre moi ? Vous êtes bien naïve ! Vous avez vu de quel poids étaient vos avis auprès du gouverneur ! Résignez-vous donc à comprendre que vous n'êtes rien en Russie, que vous n'y avez aucun crédit, aucune sympathie, aucun avenir !... Partez !...

194

Il la chassait, il la chassait de chez elle ! Le sang à la tête, elle s'entendit crier :

— Jamais ! Jamais !...

Et elle se précipita pour sortir. Mais, plus prompt qu'elle, il s'adossa à la porte. La même attitude que son père quand il voulait terroriser la petite Marie. Dans la lumière de la lampe, son visage dur avait le poli du bronze. Sa peau luisait dans l'os de la mâchoire. Il y avait dans ses yeux une extraordinaire concentration de haine.

— Vous êtes trop pressée ! dit-il. Je n'ai pas fini. J'aime que tout soit en ordre chez moi, vous le savez. Voici donc ce que j'ai décidé pour l'avenir : vous prendrez tous vos repas dans votre chambre. Cela ne vous gênera pas, puisque vous avez déjà commencé à le faire de votre propre initiative. Vous cesserez de vous occuper de la maison. Aucun domestique ne vous obéira plus. Il leur sera même interdit de vous répondre. Seule votre soubrette, Zoé, aura le droit de vous servir. A la moindre incartade de votre part, les gens coupables de vous avoir écoutée seront passés par les verges !

— Vous avez déjà essayé, une fois, de me faire peur avec cette lâche mesure de coercition ! dit-elle, les lèvres tremblantes.

— Oui, et j'ai eu tort d'y renoncer sur vos instances. J'y reviens aujourd'hui avec une volonté affermie. Vous pourrez vous plaindre à qui bon vous semble, écrire au gouverneur, au tsar, au pape, je ne fléchirai pas ! Vous avez eu la preuve qu'on ne vous écoutait pas en haut lieu quand vous clamiez votre indignation ! Moi, j'ai eu la preuve qu'il n'y avait pas d'autre méthode avec vous que la force ! Vous finirez par plier ! Vous demanderez, vous supplierez qu'on vous laisse partir !

— Est-ce tout ? dit-elle en soutenant son regard.

— Oui.

— Laissez-moi passer.

Il s'écarta de la porte. Elle sortit. Dans l'escalier, elle fut saisie de vertige. L'énergie qu'elle avait dépensée pour tenir tête à Serge lui faisait brusquement défaut. Elle s'appuya à la rampe, reprit son souffle et continua de monter les marches, lentement. Une fois dans sa chambre, elle se laissa tomber dans un fauteuil. La tête penchée, elle essayait de dominer sa détresse. Qu'allait-elle devenir au milieu de cet univers hostile ? Une envie de pleurer l'envahit, mais ses yeux restèrent secs. Ce n'était pas de tristesse qu'elle eût versé des larmes, mais de dépit contre elle-même, de colère contre Serge. La pâle lueur de la lampe de chevet éclairait un coin de son lit. Des flacons brillaient sur la tablette de la coiffeuse. Les vitres étaient argentées de givre. Derrière, la nuit, la neige, le silence.

A l'heure du souper, Zoé se présenta, portant un plateau chargé de viande froide et de fruits.

— Barynia, chuchota-t-elle, c'est affreux ! Le barine vient de réunir tous les domestiques dans le bureau. Il leur a dit...

— Je sais ce qu'il leur a dit, murmura Sophie.

— Moi seule devrai vous obéir...

— Je ne te donnerai pas beaucoup de travail, va !..

— Ce n'est pas ça, barynia !... Mais je voulais vous demander... pour David et pour tous les autres... vous ne ferez rien qui puisse fâcher le barine, n'est-ce pas ?...

196

Son visage rose et potelé avait une expression quémandeuse.

— Sois tranquille : aucun d'entre vous ne souffrira jamais par ma faute, dit Sophie.

— Oh ! merci, barynia ! s'écria Zoé.

Elle s'agenouilla devant sa maîtresse et lui baisa les mains. Sophie sentit sur sa peau cette haleine chaude d'animal familier. Elle tapota la joue de la fille. Zoé se releva, les yeux humides, et se mit à disposer le couvert sur une petite table. « Cette fois, pensa Sophie, je suis bien prisonnière ! »

Vers la mi-février, des tempêtes de neige iso-
lèrent la maison. De rares traîneaux venaient encore des villages voisins. Mais la grande route
était impraticable. Pskov se trouvait hors d'at-
teinte. Toutes les villes de Russie auraient pu disparaître, qu'on n'en aurait rien su. Au milieu de ce
désert de blancheur et de froid, les habitants de
Kachtanovka se repliaient frileusement dans la
vieille demeure aux fenêtres calfeutrées. Il y avait
assez de bois et de vivres pour soutenir, pendant
des mois, le siège de l'hiver. Sophie, qui avait aimé
autrefois cette solitude campagnarde, en souffrait
aujourd'hui comme d'un étouffement. Les consi-
gnes de Serge étaient suivies à la lettre par tous
les domestiques, à l'exception de Zoé. Ils évitaient
de rencontrer la barynia pour ne pas s'attirer
d'histoires. Si elle leur adressait la parole, même
sans rien leur demander, ils prenaient un air stupide et restaient cois. Parfois, ils tournaient les
talons et s'enfuyaient devant elle. Quand elle entrait à l'office, tous se taisaient d'un coup, et, sur
les figures, se lisait une telle crainte qu'elle s'en

allait pour ne pas les torturer davantage. Serge prenait ses repas seul dans la salle à manger et passait beaucoup de temps enfermé dans son bureau. Lorsqu'elle le croisait, par hasard, dans la maison, il ne la saluait pas, il ne la voyait pas. A force d'être ignorée par tant de gens, elle se demandait si elle existait encore. La notion de sa personnalité se perdait dans ce vide sans écho. Seule Zoé lui donnait encore la sensation d'être de ce monde. La pauvre fille n'avait pas grand-chose à lui dire. Mais, du moins, était-elle quelqu'un de vrai, avec des oreilles, une voix, un regard, un cœur. Par elle, Sophie savait ce qui se passait à Kachtanovka, ce que faisait le maître, de quoi on discutait aux cuisines. Combien de temps pourrait-elle se satisfaire de cette médiocre contrefaçon de la vie ? Ne succomberait-elle pas bientôt à l'accumulation de l'ennui ? « Tenir jusqu'au printemps, pensait-elle. Après, tout ira mieux ! »

Quand il ne faisait pas trop froid, elle sortait se promener dans le parc. La neige était si épaisse qu'il suffisait de s'écarter de l'allée pour enfoncer jusqu'au ventre. L'allée même était resserrée, encaissée entre deux énormes talus blancs. Marchant à petits pas dans l'étroit chemin gelé, Sophie s'emplissait les yeux du pâle rayonnement de ce monde englouti, d'où émergeaient les silhouettes funèbres des sapins. Un jour qu'elle s'abandonnait à la fascination du paysage, elle aperçut, au loin, la silhouette d'un cavalier. C'était Serge, rentrant de promenade. Il arrivait au galop. Elle vit grandir la tête du cheval, et, au-dessus, un visage animé par le vent de la course, les yeux étincelants, le bonnet de fourrure tiré sur l'oreille. Il ne ralentissait pas, il fonçait droit sur elle, il allait la bousculer. Instinctivement, elle se plaqua contre le remblai de neige. Une bourrasque noire la souffleta. Un pied botté faillit lui emporter la figure. Des mottes glacées la bombardèrent à bout portant. « Il est fou ! » pensa-t-elle quand il l'eut dépassée. Tout son corps tremblait. Elle crut que c'était de froid. Mais non, seule son émotion était responsable de ce malaise. Une phrase lui revint, que son neveu lui avait dite autrefois : « Nous devons rester dans l'indivision jusqu'à la mort de l'un de nous deux. » Puis elle se rappela Vassia, la suppliant d'être prudente, parce qu'il jugeait Serge capable d'un nouveau crime pour s'approprier Kachtanovka. « Un homme qui a tué son père, se dit-elle, ne va pas hésiter devant le faible obstacle que je représente. Mais a-t-il vraiment tué son père ? Je ne le saurai jamais... » Tout à coup, il lui fut indifférent de mourir ou de vivre. Elle reprit le chemin de la maison. Des paysannes emmitouflées balayaient le perron. Elles avaient tout vu. Sophie leur sourit. Elles détournèrent la tête. Elle monta dans sa chambre et agita la sonnette pour appeler Zoé. Mais Zoé devait être loin : elle n'entendait pas, elle ne venait pas. A l'idée de rester plus longtemps seule, une horreur s'empara de Sophie. Elle était trop malheureuse. Elle avait envie de crier. Pour se calmer, elle prit du papier et écrivit à Ferdinand Wolff une lettre où elle lui racontait tout. Mais elle ne l'enverrait pas : les censeurs l'arrêteraient au passage. Ayant noirci deux feuillets, elle les déchira. Le pas de Zoé, dans le couloir, fit battre son cœur. Elle se domina pour ne pas laisser éclater son contentement. Quoi qu'il advînt, elle devait garder ses distances, rester une vraie barynia pour les domestiques.

★

Les jours se suivaient, désespérément identiques. Assise devant sa fenêtre, Sophie s'engourdissait à regarder, des heures entières, le parc blanc, où pas une ombre ne bougeait. Un poêle en faïence chauffait sa chambre. Mais, sous la porte, passait un courant d'air glacé. Elle remontait un châle sur ses épaules, ouvrait un livre, en lisait quelques lignes, le reposait tristement, prenait son ouvrage de tapisserie. Cet hiver ne finirait donc jamais ? Quand pourrait-elle de nouveau marcher dans la campagne verte ? La dernière semaine du grand carême, il y eut encore une tempête de neige. Mais les routes furent déblayées à temps et, le samedi saint, les domestiques purent accompagner leur maître à Chatkovo pour la messe de minuit. Aucune voiture n'ayant été mise à la disposition de Sophie, elle resta à la maison. D'ailleurs, elle n'eût pas accepté de paraître à l'église avec Serge. De loin, elle écouta le tintement irréel des cloches, qui annonçaient la résurrection du Seigneur. Le lendemain, Zoé lui apporta des œufs coloriés, qui avaient été bénits par le prêtre. Elles échangèrent le triple baiser pascal.

Le printemps n'était plus loin ; une tiédeur amicale passait dans l'air, en dépit de la neige persistante ; les bourgeons des châtaigniers, des bouleaux, des trembles, des groseilliers se gonflaient de sève sur les branches humides ; des plaques gelées glissaient des toits avec un bruit mat ; par terre, la neige mollissait, fondait, libérant l'herbe verte et drue, semée de fleurs ; tout le paysage se déshabillait sous le ciel bleu. Et, au-dessus de ce monde nouveau, encore trempé de boue, s'égosillaient les alouettes qui étaient revenues, comme chaque année, le jour des Quarante-Martyrs. Sophie émergea de la mauvaise saison avec une faiblesse dans tout le corps. Peut-être avait-elle pris froid dans sa chambre ? Le soleil qui brillait dehors la rassura..Pour la première fois, elle n'endossa pas son manteau fourré et sortit, vêtue légèrement et chaussée de petites bottes.

De tous côtés, couraient des ruisseaux éblouissants. Elle les enjambait ; ses pieds enfonçaient dans la vase ; et, plus loin, elle rencontrait une pellicule de glace, qui ne cédait pas encore, mais sous laquelle on voyait, par transparence, bouger des bulles brunes. Des vanneaux criaient autour de la rivière. Une abeille perdue passa en bourdonnant. Sophie la suivit du regard et sourit. Ses yeux clignaient dans la lumière trop forte. Elle ouvrait la bouche et buvait, à grands traits, un air parfumé de neige et de mousse. Le sentier où elle s'était engagée au hasard finit en fondrière. Elle pataugea, s'échauffa et retrouva la terre ferme. Elle était en nage. Des nuages gris couvrirent le soleil. Il fit très froid, tout à coup. Elle rentra à la maison.

Le soir, après le souper, elle se sentit glacée jusqu'au cœur et un long tremblement la secoua. Toute sa peau se hérissait, dansait sur ses os douloureux. Elle claquait des dents, trouvait cela ridicule, voulait s'arrêter et ne le pouvait pas. Comme Zoé s'inquiétait, elle se mit à rire nerveusement :

— Ce n'est rien. J'ai dû prendre un rhume. Aide-moi à me déshabiller et rajoute une couverture.

Une fois couchée, elle renvoya sa servante et éteignit la lampe de chevet. Mais elle ne pouvait dormir. Au milieu de la nuit, elle constata qu'elle avait les membres rompus, la poitrine oppressée, toussa, et un point de côté lui coupa le souffle.

Elle essaya de retenir sa respiration. Des gouttes de sueur perlèrent à son front. Après avoir eu froid, elle étouffait de chaleur. « Je dois avoir beaucoup de fièvre », pensa-t-elle. Et elle se rappela Alexandrine Mouravieff, qui avait toussé, les poumons déchirés, la face exsangue, des semaines entières, avant de mourir. « Serais-je malade comme elle ? Non ! Non ! » Elle regretta d'avoir renvoyé Zoé, saisit la sonnette sur la table, l'agita d'une main faible. Le son se perdit dans la maison endormie. Alors, elle appela : « Zoé ! Zoé ! » Mais, à chaque cri, un coup de poignard lui perçait le dos, du côté gauche. Elle renonça à se faire entendre et renversa la tête sur son oreiller moite de transpiration. Sa figure flambait comme dans un brasier. Ses cheveux collaient à son front. Sa langue était sèche. Pourquoi avait-elle éteint la lampe ? Elle n'avait pas la force de la rallumer. Personne ne viendrait la voir avant l'aube. Toute son attention se fixa sur le coin de la chambre où se trouvait la coiffeuse.

Enfin, une lueur blême parut dans la glace. Le reflet du jour. Elle s'assoupit, assurée. Quand elle rouvrit les yeux, Zoé, penchée sur elle, lui essuyait le visage avec un linge frais :

— Oh ! barynia, vous êtes malade ?...

Une idée joyeuse traversa l'esprit de Sophie.

— Oui, dit-elle. Appelle le docteur Wolff !

— Qui, barynia ?

— Le docteur Wolff, vite ! Il doit être au dispensaire...

A partir de ce moment, tout se brouilla dans son esprit. Les heures tournaient tantôt très vite, tantôt très lentement ; les ténèbres succédaient à la lumière ; Zoé s'en allait, revenait ; la nuit, elle

dormait dans un fauteuil, près du lit. Sophie se
fâcha :

— Eh bien ? As-tu prévenu le docteur Wolff ?

— J'ai demandé à notre barine, balbutia Zoé.
Il dit qu'il ne veut pas de docteur dans la maison.

Alors, un voile se déchira dans la tête de Sophie.
Elle se rappela où elle était et une affreuse détresse remplaça son exaltation. La Sibérie s'éloigna devant elle avec sa charge d'amis. Elle restait seule dans la vieille demeure de Kachtanovka, aux prises avec un homme qui voulait sa mort.
Zoé sanglotait :

— Barynia, barynia ! Je ne peux pas vous laisser sans soins et je ne sais pas ce qu'il faut faire !
Qu'allons-nous devenir ?

— Nous nous passerons de docteur, chuchota
Sophie. Fais-moi des tisanes très chaudes...

Elle ne put en dire davantage. Chaque mot lui
défonçait le thorax. Une toux sèche l'ébranla et,
sous le choc de la souffrance des larmes lui jail-
lirent des yeux. Zoé lui apporta une tisane si amère, qu'elle refusa de la boire.

— C'est trop mauvais, soupira-t-elle. D'ailleurs,
il est temps que je me lève ! Depuis combien
d'heures suis-je couchée ?

— Depuis quatre jours, barynia.

Sophie trouva cette réponse très drôle, mais se
retint de rire, par prudence. Le lendemain, Zoé
lui annonça, en grand mystère :

— Le barine est parti pour la journée. J'ai de-
mandé à Julie de passer vous voir, en cachette.
C'est ma marraine. Elle connaît toutes les plantes.
Elle vous guérira...

— Oh ! oui, gémit Sophie. Fais-la venir, s'il te
plaît ! Je n'en peux plus !

Une vieille au museau de souris se glissa dans

205

la chambre. Elle apportait, dans un panier, de petits pots, des bouquets d'herbes sèches, des linges, qu'elle étala sur la commode. Zoé l'aida à retirer la chemise de la barynia et à la frictionner rudement. Elles lui posèrent un cataplasme. Le dos brûlé, Sophie se remit à claquer des dents. On l'obligea à boire une mixture très aigre et une autre très sucrée. Sa tête s'emplit d'un bruit de roues. Maintenant, elle était sûre de mourir. C'était stupide ! Elle avait tant de choses à dire ! Comment était-ce déjà ? Elle ne trouvait plus ses mots. Elle hoqueta :

— Personne... Personne pour vous protéger contre ce monstre !... Si on le laisse faire, il vous tuera tous sous le knout !... Vous savez que c'est lui... c'est lui qui a assassiné son père !...

Zoé et Julie échangèrent un regard effrayé et se signèrent.

— Taisez-vous, barynia ! bredouilla Zoé. Il ne faut pas parler de ces choses !

— Si... Si... Répétez-le partout !... On l'arrêtera !... On relâchera les innocents ! Ah ! j'aurais tant voulu y arriver moi-même !... Mais je n'ai pas su !... C'est ma faute !... Jurez-moi, jurez-moi qu'après moi...

Elle ne put continuer, rompue en deux par une quinte de toux. Julie se dépêcha de ramasser son attirail et de disparaître, laissant derrière elle une odeur de térébinthe. Restée seule avec Zoé, Sophie se tut. Mais son cerveau travaillait toujours à une vitesse inhabituelle. Une idée chassait l'autre. A l'extrémité où elle était parvenue, elle ne comprenait pas pourquoi elle avait refusé de présenter une demande de retour en France. N'y aurait-il eu qu'une chance sur mille de convaincre le gouvernement, elle aurait dû essayer. L'orgueil de résister aux volontés de Serge lui avait fait perdre de vue la vraie valeur de l'enjeu. Que lui était la Russie auprès de son propre pays, quitté trente-cinq ans plus tôt ? Mourir en terre étrangère, abandonnée, détestée — alors qu'elle aurait pu finir ses jours au milieu d'une nature tempérée, dans la douce musique de la langue française ! Les vers de Racine, les ponts de la Seine, le vin de Bourgogne, les bons mots, les colères politiques... Elle dit à haute voix :

— Je me demande si on dîne toujours aussi bien chez les Frères Provençaux...

Elle avait parlé en français. Zoé arrondit les yeux. Un flot de tristesse souleva le cœur de Sophie. Elle ne savait plus si c'était de douceur ou de chagrin qu'elle gémissait. Les gens pieux avaient peut-être raison : elle allait retrouver Nicolas dans l'autre monde. Mais, plus elle pensait à lui, moins elle voyait son visage. Il était mort une première fois en tant qu'être de chair, une deuxième fois en tant que souvenir. Ce n'était pas vers une promesse de rencontre lumineuse qu'elle cheminait en haletant d'angoisse, mais vers un trou noir qui avait un goût d'ossements et de terre. Et, quand elle aurait disparu, Serge éclaterait de rire. Elle s'agita dans son lit :

— Non !... Je ne veux pas !... Je ne veux pas !...

Des pelletées sonores la recouvrirent. Elle dormit un siècle. De temps à autre, une laveuse de cadavres la remuait, la frottait avec des onguents qui sentaient mauvais, lui versait des breuvages bouillants dans la bouche, puis la recouchait dans son cercueil.

Assise dans son lit, le dos calé par des oreillers, Sophie n'osait croire qu'elle était guérie. Le mal s'était enfui aussi brusquement qu'il était venu. La semaine passée, une rude sudation l'avait saisie en pleine nuit, pour la laisser, à l'aube, exténuée et heureuse. Il y avait bien eu un retour de fièvre dans la journée, avec quintes de toux, crachats rougeâtres et douleurs vagues dans le dos, mais l'alerte avait été brève. Le lendemain, elle se sentait mieux. Depuis, elle ne cessait de reprendre des forces. Déjà, elle avait pu se lever et faire quelques pas dans la chambre. La fenêtre l'attirait. Derrière, c'étaient la lumière, les feuillages tendres, les routes déroulées dans la vapeur du matin... Elle avait plus que jamais soif de vivre. Et aussi de recommencer la lutte contre Serge. Sans savoir ce qu'elle entreprendrait, elle aimait à se persuader qu'elle n'avait pas dit son dernier mot. Zoé entra, portant une tasse de thé. Le dévouement de cette fille simple la renforçait dans l'idée qu'elle devait tenter l'impossible pour améliorer le sort des serfs de Kachtanovka. Elle but le thé, croqua deux rôties et voulut se lever. Zoé lui passa un déshabillé de soie rose, et la soutint pendant qu'elle marchait, sur ses jambes vacillantes, jusqu'à la fenêtre. Arrivée là, elle se laissa glisser, épuisée, essoufflée, dans un fauteuil. Une petite toux lui vint de cet effort. Elle avait encore les côtes endolories comme par un coup de bâton. Mais cette gêne était supportable, même quand elle respirait profondément. Elle se pencha vers la croisée et s'étonna de l'agitation qui régnait dans le parc. Des domestiques balayaient l'allée centrale, d'autres jetaient du sable dans les ornières pour les niveler, d'autres encore taillaient les buissons, au bord de la grande pelouse.

— Ils arrangent tout, vite, pour recevoir les invités, dit Zoé.

— Quels invités ?

— Je ne sais pas. Des messieurs importants, sans doute. Ils viennent pour le dîner. Six couverts ! Il y a un de ces remue-ménage aux cuisines ! Vous voulez que je vous dise ce qu'on leur servira ?

Sophie ne répondit pas, plongée dans une réflexion qui la séparait du monde. Il n'était guère dans les habitudes de Serge d'accueillir des étrangers à sa table. Pourquoi cette brusque exception ? Zoé babillait au-dessus de sa tête :

— Après, il y aura des *pelménis* au fenouil ; après, du saumon et du *lavaret* fumés ; après... après, une oie farcie... Ça ne vous fait pas envie, barynia ?

— Si, dit Sophie distraitement.

— Ah ! c'est signe que la santé revient ! Bien sûr, ce ne serait pas raisonnable pour vous de manger tout ça ! Mais je vous apporterai un peu de leur dessert. Ça ne vous fera pas de mal. Une sorte de pâte sucrée, avec, à l'intérieur...

Sophie lui coupa la parole :

— Le barine t'a-t-il demandé de mes nouvelles pendant ma maladie ?

— Non, barynia, murmura Zoé en baissant le front. Mais je lui ai tout de même dit, avant-hier, que vous étiez guérie.

— Et qu'a-t-il répondu ?

— Rien.

Il y eut un silence. Zoé ressortit de la chambre sur la pointe des pieds. Sophie continua de regarder par la fenêtre. Vers midi, l'affairement cessa dans le parc, les balayeurs se dispersèrent, comme des machinistes évacuant la scène d'un théâtre avant le lever du rideau. Toute la maison devint attentive. Après un assez long temps, deux calèches se montrèrent au bout de l'allée, contournèrent la pelouse et s'arrêtèrent devant le perron. Des valets se précipitèrent pour ouvrir les portières et baisser les marchepieds. A tour de rôle, surgirent deux hommes en manteaux militaires, une forte femme en rotonde de velours lilas, une autre femme, plus petite et plus mince, coiffée d'une toque jaune, un vieillard en uniforme et chapeau à plumes. Le cœur de Sophie reçut un coup : elle venait de reconnaître le gouverneur de Pskov. Déjà, le groupe gravissait le perron et disparaissait dans le péristyle. Les calèches vides s'éloignèrent.

Renversée dans son fauteuil, Sophie essayait de comprendre le sens de cette visite. De toute évidence, en conviant le gouverneur, Serge avait voulu prouver à sa tante que, même rétablie, elle ne pouvait rien contre lui, qu'il était le plus fort, qu'elle devait partir... Mais comment un personnage aussi important que Tcherkassoff avait-il accepté de venir à Kachtanovka après ce qu'elle lui avait dit ? Même s'il était convaincu de l'innocence de Serge, il aurait dû décliner l'invitation par égard pour elle. Les yeux à demi clos, elle écouta la maison s'animer : une voix de femme haut perchée, des rires d'hommes, des tintements de vaisselle, les pas précipités de la valetaille entre la salle à manger et l'office.

Zoé servit à Sophie son repas de convalescente : un bouillon, du poulet rôti et du blanc-manger ; en supplément, une tranche de gâteau à la crème. Un souvenir d'enfance la toucha : chez ses parents, quand elle était punie, une domestique lui apportait, en cachette, des friandises dans sa chambre.

— Ils en sont au saumon fumé, chuchota Zoé. J'ai demandé à Sabel, le valet de pied, comment ça marchait, là-bas. Paraît qu'ils trouvent tous que c'est très bon... Ils causent, ils causent, on les entend du couloir, mais on ne les comprend pas : c'est tout en français. Notre barine raconte des histoires qui les font rire...

Elle repartit, laissant Sophie rêveuse devant son assiette. La conscience de ce qui se passait en bas l'empêchait de penser à la nourriture. C'était, sous ses pieds, comme une réunion de conspirateurs. Sans doute ne s'agissait-il pas d'une véritable complicité entre Serge et le gouverneur, mais de cette alliance tacite qui unit les gens heureux, arrivés, casés, contre ceux qui prétendent les déranger dans leurs habitudes. De nouveau, se dressait devant elle le bloc d'injustices et de préjugés qu'elle avait si souvent trouvé sur sa route, en Russie. Devrait-elle, comme Sisyphe, pousser, jusqu'à la fin de ses jours, ce rocher ?

Zoé revint, les joues roses, la bouche pleine de nouvelles :

— Ils attaquent l'oie farcie, maintenant ! Le gouverneur boit beaucoup ! Déjà neuf petits verres de vodka ! C'est trop pour un homme de son âge ! Ah ! mon Dieu, mais vous n'avez rien mangé, barynia !...

— Je n'ai pas faim, dit Sophie. Quels sont les autres invités, à part le gouverneur ?

Zoé prit un air important :

— Son Excellence le directeur des Postes, Son Excellence le juge du district...

Sophie eut un sourire d'ironie amère et marmonna :

— Je comprends ! Je comprends ! Et les deux femmes ?

— L'épouse du gouverneur et sa demoiselle.

— Sa demoiselle ? répéta Sophie étonnée.

— Oui, barynia.

Sophie renvoya Zoé. Tout s'éclairait dans sa tête. Si le gouverneur avait une fille à marier, il devait naturellement ménager Serge, qui était l'un des meilleurs partis de la région. Et lui, bien que n'ayant aucune intention matrimoniale, jouait les empressés pour conserver le plus longtemps possible un puissant protecteur. C'était comique et hideux ! Ah ! que n'eût-elle donné pour assister à la réunion. La mère et la fille endimanchées, empotées, radieuses, le père, digne et attendri, Serge en fiancé hésitant, le juge, le directeur des Postes... Une vraie pièce de Gogol !... Elle se demanda s'il avait été question d'elle pendant le dîner. Mais oui, pourquoi pas ? Serge avait certainement expliqué, d'un air contrit, que sa tante, relevant de maladie, n'avait pu descendre dans la salle à manger. Mais il avait bon espoir, elle se remettrait vite ! Sophie croyait l'entendre. Son sang bouillonnait. Vers quatre heures, il y eut un bruit de troupe piétinante. Les invités sortirent de la maison et s'arrêtèrent devant les calèches. Comment était la petite ? Sophie se rapprocha de la fenêtre et souleva le rideau de tulle, juste assez pour voir sans être vue. Serge, élégant et disert, pérorait, cherchant à retenir son monde. En face de lui, buvant ses paroles, se tenaient la femme du gouverneur, massive, hommasse, et sa fille, malingre, le dos rond, le coude étriqué, avec un long visage chevalin sous une toque de velours jaune. La disgrâce physique de cette enfant expliquait mieux encore la faveur dont Serge jouissait auprès de Tcherkassoff. Les dernières amabilités échangées, les visiteurs remontèrent en voiture. Serge les regarda s'éloigner, agita plusieurs fois la main, et, brusquement, leva les yeux vers la fenêtre de Sophie. Elle se rejeta en arrière. Trop tard ! Il l'avait aperçue !

★

A dater de ce jour elle fut plus impatiente encore de se rétablir. Il lui semblait que tout son avenir à Kachtanovka dépendait du prompt retour de ses forces. Chaque matin, elle faisait quelques pas dans le parc et poussait sa promenade plus loin. Après trois semaines de cet exercice, elle se sentit assez solide pour aller à pied jusqu'à Chatkovo. La distance était de sept verstes à peine. En deux heures, elle y serait. Quelle surprise pour les moujiks, lorsqu'ils la verraient reparaître. Elle avait besoin de leur parler pour reprendre confiance en elle-même. Par une claire matinée de juillet, elle se mit en route, après avoir prévenu Zoé qu'elle ne rentrerait pas pour le dîner.

Elle marchait lentement, d'un pas régulier, s'arrêtait dès qu'elle était essoufflée et s'asseyait sur un talus, la main gauche appliquée en travers du dos, à l'endroit où son poumon était encore sensible. Tant qu'elle fut dans le parc, sous les arbres, elle ne souffrit pas de la chaleur. Mais, une fois en rase campagne, la réverbération du soleil l'incommoda. Elle voulut accélérer son allure et dut y renoncer. La fatigue montait de ses jambes à ses reins. Ses yeux éblouis se fixaient jusqu'à l'hébétement sur la campagne qui s'étalait devant elle, muette, assoiffée, avec ses moissons d'or, ses douces collines, ses boqueteaux de velours vert. Des moustiques tournaient autour de son visage en feu. Dans le ciel d'un bleu cru, trois petits nuages blancs, immobiles, attendaient le retour du vent pour continuer leur voyage. Elle se dit qu'elle avait trop présumé de ses forces. Pourtant, dix minutes de repos, à l'ombre d'un groupe de peupliers, lui rendirent le courage de poursuivre. Elle couvrit les deux dernières verstes en marchant comme une automate, les mâchoires serrées, la prunelle fixe. Lorsqu'elle aperçut enfin l'écriteau : « Chatkovo : 67 feux ; hommes recensés : 215 ; femmes : 261 », elle eut un élan de joie. Mais elle arrivait à un mauvais moment. Elle aurait dû penser qu'à cette heure-là tous les travailleurs seraient loin. L'aspect à demi mort du village la déçut. Depuis le temps qu'elle rêvait à ses retrouvailles avec les moujiks, elle s'était inconsciemment préparée à l'idée d'un accueil chaleureux. Elle s'avança dans l'unique rue, attendant que, de tous cô-

215

tés, les vieux, les impotents, sortissent, comme d'habitude, à sa rencontre. Mais les maisons restaient fermées, sous le soleil brutal. Deux matrones, assises sur le pas de leur porte, rentrèrent précipitamment, avant qu'elle ne parvînt à leur hauteur ; le staroste, occupé à tailler un joug à la hache, tourna le dos pour ne pas la voir ; une fillette de dix ans, qui conduisait des oies à la mare, eut, en la croisant, un regard apeuré et ne répondit même pas à son salut. Sophie se crut reportée d'une année en arrière, au lendemain de son retour de Sibérie. Elle retrouvait exactement l'atmosphère d'hostilité anxieuse qu'elle avait connue le jour de sa première visite au village, quand tout le monde se méfiait encore de la « barynia française ». Après avoir lentement regagné l'amour, l'estime de ces gens, elle ne pouvait supposer qu'ils se fussent détachés d'elle pendant sa maladie. Que s'était-il passé depuis qu'elle ne les avait vus ? Le seul être sur qui elle pût compter, à Chatkovo, était Antipe. Elle se rendit droit chez lui, le découvrit dormant sur son four et le secoua par l'épaule. Eveillé en sursaut, il leva son bras replié comme pour se protéger d'un coup, puis, reconnaissant Sophie, sauta sur ses pieds et bredouilla :

— Ah ! barynia !... C'est vous ?... Mais je... je croyais que vous n'aviez plus le droit de venir nous voir !...

Elle s'indigna :

— Qui a pu te dire cela ?

— Les conducteurs.

— Eh bien ! ils se sont trompés ! répliqua Sophie en s'asseyant, rompue de fatigue, sur un banc.

Elle s'adossa au mur et ferma les yeux. Des

216

fleurs phosphorescentes se dessinaient sur le tissu rouge de ses paupières.

— Comment êtes-vous venue ? demanda Antipe.

— A pied.

Il ne parut nullement surpris de cette performance (pour un moujik, sept verstes, ce n'était rien !) et murmura :

— Le barine est au courant ?

— Non.

L'effarement arrondit les yeux d'Antipe et déboîta sa mâchoire :

— Aïe ! Aïe ! Alors, partez vite, barynia ! Si les conducteurs vous voient ici, je suis perdu !

Elle protesta :

— Tu es fou ! Tu n'es pas un domestique de Kachtanovka pour avoir peur ! Je ne te commande rien !...

— C'est la même chose, barynia !... Le barine nous a prévenus !... Domestique ou moujik, celui qui vous écoutera, celui qui vous parlera — les verges !... Vous ne pouvez pas vouloir cela pour votre vieil Antipe, barynia !... Vous êtes trop bonne !...

Comme elle se taisait, consternée, il poursuivit avec une grimace en coin dans les poils de sa barbe :

— Nous avons su que vous étiez malade... Nous avons prié pour votre guérison... Mais voilà, pendant que vous étiez au lit, nous étions tranquilles... Maintenant, nous allons recommencer à trembler... Vous ne pouvez rien pour nous, barynia... Laissez-nous, je vous en prie, dans notre misère et notre obéissance...

— Comment peux-tu dire cela, après t'être plaint à moi si souvent de la façon dont on vous traitait ? s'écria-t-elle.

217

— Se plaindre, ça soulage !... Je ne pensais pas que vous alliez tout remuer pour si peu !...

— Et aujourd'hui, tu voudrais que je renonce ?

— Oui, barynia... Vous nous faites plus de mal que de bien en venant... Partez... Pour l'amour du ciel, partez !...

Elle se leva et dit d'une voix détimbrée :

— C'est bon. Je m'en irai. Mais je suis trop lasse pour marcher jusqu'à Kachtanovka. Demande au staroste qu'il attelle une télègue et qu'il me ramène...

Antipe hocha la tête :

— Il ne voudra pas, barynia.

— Pourquoi ?

— Si ça se savait !...

Elle le poussa vers la porte :

— Va lui demander !... Je te l'ordonne !...

Il partit en courant. Restée seule dans l'isba, elle s'abandonna à une désillusion si amère, qu'elle ne croyait pas en avoir éprouvé de semblable. En refusant son aide, Antipe lui ôtait sa dernière raison de vivre. Elle se découvrait ridicule soudain avec, dans le cœur, cette sollicitude dont personne ne voulait. C'était tout juste si ceux à qui elle s'intéressait ne lui tenaient pas rigueur de son dévouement. D'ailleurs, répudiée avec tous ses beaux sentiments, elle ne pouvait même pas accuser les moujiks d'ingratitude. Elle n'avait rien su faire pour eux, sinon s'agiter, imaginer, parler... Leur sort était réglé par d'autres ; et ils en avaient conscience. Voilà tout ! Qu'avait-elle espéré en venant ici ? Lever une armée d'amis contre le mauvais maître. Elle qui critiquait Nicolas jadis, parce qu'il prenait ses rêves pour des réalités, voici qu'elle était plus folle que lui, à son âge et avec son expérience ! Elle eut envie de se courber, de se recroqueviller sur son désespoir. Antipe revint, la tête ballante :

— J'en étais sûr, barynia... Le staroste refuse... Tout le monde refuse...

Sophie n'insista pas. Elle sentait que, malgré sa volonté, elle ne pourrait obtenir d'elle-même un second effort.

— D'après toi, quel est le village le plus proche ? demanda-t-elle. Tcherniakovo ?

— Non. Koustarnoïé, dit Antipe. Mais il appartient aux Volkoff...

— Tant mieux ! Ce que mes propres moujiks refusent de faire pour moi, ceux des Volkoff le feront peut-être...

Antipe se tassa sous la réprimande, mais ne dit mot. Elle sortit. Après la pénombre de l'isba, la violente lumière du soleil la cloua sur place. Toute sa fatigue lui revint d'un seul coup.

— Si vous allez à Koustarnoïé, dit Antipe, le plus court, c'est de prendre par le sentier à gauche, tout de suite en sortant du village. Vingt minutes et vous y serez... Que Dieu vous garde !... Au revoir, barynia !...

— Au revoir, mon pauvre Antipe ! dit-elle, la gorge serrée.

Et elle se mit en marche, avec l'impression étrange que des centaines de personnes, cachées derrière les fenêtres, les palissades, les piles de bois, les tas de fumier assistaient à son départ honteux.

Elle arriva au village de Koustarnoïé une demi-heure plus tard, la tête vide, les genoux tremblants, s'adressa au premier moujik venu et lui demanda de la conduire, en télègue, à Slavianka, chez ses maîtres.

De tout le trajet, malgré le soleil, les cahots, la

poussière et la ronde exaspérante des mouches, elle ne vit rien, elle ne sentit rien. Une phrase d'Antipe la poursuivait : « Vous nous faites plus de mal que de bien en venant, barynia... Partez !... » Elle songea : « Pourquoi suis-je si acharnée à rester dans ce pays ? Pour défendre les moujiks ? — Ils ne veulent plus de moi ! Pour prouver que Serge est un assassin ? — Je n'en suis plus sûre moi-même. Je me bats contre des ombres. Je perds mon temps. En vérité, je me sens de plus en plus étrangère ici... » L'idée lui vint que cette rupture de contact avec la Russie avait commencé pour elle après la mort de Nicolas. Tant qu'il avait vécu, il l'avait aidée à comprendre l'âme de sa patrie ; elle avait reçu, à travers lui, l'enseignement d'un pays difficile à saisir ; elle avait pu se croire partout chez elle ; maintenant, elle supportait moins bien les déceptions que lui causaient les habitants de cette grande terre. Elle avait perdu à la fois son mari et son intercesseur auprès de la réalité russe.

Quand elle arriva à Slavianka, Daria Philippovna et Vassia avaient déjà fini de dîner et prenaient le café, sous les tilleuls. En la voyant descendre d'une télègue de paysan, ils se précipitèrent vers elle, avec des visages inquiets :

— Mon Dieu !... Que se passe-t-il ?... Avez-vous eu un accident avec votre voiture ?...

— Non, dit Sophie, en s'efforçant de sourire. C'est ma nouvelle façon de voyager !

Elle épousseta sa robe et se laissa conduire, ébahie de fatigue, jusqu'à un fauteuil en osier où elle s'écroula. Daria Philippovna lui fit boire un café très fort et très sucré.

— Remettez-vous, ma colombe, murmura-t-elle, penchée vers Sophie. Vous êtes toute pâle ! C'est une telle joie pour nous de vous accueillir ! Sans nouvelles de vous depuis des mois, nous pensions que vous ne vouliez plus nous voir !

— Ma mère vous a écrit trois fois, dit Vassia. C'est mon piqueur qui a porté les lettres à Kachtanovka.

— On ne m'en a remis aucune, dit Sophie.

— Comment ?... Mais c'est impossible !... Votre neveu aurait osé ?...

— Cela vous surprend ?

Il y eut un silence de fureur impuissante. Vassia se rongeait les ongles.

— Et vous ne vous êtes même pas demandé pourquoi nous ne vous donnions plus signe de vie ? susurra Daria Philippovna.

— J'ai été très malade, dit Sophie.

— Seigneur ? Qu'avez-vous eu ? Qui vous a soignée ?

Après les déconvenues qu'elle avait subies, cet accent d'amitié toucha Sophie aux larmes. Elle avait un tel besoin de se confier, qu'elle raconta tout, depuis sa dernière explication avec Serge jusqu'à la visite du gouverneur. Pendant le récit, Daria Philippovna respirait avec difficulté, une main sur sa poitrine, les yeux humides, les lèvres agitées de petits frémissements ; à côté d'elle, le visage doux et empâté de son fils se contractait dans une expression de fausse violence. Quand Sophie se tut, il soupira :

— Le plus terrible, c'est qu'on ne peut rien contre ce monstre !

Sophie le regarda avec surprise. Etait-ce là tout ce qu'il trouvait à dire, lui, l'intellectuel révolté, le lecteur de Saint-Simon et de Lamennais ? Sa phrase sonnait comme un écho lointain des paroles d'Antipe. Tous — moujiks incultes ou seigneurs libéraux — acceptaient les faits pour ne pas se compliquer l'existence. Daria Philippovna, cependant, était fort excitée par l'histoire de la fille du gouverneur :

— J'avais bien entendu dire, à Pskov, qu'il y avait quelque chose de ce côté-là, mais je ne voulais pas le croire ! La petite est si laide ! Et lui, il a des habitudes de garçon en ville !...

— Laisse, maman ! Cela n'a aucun intérêt ! grogna Vassia.

— Je ne suis pas de ton avis ! dit Daria Philippovna. Selon ce que Serge Vladimirovitch a dans la tête, tout l'avenir de notre amie peut être modifié !...

Elle posa une main sur le genou de Sophie et reprit affectueusement :

— Vous devez avoir hâte de vous reposer. Je vais vous installer dans la chambre de ma fille aînée. Vous fermerez les yeux un moment. Et, ce soir, notre cocher vous ramènera à Kachtanovka.

Sophie fut tentée de dire oui : des rideaux tirés, un lit moelleux. quelques heures d'oubli, dans le silence d'une maison bienveillante. Puis une pensée la traversa, si forte que, devant elle, tous les autres projets s'envolèrent.

— Je vous remercie, chère amie, balbutia-t-elle, mais je ne puis rester. Il faut immédiatement que j'aille à Pskov.

— A Pskov ? s'écria Daria Philippovna. Dans votre état ?

— Oui. C'est très important. Si votre cocher pouvait m'y conduire...

— C'est moi qui vous y conduirai, dit Vassia avec flamme. Et, de là, si vous le voulez, je vous raccompagnerai chez vous !

Daria Philippovna lui jeta un regard inquiet.

Sans doute craignait-elle qu'il ne rencontrât Serge.

— J'accepte, dit Sophie, mais à condition que vous me laissiez dans le parc de Kachtanovka.

Vassia s'inclina, soulagé dans son appréhension et préservé dans son honneur. Daria Philippovna eut pour Sophie un sourire de gratitude maternelle.

★

— D'où venez-vous ? dit Serge d'une voix rude.

Il était sorti du bureau en entendant le pas de Sophie dans l'antichambre, et se tenait devant elle, blanc de colère, les mâchoires serrées, les yeux en cabochons. Elle se félicita d'avoir insisté pour que Vassia n'entrât pas avec elle dans la maison. A quoi bon risquer une scène inutile et grotesque entre les deux hommes ?

— Eh bien ! reprit-il. Répondez ! D'où venez-vous ?

— De Pskov, dit-elle.

Il saisit une lampe sur la console et l'éleva, comme s'il avait eu besoin de voir le visage de Sophie en pleine lumière pour le croire. Boutonné dans sa redingote noire, les sourcils froncés, il ressemblait à un mari jaloux.

— Qu'alliez-vous faire à Pskov ? dit-il.

Elle était si épuisée, qu'elle l'entendit à peine.

— Qu'alliez-vous faire à Pskov ? répéta-t-il en criant.

Elle tressaillit.

— J'ai vu le gouverneur, dit-elle.

— Le gouverneur ? Pourquoi ?

— Pour lui remettre ma demande de changement de résidence.

Il eut un haut-le-corps. Ses traits se détendirent. Un sourire allongea ses lèvres.

— C'est vrai ?

Elle inclina la tête.

Serge bomba la poitrine.

— Vous ne le regrétterez pas, dit-il. J'appuierai votre requête. Toutes mes relations en feront autant. Où voulez-vous aller ? A Saint-Pétersbourg ? A Moscou ?...

— Je veux rentrer dans mon pays.

— En France ? dit-il avec un étonnement goguenard.

« En France... En France... En France !... »

Ce mot retentit aux oreilles de Sophie comme un appel répercuté à l'infini, dans la montagne. Au degré de fatigue où elle était parvenue, elle ne comprenait plus ce qui lui arrivait. La lumière de la lampe se fixa sur sa rétine, grandit, devint un soleil éblouissant. Puis tout s'éteignit, et elle tomba dans un gouffre.

TROISIÈME PARTIE

1

Sophie domina sa gêne et pria le gros monsieur chauve, assis près de la fenêtre du wagon, de changer de place avec elle. Il lui sourit avec l'ironie supérieure d'un habitué des trains et accepta.

— Serait-ce votre premier voyage par le chemin de fer, Madame ? demanda-t-il en se levant.

— Oui, Monsieur, murmura-t-elle en se levant aussi.

— C'est très impressionnant quand on ne connaît pas...

Elle acquiesça du menton. Pouvait-elle lui dire que, ce qui l'impressionnait, ce n'était pas d'être tirée par une machine à vapeur, mais de voir défiler derrière la vitre la terre de France qu'elle avait quittée trente-sept ans plus tôt ? Les autres voyageurs se tassèrent avec des visages rogues et rentrèrent leurs genoux pour permettre le chassé-croisé. Le gros monsieur passa devant Sophie en ravalant son ventre. Déséquilibrée par les cahots, elle se laissa tomber maladroitement sur la banquette et sourit à la ronde pour s'excuser. La locomotive siffla avec force. Le convoi roulait à une allure effrayante. Le plancher vibrait, les portières tressautaient, une targette claquait entre ses crampons. Dans l'encadrement de la fenêtre s'écoulait une campagne rapide comme un fleuve en crue. Parfois, un groupe de maisons blanches à toits rouges frôlait la voiture de si près, qu'instinctivement Sophie reculait la tête. Quand elle songeait que dans une heure et cinq minutes elle serait à Paris, il lui semblait que son rêve prenait la réalité de vitesse. Malgré l'appui du gouverneur, il lui avait fallu plus d'un an et demi de démarches avant que sa requête ne reçût l'approbation impériale. Une intervention de l'ambassadeur de France à Saint-Pétersbourg avait emporté la décision. Par une première mesure de faveur, on l'avait autorisée à résider à Pskov. Six mois plus tard, elle était transférée à Saint-Pétersbourg, où chaque samedi, elle devait faire viser son permis de séjour au commissariat de police du quartier. Enfin, le 7 mars dernier, le général de cavalerie comte Orloff, directeur de la IIIᵉ section de la Chancellerie privée de Sa Majesté, l'avait convoquée pour lui annoncer qu'elle pouvait quitter la Russie. Quelques semaines lui avaient suffi pour régler ses affaires et, après la débâcle de la Néva, elle avait embarqué sur un navire de commerce russe, à destination du Havre. C'était un « voilier-barque » à trois mâts et à coque de fer, qui comprenait une dizaine de cabines pour les passagers. Lorsque Sophie avait vu décliner la masse du fort de Cronstadt, elle avait ressenti une angoisse, un déchirement qu'elle s'exprimait

226

mal. Elle était à la fois heureuse de s'évader d'un pays où elle n'avait connu que la contrainte et le deuil, et malheureuse de laisser là-bas tout ce qui la rattachait à la vie : des souvenirs, une tombe, des amis. Sa séparation avec Serge avait été correcte et froide. Il était parvenu à ses fins. Restant seul à Kachtanovka, il continuerait de verser à sa tante la moitié des revenus du domaine. Un acte signé par-devant le gouverneur avait constaté cet accord. D'ailleurs, depuis qu'elle avait présenté sa demande de changement de résidence, elle avait retrouvé à la maison une vie normale et des domestiques obéissants. C'était une preuve supplémentaire que tout, dans la propriété, était soumis au pouvoir de son neveu. Maintenant, Sophie était convaincue qu'il n'y avait rien à faire pour elle sur ce coin de terre où elle avait eu la faiblesse de vouloir se rendre utile. Même l'idée de la culpabilité de Serge ne la tourmentait plus. Elle avait dépassé le temps de l'inquiétude et de la révolte. A Saint-Pétersbourg déjà, elle avait eu l'impression de commencer une autre existence. Quelques salons s'étaient timidement rouverts devant elle. Des connaissances de Nicolas l'avaient entourée de leur sollicitude. Mais, tout en acceptant leur prévenance, elle ne songeait qu'à préparer son départ. Qu'allait-elle trouver en France ? D'après ce que lui écrivait le notaire de la famille, Me Pelé, ses parents avaient liquidé tous leurs biens pour payer les dettes contractées dans les dernières années de leur vie. Il ne restait que l'hôtel de la rue de Grenelle, dont la toiture était en ruine, l'intérieur délabré et la moitié des meubles vendus. En transférant à une banque parisienne ses revenus de Kachtanovka, Sophie avait prié Me Pelé de faire exécuter dans la maison les

227

réparations les plus urgentes et d'engager deux domestiques. Ainsi pensait-elle pouvoir s'installer, tant bien que mal, à son retour. Elle allait rentrer « chez elle » et il n'y aurait personne de sa famille ni de ses amis pour l'accueillir. Elle connaissait moins de monde en France qu'en Russie. Elle avait vécu plus longtemps en Russie qu'en France. Et pourtant, une fois en France, elle se sentait profondément, farouchement française !

Ah ! tous ces gens autour d'elle ignoraient leur bonheur d'être les citoyens d'un pays libre. Il est vrai que, lorsqu'elle avait signé sa requête, en juillet 1851, la France était encore une république et qu'aujourd'hui, en mai 1853, elle était redevenue un empire. Mais cet empire-là devait être assez débonnaire ! Selon ce qu'on racontait à Saint-Pétersbourg, Napoléon III n'avait rien d'un Nicolas 1er. Son amour du peuple était sincère et, s'il avait fait arrêter et exiler quelques opposants à sa politique, après le coup d'Etat du 2 décembre, on lui prêtait l'intention de les amnistier. Autant la tyrannie paraissait naturelle en Russie, autant elle était inconcevable en France. Il suffisait de regarder des Français pour se convaincre qu'ils n'étaient pas opprimés. En mettant pied à terre, au Havre, Sophie avait été frappée de l'air désinvolte qu'affectaient les gens les plus simples. Cette même impression, elle l'avait retrouvée sur le quai d'embarquement du chemin de fer. Parmi les voyageurs qui prenaient le train de Paris, ceux de troisième classe avaient tous des paniers d'où dépassaient des pains appétissants, des saucissons, des bouteilles de vin. En première, on était plus gourmé et moins porté sur la nourriture. Mais, singulièrement, il n'y avait pas un abîme entre le bourgeois et l'homme du peuple, comme en Russie entre le seigneur et le serf. Ici, le riche et le pauvre, quoique distincts par le costume, les manières, le langage, appartenaient à la même nation, alors que, là-bas, on pouvait presque parler d'une différence de races. Tout à coup, Sophie comprit que ce qui la déroutait depuis son arrivée en France, c'était l'absence de moujiks. Leurs faces candides, barbues, craquelées de soleil, manquaient à son univers. A la pensée qu'elle n'en verrait plus un seul, jamais, une étrange tristesse altéra son bonheur. Ce fut si rapide qu'elle en eut à peine conscience. Déjà, elle retournait avidement au spectacle de son pays qui se déroulait devant elle. Comme tout était petit en France, après les immenses espaces russes ! Les champs minuscules, peignés, ratissés ; les barrières dressées entre des propriétés grandes comme des mouchoirs de poche ; les villages sagement groupés autour de leur clocher, dont la pointe effilée surprenait l'œil après les bulbes bleus, verts et or des clochers orthodoxes... Là-bas, au loin, cette vibration de brume mauve, cet amoncellement crayeux, ce miroitement de mille vitres, n'était-ce pas les faubourgs de Paris ? Les voyageurs s'agitèrent ; une dame humecta son mouchoir avec l'eau d'un flacon et essuya son visage, qui était marqué de suie ; le gros monsieur tira sur son gilet et dit :

— Nous allons traverser le pont d'Asnières. Celui-ci est encore en bois. On en construit un en fer, par-dessous, qui sera bientôt livré à la circulation. Nous aurons alors un bel ouvrage d'art !...

Sophie colla son front à la vitre. Avec une lenteur inquiétante, le train s'engagea sur une passerelle de charpente qui tremblait. Chacun retint sa respiration. En contrebas, brillait le fleuve, avec ses berges molles, ses lavandières tapant le linge et ses bateaux de pêcheurs glissant au fil de l'eau. Lorsque le dernier wagon eût touché la terre ferme, la locomotive exhala un soupir de délivrance et accéléra son allure. Les maisons s'entassaient, petites, laides, sales. Un rempart, coupé de bastions et précédé d'un robuste glacis, se dressa devant le convoi. C'étaient les nouvelles fortifications dont Sophie avait entendu parler en Russie mais dont elle ne soupçonnait pas l'importance. Le train passa entre deux demi-lunes, plongea dans un tunnel. Une diabolique odeur de fumée envahit le compartiment et tout le monde se mit à tousser. Enfin, le convoi émergea des ténèbres, les passagers s'ébrouèrent, soufflèrent, rajustèrent leurs vêtements. Le long des rails apparurent les ateliers, les magasins, les dépôts de marchandises. Encore quelques tours de roues et les quais de débarquement s'avancèrent avec lenteur. Une verrière encrassée ternit l'éclat du soleil. La locomotive s'arrêta, une forte secousse jeta les voyageurs les uns sur les autres.

De tous côtés, les facteurs accouraient pour proposer leurs services. Sophie confia ses bagages à l'un d'eux qui avait une tête ronde, des moustaches frisées et des yeux insolents. Elle le rejoignit dans la grande salle de l'octroi. Juché sur une malle, il l'appelait en agitant les bras à la façon d'un sémaphore. Soudain, elle se trouva prise dans la cohue des voyageurs. Des hommes coiffés d'un tuyau de poêle ou d'une casquette, des femmes en capeline, en bonnet, en fichu, des enfants ahuris, qu'on tirait par la main, une mer de visages et, par-dessus cela, le bourdonnement léger de la langue française. Un employé de l'octroi fit ouvrir à Sophie sa valise, son sac de nuit et se déclara satisfait. Le facteur porta ses bagages à la sortie du débarcadère. Dans la rue Saint-Lazare, des fiacres attendaient en file. Elle monta dans un cabriolet, dont le cocher n'avait pas de barbe — ce qui eût paru tout à fait anormal en Russie — veilla au chargement de ses valises, donna un pourboire trop généreux au facteur et prononça le plus naturellement qu'elle put :

— 81, rue de Grenelle.

L'attelage s'engagea dans un flot de voitures qui descendaient vers la place de la Madeleine. Dominant l'enchevêtrement des calèches à la Daumont, des coupés et des cabs, un lourd omnibus se traînait, avec, au sommet, un cocher morose enfermé dans une houppelande et coiffé d'un chapeau ciré. Les passants étaient nombreux sur les trottoirs ; les uns marchaient vite, d'un air préoccupé ; d'autres s'arrêtaient aux devantures des magasins qui, toutes, semblaient contenir des merveilles. Quand le fiacre déboucha sur la place de la Concorde, Sophie reçut en plein visage cette architecture de lumière, de blancheur et de majesté. Mais qu'y avait-il de changé, par ici ? Ah ! oui, l'affreux obélisque, planté au centre de l'esplanade comme un pivot de pierre autour duquel viraient les équipages. Quelle faute de goût ! En revanche, on avait bien fait de combler les fossés. Et ces deux belles fontaines jaillissantes, elles n'existaient pas autrefois ! Ni ces hauts candélabres ! Ni ces statues sur les pavillons de Gabriel ! Une partie des voitures se déversait à droite, dans l'avenue des Champs-Elysées, dont les feuillages sagement alignés conduisaient à l'Arc de Triomphe. De l'autre côté de l'eau, le Palais-Bourbon dressait sa fausse colonnade grecque. Le fiacre franchit le pont, remonta la rue de Bourgogne, tourna dans la rue de Grenelle, pénétra sous un porche, s'arrêta au milieu d'une cour pavée et Sophie, émue à en perdre le souffle, vit devant elle la maison de son enfance.

La façade s'était écaillée, il n'y avait pas de rideaux aux fenêtres, l'herbe avait poussé entre les dalles du perron, mais la vieille demeure gardait un air de sérénité et de noblesse. Un domestique inconnu, jeune, rubicond, avec de grandes oreilles, s'avança vers Sophie. Sa livrée marron, trop étroite, ne boutonnait pas par-devant. Une soubrette pâlotte le suivait. Ils se présentèrent : Justin et Valentine. Le notaire les avait engagés la semaine dernière. Ils avaient « fait le plus gros ». Madame voudrait bien les commander pour le reste. Elle leur dit de s'occuper des bagages et rentra seule dans la maison.

Le vestibule était désert, de rares meubles flottaient dans le salon trop vaste et, sur les murs vert d'eau, décolorés par le soleil, des taches rectangulaires, d'un ton plus foncé, rappelaient l'emplacement des tableaux disparus. En promenant les yeux sur ce qui restait du naufrage, Sophie reconnaissait avec amitié un fauteuil, un guéridon, une commode en marqueterie, une tapisserie cachant une porte. L'odeur même de la maison s'était miraculeusement conservée dans ces lieux depuis longtemps inhabités, une odeur subtile, où se mélangeaient les effluves de l'étoffe moisie, de la cire, de la peinture sèche, du bois vermoulu. Les narines ouvertes, l'esprit tendu, Sophie reculait à travers les années. En revenant à Kachtanovka, elle s'était replongée dans les souvenirs de son mariage avec Nicolas ; ici, elle se retrouvait entre ses parents, telle qu'elle était avant de

232

l'avoir connu. Une âcre tristesse l'envahit à la pensée que son père et sa mère étaient morts alors qu'elle était si loin d'eux. En gâchant sa vie n'avait-elle pas gâché la leur ? Ils l'avaient mal aimée et elle le leur avait rendu. Tout cela était lamentable ! Elle regarda l'espace entre la fenêtre et la porte, et une jeune fille, qui s'était souvent tenue là, se dressa devant elle, svelte, vêtue d'une robe bleue, le front à la vitre, un livre à la main. Personne encore dans son existence. Elle était impatiente d'agir, de se dévouer, d'admirer, d'adorer. Le tout était de découvrir un homme digne de son estime. Elle avait lu Plutarque. Elle se voulait héroïque. Une seconde Mme Roland. Derrière elle, son père et sa mère échangeaient des propos dénués d'intérêt sur leurs relations ou sur leur domestique. Le soir tombait dans le jardin. Cette heure crépusculaire oppressait Sophie. Elle se contempla dans la glace, au-dessus de la cheminée, et se vit maquillée en vieille dame. Une perruque grisonnante sur le crâne, des rides maladroitement crayonnées autour du menton, une ombre plombée sous les yeux, le regard fixe... Pourquoi s'était-elle fait cette tête ? Ramenée brutalement à la réalité, elle reconnut avec tendresse, dans ce visage las, tout ce qui témoignait des échecs, des deuils, des déceptions de sa vie. Elle eut froid. La maison était humide. Pourtant, on était au mois de mai.

— Vous allumerez du feu, dit-elle par-dessus son épaule à Justin qui entrait.

— Bien, Madame. Me Pelé a dit qu'il viendrait voir Madame dans la soirée. Valentine et moi ne savions pas où Madame voudrait avoir sa chambre. Nous avons choisi celle qui nous paraissait la mieux, au rez-de-chaussée...

— Vous avez bien fait, dit-elle.

C'était l'ancien petit salon où sa mère se tenait pendant les soirées d'hiver. On y avait apporté un lit qu'elle ne connaissait pas, une table de toilette, deux fauteuils dépareillés, une coiffeuse, une armoire, un tapis... Les bagages étaient empilés dans un coin. Il fallait les déballer. Quel ennui ! Elle chargea Valentine de ranger le linge et les robes provisoirement, et continua sa visite.

Elle entrouvrait les portes, jetait un regard indiscret à l'intérieur, comme si elle se fût promenée dans le logis d'une autre. De la chambre de ses parents, ne subsistaient que des murs nus ; la chambre où avait dormi Nicolas, lors de son séjour à Paris, avait conservé pour tout mobilier un lit défoncé, dont le baldaquin jaune tombait en loques. Elle monta l'escalier, entra dans la bibliothèque où elle l'avait vu la première fois, jeune, grand, avec sa chevelure blonde et son bel uniforme d'officier aux gardes de Lituanie. Comme elle le haïssait alors d'être russe et vainqueur ! Un canapé perdait son crin par une déchirure. Sur des rayons poussiéreux s'alignaient encore quelques livres. Les plus précieux avaient disparu. Sophie lut des noms d'auteurs, au hasard : J.-J. Rousseau, Montesquieu, Voltaire... Un peu plus loin, Champlitte. Son premier mari. Il l'avait si peu marquée, qu'elle s'en souvenait à peine. Elle était la femme de Nicolas et de lui seul. Machinalement, elle prit un petit volume relié en chagrin, le feuilleta : *Lettres sur le progrès incessant de l'esprit humain*, par le marquis de Champlitte. La naïveté du titre l'ébahit. Comment avait-elle pu admirer cela ? Elle remit l'ouvrage à sa place, redescendit l'escalier, sortit dans le jardin. Laissé à l'abandon, il était devenu un carré

234

de mauvaises herbes et de buissons épineux. De ce fouillis de verdure émergeait, gracieuse et maniérée, la statue de Cupidon. Le bout de son nez était cassé, il manquait un morceau de son arc. Dans les arbres, déjà touffus, des oiseaux chantaient. Au-delà, on entendait la rumeur de la ville. Sophie ne savait si elle était gaie ou triste. Le bonheur d'avoir retrouvé Paris s'associait en elle à la mélancolie d'être seule dans ce pèlerinage. Seule et si âgée sur les lieux où elle avait commencé sa vie ! « On s'agite, on aime, on déteste, on espère, on se passionne pour mille choses qui, le lendemain, vous paraissent insignifiantes, et on revient à son point de départ, les mains vides ! pensa-t-elle. Quel est donc le sens d'une destinée comme la mienne ? »

La fraîcheur et l'ombre du soir la chassèrent du jardin. Dans le salon, Justin avait allumé un feu de bois. Elle ordonna que le souper lui fût servi là, sur une petite table. Valentine était à la fois femme de chambre et cuisinière, aux gages de vingt-cinq francs par mois, plus le vin. Sophie revêtit une robe d'intérieur, mit ses cheveux à l'aise sous une fanchon de dentelle et s'assit devant un caneton aux olives. Elle finissait de souper quand le notaire s'annonça. Âgé d'une quarantaine d'années, rondouillard, cosmétiqué et le teint fleuri, il était le successeur de celui qu'elle avait connu. En quelques mots, il l'informa de sa situation de fortune, qui n'était pas brillante. Mais il importait peu à Sophie de n'avoir aucune source de revenus en France, puisqu'elle devait recevoir régulièrement de l'argent de Russie. Rien qu'avec la somme envoyée par elle de Saint-Pétersbourg à Paris, elle avait de quoi vivre deux ou trois ans. Au besoin, elle jouerait à la Bourse. (On disait que cela rapportait gros !) Mᵉ Pelé l'en dissuada. Il avait l'air pondéré, scrupuleux. Elle lui promit de suivre ses conseils et signa les papiers qu'il lui présentait. Avant de partir, il lui donna les meilleurs renseignements sur les domestiques qu'il avait engagés et lui demanda si elle en voulait d'autres. Elle refusa. Ces deux-là lui suffisaient amplement ; elle n'avait pas l'intention de mener une existence mondaine ; du reste, elle ne comptait plus d'amis en France.

— Il vous en viendra très vite, dit Mᵉ Pelé. Et davantage que vous ne le souhaitez !

Elle se coucha, étourdie de fatigue, dormit lourdement et s'éveilla tôt le matin, avec le sentiment d'avoir quelque chose de très important à entreprendre. Mais après avoir organisé le travail de Justin et de Valentine, elle se trouva désœuvrée. L'après-midi avançait. Il faisait beau. Elle sortit. Le mouvement de la rue l'amusa. Les concierges bâillaient sur le pas de leur porte, des vendeurs ambulants poussaient des voitures à bras dans la rue de Bourgogne et criaient leur marchandise avec des voix éraillées, un porteur d'eau la dépassa, les épaules pliées sous un cercle de bois auquel étaient suspendus des seaux pleins. Conduite par ses souvenirs, elle se rendit rue Jacob, à la librairie de son vieil ami, Augustin Vavasseur. Mais le magasin était fermé, les volets mis, l'enseigne « Au Berger fidèle » à demi effacée. Elle voulut se renseigner auprès du concierge et tomba sur un personnage à la face mafflue et à l'œil soupçonneux, le ventre ceint d'un tablier sale, une chique au coin de la bouche. Une pancarte dominait la loge : « Parlez au portier. »

— Vavasseur ? Il est parti, grogna-t-il.

— Pour où ?

— J'en sais rien.

— Y a-t-il longtemps ?...

— Ça fait plusieurs mois.

— Mais... il doit revenir ?

— Pas de si tôt ! C'est qui qui le demande ?

— Pardon ?

— Votre nom ?

Sophie pensa qu'il y avait quelque manœuvre policière là-dessous et murmura :

— Mon nom ne vous dirait rien.

Cependant, elle hésitait à s'en aller. Elle songeait à ses autres amis, les Poitevin, qui habitaient jadis dans la même maison. Mais ils étaient si âgés à l'époque où elle les avait connus, qu'ils devaient être morts depuis longtemps. Par acquit de conscience, elle demanda :

— Et M. et Mme Poitevin ?

Le concierge fronça les sourcils :

— Connais pas !

Puis il se frappa le front :

— Ah ! oui, les deux vieux ! Le mari était paralysé, je crois... Ils sont morts, lui d'abord, elle ensuite. Je venais juste de prendre mon service. Ça fait vingt-cinq, vingt-six ans !...

Sophie s'éloigna, le cœur lourd. Elle savait que les Poitevin ne pouvaient plus être de ce monde. Mais Vavasseur ? Celui-là était incorrigible ! Sans doute, ne se sentant plus en sécurité, avait-il transporté ailleurs son commerce peu florissant et son humeur séditieuse. Elle ne retrouverait jamais sa piste.

De la rue Jacob, elle se rendit à une station de voitures de remise, et choisit un beau cabriolet à quatre roues, attelé de deux chevaux robustes, qu'elle loua au mois, avec un cocher en livrée. Le surveillant lui proposa un groom en supplé-

ment. Elle déclina cette offre somptuaire. Le cocher se nommait Basile et portait un chapeau
haut de forme. Des favoris roux en côtelettes encadraient son visage bouffi de prétention. Visiblement, il voulait être pris pour un cocher de maître. Afin de faciliter l'illusion, le numéro de sa
voiture était tracé légèrement en rouge sur fond
noir. De loin, on ne le remarquait même pas.

Pour commencer, Sophie pria Basile de la conduire aux Champs-Elysées. La promenade lui
parut encore plus belle et plus animée que du
temps de sa jeunesse. Dans aucune ville du monde, les arbres n'étaient aussi nombreux qu'à Paris. Il y avait une amitié très française entre les
vieilles pierres et les feuillages neufs. L'avenue
s'ouvrait avec la majesté d'un estuaire. Un nimbe
de poussière entourait le miroitement des vitres,
des laques et des harnais d'argent. Tous les types
de véhicules, depuis le noble coupé aux portières
armoriées jusqu'à la confortable calèche bourgeoise, en passant par le colimaçon de la femme
légère et le brougham du dandy, se croisaient, se
frôlaient, et, de l'un à l'autre, s'échangeaient de
piquants regards de curiosité. Parfois, des cavaliers revenant du Bois abordaient une voiture
découverte et saluaient une grande capeline de
paille aux rubans multicolores. Sophie examinait
les toilettes avec un intérêt passionné. Elle dut
convenir que la mode était très jolie, en France,
cette saison. Subitement, elle se sentit vêtue
comme une provinciale. Sa robe lui pesait. Son
chapeau lui serrait le front. Il faudrait y remé-
dier au plus tôt. Le martèlement des sabots accompagnait ses réflexions d'une musique synco-
pée. Après un coup d'œil à l'Arc de Triomphe —
enfin achevé ! — elle se fit ramener au carré Ma-

238

rigny, mit pied à terre et s'avança dans les jardins. Là aussi, que de changements ! Enfouis sous les arbres, des bals, des restaurants, un cirque, des baraques de foire, et, grouillant autour de ces frêles édifices de toile peinturlurée, une foule de badauds ensorcelés par les flonflons des orchestres et le parfum du cidre, des gaufres et des saucisses. Quand elle remonta en voiture, son cocher, le chapeau sur l'oreille, fredonnait :

« O Pomaré, reine des cœurs sensibles !... »

Elle rentra à la maison, enchantée. Justin lui avait acheté les journaux. Elle les parcourut avec amusement. C'était le mémorial d'un pays heureux : l'empereur s'était marié au début de l'année ; son épouse était belle, spirituelle, élégante ; tout le peuple semblait éperdu d'amour pour ses souverains ; on annonçait de grands travaux dans la ville, de nouveaux spectacles dans les théâtres, un bal aux Tuileries... Sautant les nouvelles politiques, Sophie se précipita sur la rubrique de la mode, illustrée de dessins. L'air de Paris l'excitait à la coquetterie. Alors qu'à Kachtanovka elle portait des robes très simples et n'éprouvait pas le besoin d'en changer, ici, son regard caressait avec convoitise les gravures représentant d'extraordinaires toilettes de bal. « La robe ronde, en moire antique rose tendre, garnie de trois volants d'Angleterre, surmontés d'une guirlande en feuillages de crêpe rose, touchés d'argent... » Elle lisait, imaginait, approuvait, s'étonnait de prendre tant de goût à des choses si futiles. Cette gravité dans le divertissement était, à coup sûr, le signe d'une convalescence inespérée, d'un merveilleux retour aux origines. Le journal glissa de ses genoux. Elle tourna les yeux vers la glace de sa psyché. Etait-ce une ques-

239

tion de lumière, de climat ? Elle se trouvait plus jeune qu'à Tobolsk, plus dégagée, plus légère. Elle regretta que Ferdinand Wolf ne pût la voir chez elle, en Parisienne. Dire qu'elle n'avait pas eu un mot de sa main depuis qu'elle l'avait quitté ! Pas plus à Saint-Pétersbourg qu'à Kachtanovka ! Mais le courrier passait peut-être plus facilement de Russie en Sibérie qu'en sens inverse. Il était fort possible qu'il eût reçu quelques lettres d'elle, alors qu'elle était toujours sans nouvelles de lui. Cette idée absurde la soutenait dans sa solitude. Elle se donnait cette excuse pour ne pas se décourager devant le vide. Toute remuée de tendresse, elle ouvrit son secrétaire, trempa sa plume dans l'encre et écrivit à son grand ami, sans espoir de réponse, comme elle eût jeté des pages dans le vent.

Les jours suivants, Sophie fut dominée par le
souci de son installation. Aménager les pièces
du rez-de-chaussée où elle avait l'intention de vivre, laissant le premier étage à l'abandon, commander du linge de maison, de la vaisselle, des
ustensiles de cuisine, houspiller le tapissier qui
n'en finissait pas de réparer les fauteuils, courir
les magasins de modes et les couturières — il
lui semblait qu'elle n'aurait pas assez d'une année
pour prendre le vent de Paris et arranger sa nouvelle existence. Elle avait craint d'être déçue par
son retour en France, et tout lui plaisait ici, les
êtres et les pierres, le goût du pain et la couleur
du ciel. Rien que le fait d'entendre parler le français dans la rue, lui paraissait un prodige dont
elle ne se lasserait jamais. Souvent, au cours
d'une promenade, ou seule dans sa chambre, elle
était saisie d'un bonheur aigu et sans cause, comme elle en avait connu quand elle était très jeune
fille. Cette impression d'être en accord avec toute
son âme avec une vérité naturelle, aucune parole
ne pouvait en traduire la douceur. Dans cet état

d'euphorie, elle acheta, coup sur coup, pour le salon, une encoignure d'ébène et une petite bibliothèque en poirier noirci, décorée d'émaux de couleur. La satisfaction qu'elle éprouvait à contempler ces meubles modernes l'aidait à oublier que la dépense était disproportionnée à ses moyens.

Un soir, comme elle se reposait dans sa chambre, Justin lui annonça une visite : la baronne de Charlaz. D'étonnement, Sophie resta quelques secondes indécise : « Comment a-t-elle appris mon retour ? » Elle était touchée que Delphine se fût souvenue d'elle. Certes, après avoir été très liées dans leur enfance, elles avaient de moins en moins sympathisé et, les dernières années de son séjour à Paris, Sophie ne rencontrait que rarement son ancienne amie de pension. Mais elle gardait encore une image amusée de cette personne de vertu légère et d'esprit allègre, dont la réputation offusquait les honnêtes gens. Nicolas, qui n'avait pas toujours bon goût, lui avait dit autrefois qu'il trouvait Delphine jolie. Peut-être même lui avait-il fait la cour ? Il n'y avait pas d'homme, à Paris, qu'elle n'eût cherché à séduire.

Sophie se rajusta devant la glace, avec un soin particulier, vérifia sa coiffure, se composa un visage aimable et passa dans le salon pour affronter celle que ses familiers surnommaient jadis « l'ensorceleuse ».

Une petite dame sèche, toute en violet sombre, se leva d'un fauteuil à son approche. Elle avait un visage fripé, dont la peau épousait si étroitement l'ossature, qu'on eût dit une tête de mort sous un chapeau à plumes. Dans ce mélange de rides et de poudre, brillaient deux yeux bleus d'une vivacité charmante. Sa seule coquetterie était encore

242

le sourire. Sophie eut un serrement de cœur en recevant dans ses bras cette ruine friable et parfumée.

— Ah ! Sophie ! s'écria la visiteuse. Est-ce possible ? Vous ? Vous ? Après tant d'années ?...

Elles s'assirent côte à côte, sur un canapé, en se tenant par les mains, comme autrefois au couvent. C'était ridicule, mais Sophie ne pouvait se dégager sans offenser Delphine. Il n'y avait pas si longtemps, sa rencontre avec Daria Philippovna lui avait procuré le même choc pour les mêmes raisons. « Revoir, usée, fanée, une femme qu'on a connue jeune, c'est terrible ! songea-t-elle. Sans doute, Delphine éprouve-t-elle devant moi la même surprise navrée et n'ose-t-elle pas me le dire. Nous nous plaignons l'une l'autre en silence. Nous mesurons, l'une sur l'autre, les ravages des ans... » Trop émue pour trouver rien à dire, elle baissa la tête. Il y eut entre elles un silence de larmes contenues. Enfin, Delphine murmura :

— Vous avez eu bien des malheurs, ma pauvre amie !

— Comment avez-vous su ?... dit Sophie.

— D'abord par la sœur de la princesse Troubetzkoï, Mme Wanda de Kosakovska, qui habite Paris. Puis par M. Nicolas Tourguénieff (1), qui était très lié avec les décembristes ; mais il a eu la chance de se trouver hors de Russie au moment où ils ont fait leur coup d'Etat. Enfin, par les journaux, par les livres... J'ai lu *Le Maître d'Armes*, d'Alexandre Dumas !

_____

(1) Nicolas Ivanovitch Tourguénieff (1789-1871), homme politique et écrivain, longtemps exilé en France, à ne pas confondre avec le célèbre romancier russe Ivan Serguéïévitch Tourguénieff (1818-1883).

— Un tissu de mensonges !

— Peut-être ! Mais des mensonges de ce style ne sont pas à dédaigner ! Ils suscitent autour de vous et de vos amis un courant de curiosité, de sympathie. Le grand public sait qui vous êtes...

— Je ne cherche pas la notoriété, Delphine. Je vous avouerai même que je n'ai jamais autant souhaité passer inaperçue !

— Comme je vous comprends ! soupira Delphine. Le monde, le bruit, c'était bon autrefois ! Savez-vous que j'ai passé par la même épreuve que vous, ma chère ? Moi aussi, j'ai perdu mon mari, il y a quinze ans !...

Sophie dut se forcer pour paraître affligée. Pouvait-on comparer des deuils si différents ? Le baron de Charlaz étant deux fois plus âgé que Delphine, sa mort n'avait rien de surprenant, alors que Nicolas avait disparu en pleine jeunesse, en pleine vigueur... Mais peut-être, après avoir trompé son mari toute sa vie, Delphine lui vouait-elle un culte sincère par-delà le tombeau. Souvent, le souvenir d'un homme est plus utile à la femme que l'homme lui-même. C'est le moment crépusculaire où se tressent les couronnes, où naissent les légendes... « Dieu me préserve de cette maladie de respectabilité à retardement ! » pensa Sophie. Pendant quelques minutes elles parlèrent de leurs amis communs, dont beaucoup étaient morts, de Nicolas, que Delphine disait avoir fort peu connu, des parents de Sophie, des troubles politiques qu'avait traversés la France pendant ces dernières années... Delphine, qui, jadis, était légitimiste, avouait maintenant s'être ralliée de tout cœur à Napoléon III.

— La république était finie, pourrie, impuissante, dit-elle, nous courions à l'anarchie, quand il a pris les rênes de l'Etat ! Et de cela, tout le monde était conscient ! Les résultats écrasants du plébiscite en sont la preuve ! La nation entière a voté pour Napoléon, à droite comme à gauche, sauf quelques fous ! Je sais que vous avez toujours eu des idées un peu... mettons socialistes !... Eh bien ! si curieux que cela puisse vous paraître, ce serait une raison de plus pour vous d'admirer l'empereur ! Il aime le peuple, c'est le peuple qui l'a choisi et il gouvernera pour le peuple ! Sans pour cela froisser la bourgeoisie ! Depuis qu'il est là, on respire, on croit de nouveau à la paix, à la fraternité, à la justice...

— Je ne vous ai jamais connu cet engouement pour un homme d'Etat, dit Sophie en souriant.

— C'est que, celui-ci, j'ai eu la chance de l'approcher. Je puis donc parler de lui à bon escient. Oui, j'ai été invitée plusieurs fois aux Tuileries...

Elle prononça ces mots d'un ton modeste, mais, visiblement, elle était fière de son accession à la sphère du pouvoir.

— Un être de tout premier ordre, précisa-t-elle. Noble, intelligent, résolu, sensible ! Et l'impératrice, quelle grâce, quelle beauté ! Elle voudra sûrement vous connaître !

— Je me demande pourquoi !

— Parce qu'elle est curieuse de toutes les souffrances humaines. D'ailleurs, elle et moi nous intéressons aux mêmes œuvres de bienfaisance. Si je vous disais que je passe le plus clair de mon temps à m'occuper d'une Société de Charité maternelle !...

Sophie arrondit les yeux sur cette créature qui, à force de passer d'un homme à l'autre, avait fini par les aimer tous. La vertu lui était venue avec les rides. Comment retrouver la femme jolie, facile et un peu commune d'autrefois dans cette vieille personne au maintien digne et à l'esprit bienveillant ?

— Il ne tient qu'à vous d'avoir une existence aussi remplie que la mienne, reprit Delphine. Créez-vous quelques obligations qui vous réchauffent le cœur. On n'a pas encore inventé de meilleur remède que la société contre la solitude ! A ce propos, je vous signale qu'il y a beaucoup de Russes à Paris. Tous sont des gens charmants. C'est d'ailleurs par M. Nicolas Kisseleff, ambassadeur de Russie en France, que j'ai appris votre arrivée. Vous devriez peut-être lui faire une visite...

— Si vous saviez combien j'ai fait de visites aux gouverneurs, aux généraux, aux directeurs de départements ministériels en Russie, vous comprendriez que je n'ai guère envie de recommencer ici !

— Bon ! Bon ! dit Delphine en riant. Laissons donc de côté les personnages officiels. En tout cas, il y a un salon où vous ne pouvez refuser de paraître, c'est celui de la princesse de Lieven. Toute la petite colonie russe de Paris s'y réunit le dimanche pour rencontrer les plus beaux esprits français de notre temps. La princesse m'a dit qu'elle avait l'intention de vous inviter. Je vous préviens pour que vous ne soyez pas surprise...

— C'est très aimable de sa part, dit Sophie. N'est-elle pas née Benkendorff ?

— Si, son mari, le prince de Lieven, s'est distingué comme ambassadeur à Londres. Elle-même a été dame d'honneur de l'impératrice de Russie...

— Que fait-elle donc à Paris ?

— Il y a une vingtaine d'années, elle a eu un immense chagrin. Deux de ses fils sont morts de la fièvre scarlatine. Alors, elle a quitté la Cour. Elle s'est même séparée de son mari avec qui elle ne s'entendait pas très bien. Et, prétextant que le climat de Saint-Pétersbourg lui était néfaste, elle est venue se fixer ici, dans son entresol de la rue Saint-Florentin, par amour de la France. On dit qu'elle a été l'amie de Metternich et que Guizot est très épris d'elle, bien qu'elle ait soixante-dix ans. Le comte de Morny est un habitué de son salon. Lord Aberdeen lui écrit chaque semaine. Elle est aussi en correspondance suivie avec l'impératrice Alexandra Fédorovna, qui lui a conservé beaucoup de tendresse. Bref, elle est très influente ici comme là-bas. C'est une sorte d'ambassadrice officieuse de la Russie en France. On l'a surnommée la Sibylle de l'Europe. Vraiment, il faut que vous la connaissiez !...

Sophie songea aux espoirs que ses amis de Sibérie avaient placés en elle. Pouvait-elle négliger l'occasion de plaider leur cause auprès d'une personne si bien introduite à la Cour ?

— L'ennui, c'est que je n'ai rien à me mettre, dit-elle.

— Rassurez-vous, dit Delphine, chez la princesse de Lieven, on fait plus attention à l'esprit qu'à la toilette ! D'ailleurs, je suis sûre que vous vous calomniez. Telle que je vous connais, vous avez déjà dû vous commander quelques robes charmantes ! Si vous voulez de bonnes adresses de fournisseurs...

La conversation s'égara dans les chiffons. Sophie ne remarquait plus les rides sur le visage de Delphine. A se parler comme autrefois, elles rajeunissaient l'une devant l'autre. Pour elles seules, pendant une heure, elles eurent dix-huit ans.

Delphine se leva et tourna dans le salon en inspectant les meubles à travers son face-à-main.

— Vous avez arrangé votre intérieur avec un goût exquis ! dit-elle d'une voix chantante. L'encoignure est un pur chef-d'œuvre ! Et cette bibliothèque en poirier noirci, ne serait-elle pas signée Fourdinois ?

— Si ! avoua Sophie, toute heureuse que son achat fût apprécié d'une femme qui, évidemment, était experte en belles choses.

Ensuite, Delphine s'extasia sur des objets que Sophie avait rapportés de Russie : un encrier en malachite à sujet de bronze, quelques statuettes de porcelaine représentant des moujiks russes dansant, un jeu d'estampes : « Vues de Saint-Pétersbourg en 1812. »

— Quelle est cette place ? demandait Delphine. Et ce pont ?

Sophie donnait des explications avec une bizarre fierté. Elle se rappela le temps où, dans une isba sibérienne, elle collectionnait des souvenirs de Paris. Ce balancement de son esprit d'un pays à l'autre ne s'arrêterait-il jamais ? Soudain, elle fut envahie d'allégresse à l'idée d'avoir retrouvé une amie, de n'être plus seule en France, de pouvoir, désormais, échanger ses impressions avec quelqu'un de sa nationalité, de son rang, de son âge. Elle prit rendez-vous avec Delphine pour le lendemain.

★

Sophie avait tellement perdu l'habitude du monde, qu'en pénétrant dans le grand salon blanc et or de la princesse de Lieven elle fut étonnée par le nombre de gens qui s'y trouvaient réunis. Devant elle, sous la lumière des lustres, se pressaient des robes lourdement ornées, qui laissaient les épaules nues et s'évasaient vers le bas, donnant aux femmes un aspect de calices renversés. Dans ce remuement de soie, de brocart et de moire antique, les fracs des hommes tranchaient par leur teinte funèbre et leur coupe nette, inspirée de la cosse de haricot. Le parfum de la poudre chaude et du cosmétique flottait audessus des têtes et le bourdonnement continu des conversations avait quelque chose de bien élevé, de melliflue et d'intarissable. Un annonceur aboyait les noms à la porte. Des laquais à perruque et à bas blancs passaient des rafraîchissements aux couleurs variées. Laissant courir ses regards sur les visages, Sophie se demandait si elle était assez habillée avec cette robe de dentelle prune à jupes étagées, que « Madame Louise Pierson », couturière, lui avait livrée la veille. Sa garniture de cheveux, en feuillages vernis, venait de chez Alexandrine, ses gants longs de chez Mayer, son éventail de chez Duvelleroy. Il y avait longtemps qu'elle n'avait éprouvé la sensation d'une pareille harmonie. En l'apercevant, Delphine se récria d'admiration.

— Vous aussi, vous avez une toilette ravissante, dit Sophie en détaillant la robe en taffetas vert de son amie qu'égayaient des fleurs artificielles en gaze jaune pâle.

— La robe n'est pas mal, dit Delphine, mais les jupons de crin sont trop volumineux ! Cela me gêne pour marcher ! Venez vite ! On vous attend ! On est impatiente de vous voir !

Elle saisit la main de Sophie et l'entraîna vers le fond du salon, où, à demi allongée sur un sofa, se tenait une vieille femme sèche, dure, au re-

gard vif et aux cheveux blancs, coiffés d'un bon
net de dentelle. Une robe de velours noir l'enveloppait du cou aux chevilles. Sur son corsage
brillait le chiffre de diamants des dames d'honneur de l'impératrice Alexandra Fédorovna. Une
petite cour de messieurs âgés et graves l'entourait. Delphine lui présenta Sophie et s'éclipsa
sur un semblant de révérence. La princesse examina la nouvelle venue des pieds à la tête avec
une tranquillité souveraine, la pria de s'asseoir
près d'elle sur une chaise et dit, en français, d'une
voix fêlée :

— Je suis bien aise de vous voir chez moi, Madame. Vous allez me donner des nouvelles de
mon pays.

— Je crois, princesse, que vous en savez davantage que moi sur ce qui se passe en Russie, dit
Sophie avec un sourire.

— Je sais ce qui se passe à Saint-Pétersbourg
mais la vraie Russie est ailleurs. Certains prétendent même que, de nos jours, il faut la chercher de l'autre côté de l'Oural !

Il y eut des rires dans le groupe des messieurs.
Contente de son effet, la princesse ajouta :

— Des êtres chers à mon cœur se trouvent encore là-bas : les Troubetzkoï, les Volkonsky. Que
savez-vous d'eux ?

Sophie répondit qu'elle ignorait ce qu'ils étaient
devenus depuis son départ de Sibérie, mais raconta, le plus simplement qu'elle put, leur vie
commune, jadis, à Tchita et à Pétrovsk. Ce récit
émut la princesse.

— C'est abominable ! dit-elle. Quelle qu'ait été
la faute de ces garçons, l'empereur aurait dû les
gracier, depuis le temps ! Son entêtement est absurde, inique, antichrétien !

Les hommes qui l'encadraient firent chorus avec elle. Sophie s'étonna qu'une personne si proche de la famille impériale portât publiquement sur le tsar un jugement si sévère. Craignant un piège, elle se garda de renchérir. Comme piquée de cette méfiance, la princesse se pencha vers elle et poursuivit à mi-voix :

— Vous savez, Madame, d'une certaine façon, je suis, moi aussi, une persécutée. Le tsar est furieux que je refuse de rentrer en Russie. Il a tout fait pour contraindre mon mari à me ramener. Comme je m'obstinais, il l'a sommé de rompre. Maintenant, Nicolas Ier s'est résigné : il me laisse là où je suis, il lit les lettres que j'écris à l'impératrice, il en fait son profit, mais, au fond, il me déteste !

— J'ai peine à le croire, princesse, dit Sophie.

— Si, si, il me déteste ! C'est un homme extraordinaire, plus intelligent et plus fort qu'on ne le suppose, mais sa rancune l'étouffe. Il ne sait pas pardonner ! Vos amis décembristes ne me démentiraient pas !

— Vous pensez qu'il n'y a plus aucune chance pour eux ?

— J'en ai parlé cent fois dans mes lettres à l'impératrice. Je vous promets de le faire encore. Ce sera en pure perte, hélas !

Leur conversation fut interrompue par d'autres invités qui venaient saluer la maîtresse de maison. Elle en présenta quelques-uns à Sophie. Les grands noms français alternaient avec les grands noms russes. Sophie entendait : Dolgoroukoff, Tourguénieff, Ermoloff, Chouvaloff, Démidoff, et s'étonnait que tant de sujets du tsar fussent domiciliés à Paris. Tous étaient vêtus à la dernière mode et parlaient le français avec volupté, avec ivresse, en roulant les r. Visiblement, ils forçaient leur talent pour paraître très parisiens. Il en résultait une impression de comédie assez pénible.

Un homme âgé, voûté, au visage glabre et aux yeux pensifs, s'approcha de Sophie en s'appuyant de tout son poids sur une canne à pommeau d'or. Sophie reconnut Nicolas Tourguénieff, que la princesse lui avait présenté cinq minutes auparavant. Il la prit à part pour lui parler de ses amis de Sibérie. On eût dit qu'il voulait se justifier devant elle de s'être trouvé à l'étranger au moment de la révolte. En l'écoutant, Sophie pensa aux explications embarrassées de Vassia Volkoff. Tous deux étaient atteints de la même maladie. Après avoir échappé au châtiment des conjurés, ils vivaient dans le remords d'avoir eu plus de chance que leurs camarades. Mais Nicolas Tourguénieff était d'une autre envergure que le misérable Vassia. Son regard brillait d'intelligence, il émanait de lui un air de calme, d'honnêteté et de résolution. En quelques mots, il raconta comment, réfugié à Edimbourg, il avait reçu l'ordre du tsar de comparaître devant la commission d'enquête pour complicité avec les décembristes, comment il avait refusé de quitter la Grande-Bretagne et comment il avait été condamné à mort, puis aux travaux forcés, par contumace. Depuis, il s'était installé en France, dans une villa, près de Bougival. Son idée fixe était l'abolition du servage en Russie. Il espérait contribuer à cette réforme par ses écrits.

— Il y a six ans, j'ai publié en français un ouvrage qui a fait quelque bruit. *La Russie et les Russes*, dit-il. Je vais vous l'envoyer. J'y étudie tout ce qui ne marche pas dans notre pays. Cela

252

me permet, en passant, de rendre hommage à mes amis les décembristes...

La rose et blonde Mme Griboff, entendant ces paroles, joignit les mains et s'écria .

— Ah! oui, lisez-le, c'est un livre admirable! Seul un homme aimant profondément son pays pouvait le critiquer ainsi!

Et, tournée vers Sophie, elle ajouta :

— Savez-vous que, moi aussi, je suis très proche de certains décembristes? Vous avez certainement connu Youri Almazoff, en Sibérie. Je suis sa nièce. Evidemment, j'étais trop jeune lorsqu'il a été arrêté pour me souvenir de lui. Mais ma mère m'en a beaucoup parlé. Je voudrais vous demander une faveur : faites-moi le plaisir de venir souper à la maison le 18 juin prochain.

En souvenir de Youri Almazoff, Sophie accepta de grand cœur. Quand Mme Griboff se fut éloignée, ravie d'avoir si facilement obtenu gain de cause, Nicolas Tourguénieff chuchota :

— Elle est catholique!

— Ah! oui? murmura Sophie sans marquer la moindre surprise.

— Je veux dire qu'elle était orthodoxe et qu'elle s'est fait baptiser catholique. Elle, son mari, son fils... et ils ne sont pas les seuls! Le prince Gagarine, le comte Chouvaloff, Nicolaï... Il y a en France tout un petit clan de Russes qui ont changé — Dieu sait pourquoi! — de religion. Sur eux règne la très vertueuse Mme Swetchine. Vous avez sûrement entendu parler d'elle!

— Oui, dit Sophie, sa renommée est venue jusqu'en Russie. C'est, dit-on, une sorte de sainte...

— Une sainte très entreprenante. Elle fait du prosélytisme. Quand on va chez elle, elle vous demande des nouvelles de votre âme comme elle vous demanderait des nouvelles de votre rhume de cerveau !

Sophie décela une pointe d'acrimonie dans l'opinion de Nicolas Tourguénieff sur les orthodoxes convertis au catholicisme. Cela se comprenait de la part d'un homme, qui, bien qu'émigré en France, se croyait plus russe que ses compatriotes restés chez eux. Il y avait certainement, dans cette petite colonie brillante et oisive, des rivalités, des jalousies, des divergences d'idées, que recouvrait tant bien que mal le vernis de la politesse française. Tous ces boyards travestis en dandys, tous ces propriétaires de terres et de serfs, devaient chercher à Paris une culture plus raffinée, une vie plus douce, une plus grande liberté ; mais ils trichaient avec eux-mêmes ; le fond de leur caractère était russe ; en s'expatriant, ils adoptaient les façons de la société cosmopolite et demeuraient asservis aux préjugés de leur lointaine patrie... Sophie s'arrêta au milieu de ses réflexions, surprise de leur incohérence et de leur sévérité. Devant ces exilés plus ou moins volontaires elle se sentait tantôt intransigeante comme une vraie Russe qui ne pardonnerait pas à ses concitoyens de préférer les plaisirs de l'Occident à ceux de son pays natal, tantôt méfiante comme une Française xénophobe qui souffrirait de voir des étrangers s'installer sur son sol. Un vieux monsieur très distingué l'ayant interrogée sur la dernière saison théâtrale à Saint-Pétersbourg, elle crut avoir affaire à un Russe et apprit avec confusion qu'il s'agissait du comte de Sainte-Aulaire ; en revanche, une dame entre deux âges, exubérante et emplumée, qu'elle prenait pour une Française, se retourna d'un bloc en s'entendant appeler Nastassia Constantinovna. La France et la Russie échangeaient leurs masques. C'était un jeu de société dont Sophie était la devineresse. Il y eut un grand mouvement dans la salle : on chuchota que le comte de Morny arrivait. Mais l'annonceur détrompa tout le monde en clamant un nom inconnu, sans particule.

— Il avait pourtant promis de venir ? se lamentait Delphine. Je voulais lui demander s'il était exact que l'impératrice s'apprêtait à distribuer cent mille francs aux Sociétés de Charité maternelle.

— S'il ne vient pas, Guizot, lui, viendra, dit Nicolas Tourguénieff.

— Que voulez-vous que je fasse de Guizot ? Guizot, c'est le passé...

— Un passé qui pourrait renaître de ses cendres !

— Chut ! si on vous entendait !...

— Est-il possible que M. Guizot rencontre ici le comte de Morny ? demanda Sophie.

— Eh ! oui, chère Madame, dit Nicolas Tourguénieff. C'est un miracle de notre princesse. Tous ses amis d'autrefois, Guizot en tête, étaient parmi les vaincus du coup d'Etat du 2 décembre. Après la proclamation de l'empire, elle aurait pu refuser sa porte aux triomphateurs. Mais elle est trop avide d'informations. Elle ne saurait vivre sans respirer le fumet des affaires publiques. Elle a donc invité chez elle les nouveaux dirigeants, sans répudier les anciens. Pour les contraindre tous à se réunir autour de son canapé, il fallait un tact, une diplomatie, dont bien peu de femmes eussent été capables !...

En parlant, il s'était rapproché du sofa sur lequel se tenait la princesse de Lieven, toujours à demi étendue, un éventail de jais palpitant devant son thorax squelettique.

— Que complotez-vous encore ? dit-elle en dressant sa petite tête de serpent au bout d'un long cou décharné.

— Je faisais à Mme Ozareff les honneurs de notre société russe de Paris, dit-il.

— Il n'y a pas de quoi en être fier ! répliqua la princesse. Les défauts de chacun s'accusent à l'étranger. J'en sais quelque chose, moi qui ai passé les trois quarts de ma vie hors de mon pays. Mais que voulez-vous ? Je ne me sens bien qu'en France. Est-ce ma faute, si je ne suis pas née ici ?

Elle soupira, posa une main froide comme une grenouille sur la main de Sophie et poursuivit :

— Je regrette que notre chère Wanda de Kosakovska n'ait pu venir aujourd'hui ! Vous lui auriez parlé de sa sœur, la princesse Troubetzkoï !...

— Où est Wanda ? demanda le comte de Sainte-Aulaire.

— A Nice, je crois.

— En cette saison ?

— Oui, c'est une drôle d'idée ! Elle nous reviendra cuite comme une galette. Savez-vous, Madame, que c'est elle qui a incité M. Alfred de Vigny à écrire son poème sur les décembristes ?

— Un poème sur les décembristes ? murmura Sophie. Je n'en ai jamais entendu parler.

Son ignorance enchanta la princesse de Lieven. Elle exultait, la bouche grande et mobile, l'œil enflammé :

— Vous, l'une des principales intéressées ?... C'est un comble !... Pourtant, ce poème date de cinq ou six ans !... Il est vrai qu'il n'a pas encore été publié !... J'en ai une copie manuscrite. Vous plairait-il d'en prendre connaissance ?

Sans attendre la réponse de Sophie, elle l'obligea à s'asseoir près d'elle et dit à une jeune fille, qui devait être sa secrétaire :

— Allez vite dans mon cabinet de travail. Ouvrez le tiroir de gauche. Vous trouverez, sur le dessus, un grand papier...

La jeune fille revint avec le poème et la princesse pria Nicolas Tourguénieff de le lire. Il s'affala dans un fauteuil et allongea sur un tabouret sa jambe malade. Quelques invités firent cercle autour de lui. Après avoir toussoté pour s'éclaircir la gorge, il commença d'un ton emphatique. Le poème était une sorte de dialogue, au bal, entre un poète français et une jeune Russe, Wanda. Questionnée par le poète, Wanda lui racontait comment sa sœur, une princesse, avait décidé d'accompagner son mari en Sibérie, pour y boire « chaque matin, les larmes du devoir ». Les souffrances du prisonnier étaient décrites en termes véhéments :

La fatigue a courbé sa poitrine écrasée ;
Le froid gonfle ses pieds dans ces chemins mau-
*   [vais ;*
La neige tombe en flots sur sa tête rasée,
Il brise les glaçons sur le bord des marais...

A mesure que le poème se développait, Sophie était de plus en plus gênée par l'enflure du style et la fausseté de l'image. D'avoir partagé l'exil des décembristes la rendait maladivement sensible à toute altération de la vérité. Elle savait bien que cette œuvre avait été écrite pour glorifier ses amis, mais l'exagération lyrique, en cette affaire, la choquait davantage que ne l'eût fait l'indifférence. Quand elle entendait parler du « tombeau

257

du mineur », de la femme soutenant le bras de
son mari qui maniait « l'épieu », du lin tissé par
elle pour un « linceul mortuaire », les souvenirs
de Tchita se levaient, tous chauds, dans sa mémoire et protestaient. Elle revoyait le départ des
décembristes pour les corvées, avec leur attirail
de pique-nique, Nicolas et Youri Almazoff jouant
aux échecs sur une pierre, au bord de l'eau, le
général Léparsky prenant le thé avec ses détenus,
les promenades en calèche avec Pauline Annenkoff,
Marie Volkonsky, Nathalie Fonvizine — tout ce
mélange d'amitié, de nostalgie, d'espoir, de contrainte, tout ce bonheur dans le malheur, que
seul un être ayant vécu là-bas pouvait comprendre.

Cependant, Nicolas Tourguénieff, fronçant les
sourcils et haussant la voix, lisait à présent la réponse du poète indigné aux révélations de
Wanda :

Tandis que vous parliez, je sentais dans mes
[veines
Les imprécations bouillonner sourdement.
Vous ne maudissez pas, ô vous, femmes ro-
[maines :
Vous traînez votre joug silencieusement.
Eponines du Nord, vous dormez dans vos
[tombes,
Vous soutenez l'esclave au fond des cata-
[combes...

Les regards convergeaient sur Sophie. Chacun
guettait ses impressions. Elle en avait conscience
et souffrait d'être ainsi livrée en spectacle.
C'étaient toutes les épouses des décembristes,
c'était elle-même qu'à travers la sœur de Wanda

l'auteur comparait aux héroïnes de l'antiquité. Elle se sentait indigne de cet hommage. Qu'avait-elle fait d'extraordinaire en rejoignant son mari sur les lieux de sa déportation ? Pourquoi transformer Catherine Troubetzkoï et ses compagnes en statues du devoir, alors qu'elles étaient des êtres de chair et de sang, avec leur courage et leur faiblesse ?

Soudain, elle eut envie de crier : « Ce n'est pas vrai ! Nous n'étions pas si grandes, si nobles, si désintéressées ! Notre vie était moins tragique ! Moins tragique et plus triste dans la simplicité, la médiocrité, les petites jalousies, l'ennui quotidien, la dégradation des sentiments, l'usure des caractères ! De quoi se mêle-t-il, M. Alfred de Vigny, avec son inspiration pompeuse ? Qu'il nous laisse en paix ! Qu'il se taise ! » Mais elle n'avait plus le droit de détruire cette légende qui l'irritait. Elle n'était pas seule en cause. Ses amis, restés là-bas, avaient besoin de l'auréole des martyrs. Leur pardon, leur retour en Russie, seraient peut-être dus, quelque jour, à la publicité poétique faite autour de leur infortune. A cet égard, tout ce qui pouvait les rendre sympathiques, pitoyables, sublimes, méritait l'encouragement. « Tant pis pour la vérité pensa-t-elle, si leur bonheur est au prix d'un mensonge ! » Une fois de plus, comme à Tobolsk, par solidarité avec eux, elle renonçait à être elle-même. Prisonnière d'un mythe, il fallait qu'elle subît jusqu'au bout la honte d'être surestimée. Maintenant, dans une péroraison vengeresse, le poète s'en prenait à Nicolas Ier qui, malgré le temps passé, refusait l'amnistie aux rebelles :

Silencieux devant son armée en silence

Le Czar, en mesurant la cuirasse et la lance,
Passera sa revue et toujours se taira.

C'était fini. Des dames soupirèrent derrière leurs éventails. Delphine se moucha avec émotion. Puis des exclamations se croisèrent :

— C'est génial ! Déchirant !
— Il faudra que je le recopie !
— Vigny est un grand poète !
— Je préfère Hugo !
— Parce qu'il s'est exilé ?
— Eh bien ! qu'en pensez-vous ? demanda la princesse de Lieven à Sophie. Le tableau est-il ressemblant ?

Sophie banda sa volonté, essaya de sourire et murmura :

— C'est un très beau poème... Trop beau, peut-être... Enfin, je veux dire... nous ne méritons pas cet honneur... Après tout, nous n'avons fait que notre devoir de femmes...

— Allons donc ! s'écria la princesse de Lieven. Vous avez été admirables. Mais il ne vous appartient pas d'en juger. Pour ce qui est du récit, je pense que vous avez fait la part de la transposition poétique. M. Alfred de Vigny a mis bonne mesure de romantisme dans son propos. Il serait sûrement très touché d'apprendre que vous, une réchappée des geôles sibériennes, vous appréciez ses vers. Voulez-vous que je vous ménage une entrevue avec lui ?

— Non, non, je vous remercie, balbutia Sophie.
— Pourquoi ?
— Je ne sais pas... Cela m'embarrasserait plutôt...

Elle était furieuse de ne pas trouver de meilleure excuse à sa dérobade. Ces hommes, ces femmes, inconnus d'elle, et qui la considéraient avec avidité, lui ôtaient soudain toute assurance. Heureusement, la princesse de Lieven, prenant en pitié son désarroi, orienta la conversation vers un autre thème : les récents désaccords de la Russie et de la Sublime Porte, au sujet du protectorat du tsar sur les chrétiens grecs de l'empire ottoman. Bien que le prince Menschikoff eût présenté un ultimatum au sultan sur ce point et que l'ultimatum eût été rejeté, rien ne laissait croire à un risque de guerre.

— Les Turcs ne bougeront pas s'ils ne sont pas soutenus par la France, disait la princesse de Lieven. Et la France ne bougera pas, parce qu'il est sans exemple qu'un régime qui vient de s'installer et qui n'a pas encore consolidé ses assises se lance dans une aventure militaire alors que ses frontières ne sont pas menacées.

Ce raisonnement était si clair, que tout le monde en parut convaincu. Seul, le comte de Sainte-Aulaire osa dire :

— Vous parlez de la France et vous oubliez l'Angleterre, princesse. L'Angleterre n'a pas les mêmes soucis intérieurs que nous. Lord Stratford de Redcliffe me semble tout à fait résolu à contrecarrer, à Constantinople, les desseins de la Russie. Ce faisant, il n'obéit pas seulement à la ligne générale de la diplomatie britannique, mais à une haine personnelle contre Nicolas Ier qui lui avait, si je ne m'abuse, refusé son agrément comme ambassadeur à Saint-Pétersbourg...

— J'en aurais fait autant à la place du tsar ! s'écria la princesse de Lieven. Ce Redcliffe est un personnage sinistre. Quand il est passé par Paris, sa vue m'a donné le frisson. Sans compter qu'il portait une cravate noire et verte, le dimanche, dans mon salon, alors que vous avez tous, Messieurs, le bon goût de porter une cravate blanche !

Le rire de l'assistance alla en s'élargissant et la princesse reprit :

— Non, il n'y aura pas de conflit armé. Simplement, un marchandage de diplomates. Lord Aberdeen me l'a confirmé dans sa dernière lettre.

Sachant que la princesse entretenait une correspondance suivie avec le premier ministre d'Angleterre, quelques hommes, assoiffés de politique, la cernèrent de près, comme s'ils se fussent penchés sur une source. Sophie profita de ce mouvement pour s'éloigner. Par-delà un barrage de fracs sombres, elle entendait monter des noms, toujours les mêmes : Menschikoff, Redcliffe, Nesselrode, Abdul-Medjid... On avait oublié les décembristes. Ils comptaient si peu aujourd'hui, dans l'immense remuement des peuples !

Elle retrouva Delphine dans un cercle de dames qui devisaient de mode et de théâtre. Là non plus, elle ne se sentit pas à l'aise. Elle en conclut qu'elle était trop fraîchement arrivée en France pour ne pas souffrir de dépaysement. Comme on s'impose une discipline, elle se contraignit à rester une demi-heure encore, parlant aux uns et aux autres, souriant, l'œil attentif et l'esprit distrait. Enfin, elle prit congé de la princesse de Lieven, qui lui fit de grands compliments et la pria de revenir, aussi souvent qu'elle le voudrait. Elle se préparait à franchir la porte, lorsque l'annonceur cria :

— Son Excellence, monsieur le comte de Morny.

Un frémissement parcourut le salon, les invités se rangèrent sur deux haies et Sophie aperçut un homme en habit noir, la figure mince et pâle, le front dégarni, qui cambrait la taille en marchant, à la façon d'un militaire. Sur le passage du demi-frère de l'empereur, les messieurs s'inclinaient un peu, les dames souriaient d'un air attirant. Il alla droit à la princesse de Lieven et lui baisa la main. Puis la foule les déroba aux yeux de Sophie. La soirée battait son plein. Sur les sièges bas, les femmes se réunissaient, semblait-il, non par affinité, mais par couleurs de robes ; les hommes, debout dans leurs fracs, le buste empesé, toutes décorations dehors, se rengorgeaient et parlaient d'abondance. Tous les visages, mêmes les plus vieux, portaient une expression tendue, surexcitée, d'acteurs en représentation. Sophie se faufila entre les groupes et déboucha au sommet du grand escalier, que bordaient des corbeilles de fleurs et des plantes vertes. Le brouhaha des conversations s'éteignit dans son dos. Une agréable fraîcheur l'enveloppa. Deux couples, qui venaient d'arriver, montaient les marches à sa rencontre. Elle admira une jeune femme au décolleté royal, dont la traîne soyeuse glissait en sifflant à chaque pas, détourna la tête en passant elle-même devant une glace, et pria un valet de lui appeler sa calèche.

Après une semaine d'attente, Sophie se persuada que Nicolas Tourguénieff avait oublié sa promesse et décida d'acheter elle-même ce livre sur la Russie et les Russes dont il lui avait parlé. Ne sachant à quel libraire s'adresser, elle repassa, sans espoir, par la rue Jacob. A sa grande surprise, elle trouva le magasin ouvert. Derrière la vitre poussiéreuse de la devanture, s'alignaient, comme autrefois, des volumes aux reliures détériorées. Il était impossible de voir ce qui se passait à l'intérieur. Elle poussa la porte, reçut, comme une goutte d'eau sur le crâne, le tintement de la clochette, et découvrit une jeune femme au visage maladif et à la mise négligée, entourée de quatre enfants ; le cadet pouvait avoir deux ans et l'aîné douze à peine.

— M. Vavasseur est-il là ? interrogea Sophie.

— Non, Madame, dit la jeune femme en s'avançant pour l'accueillir.

— Je suis une de ses vieilles amies. J'aimerais avoir de ses nouvelles. Peut-être pourriez-vous ?...

La jeune femme secoua la tête négativement,

le regard craintif. Deux de ses enfants se collèrent contre ses jupes. Comme elle continuait à se taire, Sophie se demanda qui elle était : une parente, une voisine chargée de garder la boutique ?

— M. Vavasseur vous a bien dit où on pouvait le joindre ! reprit-elle. Vous êtes de sa famille ?

— Je suis sa femme.

Sophie tomba de haut : son interlocutrice devait avoir vingt-huit ans, alors que Vavasseur marchait sur la soixantaine. De toute façon, il était surprenant que ce célibataire farouche se fût résigné au mariage.

— Comme je suis heureuse de vous connaître ! dit Sophie. Peut-être vous a-t-il parlé de moi ? Je suis Sophie Ozareff... Sophie de Champlitte, si vous préférez...

Un sourire détendit les traits fatigués de Mme Vavasseur.

— Oh ! s'écria-t-elle, bien sûr qu'il m'a parlé de vous ! Il sera si content quand il saura que vous êtes revenue ! Mais comment avez-vous fait pour quitter la Russie ?

— Ce serait trop long à vous expliquer. L'essentiel est que j'y sois parvenue. Maintenant, me voici en France, et libre pour toujours ! Où est votre mari ?

— En prison, dit Mme Vavasseur.

Sophie ne fut qu'à demi étonnée.

— Ah ! mon Dieu ! dit-elle. Qu'a-t-il fait ?

Mme Vavasseur leva les yeux au plafond et soupira.

— Vous le demandez ? Toujours la même chose ! Il a conspiré contre le gouvernement !

— Contre quel gouvernement ?

— Contre tous. Mais c'est le dernier en date qui l'a fait coffrer ! A partir du moment où Louis-Na-

266

poléon a été élu Président de la République, Augustin est entré en guerre contre lui. En a-t-il imprimé des pamphlets. des journaux clandestins, des proclamations révolutionnaires ! C'est sûrement notre concierge qui l'a dénoncé !

— Il a, en effet, une tête de mouchard, dit Sophie. Je comprends qu'il m'ait si mal reçue quand je suis venue la première fois !

— Vous êtes déjà venue et le magasin était fermé ? c'est stupide, je n'ouvre plus que deux ou trois fois par semaine ! Il y a si peu de clients, que c'est plutôt pour aérer que pour vendre ! Quand mon mari reviendra, il faudra qu'il se refasse un achalandage.

— Il n'a pas été condamné pour longtemps, j'espère ?

— On ne sait pas au juste. Une première fois, il a été arrêté avec ses amis après le coup d'Etat du 2 décembre et libéré au bout de six mois. Aussitôt, il a récidivé. Et je t'écris, et je te complote !... En octobre dernier, ils l'ont repincé. Là, il en a pris pour un an et un jour. Mais j'ai fait une demande. Je pense qu'on le relâchera avant terme. Ça m'arrangerait bien ! Un père de famille ! Un homme âgé ! Un commerçant payant patente !...

— Où l'a-t-on incarcéré ?

— A Sainte-Pélagie. Je vais le voir là-bas régulièrement.

— Ne pourrais-je le voir, moi aussi ?

— C'est bien facile ! Evidemment, il vous faudrait une autorisation spéciale, parce que vous n'êtes pas une parente. Mais je connais un commis à la Préfecture de Police qui m'arrange tous les laissez-passer que je veux en vingt-quatre heures. Après-demain, cela vous conviendrait ?

267

— A merveille ! Si je pouvais faire quelque chose pour lui !....

— Oh ! oui, dit Mme Vavasseur en joignant les
mains, vous avez sûrement des relations dans
les hautes sphères !

Elle était simplette et touchante, parmi ses
bambins mal tenus. Vraisemblablement, elle ne
comprenait rien à la politique, béait d'admiration devant la science de son mari et tremblait
qu'il ne finît plus mal encore, la laissant sur la
paille avec sa nichée.

— J'irai donc vous chercher, après-demain, à
deux heures, reprit-elle. Où habitez-vous ?

— 81, rue de Grenelle, dit Sophie.

Et, se souvenant du but de sa visite, elle demanda :

— Pendant que j'y pense, n'auriez-vous pas un
livre de Nicolas Tourguénieff : *La Russie et les
Russes* ?

— Peut-être bien. Je remplace mon mari au
magasin, mais je ne suis guère au courant. Tous
les livres sur la Russie sont dans ce coin. Regardez vous-même...

Pendant que Sophie se dirigeait vers le fond de
la boutique, le plus jeune fils de Vavasseur, qui
rampait par terre, se cogna le front au comptoir
et éclata en sanglots. Sophie le ramassa, le berça
et le rendit à sa mère. C'était un bambin bouffi
et triste. Mme Vavasseur le moucha et, énervée,
donna une taloche au plus grand, qui attachait
des chaises ensemble avec une ficelle.

— Vous avez de beaux enfants ! dit Sophie.
Comment se nomment-ils ?

— Le petiot, c'est Maximilien-François-Isidore...

Sophie eut un sourire amusé.

— Oui, reprit Mme Vavasseur, à cause de Robespierre, le moyen c'est Pierre-Joseph, à cause de Proudhon ; l'aîné c'est Claude-Henri, à cause de Saint-Simon...

Sophie contempla avec attendrissement ces grands hommes retombés en enfance.

— Et la fille ? dit-elle.

— Anne-Joseph. Comme Théroigne de Méricourt !

— Un héritage lourd à porter !

— Moi, je n'aime pas tellement ces prénoms ! J'ai dit à mon mari que c'était ridicule ! Mais allez donc lui faire entendre raison !...

Sur un rayon, à hauteur d'homme, Sophie découvrit l'ouvrage de Nicolas Tourguénieff, en trois volumes. Elle les mit de côté et continua de fouiller parmi les bouquins, dont la poussière lui veloutait les doigts. Plus loin, s'alignaient quelques exemplaires d'un opuscule à couverture bleue : *Le peuple russe et le socialisme, lettre à Monsieur J. Michelet, professeur au Collège de France.* Elle sortit l'une de ces brochures et la feuilleta.

— Mon mari connaissait l'auteur, dit Mme Vavasseur. Alors, il a pris beaucoup de ces petits livres en dépôt. Mais ça ne se vend pas du tout !

Sophie lut le nom sur la couverture : Iscander.

— Il a signé Iscander, mais son vrai nom c'est Herzen, reprit Mme Vavasseur. Alexandre Herzen... Un Russe... Il est venu souvent au magasin. Un homme gentil, distingué, qui a dû quitter son pays à cause de ses opinions politiques. Vous n'en avez pas entendu parler, là-bas ?

— Si, dit Sophie. A Tobolsk, en Sibérie. Mais je n'ai rien lu de lui.

Elle revit les jeunes exaltés du complot de Pétrachevsky discutant de Bakounine, de Proudhon, de Herzen, dans le salon de l'inspecteur de la prison. Tout se tenait. De pays en pays, d'année en année, le même fil liait ceux qui combattaient pour une liberté insaisissable et changeante.

— Habite-t-il encore la France ? demanda-t-elle.

— Plus maintenant, dit Mme Vavasseur. On l'a expulsé, voilà bien deux ans, parce qu'il avait publié des choses contre le gouvernement. Vous savez qu'il a perdu sa mère et son fils dans un naufrage, au large d'Hyères ? Puis c'est sa femme qui est morte. Entre nous, elle lui avait fait porter les cornes ! Maintenant, il est comme fou de chagrin. Il vit à Londres. Vous prenez ce livre ?

— Oui, dit Sophie.

Elle dut insister pour payer son acquisition. Mme Vavasseur la retint et l'obligea à boire un doigt de madère. Anne-Joseph et Pierre-Joseph se disputaient, tirant chacun sur la jambe d'une poupée. Maximilien-François-Isidore avait trouvé une épingle dans une rainure du parquet et il fallut la lui confisquer, malgré ses cris. A l'écart de la bousculade, Claude-Henri, un livre sur les genoux, coloriait des images en chantonnant. Maintenant que les enfants s'étaient habitués à la visiteuse, leur naturel reprenait le dessus. Mme Vavasseur, toujours l'œil sur l'un ou sur l'autre, pouvait difficilement soutenir une conversation. Elle finit par gémir :

— Il leur faut un père à ces petits ! Ils me rendront folle !

Et, comme Sophie s'apprêtait à prendre congé, elle la pria de l'appeler désormais Louise.

★

A peine rentrée chez elle, Sophie parcourut

270

l'ouvrage de Nicolas Tourguénieff, qu'elle trouva sérieux, documenté, équitable. Les pages consacrées à ses camarades décembristes témoignaient d'une amitié sincère. Son plan d'émancipation des serfs était cohérent. Mais elle avait l'impression que, tout cela, elle le savait avant de l'avoir lu. En revanche, la brochure de Herzen lui procura le choc d'une révélation. Répondant à Michelet qui accusait la Russie d'être un Etat barbare, il se déclarait d'accord avec l'auteur sur toutes les critiques adressées au gouvernement, mais prenait avec fureur la défense du peuple. Pour lui, la seule force qui pouvait s'opposer à l'autocratie délirante du tsar, c'était la masse paysanne. Et cela parce que les serfs ignoraient la propriété individuelle et vivaient en associations communales sur les terres d'autrui. Ainsi, avaient-ils dans leur sang la notion du « communisme », qui, un jour, changerait la face du monde. « Quel bonheur pour le peuple russe d'être resté en dehors de tout mouvement politique, en dehors même de la civilisation européenne, qui, nécessairement, lui aurait miné sa commune, écrivait Herzen... L'Europe, à son premier pas dans la révolution sociale, rencontre ce peuple qui lui apporte une réalisation rudimentaire, demi sauvage, mais enfin une réalisation quelconque du partage continuel des terres parmi les ouvriers agricoles... L'homme de la Russie future c'est le moujik, comme l'homme de la France régénérée sera l'ouvrier... » En fin de compte, tout en préconisant de jeter bas le régime actuel, Herzen n'indiquait pas par quoi le remplacer. Son seul espoir, il le mettait dans la communauté agraire. N'était-ce pas une gageure d'intellectuel ? Sophie reposa le livre. Le calme de sa demeure parisienne

271

l'étonna, après les sentiments qui l'avaient agitée. L'abat-jour de la lampe dessinait un cercle de lumière, au milieu duquel elle était assise. Par la fenêtre entrouverte sur le crépuscule du jardin entraient les pépiements des oiseaux qui tournoyaient autour de leurs nids. Bientôt, Justin viendrait annoncer à Madame qu'elle était servie. Elle passa la main sur ses yeux fatigués. « C'est étrange, songea-t-elle, j'arrive en France, tout heureuse d'avoir quitté la Russie, et les premiers livres que je lis sont précisément des livres sur la Russie !... »

★

Louise vint à l'heure dite, flanquée d'Anne-Joseph et de Claude-Henri. Comme Sophie s'étonnait qu'elle ne fût pas seule, elle expliqua :

— Les enfants ont l'habitude. Je les emmène toujours là-bas, à tour de rôle, pour que leur père les voie...

Elle tenait un paquet sous chaque bras. Sa capote de paille, aux crevés garnis de rubans cerise, était deux fois trop grande pour son visage émacié. Claude-Henri portait une longue blouse bleue sur un pantalon court et une casquette de velours à visière vernie. Anne-Joseph se guindait dans une jupe rose évasée, d'où dépassaient des pantalons à festons. Visiblement, ils s'étaient tous endimanchés pour cette visite. Sophie prit deux bouteilles de champagne qu'elle avait fait monter de la cave.

— Oh ! il ne faut pas ! susurra Louise. Vous le comblez !...

On se serra, à quatre, dans la calèche. Quand Sophie ordonna à Basile de les conduire à Sainte-

Pélagie, il arrondit un œil scandalisé et se fit répéter l'adresse. Pendant tout le trajet, à travers les rues ensoleillées, les enfants jabotèrent comme s'ils s'étaient rendus à la promenade. Dans la rue du Puits-de-l'Ermite, la prison les prit sous son ombre. C'était une bâtisse grise, massive, dont la façade menaçait ruine, malgré les grossiers raccords de maçonnerie qui en rompaient la continuité. Par endroits, s'ouvraient des fenêtres étroites et fortement grillagées. La calèche s'arrêta. On mit pied à terre. Des passants se retournèrent en chuchotant. Louise frappa la porte avec son lourd marteau de fer.

— Il y a de tout à Sainte-Pélagie, dit-elle. Même des condamnés de droit commun. Mais on ne mélange pas les genres. Les politiques sont groupés au Pavillon des Princes !

Ces derniers mots furent prononcés par elle avec une nuance de fierté. Des pas se rapprochèrent. Un judas s'ouvrit sur un gros œil luisant. Louise montra les permis de visite et le vantail pivota sur ses gonds avec un bâillement affamé. Dans le vestibule, le guichetier, bonhomme, examina encore une fois les papiers, tapota la joue des enfants qu'il avait l'air de bien connaître, toisa Sophie de la tête aux pieds et chargea le gardien de conduire « la petite famille » jusqu'à M. Vavasseur.

On s'engagea dans une galerie sombre et fraîche, aux murs suintants d'humidité. De part et d'autre de ce passage s'alignaient des portes énormes, dont les verrous occupaient le quart de la surface. Avant même de s'en être rendu compte, Sophie fut saisie par l'odeur de la prison. Les narines ouvertes, elle se crut revenue en Sibérie, dans quelque centre de triage. Partout, la misère humaine sentait mauvais. Mais, sur ce fond de puanteur internationale, jouaient des variations infinies. Ainsi, les relents de cuisine étaient différents. Les exhalaisons du chou aigre et du kwass, caractéristiques de la Russie, étaient remplacées ici par celles du pot-au-feu et de la piquette. On entendait des grognements, des toux, derrière les parois aveugles. Cette termitière était habitée dans ses moindres alvéoles.

— C'est par là qu'on va au Pavillon des Princes, dit Louise. Au début, mon mari couchait dans un dortoir, avec vingt autres détenus, ensuite, on l'a logé à la Grande Sibérie.

— La Grande Sibérie ? dit Sophie intriguée. Qu'est-ce que c'est ?

— Une salle importante, au cinquième, pour plusieurs prisonniers. On l'appelle ainsi parce qu'elle est la plus froide. Mon époux, qui est fragile des bronches, a demandé à changer. Maintenant, il a sa chambre particulière, au quatrième. Je l'ai meublée avec des objets de la maison, pour qu'il se sente un peu chez lui...

Sophie songea aux femmes des décembristes arrangeant les cellules de leurs maris dans le bagne de Pétrovsk. Décidément, il existait des similitudes troublantes entre les régimes pénitentiaires des pays les plus éloignés.

Elles abordèrent un large escalier de pierre. On était chez les politiques. L'atmosphère changea. Si le premier étage, réservé à l'administration, était calme, au deuxième, déjà, Sophie remarqua une grande agitation. Toutes les portes sur le couloir étaient ouvertes. Des jeunes gens barbus fumaient la pipe autour d'un poêle en fonte, sur lequel mijotait une marmite. Sans doute mangeait-on à n'importe quelle heure dans cette mai-

son — quand l'ennui vous prenait. Quelques détenus saluèrent avec empressement Mme Vavasseur. Elle leur demanda :

— Mon mari est-il là-haut ?

— Probablement, nous ne l'avons pas vu de la
journée.

Au-dessus, éclatèrent des rires de femmes. Deux
lorettes effrontées coquetaient, dans l'encadrement d'une porte, avec un prisonnier invisible.
Dans le même corridor, une vieille mère, en capeline de veuve, se promenait à petits pas avec son
fils, qui baissait la tête. Au troisième, toute une
chambrée se disputait Sophie entendit :

— ... Liberté étranglée... la personnalité du tyran... Tant que le peuple... je te dis que tant que le
peuple !... Non, non, il faut renverser et recons-
truire !...

Puis les clameurs se turent. Une femme chanta.
Elle avait une belle voix triste. Sophie s'arrêta, essoufflée. Ce malaise lui rappela son âge. Elle posa
une main sur sa poitrine.

— Encore un étage, dit Louise.

Elles reprirent leur ascension. Une créature très
peinte et très parfumée descendait les marches à
leur rencontre. Les enfants la regardèrent avec
stupeur, comme si elle eût été un cerf-volant qui
passait.

— C'est inadmissible ! siffla Louise.

Le gardien qui la précédait soupira :

— Eh ! oui, que voulez-vous ? Il n'y a plus de
moralité dans cette maison ! On devrait pouvoir
y venir en famille ! Et c'est tout juste si on ne s'y
fait pas raccrocher pis que dans la rue des Fossés-
du-Temple ! Vous voilà arrivées. Je vous laisse...

Louise arrangea son chapeau, tira la blouse de
son fils, défripa la jupe de sa fille et, rayonnante

d'allégresse conjugale, tapa d'un doigt léger à la porte d'une cellule.

— Entrez ! grogna une voix rogue.

Elle ouvrit le battant, poussa ses enfants devant elle, attendit qu'ils eussent fini d'embrasser leur père, et annonça :

— Augustin, j'ai une surprise pour toi ! Regarde !...

En franchissant le seuil, Sophie aperçut, dans un fauteuil, un vieillard décharné, le col de la chemise ouvert, les cheveux gris en désordre, la prunelle brillante comme un tesson de bouteille. Il se leva et considéra Sophie longuement. Ses rides tremblaient, s'envolaient. Il rajeunissait à vue d'œil. Enfin, il grommela :

— Je savais que vous étiez arrivée à Paris !

— Est-ce possible ? dit-elle.

— A Sainte-Pélagie, on est mieux renseigné que partout ailleurs ! Les nouvelles se télégraphient vite du monde extérieur à la prison ! Ah ! chère Sophie ! confidente et alliée de mes premiers combats, quel bonheur de vous revoir ! J'ai su votre tragique aventure ! Vous êtes restée fidèle, en Russie, à votre vocation révolutionnaire, comme je suis resté fidèle à la mienne, en France ! Mais vous êtes libre, et je suis encore au cachot ! Vous allez tout me raconter ! Il me faut des détails !...

Il lui avait saisi les mains et plongeait un regard exigeant dans ses yeux. Elle était lasse de se répéter. D'un jour à l'autre, sa relation des faits lui semblait moins sincère. Comme si elle eût récité un monologue, dont elle connaissait d'avance l'effet sur le public. Elle se demandait même si, à force de parler d'elle et de ses amis, elle ne versait pas dans cette fausse littérature

276

qu'elle reprochait aux thuriféraires des décembristes. A contrecœur, elle évoqua pour Vavasseur la révolte du 14 décembre, les années de bagne et d'exil, la fraternité qui liait entre eux les prisonniers, la mort de Nicolas... Il l'écoutait avec passion. Son visage était secoué de tics. Enfin, il s'écria :

— Votre sacrifice n'aura pas été vain !

— C'est ce qu'on dit toujours quand on veut consoler quelqu'un d'une défaite ! murmura-t-elle.

— Dans une affaire pareille, il n'y a pas de défaite, il n'y a que des temps de répit, pendant lesquels de nouveaux combattants relèvent les anciens !

— Peut-être, mais je constate que les années passent, que les générations se succèdent, et qu'on trouve toujours la même race de gens au pouvoir et la même race de gens en prison.

— Patience ! Nous avançons !...

— En tournant en rond dans vos cellules ?

— Non, non, assez de politique ! s'exclama Louise avec une brusque énergie.

Elle obligea son mari et Sophie à s'asseoir et déballa les paquets, qui contenaient, l'un des livres, l'autre une tarte. Anne-Joseph alla chercher des assiettes et des verres dans un buffet qui, certainement, n'avait pas été fourni par l'administration. Pour le reste, le mobilier se composait de sièges dépareillés, d'une table à écrire, d'un lit de sangles. d'une cuvette et d'un pot à eau. Dans un coin, par terre, s'élevaient des piles de papiers. Le jour venait par une fenêtre carrée aux gros barreaux de fer. La cellule pouvait mesurer cinq pas sur six. Aux murs, pendaient quelques estampes de 1848 représentant des combats de barricades et une caricature de Napoléon III.

— Comment se fait-il qu'on vous autorise à garder ces gravures ? demanda Sophie.

— Je suis ici chez moi, répliqua fièrement Vavasseur. On a le droit de m'incarcérer, mais pas de m'arracher mes convictions !

— Décidément, l'empire français est plus tolérant que l'empire russe ! Au bagne de Pétrovsk, nous pouvions meubler nos cellules à notre guise, mais il eût fait beau voir que l'un de nous accrochât aux murs des images subversives ! Etes-vous astreints à des corvées ?

— Il ne manquerait plus que ça ! Notre statut est celui des prisonniers de guerre ! Pour le ménage, ce sont des auxiliaires, des prisonniers de droit commun, qui s'en chargent, moyennant quinze francs par mois.

— Et la nourriture ?

— Elle est convenable. Si nous ne voulons pas de l'ordinaire, nous pouvons manger à la cantine ou nous faire apporter des repas du restaurant.

— Mais votre correspondance est surveillée ?

— Je le suppose. En tout cas, on nous laisse écrire ce que bon nous semble et les lettres arrivent à destination.

— Chez nous, les cellules n'étaient bouclées que pour la nuit.

— Chez nous aussi. Le reste du temps, nous pouvons nous promener dans la prison, aller d'une cellule à l'autre, descendre dans la cour à n'importe quelle heure, organiser des réunions, recevoir des amis, donner des dîners de plusieurs personnes dans notre cellule...

— En somme, il ne vous manque que de pouvoir sortir !

— Nous le pouvons, de temps en temps, à condition d'être rentrés pour minuit.

278

Sophie hocha la tête d'un air entendu : le général Léparsky n'avait rien inventé.

— A quand la prochaine sortie ? demanda-t-elle.

— Dans un peu plus d'un mois, dit Louise vivement. On fera une petite fête à la maison !

Ses yeux brillaient d'un bonheur timide. Longtemps, Sophie et Vavasseur discutèrent de leurs expériences pénitentiaires respectives, comparant les geôles russes et françaises, appréciant ceci, critiquant cela, gravement, en connaisseurs. Puis pendant que Anne-Joseph disposait les assiettes et les verres sur la table, Sophie se leva pour lire les inscriptions taillées dans la pierre des murs. Parmi une confusion de noms et de dates, elle déchiffra quelques citations vengeresses : « Presque toujours, c'est par la loi qu'on persécute et qu'on tyrannise. — Lamennais. » « Meurs s'il le faut, mais dis la vérité ! — Marat. » « Parler sans agir est la forme la plus vile de la trahison... — Vavasseur. »

Elle se rassit en pensant : « Il n'a pas changé. » Et elle en éprouva une gêne, comme si elle se fût essoufflée à marcher aux côtés d'un homme plus jeune qu'elle.

— Comment avez-vous trouvé la France ? demanda-t-il soudain.

— Merveilleuse ! dit-elle, prise au dépourvu.

Il fronça les sourcils.

— Ça y est, tu recommences ! dit Louise. Ne peux-tu parler d'autre chose ? Regarde ce que Madame t'a apporté !

Sophie avait oublié les deux bouteilles de champagne. Elle les posa sur la table. Vavasseur empoigna l'une d'elles et se mit à la décapuchonner, en marmonnant :

— C'est bien aimable...

Puis il reprit :

— Ainsi, vous avez trouvé la France merveilleuse ?

— Par comparaison avec la Russie, oui, dit Sophie.

— Ce régime ?...

— Je ne peux pas le juger encore. Mais je suis obligée de constater qu'après avoir goûté de la république, la majorité des Français a voté le retour à l'autocratie. Pour quelqu'un qui met la volonté du peuple au-dessus de tout, il est difficile de négliger ce fait !

Le bouchon sauta au plafond ; la mousse déborda du goulot, les enfants battirent des mains ; Vavasseur inclina la bouteille au-dessus des verres.

— Je ne sais qui vous avez rencontré depuis votre arrivée ici, mais permettez-moi de vous dire qu'on vous a mal renseignée ! gronda-t-il. Le peuple a été dupé par un aventurier qui, tout en se proclamant fidèle au principe du suffrage universel, n'a jamais eu d'autre ambition que de gouverner seul. S'il a réussi son coup d'Etat du 2 décembre, c'est qu'il avait préalablement endormi les masses ouvrières par des promesses. Et puis, il avait l'armée pour lui. En un tournemain, tous les chefs de l'opposition ont été arrêtés, expulsés... Edgar Quinet, Victor Hugo, Dussoubs et j'en passe... On a déporté des hommes par centaines, à Cayenne, en Algérie... Journaux interdits, organisations secrètes démantelées, la police fourrant son nez partout ! La paix par le vide, la sagesse par la menace !...

— C'est terrible ! dit Sophie. Je n'ai pas su cela...

280

— Parce que vous n'avez pas frappé à la bonne porte en arrivant à Paris !

— S'il en est ainsi, le pouvoir impérial ne compte plus d'opposants !

— On ne peut faucher d'un seul coup toutes les têtes qui dépassent. La république a été pendant quatre ans le gouvernement légal du pays. Grâce à elle, des doctrines se sont propagées dans la masse, des espérances sont nées, que le despotisme, si brutal soit-il, ne parviendra plus à étouffer. La police nous traque, les mouchards sont partout. Mais, déjà, un mouvement se dessine parmi la jeunesse du Quartier latin, dans les ateliers, dans les usines et même dans certains salons !...

Il leva son verre.

— A la république ! dit-il.

— Tu en as donné trop aux enfants ! dit Louise.

— Un jour pareil, ça ne pourra pas leur faire de mal !

On trinqua, on but, et Vavasseur s'essuya la moustache. Ses yeux scintillaient d'une joie haineuse.

— Un de ces quatre matins, tout pétera ! dit-il.

Louise découpa la tarte. Sophie pensa que la France avait un visage bien différent suivant qu'on la regardait du salon de la princesse de Lieven ou d'un cachot de Sainte-Pélagie. Où était la vérité ? Entre les deux extrêmes, sans doute. L'humeur du pays n'était ni aussi claire que le prétendaient les partisans de l'empereur ni aussi sombre que l'affirmaient ceux de la république. Et pourtant, irrésistiblement, c'était à ces derniers qu'elle était tentée de donner raison. Elle écouta avec intérêt Vavasseur lui parler de certains professeurs de l'Université qui refusaient de prêter serment, des étudiants qui transportaient des brochures illégales publiées à l'étranger, des jeunes avocats qui organisaient entre eux des conférences politiques hebdomadaires...

Parfois, un prisonnier frappait à la porte, entrebâillait le battant, disait : « Oh ! pardon ! Tu es occupé ! » et s'en allait. Anne-Joseph, ayant fini sa tarte, recousait des boutons aux chemises de son père. Claude-Henri se balançait sur sa chaise au risque de la casser. Sa mère lui allongea une claque. Il se mit à pleurer. Elle le menaça de le donner au guichetier s'il n'était pas sage.

— Ça m'est égal ! dit-il.

Vavasseur l'envoya au coin, pour insolence. Puis il remplit les verres, une seconde fois. Le champagne l'attendrissait. Il passa un bras autour des épaules de sa femme.

— Ah ! ma petite Louise ! dit-il. Je t'en fais voir ! Mais avant trois ans, nom de Dieu, nous aurons gain de cause !...

— Depuis le temps que tu me répètes ça, murmura-t-elle.

— J'y pense, pour ma prochaine sortie, j'inviterai Proudhon à la maison ! Je veux que notre amie fasse sa connaissance ! Ça c'est un homme ! Un génie ! Un voyant ! Je me prosterne devant lui !...

Il vida son verre, clappa de la langue et rectifia :

— Je me prosterne devant lui, mais je ne suis pas toujours d'accord avec ses idées. Vous savez qu'il a passé un bon bout de temps à Sainte-Pélagie ? C'est même là qu'il s'est marié ! On l'a libéré l'année dernière. Depuis, il se tient coi !

Un souffle d'air tiède entra par la fenêtre, portant un parfum si capiteux, que Sophie demanda :

— Qu'est-ce que ça sent ?

— Nous sommes à deux pas du Jardin des Plantes, dit Louise. Dès qu'il fait chaud, l'air embaume !

— Une délicate attention de plus à notre égard ! s'écria Vavasseur. Et malgré ça, je ne suis pas content !...

— Je peux revenir du coin ? demanda Claude-Henri.

— Non, dit le père.

Des pas précipités retentirent dans l'escalier. Un chœur de voix fortes entonna *la Marseillaise*. Au loin, d'autres voix, moins nombreuses, répondirent par *O Richard, ô mon roi !* Les deux hymnes ennemis se mêlèrent en une cacophonie, coupée de hurlements. Vavasseur éclata de rire :

— Vous entendez ? Quel charivari ! C'est devenu une tradition ! Il y a encore quelques orléanistes à Sainte-Pélagie. Chaque soir, à la même heure, les républicains leur donnent l'aubade et ils répondent. A part ça, on s'aime bien, on se respecte, vu qu'on est tous des victimes de ce Robert-Macaire couronné !

— Que faites-vous toute la journée ? demanda Sophie.

— J'écris, j'écris pour mettre au point ma théorie de l'Etat, dit-il. Une grosse affaire ! Entre nous, je n'ai jamais aussi bien travaillé qu'en prison !

— Il est pourtant grand temps que tu en sortes ! dit Louise. Madame m'a promis qu'elle verrait, de son côté, si elle pouvait faire quelque chose pour toi...

— Je n'ai pas tellement de relations ! dit Sophie. Peut-être que, par la princesse de Lieven...

— Celle-là, ricana Vavasseur, c'est une drôle de citoyenne ! Elle ménage la chèvre et le chou. Une risette à l'empire, une à la république, une à la

France, une à la Russie... Tous ces Russes riches, séduisants, cultivés, me paraissent trop aimables pour être honnêtes. Ils sont à Paris par amour de la démocratie ou de l'art, mais tel conseiller de commerce en off ou en sky étudie avec soin nos usines, tel officier d'artillerie à la retraite examine nos fonderies par curiosité personnelle et, de là, va à Liège et à Seraing continuer ses investigations, telle femme du monde donne des réceptions pour faire bavarder nos ministres...

— Dites tout de suite que vous prenez tous les Russes de Paris pour des espions !

— Ce n'est pas pour rien que le tsar les laisse séjourner à l'étranger !

Sophie se domina. Elle ne comprenait plus pourquoi elle s'était emportée. N'avait-elle pas été agacée elle-même par quelques Russes trop francisés qu'elle avait rencontrés chez la princesse de Lieven ? En vérité, si elle était disposée à critiquer ces expatriés somptueux, elle ne tolérait pas qu'un autre le fît à sa place. Comme s'il y avait eu entre elle et eux des liens de famille qui l'autorisaient à les juger sévèrement tout en leur gardant sa sympathie, alors qu'un Vavasseur, qui les considérait d'un point de vue strictement français, ne pouvait émettre à leur égard que des avis entachés d'ignorance, de sottise et d'aigreur. Louise était consternée.

— Tu vois, Augustin, dit-elle, tu as fait de la peine à Madame ! Cette princesse aurait pu t'aider...

— Mais je ne demande pas mieux ! dit-il en riant. Même si Arsène Houssaye me proposait ses services pour me tirer de Sainte-Pélagie, je lui tendrais les deux mains !

Sophie rit à son tour.

284

— Je m'étonne, dit-elle, que vous attaquiez les Russes de France après avoir connu Herzen.

— C'est vrai, convint Vavasseur. Celui-là, c'est un pur, un frère. Mais citez m'en d'autres qui lui ressemblent ?

On rappela Claude-Henri de son coin. Une cloche sonna. Il était temps de partir. Les adieux des époux furent tendres.

— Tu n'as besoin de rien ? disait Louise. Je t'ai laissé de la tarte... La prochaine fois, je te rapporterai tes chaussettes raccommodées...

Il souleva son fils et sa fille, ensemble, dans ses bras, les embrassa, les reposa à terre, puissant, fatigué et doux — père de famille en même temps que lutteur politique.

En sortant de la prison, Sophie retrouva avec plaisir la lumière et l'animation du monde libre. Le crépuscule n'avait pas encore assombri les rues. Un soleil rouge brillait dans les plus hautes fenêtres des maisons. Le cocher bavardait avec un factionnaire nonchalant, adossé à sa guérite. Louise suggéra de rentrer à pied pour donner de l'exercice aux enfants. Cette proposition enchanta Sophie et elle renvoya Basile, qui partit, vexé, conduisant les chevaux du bout des doigts.

Les deux femmes prirent par les quais de la Seine. Anne-Joseph et Claude-Henri marchaient devant elles en se tenant par la main. A hauteur de Notre-Dame, Louise soupira.

— Que c'est beau ! Dire qu'il ne voit pas ça !

— Le voyait-il quand il était libre ? demanda Sophie.

L'enveloppe avait été timbrée en Prusse ; l'écriture de l'adresse était inconnue de Sophie ; elle fit sauter le cachet et trouva une lettre de Ferdinant Wolff. L'étonnement, la joie, la crainte l'attaquèrent avec une violence telle, que sa raison, un instant, vacilla. Que faisait-il en Allemagne ? Avait-il été libéré ? S'était-il enfui ? Mais non, la lettre portait en tête : « Tobolsk, le 23 mars 1853. » Des nouvelles vieilles d'à peine trois mois ! C'était inespéré. Elle se précipita dessus, comme une affamée :

« Chère grande amie,

« Je vous ai écrit plus de dix fois à Kachtanovka, mais, sans doute, aucune de mes lettres n'est-elle arrivée jusqu'à vous comme aucune des vôtres n'est arrivée jusqu'à vos amis. Si, pourtant : Marie Frantzeff, qui, en sa qualité de fille du procureur du gouvernement est, plus ou moins, à l'abri de la censure, a reçu le mot que vous lui avez envoyé quand vous avez décidé de quitter la

Russie. C'est ainsi que j'ai su votre future adresse à Paris. Convaincu que vous y êtes maintenant, je profite d'une occasion exceptionnelle : un jeune diplomate allemand, de passage à Tobolsk, veut bien se charger de vous faire parvenir ces quelques lignes, que j'écris en hâte. Le fait que vous soyez en France facilitera la correspondance entre nous. Vous pourrez me répondre à l'adresse ci-dessous, à Berlin, aux bons soins du Dr Gottfried August König. Comme vous devez être heureuse, chère Sophie, d'avoir retrouvé votre pays ! Vous l'aimez tant ! Vous en parliez si bien ! Je me rappelle encore ce que vous m'en disiez, lorsque nous visitions ensemble cette maison de Tobolsk, aujourd'hui transformée, grâce à vous, en dispensaire. Les minutes passées près de vous, dans ces pièces glacées, délabrées, sont parmi les plus belles de mon existence. Je reviens souvent à ces souvenirs pour reprendre courage et pour m'attrister tout à la fois. Egoïstement, je regrette que vous vous soyez davantage éloignée de moi en vous fixant à Paris. J'ai peur que la distance, le changement de vie, le brillant de la civilisation occidentale, ne vous fassent oublier vos amis de Sibérie. Dites-moi ce que vous devenez ! Décrivez-moi votre maison, vos meubles, vos robes, votre coiffure !... C'est très important pour un vieil ours dans mon genre ! Avec ces détails, je me fabriquerai des rêves délicieux pour les longs hivers sibériens ! Parlez-moi aussi de vos amis. Car vous en avez sûrement ! Et ils doivent être plus divertissants que les braves lourdauds de Tobolsk ! Voilà que je suis jaloux ! Ah ! les spectacles, les bals, les salons parisiens... Ici, tout est gris, monotone, provincial ; nos amis vieillissent paisiblement ; les jeunes se marient, se dispersent ; je travaille quatorze heures par jour et projette d'agrandir le dispensaire. Et, au milieu de tout cela, je pense constamment à vous... »

L'écriture, au bas de la page, devenait si serrée, que Sophie ne put déchiffrer la suite. Elle s'était acheté un face-à-main, la semaine dernière. Vite, elle le sortit d'un tiroir et le porta à ses yeux :

« Votre cher souvenir ne me quitte pas. Je vous parle chaque nuit en secret. Lorsque j'ai une décision à prendre, je vous demande votre avis, lorsque je suis content de la guérison d'un malade, je vous associe à mon bonheur, lorsque je suis fatigué (cela m'arrive souvent) je m'imagine que vous me grondez, et c'est très agréable... »

Les yeux de Sophie se voilèrent. Un émoi juvénile la pénétrait, qu'elle jugeait absurde sans pouvoir le combattre. Elle n'était plus seule dans l'existence. La conscience d'une amitié masculine lui redonnait le goût d'elle-même. A mille lieues de Ferdinand Wolff, elle s'épanouissait dans la chaleur de son admiration.

Quand elle sut chaque phrase de la lettre par cœur, elle songea à répondre. Son cœur débordait. Elle raconta à Ferdinand Wolff sa vie à Paris, ses achats, ses sorties, mais l'assura qu'elle n'en oubliait pas, pour autant, les êtres chers qu'elle avait laissés à Tobolsk. « Un jour, vous serez libéré, écrivit-elle. Alors, peut-être viendrez-vous ici. Je vous ferai connaître cette ville que j'aime, je vous présenterai à mes amis... » Elle se berça de ce rêve qu'elle savait irréalisable. Puis, après une courte hésitation, elle ajouta : « Vous voyez, moi aussi, je pense à vous constamment, parmi toutes les occupations qui me sollicitent sans me distraire. »

Un accès de pudeur l'empêcha d'en dire plus. Elle termina par une formule de politesse banale et signa : « Sophie Ozareff. »

Six pages ! Elle les relut, les glissa dans une première enveloppe au nom du Dr Wolff et enferma le tout dans une seconde enveloppe plus grande, adressée au Dr Gottfried August König. L'importance de l'envoi était telle, qu'elle décida de se rendre elle-même à la poste centrale de la rue Jean-Jacques Rousseau, pour être sûre que sa lettre serait bien affranchie et partirait pour Berlin dans les plus brefs délais.

En ressortant du bureau, elle rayonnait : le contact était rétabli entre elle et ses amis de Sibérie. Même si elle ne recevait qu'une lettre par an de Ferdinand Wolff, elle serait contente. Dans une âme habituée à la méditation, les sentiments n'ont pas besoin de beaucoup d'aliments matériels pour survivre. Marchant dans la rue, Sophie s'estimait plus riche que n'importe quelle jeune femme qui la croisait.

Elle était invitée à souper, ce jour-là, chez Mme Griboff. Ce fut en pensant à Ferdinand Wolff qu'elle choisit sa robe. A table, elle fut particulièrement brillante. Cependant, ce n'était pas pour les personnes présentes qu'elle souriait, plaisantait, ou laissait partir son regard dans le vide avec une expression mélancolique. A part un vieil abbé aux cheveux longs et elle-même, il n'y avait que des Russes parmi les convives. Mais tous ces Russes étaient convertis au catholicisme. Ils formaient, selon l'expression de la maîtresse de maison, « le petit troupeau ». Tandis que des valets en bas blancs servaient un chaud-froid de perdreau, Mme Griboff exposa un projet qui lui était venu en tête : la création à Paris d'un pensionnat pour les enfants russes, où ils pussent être élevés dans la connaissance de leur langue natale, le respect de leur lointaine patrie et l'attachement à l'Eglise romaine.

— Car il ne saurait être question pour nos fils et nos filles d'être moins russes en devenant catholiques ! précisa-t-elle.

Les autres convives approuvèrent cette affirmation avec bruit. Visiblement, ils avaient tous peur de passer pour des gens qui renient leurs origines. Séparés de leurs compatriotes par leur confession, ils ne s'en accrochaient qu'avec plus de ferveur au seul sentiment qu'ils eussent encore en commun avec eux, l'orgueil national, l'espoir d'un avenir glorieux pour leur pays. Sophie se pencha vers son voisin de gauche, M. Krestoff, ancien secrétaire d'ambassade, qui, sa carrière terminée, était resté à Paris, et demanda à mi-voix :

— De quel œil le tsar voit-il certains de ses sujets se détourner de la tradition orthodoxe ?

Au même instant, il se fit un silence autour d'elle. Ce qu'elle destinait à un seul, tous l'avaient entendu. Les visages se figèrent. Dans cette salle à manger parisienne, où le cuir rouge des sièges tranchait sur la verdure profonde des tapisseries, l'ombre de Nicolas Ier venait d'entrer, toute sanglée, toute bottée.

— Pourquoi le cacher ? dit M. Krestoff. Le tsar est furieux. Il nous considère presque comme des traîtres. Il refuse de comprendre que, placés dans l'alternative d'obéir à ses ordres ou à ceux de notre conscience nous n'ayons pas hésité !

La réponse toucha Sophie par sa franchise. Elle regardait ces gens graves, paisibles, un peu tristes, et comprenait leur drame.

— Mais il ne vous est pas interdit de retourner en Russie ? dit-elle.

— Non, pas précisément, répondit M. Krestoff. Cependant, si nous y allions. l'accueil serait probablement réservé, voire hostile...

— Et nous sommes si bien en France ! soupira une jeune femme enceinte au regard bleu ciel.

— Pourvu que ces satanés Turcs ne brouillent pas les relations entre nos deux pays ! dit M. Griboff.

Il avait une barbiche en forme de pinceau et huit cheveux noirs barraient sa calvitie.

L'abbé, qui avait eu, la veille, une entrevue avec un sénateur important calma tout le monde. La paix ne serait pas troublée à propos des affaires d'Orient. Bien que la flotte anglaise de Malte eût rejoint la flotte française dans le voisinage des Dardanelles et que les Russes fussent à quelques lieues des frontières de la Moldavie, sur la rive du Prut, jamais on n'avait été si près d'un règlement amiable.

— Il ne faut pas se laisser fasciner par la balançoire diplomatique, renchérit M. Krestoff. La baisse des fonds publics à la Bourse n'est pas autre chose qu'une manœuvre pour asphyxier les petits épargnants. Il paraît que certains ont été ruinés en dix minutes !

Sophie se félicita d'avoir suivi les avis de Me Pelé qui lui avait déconseillé de jouer à la Bourse. A coup sûr, elle eût tout perdu. Après le dessert, on passa au salon, pour prendre le café, à la française. Il y avait là des fleurs dans des vases sang de bœuf, des plaques de faïence incrustées dans le plafond, des trumeaux décorés par un émule maladroit de Boucher, des vitrines pleines de menus objets poussiéreux, des tentures de lampas, des tapis persans, le tout baignant dans la lumière jaune d'une dizaine de lampes à modérateur. Mme Griboff entraîna Sophie à l'écart, dans l'embrasure d'une fenêtre, afin de la questionner sur Youri Almazoff, dont elle ne devait guère se soucier, l'ayant à peine connu. Puis elle prit la tasse vide des mains de Sophie, la posa sur un guéridon et soupira :

— C'est une condition bien étrange que d'être russe de cœur, catholique de religion et de vivre en France sans pouvoir renoncer à la Russie ! Certains de nos compatriotes nous jugent sévèrement. J'espère que, vous, vous nous comprenez, Madame.

— Bien sûr ! dit Sophie avec effort. Y a-t-il longtemps que vous avez embrassé la foi catholique ?

— Neuf ans. Ce fut, pour mon mari et pour moi, un cas de conscience terrible. Mme Swetchine nous a aidés. Et le R.P. Gagarine aussi...

Tandis qu'elle parlait, Sophie observait, du coin de l'œil, le vieil abbé, qu'entourait un cercle d'ouailles déférentes. Mme Griboff surprit son regard et dit, soudain :

— Auriez-vous préféré voir un prêtre orthodoxe à ma table ?

Sophie tressaillit et murmura :

— Mais non ! Pourquoi ?

Et elle pensa qu'en effet elle eût été plus a l'aise si un pope barbu l'avait accueillie parmi ces Russes exilés.

5

A l'approche des vacances, une fièvre de soirées mondaines s'empara des Parisiens, comme si, avant de partir pour la campagne, le château familial ou la ville d'eau, chaque maîtresse de maison eût tenu à rendre au plus vite les invitations qu'elle avait acceptées dans l'année. Delphine de Charlaz organisa un grand *raout* chez elle, avec pianiste, cantatrice, diseur de poèmes et tombola de charité. Sophie donna, elle aussi, une réception. Elle attendait une cinquantaine de personnes ; elle en vit deux cents. Toutes étaient évidemment poussées par la curiosité de voir où habitait cette réchappée des bagnes tsaristes et comment elle traitait ses amis. De la première à la dernière minute, elle eut l'impression de subir un examen. Elle avait engagé des domestiques pour la journée et souffrait de constater que leur livrée était défraîchie. Il y avait de la presse autour du buffet : le punch et la glace n'allaient-ils pas manquer ? Dix fois, elle gourmanda des valets somnolents qui tardaient à repasser les sandwiches et les petits fours. Tout en

295

surveillant à la dérobée le déroulement du service, elle évoluait de groupe en groupe, feignait de se passionner pour des conversations décousues, lançait un compliment, en recevait un autre et souriait à s'en fatiguer les mâchoires. La princesse de Lieven, qui lui avait fait l'honneur de se déranger, la félicita sur le charme discret de son intérieur et resta l'une des dernières, ce qui était un signe de succès.

Après le départ de ses invités, Sophie inspecta philosophiquement son salon saccagé où des verres et des assiettes sales traînaient sur la cheminée, le rebord des fenêtres et les guéridons de marqueterie, rentra dans sa chambre et se mit à sa correspondance : Daria Philippovna, Marie Frantzeff, Pauline Annenkoff — en bavardant avec ses amis de Russie, elle quittait un vêtement d'emprunt et redevenait elle-même. Bien qu'elle n'eût aucune réponse de Ferdinand Wolff, elle lui écrivit de nouveau, à Berlin. Cette fois, elle osa dans la formule terminale, l'assurer de son « affectueux souvenir ». Longtemps, elle ne put s'endormir et se retourna dans son lit, oppressée, énervée, en songeant à l'audace de cet aveu.

Le lendemain, Delphine la surprit à sa toilette et lui affirma qu'il n'était question en ville que de la réception offerte par « la séduisante Mme Ozareff ». Sophie devina la flatterie mais s'y laissa prendre. A mesure qu'elle élargissait le cercle de ses relations, elle s'étonnait que ses compatriotes fussent aussi mal renseignés sur la Russie. Les mieux informés avaient lu le récit du voyage de Custine, croyaient que Moscou restait ensevelie sous les neiges neuf mois sur douze, et ne connaissaient Pouchkine que parce qu'il avait été tué, seize ans plus tôt, en duel, par un Français, le baron Georges de Heeckeren d'Anthès. Celui-ci se trouvait d'ailleurs maintenant à Paris, où son crédit politique fleurissait. Le brillant chevalier garde, qui avait privé la Russie de son plus grand poète, était devenu sénateur d'Empire. On proposa à Sophie de le lui présenter. Elle refusa, prenant d'instinct le parti des Russes dans cette querelle. En revanche, elle considéra comme un honneur d'approcher certains phénix artistiques, philosophiques, littéraires, dont tout le monde parlait dans son entourage. Chez Mme d'Agoult, elle rencontra Littré, qui était si laid et si savant, qu'elle n'osa échanger deux mots avec lui ; chez Mme Swetchine, petite vieille douceâtre, habillée de bure brune, coiffée de dentelle et parfumée à la violette, elle eut l'impression que la perfection morale de l'hôtesse incitait tous ses familiers à prendre des visages d'anges ; chez Jules Simon, elle écouta Hippolyte Carnot jurer la fermeté de ses convictions démocratiques. Vavasseur n'avait pas menti : l'espérance républicaine demeurait chevillée au cœur de certains, qui se souvenaient des beaux jours de 1848. Pourtant, cette constatation, qui aurait dû la réjouir, la laissait indifférente. Il lui semblait qu'un ressort s'était brisé en elle et qu'elle avait perdu la faculté de vibrer aux sollicitations de la politique. Elle retourna néanmoins chez la princesse de Lieven et lui parla du cas de Vavasseur. La princesse promit d'user de son influence auprès du comte de Morny pour hâter la libération du prisonnier. Par malchance, trois jours plus tard, le 5 juillet, la police découvrit un complot contre la vie de l'empereur. Tous les journaux mentionnèrent l'arrestation d'une douzaine de membres d'une société secrète, en plein Opéra-Comique, pendant une représentation

297

à laquelle assistaient les souverains. La princesse
de Lieven fit savoir à Sophie que le moment était
mal choisi pour intercéder en faveur de son protégé.

Delphine de Charlaz se préparait à partir pour
Vichy ; d'autres, parmi les relations de Sophie,
avaient jeté leur dévolu sur Trouville, sur Etretat,
sur Biarritz. Il semblait que le fait de rester à
Paris à l'époque de la canicule fût considéré par
tous comme un signe de mauvais ton. Brusquement, les beaux quartiers se vidèrent de leurs habitants et les provinciaux envahirent les rues. Les
théâtres affichèrent de grosses comédies ou des
drames larmoyants, à l'usage du public le plus
bas. Aux heures chaudes, des hommes s'alignaient
en file devant le guichet des bains Deligny, sur la
Seine. Le bal Mabille et le Château des Fleurs refusaient du monde. Au Théâtre impérial du Cirque, les lycéens et leurs parents s'instruisaient en
regardant une pièce à grand fracas sur les victoi-
res du Consulat et l'Empire. Le 15 août, pour la
fête de l'empereur, il y eut un défilé militaire, des
feux d'artifice, et Sophie, terrée dans son salon,
entendit longtemps la rumeur de la foule satisfaite. Ce Paris d'où tous les gens importants avaient
fui la reposait de l'autre.

Le samedi 20 août, l'empereur et l'impératrice
partirent pour Dieppe par train spécial et la capitale, écrasée de soleil, entra en léthargie. Sophie
se proposait d'aller prendre le frais au bois de Bou-
logne, en calèche, quand Mme Vavasseur se fit
annoncer : après quelques ajournements dus à la
malveillance de l'administration pénitentiaire, son
mari venait enfin d'obtenir une permission de minuit pour le lendemain dimanche. Ses amis avaient
improvisé une petite fête en son honneur, à la librairie de la rue Jacob. Sophie promit de s'y ren-

dre et offrit d'apporter des plats préparés et des boissons. Mais Louise affirma, du haut de sa dignité ménagère, qu'elle n'avait besoin de rien.

En effet, quand Sophie pénétra, le jour suivant, dans la boutique, elle trouva le comptoir recouvert d'une nappe et garni de viandes froides, de salades diverses et de bouteilles de vin. Une trentaine de personnes se pressaient dans cet espace réduit. Peu de femmes — quatre ou cinq au plus ; les hommes étaient, dans l'ensemble, pauvrement vêtus, portaient la barbe et avaient le verbe sonore. Au milieu de ce tohu-bohu, trônait Augustin Vasseur, en manches de chemise, la face luisante de transpiration, une gaieté insensée dans les yeux. Dès qu'il se fut emparé de Sophie, elle n'eut plus rien à dire. Elevant la voix pour être entendu de tous, il raconta ce qu'elle avait fait en France d'abord, en Russie ensuite, pour la cause de la république. A l'en croire, c'était elle qui avait transplanté l'idée de liberté à Saint-Pétersbourg ; le mouvement décembriste était son œuvre ; et, même au bagne, elle n'avait cessé de prêcher la lutte contre le tsar. Les jeunes, autour d'elle, la regardaient comme si elle eût été un personnage historique, la grand-mère de la révolution. Elle eut beau protester contre l'exagération de ces éloges, la légende était lancée. Alors que, dans le salon de la princesse de Lieven, on l'admirait pour son dévouement conjugal, ici c'était son dévouement politique qui était porté aux nues. Dans un cas comme dans l'autre, les gens se trompaient sur elle. Cette réputation usurpée lui était intolérable. Après en avoir ri, elle souhaitait rentrer dans un trou. Mais on l'interrogeait maintenant, on écoutait ses moindres propos avec une déférence absurde. Que pensait-elle de l'avenir du tsarisme ?

Croyait-elle que la France évoluerait, sans à-coups, vers un régime démocratique ? Elle avait envie de dire qu'elle n'en savait pas plus que ses questionneurs et que, du reste, elle était fatiguée, depuis longtemps, du vain bourdonnement des parlotes politiques. Mais elle ne voulait pas blesser les amis de Vavasseur, qui étaient tous des socialistes sincères. En vérité, leurs convictions ressemblaient fort à celles des jeunes gens du complot de Pétrachevsky. Pour les uns comme pour les autres, la grande idée n'était plus le libéralisme né de la Révolution française, mais une association populaire en vue de partager les dons de la nature. Leur soif d'égalité et de justice, leur mépris pour les distinctions qui ne venaient pas du mérite, les conduisaient tout droit au rêve d'une société uniforme, où personne ne posséderait rien et où chacun bénéficierait du travail de tous. La lutte contre le despotisme, qu'avaient menée leurs devanciers, devenait pour eux une lutte contre la propriété. Ils se réclamaient de Herzen, de Fourier, de Proudhon et d'un certain Karl Marx, dont Sophie n'avait jamais entendu parler. Comme ils s'échauffaient en discutant, Sophie demanda à Vavasseur s'il ne craignait pas que le concierge, qui certainement était aux écoutes, les dénonçât. Il répondit fièrement que ce qui se disait chez lui, entre quatre murs, ne pouvait lui être imputé à crime. Elle admira que, tout en dénigrant le régime, il fit confiance à la police au point de se croire protégé par la règle du jeu.

Louise passait entre les invités et les priait de se servir. Comme il n'y avait pas assez de sièges pour tout le monde, beaucoup mangeaient et buvaient debout, adossés aux rayons pleins de livres. Les lampes à pétrole fumaient dans une atmosphère méphitique. Un faible courant d'air entrait par l'imposte en demi-lune ouverte sur la rue. Incommodée par la chaleur, Sophie s'assit près du comptoir, déplia son éventail et l'agita devant son visage. Une colonnade de pantalons l'entourait. Soudain, au milieu des voix, retentirent quatre coups secs, frappés à la porte.

— C'est lui ! cria Vavasseur avec joie.

Il tira la targette, ouvrit le battant et fit entrer un homme massif et souriant. Le nouveau venu portait une redingote verte. Il ôta son chapeau et serra les mains qui se tendaient vers lui. Son grand front d'ivoire surplombait de petits yeux myopes, déformés par des besicles ; un épais nuage de barbe entourait son menton ; il ressemblait à un rude instituteur de campagne. Vavasseur le conduisit vers Sophie et annonça d'un ton superbe :

— Je vous présente Proudhon ! Vous savez qui il est, je veux qu'il sache qui vous êtes !

Et il recommença, à l'intention de Proudhon, le panégyrique de celle qui, disait-il, avait été l'égérie des décembristes. Elle dut le prier de se taire, tant il l'agaçait par son emphase. Les autres invités, cependant, avaient formé un cercle autour d'eux. Pour changer de conversation, Sophie demanda à Proudhon ce qu'il était en train d'écrire.

— Bien des choses ! dit-il. Une histoire de la démocratie, des notes pour une étude sur Napoléon...

Il avait l'air ennuyé, distrait. Un jeune énergumène chevelu l'ayant questionné, avec un rien d'insolence, sur ses « nouveaux rapports avec le pouvoir », il marmonna :

— Je n'ai pas à me plaindre... On me laisse tranquille...

— Et pour cause ! Vous avez fait, dit-on, soumission au régime !

— Vous êtes mal renseigné, jeune homme ! gronda Proudhon. C'est précisément parce que je n'ai aucune estime pour Louis-Napoléon que je ne veux pas le combattre ouvertement. Par son incapacité, il servira mieux nos desseins que nous ne saurions le faire par notre talent. En essayant de le renverser avant que l'opinion publique entière ne l'ait pris en exécration, nous le transformerions en martyr et l'autorité de son successeur sur le pays serait renforcée. Au contraire, en le laissant se compromettre de mensonge en mensonge, trébucher d'erreur en erreur, nous gagnerons à coup sûr !

— Ainsi, d'après-vous, il est absurde de vouloir rester en prison, en exil, par fidélité à l'idéal démocratique ? demanda un autre adolescent dressé sur ses ergots.

— Parfaitement ! Tous ceux qui refusent l'amnistie sont des sots ! Je n'ai pas hésité une seconde, moi, à profiter de la liberté qui m'était offerte ! Je me conduis bien en apparence. Je publie avec l'autorisation du gouvernement. J'attends l'heure où le misérable mannequin poussé sur la scène par le coup d'Etat du 2 décembre s'écroulera de lui-même...

— C'est une notion bien bourgeoise de la révolution !

— Et puis après ? Je veux, en effet, concilier la bourgeoisie et le prolétariat, le salaire et le capital, dans un communisme sans haine. Je veux faire rentrer dans la société, par une combinaison économique, les richesses qui en sont sorties par une autre combinaison économique. Je veux brûler la propriété à petit feu, par crainte de lui redonner une certaine valeur mystique en organisant une Saint-Barthélemy des propriétaires !

Ces paroles modérées jetèrent la consternation dans l'auditoire.

— Libre à vous de croire que l'empire s'achèvera dans la lassitude et la pourriture, dit Vavasseur. Mais moi, je ne peux plus attendre. De génération en génération, des théoriciens prudents remettent à plus tard l'instant de l'action décisive. Il me semble que si quelques hommes courageux s'unissaient pour culbuter le régime...

Proudhon haussa ses lourdes épaules :

— Je ne serai pas des vôtres dans cette entreprise. La violence politique est une notion périmée. Le socialisme a besoin d'économistes et non de bouchers !

— Si l'empereur vous appelait demain en consultation, vous iriez donc le voir ?

— Sans doute ! Et, comme il se prétend féru de progrès social, je l'encouragerais à améliorer par mille mesures généreuses le sort des petites gens, je ferais en sorte qu'il prît à sa charge un chapitre de notre programme et se brouillât ainsi avec les vieux partis, bref je me servirais de lui pour préparer l'avènement de la démocratie !

— Je vous admire, dit Vavasseur. Moi, si j'étais appelé demain en consultation par Napoléon III, j'irais peut-être, mais je dissimulerais une bombe sous les pans de ma redingote !

Il y eut un éclat de rire unanime, qui désarma les esprits tendus jusqu'au malaise. Puis quelqu'un fit allusion aux risques de guerre et Vavasseur déclara :

— Ce serait éminemment souhaitable !

— Comment pouvez-vous dire cela ? s'écria Sophie indignée.

— Mais voyons, chère amie, réfléchissez ! rétorqua Vavasseur. La guerre constituerait une épreuve fatale pour Napoléon III. Ayant envoyé ses troupes au diable, du côté de la Turquie, il n'aurait plus grand monde pour le protéger en cas de soulèvement populaire ! Tout vrai révolutionnaire doit espérer qu'on s'étripera ferme en Orient ! Malheureusement, les diplomates sont en train d'arranger les choses. La France met de l'eau dans son vin et la Russie dans sa vodka. Pour occuper nos généraux, on se bornera à poursuivre la pacification de l'Algérie. Les braves Kabyles continueront à se faire massacrer pour la gloire de Mac-Mahon et le public, en lisant les journaux, se persuadera de la force invincible de l'empire !

L'ironie amère de Vavasseur indisposait Sophie. Etait-ce un effet de l'âge ? — elle avait l'impression qu'aucune idée politique ne méritait une effusion de sang. Autrefois, le choix des moyens l'embarrassait peu, lorsque la fin lui semblait juste. Aujourd'hui, elle était comme malade de tendresse envers le genre humain. Proudhon, avec son solide bon sens, était-il le seul ici à pouvoir la comprendre ? Il s'était tu, pensif, mécontent, retiré dans sa barbe. Vavasseur et ses amis parlaient maintenant des proscrits de Londres. Ensuite, on en vint à échanger des histoires drôles sur Sainte-Pélagie. La porte conduisant à l'arrière-boutique s'entrebâilla et des têtes d'enfants s'étagèrent dans l'ouverture. Les prunelles écarquillées, ils suivaient le jeu incompréhensible des grandes personnes. Louise les renvoya dans leur domaine avec une tranche de brioche pour chacun. Peu après, Proudhon dit que sa femme était souffrante, qu'il lui avait promis de rentrer tôt et s'en alla, les épaules rondes.

Dès qu'il eut refermé la porte, le ton monta, comme dans une classe après le départ du surveil-

304

lant. Manifestement, cet homme intelligent et fort gênait les autres dans leur désir de folie révolutionnaire. Certains se mirent à discuter des chances d'un attentat contre Napoléon III. Sophie observa Vavasseur qui jubilait, une lumière d'explosion dans les yeux. Sans doute était-il de ces éternels révoltés pour qui tout régime politique est insupportable. Si demain la France était conforme à ce qu'il désirait aujourd'hui, il trouverait un prétexte pour passer de nouveau dans l'opposition. Il n'était heureux que dans le dénigrement, le complot, la haine. Au milieu de ces menaces de mort, Louise, souriante, allait, venait, proposait des sucreries. Sophie voulut prendre congé à son tour : elle manquait d'air. Louise la supplia de patienter quelques minutes encore : la permission d'Augustin expirait à minuit. On le raccompagnerait tous ensemble à la prison... Elle était si touchante dans son effort de persuasion, que Sophie se laissa convaincre.

Il ne restait plus que huit personnes dans le magasin, quand Vavasseur, ayant lorgné sa montre, annonça :

— Il est temps que je parte, mes amis ! J'ai donné ma parole !

Louise éteignit les lampes et le petit groupe se retrouva dans la rue. Augustin et sa femme montèrent dans la calèche de Sophie, les autres invités se répartirent dans deux fiacres, et la caravane s'ébranla au trot. Les sabots des chevaux secouaient des morceaux de ville endormie. Toutes les fenêtres étaient éteintes, mais, de loin en loin, brillait une pâle lanterne. Les ombres des voitures se traînaient, en se déformant, sur les murs couleur de lune. Parfois, se lisait une inscription au charbon : « Vive Barbès ! » ou « A bas Bonaparte ! » On mit pied à terre au coin de la rue de la Clef. Vingt-cinq minutes de retard. Ce n'était pas grave. Un factionnaire dormait debout dans sa guérite. Vavasseur embrassa sa femme, serra les mains de Sophie, tapota l'épaule de ses amis et soupira :

— Vous qui entrez ici, laissez toute espérance !

On le réconforta :

— Allons ! Courage ! Tu n'en as plus pour longtemps !

— Quand tu seras sorti du trou, nous entreprendrons de grandes choses !

— Es-tu sûr que tu n'as rien oublié ? demanda Louise.

Il se ragaillardit, frappa du marteau contre la porte et croisa les bras sur sa poitrine, dans la pose d'un homme qui attend avec sérénité la venue du bourreau. Le judas s'ouvrit. Une voix rogue demanda :

— Qu'est-ce que vous voulez ?

— Je rentre, dit Vavasseur.

— Votre nom ?

— Vavasseur, Augustin-Jean-Marie.

— Attendez une seconde.

Le guichetier s'éloigna. Sans doute allait-il consulter son registre.

— Pour un peu, il refuserait de me recevoir ! dit Vavasseur furieux.

Deux minutes passèrent. Dans la maison d'en face, une fenêtre s'ouvrit, au second étage, quelqu'un vida une cuvette sur le pavé. Le guichetier revint et dit :

— C'est d'accord.

La porte tourna sur ses gonds. Vavasseur franchit le seuil, tête haute.

6

La poste russe avait des fantaisies inexplicables : après des mois de silence, Sophie reçut tout à coup une lettre de Vassia Volkoff. Il s'excusait de lui répondre à la place de sa mère, qui était au lit avec une jaunisse :

« ... Sans doute aimeriez-vous avoir des nouvelles de Kachtanovka ? Eh bien ! votre neveu est devenu tout à fait étrange : plus question de mariage entre lui et la fille du gouverneur. La petite l'a échappé belle ! J'ai d'ailleurs l'impression qu'il n'épousera jamais personne. Son domaine lui tient lieu de femme. L'idée de son pouvoir sur sa terre et sur ceux qui l'habitent le grise. Cela tourne à la mégalomanie. Me croirez-vous si je vous dis qu'il a fait peindre toutes les maisons des paysans en blanc cru, avec un numéro noir sur le côté, que les serfs de chaque village portent des chemises de couleur différente (bleues pour Chatkovo, vertes pour Bolotnoïé, etc.), qu'ils se rendent au travail au son du tambour, sous les ordres de quelques « conducteurs » armés de gourdins, bref que la propriété entière prend l'allure d'un champ de manœuvres, avec des hameaux pour casernes et des moujiks pour soldats ? Tout cela serait simplement comique, si tant de malheureux n'étaient victimes de cette lubie ! Notez qu'ils ne s'en plaignent pas : ils sont bien nourris, bien logés, assurés de ne manquer de rien dans l'avenir... Je disais hier à ma mère combien j'étais heureux que vous n'ayez pas assisté à cette enrégimentation de vos serfs. Impuissante à vous y opposer, vous en seriez tombée malade... Je rêve de votre vie à Paris, capitale de l'esprit et de l'élégance. Vous ne devez pas avoir une minute à vous... Ici, l'existence est monotone, comme un de ces larges fleuves russes que vous connaissez. Ma journée est un long bâillement. Même lire ne m'intéresse plus. J'échange, entre le matin et le soir, quatre phrases banales avec ma mère, je mange trop, je bois sans soif... Il y a eu, avant hier, un gros orage... Notre jument noire est morte en mettant bas... La dernière récolte de pommes de terre a été excellente... »

Sophie lisait et changeait de monde. Peu à peu, elle était reprise par ses préoccupations d'autrefois : le sort des moujiks, la moisson, les menaces de grêle... C'était comme si, sur le point de s'acclimater en France, elle eût respiré une bouffée d'air russe. Elle en voulut soudain à ce pays lointain de ne pas mieux se laisser oublier. Qu'avait-elle à voir encore avec les gens de Kachtanovka ? Serge, Antipe, David le cocher, Zoé la femme de chambre, Daria Philippovna, Vassia. Des ombres ! Elle posa son face-à-main et referma la lettre dans ses plis. Son trouble augmentait. La joie qu'elle avait d'abord éprouvée se muait en une mélancolie stérile. Au lieu de sortir se promener, comme elle en avait formé le projet, elle resta chez elle, resassant des souvenirs, ouvrant des tiroirs et classant des feuillets jaunis. Quel étrange résidu de factures, d'attestations administratives, de passeports, de programmes de théâtre, de lettres oubliées laissait derrière elle une existence humaine ! Serge ne lui avait pas écrit une seule fois depuis qu'elle avait quitté la Russie, mais ses envois d'argent tombaient avec une régularité irréprochable. Elle n'avait pas, non plus, de nouvelle lettre de Sibérie. Que le courrier des décembristes fût intercepté par la censure n'aurait pas dû empêcher Marie Frantzeff, protégée par les hautes fonctions de son père, de correspondre avec la France. Comment vivait Ferdinand Wolff ? Sophie l'évoqua dans sa petite chambre, parlant à un malade, rédigeant une ordonnance. Un bonheur aigu la pénétra. Elle se sentit aimée, à distance, pour toujours. Jusqu'au soir elle demeura ainsi, rangeant des documents inutiles. A neuf heures, lasse de tout ce passé remué à la fourche, elle soupa, frileusement, devant le feu allumé dans la cheminée.

Le mois de septembre était humide et froid. Déjà, de nombreux Parisiens rentraient de vacances. Delphine débarqua, régénérée par les eaux de Vichy, et voulut immédiatement reprendre la vie mondaine. Sophie l'accompagna à un bal masqué, donné par un riche armateur, à la Porte Saint-Martin, après le spectacle. On dansait sur la scène, au son d'un orchestre dont les musiciens étaient costumés en pompiers. Entre les panneaux de toile peinte représentant un jardin à la française, s'agitaient des mousquetaires, des geishas, des mignons, des grognards, des sylphides, des colombines, des marquises et des gladiateurs. Sophie, assise dans une loge, s'amusait de ce remue-ménage. Beaucoup parmi les invitées lui paraissaient jolies, les yeux scintillant dans les trous du masque, la gorge ronde, provocante, le pied leste. L'âge venant, elle était de plus en plus sensible à la beauté des femmes. La fraîcheur d'un visage, la grâce d'un mouvement, excitaient sa sympathie. Tout être qui débutait dans l'existence l'attirait irrésistiblement et appelait son soutien. Jusqu'aux premières lueurs de l'aube, elle ne sentit pas sa fatigue. Quand elle quitta la salle avec Delphine, les boutiquiers ôtaient les volets de bois de leurs magasins ; des ménagères en papillottes descendaient dans la rue ; aux portes des restaurants, les enleveurs d'ordures chargeaient les écailles d'huîtres dans des tombereaux ; une clarté rose montait dans le ciel et coulait sur les toits, entre les créneaux noirs des cheminées. La calèche roulait à vive allure dans ce Paris somnolent et mal lavé. Sophie songeait à son lit, avec délices. Elle se croyait exténuée pour la semaine, mais, le lendemain, elle se rendit, d'un bon pied, au Gymnase pour voir *le Pressoir*, une pièce paysanne de George Sand, et, le surlendemain, au Théâtre Français, où une comédie-ballet de Molière, *le Mariage Forcé*, l'enchanta par la légèreté du texte et l'aisance des acteurs. Au foyer, les habitués parlaient avec dépit du récent départ de Mlle Rachel, que le tsar avait engagée au Théâtre impérial de Saint-Pétersbourg pour une centaine de représentations. On chuchotait qu'elle toucherait quatre cent mille francs sur la cassette particulière de l'empereur. De ces rumeurs, Sophie ne retenait qu'une chose : si le tsar appelait Mlle Rachel en Russie, c'était que la guerre n'était pas pour demain. Pourtant, après une période d'accalmie, les journaux se remplissaient de nouvelles alarmantes. La Turquie raidissait son attitude. La conférence d'Olmütz entre le tsar et ses alliés prussiens et autrichiens n'avait rien donné. Seul un miracle pouvait détourner l'orage. Tel n'était pas, cependant, l'avis du comte Kisseleff, chargé d'affaires de Russie à Paris, que Sophie approcha un soir, chez la princesse de Lieven. Il affichait un optimisme béat. A peine rassurée par les propos de ce haut personnage, Sophie lut, dans le *Journal des Débats,* que les hostilités entre Russes et Turcs avaient commencé.

Au début du mois de novembre, les gazettes publièrent la proclamation de Nicolas Ier, répondant à la déclaration de guerre de la Turquie : il demandait au Très-Haut de bénir ses armes dans « la sainte et juste cause » que ses « pieux ancêtres » avaient toujours défendue. Malgré cette profession de foi, les Russes de Paris se raccrochaient à l'espoir que rien ne troublerait les rapports de leur patrie avec la France. « Les motifs de cette guerre sont trop ridicules pour être soutenus par des pays civilisés, disait la princesse de Lieven. De quoi s'agit-il, au fait ? De la plus ou moins grande protection à accorder par le tsar à quelques prêtres dont la religion n'est ni celle de la France ni celle de l'Angleterre ! Et, pour cette question qui ne les concerne en rien, l'Angleterre et la France iraient verser leur sang ?... » Des commentateurs plus sérieux faisaient observer que, si la France n'était pas directement intéressée dans cette affaire, l'Angleterre, elle, enviait les progrès du commerce moscovite et la pénétration toujours plus accentuée des Russes dans la région danubienne, dans l'Asie Centrale et dans l'Extrême-Orient. Sophie qui, naguère, lisait peu les journaux, les achetait tous maintenant et s'énervait de leurs nouvelles contradictoires. Au cours d'un engagement à Oltenitza, sur le Danube, les Russes du prince Gortchakoff avaient, disait-on, subi une sanglante défaite devant les Turcs d'Omer-Pacha ; en revanche, le 30 novembre, l'amiral Nakhimoff, à la tête de six vaisseaux de ligne, avait forcé l'entrée de la rade de Sinope et détruit en une heure une puissante escadre ottomane. Ces premières actions, menées de part et d'autre avec fureur, laissaient présager que la guerre serait longue et meurtrière. Déjà, insensiblement, l'opinion publique, à Paris, se déclarait hostile à la Russie. Dans les milieux bien pensants, on estimait que l'attitude de la France dans l'affaire des Lieux Saints était inspirée par une haute pensée religieuse. Victor Hugo, dont le livre *Les Châtiments* passait clandestinement la frontière traitait Nicolas Ier de « tyran », de « vampire » et plaignait le peuple russe asservi à sa volonté.

Il faisait très froid. Sophie était dépaysée par cet hiver grisâtre. Ce serait la première fois, depuis une trentaine d'années, qu'elle ne verrait pas de neige pour Noël et la Saint-Sylvestre. Il lui semblait que les fêtes y perdraient de leur poésie. Elle s'était si bien habituée à la coutume nordique des sapins décorés de jouets et de bougies, qu'elle regrettait l'indifférence des Parisiens à cet égard. Ici, on ne pensait qu'à la messe de minuit, aux étrennes et aux bals. Dans les quartiers élégants, les étalages des magasins rivalisaient de richesses. Les gens s'abordaient avec des mines réjouies. Mais où était le mystère léger — mi-chrétien, mi-païen — fait de gel, de légende et d'intimité familiale, des Noël de là-bas ? Souvent, au cours de ses sorties en ville, elle levait les yeux vers les fenêtres et s'attristait de ne pas apercevoir, derrière le voile des rideaux, la silhouette sombre et conique de l'arbre dont rêvaient tous les enfants de Russie. A Kachtanovka, songeait-elle, la nais-

312

sance dù Christ ne serait célébrée que douze jours plus tard, à cause du décalage entre les calendriers grégorien et julien. En ce moment, dans toutes les villes et dans tous les villages orthodoxes, les ménagères préparaient des provisions maigres pour la dernière semaine du carême. Elle accompagna Delphine à la messe de minuit, mais refusa de réveillonner avec elle et resta le jour de Noël, seule, à la maison, entourée de livres.

Le lendemain, elle était encore au lit, lorsque Valentine lui apporta, sur un plateau, sa collation du matin et son courrier. L'une des lettres était timbrée de Tobolsk. Sophie la décacheta avec des mains tremblantes. Pouvait-elle espérer un meilleur cadeau de fin d'année ?

C'était Marie Frantzeff qui lui écrivait. Elle parcourut le début, puis son regard, comme attiré par un accident de terrain, se posa sur une ligne au milieu de la page : « Notre cher Dr Wolff... » Plus loin, le mot : « mort ». Un choc ébranla le cerveau de Sophie. Il ne pouvait y avoir de rapport entre ces deux membres de phrase. L'angoisse au cœur, elle revint en arrière et lut : « Notre cher Dr Wolff, qui a fait tant de bien autour de lui, est mort le 14 mai dernier. Une fièvre cérébrale a eu raison de son organisme miné par la fatigue. Il travaillait trop ; il ne se réservait pas une heure de repos dans la journée ; pour nous tous, cette perte a été horrible... » Sophie renversa la tête sur l'oreiller et, pendant quelques secondes, il lui sembla qu'elle baignait dans un grand espace désert, lugubre et solennel. Tout son corps était comme rompu par une catastrophe. Une amertume lui vint dans la gorge. Des larmes piquèrent ses yeux. Elle haletait, elle tremblait, elle se mordait les lèvres jusqu'au sang. Soudain, elle se précipita

313

vers son secrétaire, ouvrit un tiroir, y prit la lettre de Ferdinand Wolff et la considéra d'un air égaré, à travers son face-à-main. Quand elle l'avait reçue, au mois de juin, il était déjà mort. C'était à un mort qu'elle avait répondu, avec allégresse, avec espoir, avec coquetterie ! A un mort qu'elle avait adressé l'aveu déguisé de sa tendresse ! A un mort qu'elle avait écrit, dernièrement encore, pour raconter ses visites, ses projets ! « Pauvre ! Pauvre ! se disait-elle. Comme c'est bête ! Si j'étais restée près de lui, si j'avais veillé sur sa santé, peut-être vivrait-il aujourd'hui ? » Elle l'imaginait, râlant, seul, sur son petit lit de fer, dans la chambre mal éclairée. L'avait-il appelée dans son délire ? Elle eût voulu connaître sa dernière pensée. Puis elle se résigna : à quoi bon ? Des souvenirs décousus flottaient dans sa mémoire : une attitude familière de Ferdinand Wolff, la tête penchée sur l'épaule, la calotte de velours repoussée sur la nuque, son sourire sceptique, ses mains fines rongées par les acides... Lentement, le visage du médecin se déformait, rajeunissait, devenait celui de Nicolas. Et cette métamorphose n'étonnait pas Sophie. « Ferdinand Wolff, c'est Nicolas », pensa-t-elle avec l'impression de réfléchir très vite et de n'être pas tout à fait dans son état normal. De deuil en deuil, la surface sensible de son âme se rétrécissait. Bientôt, il ne lui resterait même plus assez de conscience pour souffrir.

Elle passa toute la matinée au lit, engourdie, stupéfaite. A midi, Valentine l'aida à s'habiller. Elle déjeuna machinalement, sur une petite table, dans le salon. La pluie ruisselait sur les vitres. Il n'y avait pas de neige, il n'y en aurait plus jamais. Elle but trois tasses de café, très noir. Son regard s'arrêta sur les flammes qui dansaient dans la cheminée. Il se déroulait là d'extraordinaires histoires de chevalerie dont les personnages étaient des étincelles et les décors des châteaux d'or, de pourpre et de charbon fumant. Au milieu de sa rêverie, Justin entra et dit :

— M. Vavasseur fait demander à Madame si elle peut le recevoir.

Sophie eut un mouvement de contrariété. Elle eût aimé rester seule avec sa peine. Mais sans doute Augustin avait-il obtenu quelques heures de permission pour les fêtes. Elle ne pouvait refuser de le voir.

— Faites entrer, dit-elle avec ennui.

Et elle se composa un visage.

Du seuil, Vavasseur cria :

— Ça y est ! Je suis libre ! Un cadeau de l'empereur pour le nouvel an des prisonniers méritants !

Sa vieille face craquait de joie sous sa tignasse hirsute et grise.

— C'est magnifique ! dit Sophie avec un faux entrain. Nos démarches à tous n'auront donc pas été inutiles. Quand vous a-t-on relâché ?

— Ce matin. Et, vous voyez, ma première visite a été pour vous !

— Je suis très touchée ! J'imagine avec quel bonheur vous avez retrouvé votre femme, vos enfants ! Maintenant, il s'agit de vous faire oublier !

Vavasseur fronça les sourcils et dit, du coin de la bouche :

— Il s'agit surtout de préparer l'avenir. Je suis là pour vous parler affaires. Vous savez que nos amis sont prêts à l'action !

— Quels amis ? Quelle action ? dit-elle avec brusquerie.

Il s'assit près de la cheminée et tendit les mains vers les flammes. La pointe de son nez, son menton, sa lèvre supérieure, éclairés par en dessous, avaient le brillant du cuivre. Il remuait les doigts, doucement, dans la chaleur du foyer.

— Le moment est venu de jeter bas ce César de Carnaval ! dit-il. Une organisation est en train de se créer, qui groupera les républicains sincères. J'ai tout de suite pensé à vous pour en faire partie...

Elle soupira :

— Je suis fatiguée, Vavasseur. N'avez-vous pas entendu ce que vous a dit Proudhon ? Il est préférable de laisser les événements suivre leur cours et la situation de dégrader d'elle-même...

Il bondit sur ses jambes et se mit à marcher de long en large, d'un pas sec de héron. Son regard balayait la pièce avec une violence exterminatrice.

— Les conceptions de Proudhon sont dépassées, dit-il. C'est un apôtre, non un technicien. Abandonné à lui-même, il tournerait en rond dans un cercle d'axiomes admirables. Les vrais ouvriers de la révolution ne sont pas ceux qui rêvent, mais ceux qui risquent leur peau dans des entreprises aussi peu idéales que possible. Vos décembristes n'ont pas hésité à prendre les armes. Pourquoi serions-nous moins courageux que les Russes ? Seulement nous ne commettrons pas l'erreur de débuter par une sédition militaire. Avant de s'attaquer à l'empire, il faut supprimer l'empereur. C'est facile. On peut le tuer à l'Hippodrome, lancer une bombe sur lui à l'Opéra, faire sauter son train pendant un voyage officiel. J'ai des amis chimistes qui sont très capables de confectionner une machine infernale !...

Elle l'écouta d'abord avec étonnement, puis une

316

colère la secoua devant tant de fanatisme. Tuer, toujours tuer, soulever des foules aveugles, renverser un pouvoir pour le remplacer par un autre qui, à l'usage, ne vaudrait guère mieux... Elle en avait assez de ce jeu absurde et sanglant, où les meilleurs des hommes usaient leur intelligence ! D'ailleurs, que lui parlait-on de politique, alors qu'elle venait d'apprendre la disparition de son seul ami ? Cette mort lui en rappelait d'autres, dont elle ne guérirait jamais. Du haut de sa tristesse, elle voyait Vavasseur comme un affreux pantin, ridicule et malfaisant. Tout ce qu'il disait était mesquin, stupide, en comparaison des deuils qui la frappaient sans cesse. Quand donc comprendrait-il que ce qu'il y avait d'important dans la vie ce n'était pas Napoléon III ou Nicolas Ier mais des gens dont l'Histoire ne retiendrait pas le nom, des gens simples, honnêtes, admirables, qui s'appelaient Ferdinand Wolff, Nicolas Ozareff, Nikita ? Elle s'entendit prononcer d'une voix calme :

— Vavasseur, vos histoires ne m'intéressent plus.

Il fit un écart et la regarda sévèrement :

— Pardon ?... Que voulez-vous dire ?...

— J'ai passé l'âge des complots, des batailles !...

— Ah ! non s'écria-t-il. Vous n'avez pas le droit de refuser ! Pas vous ! Tous ceux qui, en Russie, sont morts pour la même cause vous poussent dans le dos. Nous avons besoin d'un porte-étendard. Votre passé vous désigne pour ce rôle. Que vous le vouliez ou non, vous serez des nôtres, vous êtes déjà des nôtres !

— Si je viens parmi vous, ce sera pour prêcher la tolérance, dit-elle.

Il ricana :

— Est-ce votre séjour en Sibérie qui vous a rendue si respectueuse de l'ordre établi ?

— Peut-être. Tant de gens ont souffert, sont morts devant moi, en vain, que, maintenant, la politique me répugne !

— En parlant ainsi vous faites le jeu de l'autocratie ! Seriez-vous pour Napoléon III contre le peuple ?

— Je suis pour la paix, pour l'oubli, au bout d'une existence gâchée.

Il baissa la tête :

— Je suis consterné !

Sophie le plaignit pour la déception qu'elle lui causait et murmura :

— Il ne faut pas, Vavasseur. Vous me placiez trop haut. C'était ridicule ! Laissez-moi vivre mes dernières années, non selon vos désirs, mais selon mes moyens.

Dans le silence qui suivit, une bûche s'écroula. Vavasseur, immobile, tendait vers le feu sa face de vieux diable pensif. Tout à coup, il lança un regard furibond à Sophie et dit avec violence, comme s'il eût craché sur elle :

— J'aurais dû m'y attendre ! Vous n'êtes qu'une femme !

Il sortit et claqua la porte. Elle prit la lettre de Marie Frantzeff et relut lentement le passage qui avait trait à la mort de Ferdinand Wolff.

Les navires, alignés à l'entrée de la rade avaient ouvert le feu, tous en même temps. A leurs flancs se gonflaient des nuages de fumée blanche. Au loin, dans la ville étagée sur une hauteur, des batteries côtières ripostaient faiblement. Un incendie s'était déclaré dans un entrepôt. Sur la gauche, une poudrière venait d'exploser, lançant au ciel des débris incandescents, au milieu d'un formidable crachement de vapeur. Cette image du journal *l'Illustration* fascinait Sophie. Pour la dixième fois, elle relut la légende : « Bombardement du port d'Odessa. » Elle ne pouvait se résoudre à accepter une conjoncture aussi monstrueuse que l'état de guerre entre la Russie et la France. Deux mois, déjà, que les diplomates avaient donné la parole aux militaires ! Ce qui paraissait impossible s'était déroulé le plus naturellement du monde : le 7 février 1854, le comte Nicolas Kisseleff et tout le personnel de l'ambassade de Russie avaient bouclé leurs malles et pris le train. Si leur départ s'était effectué de façon très discrète, il n'en avait pas été de même pour la petite colonie russe de Paris. Considérés du jour au lendemain comme citoyens d'une nation ennemie, ils avaient dû, eux aussi, repasser la frontière. Leur séparation d'avec la société française avait donné lieu à des scènes déchirantes. La plupart d'entre eux avaient préféré ne pas retourner dans leur pays, mais se fixer le plus près possible de la France, en attendant la chance d'y revenir. Ainsi, réfugiés en Belgique, en Allemagne, en Suisse, des sujets de Nicolas Ier continuaient de correspondre avec leurs amis de Paris et déploraient dans leurs lettres la dureté d'une guerre que ni les uns ni les autres n'avaient voulue. La princesse de Lieven, après avoir essayé d'obtenir, par le comte de Morny, le droit de rester dans son appartement de la rue Saint-Florentin, avait été obligée elle-même de s'installer à Bruxelles. On disait que, de là, elle s'efforçait encore d'agir sur le cours des événements, en écrivant chaque jour à Paris, à Saint-Pétersbourg et à Londres.

La disparition de tous ces Russes avait un peu désemparé Sophie. Certes, elle ne les fréquentait guère depuis quelque temps. Mais l'idée qu'elle pouvait, n'importe quand, les rencontrer dans un salon et les entendre parler français avec l'accent slave, lui apportait une sorte de tranquillité morale. Elle lut machinalement le récit de la brillante action des flottes anglaise et française contre le port d'Odessa, passa le courrier de Paris, la causerie littéraire et se plongea dans un article qui racontait en détail la façon dont la déclaration de la guerre avait été annoncée aux escadres combinées de la mer Noire ; « Midi sonne et le signal de *Guerre à la Russie* paraît aux mâts des vaisseaux. Les couleurs des nations alliées se déploient aux trois mâts de tous les navires. Les cris trois fois répétés de la flotte française : *Vive l'Empereur !* se mêlent aux hurrahs éclatants des équipages anglais ; c'est à qui acclamera avec plus d'enthousiasme cet événement si désiré. » Un sourire mélancolique monta aux lèvres de Sophie. Le mensonge de ce journalisme patriotique l'écœurait. « Un événement si désiré ! » Par qui ? se demanda-t-elle. Il était peu probable que ce fût par les braves marins français qui, demain, après-demain, allaient risquer leur vie pour la défense des droits de la Sublime Porte ! Elle regarda, sur la gravure qui accompagnait le texte, les minuscules silhouettes des matelots, rangés debout le long des vergues, pour saluer l'annonce des prochains combats. Les pavillons français, anglais et turc flottaient côte-à-côte dans le vent. Une neige serrée tombait du ciel bas et gris sur une mer agitée. Sophie referma le journal, plia son face-à-main et tourna les yeux vers la fenêtre. Triste printemps. Il pleuvait. Des branches noires, à peine feuillues, s'égouttaient dans le jardin. Delphine avait promis de passer, vers cinq heures. Elles parleraient encore de la guerre. Bien entendu, depuis la rupture des relations diplomatiques entre la France et la Russie, Sophie ne recevait plus d'argent de son neveu. Il aurait pu continuer à lui en envoyer par l'intermédiaire d'une tierce personne résidant dans un pays neutre, mais il était trop heureux sans doute, d'avoir cette excuse pour ne plus l'aider. Privée de revenus, elle avait calculé qu'il lui resterait de quoi vivre pendant une année. D'ici là, vraisemblablement la guerre serait finie. C'était du moins ce qu'on disait dans les salons où elle se rendait encore, par habitude. Là, les nouvelles du théâtre des opérations n'empêchaient pas les gens de s'intéresser aux toilettes, aux tables tournantes et aux courses du Champ de Mars et de Chantilly. Le bon usage voulait même qu'on évitât de médire des Russes. On les traitait en ennemis honorables. Mais Sophie avait le pressentiment que, tôt ou tard, la haute société se laisserait gagner par l'enthousiasme patriotique. Elle ne pouvait oublier qu'au lendemain de la déclaration de la guerre le peuple de Paris avait accompagné en chantant, pendant trois lieues, les régiments qui partaient pour rejoindre leur corps d'armée. L'archevêque Sibour avait lancé un mandement dans lequel il déclarait : « La guerre est une nécessité ; il en sortira assurément quelque bien ! » Les théâtres affichaient des pièces de circonstance où l'adversaire était ridiculisé. Ici, on jouait *Les Russes*, là *Les Cosaques*, ou *La Rencontre sur le Danube* ou *les Russes peints par eux-mêmes*, cette dernière comédie n'étant d'ailleurs qu'une grossière adaptation du *Révizor* de Gogol. Chaque jour voyait paraître des libelles haineux sur « le pays du knout » ; les caricaturistes s'en prenaient au « tsar sanguinaire » et à ses « boyards dépravés » ; Adrien Peladan publiait un ouvrage intitulé *La Russie au ban de l'univers et du catholicisme ;* dernièrement encore, en passant par le boulevard des Italiens, Sophie avait remarqué, à l'étalage de la « Librairie nouvelle », un opuscule édité par cette maison : *La Vérité sur l'Empereur Nicolas*. C'était signé : *Un Russe*. Interrogé par Sophie, le marchand, avec un sourire entendu, lui avait confié que, derrière cet anonymat, se cachait M. Alexandre Herzen. Elle avait acheté le livre, l'avait lu d'une traite et en gardait l'amertume que donne le spectacle d'une mauvaise action. Tout en partageant l'animosité de Herzen contre le tsar, elle déplorait que l'auteur eût osé élever la voix en pleine guerre pour approuver ceux qui, à Paris et à Londres, calomniaient son pays. Il y avait là, pensait-elle, une trahison qu'aucune intention politique ne suffisait à justifier. Le seul parti digne d'un exilé était le silence. Elle s'aperçut que, depuis un moment, elle avait oublié *l'Illustration* sur ses genoux et qu'elle souffrait, les yeux grand ouverts, de ne pouvoir être, à fond, ni pour les Français ni pour les Russes. Chaque moquerie, chaque injure dirigée contre la Russie la blessait au plus vif de ses souvenirs. Elle avait connu la même colère jadis, quand son beau-père critiquait la France, par taquinerie. Mais alors elle n'avait devant elle qu'un seul contradicteur. Aujourd'hui, une nation entière partait dans la folie du dénigrement. Cette guerre, dont d'aucuns cherchaient à exalter les motifs et à célébrer les hauts faits, avait pour elle l'horreur d'une guerre fratricide. Et encore, pour l'instant, il ne s'agissait que de lointaines opérations du côté du Danube ! Que serait-ce si, mettant leurs plans à exécution, les flottes française et anglaise attaquaient la Russie, au nord, par la Baltique ? Une tuerie aux portes de Saint-Pétersbourg !...

Elle était si absorbée dans ses méditations, que Delphine arriva sans qu'elle se fût avisée de l'heure. Valentine leur servit du thé sur une petite table, dans le salon. Comme d'habitude, Delphine était pleine d'histoires : Mlle Rachel, la tête tournée par le succès qu'elle avait remporté en Russie, venait de donner sa démission au Théâtre Français ; l'élection de Mgr Dupanloup à l'Académie était, disait-on, assurée ; on parlait de créer des trains de plaisir pour Constantinople ; la mode était, de nouveau, à la dentelle et aux coloris sévères... Sophie écoutait, approuvait, souriait, distraite un instant de son principal souci. Soudain, Delphine prit un visage important et évoqua un projet dont elle avait déjà entretenu Sophie : elle voulait organiser chez elle une loterie au profit des familles de soldats de l'armée d'Orient,

— Après les fêtes de Pâques, ce sera la meilleure époque ! dit-elle. Je réunirai une société très brillante ! Il faut absolument que vous fassiez partie du comité !

— Oh ! non, Delphine ! supplia Sophie. Vous savez que le monde m'attire de moins en moins !

— Cependant, vous devriez avoir à cœur d'y paraître de plus en plus.

— Pourquoi ?

— Pour dissiper certains bruits qui circulent sur votre compte. Trop de gens s'imaginent que votre sympathie pour les Russes vous fait oublier que vous êtes française !

Sophie rougit et murmura :

— C'est indigne !

— Croyez bien que je prends chaque fois votre défense ! dit Delphine en croquant un biscuit. Mais on ne sauve pas une réputation par des paroles.

— Je suis, en effet, très malheureuse de cette guerre ! dit Sophie. Je souhaite qu'elle finisse au plus vite ! Quelle que soit l'issue des combats, il n'y aura pour moi ni vainqueur ni vaincu !

Delphine poussa un soupir de reproche :

— Voilà des choses que vous ne devriez pas dire autour de vous, Sophie !

— Vous ne pouvez pas comprendre !...

— En tout cas, votre vie russe est terminée. Vous êtes revenue parmi nous, pour toujours. Il faut vous efforcer de nous suivre dans nos élans !

— Même si vous vous trompez ?

— Oui, Sophie.

Il y eut un silence pesant. Sophie éprouvait jusque dans sa chair la sensation d'un impossible partage.

— Ma loterie est une œuvre non de politique mais de charité, reprit Delphine. Vous ne renoncerez pas à vos idées en m'aidant. Il y aura beaucoup à faire. Recueillir les dons en nature, vendre les billets... Mon lot le plus important sera un bon pour un portrait par Winterhalter...

Peu à peu, Sophie se laissait prendre par l'enthousiasme de Delphine. Elle n'avait jamais su résister à un certain ton d'amitié et de décision.

— Eh bien ! soit, dit-elle, je serai des vôtres.

★

Delphine avait bien fait les choses. Au-dessus de la table qui supportait les lots — pendulettes, pantoufles brodées, boîtes à musique, bonnets de dentelle, tabatières... — s'étirait une banderole avec cette inscription : « Gloire à notre vaillante armée d'Orient ». Des figures en carton peint, de grandeur naturelle, représentant des soldats au garde-à-vous, s'adossaient à chaque colonne du salon. Les trumeaux étaient décorés de drapeaux français, anglais et turcs liés en faisceaux. Un portrait de Napoléon III pendait devant la glace de la cheminée. Le buffet était flanqué de deux petits canons prêtés par un antiquaire. Sur une estrade, une fillette, aux cheveux ornés de cocardes tricolores, sortait des billets d'une corbeille. C'était M. Samson, du Théâtre Français, qui annonçait les numéros gagnants au fur et à mesure du tirage. Il avait une voix de tonnerre, mais personne ne l'écoutait. On n'était pas venu dans l'espoir de se voir attribuer quelque babiole, mais pour se rencontrer entre gens d'un certain milieu. Il eût même été du plus mauvais ton de paraître s'intéresser aux objets exposés. Tout le faubourg Saint-Germain était là. Abasourdie par le brouhaha des conversations, Sophie évoluait entre des sénateurs en tenue — l'habit bleu brodé d'or, le pantalon de casimir blanc et l'épée au côté — des curés dodus, roses et rasés de près, des officiers roides comme des tiges d'acier avec une impériale et des moustaches passées à la pommade hongroise, des hommes de lettres, de science ou de haut négoce, en frac noir et cravate blanche, et toutes sortes de femmes, jeunes, vieilles, jolies, laides, en jupes ballonnées, châles multicolores et diadèmes de fleurs artificielles. Un parfum sucré se dégageait d'elles et leurs voix résonnaient sur un registre aigu. Au milieu de tout ce monde, Delphine, en robe couleur de miel, savourait le succès de son entreprise. Elle se déplaçait continuellement, appelait beaucoup de gens par leur prénom et mêlait la mode, le théâtre, la guerre et la charité dans un babillage étincelant et futile. A un moment, comme elle se trouvait près de Sophie, un cercle se forma autour d'elles et les emprisonna. Un lieutenant de la garde, fier de son nouvel uniforme, expliquait à deux jeunes filles pâmées combien il était impatient d'être expédié avec son régiment sur les lieux des combats.

— Il nous faut effacer la honte de la retraite de 1812 ! disait-il. La leçon que Napoléon Ier n'a pas donnée aux Russes, Napoléon III la leur donnera !

Il avait un visage d'enfant au-dessus de son habit bleu, à parements rouges, plastron blanc et épaulettes d'or.

— Je vous présente le vicomte de Caillelet, dit Delphine à Sophie.

Il claqua des talons et s'inclina avec une sécheresse militaire. Sophie ne put résister au désir de le plaisanter sur son ardeur belliqueuse.

— Vous êtes bien jeune, Monsieur, pour nournir une telle rancune contre les Russes ! lui dit-elle en souriant.

— J'ai les souvenirs de mes parents pour héritage, Madame ! répliqua-t-il.

Elle hocha la tête dans un mouvement qu'elle savait gracieux :

— Aucune querelle ne finirait jamais, si les fils continuaient à penser comme leurs pères.

— En temps de guerre, il faut détester pour vaincre !

— Détester qui ? Le tsar, le peuple russe, les moujiks de là-bas ?...

Le vicomte de Caillelet se troubla et fronça les sourcils, qu'il avait minces et blonds.

— Sa Majesté l'empereur nous a tracé notre devoir, Madame, dit-il. J'obéis, je ne discute pas.

— Bien répondu, lieutenant ! s'écria un vieillard à face de lune, que Sophie avait déjà rencontré plusieurs fois dans des salons.

Et tourné vers elle, il ajouta sévèrement :

— Comment pouvez-vous, Madame, vous complaire à démoraliser par vos propos un défenseur de la patrie ?

— Est-ce démoraliser un défenseur de la patrie que de le rappeler à des sentiments humains ? demanda-t-elle.

— Parfaitement ! En temps de guerre, il faut

avoir des idées nettes comme le tranchant d'un sabre !

— Et bêtes comme des boulets de canon !

Le vieillard eut un haut-le-corps et son visage s'empourpra.

— Madame, dit-il, si vous ne savez qui je suis, je sais, moi, qui vous êtes. Les épreuves que, dit-on, vous avez subies en Russie, auraient dû vous rendre deux fois plus française !

— Mais je suis française ! Autant que vous, plus que vous, peut-être ! s'exclama-t-elle.

— On ne le dirait pas ! siffla quelqu'un dans son dos.

— L'ambassadeur de Russie est parti, mais il nous a laissé une ambassadrice ! observa un autre.

Sophie fut brusquement suffoquée de colère. Une vague de sang lui sauta aux joues. Elle parcourut du regard les figures hostiles qui l'entouraient. Delphine lui serra la main et chuchota :

— Ma chérie, ce n'est rien !... Calmez-vous !...

Dominant le tumulte, la voix de Samson annonçait :

— Le numéro 187 gagne une statuette en bronze représentant le sacrifice du jeune Bara. Le numéro 12, une boîte à ouvrage...

Sophie tourna les talons et se dirigea vers la sortie. Sur son passage, les gens s'écartaient de mauvaise grâce. « Et je suis en France ! pensait-elle. En France ! Chez moi ! » Des larmes de rage lui brouillaient les yeux. A travers un voile déformant, elle revit la grande banderole : « Gloire à notre vaillante armée d'Orient », des plantes vertes, des drapeaux... Delphine la rattrapa :

— Vous n'allez pas partir maintenant ? C'est un malentendu ! Une sottise !...

328

— Non ! gémit-elle. Laissez-moi ! J'ai eu tort de venir ! Vous voyez bien que ma place n'est pas ici !

Elle se dégagea et se jeta dans le vestibule, où des valets somnolents veillaient sur une jonchée de manteaux.

Les journaux chantaient victoire : à peine débarquées à Gallipoli et à Varna, l'armée française du maréchal Saint-Arnaud et l'armée anglaise de lord Raglan avaient contraint les Russes à lever le siège de Silistrie et à évacuer les principautés danubiennes. Malheureusement, le choléra et le typhus menaçaient d'entamer le courage des troupes. L'été commença dans l'angoisse, car d'après les rares renseignements qui passaient dans la presse, l'état sanitaire des soldats s'aggravait avec la chaleur. Le 15 août, la Saint-Napoléon fut célébrée avec plus de solennité encore que l'année précédente, en l'absence de l'empereur qui voyageait dans le Midi : salves d'artillerie, *Te Deum*, joutes nautiques sur la Seine et grand concours de voitures publiques décorées de drapeaux tricolores, d'aigles dorées et de bouquets de fleurs. Tous les théâtres jouaient gratis. La Porte Saint-Martin donnait une pièce sur *Schamyl*, le chef circassien, l'irréductible ennemi de Nicolas Ier ; le Cirque Impérial — une pantomime militaire représentant la levée du siège de Silistrie et la mort glorieuse de Mussa Pacha. Partout, les musulmans étaient à l'honneur et les Russes villipendés. A cinq heures, Sophie, qui s'était réfugiée au fond de son jardin pendant les réjouissances patriotiques, vit s'élever dans les airs un immense ballon portant l'inscription : « Turquie, Angleterre, France. » Le lendemain matin, elle lut avec émotion, dans les journaux, la proclamation de l'empereur à l'armée d'Orient. Tant de Parisiens avaient leurs fils sous les drapeaux ! « Ils se couvrent de gloire, écrivait un chroniqueur, mais leurs souffrances sont grandes. » Puis ce fut l'annonce du rembarquement des troupes franco-anglaises, de leur transport à Eupatoria et des premiers combats en Crimée. Le 20 septembre, les alliés, lancés dans une charge héroïque, enlevaient les hauteurs de l'Alma ; aussitôt après, commençait le siège de Sébastopol. Les fausses nouvelles se multipliaient. Un jour, la citadelle était prise, le tsar demandait la paix ; le lendemain, rien n'avait changé, les adversaires s'enterraient face à face, la guerre serait longue... Depuis l'altercation survenue au cours de la loterie, Sophie refusait toutes les invitations. Quand Delphine passait la voir, elles évitaient, d'un commun accord, les conversations politiques. Il en résultait entre elles une gêne qui ressemblait à de la dissimulation.

Un matin, comme Sophie s'apprêtait à sortir, Justin vint l'avertir, dans sa chambre, que deux messieurs désiraient lui parler. Il avait l'épaule basse, le regard fuyant.

— Je n'attends personne, dit-elle étonnée. Leur avez-vous demandé leurs noms ?

— Je n'ai pas cru devoir, Madame...

— Eh bien ! vous avez eu tort. Allez-y !

— C'est que, Madame... ils m'ont dit qu'ils étaient de la police ?

Une appréhension effleura Sophie. Que lui voulait-on encore ?

— Faites-les entrer au salon, dit-elle brièvement.

Elle avait déjà le chapeau sur la tête. Au moment de le retirer, elle se ravisa. En se montrant ainsi à ses visiteurs, elle leur prouverait qu'elle était sur le point de partir, qu'ils la dérangeaient.

Elle les trouva déambulant dans la pièce, le nez fureteur, les mains dans le dos. Ils se tournèrent vers elle avec un ensemble comique. L'un était grand et maigre, l'autre petit et gros ; tous deux portaient une longue redingote sombre boutonnée jusqu'au cou. Un chapeau haut de forme et un gourdin complétaient cet accoutrement. Avant que Sophie eût pu prononcer un mot, le plus grand des deux lui dit d'un ton rogue :

— Nous avons ordre de perquisitionner chez vous, Madame.

Et il lui mit sous les yeux un papier à en-tête de la Préfecture de Police. Sophie lut son nom écrit en lettres grasses, au milieu de la page. Des signatures gribouillées et un cachet authentifiaient le document. Elle resta un instant suspendue dans le vide, incapable de comprendre ce qui lui arrivait ni de déterminer ce qu'elle devait dire pour se défendre. Enfin, elle s'écria :

— C'est impossible, Monsieur ! Que me reproche-t-on ?

— Vous le saurez en temps voulu. Laissez-nous travailler, je vous prie...

L'un des hommes se dirigea vers un secrétaire, l'autre vers une commode. Sophie ne songea même pas à protester. Elle savait, par expérience, qu'il est superflu de parler raison à un policier chargé d'exécuter un ordre.

— Les clefs ? demanda l'homme.

— C'est inutile, Monsieur, dit Sophie. Tout est ouvert.

Ils plongèrent leurs bras jusqu'aux coudes dans les tiroirs, remuant des papiers avec une dextérité professionnelle. Ce fut comme s'ils eussent touché la peau de Sophie à pleins doigts. Elle se raidit de répulsion. Tout recommençait, en France comme en Russie. Une fatalité administrative au visage stupide la poursuivait d'âge en âge, de pays en pays. Soudain, elle vit, dans les mains des policiers, les lettres de Nicolas, de Ferdinand Wolff, de Pauline Annenkoff, de Nathalie Fonvizine... Elle les avait relues et classées dernièrement. Son sang bondit. Elle balbutia :

— Messieurs ! Laissez cela ! Ce sont des lettres personnelles !

Sans sourciller, le petit gros empocha une liasse de feuillets, en donna autant à son collègue et dit :

— On vous les rendra après en avoir pris connaissance. Passons à côté. Si vous voulez nous montrer le chemin...

Guidés par elle, ils ouvrirent toutes les portes, fouillèrent toutes les armoires, retournèrent le linge, secouèrent les robes, tapotèrent les murs, examinèrent les livres dans la bibliothèque. Puis le grand maigre, ayant noté quelques mots dans son calepin déclara :

— Veuillez nous suivre.

— Où ? demanda-t-elle.

— A la Préfecture de Police.

Une terreur la saisit au ventre. On allait l ar-

334

rêter, l'emprisonner. Pourquoi ? Le fait d'être complètement innocente, loin de la rassurer, l'inquiétait vaguement. Au degré d'absurdité où elle était parvenue, il lui semblait qu'elle se fût mieux défendue si elle avait eu quelque crime précis sur la conscience.

— Mais puisque je vous répète que je n'ai rien fait ! dit-elle.

Pour toute réponse, le petit gros lui prit rudement le bras. Elle se dégagea d'un mouvement vif. Dans l'antichambre, Justin et Valentine, perclus de crainte, la regardèrent passer entre deux policiers comme une voleuse. Elle leur dit :

— Ce n'est rien ! Je serai bientôt de retour !

Et elle s'efforça de sourire, par crânerie. Un coupé l'attendait au milieu de la cour. Elle monta dedans, sans l'aide de personne. L'un des hommes s'assit près d'elle sur la banquette, l'autre se jucha à côté du cocher. Pendant tout le trajet, le voisin de Sophie ne lui adressa pas la parole. Enfermée dans une boîte avec cet inconnu qui sentait le vin et le tabac, elle manquait d'air. A chaque cahot, elle touchait un coude, un genou. Enfin, les roues tressautèrent en franchissant un profond caniveau.

La cour pavée de la Préfecture de Police, de longs couloirs gris encombrés de solliciteurs ou de coupables, des ouvriers en casquette, des filles en bonnet de Saint-Lazare, des crachoirs blancs, des portes vitrées, des écriteaux — en traversant cet univers sinistre, Sophie se rappela que Nicolas était venu la chercher, ici même, un jour qu'elle avait été arrêtée par erreur. C'était en 1815, peu de temps avant leur mariage. Il était en grand uniforme de garde de Lithuanie. Son air amoureux et inquiet l'avait touchée. Nul n'accourrait pour la défendre aujourd'hui. Elle ne pouvait compter que sur elle-même. Qu'avait-il dit en la voyant ?

— Entrez, grommela le petit gros en poussant une porte.

Elle pénétra dans une pièce aux murs vert pâle, dont le fond était occupé par un cartonnier. Un homme, tout en front et en mâchoires, était assis derrière un bureau de chêne. Des favoris laineux, d'un gris jaunâtre, pendaient le long de ses joues. Il leva les yeux sur Sophie et ressembla soudain à un batracien attentif. Les deux policiers déposèrent sur sa table les lettres, les papiers qu'ils avaient saisis. Il les renvoya d'un mouvement de tête. Resté seul avec Sophie, il se présenta comme étant l'inspecteur Martinelli et l'invita à prendre place, devant lui, sur une chaise de paille.

— Monsieur, dit-elle, je suis stupéfaite, je ne comprends pas...

Il l'arrêta d'un geste de la main :

— Vous allez tout comprendre, Madame, mais, auparavant, il me faudra vous poser quelques questions. Vos nom, prénoms, date de naissance...

Tandis qu'elle répondait, il l'écoutait à peine. Visiblement, il savait déjà tout cela. Elle remarqua, dans un coin de la pièce, un scribe bossu, juché sur un tabouret, devant un haut pupitre. Il notait ses moindres mots d'une plume aux barbes frémissantes. Brusquement, Martinelli se pencha en avant et demanda :

— Vos moyens de subsistance vous venaient de Russie, n'est-ce pas ?

— Oui, dit-elle. Est-ce contraire aux lois ?

— Nullement ! Cependant, si mes renseignements sont exacts, vous n'étiez pas très bien vue dans ce pays. Votre mari avait été condamné pour son appartenance à une société secrète. Au lieu de le désavouer, vous l'aviez suivi en Sibérie...

— Aurait-on l'intention de rouvrir en France le procès des décembristes ?

— Non, mais cela nous fournit une indication.

— Sur quoi ?

— Sur vos préférences politiques.

Elle éclata :

— C'est insensé ! Nous sommes en guerre contre la Russie et vous me poursuivez de vos soupçons, alors que je suis victime de l'impérialisme russe ! Etes-vous aux ordres de Nicolas Ier ou de Napoléon III ?

Martinelli sourit et sa face de caoutchouc changea de forme. Plus large que haute, elle s'évasait, à la base, sur le socle d'un col blanc.

— Une distinction s'impose, Madame ! dit-il. Sur le plan de la politique extérieure, nous sommes évidemment contre les Russes. Mais, sur le plan de la politique intérieure, nos intérêts et nos soucis rejoignent les leurs. Comme eux, nous luttons pour le maintien de l'ordre et la défense de la légalité. Le fait d'avoir été un agitateur à Saint-Pétersbourg ne constitue pas une recommandation pour la police de Paris. Au contraire ! Vous nous arrivez de là-bas avec un dangereux bagage d'habitudes subversives. Une légende vous entoure...

Enfin, il éclairait sa lanterne. Elle reprit espoir.

— Je ne sors presque jamais ! dit-elle. Je ne vois personne ! Je ne m'occupe pas de politique !...

— On vous a cependant entendue tenir en public des discours déprimants, pour ne pas dire antifrançais !

Immédiatement, elle pensa que des mouchards avaient rapporté, en le déformant, ce qu'elle avait dit chez Delphine. Un dégoût la prit de cette fausse liberté, si peu conforme à ce qu'elle attendait de la France.

— En Russie, on m'accusait d'être une espionne française, dit-elle, en France, on m'accuse d'être une espionne russe !

Martinelli croisa ses mains sur son ventre et un regard mince et froid coula entre ses paupières adipeuses.

— Remplacez le mot « russe » et le mot « française » par le mot « révolutionnaire » et vous comprendrez, dit-il.

— Pourquoi révolutionnaire et non républicaine ?

— Excusez-moi, je ne distingue pas très bien la nuance !

— La révolution est un moyen, la république est une fin, dit-elle.

— Et l'empire ?

Elle ne répondit pas.

— A propos, reprit-il, n'êtes-vous pas en relation avec un certain Vavasseur ?

« Nous y voilà ! » songea-t-elle. Et elle murmura :

— Si.

— Vous lui avez rendu visite à Sainte-Pélagie ; puis chez lui, à la librairie du « Berger fidèle ».

— C'est exact.

— Il vient d'être arrêté. Nous le soupçonnons d'avoir participé à un complot contre la vie de l'empereur. Je suppose que vous n'êtes au courant de rien.

— Absolument de rien ! dit Sophie.

Et son cœur faiblit.

— Il ne vous a pas proposé d'entrer dans la conspiration ?

— Non.

— Vous représentez pourtant un symbole vivant pour lui et pour ses camarades.

— Il a dû se rendre compte que j'étais devenue hostile à ses idées !

— Le lui avez-vous dit ?

— Oui, je crois.

— Donc, il vous a entretenue de son projet ?

Elle rougit et balbutia :

— Jamais de façon précise.

— Mais en passant... à mots couverts ?...

— Peut-être, je ne m'en souviens plus...

Martinelli se renversa dans son fauteuil :

— Vous auriez intérêt à me parler franchement.

— C'est ce que je fais.

— Non, Madame.

Sophie tressaillit. Le cycle des accusations reprenait, alors qu'elle avait cru y échapper en quittant la Russie. Elle se vit traînée devant des juges, confondue sur de faux témoignages, emprisonnée, exilée. Cette fois, ce ne serait pas pour rejoindre son mari qu'elle abandonnerait tout. Qu'avait-elle de commun avec Vavasseur ? Elle le détestait, elle condamnait sa politique aventureuse, elle ne vivait plus que pour les habitudes sereines de l'âge mûr, pour la chaleur de la maison retrouvée.

— Je vous jure, affirma-t-elle, que je ne sais rien de plus !

Et elle eut honte de se défendre ainsi. Pourquoi fallait-il que, dans la majorité des cas, la rançon de la paix fût l'humiliation ?

— Dites-moi qui était dans le coup avec lui et je vous relâche ! grommela Martinelli d'un ton radouci.

Elle haussa les épaules :

— Je ne peux pas... Il faudrait que j'invente !

339

— Je vais vous guider : Antonin Lacroix, Marcel Pièdeferre, Georges Klaus...

— Je n'en ai jamais entendu parler !

— Et Proudhon ? Vous l'avez bien rencontré, rue Jacob ?

— En effet !

— Que disait-il ?

— Rien que de très sensé.

— Bref, tout le monde était d'accord pour se réjouir des premiers résultats du régime ?

— Je n'ai pas prétendu cela, Monsieur. Certains invités avaient des idées sociales avancées. Mais ils les exposaient posément, sans violence. L'empereur même, s'il les avait entendus, n'aurait pu en prendre ombrage.

— Ce n'est pas ce qu'on m'a rapporté !

— Eh bien ! admettez qu'on vous ait mal renseigné, pour une fois !

Elle s'était ressaisie, peu à peu. Son expérience des interrogatoires l'aidait à dominer la situation. Martinelli passa la main à rebrousse-nez sur son visage. Il paraissait excédé par l'obstination de Sophie. Elle devina que son avenir se jouait à pile ou face derrière ce front volumineux. Elle était encore libre. Et dans une minute ? Les battements de son cœur sonnaient jusque dans ses mâchoires. Lentement, Martinelli prit les lettres de Nicolas sur la table et les déplia, l'une après l'autre. Elle pensa aux mots d'amour qui défilaient sous cet œil d'argousin.

— De qui sont ces lettres ? demanda-t-il.

— De mon mari.

— Et celle-ci ?

— D'un ami de Sibérie.

— Un décembriste, lui aussi ?

— Oui, Monsieur.

340

Il se replongea dans sa lecture. Une lumière sous-marine entrait par la fenêtre. La plume du scribe grinçait. Une odeur de poussière arrosée montait du plancher raboteux. Soudain, Martinelli repoussa le tas de lettres vers Sophie :

— Reprenez ça !

Elle les glissa dans son sac à main. Le paquet était si gros, qu'elle dut laisser le fermoir entrouvert.

— Je verrai s'il y a lieu de donner une suite à cette affaire, dit-il encore. Pour l'instant, vous êtes libre !

Elle ressentit un soulagement dans sa poitrine. Pourtant, elle savait que la police ne renonce pas facilement à ses soupçons. Si cet inspecteur la laissait partir, c'était assurément pour la faire filer à distance et tâcher d'en apprendre davantage sur les gens qu'elle fréquentait. Le scribe s'était arrêté d'écrire. Elle se leva. Martinelli la raccompagna jusqu'à la porte avec beaucoup d'amabilité.

Elle retraversa l'enfer monotone des corridors. Des sergents de ville bavardaient, bicorne à bicorne, dans la cour. Par la moustache et la barbiche, ils ressemblaient tous à Napoléon III. Un panier à salade passa sous le porche, avec fracas, et se rangea devant le perron principal. Dans la rue de Jérusalem, la lumière et le bruit étourdirent Sophie et elle sourit à la vie qui reprenait. Sur le Pont Neuf, elle se retourna pour voir si elle n'était pas suivie. Mais il y avait trop de monde autour des étalages. Tous les visages se confondaient. Tondeurs de chiens, décrotteurs, rétameurs, fondeurs de cuillères, marchands de chapeaux, de rubans, de mort aux rats, de pastilles du sérail criaient à qui mieux mieux pour attirer le

341

chaland. Elle se hâta d'échapper à la cohue. Une inquiétude restait collée à son dos. Elle se redressa par discipline. Il y avait longtemps qu'elle n'avait connu cette impression de poursuite. Même en Russie, les derniers mois, il lui arrivait d'oublier qu'elle était suspecte. Valentine et Justin l'attendaient à la maison, la mine compatissante.

— C'était une erreur ! leur dit-elle.

Ils firent semblant de la croire. Pendant son absence, ils avaient rangé la chambre. Il n'y avait plus trace du passage de la police dans l'appartement. Sophie regarda les meubles, autour d'elle, avec gratitude, comme on retrouve des amis après un accident qui aurait pu vous coûter la vie. Valentine lui proposa de l'aider à se déshabiller, à se mettre au lit.

— Pourquoi ? Je ne suis nullement fatiguée ! dit Sophie avec vivacité.

Elle renvoya la soubrette, s'assit dans un fauteuil, et ses nerfs, longtemps crispés, la trahirent. Un tremblement la secouait, elle souhaitait verser des larmes et ne le pouvait pas. Plus jeune, pensait-elle, elle se fût mieux défendue contre l'émotion. Etait-ce parce qu'elle avait failli être emprisonnée elle-même, qu'elle était si préoccupée soudain du sort de Vavasseur ? Elle le condamnait et elle le plaignait à la fois. Un fou, un illuminé. Poussé par son idée fixe, il ne pouvait finir autrement. Elle l'avait prévenu. Il s'était moqué d'elle : « Vous n'êtes qu'une femme ! » Cette exclamation sonnait encore dans la tête de Sophie. Elle réfléchissait à tous ceux qui, comme Vavasseur, avaient sacrifié leur liberté, leur sécurité, leur famille, à une conviction politique. Décidément, les hommes avaient dans le sang le goût des perspectives grandioses. Neuf fois sur dix, leur agitation n'aboutissait à rien. Le seul bien qui se faisait au monde provenait d'initiatives modestes, quotidiennes, féminines. Elle-même, quand avait-elle été le plus utile à ses semblables ? Quand elle se grisait de théories politiques violentes, à Paris, ou quand elle se contentait de soigner les moujiks de Kachtanovka ? C'était là-bas, sur le terrain de la misère et de l'ignorance, qu'elle aurait pu, le mieux, accomplir son destin de femme. Serge s'y était opposé. A cause de lui, elle avait dû renoncer à une existence qui l'eût rendue fière d'elle-même. Elle rêva un instant à tout le bonheur qu'elle aurait distribué à ces êtres simples, s'il n'avait été là pour l'en empêcher. Dommage. La route était coupée. Il fallait songer à autre chose. Tout à coup, elle s'inquiéta de Louise. La malheureuse devait être aussi bas que possible. Sur-le-champ, la fatigue de Sophie s'envola. Elle remit son chapeau, son manteau, et ressortit dans la rue.

Elle trouva Louise en larmes, dans la librairie. Une femme épaisse et âgée — sa mère, sans doute — était assise près d'elle et lui tapotait les mains. Les enfants jouaient à la toupie derrière le comptoir. Louise leva sur Sophie un regard noyé et dit :

— Ah ! je n'ai pas de chance ! Il m'avait pourtant promis que, cette fois, il serait prudent !

Bien que l'accusation eût été incapable de prouver l'existence d'un complot contre l'empereur, Augustin Vavasseur fut condamné à cinq ans de prison ferme et incarcéré à Belle-Ile, où se trouvaient déjà de nombreux détenus politiques. Désemparée par ce nouveau coup, Louise prit l'habitude de rendre visite, plusieurs fois par semaine, à Sophie, pour lui parler de son chagrin, lui demander conseil et lui lire les lettres qu'elle recevait de son mari. Il ne se plaignait pas trop du régime pénitentiaire, disait le plus grand bien de ses camarades, affirmait que ses convictions républicaines s'étaient renforcées dans l'épreuve et racontait comment il employait ses loisirs à travailler la terre et à étudier la musique.

— Il me semble qu'il est plus heureux en prison avec des hommes de son parti qu'à la librairie avec moi ! soupirait Louise.

Elle avait un petit air peuple qui amusait Sophie et la reposait des mensonges du monde. Leurs deux solitudes s'accordaient en de paisibles rencontres. Elles prenaient le thé ensemble et, ensuite, Louise bavardait de mille riens, devant Sophie qui l'écoutait, penchée sur sa tapisserie. Pas une fois, Delphine de Charlaz ne vint troubler leur tête-à-tête. Sans doute ne pouvait-elle se permettre, dans sa situation, de continuer à fréquenter une personne politiquement compromise. Tous les salons honorables avaient d'ailleurs suivi son exemple. Sophie était heureuse de n'être plus invitée nulle part. Le manque d'argent l'obligeait à se restreindre. Eût-elle voulu sortir, qu'elle n'aurait pu se payer les toilettes nécessaires pour tenir son rang. De temps à autre, Louise amenait un de ses enfants, et il demeurait dans un coin à feuilleter des livres d'images. C'était sa mère qui s'occupait du reste de la famille et gardait le magasin. Les clients étaient rares, les gains médiocres, mais il fallait à tout prix assurer un petit courant de commerce pour que Vavasseur pût reprendre l'affaire à son retour. Sophie avait bien essayé d'aider Louise ; mais celle-ci avait toujours refusé son offre, disant qu'elle avait des économies ; sa dignité était de ne rien devoir à personne. En arrivant, elle annonçait :

— Aujourd'hui, j'ai été suivie.

Ou bien :

— Je ne sais ce qu'est devenu mon mouchard ; je ne l'ai pas vu, ce matin !

Sophie, elle aussi, avait un mouchard attaché à ses pas. Elle s'y était accoutumée et le saluait d'un hochement de tête quand elle le surprenait à un tournant de rue. Le lendemain, il était remplacé par un autre, tout aussi reconnaissable par ses vêtements sévères et son expression chafouine. On s'occupait beaucoup d'elle, à la police. Mais elle avait le sentiment que, peu à peu, ces messieurs se fatigueraient de la soupçonner. L'essentiel était que la guerre finît vite !

Cependant, le siège de Sébastopol s'éternisait, suscitant de part et d'autre des prodiges d'héroïsme. On racontait qu'il y avait une telle courtoisie entre les adversaires, qu'après s'être battus à mort pendant des heures, ils profitaient de la trêve pour bavarder amicalement et échanger de menus cadeaux. Chaque fois qu'elle entendait rapporter un trait de chevalerie chez un officier russe, Sophie en était émue. Elle eût voulu faire partager à tous ses compatriotes l'estime que lui inspiraient les actuels ennemis de la France. Souvent, elle parlait à Louise de ses souvenirs de Sibérie. Lorsqu'elle prononçait le nom de Nicolas ou de Ferdinand Wolff, son cœur changeait de rythme. Louise l'écoutait, subjuguée, la bouche entrouverte dans une moue d'enfant. Elle était charmante dans son ignorance. Quand elle ne venait pas pendant un jour ou deux, Sophie s'ennuyait. « Pourquoi me suis-je attachée à cette petite ? pensait-elle. Je ne sais rien d'elle, ou si peu de chose ! Je n'ai même pas l'impression de l'avoir choisie ! Elle n'est là que pour m'empêcher d'avoir le vertige devant le vide... » Le samedi 3 mars, pendant qu'elles prenaient le thé, face à face, Justin apporta les journaux. Il avait un visage papelard.

— Madame sait la nouvelle ? chuchota-t-il. Le tsar est mort !

— Que dites-vous là ? s'écria Sophie.

Et elle prit *le Moniteur Universel*, qu'il lui tendait sur un plateau. La nouvelle s'étalait en première page, à la rubrique « Non officielle ». Une joie grave frappa Sophie et se répercuta en elle profondément. L'empereur avait succombé, disait-on, à une sorte de paralysie du poumon. En réalité, les revers subis par ses troupes en Crimée avaient dû miner sa résistance. Quelles seraient les conséquences politiques de l'événement ? Sophie voulait croire que la guerre s'arrêterait par la disparition de celui qui en avait été le principal instigateur. Elle développa ce point de vue devant Louise, qui l'écouta, en buvant son thé à petites gorgées. Pour la première fois, cette passivité souriante irrita Sophie.

Après le départ de la jeune femme, elle se retrouva seule dans le salon, parmi des gazettes chiffonnées. L'ombre venant, elle commençait tout juste à comprendre que Nicolas Ier n'était plus. Ainsi, ce bloc de marbre inébranlable avait fini, lui aussi, par s'effacer de l'horizon. Combien d'hommes avaient souffert par sa faute ! Avant-hier, les décembristes enterrés vivants en Sibérie, hier, les « pétrachevtsy », aujourd'hui, les soldats sacrifiés à Sébastopol ! La volonté aveugle de ce potentat, son intelligence rude et limitée, son absence de pitié, de finesse, de cœur, avaient infléchi, pendant trente ans, le destin de millions d'êtres. Elle-même avait eu sa vie écrasée par l'orgueil et la cruauté du maître de la Russie. Qui pouvait le pleurer, hormis quelques courtisans dont il avait fait la fortune ? De la Baltique au Pacifique, de l'Océan glacial aux frontières du sud, le peuple russe tout entier devait pousser un soupir de soulagement. C'était surtout en Sibérie, pensait-elle, que ce deuil national serait accueilli avec joie. Malheureusement, la plupart des condamnés politiques étaient morts dans l'attente de l'amnistie : Nicolas depuis plus de vingt ans, Ferdinand Wolff depuis deux ans à peine. Elle imagina les survivants réunis chez l'un ou chez l'autre, à Irkoutsk, à Tobolsk, à Kourgane, pour commenter l'événement autour d'un samovar. Un conciliabule de squelettes. Sûrement, le nouveau tsar, Alexandre II, allait leur pardonner. On le disait cultivé, indulgent, sincère. Elle se rappelait avec quelle émotion elle l'avait aperçu, jeune tsarévitch timide, lors de sa visite à Kourgane, en 1837. Son signe de croix devant les décembristes, au moment de la prière pour les réprouvés... Il libérerait les condamnés politiques et conclurait l'armistice. A moins qu'il ne fût mal entouré. Pourvu qu'il n'eût pas conservé les conseillers de son père ! Elle regretta de n'avoir pas un Russe auprès d'elle avec qui elle pût échanger des idées. Les Français étaient incapables de la comprendre. Pour eux, la mort de Nicolas Ier, c'était une affaire de politique étrangère. Pour elle, une affaire de famille.

Elle passa une mauvaise nuit et, les jours suivants, guetta avec une impatience croissante le déroulement des opérations. Mais, si les gazettes multipliaient les dépêches retraçant l'agonie édifiante de Nicolas Ier, il ne semblait pas que son héritier fût pressé de mettre un terme aux combats. Sans doute Alexandre II attendait-il d'être couronné empereur au Kremlin pour prendre une décision aussi importante. Cela risquait de durer plusieurs mois ! Pour l'instant, on se bornait, en Russie, à changer de généraux. Dans le camp des alliés, pour marquer solennellement l'accord franco-britannique, Napoléon III et l'impératrice se rendaient en Angleterre. A leur retour, l'empereur échappait aux balles d'un assassin sur les Champs-Elysées, et tous les journaux bénissaient la Providence. En lisant les éloges adressés par la presse au souverain, Sophie aurait pu se croire en Russie. Il est vrai que les Français avaient sujet d'être fiers de leur chef, puisque le gouvernement menait de front avec succès les entreprises de la guerre et celles de la paix. L'effort militaire déployé autour de Sébastopol n'empêchait pas les démolitions et les reconstructions dans la capitale, ni les fêtes en l'honneur de l'armée ou des monarques étrangers. De toutes parts s'ouvraient des chantiers de pierre de taille. L'édification du nouveau Louvre se poursuivait en même temps que la rue de Rivoli était prolongée jusqu'à l'Hôtel de Ville et que des maisons géantes, de six étages, poussaient au bord du boulevard de Strasbourg. Mais c'était dans les Champs-Elysées que les ouvriers travaillaient le plus fiévreusement, pour achever le bâtiment du Palais de l'Industrie où devait se tenir l'Exposition Universelle de 1855. Le 15 mai enfin, le monument fut débarrassé de ses derniers échafaudages et reçut la visite des souverains. Il n'était question dans les journaux que des merveilles assemblées en ces lieux par vingt mille exposants, tant français qu'étrangers. La Russie elle-même avait été invitée à envoyer les produits de son agriculture et de ses usines, mais avait décliné cette offre « pour cause de guerre ».

Louise, très excitée par les comptes rendus des gazettes, voulut absolument visiter l'Exposition avec Sophie. Elles s'y rendirent un matin et furent à demi étouffées par la foule. Le courant des badauds les poussait devant des étalages qu'elles avaient à peine le temps d'entrevoir. Dans l'immense nef, grouillante, bourdonnante, surchauffée par les rayons du soleil qui tombaient droit des verrières, les tissus de laine voisinaient avec la céramique et les bronzes d'ameublement avec la petite bijouterie. Des noms de pays lointains se lisaient sur des écriteaux énormes : Etats-Unis, Egypte, Grèce, Chine... Le monde entier avait donné son amitié à la France. L'absence de la Russie passait inaperçue. Sophie eût aimé parcourir toute l'Exposition, mais, après deux heures de cheminement laborieux dans la cohue et la poussière, elle se sentit fatiguée et s'assit sur une banquette. Ce fut à ce moment que Louise découvrit quelqu'un de sa connaissance, près du trophée de l'ébénisterie : un homme jeune et mal vêtu, au visage agréable entouré d'une barbe blonde, légère comme de la dentelle. Il semblait attendre qu'elle le remarquât. Elle le présenta comme étant Martial Louvois, artiste peintre, un ami de Vavasseur. Sophie se rappela confusément l'avoir rencontré à la librairie du « Berger fidèle », le soir où tous les camarades d'Augustin s'y trouvaient réunis. Il s'offrit à guider les deux femmes dans l'annexe des Beaux-Arts. A cette proposition, la figure de Louise s'anima d'une gaieté un peu suspecte. Soudain, la peinture moderne la passionnait.

— Oh ! oui, allons-y ! s'écria-t-elle.

Amusée par cette métamorphose, Sophie accepta. De tous côtés, le monde affluait dans les salles où les chefs de l'Ecole française avaient exposé leurs tableaux. On se pâmait devant l'*Odalisque couchée*, de M. Ingres, *le Massacre de Scio*, de M. Delacroix, *le Grand Bazar Turc*, de M. Decamps, ou *le Pilori*, de M. Glaize. Les commentaires du public irritaient Martial Louvois, qui avançait d'une toile à l'autre, les mains dans les poches, l'œil mauvais. Il se prétendait « naturaliste » et ne jurait que par des peintres dont Sophie n'avait jamais entendu parler. Au milieu de la visite, il conclut : « Tout cela est sordide ! »

Quelques personnes se retournèrent sur lui avec indignation.

— Sortons, dit-il. Nous serons mieux dans un café. Je vous expliquerai ce que c'est que la vraie peinture !

Louise acquiesça d'emblée, avec un grand élan qui fit palpiter les fleurs de son chapeau. Mais Sophie était trop lasse : elle préféra rentrer chez elle.

Le lendemain, en revoyant Louise, elle lui demanda des nouvelles de Martial Louvois.

— Il m'a ennuyée toute la soirée, à me parler d'art et de philosophie, dit Louise. Vous avez bien fait de ne pas rester !

Pourtant, à dater de ce jour, elle s'habilla avec plus de recherche. La venue de l'été la rendait coquette. Ses visites à Sophie s'espacèrent. Evidemment, elle était occupée ailleurs. Sophie plaignit Vavasseur, mais ne se reconnut pas le droit de morigéner la coupable. Cette passionnette lui semblait ridicule, auprès de l'immense angoisse qui l'étreignait chaque jour davantage à la lecture des journaux. Les commentaires ampoulés que suscitaient, dans toutes les feuilles, la visite de la reine Victoria à Paris, les concerts aux Tuileries ou les spectacles des théâtres parisiens, ne parvenaient pas à masquer la réalité affreuse de la guerre. De temps à autre, un communiqué laconique précisait que l'enlèvement des blessés sur les champs de bataille s'était amélioré ou que le nombre des morts du côté français n'était pas très considérable. Bien entendu, les Russes, eux, étaient plus durement touchés. Les prisonniers faits dans leurs rangs avouaient qu'à présent, personne, à Sébastopol, ne croyait à la victoire. On se battait et on mourait pour l'honneur. Prise du

352

Mamelon-Vert, affaire de Tchernaïa, attaque de la tour de Malakoff, derrière ces expressions banales, quelles montagnes de cadavres ! « Tout va bien, tout marche, nous avançons », télégraphiait le général Pelissier, nouveau commandant de l'armée d'Orient, au ministre de la Guerre. Les journaux illustrés publiaient des dessins terribles, représentant des combats au corps à corps, parmi les fumées en choux-fleurs des explosions. Les zouaves avaient de nobles visages sous leur chéchia, les Russes, des mufles de tigres. Soudain, le 10 septembre, dans *le Moniteur Universel*, une dépêche imprimée en première page : « Korabelnaya et la partie sud de Sébastopol n'existent plus. L'ennemi, voyant notre solide occupation à Malakoff, s'est décidé à évacuer la place, après en avoir ruiné et fait sauter par la mine presque toutes les défenses. »

Le lendemain, la prise de Sébastopol était confirmée et l'empereur ordonnait qu'un *Te Deum* fût célébré à Notre-Dame, tandis que tous les théâtres de Paris joueraient gratis. Un débordement d'enthousiasme salua cette nouvelle. Sophie se dit qu'après un tel coup le tsar mettrait bas les armes. La pensée de la paix prochaine la réconciliait avec l'allégresse délirante de la foule. Mais combien de temps faudrait-il aux Français et aux Russes pour oublier le sang versé ? La journée du 13 septembre fut vouée à la liesse populaire. Justin et Valentine demandèrent à Sophie la permission de sortir pour fêter la victoire. Elle les y autorisa volontiers, heureuse de rester seule à la maison. Une grosse rumeur de foire battait les murs. Sur le tard, Louise arriva, rose, froissée, décoiffée, et raconta qu'elle avait assisté à un spectacle en matinée, à l'Opéra. Devant une toile de fond représentant Sébastopol, un chanteur avait récité un poème à la gloire de l'armée française.

— C'était beau ! J'en avais les larmes aux yeux ! J'ai crié avec tout le monde ! Ce soir, il y aura des illuminations. M. Martial Louvois a un ami qui habite à côté de l'Hôtel de Ville. De ses fenêtres, on verra le feu de Bengale. Ne voulez-vous pas venir avec nous ?

Sophie remercia, refusa, un peu honteuse de son manque d'entrain devant cette petite femme échauffée. Louise s'envola, ailée de patriotisme et d'amour. La prise de Sébastopol lui était une excuse de plus pour tromper son mari.

Le dimanche 30 mars 1856, à deux heures de l'après-midi, le canon des Invalides tonna pour annoncer la signature de la paix. Depuis plus d'un mois que les pourparlers se déroulaient à Paris entre les plénipotentiaires des pays alliés et de la Russie, le public attendait cette nouvelle d'un jour à l'autre. Les drapeaux, les lampions, étaient prêts dans chaque maison. Immédiatement, ils apparurent aux façades. Sur l'ordre de Sophie, Justin se précipita pour pavoiser le porche de l'hôtel. Cet événement, tombant deux semaines après la naissance du prince impérial, portait l'exaltation populaire à son comble. Sophie sortit dans la rue et vit un attroupement devant une affiche fraîchement collée : « Congrès de Paris. La paix a été signée aujourd'hui à une heure, à l'hôtel des Affaires étrangères... » L'émotion lui coupait les jambes. Elle se dit que son bonheur était sans commune mesure avec celui des gens qui l'entouraient, puisqu'elle se réjouissait à la fois pour la France et pour la Russie. Cette double félicité, provenant d'un double amour, lui donnait envie

de pleurer. Des vendeurs de journaux la bouscu-
laient. A côté d'elle, un soldat amputé d'un bras
riait dans sa barbe rousse, une femme en deuil
s'appuyait contre l'épaule de son mari qui soulevait son chapeau d'un geste théâtral. Des cloches
sonnaient au loin. Sophie se dépêcha de rentrer
chez elle, comme si elle eût craint de dissiper son
allégresse dans la foule.

Les jours suivants furent marqués par des revues et des réceptions officielles. On racontait
que Napoléon III se montrait particulièrement
aimable avec le comte Alexis Orloff, représentant
la Russie. Des deux côtés, le désir de recoudre ce
qui avait été déchiré par la guerre semblait évident. Aussitôt le traité de paix ratifié, le tsar et
l'empereur échangèrent des congratulations fra-
ternelles ; l'ambassade de Russie à Paris entrebâilla ses portes en attendant le retour du ministre, comte Kisseleff ; le comte de Morny, nommé
ambassadeur extraordinaire de France en Russie,
s'apprêta à partir pour Saint-Pétersbourg où le
palais Vorontzoff-Dachkoff avait été loué à son
intention. Avant même la fin de la guerre, la princesse de Lieven avait obtenu l'autorisation de se
réinstaller dans son entresol de la rue Saint-Florentin. Peu à peu, d'autres Russes, timides, crain-
tifs, reparurent à Paris et leurs amis français
accueillirent à bras ouverts ces convalescents,
étonnés. Sophie reçut la visite inopinée de Delphine, qui comptait absolument sur elle pour son
prochain *raout* :

— C'est absurde ! Nous nous sommes perdues
de vue ! Il y aura chez moi beaucoup de gens que
vous connaissez et qui n'ont cessé de me demander de vos nouvelles !

Devant ce retour d'intérêt, Sophie conclut qu'elle n'était plus une pestiférée. Du reste, depuis quelque temps, elle pouvait sortir sans être suivie. Dédaignée par la police, il était naturel qu'elle rentrât en grâce auprès des honnêtes gens. Elle se rendit, par curiosité, à la réception de Delphine et en revint étourdie par le chatoiement des toilettes et la banalité des propos. Elle avait perdu l'habitude de ces grandes parades de l'élégance, de la médisance et de la fatuité. Sa robe était démodée. Cette circonstance la contrariait. Il eût fallu qu'elle renouvelât tout son équipage. Mais, bien que les correspondances postales eussent repris normalement avec la Russie, elle ne recevait toujours pas d'argent de son neveu. Elle s'était adressée en vain au gouverneur et au maréchal de la noblesse de Pskov. Fallait-il qu'elle écrivît à Serge directement ? Elle ne pouvait s'y résoudre ! De toute évidence, il avait trouvé si commode de ne plus lui verser de revenus pendant la guerre, qu'il allait continuer à l'ignorer maintenant. Elle était trop fière pour lui réclamer son dû en le menaçant d'un procès. Au fond, cet argent, elle n'avait jamais eu l'impression d'y avoir droit. Il lui venait de son beau-père qu'elle détestait. L'idée d'être, en quelque sorte, entretenue par un mort, la gênait davantage depuis que Nicolas n'était plus auprès d'elle. Après tout, Serge était le seul descendant de Michel Borissovitch. Kachtanovka devait lui appartenir en entier. Toute disposition contraire n'était que jeu d'écritures... Il l'avait bernée ? La belle affaire ! Elle n'en était pas à une avanie près. Restait à décider quels seraient à présent ses moyens d'existence. Elle envisagea la situation froidement : le plus simple serait de mettre en location le premier étage de la maison. Ses goûts étaient assez modestes pour qu'elle pût vivre sur les sommes que lui rapporterait le loyer. Au besoin, elle donnerait des leçons de français, d'histoire, de géographie, comme à Tobolsk. La perspective de la pauvreté et du travail ne l'effrayait pas. Elle retrouvait en y songeant son ardeur de jadis et presque une raison d'espérer. Pour commencer, elle renvoya le cocher et la voiture de remise. Puis elle signifia son congé à Justin. Il le prit très mal, vexé et dédaigneux à la fois, chipotant sur les gages. Valentine pleurait en attendant son tour. Sophie lui promit de ne se séparer d'elle qu'à toute extrémité. Elle se disait que Serge eût bien ri s'il l'avait vue si embarrassée devant ses domestiques. Ces derniers temps, elle pensait souvent à son neveu. Quand elle l'évoquait, il avait toujours un pli sarcastique aux lèvres et de la haine dans les yeux. Elle n'avait même plus Louise pour la distraire. Absorbée par ses amours coupables, la jeune femme avait oublié le chemin de la rue de Grenelle. En vérité, Sophie eût été gênée de la recevoir. La franchise entre elles étant devenue impossible, de quoi auraient-elles parlé ?

Un matin, Valentine remit à sa maîtresse une lettre portant l'en-tête officiel du maréchal de la noblesse de Pskov. Elle l'ouvrit avec appréhension, essuya les verres de son face-à-main et lut :
« Madame,
« J'ai le pénible devoir de vous annoncer que votre neveu, Serge Vladimirovitch Sédoff, est décédé le 7 février dernier, dans des circonstances tragiques. Des troubles ayant éclaté dans le domaine, il a voulu haranguer ses paysans et a été lâchement massacré par eux. Bien entendu, les misérables ont été immédiatement arrêtés, jugés

et envoyés en Sibérie. L'interruption des relations postales pendant la guerre m'a empêché de vous tenir au courant de ces faits, ce dont vous voudrez bien m'excuser. D'après les dispositions testamentaires de Michel Borissovitch Ozareff, la disparition de Serge Vladimirovitch vous laisse seule héritière de la propriété. Les papiers constatant cet état de choses ont été expédiés au consulat général de Russie à Paris, qui les transmettra à la chancellerie du ministère des Affaires étrangères. Sans doute serez-vous convoquée sous peu par cette haute administration française. Ai-je besoin de vous dire que, d'accord avec le gouverneur, j'ai placé un intendant à Kachtanovka pour diriger l'exploitation de vos terres dans l'attente des décisions que vous ne manquerez pas de prendre à cet égard ?... »

Jusqu'à la fin de la lettre, elle eut le sentiment de n'être pas tout à fait éveillée. L'atmosphère de cauchemar, dont elle s'était évadée en quittant Kachtanovka, la reprenait ; cette impression d'appartenir à un monde illogique où toutes les violences sont à craindre, où maîtres et serfs sont liés par un étrange contrat de cruauté, où la fortune et la misère se nourrissent l'une de l'autre, où l'âme des morts pénètre la chair des vivants. Quand Serge faisait battre ses paysans, il savait que chaque coup lui serait compté. Il le savait et il ne pouvait s'empêcher d'être toujours plus dur. Comme s'il avait hâte de voir se déchaîner la catastrophe qui l'emporterait. La fascination du gouffre. Les seigneurs de Kachtanovka y plongeaient tous, l'un après l'autre. Une malédiction planait sur la famille. Cette idée superstitieuse agaçait Sophie, qui la récusait et y cédait tour à tour. Elle songeait à Serge, défiguré, ensanglanté, aux moujiks expédiés en Sibérie, au désordre des esprits dans les villages et marchait de long en large, à travers le salon, pour tâcher de calmer ses nerfs. Soudain, elle se dit qu'elle avait sans doute accusé son neveu à la légère. En succombant sous les coups de ses paysans, il démontrait que son père avait pu être tué de la même façon. Maintenant, malgré qu'elle en eut, elle devait convenir que des serfs, poussés à bout, étaient capables d'assassiner leur maître. Et après ?... Les soupçons qui pesaient sur Serge étaient trop lourds pour être levés par ce seul argument. Qu'il fût ou non un parricide ne modifiait en rien ses torts envers les moujiks. Elle n'allait pas s'attendrir sur lui après ce qu'elle avait vu à Kachtanovka ! Comment faire pour en savoir davantage sur les circonstances du meurtre ? Le mieux était encore de se rendre au consulat général de Russie.

Un fiacre la conduisit, en deux tours de roues, au numéro 33 du faubourg Saint-Honoré. Elle traversa une cour sablée et gravit un perron que protégeait une marquise de verre en rotonde. Le suisse, à large baudrier d'or, l'accueillit au haut des marches, lui demanda ce qu'elle désirait et la remit entre les mains d'un huissier à chaîne. Le consulat et l'ambassade, logés dans le même hôtel, étaient sens dessus dessous. Après une absence de deux ans, les fonctionnaires se réinstallaient. Il y avait des caisses de bois blanc et des monceaux de paille dans l'antichambre, vaste comme une nef. Des ouvriers fixaient le tapis rouge de l'escalier d'honneur. Arrivée au palier du premier étage, Sophie dut attendre que l'huissier l'eût annoncée. Il revint bientôt et lui expliqua, en mauvais français, que M. le Consul général n'était pas là, mais que son secrétaire particulier, M. Scriabine, se ferait un plaisir de la recevoir.

Elle croyait trouver un personnage important et tomba sur un petit jeune homme, blondin et poupin, assis sous un grand portrait d'Alexandre II. Ce devait être le premier poste de Scriabine à l'étranger, car il paraissait grisé d'être à son bureau, accueillant une femme. Quand Sophie lui eut exposé le but de sa visite, il exulta. Justement, il avait reçu, la veille, un rapport sur l'affaire. Il n'en revenait pas de pouvoir, sur-le-champ, prouver sa compétence. En une minute, il exécuta la pantomime du diplomate surchargé de besogne, fouillant dans ses archives et découvrant le document voulu. Puis, se rappelant qu'il s'agissait en somme d'un assassinat, il prit un air funèbre et confirma que Serge Vladimirovitch Sédoff avait rendu l'âme à Dieu, le 7 février dernier.

— Une bien pénible conjoncture ! dit-il en soupirant.

— Comment cela s'est-il passé ? demanda Sophie.

— D'après le compte rendu que j'ai sous les yeux, Serge Vladimirovitch Sédoff avait voulu imposer à ses paysans un travail de nuit, pour déblayer des neiges la route qui traverse le domaine. Les moujiks ont refusé de lui obéir. Il est allé à cheval, à leur rencontre. Une altercation a suivi. Les misérables ont osé lever la main sur leur maître... Je suis désolé, Madame, de vous donner des détails si cruels !... Permettez-moi, en tout cas, de vous présenter mes condoléances !...

Ce témoignage de compassion rencontra un tel vide dans le cœur de Sophie, qu'elle en fut gênée. Il n'était pas dans son caractère de feindre le chagrin quand tout était calme en elle. Pourtant, elle devait sauver les apparences. Elle remercia et dit :

— De quel village étaient les meurtriers ?

— De Krapinovo et de Chatkovo.

— Savez-vous quels moujiks, au juste, ont été condamnés ?

— Oui... attendez une seconde...

Il lut une liste de six noms. Elle n'en connaissait aucun. Cette constatation la soulagea.

— A présent, reprit-il, tout est rentré dans l'ordre. Comme vous l'a écrit, sans doute, le maréchal de la noblesse de Pskov, un intendant dirige votre domaine. Vous avez donc le temps de réfléchir avant de vous déterminer.

Sophie le regarda, interloquée. Elle n'avait pas encore pris conscience qu'elle était seule propriétaire de Kachtanovka. Tous ces champs, tous ces villages, tous ces moujiks ! Qu'allait-elle en faire, maintenant qu'elle habitait la France ? Emanciper les serfs ? Bien sûr, mais, libérés du jour au lendemain après une vie entière d'obéissance, ils auraient encore plus besoin d'elle pour veiller sur eux, les aider, les instruire dans l'apprentissage de leur nouveau destin. Laisser les choses en état et charger un intendant d'administrer son domaine et de lui en expédier les revenus ? Elle avait trop le respect du travail humain pour considérer Kachtanovka comme une simple source de profit. Puisqu'il lui était impossible de s'occuper elle-même de ses gens et de ses terres, elle préférait les vendre. Ses paysans seraient plus heureux sous les ordres d'un autre maître que sous la froide surveillance d'un gérant appointé par elle. Peut-être faudrait-il qu'elle se rendît en Russie pour réaliser cette opération ? Eh bien ! un tel voyage ne l'effrayait pas. Elle irait, elle reviendrait... Parvenue à ce point, elle se demanda si la vente était

362

praticable dans l'état actuel de la succession. N'existait-il pas des délais légaux à observer ? Interrogé à ce sujet, Scriabine la rassura. Rien ne s'opposerait à une cession de la propriété, aussitôt qu'elle en aurait exprimé le désir. Néanmoins, pour le voyage en Russie, il lui conseillait d'attendre la fin des fêtes du couronnement, qui devaient commencer le 26 août prochain.

— C'est un événement d'une telle importance, en Russie, dit-il, qu'actuellement le pays entier s'y prépare avec fièvre. Du plus haut gouverneur de province au dernier des assesseurs de collège, personne n'a plus la tête à son travail. Vous vendriez votre bien dans de mauvaises conditions. Laissez donc passer le temps des réjouissances !...

Elle convint qu'il avait raison. Rien ne pressait. En la raccompagnant, il la félicita d'avoir choisi la solution la plus raisonnable : celle de la vente.

— Vous savez, quand on n'est pas sur place pour diriger une exploitation agricole, mieux vaut y renoncer ! dit-il. D'autant que, d'après les indications que je possède, votre propriété représente un beau capital. Ne vous laissez pas faire par les marchands. Maintenez vos prix. Et revenez me voir, pour le visa. On vous le délivrera en quarante-huit heures.

Pendant qu'il parlait, Sophie respira, dans la galerie, une odeur de plat russe venue de quelque lointaine cuisine : un hachis de viande parfumé au fenouil et noyé de crème, sans doute. Ses idées se brouillèrent. Scriabine lui baisa la main. L'huissier étant occupé ailleurs, ce fut un valet de pied, en culottes courtes et livrée bleue et or, qui la reconduisit, par le grand escalier, jusqu'à l'antichambre. Elle le regarda à la dérobée. Sous sa perruque poudrée à marteau, il avait une face de paysan sibérien, aux pommettes saillantes et au nez camard.

En sortant du consulat général, elle se sentit dépaysée comme après un long voyage. Devant elle, un soleil cru blanchissait la chaussée et allumait des couleurs de papillon dans les toilettes des femmes. Le bruit de la ville l'entoura, sans la distraire de ses pensées. Elle traversa la place de la Concorde, avec, sur ses talons, tous les moujiks de Kachtanovka.

Le lendemain matin, elle trouva, dans son courrier, une lettre de Daria Philippovna qui lui racontait, à peu de choses près, ce qu'elle savait déjà :

« Je n'ai pas voulu vous écrire à ce sujet tant que l'affaire ne serait pas jugée, par crainte de me mettre dans un mauvais cas. A présent que votre neveu est sous terre (Dieu ait son âme !) et ses assassins aux travaux forcés (Dieu leur pardonne !), je ne puis résister au désir de vous dire combien tout cela nous a bouleversés, mon fils et moi. Une histoire horrible ! Savez-vous que les moujiks l'ont tiré à bas de son cheval, roué de coups, étranglé, noyé dans la rivière en le poussant par un trou de la glace ? Les « conducteurs », sur lesquels il comptait pour le protéger, se sont croisés les bras. Eux aussi avaient fini par le détester. Et pourtant, il les payait bien ! Je n'en ai pas dormi pendant deux nuits ! Depuis la guerre, les émeutes de moujiks sont nombreuses dans notre région. Même à Slavianka, ils boivent et relèvent le nez ! Quelle triste époque ! L'intendant qui a été placé chez vous est un homme de premier ordre, un Allemand. D'après Vassia, vous pouvez avoir confiance en lui. Sans doute, maintenant que vous êtes fixée à Paris, votre maison de Kachtanovka ne présente-t-elle plus d'intérêt pour vous ! Tout le monde, ici, pense que vous allez vendre ce beau domaine. Cela m'afflige fort, car, vous le savez, Vassia et moi aimions beaucoup vous avoir pour voisine ! Nous en parlons, parfois, à la veillée ! Mais, entre nous, je crois que vous avez raison. L'avenir des grandes propriétés foncières est bien sombre. La culture ne rapporte plus rien, le paysan se fait paresseux, difficile. Partout, règnent l'insécurité et le manque d'argent. On raconte que notre nouveau tsar — un ange de douceur et de générosité ! — est fermement résolu à émanciper les serfs dans les prochaines années. C'est une noble intention et Vassia en est tout ému. Il dit que ce sera l'aube d'une ère nouvelle pour la Russie, la réalisation du vœu de ses amis. Dieu l'entende ! Mais, j'ai peur, pour ma part, qu'une fois libérés, nos moujiks ne sachent pas se conduire et que l'économie du pays n'en soit perturbée. « Raison de plus pour me séparer de Kachtanovka ! » me direz-vous. Eh ! oui, je suis ainsi, je prêche contre mon saint. Quoi que vous décidiez, j'espère que vous viendrez régler toutes ces questions sur place. Vous revoir, ne fût-ce que quelques jours, adoucirait le chagrin que j'éprouve à l'idée qu'un étranger s'installera bientôt, peut-être, sur vos terres... »

La nouvelle de l'héritage de Sophie se répandit très vite dans les salons parisiens. Delphine en conçut autant de joie que si cette chance lui fût échue à elle-même. Elle ne quittait plus son amie et prétendait la conseiller sur tout. A l'entendre, il fallait restaurer l'hôtel de la rue de Grenelle, acheter des meubles de qualité, rafraîchir tentures et peintures, embaucher des domestiques. Sophie, qui venait à peine de toucher les arriérés des revenus du domaine, refusait d'engager de grosses dépenses avant d'avoir vendu Kachtanovka. Il lui semblait que ces aménagements pouvaient attendre son retour de Russie et qu'elle aurait même l'esprit plus libre, à ce moment-là, pour en décider. Néanmoins, elle accepta de se commander quelques robes. Encore s'agissait-il de toilettes de voyage et non de réception. Delphine, qui assistait à tous ses essayages, lui dit un jour, pendant qu'elle s'abandonnait, devant la glace de sa chambre, aux mains d'une couturière hérissée d'épingles :

— Vous avez tort de remettre à demain l'embellissement de votre intérieur. Des travaux de ce genre sont longs à exécuter, et il faut absolument que votre maison et vous-même soyez prêtes pour la saison d'hiver !

— Le mal ne sera pas grand si je suis de quelques mois en retard ! dit Sophie.

— Si, ma chère ! Vous ne pouvez plus vous permettre d'être à la traîne des mondanités !

— Allons donc ! s'écria Sophie. Je vis loin de tout, je n'intéresse personne !...

— C'est ce qui vous trompe ! Les temps ont changé ! Votre situation promet de devenir exceptionnelle...

Comme Sophie ne réagissait pas, Delphine tendit le visage et poursuivit, à voix basse, d'un air de conspiration :

— Vos attaches avec la Russie d'une part, avec la France de l'autre, vous désignent tout naturellement pour un rôle de médiation entre ces deux mondes. La princesse de Lieven est vieille. Elle ne reçoit guère. On ne l'écoute plus. Je vous vois très bien prenant sa place !

Sophie éclata de rire :

— Vous plaisantez ! Je n'ai ni l'envergure ni le goût de ce genre d'emploi !

— Pour ce qui est de l'envergure, vous vous mésestimez ! Pour ce qui est du goût, il vous viendra peu à peu ! N'aimeriez-vous pas peser sur l'opinion de vos concitoyens en ce qui concerne leurs rapports avec la Russie ?

Sophie haussa les épaules ; la couturière, à genoux sur le tapis, se plaignit de ne pouvoir travailler dans ces conditions ; Delphine lui fit observer que la manche était trop plate du haut, puis s'exclama en battant des paupières :

— Ah ! Sophie comme je voudrais vous convaincre ! Vous n'allez pas, après ce que vous avez
vécu, vous désintéresser des affaires publiques !
J'en causais, l'autre jour, avec Mme d'Agoult. Elle
est tout à fait de mon école. Elle estime...

Delphine parla longtemps ainsi, exaltant les mé-
rites de la femme du monde auprès de qui des
hommes éminents cherchent l'inspiration de leur
carrière en fumant des cigares et en buvant du
punch. Quelle meilleure utilisation Sophie pouvait-elle faire de sa fortune qu'en la consacrant
à créer, au cœur de Paris, une sorte de foyer intellectuel franco-russe ?

— Tournez-vous, je vous en prie, Madame, dit
la couturière. La manche vous convient-elle maintenant ?

Sophie pivota sur ses talons. Sa psyché lui montra une dame mûre, les cheveux bruns striés d'argent, le front bombé, le sourcil net, l'œil noir et
vif, le nez finement aquilin, le menton maigre et
carré, la bouche serrée dans une expression
d'énergie féminine. Une robe aubergine bâtie à
gros points de fil blanc, lui moulait le buste et
s'évasait en ballon dans le bas.

— Oui, c'est très bien, dit-elle.

Et elle pensa : « Prendre rang dans la société
parisienne. Essayer d'expliquer la Russie aux
Français. Pourquoi pas ? L'argent que me rappor-
tera la vente de Kachtanovka me permettra de
recevoir beaucoup de monde. Je m'imposerai. Je
me rendrai utile, enfin ! » Un choc l'arrêta dans
sa méditation. De nouveau, elle butait sur l'idée
de vendre le domaine. Céder à des étrangers cette
terre pleine de souvenirs négocier le prix des
moujiks — tant par tête — comme pour du
bétail — en aurait-elle la force ? « Et pourtant,

il le faut, se dit-elle. La mort de Serge ne change rien. Je n'ai plus à connaître de ce pays, de ces serfs. Ils ne m'aiment pas, ils me l'ont prouvé. Et moi, je ne me sens plus capable de m'occuper d'eux, émancipés ou non, comme j'avais tenté de le faire autrefois. L'obstacle est tombé trop tard. On ne réchauffe pas une passion déçue. Si seulement mon enfant avait vécu, j'aurais eu quelqu'un à qui laisser ce bien en héritage. Mais moi disparue, que deviendra la propriété ? Personne pour me succéder. C'est affreux ! Ah ! vite, vite, que tout cela finisse, que je n'entende plus parler de Kachtanovka ! » Elle se pencha vers Delphine, qui l'observait du fond d'un fauteuil, et murmura :

— Vous voyez grand ! Mais, peut-être avez-vous raison ! J'aimerais me dévouer, en France, à ce rapprochement de deux peuples que je connais bien ! Surtout après une guerre si sanglante ! Nous en reparlerons à mon retour de voyage...

Delphine se leva et lui saisit les deux mains en disant :

— Je suis contente de vous retrouver ainsi, résolue et lucide, pleine de confiance en l'avenir ! Cette robe vous sied à merveille !

Le visage de la couturière s'éclaira : enfin on parlait son langage ! Elle suggéra de rajouter un volant, très léger, en bas. Une discussion s'engagea entre les trois femmes.

L'excitation qui préludait aux fêtes du couronnement, en Russie, semblait, peu à peu, gagner la France. La presse parisienne relatait avec complaisance les préparatifs de ces journées extraordinaires, la décoration somptueuse de Moscou,

l'ordonnance probable du cortège et la signification de certains rites orthodoxes. Les mêmes chro-
niqueurs qui avaient prêché la guerre à outrance
contre les barbares s'attendrissaient maintenant
sur les mœurs pittoresques de ce grand peuple et
louaient la noble figure d'Alexandre II. C'était le
comte de Morny en personne qui devait conduire
la délégation française. Un tel honneur était, disait-on, amplement ressenti à Saint-Pétersbourg.

Au lendemain du sacre, Sophie lut dans *le Moniteur Universel*, une dépêche qui la troubla. Parmi les dispositions du manifeste promulgué par
le nouveau tsar à l'occasion de son avènement au
trône, le correspondant du journal avait noté
ceci : « On gracie complètement 31 conjurés de
1825, qui étaient encore exilés en Sibérie. » Ainsi,
le châtiment des décembristes était enfin terminé !
Après trente ans de travaux forcés et de bannis-
sement, ils allaient recevoir le droit de revenir sur
les lieux de leur jeunesse heureuse. Sophie parcourut plusieurs fois ces lignes imprimées en petits caractères et ses yeux s'emplirent de larmes
au souvenir de ses amis.

A quelque temps de là, elle reçut une lettre de
Marie Frantzeff, lui confirmant la nouvelle :

« Nous ne savions rien encore en Sibérie. Mais
Michel, le fils des Volkonsky, se trouvait à Moscou au moment du couronnement. Ce fut lui que
l'empereur, dans une pensée délicate, chargea
d'apporter le message de grâce aux décembristes.
Il partit comme un fou et ne mit que quinze
jours pour parcourir son long chemin. En arrivant chez son père, il ne pouvait plus se tenir sur
ses jambes et, de fatigue, avait perdu la voix.
Vous imaginez la joie de nos amis ! Une joie qui,
d'ailleurs, assez rapidement se tempéra de tristes-

se. A leur âge avancé, il est difficile de changer d'habitudes. Ils se préparent, en soupirant, à quitter un pays qu'ils connaissent bien pour une patrie incertaine. D'ailleurs, il leur sera interdit de résider à Moscou et à Saint-Pétersbourg. Les journaux parlent de 31 proscrits ! En réalité, ils ne sont plus que 19. Ceux qui ont des enfants se félicitent, par esprit de famille, que l'honneur et la liberté leur soient rendus. Mais les autres, je vous le dis entre nous, se seraient volontiers passés de cette tardive mesure de clémence. Ils se sentent moralement tenus d'accepter la grâce qui leur est faite et pleurent quand je leur parle de leur départ. Moi aussi, je suis très malheureuse. Que vais-je devenir quand ils seront loin ?... Des événements plus récents, plus tragiques, repoussent déjà leur histoire au second plan. Après la guerre de Crimée et ses sanglantes séquelles, le passé auquel nous tenons recule d'un siècle ! Comment avez-vous vécu ces abominables années ? Quels sont aujourd'hui les sentiments des Français à notre égard ?... »

Sophie répondit à cette lettre avec chaleur. Elle écrivit également à Pauline Annenkoff et à Marie Volkonsky pour les féliciter de leur prochain retour en Russie. Au moment de cacheter la dernière enveloppe, elle tomba en rêverie, les mains inertes, le regard lointain. Une lampe à globe éclairait la tablette du secrétaire. Derrière les fenêtres noires, le vent d'automne soufflait. Elle calcula que, dans neuf jours, elle serait partie. Cette fois, elle avait changé d'itinéraire. Le chemin de fer la conduirait de Paris à Stettin, par Cologne et Berlin ; et, à Stettin, elle prendrait un bateau à vapeur jusqu'à Saint-Pétersbourg. C'était, aux dires des connaisseurs, le trajet le plus rationnel.

Il ne lui faudrait guère plus d'un mois pour régler ses affaires à Pskov. Débarrassée de Kachtanovka, comme elle se sentirait légère ! Elle repensa aux transformations qu'elle avait décidé d'apporter à son hôtel de la rue de Grenelle. A côté du grand salon meublé à l'ancienne, elle aurait un boudoir de goût moderne, avec des sièges capitonnés, une fontaine murale en porcelaine, un sofa, des coussins à pompons, des rideaux épais à franges. Elle avait déjà choisi les tons dominants de l'ensemble : rose et gris de perle. On disait que c'étaient les couleurs préférées de l'impératrice. Ne serait-ce pas trop fade ? Des soucis infimes l'envahirent en tourbillonnant. Tout à coup, elle s'imagina recevant chez elle, à Paris, les Fonvizine, les Annenkoff, les Volkonsky, tous ses amis de Sibérie. Ils la regardaient tristement sans la comprendre. Elle se remémora une phrase de la Bible, que certains décembristes citaient parfois avec complaisance : « La lumière des Justes donne la joie. La lampe des méchants s'éteindra. » La lampe des méchants s'était éteinte avec la mort du tsar. Mais où était la joie des Justes ? Ils étaient trop vieux pour se réjouir ; ils avaient tout perdu à cause d'une idée ; et d'autres, après eux, allaient tout perdre, pour rien, pour rien ! L'air était plein de grands rêves morts, de nobles projets avortés. Mais peut-être ce désir obstiné de changer la face du monde était-il la marque même de l'homme, dans la fantasmagorie gigantesque où chaque génération effaçait l'ancienne et où tout était toujours à recommencer ? Peut-être le besoin de se passionner était-il plus important que le besoin d'être heureux ? Peut-être n'y avait-il d'existence gâchée que celle qui avait été conduite prudemment ? Nul n'avait le droit de se plaindre tant qu'il voyait devant lui une route ouverte. L'effort, qu'il fût ou non couronné de succès, payait celui qui l'avait accompli. S'il en était ainsi, qui pouvait affirmer que les décembristes s'étaient battus en vain, que Nicolas avait manqué sa vie ? Sophie se leva, remuée par toutes ces pensées contradictoires, ouvrit le tiroir d'une commode, y prit de vieilles lettres, un portrait en médaillon. Des souvenirs tendres se ranimaient en elle. Un jeune officier ennemi entrait dans le salon. Grand et blond, les dents blanches dans une face hâlée. Il la regardait avec respect, avec admiration. De ces belles années, il ne restait pas plus que de la courbe tracée dans le ciel par la pierre que jette un enfant. Elle serra les mains sur sa poitrine. Un volet claquait dans le vent. Elle se rappela certaines nuits de Kachtanovka, le bruit furieux des arbres autour de la maison, l'allée des sapins noirs sous la neige, les grelots d'une troïka au loin... Des voix joyeuses criaient : « Barynia ! Barynia ! Quelqu'un arrive !... » Il y avait longtemps que personne ne l'avait pas appelée barynia.

Valentine frappa à la porte et parut, souriante, avec une tasse de bouillon sur un plateau. Sophie lui fit signe d'approcher. Tout était si calme dans sa vie ! Etait-ce vraiment la fin des combats ?

Malgré les protestations de Sophie, Delphine avait voulu l'accompagner à la gare du Nord. Arrivées trois quarts d'heure avant le départ du train, elles s'étaient réfugiées dans la salle d'attente des premières classes et, assises côte à côte, les jupes bouffantes, le dos roide, elles se taisaient. C'était le soir. La lumière blanche du gaz tombait de quelques lampes haut suspendues. A tout moment, la porte s'ouvrait pour laisser pénétrer de nouveaux voyageurs. Messieurs coiffés du noir tuyau de poêle, dames emmitouflées dans des cache-poussière, enfants sages, enrubannés, et grooms en bottes à revers et casquette galonnée, portant les sacs de nuit et les paniers à provisions de la famille. Ayant installé leur nichée sur des banquettes, les hommes s'assemblaient pour parler et fumer, l'esprit libre, devant les deux cheminées monumentales qui donnaient à ce lieu de passage un air de château de la Renaissance. Partout, le fer forgé répondait au bois chantourné et au stuc. Derrière une baie vitrée, des convois manœuvraient, dans une curieuse effusion de vapeur. Le plancher vibrait comme dans un moulin. A chaque coup de sifflet, les femmes sursautaient, inquiètes. Delphine tenait un mouchoir devant sa bouche, à cause de l'odeur du charbon. Quand il ne resta plus que vingt-cinq minutes à attendre, elle répéta à Sophie les recommandations que lui inspiraient son amitié et son expérience.

Un employé vint les avertir qu'il était temps de monter en wagon. Elles sortirent et se mêlèrent à la cohue de l'embarcadère. Là, plus de distinction de classes. Des têtes ahuries roulaient, toutes dans le même sens, comme des pommes hors d'un panier. A la lueur des becs de gaz, Sophie entrevit une file de voitures, dont des ouvriers vérifiaient les roues, une locomotive qui fumait. Quelqu'un criait dans un porte-voix :

— Les voyageurs pour Cologne, Berlin, Stettin !...

La pluie tombait sur la verrière inclinée. Des bouffées de vent sautaient à la figure des deux femmes. Un facteur marchait devant elles, portant les bagages. Il aida Sophie à monter dans le wagon. Sa crinoline la gêna pour escalader le marchepied. Une fois enfermée dans son compartiment, elle se pencha par l'ouverture de la portière. Delphine se tenait sur le quai, les mains enfouies dans un manchon de fourrure, son visage poudré, momifié, s'encadrait entre les brides d'un cabriolet tout en coques de rubans mauves et citron. Elle avait cent ans !

— Promettez-moi que vous reviendrez très vite, dit-elle.

— Mais oui !

— Vous savez que, le 25 novembre, j'ai cette soirée musicale chez moi !

— Je n'aurais garde de l'oublier !

— Alors, à bientôt !

— A bientôt !...

Elles se souriaient, agitaient doucement leurs mains gantées, mais le train ne partait pas encore. L'aiguille des minutes se traînait sur le cadran de l'horloge qui dominait la galerie de l'Ouest. Enfin, il y eut un coup de sifflet déchirant. Les wagons frémirent, s'entrechoquèrent, tirés par une force aveugle. Une rangée de visages inconnus défila lentement devant Sophie. Elle vit Delphine qui s'éloignait en secouant un petit mouchoir. Des gens hurlaient :

— Au revoir ! Au revoir ! Bon voyage ! A bientôt !

— A bientôt ! cria Sophie.

Mais, au fond d'elle-même, elle savait déjà qu'elle n'aurait pas le courage de vendre ses paysans et qu'elle finirait sa vie à Kachtanovka.

Ainsi s'achève le cycle romanesque de
LA LUMIÈRE DES JUSTES
qui comprend, dans l'ordre chronologique,
les volumes suivants :

LES COMPAGNONS DU COQUELICOT
LA BARYNIA
LA GLOIRE DES VAINCUS
LES DAMES DE SIBÉRIE
SOPHIE OU LA FIN DES COMBATS

Henri Troyat

Né à Moscou en 1911, il est arrivé en France en 1920 et est devenu l'un des plus grands écrivains français. En 1959, il est élu à l'Académie française. Les éditions J'ai lu ont vendu plus de douze millions d'exemplaires de ses livres.

La neige en deuil
10/1

La lumière des justes

1 - Les compagnons du coquelicot
272/4

En arrivant à Paris en 1815, avec les troupes d'occupation russes, Nicolas Ozareff découvre avec enthousiasme les théories démocratiques et tombe amoureux de Sophie, la fille de ses hôtes. L'aventure malheureuse des «décembristes», conspirateurs libéraux, qui tentèrent d'instituer un régime libéral en Russie, en 1825.

2 - La barynia
274/4

3 - La gloire des vaincus
276/4

4 - Les dames de Sibérie
278/4

5 - Sophie ou la fin des combats
280/4

Le geste d'Eve
323/2

Les Eygletière

1 - Les Eygletière
344/4

Avocat parisien fortuné, Philippe Eygletière se remarie avec une femme ravissante, qui n'a que dix ans de plus que l'aîné de ses fils. Peu à peu, la façade de respectabilité bourgeoise de cette grande famille va se désagréger, minée par l'hypocrisie et les compromis.

2 - La faim des lionceaux
345/4

3 - La malandre
346/4

La pierre, la feuille et les ciseaux
559/3

Anne Prédaille
619/3

Grimbosq
801/3

Le Moscovite

1 - Le Moscovite
762/3

Moscou, 1812 : la Grande Armée arrive aux portes de la ville, qui s'embrase dans un gigantesque incendie. Armand de Croué, un jeune émigré français dont la famille s'est réfugiée en Russie à la Révolution voit alors, avec épouvante, les troupes napoléoniennes déferler sur sa terre d'adoption.

2 - Les désordres secrets
763/3

3 - Les feux du matin
764/2

Le front dans les nuages
950/2

Le pain de l'étranger
1577/2

La Dérision
1743/2

Marie Karpovna
1925/1

Viou

- Viou
1318/2

A huit ans, dans la grande maison du Puy qu'elle habite avec ses grands-parents, Viou rêve à son père mort au combat à la Libération et à sa mère qui l'a abandonnée.

- A demain, Sylvie
2295/2

- Le troisième bonheur
2523/2

Le bruit solitaire du cœur
2124/2

Un si long chemin
2457/3

Toute ma vie sera mensonge
2725/1

La gouvernante française
2964/3

La femme de David
3316/1

Aliocha
3409/1

A Paris, en 1924, un adolescent d'origine russe vit difficilement sa condition d'émigré. Il va pourtant retrouver peu à peu la fierté de ses origines, grâce à la littérature et à l'amitié d'un de ses compagnons de lycée.

Nicolas II
3481/5

Le destin tragique du dernier des tsars et de la famille impériale, dans la Russie tumultueuse du début du siècle, déchirée par la guerre, les grèves et l'agitation révolutionnaire. En évoquant la poussée des nationalismes, les affrontements idéologiques, les timides essais de parlementarisme, Henri Troyat éclaire les problèmes actuels de l'ex-URSS.

Youri
3634/1 (Mars 94)

1917. Youri est le fils des riches Samoïlov, Sonia la fille d'une servante. Emportés dans la tourmente de la révolution russe, les deux enfants découvrent le monde des adultes, sans comprendre que ce désordre qui leur semble de grandes vacances va changer irrémédiablement le cours de leur existence.

Grands romans

La littérature conjuguée au présent, pour votre plaisir. Des œuvres de grands romanciers français et étrangers, des histoires passionnantes, dramatiques, drôles ou émouvantes, pour tous les goûts...

ADLER Philippe
Bonjour la galère !
1868/1
Les amies de ma femme
2439/3
Mais qu'est-ce qu'elles veulent ces bonnes femmes ? Elles passent des heures au téléphone, boudent ou pleurent des amants qui les ignorent. Quand il rentre chez lui, Albert aimerait que Victoire s'occupe de lui mais rien à faire : les copines d'abord. Jusqu'au jour où Victoire se fait la malle et où ce sont ses copines qui consolent Albert.

Qu'est-ce qu'elles me trouvent ?
3117/3

ANDREWS™ Virginia C.
Fleurs captives
Dans un immense et ténébreux grenier, quatre enfants vivent séquestrés. Pour oublier leur détresse, ils font de leur prison le royaume de leurs jeux, le refuge de leur tendresse, l'abri du monde. Mais le temps passe et le plaisir devient un enfer. Et le seul désir de ces enfants devenus adolescents est désormais de s'évader... à n'importe quel prix.

- Fleurs captives
1165/4
- Pétales au vent
1237/4
- Bouquet d'épines
1350/4
- Les racines du passé
1818/4
- Le jardin des ombres
2526/4

La saga de Heaven
- Les enfants des collines
2727/5
Les enfants des collines, c'est l'envers de l'Amérique : la misère à deux pas de l'opulence. Dans la cabane sordide où elle vit avec ses quatre frères et sœurs, Heaven se demande comment ses parents ont eu l'idée de lui donner ce prénom : «Paradis». Un jour, elle apprendra le secret de sa naissance, si lourd que la vie de son père en a été brisée, mais si beau qu'elle croit naître une seconde fois.

- L'ange de la nuit
2870/5
- Cœurs maudits
2971/5
- Un visage du paradis
3119/5
- Le labyrinthe des songes
3234/6
Ma douce Audrina
1578/4
Aurore
- Aurore
3464/5
- Les secrets de l'aube
3580/6

ATTANÉ Chantal
Le propre du bouc
3337/2

AVRIL Nicole
Après des études de lettres, elle s'est imposée dès ses premiers livres. D'autres ont suivi qui furent autant de succès.

Monsieur de Lyon
1049/2
La disgrâce
1344/3
Un père doux et bon, une mère si belle, une grande maison face à l'océan : Isabelle est heureuse. Jusqu'au jour où elle découvre qu'elle est laide. A cette disgrâce qui la frappe comme une malédiction, elle survivra, lucide, dure, hostile, adulte soudain.

Jeanne
1879/3
Don Juan aujourd'hui pourrait-il être une femme ? La belle Jeanne a appris à jouir d'une existence qu'elle sait toujours menacée. D'homme en homme, elle poursuit sa quête de l'éternel masculin.

L'été de la Saint-Valentin
2038/1
La première alliance
2168/3
Sur la peau du Diable
2707/4
Dans les jardins
de mon père
3000/2
Il y a longtemps
que je t'aime
3506/3
L'amour impossible entre Antoine, 14 ans, et Pauline, sa belle-mère.

BACH Richard
Jonathan Livingston
le goéland
1562/1 Illustré
Illusions/Le Messie
récalcitrant
2111/1
Un pont sur l'infini
2270/4
Un cadeau du ciel
3079/3

Grands romans

BELLETTO René
Le revenant
2841/5
Sur la terre comme au ciel
2943/5
La machine
3080/6
L'Enfer
3150/5

Dans une ville déserte et terrassée par l'été, Michel erre. C'est alors qu'une femme s'offre à lui, belle et mystérieuse...

BERBEROVA Nina
Le laquais et la putain
2850/1

Dans le Paris des années folles, une jeune émigrée russe s'étourdit dans les cabarets tziganes et cherche désespérément celui qui la tirera de la misère. Une écriture implacable et glacée.

Astachev à Paris
2941/2
La résurrection de Mozart
3064/1
C'est moi qui souligne
3190/8
L'accompagnatrice
3362/4

Fascinée par la cantatrice qui l'a engagée, une jeune pianiste russe découvre un monde qu'elle ne soupçonnait pas. Peu à peu, elle se laisse submerger par la jalousie que lui inspire la gloire, la beauté et le bonheur d'une autre.

De cape et de larmes
3426/1
Roquenval
3679/1 (Mai 94)

BERGER Thomas
Little Big Man
3281/8

BEYALA Calixthe
C'est le soleil qui m'a brûlée
2512/2
Le petit prince de Belleville
3552/3

BLAKE Michael
Danse avec les loups
2958/4

BULLEN Fiona
Les amants de l'équateur
3636/6 (Mars 94)

CATO Nancy
Lady F.
2603/4
Tous nos jours sont des adieux
3154/8

CHAMSON André
La tour de Constance
3342/7

CHEDID Andrée
La maison sans racines
2065/2
Le sixième jour
2529/3

Lorsque le choléra frappe Le Caire, ce sont les quartiers pauvres les plus touchés. Ignorante et superstitieuse, la population préfère cacher les malades car, lorsqu'une ambulance vient les chercher, ils ne reviennent plus. Il faut attendre le sixième jour. L'instituteur l'a dit : «Le sixième jour, si le choléra ne t'a pas tué, tu es guéri.»

Le sommeil délivré
2636/3
L'autre
2730/3
Les marches de sable
2886/3
L'enfant multiple
2970/3

Le survivant
3171/2
La cité fertile
3319/1

CLANCIER Georges-Emmanuel
Le pain noir
651/3

Le pain noir, c'est celui des pauvres, si dur, que même les chiens n'en veulent pas. Placée à huit ans comme domestique chez des patrons avares, Cathie n'en connaîtra pas d'autre. Récit d'une enfance en pays Limousin, au siècle dernier.

COCTEAU Jean
Orphée
2172/1

COLETTE
Le blé en herbe
2/1

COLOMBANI Marie-Françoise
Donne-moi la main, on traverse
2881/3
Derniers désirs
3460/2

COLLARD Cyril
Cinéaste, musicien, il a adapté à l'écran et interprété lui-même son second roman Les nuits fauves.
Le film 4 fois primé, a été élu meilleur film de l'année aux Césars 1993. Quelques jours plus tôt Cyril Collard mourait du sida.
Les nuits fauves
2993/3
Condamné amour
3501/4
Cyril Collard : la passion
3590/4 (par Guerand & Moriconi)

Grands romans

CONROY PAT
Le Prince des marées
2641/5 & 2642/5

Dans une Amérique actuelle et méconnue, au cœur du Sud profond, un roman bouleversant, qui mêle humour et tragédie.

CORMAN AVERY
Kramer contre Kramer
1044/3

Un divorce et des existences se brisent : celle du petit Billy et de son père, Ted Kramer. En plein désarroi, Ted tente de parer au plus pressé. Et puis un jour, Joanna réapparaît...

DENUZIÈRE MAURICE
Helvétie
3534/9

A l'aube du XIXᵉ siècle, le pays de Vaud apparaît comme une oasis de paix au milieu d'une Europe secouée par de furieux soubresauts. C'est cette joie de vivre oubliée que découvre Blaise de Fonsalte, soldat de l'Empire, déjà las de l'épopée napoléonienne. De ses amours clandestines avec Charlotte, la femme de son hôte, va naître une petite fille aux yeux vairons. Premier volume d'une nouvelle et passionnante série romanesque par l'auteur de Louisiane.

La trahison
des apparences
3674/1 (Mai 94)

DHÔTEL ANDRÉ
Le pays où l'on n'arrive jamais
61/2

DICKEY JAMES
Délivrance
531/3

DIWO JEAN
Au temps où la Joconde parlait
3443/7

1469. Les Médicis règnent sur Florence et Léonard de Vinci entame sa carrière, aux côtés de Machiavel, de Michel-Ange, de Botticelli, de Raphaël... Une pléiade de génies vont inventer la Renaissance.

DJIAN PHILIPPE
Né en 1949, sa pudeur, son regard à la fois tendre et acerbe, et son style inimitable, ont fait de lui l'écrivain le plus lu de sa génération.

37°2 le matin
1951/4

Se fixer des buts dans la vie, c'est s'entortiller dans des chaînes... Oui, mais il y a Betty et pour elle, il irait décrocher la lune. C'est qu'ils commencent à souffrir. Car elle court derrière quelque chose qui n'existe pas. Et lui court derrière elle. Derrière un amour fou...

Bleu comme l'enfer
1971/4
Zone érogène
2062/4
Maudit manège
2167/5
50 contre 1
2363/2
Echine
2658/5

Dan a sacrifié ses jours, ses amis, ses amours à l'écriture. Il avait du talent, du succès. Et puis plus rien : la source est tarie. Depuis, Dan écrit des scénarios pour la télévision, sans honte et sans passion. Mais il y a son fils Herman, la bière mexicaine et les femmes, toujours belles, qui s'en vont parce qu'on les aime trop, ou trop mal...

Crocodiles
2785/2

Cinq histoires qui racontent le blues des amours déçues ou ignorées. Mais c'est parce que l'amour dont ils rêvent se refuse à eux que les personnages de Djian se cuirassent d'indifférence ou de certitudes. Au fond d'eux-mêmes, ils sont comme les crocodiles : «des animaux sensibles sous leur peau dure.»

DORIN FRANÇOISE
Elle poursuit avec un égal bonheur une double carrière. Ses pièces (La facture, L'intoxe...) dépassent le millier de représentations et ses romans sont autant de best-sellers.

Les lits à une place
1369/4

Pour avoir vu trop de couples déchirés, de mariages ratés (dont le sien !), Antoinette a décidé que seule le lit à une place est sûr. Et comme elle a aussi horreur de la solitude, elle a partagé sa maison avec les trois êtres qui lui sont les plus chers. Est-ce vraiment la bonne solution ?

Les miroirs truqués
1519/4
Les jupes-culottes
1893/4
Les corbeaux et les renardes
2748/5

Baron huppé mais facile à duper, Jean-François de Brissandre trouve astucieux de prendre la place de son chauffeur pour séduire sa dulcinée. Renarde avisée, Nadège lui tient le même langage. Et voilà notre corbeau pris au piège, lui qui croyait abuser une ingénue.

Nini Patte-en-l'air
3105/6

Grands romans

DORIN FRANÇOISE (SUITE)
Au nom du père
et de la fille
3551/5

Un beau matin, Georges Vals aperçoit l'affiche d'un film érotique, sur laquelle s'étale le corps superbe et intégralement nu de sa fille. De quoi chambouler un honorable conseiller fiscal de soixante-trois ans ! Mais son entourage est loin de partager son indignation. Que ne ferait-on pas, à notre époque, pour être médiatisé ?

DUBOIS JEAN-PAUL
Les poissons me regardent
3340/3
Une année sous silence
3635/3 (Mars 94)

DUNKEL ELIZABETH
Toutes les femmes
aiment un poète russe
3463/7

DUROY LIONEL
Priez pour nous
3138/4 (Février 94)

EDMONDS LUCINDA
En coulisse
3676/6 (Mai 94)

FOSSET JEAN-PAUL
Chemins d'errance
3067/3
Saba
3270/3

FOUCHET LORRAINE
Jeanne, sans domicile fixe
2932/4
Taxi maraude
3173/4

FREEDMAN J.-F.
Un coupable sur mesure
3658/9 (Avril 94)

FRISON-ROCHE
Né à Paris en 1906, l'alpinisme et le journalisme le conduisent à une carrière d'écrivain. Aujourd'hui il partage son temps entre de grands reportages, les montagnes du Hoggar et Chamonix.

La peau de bison
715/2
La vallée sans hommes
775/3
Carnets sahariens
866/2
Premier de cordée
936/3

Le mont Blanc, ses aiguilles acérées, ses failles abruptes, son pur silence a toujours été la passion de Jean Servettaz, l'un des meilleurs guides de Chamonix. C'est aussi pour cela qu'il a décidé d'en écarter son fils. Pierre s'est incliné, la mort dans l'âme. Mais lorsque la montagne vous tient, rien ne peut contrarier cette vocation.

La grande crevasse
951/3
Retour à la montagne
960/3
La piste oubliée
1054/3
La Montagne
aux Écritures
1064/2
Le rendez-vous
d'Essendilène
1078/3
Le rapt
1181/4

Djebel Amour
1225/4

En 1870, une jolie couturière, Aurélie Picard, épouse un prince de l'Islam. A la suite de Si Ahmed Tidjani, elle découvre, éblouie, la splendeur du Sahara. Décidée à conquérir son peuple, elle apprend l'arabe, porte le saroual et prend le nom de Lalla Yamina. Au pied du djebel Amour se dresse encore le palais de Kourdane où vécut cette pionnière.

La dernière migration
1243/4
Les montagnards de la
nuit
1442/4

Frison-Roche, qui a lui-même appartenu aux maquis savoyards, nous raconte le quotidien de ces combattants de l'ombre.

L'esclave de Dieu
2236/6
Le versant du soleil
3480/9

GEDGE PAULINE
La dame du Nil
2590/6

L'histoire d'Hatchepsout, qui devint reine d'Egypte à quinze ans. Les splendeurs de la civilisation pharaonique et un destin hors série.

GEORGY GUY
La folle avoine
3391/4
Le petit soldat de
l'Empire
3696/4 (Juin 94)

GOLDSMITH OLIVIA
La revanche
des premières épouses
3205/7

Grands romans

GOLON ANNE ET SERGE
Angélique
Marquise des Anges
2488/7
Lorsque son père, ruiné, la marie contre son gré à un riche seigneur toulousain, Angélique se révolte. Défiguré et boiteux, le comte de Peyrac jouit en outre d'une inquiétante réputation de sorcier. Derrière cet aspect repoussant, Angélique va pourtant découvrir que son mari est un être fascinant...

Le chemin de Versailles
2489/7
Angélique et le Roy
2490/7
Indomptable Angélique
2491/7
Angélique se révolte
2492/7
Angélique et son amour
2493/7
Angélique et le Nouveau Monde
2494/7
La tentation d'Angélique
2495/7
Angélique et la Démone
2496/7
Le complot des ombres
2497/5
Angélique à Québec
2498/5 & 2499/5
La route de l'espoir
2500/7
La victoire d'Angélique
2501/7

GROULT FLORA
Après des études à l'Ecole des arts décoratifs, elle devient journaliste et romancière. Elle écrit d'abord avec sa sœur Benoite, puis seule.

Maxime ou la déchirure
518/1
Un seul ennui, les jours raccourcissent
897/2
A quarante ans, Lison épouse Claude, diplomate à Helsinki. Elle va découvrir la Finlande et les trois enfants de son mari. Jusqu'au jour où elle se demande si elle n'a pas commis une erreur.

Ni tout à fait la même, ni tout à fait une autre
1174/3
Une vie n'est pas assez
1450/3
Mémoires de moi
1567/2
Le passé infini
1801/2
Le temps s'en va, madame...
2311/2
Belle ombre
2898/4
Le coup de la reine d'Espagne
3569/1

HARVEY KATHRYN
Butterfly
3252/7 Inédit
A deux pas d'Hollywood, un monde réservé aux femmes riches en mal d'amour, qui s'y choisissent des compagnons à la carte. Pendant ce temps, une vague de puritanisme déferle sur l'Amérique. Le vice et la vertu vont s'affronter.

TERROIR
Romans et histoires vraies d'une France paysanne qui nous redonne le goût de nos racines.

CLANCIER G.-E.
Le pain noir
651/3

GEORGY GUY
La folle avoine
3391/4
Orphelin, Guy-Noël vit chez sa grand-mère, une vieille dame qui connaît tout le folklore et les légendes du pays sarladais. Dans ce merveilleux Périgord, où la forêt ressemble à une cathédrale, l'enfant s'épanouit comme la folle avoine.

JEURY MICHEL
Le vrai goût de la vie
2946/4
Le soir du vent fou
3394/5
Un soir de 1934, alors que souffle le vent fou, un feu de broussailles se propage rapidement et détruit la maison du maire. La toiture s'effondre sur un vieux domestique. Lolo avait si mauvaise réputation que les gendarmes ne cherchent pas plus loin...

LAUSSAC COLETTE
Le sorcier des truffes
3606/1 (Février 94)

MASSE LUDOVIC
Les Grégoire/
Le livret de famille
3653/5 (Avril 94)

VIGNER ALAIN
L'arcandier
3625/4

Achevé d'imprimer en Europe (France)
par Brodard et Taupin à La Flèche (Sarthe)
le 6 mai 1994. 6010J-5
Dépôt légal mai 1994. ISBN 2-277-13280-2
1er dépôt légal dans la collection : février 1974

Éditions J'ai lu
27, rue Cassette, 75006 Paris
Diffusion France et étranger : Flammarion

280